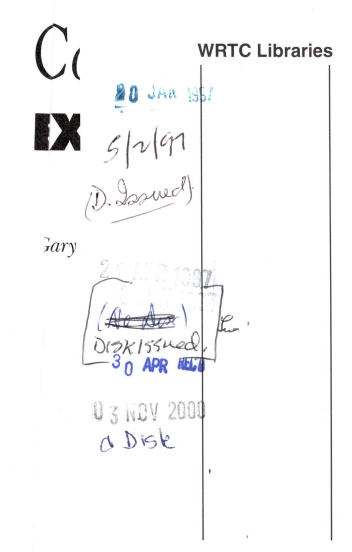

C(

EX

Gary

New Riders

New Riders Publishing, Indianapolis, Indiana

CorelDRAW!™ 6 Expert's Edition

By Gary David Bouton

Published by:
New Riders Publishing
201 West 103rd Street
Indianapolis, IN 46290 USA

Copyright © 1996 by New Riders Publishing

Printed in the United States of America 1 2 3 4 5 6 7 8 9 0

CIP data available upon request

Warning and Disclaimer

This book is designed to provide information about the CorelDRAW computer program. Every effort has been made to make this book as complete and as accurate as possible, but no warranty or fitness is implied.

The information is provided on an "as is" basis. The author and New Riders Publishing shall have neither liability nor responsibility to any person or entity with respect to any loss or damages arising from the information contained in this book or from the use of the disks or programs that may accompany it.

Publisher	Don Fowley
Publishing Manager	David Dwyer
Marketing Manager	Ray Robinson
Managing Editor	Tad Ringo

Development Editor
GAIL BURLAKOFF

Production Editor
STACIA MELLINGER

Copy Editors
MARGARET BERSON
CARLA HALL
PATRICE HARTMANN
PETER KUHNS
CLIFF SHUBS

Technical Editor
WILLIAM SCHNEIDER

Associate Marketing Manager
TAMARA APPLE

Acquisitions Coordinor
STACEY BEHELER

Publisher's Assistant
KAREN OPAL

Cover Illustrator
GARY BOUTON

Cover Designer
KAREN RUGGLES

Book Designer
SANDRA SCHROEDER

Manufacturing Coordinator
PAUL GILCHRIST

Production Manager
KELLY DOBBS

Production Team Supervisor
LAURIE CASEY

Graphics Image Specialists
CLINT LAHNEN, LAURA RBBINS,
CRAIG SMALL, TODD WENTE

Production Analysts
ANGELA BANNAN
JASON HAND
BOBBI SATTERFIELD

Production Team
KIM COFER, TRICIA FLODDR,
DAVID GARRATT, ALEATA
HOWARD, BETH RAGO,
ERICH J. RICHTER, CHRISTINE
TYNER, KAREN WALSH

Indexer
CHRIS CLEVELAND

About the Author

Gary David Bouton is the author of eight books by New Riders, and although the books cover different software applications, they all concentrate on a single idea: how a traditional artist ports his or her skill and sensitivity to the virtual canvas of computer graphics. A professional designer and art director for over twenty years, Gary has found the new medium of digital art to be a different means of communication, and one that continually branches into other areas of creative expression.

"With the version 6 suite of tools, Corel Corporation has broadened its traditional focus on drawing and painting applications to include 3D design tools," says the author. "Adding DREAM 3D and MOTION 3D to the suite expands the horizons for computer illustrators by providing *authoring tools* for Web documents and multimedia creation, as a complement to Corel's superb design tools." *CorelDRAW! 6 Expert's Edition* is Gary's third Corel book, and the first targeted at the more experienced CorelDRAW user.

The author has won several international awards for his work as an illustrator and publisher, including two CorelDRAW! World Design Contests, the InterGalactic Newsletter Competition sponsored by NYPC, InfoWorld, and Lotus, and the Macromedia MacroModel Art Contest. Gary and his wife Barbara, also a New Riders author, are partners in Exclamat!ons, a firm that "polishes rough ideas," and creates electronic and physical documents as diverse in scope as brochures, program interfaces, Web pages, and corporate annual reports.

Gary's other books include *CorelDRAW! 5 for Beginners, Inside Adobe Photoshop 3,* and *Adobe Photoshop 3 Filters and Effects,* all published by New Riders, and which make a splendid addition to the *Expert's Edition* on your bookshelf in the den.

The author can be reached at CIS: 74512,230, or on the Internet at bbouton@future.dreamscape.com.

Trademark Acknowledgments

All terms mentioned in this book that are known to be trademarks or service marks have been appropriately capitalized. New Riders Publishing cannot attest to the accuracy of this information. Use of a term in this book should not be regarded as affecting the validity of any trademark or service mark. CorelDRAW is a registered copyright of Corel Systems Corporation.

Dedication

This book must be dedicated to the individuals who tested the Corel 6 applications in advance of the product's commercial release. These folks became a community of friends during the development cycle, and are some of the pickiest, most hard-working souls you'd ever care to meet. Jose Camara, above all the testers, should be commended for the phenomenal persistence and dedication with which he has, and continues to, pursue "unexpected enhancements" with the product.

It should be known that folks who *test* a product never cast the deciding vote in the features *contained* in the final version; they dutifully report a problem or anomaly to the manufacturer. It's then the responsibility of the manufacturer to take further steps. The Corel 6 application testers are the finest collection of skilled professionals I've ever had the privilege of working with, and several of the techniques you'll find in this book are the product of their research.

Acknowledgments

If you speak with an author whose book you've read, face to face or through e-mail, you might be disappointed on occasion that the author doesn't seem as bright or deep as they do in print. The reason for this is that books such as the *Expert's Edition* are a *collective* effort; there is an under-thanked group of talented individuals who turn mere writing into the tome you hold before you.

In no particular order, I'd like to acknowledge the folks who put the wind in the sails, and guided the examples, information, and insights down a path that's more precise than a Pencil tool can create:

Thanks to:

David Dwyer, Publishing Manager at New Riders, for encouraging me to drop the kid gloves with the *Expert's Edition*, and show the experienced user that it takes something more than understanding a tool's properties to produce outstanding work. Thanks, David, for believing in me, and the manuscript.

Lead Editor Stacia Mellinger, for her patience, her sense of humor, and willingness to put the extra effort (and additional hours!) into creating a well-organized, information-packed book. Thanks, Stacia, and I hope the candy in the FedEx packages was dutifully passed around, and too much didn't get stuck between the chapters.

Technical Editor William Schneider, a very gifted CorelDRAW artist, helped create several of the example steps in this book, which goes above and beyond proofreading for technical accuracy. It generally helps if a Technical Editor understands the program, but William's willingness to also share his insights on digital art and pre-press came as nothing short of a blessing for the author and readers of this book. William, can we log a date for version 7?

Developmental Editor Gail Burlakoff, for putting up with me—again—on yet another strange, wonderful excursion into the art of twisting pixels. Gail, I hope I broke old patterns in the first drafts (I know I certainly *introduced* a few!), and what can I say other than the pleasure was mine, welcome to New York, and Barbara thinks you're funnier on paper than I am. You made this thing sing, Gail—thank you from the bottom of my heart.

Margaret Berson, Peter Kuhns, Patrice Hartmann, Cliff Shubs, and Carla Hall, who gave at least 300% to making this book easy to understand, adding actual punctuation where there was the author's own creative use of extended characters, and for contributing organization and connective threads where there were potholes the size of Rhode Island in the chapters. Thank you all for doing this with a constructive, lighthearted approach; one that a "technical" book always needs.

Software Specialist Steve Weiss, the guy who puts the *non*-printed materials together on CD for our books. Steve, thanks for scrounging for the very best Windows 95 shareware and utilities, and I only wish that surfing the Web entitled you to commercial airline bonus miles. You went the extra one for us, buddy. Thanks for being a part of yet another CorelDRAW epic!

Acquisitions Coordinator Stacey Beheler, who does unthinkable things. Let me clarify this one: Stacey *remembers* the things everyone else has forgotten, prompts us to include little things in the book like chapter figures, and generally makes the writing the prime focus of an author, by handling the peripheral distractions. Thank you Stacey; I'd be lost on page one without your help.

The following individuals must be thanked for support that directly relates to the *Expert's Edition,* beyond coordination, editing, and proofing of the materials:

Beta Coordinator Kelly Greig at Corel Corporation, for her assistance in working with preliminary releases of Corel 6 during the summer of 1995. Kelly, thanks for the sneak preview, and congratulations to your and your husband on your newborn daughter. Beta sites are like members of one big family; and we wish you the best from ours.

Bill Cullen at Corel Corporation, who headed up the QA group for CorelMOTION 3D. Bill, thanks for continually posting advice and tips during the development cycle of version 6. You made working with a completely new Corel application more of a pleasure than a challenge.

Kim Connerty, QA leader for the CorelDRAW group. Kim responded to many of the questions we had about CorelDRAW during the development cycle of version 6 on her own time—it wasn't her appointed duty, and I believe we're all thankful for her input. Thank you Kim, for the honest answers and quick replies. You made writing this book ten times easier than it might have been, and we all wish Corel Corporation the best with version 7.

Steve Rindsburg, of Rindsburg Digital Photography, for his advice on the finer points of PostScript mentioned in this book. I believe Steve coined the phrase "PostScript Weenie," a term that indicates advanced expertise in PostScript hacking and language; a little more evocative than "guru" or "power user." I don't think he has conferred the title upon *himself,* but I am deeply grateful for the wisdom and spirit of sharing that Steve has shown me in the brief time I've known him. And I definitely want to challenge his film recorder with a few images in the near future. Thanks, Steve.

Robin Henson and Costas Kitsos at Ares Software, for invaluable digital font assistance. Many of the fonts you'll find in the BOUTONS folder on the Bonus CD were checked for errors by the best—the folks who make FontMonger and FontMinder. Thank you, kind folks and fellow CorelDRAW users.

Rick Brown at Adobe Systems, for the use of Acrobat Pro, which was used to compile the Acrobat documents on the Bonus CD.

Peter Card at Adobe Systems, for the use of PageMaker 6 in this book's examples, and as a compiling front end for the Acrobat documents.

Scott Brennan at Dreamscape On-Line, Inc., for the Internet connections used to get the manuscripts between Indy and Liverpool, and to find some of the very special shareware we've included on the Bonus CD.

Rafael Arboleda, at Compulink Electronics, Inc., for a very atypical SCSI cable, created on short notice. Compulink still builds custom cables by hand, and for this reason, it's doubtful that my scanner will ever be at "loose ends" the next time I decide to redecorate the game room.

Spousal Editor Barbara Bouton, for putting up with my idea of "a quick dinner"—a Little Caesar's Meat Lover's Special—all too frequently during the writing of this book. Little Caesar's pizzas are terrific, mind you, and Kurt, our Little Caesar's Delivery Specialist has been prompt and friendly. But it's my wife's belief in what I'm doing, the hours, her understanding of the general condition in which I leave our home during the writing, that make a seemingly impossible feat happen with grace, dignity, and a sense of humor. Thank you, Barbara, for your help, and for being you.

Thanks to my folks, friends, and business acquaintances, for understanding why I didn't answer the door for 3 months. And thanks to my brother, David Brian Bouton, for allowing me to use him as a target image on CorelDRAW's color sample area.

Contents at a Glance

Table of Contents

Introduction

Perhaps you've seen, or own, a computer book that labels a program's tools, mentions what a tool does, then leaves it up to you to figure out how to *use* the tools and the programs together to get your work done. This book is different—it's not an owner's manual, and it's not a beginners book—it's the next step up. The *CorelDRAW! 6 Expert's Edition* was written to help you make the transition from "knowing your way around," to being able to put all the pieces together to create exciting, professional, printable work.

- ✔ If you've become proficient at drawing basic shapes and are hungry for directions on how to build the "really cool stuff," this book is for you.

- ✔ If you're excited about the new 3D and multimedia programs you discovered in the CorelDRAW! 6 box—but wonder how you're ever going to transfer the knowledge and the skills you've developed working in CorelDRAW's 2D space to a 3D environment—then simply read on.

- ✔ If you've ever been told that your design is too complex to output, then this book is *definitely* for you!

- ✔ If you've ever looked at all the applications and utilities in the CorelDRAW package and wondered if it is possible to make them work together, you're presently in search of expert techniques, and you need look no further.

The *CorelDRAW! 6 Expert's Edition* zeros in on *key concepts* relating to color theory, path construction, font construction, as well as the *principles* behind Corel's core special effects capabilities.

But don't think for a minute that this is a stuffy theory book—this book is *hands-on from* cover to cover. You put the concepts and principals to work as you are guided through the *entire* process of a design's creation, from the concept to the completed work. Step-by-step, you'll work through the process, just as you do in your everyday work; you'll gain the insights and experience that make producing stunning, award-winning design work an attainable goal.

Something Old, Something New

Version 6, like each preceding version of the CorelDRAW suite of applications, breaks a lot of new ground. There are new applications, different ways to perform tasks you've grown accustomed to performing, and *everything* about the Corel version 6 applications operates under a new operating system—Windows 95. Even if you've worked extensively with versions 3, 4, and 5 of the Corel applications, the host of new conventions and features can be a little disorienting. The *CorelDRAW! 6 Expert's Edition* will guide you over the rough spots that might catch you by surprise by making specific recommendations for working smarter and faster in both CorelDRAW! 6 and Windows 95. You'll learn how to infuse your present CorelDRAW expertise with new techniques to enhance your compositions and extend your capabilities as a designer and artist.

Note   *CorelDRAW! 6 Expert's Edition* assumes that you are familiar with drawing and painting programs. If this is your first graphics application or the first version of the Corel applications you've worked with, we recommend that you spend some time with Corel's own documentation, printed and online, before diving into the examples in this book.

Set aside some time to do the Corel-provided tutorials, and to explore on your own. As you get acquainted with Corel 6, you'll find that its basic tools, commands, and features are *fairly* intuitive, and that the real hurdles might come when you want to *integrate* your knowledge of the tools to make your design concept spring to life.

When you're comfortable with the tools, we'll take you through the integration of the tools and features in CorelDRAW, and also show you how CorelPHOTO-PAINT, CorelMOTION 3D, CorelDREAM 3D, and CorelDEPTH can be effectively used in combination with CorelDRAW.

About the Organization of the Expert's Edition

The *CorelDRAW! 6 Expert's Edition* is divided into three parts, each part relating to a different aspect of the Corel applications. In sequence, the parts cover the following:

✔ In Part I, you'll discover how to work more efficiently in Win95, and how to put the features in CorelDRAW at your fingertips by taking advantage of Corel's customizable interface. You'll also master the Bézier tool, and learn how to create correct, printable paths and nodes in any design. Part I also covers the advanced core topics of color theory, using color models, and how to create and apply the complex fills and blends that give your work a realistic, dimensional look.

✔ Part II focuses on how to integrate the output from other Corel applications into a CorelDRAW design. You'll learn how to use CorelDRAW and PHOTO-PAINT together in a single design by tapping into the strengths of each program. You'll see how the OCR-Trace conversion program can be used as a design tool, and take a long look at designing your own fonts, and how a font can become a graphic and vice versa.

✔ In Part III, we pull out all the stops and take you on exciting exploration of 3D graphics, animation, and Web page design. You'll learn how to use CorelDRAW and PHOTO-PAINT to create materials that are used in CorelDEPTH to create 3D images, and then how to bring them back into a CorelDRAW design. You'll take a seat in the director's chair and design, score, and generally have a ball creating a movie clip with CorelMOTION 3D. Your last stop in Part III isn't Hollywood, but rather it's the World Wide Web. Designing stunning Web pages takes a different design approach than you might be used to, and we'll show you how to do it right.

✔ Parts I, II, and III simply weren't big enough to hold all of the information we wanted to share with you. So if you take a peak on the *CorelDRAW! 6 Expert's Edition Bonus CD*, you'll find "Outputting Your Input," a comprehensive guide to traditional printing, electronic publications, and export file formats from CorelDRAW to other applications. "Outputting Your Input" is in Acrobat format, and it's stocked with information that you need to know to ensure that what you design can be rendered to today's media formats, including film recorders.

Part I: Getting Up and Running with CorelDRAW!

The chapters in Part I focus on CorelDRAW! 6. Even if you've used every version of CorelDRAW since Corel Headliner, be sure to take a look through Chapter 1, "Welcome to Win95 and a Whole New CorelDRAW!". Because CorelDRAW! 6 is a Windows 95 native application, there are Windows 95 and new Corel features and conventions you need to be come acquainted with before you'll be able to work comfortably in this new version. The following sections detail what's in store for you in each chapter of Part I.

Chapter 1: Welcome to Win95 and a Whole New CorelDRAW!

Corel 6 is a Windows 95-compliant application, and as such, it's important to understand a little about the operating system *before* investing the time in CorelDRAW! 6 design work. An object-oriented workplace means that you can drag and drop files to relocate them, but you can also accidentally *lose* valuable program files unless you understand the new rules! Right-click shortcuts, long file names (and when not to use them), and other features that impact on the new 32-bit CorelDRAW are discussed in this chapter.

Chapter 2: Customizing CorelDRAW!

Once you get used to the reality that everything is an object under Windows 95, you'll soon discover that screen elements—including CorelDRAW tools and menus—can be arranged to your personal work preferences. You have your choice of Zoom tools, how to edit paths, which buttons appear on the toolbox and toolbar, and how each tool works. Chapter 2 shows the best way to arrange CorelDRAW's workspace, and provides valuable insights into accessing special features that are *not* documented in Corel's reference manuals.

Chapter 3: Beating Nodes and Paths into Submission (The Easy Way)

In Chapter 3, we take a detailed look at the basic elements that make up a CorelDRAW design: nodes and paths. Although you can design anything you like with the Pencil tool, there is most definitely a "right" and a "wrong" way for path construction. If you've ever designed a CorelDRAW piece that refuses to print, it might very well have to do with the construction of a path, or the property of nodes along the path. This chapter provides the answers to shaping a path the way *you* intended it, and adding PostScript compliance, accuracy, and detail to your CorelDRAW document. The Node Edit Roll-Up has changed in version 6; check out Chapter 3 to make working with nodes and paths a breeze.

Chapter 4: Mastering Color Models and the Fill Tool

Much more so than in previous versions, CorelDRAW is a *color* tool; you have several color models upon which to base your design work, and each color model was created for a specific type of output. CMYK, RGB, color-matching systems such as PANTONE, and more are all featured in CorelDRAW's workspace, but which is the right one for the design assignment you have today? Chapter 4 covers the *principles* behind the light you see on-screen, how printed colors correspond to monitor colors, and how to specify the correct color model for use in your own work. What You See *Isn't* Always What You Get, unless you work with color models appropriate for a specific medium in Windows and CorelDRAW. Chapter 4 shows you the menus, the palettes, and the options for ensuring that the world sees your finished piece the way you do.

Chapter 5: Complex Fills and Blend Shading

Texture fills, blend groups, fountain fills, tiling bitmaps, and CorelDRAW's other special fills can lend a quality of realism to even the simplest of designs. Chapter 5 takes you past the perfunctory steps of filling an object, to *shading* an object, and creating photorealistic illustrations. Highlights, reflections, shadows, and surface texture are as important as the outline shape of an object in attaining the goal of a graphic that immediately communicates to an audience. Learn the secrets of using special fills and blend objects to make *your* CorelDRAW design the one that commands the most attention.

Part II: Document-Centricity: Using CorelDRAW! as the Design Hub for Assignments

The second part of *CorelDRAW! 6 Expert's Edition* takes an artist's look at how qualities of an illustration you might have in mind can be best accomplished *outside* CorelDRAW. If you've always wanted to create a typeface from your designs, CorelDRAW can assist, and the complete instructions are contained in Part II. Additionally, you'll see the relationship between bitmap and vector graphics, and learn how to meld the two different formats of computer graphics into a single composition. Part II puts the different types of PC files in perspective, and shows you how to use CorelDRAW as the "home base" for specialized design needs.

Chapter 6: Bitmaps and Vector Designs

Between CorelPHOTO-PAINT and CorelDRAW, you have 99 percent of the design tools you need to create almost anything. However, it's sometimes difficult to decide when a design needs to be saved as a bitmap image or in CorelDRAW's vector format, and the finished format does indeed play a factor in your choice of design tools. In Chapter 6, you'll learn two different ways to arrive at a design that uses the best features of CorelDRAW and PHOTO-PAINT to make a "hybrid" composition. Bitmap images and vector objects are easily melded when you understand the capabilities of the programs discussed in Chapter 6.

Chapter 7: Corel OCR-Trace: Converting Bitmaps to Vectors

Corel OCR-Trace is often overlooked as a design tool, but it can actually bridge the gap between the bitmap and vector properties of these different file formats. If you've ever wanted to work with a physical pen-and-ink sketch in the same way as you bend and shape CorelDRAW paths, Corel OCR-Trace is the key. Chapter 7 shows how to take photos, physical illustrations, and even scans of text, and turn them into copies that can be edited in CorelDRAW in the same way as any path you've drawn with the Pencil tool. Achieve the ultimate in computer graphics flexibility by using OCR-Trace and learning the technique found in this chapter.

Chapter 8: Creating Your Own Fonts

What is a font? It's simply a collection of designs with which you can type, right? Although we frequently take digital fonts for granted, there is a marvelous wealth of technology behind a font's construction and the programs that enable you to work with fonts as text and as objects. Chapter 8 shows you how to create your own font by using CorelDRAW's PFB and TTF export filters, how font construction can be optimized, and how fonts created with CorelDRAW can be used in CorelDEPTH and CorelDREAM 3D. You can even create a logotype font for clients who want their logos to appear in word processing documents. Additionally, Chapter 8 discusses other applications that can help refine a CorelDRAWn font. You're closer than you think to offering the business community professional type foundry results as a service, courtesy of this chapter and CorelDRAW's font-creation features.

Part III: Beyond CorelDRAW!

Part III doesn't actually leave CorelDRAW behind, but we *do* use CorelDRAW extensively as a launching pad to other applications, most notably the 3D programs found in the version 6 box. If you've ever wanted to express a design idea in a photorealistic fashion, produce a mini-movie with tools you already have, or design a Web page for the Internet, Part III is your guide.

Chapter 9: Working between CorelDRAW! and CorelDREAM 3D

CorelDREAM 3D adds a third graphics type to the Corel bundle's capabilities. Beyond vector and bitmap illustration lies a combination of the two, in the form of modeling and rendering dimensional scenes. Chapter 9 takes you from the familiar CorelDRAW workspace to the not-so-intuitive DREAM 3D viewport, where anything you design can be rotated, shaded with virtual lights, and covered with user-defined, realistic textures.

Although Corel has provided many clip objects and preset shaders (materials) for working with CorelDREAM 3D, this chapter shows you how to create your own wireframes. Additionally, you'll see how to use your own CorelDRAW designs as CorelDREAM 3D shading materials, and how to make transparency masks for surfaces that will look like you placed a decal on a 3D object. If you've ever wondered how to take the first artistic step into the next dimension of computer graphics, Chapter 9 opens the door.

Chapter 10: Adding DEPTH and MOTION

Chapter 9 continues with the topic of dimensional modeling, and adds the dimension of time to your repertoire of graphics tools, as we explore CorelMOTION 3D. CorelMOTION 3D is a full-fledged animation program that works with wireframe models of text, or objects you import from CorelDRAW. The results can be photorealistic, with reflections and highlights moving through time in a CorelMOTION composition. Learn how to create an animated logo that can be played back using Windows 95's Media Player!

Additionally, you'll see how to get into illustrating, 3D style with CorelDEPTH. CorelDEPTH is *not* simply a "font extruder"; you can create stunning compositions from within CorelDEPTH that can be exported and enhanced in PHOTO-PAINT or CorelDRAW. There are absolute gems to be found in the "other applications" in the Corel 6 box, and this chapter shows you how to uncover and polish these gems.

Chapter 11: Special Effects for Web Pages

The World Wide Web is quickly becoming a combination tourist attraction and commercial billboard. And if you want the quickest, most widespread means of letting the world know you have goods to sell or services to promote, having a Web page is a must. Chapter 11 takes you through the steps of creating a Web graphic, proportioning it and assigning it a GIF transparency color, and how to tap into the latest HTML specifications to add a tiling background to your Web page. Additionally, the source code for HTML documents is provided on the *CorelDRAW! 6 Expert's Edition Bonus CD* in completely annotated format, so Chapter 11 shows you *the structure*, not simply the graphics-creation process, for designing your own Web page.

Chapter 12: Outputting Your Input (on the CD)

Chapter 12 contains the secrets, rules, tricks, and techniques for outputting your Corel work to a number of different and exciting media. Oddly enough, Chapter 12 *itself* is in a new type of output, the Acrobat Portable Document Format (PDF), which is an electronic, online chapter that can be read on-screen or printed as hard copy. You'll find Chapter 12 on the *CorelDRAW! 6 Expert's Edition Bonus CD* in the CHAP12 folder, and you'll find instruction for installing the Acrobat Reader v2.1 in the back of this book.

"Outputting Your Input" is an invaluable guide to getting high-quality hard copy and electronic versions of your Corel designs and page layouts. In this chapter, you'll learn how to build an Acrobat document, get honest information on the importance of PostScript in your design work, and learn workarounds to ensure accurate printing from within CorelDRAW. Also, we take a look at color management, how fonts can become an output problem, and how to correct and enhance a file so it always looks its best when displayed in any medium.

Additional Reference Material

The Disk Install pages in the back of *CorelDRAW! 6 Expert's Edition* contain all the steps you need for installing the Adobe Acrobat Reader v2.1 on your system. If you install the Reader, you'll unlock more valuable information about CorelDRAW that we simply couldn't pack into this book! Acrobat technology enables a user to compose a document that can be viewed and printed exactly as the author created it, as described in Chapter 12. For example, using CorelDRAW! 6 and Adobe PageMaker 6, we created several Acrobat PDF pieces that reside in sections of the Bonus CD. The fonts we used, the color images, and layout will appear in Acrobat Reader *exactly* the same as it does in the PageMaker file where the document was composed. Additionally, the same Acrobat document can be read by Macintosh, DOS, Windows, and Unix users. Acrobat technology will become more prevalent as Internet Web sites adopt the technology, and you'll become one more subscriber to electronic documents if you'll read the instructions for installing the Reader v2.1 in the back of the book.

The Acrobat Online Glossary

You'll notice that there isn't a hard copy glossary in the back of *CorelDRAW! 6 Expert's Edition*. We've ported more than 150 entries to Acrobat format, and you'll find the CEE6-GL.PDF file in the ACRODOCS folder of the Bonus CD. We recommend that you copy this file to your hard disk for quicker access, but you'll also need to copy the *.AVI files in the ACRODOCS folder to the same location as the Glossary PDF file. The AVI movies are linked to the Acrobat Online Glossary, so when you need to actually see an effect described on a glossary page, clicking on the movie icon will call Win95's Media Player, and you can watch the AVI file, as shown in figure I.1. The movie icons are external links to the PDF document; if the PDF document is moved to your hard disk without the linked AVI files, you won't be able to see the movies.

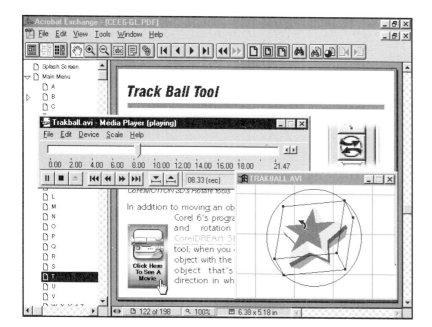

Figure I.1
The *CorelDRAW! 6
Expert's Edition*
Online Glossary is a
hypermedia and
hypertext electronic
document.

CEE6-GL.PDF is also loaded with hypertext links, so you can scoot between pages to arrive at a concept, feature, or new CorelDRAW technique you're looking for in lightning time. It's illustrated in full color, and if you want hard copy of some of the pages, you can print them out from Acrobat Reader.

Bonus, Bonus CD Guide

As an extra, added attraction, we've assembled the *CorelDRAW! 6 Expert's Edition* Resource Guide—almost 90 entries of hardware, software, and service contacts that you'll surely find handy in your continuing imaging adventures—also in the Acrobat format. Need high-resolution output? Need a filter you can't find in mail-order catalogues? Need a driver for your video card? Go directly to the source in the convenient collection of resources the authors frequently use.

What's on the Bonus CD?

In addition to the example images you can work with in the Experts Edition's chapters, the Bonus CD contains many shareware utilities for Windows 95, demoware of graphics applications, and some private stock materials found in the BOUTONS folder. The WHATCD.PDF document in the ACRODOCS folder of the Bonus CD gives a detailed description of what you'll find on the Bonus CD, so if you crack this document before exploring the CD's contents, you'll have a better idea of what might appeal to you, and what you'd like to copy to your hard disk.

However, there *are* rules and regulations that New Riders and the author had to play by in order to bring you a treasure trove of sample programs and files on the Bonus CD. Please read the accompanying README files or Acrobat documents located in the folders of each company's product or service before using the contents commercially, or deciding something is cool and a friend would like a copy.

Note Because the *CorelDRAW! 6 Expert's Edition Bonus CD* is read-only media, we include steps in the example assignments in this book to save *copies* of renamed files to your hard disk. However, you might find occasionally that if you don't edit a file before saving it to hard disk, the read-only attribute stays with the file, and that Windows 95 or CorelDRAW alerts you to this fact.

To remove the read-only attribute of a file you've copied to hard disk in Win95, right-click on the file from within a folder window on Windows Desktop. Choose P**r**operties, then uncheck the **R**ead-only check box in the Attributes field of the file's Properties dialog box.

You cannot modify a file that's located on the CD this way, because a CD-ROM is *Read-Only Memory*.

Conventions Used in This Book

This section tackles the various conventions used in *CorelDRAW! 6 Expert's Edition.*

When Is a Toolbox Not a Toolbox?

We make mention of both *toolbars* and *toolboxes* in this book. A toolbar in Corel applications, by default, is configured horizontally across the top of a document window, beneath the menu. A toolbox generally is configured vertically, to the left of a document window, although both toolbars and the toolbox in Corel applications can be detached from their docked positions in the workspace and can be resized to create a more rectangular shape.

The *Expert's Edition* References Default Settings

Although Chapter 2, "Customizing CorelDRAW!," shows about a billion ways you can fine-tune Corel's workspace so it becomes more convenient and familiar, we use the default settings for CorelDRAW's workspace in the other 11 chapters. We needed to establish a common ground for all the examples, and the default configuration is the most accessible one for all who read this book.

For example, if you're stumped that a chapter step tells you to right-click, then select Zoom Out from the shortcut menu, but you don't see this option on the shortcut menu, your Zoom tool Preferences are probably defined as use tradition zoom flyout or Mouse button 2 for the Zoom tool, Zoom out. We do not lend specific advice on zooming a lot in the *Expert's Edition*, because zooming is more of a procedure than an artistic step, and our prime focus is on how you can create the best artwork using the new features and tools.

Techniques versus "Proper Methods"

The *Expert's Edition* has been designed to provide you with the keys to the quickest results in the Corel applications, and this means occasionally breaking rules, adopting unconventional practices, and generally treating CorelDRAW and other applications as *tools*. We don't make much mention of CorelDRAW's Multiple Document Interface (MDI), because there are alternative methods for copying objects to documents more quickly.

Additionally, you'll see that we endorse the technique of marquee-selecting all nodes in a path to lines, converting the straight lines to curves, then converting one or two curves back to path segments. This is an example of taking the most time-effective route to accomplishing a task, although Corel's documentation might recommend that each path is converted individually.

You will find a lot of new techniques in this book, and our recommendations are based on months of testing CorelDRAW prior to its commercial release for the best ways to design professional pieces. For example, you might find that the shortcut menu works better for you than the Node Edit Roll-Up for editing nodes and paths. In this case, we've provided steps for working with each technique in the chapters in this book.

Working with the *Expert's Edition* and the *Current* CorelDRAW! 6

At the time *CorelDRAW! 6 Expert's Edition* was written, version 118 was the current release version. Corel Corporation had previously released a version 112, and there are more than 20,000 copies of this version in distribution that contain program errors. By the time you read this, it is expected that a maintenance release will be in distribution.

Throughout this book, you'll see tips that recommend that you contact Corel Customer Service at 613/728-8200 to obtain the latest update to the Corel 6 applications. If you look at the Help, About CorelDRAW box in CorelDRAW, you'll see which version is currently installed on your machine. Corel Corp. has no way of knowing which version you currently own, because there is no version number on your registration card. It is up to you to contact Corel Corporation to obtain an update.

The initial release of the Corel 6 applications contain program errors that have been addressed, or will be addressed in future updates. We've made note of some of the more relevant, obvious flaws in the applications in the chapters, and we make recommendations for workarounds. In all probability, any and all of the errors mentioned will be eliminated in future updates, but as of version 118, all steps in this book can be performed without unexpected occurrences. If you know of any features that you're unhappy with, or might not perform as specified in Corel's documentation, do yourself a favor and call Customer support, or leave CompuServe e-mail in the Customer Service section of the CorelAPPS forum.

To get the most out of this book, you should make certain that you have the most current update to the Corel 6 applications.

Nicknames for Applications

We frequently use a shorthand description of the programs and operating system. Win95 is used in place of Windows 95, and because all the Corel applications are preceded by the Corel name, we'll often call CorelDRAW simply DRAW. Additionally, we've dispensed with the exclamation mark after Corel product names, because this interferes with the punctuation of sentences!

Therefore, when "MOTION" is mentioned, we refer to "CorelMOTION 3D!," and the other applications are similarly abbreviated.

Mouse Notes

Because Windows 95, and therefore CorelDRAW, supports two-button mouse commands, we make special note in the examples in this book of when the primary mouse button is used, and when you need to access extended features by clicking on the secondary mouse button.

✔ The primary button is typically the left mouse button, although left-handed designers (the author being one) might decide to reverse mouse button functionality through the Windows Control Panel. For the purposes of example in this book, left-clicking means clicking the primary, most-used mouse button, and right-clicking means clicking on the secondary mouse button.

✔ *Double-clicking* is performed by clicking on the left mouse button very quickly. In CorelDRAW, you double-click to select and open a file from the common dialog box, but double-clicking is not used, overall, very often because Windows 95 is more of a "single click" environment.

✔ *Hovering* describes the action you perform when you allow the cursor to remain stationary over a tool or button. Pop-up help for Corel application tools is accessed by hovering your cursor, and the Windows Start menu can be navigated by hovering.

✔ *Clicking twice*—not to be confused with double-clicking—is an action reserved for CorelDRAW and CorelPHOTO-PAINT applications. Clicking twice means to click once in a definitive motion, then repeating the motion. This action causes an object to be selected, then sent to a special mode. In CorelDRAW, clicking-twice puts an object in Rotate and Skew mode, and you'll note that the selection handles take on a different appearance. In PHOTO-PAINT, successive clicking selects an area, then places it in Rotate and Skew mode, then places the selection in Distort mode. In both applications, clicking again puts the selection or object back in normal selection mode.

✔ *Click-and-dragging* refers to clicking on an object with the primary (left) mouse button, then moving the selection while holding the button.

✔ *Drag-and-dropping* refers to the action of selecting an object, moving the object while holding the left mouse button, then releasing the mouse button. This action is frequently used when you want to copy a file from the Windows Desktop into the workspace of an application as a means for opening the file or adding the file contents to a document. See Chapter 10, "Adding DEPTH and MOTION," for an example of drag-and-dropping.

✔ *Click-and-drag, then right-click* is an action reserved for CorelDRAW, and this is a shortcut for placing a duplicate of an object elsewhere in the document.

✔ *Right-clicking* is a context-sensitive feature in Corel applications and Windows 95. Right-clicking produces, usually, a shortcut menu with options that are context-sensitive to the tool that you currently are using. For example, right-clicking with the Shape tool over a selected object in CorelDRAW produces a shortcut menu with options for editing node and path segment properties, while right-clicking over an object with the Pick tool produces a different shortcut menu containing selection options.

✔ *Ctrl+click-and-dragging* copies files in Windows Desktop. It also copies a selected object between document windows in CorelDRAW, and Ctrl is the constrain key for creating circles with the Ellipse tool, squares with the Rectangle tool, for creating word spacing in Artistic text (using the Shape tool), and for limiting the direction of other drawn and moved objects using other CorelDRAW tools.

✔ *Ctrl+Shift+click-and-dragging* places a shortcut to a file at the location where you release the mouse button. This action is not used in CorelDRAW, but instead in Win95 folder windows and the Desktop.

New Riders Publishing

The staff of New Riders Publishing is committed to bringing you the very best in computer reference material. Each New Riders book is the result of months of work by authors and staff who research and refine the information contained within its covers.

As part of this commitment to you, the New Riders reader, we invite your input. Please let us know if you enjoy this book, if you have trouble with the information and examples presented, or if you have a suggestion for the next edition.

Please note, though: New Riders staff cannot serve as a technical resource for CorelDRAW! or for other questions about software- or hardware-related problems. Please refer to the documentation that accompanies CorelDRAW! 6 or to the applications' Help systems.

If you have a question or comment about any New Riders book, there are several ways to contact New Riders. We will respond to as many readers as we can. Your name, address, or phone number will never become part of a mailing list or be used for any purpose other than to help us continue to bring you the best books possible. You can write us at the following address:

New Riders Publishing
Attn: Publisher
201 W. 103rd Street
Indianapolis, IN 46290

If you prefer, you can fax New Riders at (317) 581-4670.

You can also send electronic mail to New Riders at the following Internet address:

ddwyer@newriders.mcp.com

New Riders is an imprint of Macmillan Computer Publishing. To obtain a catalog or information, or to purchase any Macmillan Computer Publishing book, call (800) 428-5331.

Thank you for selecting *CorelDRAW! 6 Expert's Edition*!

Final Word

If you remember the feeling the first time your drove your dad's car, then compare that feeling to the first time you took your *own* car for a spin, this is the sort of difference that the *CorelDRAW! 6 Expert's Edition* will create in your attitude and approach to working with the new tools.

The ignition is on the following page.

Part I

Getting Up and Running with CorelDRAW!

Welcome to Win95 and a Whole New CorelDRAW!

I f application software ran by itself, there would be no need for an operating system. This fictitious situation would make it extremely difficult for programmers, because there would be no common framework within which to work. Without common dialog boxes and conventions, every program would look, feel, and operate in entirely different ways, which would become a user nightmare! Fortunately, this is not the case. Microsoft's Windows 95 (Win95), the new operating system for Intel-based PCs, provides an exciting new foundation for companies like Corel Corporation to build better, more robust versions of software.

The Win95 operating system keeps a tight rein on programs, drivers, and background utilities that load upon Win95 startup (such as font managers) to ensure crash-resistant computing. Under the Win95 operating system, CorelDRAW! 6, other native Win95 applications, and even older applications, run about 40% faster. If a program hangs, it is less likely to crash the operating system or another open application than previous versions of Windows; your system and other open applications are usually affected by the event. Also, because Win95 is a true 32-bit operating system, Corel and other native Win95 applications can do things they never could before under Windows 3.1x.

To obtain all this new functionality, however, Microsoft made a "clean sweep" of the familiar Windows operating system—from the way it works, to the way *you*, the user, work *within* it. This chapter is designed to provide you as a Corel artist with the information you need to know about Win95's impact on the way you manage files, create an efficient working environment, and perform chores outside of CorelDRAW. Win95 can make computer graphics a more productive and enjoyable experience. We're working "from the outside in" in this chapter to better arrive at the wondrous new things you can do later in the core application, CorelDRAW.

Before You Install Anything...

Most people approach installing something as critical as an operating system or a major software package with some trepidation. If you haven't installed Windows 95 or CorelDRAW! 6 yet, this chapter contains valuable pre-setup information that could save you some grief later. And if you *have* installed either or both Win95 and Corel 6, read on, because there are some key concepts and features contained here that make the transition to 32-bit computing a little less stressful.

The Advantages to a Dual Boot System

You can indeed install Win95 and keep your existing Windows 3.1x setup as a fully functional, alternative operating system. Why would you want to preserve Win3.1 when CorelDRAW! 6 runs only on Win95? Although Corel 6 will not run under Windows 3.1x, you might have other applications that will not work properly under Win95 in their current version. 16-bit scanner drivers, some third-party print drivers, Adobe standard 16-bit plug-in filters, and programs that write directly to hardware (some modeling and imaging applications do this) are a few examples of Win95 non-compliant programs. Versions don't upgrade overnight, and you might want to make a gradual migration to a completely 32-bit operating system. Then when you've upgraded every piece of software you used to run under Win95, you can safely delete Windows 3.1x from your computer.

Defragmentation and Compression: New Rules

Before installing Windows 95, it's prudent to *defragment* your hard disk(s).

If you are running third-party "on-the-fly" hard disk compression programs such as Stac Industry's Stacker (discussed in detail in the next section), you must use Stacker's proprietary defragmentation routine before installing Win95, and not afterwards. Win95 comes with a defrag program, but it will make gibberish out of Stacker-compressed drives because the utility doesn't understand the structure of the Stac volume. Conversely, versions of Stacker before 4.0 are 16-bit programs, and the 16-bit defragging utility messes up Win95 because it doesn't understand the new vfat (virtual file allocation) table, which uses long file name structures. Only if you use genuine Microsoft DriveSpace (from version 3.1x or Win95), or a third-party program explicitly designed for Win95, can you safely defragment a hard disk written to Win95's structure.

Before defragmenting your hard disk, delete your "trash"; *.BAK and *.TMP files with dates from more than a year ago are likely candidates. Also, evaluate the need for unregistered shareware programs whose evaluation dates have expired, and programs that you haven't used since high school (unless you are in high school). This stuff accumulates, and the more free space you have before defragging, the more sectors on your hard disk can be optimized (you can gain significant MB). Win95 can take up 60 MB of free disk space, and Corel 6 is no slouch, either. In addition to reclaiming hard disk space, a defragmenting program can speed up disk access, because read/writes happen faster when a file is in one physical place on a hard disk's platters. Before using the DEFRAG command, you should run either CHKDSK or DOS 6.2's ScanDisk on all drives, to ensure that there are no lost hard disk clusters or truncated files. It's not a good idea to port previous operating system problems to your future one!

Third-party disk compression has been available far longer for Windows users than Microsoft's DriveSpace. It *probably* won't (and "probably" is emphasized here) hinder your Win95/CorelDRAW! 6 experience to leave as-is a hard disk compressed with a third-party program.

You should seriously consider one of the following strategies before installing Win95. If, for example, you have a large drive compressed using Stacker version 4.0 or later (don't even *think* of installing to a Stacker version 3 or earlier compressed drive), you can do one of the following:

✔ Install Win95 on a disk compressed with a third-party utility. Be sure to check with Microsoft *and* the third-party vendor about how the two interact, and how the user can *maintain* the drive (defrag and correct errors) after Win95 installation. This strategy means that you don't have to back up and reformat your present hard disk, but you are assured of performance loss in accessing the disk. Why? The non-Win95 compression utility operates in *real mode*, while Win95 operates in *enhanced mode*, and your drive is structured so that Win95 must read and write in a compatible mode.

✔ Upgrade to a Win95 version of the third-party software if available. As of this writing, Win95 versions of everything are either in the distribution pipelines, or promised for the 4th quarter of 1995.

✔ Back up everything (which you should do any time you're installing a new operating system), remove the compression scheme (check with the vendor on the procedure), and then format and repartition the hard disk, if necessary, to create enough room for Win95. Then restore your files using DriveSpace, and finally, install Win95. This method is a time-consuming process, and not for the technically challenged, but overall it is the best route if the first strategy doesn't suit you.

Whether you have disk compression or not, these considerations are only the top of your Windows 95 "pre-flight" check list. Before you install Win95, you should run a virus-checking program, and then turn the virus checker off. The BIOS of some computers, and some network cards, have virus-checking built in. This feature needs to be *turned off* before installing Win95. Consult the virus-checking program's documentation to learn how to remove the virus-checking routine.

Also, make sure that all of the equipment you have (CD-ROM drive, digitizing pad, scanner, sound cards, external modems, printers) is properly connected and working in Windows 3.1 before installing Win95. Check with manufacturers for Win95 drivers, and have the drivers available at the time of installing Win95.

Win95 is like a new tenant to your computer's "apartment"; you, as the landlord, hear a lot less complaining if you get everything in shape before the tenant moves in!

Tips for Making a Dual Boot System

When Win95's setup begins, it looks for a previous version of Windows on your machine, and presents you with the option of *overwriting* your current Windows, or installing to a new directory. To keep your Windows 3.1 setup intact, you must choose to install Win95 to a new and different directory (X:\Win95 is a good choice) than your current Windows 3.1 directory (usually C:\WINDOWS).

There are pros and cons to installing over your existing Windows 3.1x directory. The disadvantage to replacing your current version with Win95 is that native 16-bit applications must be run using a special translation mode (*virtual machine* mode, or *VXM*) under Win95, which is not as sound a method when compared to running an application under the operating system for which it was originally written. Win95 runs 16-bit applications quickly and to most users' satisfaction, but not always flawlessly.

The advantages to installing on top of Windows 3.1x are that you'll be conserving hard disk space, and that you won't have to set up new program groups in Win95. Win95 can detect Win3.1x program groups if you install Win95 to the same directory.

If you have hard disk space to spare, you can have the best of both worlds by creating a *dual boot machine*—a system that gives you the option to load either Win95 or Windows 3.1x through a previous version of DOS.

It's not a great idea, but not a fatal one either, to install Win95 to the same drive where Windows 3.1 resides. Because Win95 has a very different way of presenting directory structures on your hard disk (covered later in this chapter), you can easily specify a path to a program, or copy a file to the wrong place with similar operating system names (and subdirectories) located on the same hard disk partition.

You need to choose a drive for Win95 that has least 100 MB of free disk space on it. Win95 itself can take up to 60 MB if you install all the bells and whistles, and the additional space is needed for swap file space and temp space for the install itself. Win95 can be installed to a compressed disk partition, but you should probably choose a 32-bit compression program. Win95 uses Enhanced mode disk access, while a 16-bit disk compression utility that reads/writes DOS is confined to Real mode. And Win95 has to take time to interpret Real mode calls.

Virus Warnings and EIDE Hard Disks

You may find that you need to purchase a new hard disk to accommodate Win95 (100 MB minimum), CorelDRAW! 6 (more than 75 MB if you install everything), and for all the artwork you create! If you're considering one of the new *enhanced IDE* (EIDE) drives that is larger than 540 MB and you have a computer manufactured before 1995, please continue reading. And if your *present* machine uses a pre-load "overlay" program to access an EIDE drive that exceeds 540 MB in size, read on...

BIOS chips in most IBM PCs built before 1995 used with DOS 6.2 and earlier *cannot address* a hard disk larger than 540 MB. SCSI hard disks get around this limitation because bootable SCSI controller cards have their own BIOS, and this BIOS "fibs" to DOS about the size of the hard disk. Now that large EIDE disks are commonly available, a similar strategy must be employed. One way to trick DOS about hard disk size is through the use of an "overlay" program provided by hard disk manufacturers, such as OnTrack Computer System's Disk Manager. The overlay program loads before DOS and tells DOS the drive is smaller than it really is. The overlay is then responsible for making this slick bit of trickery work.

Although Win95 natively supports EIDE disks, older computer BIOS chips do not, and you will still require the services of the overlay program you might be using with Win3.1x. Unfortunately, Win95 often interprets the action of the overlay program as an indication that your computer has been infected by a virus. This occurs because the overlay must alter the Master Boot Record on the hard disk to make your drive work. Many viruses do their harm by making destructive changes to the Master Boot Record.

If Win95 pops up a warning saying that your computer may have a virus, you can safely ignore the warning if *both* of the following conditions apply:

1. You are using an overlay program to make a large hard disk work, and...

2. You practice "safe disk" and inspect diskettes you swap (or purchase) with a virus detection and cleanup program such as MacAffee's VIRUSCAN.

You must either find a 32-bit virus detector (MacAffee's is currently 16-bit and must be run from DOS 6.x), or run a virus scan from your previous version of DOS to ensure that your system contains no viruses.

Your other options for using a large EIDE hard disk without heeding Win95's virus message are:

✔ Buy a BIOS upgrade for your motherboard or…

✔ Buy a new EIDE controller card that will directly support EIDE hard disks

Clear the Deck for Win95 SETUP.EXE

Before performing the Win95 install, make certain that your current Windows session is configured to the bare essentials and that you have no other programs or "auto-load" utilities running. Also, turn off any screen savers; you've probably become so accustomed to, say, *After Dark* loading before Program Manager when you start Windows, that you tend to ignore its existence. If you use Adobe Type Manager, shut it off before installing, too.

If you use a third-party desktop manager such as Norton Desktop or Dashboard, switch back to Program Manager before installing Win95 by making sure that the following line is in SYSTEM.INI:

    SHELL=PROGMAN.EXE

If it is not, use a text editor to edit the SHELL= line. Save the file and while you have a text editor open, take a look at WIN.INI. In your WIN.INI file, place a semicolon (;) at the beginning of all lines that begin with RUN= and LOAD= (to remark them out), then save the file. You need to restart Windows to make the changes you made in SYSTEM.INI and WIN.INI take effect.

Before you restart, you should consider changing the video driver you are currently using. To be on the safe side, you should also go to Windows 3.1x Setup (**F**ile, **R**un, SETUP.EXE in Program Manager) and change your video display to VGA. Changing to a less demanding, "vanilla" video driver reduces your chances of installation problems.

When you restart Windows after making the changes to your configuration, and you're confident that everything is in order, you're *almost* ready to install Win95. It's *very* important to actually *read* the READ.ME file on the Win95 installation disks (or CD), along with any last-minute flyers Microsoft may have tucked into the box.

> **➔ Tip** There is a switch you might want to use to ensure that Win95's SETUP.EXE runs without "stumbling" over any third-party, pre-Win95 disk compression programs. In Program Manager's **F**ile, **R**un..., type:
>
> ```
> X:\Setup.exe /is
> ```

Adding the /is switch tells Win95 setup *not* to run ScanDisk before installing. ScanDisk is a new utility you can run within Win95 to check for logical and physical hard disk errors, and it might report a compressed hard disk as a "problem."

Microsoft does not officially condone the **/is** switch, because it might create *other* installation problems, but if you cannot install Win95, this switch is worth a try.

Modifying the MSDOS.SYS to Accept a Dual Boot

There is really nothing intellectually challenging about the Win95 setup. Before installing, you should gather together as much original documentation for your peripherals as possible, because many name brand devices are already listed in Win95 setup. When queried, definitely check Backup in Accessories, System Tools—until Win95-specific backup programs ship from third parties, Win95 Backup is the only program that can archive Win95 files.

> **Stop** Do *not* use a pre-Win95 backup program to back up user files with long file names, or any of the folders or files that Win95 (or any Win95 native application such as CorelDRAW) installs or creates. Doing so may destroy or damage data, and at the very least will make your backup worthless.

After you've recovered from the ocean of new utilities Win95 Setup offers, the most stunning thing about Win95 is that it will configure most peripheral devices such as SCSI cards and fax/modems that pre-date Microsoft "Plug and Play" standards. You no longer need to remember jumper settings and IRQ addresses. However, once you've installed Win95, you might not be able to get to Windows 3.1!

By default, Win95 will begin loading as soon as you power on your PC. If you *don't* want to launch Win95 (and have the option to boot into DOS 6 and Win 3.1), you'll need to make a small change to Win95's MSDOS.SYS. From Windows 95, use a text editor such as Notepad (*not* a word processor), to open MSDOS.SYS (in the root of your boot drive). If an Options section is not already present in the MSDOS.SYS file, create one by typing **[Options]** on a new line. Then type in the following changes in the [Options] section, each addition on its own line, exactly as they appear:

```
[Options]
BootMulti=1
BootMenu=1
BootMenuDefault=1
```

The first line tells the system that it's okay to pause before the operating system loads to allow you to choose a configuration for the machine. The second line provides an on-screen menu with boot options, which you can also access by pressing F8 as soon as the `Starting Windows` message appears during system startup. The third line means that your computer will default to Win95 as the operating system if you don't touch your keyboard within 30 seconds. The value after `BootMenuDefault=` can be changed to any of the following configurations, as shown in the following list:

Normal (Win95)

Logged (\BOOTLOG.TXT)

Safe Mode (Loads Win95 with minimal set of drivers; good for troubleshooting)

Safe Mode with Network Support (If the CD you use to install Win95 is on a network, you might need this configuration if you want to reinstall or update Win95.)

Step-by-step configuration (Allows you to check each line as Win95 is loaded. Also good for troubleshooting.)

Command Prompt Only (This is Win95 without the graphical interface. It might look like DOS 6, but it's actually DOS 7. Don't expect familiar DOS utilities such as EDIT.COM to work.)

Safe Mode Command Prompt Only

Previous Version of DOS (This is the only setting that will allow you to boot into Windows 3.1x.)

Consult the Microsoft Resource Kit, located on the Win95 CD, for a complete set of switches for the Options section of MSDOS.SYS.

After You've Booted...

Regardless of whether you want to keep your previous 16-bit version of Windows or not, you'll probably want some semblance of your previous desktop within which to work. If you've installed over Win 3.1, your program groups and icons will most likely make the transition automatically. You can find them under the Start menu in Win95 (covered later in this chapter). The only thing that would thwart the restoration of program groups is if you've used a third-party shell for Windows (for example, New Wave or Norton Desktop). If you've done so, there are two approaches, one of which requires that you still have a previous version of Win3.1 installed. These two approaches are addressed in the following sections.

Migrating Your Win 3.1 Groups

If you've kept Windows 3.1 on your system as an alternative OS, but have adopted a third-party Program Manager replacement, there is no way to convert third-party program groups to MS Program Manager groups. The easiest way to take every executable program on your hard disk and make a makeshift Program Manager desktop to use in Win95 is described in the following steps.

Restoring Win 3.1 Program Groups

1. In Windows 3.1, from your third-party desktop shell, open NOTEPAD.EXE or SYSEDIT.EXE.

   These are text editors that allow you to change system files without inadvertently introducing text attributes such as formatting and extended characters.

2. Open SYSTEM.INI (located in the WINDOWS subdirectory).

   This is the file that contains information about the Windows desktop.

3. Find the line SHELL=.

   This is SYSTEM.INI's attribute for the graphical interface that appears when Windows 3.1 loads.

4. Type a **;** (a semicolon) at the beginning of this line, then place your cursor at the end of the line and press Enter.

   The ; character remarks out the line so Windows ignores it upon startup; you've created a new, blank line by pressing Enter.

5. Type **SHELL=PROGMAN.EXE** in the blank line.

   Specifies that Windows should load Program Manager instead of your third-party shell.

6. Choose **F**ile, **S**ave, then exit the text editor, and exit Windows.

   You've instructed Windows to load Program Manager the next time you start Windows.

When you want to restore your third-party shell, simply delete the SHELL=PROGMAN .EXE line in SYSTEM.INI, and remove the ; from in front of the SHELL= Whatever Third-Party Shell line, then restart Windows.

7. Launch Windows, and then launch File Manager.

File Manager displays the directory tree of any drive or partition located on your system or a network.

8. Choose a drive from File Manager's drop-down list that contains a lot of executable programs you want to have in a group in Win95.

   Displays the directory tree in the left File Manager window pane, and the list of subdirectories in the right pane.

9. Locate the *.EXE file within a subdirectory for the program you want to move to Win95's Start menu.

   This example uses CorelDRAW version 5.F2. Use any executable program you like.

10. Open and resize a group window so you can see both it and File Manager on the desktop.

    Positions both windows so you can drag-and-drop between them.

11. Click-and-drag the executable file name into the open group window.

    Creates an icon in the group. See figure 1.1.

Figure 1.1

You can quickly copy executable programs to Program Manager Groups by dragging and dropping from File Manager.

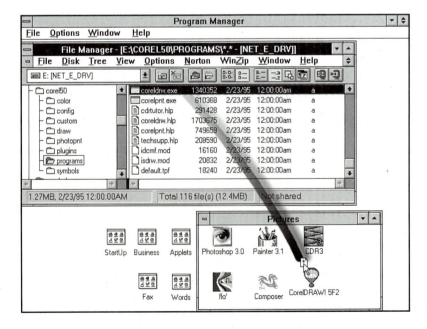

12. Repeat the preceding steps for other programs you want represented in groups in Win95.

Copies the default name and icon to the specified group.

When you're done, change the SYSTEM.INI **shell= line** (if you're running a third-party shell instead of Program Manager), so Windows 3.1x looks and operates exactly as before you read this chapter, and then exit Windows. You can drag programs you want to relocate to other groups into different Program Manager windows, and you can delete possible duplicates by clicking on an icon, then pressing Delete.

Stop Deleting an icon in Windows 3.1 simply deletes a graphic button that starts a program, and has no impact on the executable file that the icon refers to. *Do not* perform this same move to an icon in Win95. Windows 95 is a completely *object-oriented* environment, in which an icon is sometimes a graphical representation of an actual user or program file.

Read the rest of this chapter if you're unsure of whether an icon in Win95 is a *shortcut* (a path to a program) or whether the icon *is* the program.

If you've already installed Win95, the following steps detail how to convert Win 3.1x program groups to Win95 groups, and if you haven't taken the plunge yet, put a bookmark between these pages for immediate reference!

Populating Your Win95 Workspace

In the preceding exercise, you saw how to move CorelDRAW version 5.F2 to a Pictures folder (group), which contains some of the author's favorite graphics programs. The decision to keep the previous version of Corel on your machine isn't such a bad idea if you have the room on your hard disk, because version 5 "communicates" a little more easily with other programs you may have that are still in 16-bit versions than CorelDRAW! 6 does. For example, PageMaker 5 has a little trouble deciphering a Clipboard copy of a CorelDRAW version 6 graphic; on the other hand, a CorelDRAW! 5 graphic drops into a PageMaker or WinWord page without complaints from the host application. "Migration" is key to moving to a totally new program, CorelDRAW! 6, and a completely redesigned operating system.

Coming up is the abbreviated version of the Win95 Quick Tour—a compendium of life, career, and ego-saving tips designed for the graphic artist who is coping with both a new Windows and an expanded CorelDRAW. First, here's how to get the program groups you've arranged in Win 3.1 Program Manager to appear the same way in Win95's Start menu.

Setting Up the Startup Menu

1. In Windows 95, click on the Start button, then move your cursor (do not click) over **F**ind, then click on **F**iles or Folders.

   Displays Windows 95 Find, a global search engine. Win95 menus do not require clicking to expose submenus.

2. On the Name & Location tab, in the **N**amed field, type ***.grp**, then click on the **L**ook in: drop-down menu and choose the drive where Windows 3.1 is located.

   Selects the drive where Windows 3.1 stores Program Manager group information; instructs Find to search for this system file extension.

3. Click on F**i**nd Now.

   Begins search; file names begin to appear in drop-down window.

4. When Find is finished, double-click on a file with the GRP extension in the drop-down window.

   Launches conversion feature and Start Menu Shortcuts dialog box shows status of conversion. DOS programs might surface while trolling for programs and program groups, but if you have a DOS program you need to continue to use under Win95, the most fail-safe method of adding it to the Start menu is to manually add it. Certain DOS programs use the COM extension instead of EXE, and you might wind up with a labeled, empty folder on your Start menu for such a program.

5. Repeat the procedure with every group listed in Find that you want to appear on Win95's Start menu.

Now, every program you wanted arranged in specific groups for use in Win95 is located on the **P**rograms menu, which you access by clicking on the Start button on the Taskbar.

An alternate process, which requires more work, can be performed entirely within Win95. In the next section—as we explore Explorer, and take the Taskbar to task— you'll see how to work with advanced features, and make your desktop highly personal and productive.

An Orientation on Objects

Whether you call it a *model*, a *representation*, or an *icon*, Windows computing has always been based upon the user's acceptance that click-and-dragging something to someplace on the screen results in an *event*. The graphical nature of Windows insulates the user from mind-bending calculations stored in memory and hard disk. But Win 3.1x contains many graphical elements that aren't "live"; the representation of a program as an icon, for example, is merely a *path reference* to the program's executable. In other words, the icon isn't really the program code, and if you delete the icon, you've only deleted a reference to the program.

Use great caution when deleting things in Win95. Objects are actually bundled program code, and an icon of a program or file *is* the graphical representation of the program or file itself. Delete this kind of icon, and you've deleted the file itself, not simply a bitmap graphic that represents a file that is still present on your system.

You create an event when you make a change to a Win95 object.

Path reference icons (*shortcuts*) have a different appearance (little arrows in the corner) than program icons in Win95, and it is far better to create and work with shortcuts than with original file and program icons. A little later in this chapter, you learn about methods for creating shortcuts to "live" hard disk data. Figure 1.2 shows the visual difference between a program icon and a shortcut icon.

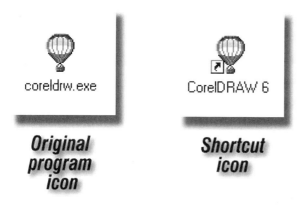

Figure 1.2
The arrow in the lower left of an icon indicates a shortcut, not the original application or file.

coreldrw.exe

Original program icon

CorelDRAW 6

Shortcut icon

Contents, Folders, and the Explorer

Win95 is going to change the terminology most users of previous versions of Windows have grown familiar with. Gone are directories and subdirectories. In their place, you will find *folders*. Folders are for all intents and purposes the same as directories and subdirectories, except that now they may also contain objects *other* than files. A Win95 folder might contain shortcut icons to files that are scattered across different drives or even on network drives. Folders can also contain icons that represent things like printers and modems that you can connect to and use.

Because the graphical metaphors Win95 uses for a hard disk's contents are *objects* and *places*, it can sometimes become confusing when trying to locate a specific file. This is where Win95 Explorer can come in handy.

Explorer is both a name for Win95's graphical shell, and for a program located in the Start menu. Explorer, the program menu, is basically a directory window with a few additional tools you use to get more information about your hard disk and network connections. You can see the same information about your hard disk by double-clicking on the My Computer icon on the desktop, but Microsoft wanted to ensure that—one way or another—users could discover a file structure in Win95.

The Desktop in Win95 is a physical location on your hard disk. When you copy or move an object to the Desktop by click-and-dragging it, you move that object, physically, to the X:\Windows\Desktop folder, where *X* is the letter of the hard disk that contains Win95.

The exception to this "rule" is that many of the icons that Win95 placed on the desktop during installation aren't exactly on the desktop. My Computer, Neighborhood Network, and the Recycle Bin are "hardwired" connections to other views and features of Win95. You should *not* try to delete these icons as you would icons you've copied to the desktop.

> **Tip**   You can, and *should*, however, find new names of less adolescent inspiration than My Computer and Neighborhood Network for your local and network connections. To change the names of these "don't move" objects, click on the name, insert the text cursor, then type the name you prefer.

Different Procedures for a Different Interface

The first thing you'll notice in Win95's Explorer workspace is that the desktop doesn't contain your program groups. Programs, documents you've recently modified, system tools, and Help information are all *nested* within the Start menu. Actions relating to running programs and accessing files begin by clicking on the Start button.

You can quickly access the shortcut options in Win95's context-sensitive menus by right-clicking on any object on the Desktop. For example, if you right-click over My Computer on the desktop, you'll see options relevant to this icon, as shown in figure 1.3.

My Computer contains a list of local and network connections, Control Panel, and printer connections. Therefore, the Options menu offers network mapping, options for opening the "place" called My Computer, and properties. You'll notice that, where appropriate, Cut, Copy, and Paste commands are available on some icons' shortcut menu; you can copy a file from a hard disk view as easily as copying a selected object from within CorelDRAW using the right mouse button menu; everything is an object in the Win95 environment. *Properties* is a new feature supported by programs designed for

Win95, and as a native Win95 application, CorelDRAW! 6 supports this feature within the program. If you need to find out quickly what something is or does, or you want to change the settings for an object, go to its property sheet by choosing Properties from the shortcut options menu.

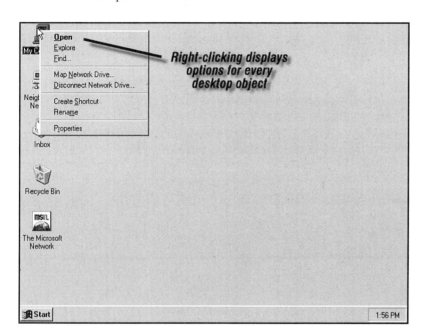

Figure 1.3
Right-click on any object on the desktop to display the shortcut options menu.

You'll also notice that the right mouse button menu contains Open and Explore commands. We'll get to what *exploring* means in a moment, but opening an object can still be performed in Win95 the same way as you would do in Windows 3.1x—you double-click on the icon.

Customizing Win95's Explorer

Explorer is Microsoft's name for the graphical shell for Win95. Although users who are completely confused and unhappy with the new Explorer interface can display the familiar Windows 3.1x Program Manager shell by changing a line in Win95's SYSTEM.INI file—substituting SHELL=PROGMAN.EXE for the SHELL=EXPLORER.EXE—that change is not recommended. You'd be ill-advised to do this because native Win95 applications will be "looking" for Explorer upon Setup.

Still, there are a lot of things you can do to the Explorer interface to organize it in a way you're comfortable with, and take advantage of file management capabilities to make your work an inspired task.

Refining the Taskbar

The Taskbar in Win95 is sort of a "persistent state" Task List, which was Windows 3.1x's menu of applications that are active in a Windows session. You can still work your way through active applications by pressing Alt+Tab (a process called *cool-switching*) to bring up a different foreground application, but the Taskbar, by default, is always present within an application, so you might not want to cool-switch. However, the Taskbar takes up room that you might prefer to use for something else, and although you can't remove it from the Explorer shell, you can make it less obtrusive.

The following exercise shows how to customize the Taskbar.

Accessing the Taskbar Options

1. Right-click on the Taskbar.

   Displays a shortcut options menu.

2. Click on Properties.

   Displays a tabbed window of Taskbar Options.

3. Uncheck the Always on Top check box (see fig. 1.4).

   Allows a program to open full-screen, without a view of the Taskbar.

4. Click on OK.

   Closes the Taskbar Properties menu and returns you to the Explorer shell.

Notice that the other tabbed menu in Properties is Start Menu Programs. This is where you can adjust Win95's Start menu, a feature covered next.

 If you hover your cursor above the Taskbar clock, it displays the date in a pop-up box.

 You can move the Taskbar to any side of the desktop by click-and-dragging. Desktop icons automatically move out of the way of the Taskbar's position.

We've covered the migration of program groups from Win 3.1 to Win95, but you'll probably add *more* programs and groups after the upgrade. The next section shows the ins and outs of creating shortcuts, making new groups, and moving ones like Corel 6 to the Start menu location of your choice.

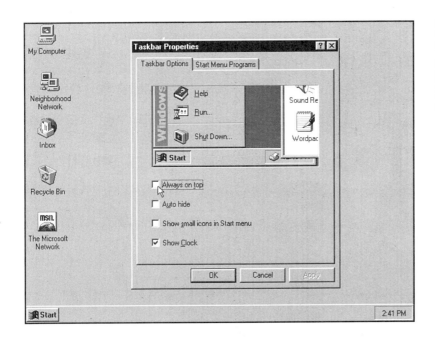

Figure 1.4
Uncheck the Always
on top check box to
keep the Taskbar
from intruding on
open applications.

Customizing Win95's Start Menu

Because Win95 generally enforces the routine of installing programs through the Add/Remove Programs feature in Control Panel, you have very little say in exactly what group, or nested group, a program is located. Although setup programs are sometimes *written* to prompt you for a program group of your choosing, experienced users know that this almost never happens.

In figure 1.5, you can see how the installation of several new applications has created a visual mess of the Start menu. The randomness of program location is compounded by the reality that Win95 lists groups and subgroups in alphabetical order, and 16×16 pixel Start menu icons are *not* a clear indicator of a program or group.

Win95 routinely "dumps" every program folder and subfolder into the Program folder on the Start menu. However, you can change this by creating a Start folder of your own. The following exercise shows you how to create a unique, private space on the Start menu—a space you can build upon, that's easy to branch from, and from which you can launch the applications you use most often.

The following exercise shows how to add a practical, personalized folder structure for the Start menu.

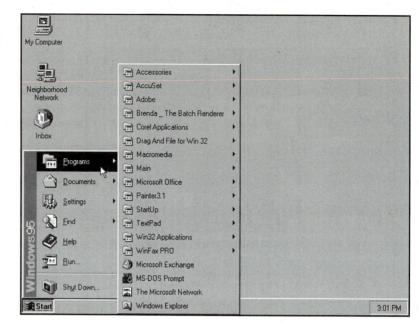

Figure 1.5
There is little or no
user input as to the
order in which
Win95 displays
program groups on
the Start menu.

Adding an Artist's Submenu

1. Right-click on the Taskbar.

   Displays a shortcut menu relating to the Taskbar.

2. Choose P**r**operties, click on the Start Menu Programs tab, then click on
   A**d**vanced.

   Opens the Start menu for exploration (editing).

3. Right-click in the right pane of the window, beneath Programs.

   Displays a context-sensitive menu for the blank space in the window pane.

Because every square inch of Win95 is "live"—it's an object—the context-sensitive
shortcut menu gives you options for what you'd like to do with this empty area beneath
the Programs folder (the submenu in the Start menu). Hint: you're going to fill this
blank space with a program folder of your own!

4. Move your cursor (don't click) to Ne**w**, then click on **F**older (see fig. 1.6).

   Creates a new icon, entitled New Folder, within the pane that represents the
   Start menu's contents.

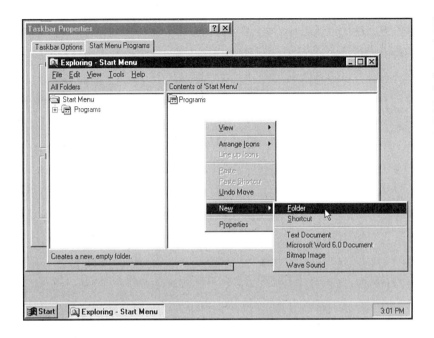

Figure 1.6
You can add to a folder's contents by choosing New from the pop-up menu, or you can drag-and-drop objects into a folder.

5. Type **Design Toolkit** (or any evocative name), then click on the icon to the left of the new title.

   You rename a folder (directory) when you type a different name in the highlighted text next to an icon.

Because the word **Design** alphabetically precedes **Programs**, you've "forced" your private program folder to the top of the Start menu.

6. Double-click on the **Design Toolkit** icon (not the name).

   This sends the Design Toolkit icon to the left window; the right window now represents the contents of Design Toolkit, which is empty because you haven't added tools yet.

Double-clicking on a folder title can sometimes highlight the title instead of moving to a view of a folder's contents, so make sure you create an event with an icon, and not its title.

7. Right-click in the right pane, choose Ne**w**, then **F**older.

   New Folder and its icon appear in the right window pane. This folder will appear as nested within the Design Toolkit folder on the Start menu.

The New Folder title is highlighted, which means you can now type in a new name.

8. Type **Utilities**.

Names the subfolder.

In the next section, you'll see how to copy and move applications to folders you've created for the Start menu.

Copying and Moving Programs

Earlier in this chapter, the term *shortcut* was used to describe a path reference to an application or file. Now that you have a group folder at your disposal for programs arranged the way you want them, it's time to populate the Design Toolkit folder. The Start menu's folders are okay to move, because the program files contained within the Start folders are shortcuts (path references to a program), and not the actual executable program. You can also copy program shortcuts.

For this example, Brenda—The Batch Renderer, a shareware utility included on the *CorelDRAW! 6 Expert's Edition Bonus CD*, is moved from its installation location of the Program folder to the Design Toolkit's Utilities folder. If you haven't installed Brenda, feel free to substitute an application to which you want easy access in the following example.

Setting Up a Design Toolkit

1. Click on the + to the left of the Programs folder.

   This expands your view of the Program folder's contents.

2. Click on the + to the left of the Design Toolkit folder.

   This expands your view of the Design Toolkit's contents. You should be able to see the Utilities folder now in the left window pane.

3. Choose a folder that you'd like nested under your Utilities folder.

   The folder's contents will branch from Utilities on the Start menu.

4. Drag the folder on top of the Utilities folder, then drop it.

   The folder you've chosen is moved to the Design Toolkit\Utilities folder (see fig. 1.7).

New folder names behave a little differently than existing folder names. New folders come into existence with highlighted text. "Brenda—The Batch Renderer" is a good, yet ponderously long name to appear in the Start menu. Here's how to edit an existing name and correct the problem...

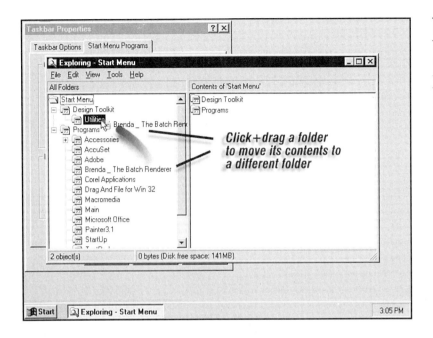

Figure 1.7

To move a Start menu folder (group) of programs to a nest within a different folder, click-and-drag to the new location.

5. Click on the Utilities' + sign.

    Expands the Utilities folder to display its contents

6. Single-click on the "Brenda…" title, then single-click in the highlighted text.

    Opens the title for editing. A box a single pixel wide surrounds the highlighted name.

7. Type a shorter name in the highlighted text, then click on the folder icon.

    Renames the (group) folder; closes the text box (protects from further or accidental editing). See figure 1.8.

While you're in the Start menu Explorer window, suppose that you want to copy Word for Windows to the Design Toolkit, leaving the original shortcut in the Programs folder. Follow these steps…

8. Click on the Microsoft Office folder.

    Opens the folder to display the program shortcut icons within the folder in the contents (right pane) window.

9. Press Ctrl while you click-and-drag the Microsoft Word shortcut icon to its new location in a subfolder under Design Toolkit in the left window pane (see fig. 1.9).

Figure 1.8

A thin box around an icon's title indicates that the name is available for editing.

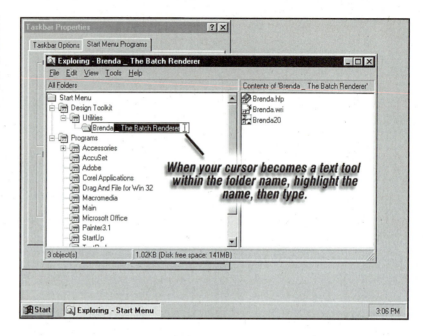

Copies the shortcut to a different folder.

Repeat any of the steps in this example to organize and populate your new Start menu folder.

Figure 1.9

The plus sign next to a cursor indicates that you're copying a folder, file, or program.

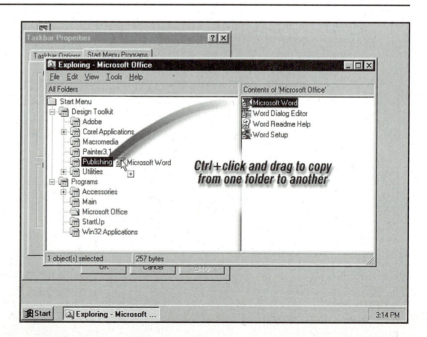

In the preceding exercise, you learned that any graphical object could be copied or moved to a different location in the Start menu. User files, such as CorelDRAW (*.CDR) designs, folders containing shortcuts, and shortcuts to programs are all legitimate targets for Start menu editing. Take care, however, not to copy an actual application icon. There is very little reason to copy an executable file; programs generally have associated files (such as a Dynamic Link Library—a *DLL*) and *.INI files that look for a specific program's physical location on your hard disk. Without the support files, an "orphaned" executable may not launch the program. And if you *move* an executable, your program will not run.

Always look for the tiny arrow in the lower left of an icon to make sure the icon is a shortcut, not an actual file, before you relocate it.

Re-Ordering the Appearance of Start Menu Items

Although the Start menu insists on displaying folders in descending alphabetical order, you can change the order in which a folder appears by renaming it. This is why Design Toolkit is a good name for your private stash of programs; "Programs" can be preceded by any folder name beginning with "A" through "P." Sometimes, however, you want to preserve the name of a program or folder.

The following example illustrates how you can precede a folder name with a single character to force it to display at the top of your Start menu list. For this example, suppose that you've already installed Corel 6, and you want the group of applications to appear at the top of your Design Toolkit list of groups.

Changing the Order of Program Folders

1. Right-click the Start button and choose **E**xplore. In the Start menu Explorer window, single-click on the Corel Applications title (or other name) in the left window pane.

   Opens the title for editing.

2. Click on the highlighted text, insert the text tool at the beginning of the folder name, highlight the entire name, then type **!Corel6.**

   Shortens the name of the folder; the ! forces the group to the top of the Design Toolkit list (see fig. 1.10).

Figure 1.10
Special characters can "force" an application to the top of a folder list.

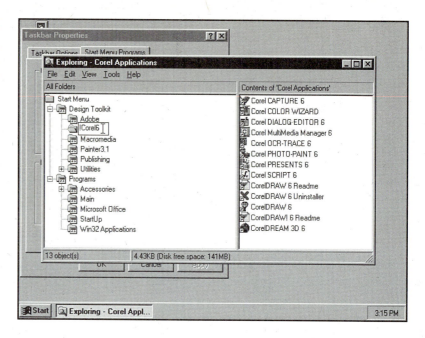

As you can see in figure 1.11, the "!Corel6" program subfolder now is at the top of the Design Toolkit's list. In this example, you could have created an "Acorel6" subfolder that still would appear before the Adobe subfolder, but at the price of quickly and easily identifying the programs.

Figure 1.11
Strive to keep subfolder names short, and create a different order for them by editing their names.

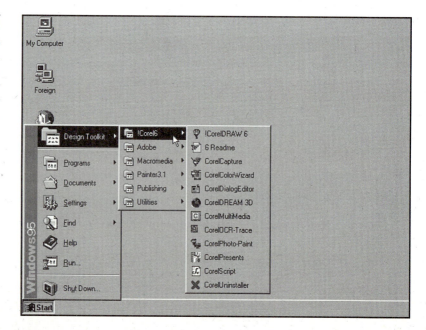

In addition to letters and numbers, punctuation marks can be used in Win95 to change the order of names as they appear in the Start menu. However, the following characters are reserved for Windows' use, and cannot be used in folder names, Start menu names, or file names:

\	(backslash)
:	(Semicolon)
*	(Asterisk)
?	(Question Mark)
"	(Double-quote; inches)
<	(Less than)
>	(Greater than)
|	(Pipe)

As mentioned earlier, everything is an object on the desktop, including the desktop itself. The next section covers the settings you can make with just a simple right-click on your Windows wallpaper to change the way you view Windows and your programs.

Changing Monitor Settings in Win95

Windows 3.1's Desktop and Colors Control Panel settings have merged with a few other features to make up the Desktop Display Properties menu in Win95. If you need to load a different video driver (to change the screen or color resolution) or you simply want a desktop wallpaper other than the one Win95 provides, a right-click on the desktop is your starting point.

The following example shows you how to customize Win95's appearance.

Changing Desktop Settings

1. On the Win95 desktop right-click, then choose P**r**operties.

   Calls the Display Properties tabbed menu.

2. On the Background menu, scroll in the **W**allpaper list until you see a preview of a design you'd like displayed on the desktop, then click on **A**pply.

   Changes the wallpaper to the design of your choice (see fig. 1.12).

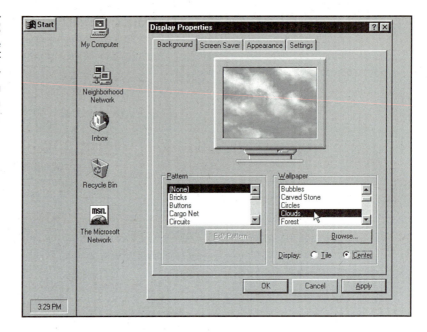

Figure 1.12
You can change the
appearance of
Win95's desktop by
choosing a
wallpaper, or pattern
bitmap.

Alternatively, you can choose Browse to search for an image located in a folder (directory) other than Win95. The image should be the size of your video display (for example, 640×480, 800×600), and ideally, should consist of an indexed, 256-color bitmap. All wallpaper candidates must be saved in Windows BMP format.

Win95 also ships with screen savers, and you can load one by clicking on the Screen Savers tab of the Display Properties menu. Screen savers, Microsoft's or those manufactured by third parties, can amuse coworkers, provide marginal system privacy while you're away, and help prevent screen burn-in if your system is unattended for more than an hour at a clip.

Note The notion that modern monitors don't suffer from screen burn-in is a myth; the author has a Sony Trinitron monitor hooked to a network server that was left inactive, displaying Program Manager for approximately two weeks, and the monitor now displays "ghosting."

Sony is not to be singled out for this problem; in fact, many different monitor brands can suffer screen burn-in.

Screen savers, therefore, serve a legitimate, although somewhat limited use in your business life, but if you choose to use one, make certain this feature is turned off before installing programs. A screen saver that "kicks in" during a program setup will cause conflict between the two programs, and the setup may fail to install the program properly.

Win95's desktop color scheme is displayed in every program. If you intend to work in CorelDRAW or any other program for hours on end, it might be a good idea to set a scheme, or create one, that's relaxing on the eyes. Or you might want a monochrome color scheme to remove the possibility of colors outside of your document influencing your color perception of the document. You also might be running programs on a notebook system whose colors don't display enough contrast. The following short example shows how to create a different color scheme for title bars, highlighted text, windows, and message boxes.

Defining/Selecting a Color Scheme

1. Click on the Appearance tab of the Display Properties menu.

   Displays the controls for choosing and modifying a color scheme for Windows and applications.

2. Click on the **S**cheme drop-down list, then scroll down.

   Displays a list of pre-defined color schemes.

3. Click on a pre-defined scheme. If you like it, click on Apply. If not, continue.

   Displays the color scheme in the proxy window at the top of the menu. See figure 1.13.

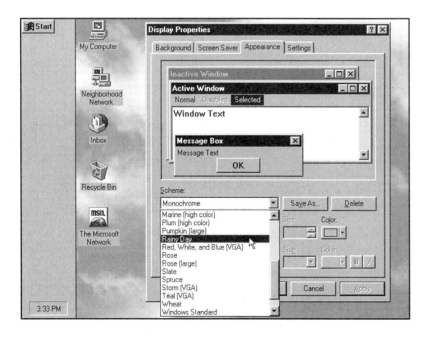

Figure 1.13
Win95 ships with several preset color schemes that can be used with a variety of computers and display systems.

You don't commit to a different color scheme until you click on **A**pply, so take your time in selecting screen colors. Some of the presets are defined for VGA (16 color) video drivers. Schemes such as teal display terribly when running TrueColor, which is what you should be running when working in CorelDRAW, so if you're fond of the color teal, follow the next steps to create your own desktop color scheme...

4. Click on the proxy window area with "Active Window" text inside it.

   This selects the title bars in Win95 as the target for color change. The **I**tem field in the Display Properties menu shows that you've selected the Active Title Bar for color change.

5. Click on the Co**l**or drop-down list, and choose a different color.

   Changes the proxy windows display to reflect the change you propose to the current color scheme.

6. Repeat the last two steps with as many areas of the proxy window as you like, then click on Sa**v**e As, and enter a name for your color scheme.

   Win95 records your color scheme and enters it in the **S**cheme list.

Many users accept Windows' default color scheme settings, which is usually fine for a lot of black-text-on-white word processing. As you work extensively in CorelDRAW and other graphics programs, however, you'll find that you eventually get eye fatigue. It's a good idea to set your color scheme to a collection of neutral shades that don't resonate with the colorful work you're creating. Rainy Day and Slate are two color scheme presets that won't distract you from your work and would never be considered the visual equivalent of caffeine.

Changing Display Settings

The Display Properties dialog box has a tab marked "Settings" that's perhaps the most important of the display qualities you have control over. Unlike Win 3.1x, changing video drivers is *not* performed by a proprietary OEM (Original Equipment Manufacturers) program or through Win Setup; adjustments to monitor resolution and color depth are both performed on the Settings menu, and in many cases, the video driver swap is performed instantly.

If, for some reason, your video driver is displaying inadequate color depth, or you have a 21" monitor displaying a 640×480 pixel desktop, here's an example that shows how to change monitor settings...

I

Changing Monitor Resolution

1. Right-click on the desktop, choose P**r**operties from the shortcut menu, then click on the Settings tab of the Display Properties menu.

   Displays the controls for your monitor's video drivers.

2. If True Color (32-bit) or (24-bit) is not the choice in the **C**olor palette drop-down list, click on the down arrow, then select it from the list.

   Selects the color depth your monitor should display.

If TrueColor (24-bit or 32-bit) is not available for your monitor, there could be one of two reasons for this: your screen resolution (**D**esktop area) is set too high, or Win95 didn't detect the appropriate video driver upon install. Screen resolution and color depth are directly proportional to the amount of VRAM on your system's video card. If your video card has 1 MB or less of VRAM, TrueColor display at resolutions higher than 640×480 are not possible. Alternatively, you may have to install your card's video drivers to access a higher color mode. Try the following:

3. Click-and-drag the desktop area slider to the left (see fig. 1.14).

   Decreases the screen resolution; you may now have the option to display higher color capabilities on your monitor.

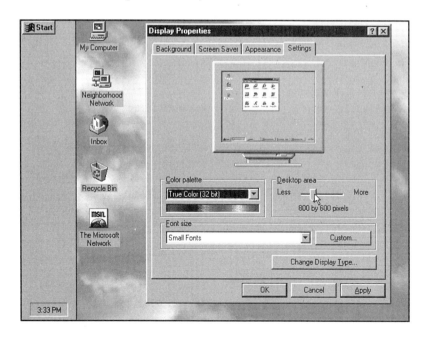

Figure 1.14

You control the size and color depth of your display by changing the Display Properties Settings.

If you are still limited to an inadequate choice of display palettes and resolutions, you might have to install new video card drivers. Check the manufacturer's bulletin board, Internet site, or online service for the latest ones, then if you've determined that it's your only option for increasing display properties...

4. Click on C**h**ange to the right of **A**dapter Type, then click on the Show **a**ll devices radio button.

   Tells Win95 to search in its own directory for a configuration for your card. The Select Device dialog box is then displayed.

The preceding step is a "last hope" measure to avoid having to reinstall a video driver. Microsoft has an extensive, although not complete, collection of compatible drivers from most video cards. If you fail to find your card listed here...

5. Click on **H**ave Disk, then choose **B**rowse, specify the path in the Install From Disk dialog box to the location of your video drivers.

   Shows the setup program where your video card's drivers are located.

6. Select the screen resolution and color depth of your choice in the Select Device dialog box, then click on OK.

   Win95 installs the video card's drivers.

➡Tip Many peripheral manufacturers maintain a number of online sites where you can obtain the latest drivers for their products. Check the CorelDRAW! 6 Expert's Edition Resource Guide (the Acrobat document RESOURCE.PDF on the Bonus CD) for a list of mailing addresses, phone numbers, and online sites for most of the major manufacturers of video cards and other devices. Always keep an eye on these sites for new drivers. Using the latest drivers ensures the best possible Win95 compatibility for programs and peripherals.

Your **M**onitor Type is also listed in the Display Properties Settings menu, and if the specific make and model of monitor you use is not listed here, you're fairly safe selecting a generic SVGA 800×600 type if your monitor was purchased in the past two years. Additionally, at high screen resolutions, you might want to display larger-than-average screen fonts. To do this (on the Settings menu), click on C**u**stom to the right of **F**ont Size, then click-and-drag the ruler to set a font size with which you're comfortable.

Most individuals who use a PC for professional purposes generate a lot of files on any given day, and the key to successful delivery of said files is being able to locate and manage them! In the next section, you'll take a look at Win95's directory structure, and alternative methods for accessing your hard disk more effectively.

Alternative File and Program Management

It seems as though the more seasoned we get as computer people, the more we resist change. This is a charitable way of saying that folks who are comfortable with Win 3.1 conventions might not like the "folder/object" metaphor that Explorer now presents us with!

Fortunately, Microsoft has made provisions for diehard fans of the previous Windows interface, and many third-party manufacturers have designed Explorer enhancements to keep users oriented and productive. This chapter examines the alterations you can make to the Explorer interface to make it a more productive place.

Navigating a Folder Window

Because subdirectories and files are now in nested folders, you might suffer some serious screen congestion while rummaging through nests to find a file. Win95's defaults for displaying drive windows might not be the most efficient for your work methodology, so the following example provides you with options for changing the defaults.

Here's a quick walkthrough that concentrates upon folder options that you can take advantage of.

Folder Viewing Options

1. On the Win95 desktop, double-click on My Computer.

   Opens the My Computer folder to display its contents.

2. Double-click on a drive icon in the My Computer window.

   Opens a drive to display its contents.

3. On the drive menu, choose View, then click on **D**etails.

   Minimizes the icons of the folders and programs, and arranges them in a column, more reminiscent of File Manager.

4. On the drive menu, choose **V**iew, Arrange **I**cons, then click on by **N**ame.

   Lists the contents of the drive in alphabetical order (see fig. 1.15).

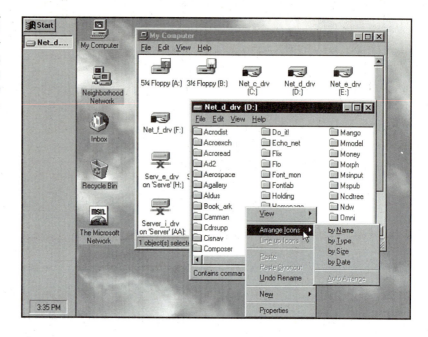

Figure 1.15
You can change your view of a hard disk's contents by choosing options from the View menu.

Alternatively, you can right-click in an empty area of a folder window to display menu options on the ubiquitous shortcut menu.

When you progressively open nested folders to locate a specific file, you can leave an excess of unused windows on your desktop. Here's how to fix this…

5. Choose **V**iew, **O**ptions from the hard disk Window (**O**ptions is not on the shortcut menu).

   Displays a tabbed Options menu with the Folder tab presented by default.

6. Click on the radio button labeled Browse folders using a si**n**gle window that changes as you open each folder.

   Changes the display on the desktop of folders from nested to a single foreground folder that changes to reflect the current folder's contents.

7. Click on **A**pply, then click on OK.

   Confirms and activates your choice. You will have only a single folder window open on the desktop until you care to change this option.

Naturally, with the single folder option activated, you can't drag-and-drop to copy and move files and folders between windows, but you can always copy and move by right-clicking on a window object and choosing **C**opy or Cu**t** from the pop-up menu. You'd then switch to the target window folder, then right-click and choose **P**aste.

> **Tip** Don't forget that folder windows include a toolbar, which is not displayed by default when you open a window. You can copy, paste, delete a file, and so on by clicking on the Toolbar icons. To display the Toolbar, choose **V**iew, **T**oolbar from the window menu.

Remember File Manager?

Most of us weren't thrilled with File Manager's inflexibility, and many Windows 3.1x users augmented their desktops with shell replacements such as Norton Desktop. However, it could never be said that WINFILE.EXE didn't provide a quick and self-explanatory visualization of a drive's contents.

Microsoft has included a semi-optimized File Manager in Win3.1, and the next example shows you how to add File Manager to your desktop so you can access and arrange hard disk information in Win95 in more than one way.

Win 3.1 File Management in Win95

1. Double-click on My Computer on the desktop, then double-click on the drive folder where Win95 is located.

   Opens the Win95 folder to display program files and other contents

2. Find WINFILE.EXE in the Win95 folder.

   This is the executable file that runs File Manager.

2. Hold Ctrl+Shift, then click-and-drag the WINFILE folder onto the desktop.

   The Ctrl and Shift keys create a shortcut to the file you've dragged (see fig. 1.16); a shortcut menu appears.

You don't have to use any key combinations to cause executable files to create shortcuts. An EXE file automatically creates shortcuts when you drag it to the desktop. But holding Shift+Ctrl is a good practice to get into while you're experimenting with the new OS. Why? Because a non-executable file, such as a CorelDRAW user file (your favorite design piece, for example) is automatically moved to the desktop unless you hold Ctrl+Shift. To finalize your shortcut to File Manager…

3. Click on Create **S**hortcut(s) Here on the shortcut menu.

   The familiar File Manager icon, with a shortcut arrow in its lower left corner, appears on the desktop, with the title "Shortcut to Winfile.exe."

Figure 1.16
A path reference (shortcut) is created when you drag-and-drop a file while holding Shift+Ctrl.

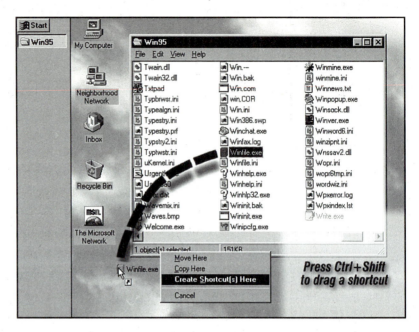

4. Click inside the File Manager icon's title, then type **FileMan**, or some other name you like.

   Shortens the title, improves recognition of it at a glance.

5. Click on the icon to close the icon's title.

   Ensures that you don't accidentally continue typing in the icon title.

As you can see in figure 1.17, Win95's presentation of File Manager offers an "at home" familiarity that experienced users can immediately put to work. Long file names and right-click shortcuts are not supported from this view of your hard disk, however; WINFILE.EXE is a 16-bit application.

An Alternative Program Manager

If you are working with program icons the size of a flyspeck on-screen, and you believe that a "program launcher" should confine its capabilities to launching programs, you might want to consider a "Program Manager *helper*." It's unwise to remove the Start menu from Win95's desktop (by specifying SHELL=PROGMAN.EXE in SYSTEM.INI); you miss out on right-button shortcuts, long file names, and Microsoft tools that were installed to Startup during Win95 Setup.

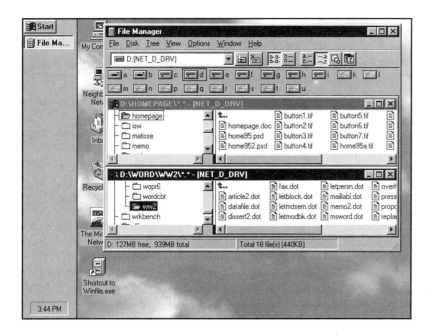

Figure 1.17

Whether you call it a tree or a nested folder, when you need access to your data, File Manager is a trusted standby.

But you can *add*, not replace, easy accessibility to programs through the use of a third-party shell. The ClySmic icon bar, a shareware Program Manager, is on the Bonus CD, and it's yours to evaluate for 30 days for free. The ClySmic icon bar was written for a 32-bit operating system such as Win95 and Windows NT. From the ClySmic icon bar menu (see fig. 1.18), you can access programs and nested program groups from the desktop at all times. The menu can be configured to disappear when you're in an application, and you can cool-switch to it from any program. You can also configure ClySmic to display horizontally or vertically along the edge of the desktop.

To modify any and all options on the ClySmic icon bar, you simply click on the Main menu icon on the top of the icon bar. In figure 1.18, you can see that the controls for adding programs and configuring the icon bar are exceptionally straightforward. Is it as functional as Win95's Start menu? No, but your applications are right there in front of you, represented by adult-sized icons, and you can launch a program by dragging and dropping a file onto a program on the icon bar.

Other Program Manager/File Manager programs are being introduced by third-party vendors, and you should soon have the option to go with Microsoft's vision of file and program management, or pick from a crop of programs that might address your personal tastes and needs. You spend a lot of time in front of your computer; you should make it as attractive, inspiring, and as well-organized as a real life, physical desktop.

Figure 1.18
The ClySmic icon bar happily co-exists with Win95's Start menu, at a minimum of screen "real estate."

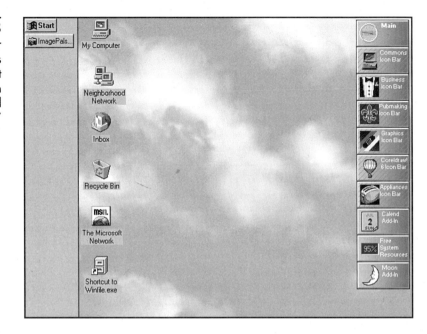

Figure 1.19
Simple, straightforward program launching is something to look for in a Win95 Start menu augmentation program.

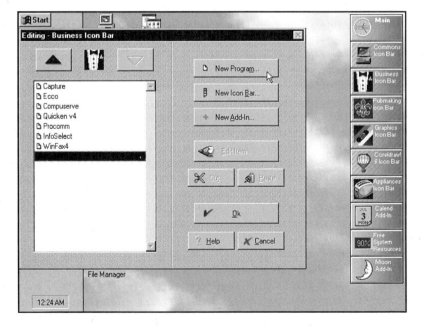

Win95 Options That Affect Your Work Indirectly

Up to this point, the chapter has concentrated on the ways you can ensure a successful setup, and configure Win95 to meet you at least half way in your quest for more powerful computing. There are a few loose ends that need to be tied up before proceeding to Chapter 2, "Customizing CorelDRAW!," however. We've yet to address this new Recycle Bin on your desktop, how long file names can ruin your day, or put a few new and old shortcuts at the tip of your fingers. This section takes you on a tour of things in Win95 that can have an impact on your work, even if you think you're not using them.

In the Macintosh World, It's Called a "Trash" Icon

And in the OS/2 World, folks call it the Shredder—the icon that you drop folders into, never to return. Microsoft, like the other players in graphical operating systems, has seen the need in this Windows version to offer a program that *sort of* deletes files and folders you feel you no longer need on your system.

The Recycle Bin is a permanent fixture on the desktop; by default, any object that's dropped in here is no longer listed from any view of your hard disk. The object is not necessarily *deleted*, mind you, because you haven't *emptied* the Recycle Bin.

The Recycle Bin is occasionally a lifesaver; by conditioning yourself to drop an unwanted folder in it, you're assured that if you change your mind, you can retrieve it, even after you've restarted Win95 within the next day or week.

How does such a modern miracle work? It's really quite simple—Win95 "tricks" the way you see the contents of your hard disk. A percentage of your hard disk is reserved for items you've tossed out. You won't see discarded folders from a view of Win95's folder Windows or Explorer; they're kept hidden from view until you decide you need them. When the percentage you set on a hard disk for Recycle Bin items has been exceeded, Win95 will start to overwrite "the bottom of the barrel"—the oldest files still kept in the Recycle Bin.

Despite its terminal cuteness, Recycle Bin might play an important part of your Win95 computing experience, particularly if you've used previous versions of Windows, and own any file-recovery programs. In a nutshell, 16-bit applications that address DOS directly in terms of file recovery *don't work* under Win95; even DOS 6.2's Undelete won't retrieve a file you've deleted, because Win95 uninstalls this program during Win95 Setup. Given the structure and order of the new Win95 operating system, applications have to have a pretty good excuse to "talk" directly to hardware. Very few exceptions are granted by Microsoft to manufacturers who want their applications to "trick" Win95, and still qualify to display the Win95 logo on the package.

Evaluate your work practices seriously before reading the next example on how to change the settings for the Recycle Bin. If you're the type who deletes things somewhat impetuously, you're best off leaving the Recycle Bin settings the way they are (or even increasing the Recycle's saved percentage). On the other hand, if you value hard disk space, and don't purge files until your client has retired, read on to learn how to optimize disk space and dispense with the waste can.

The following exercise shows how to customize Win95's Recycle Bin's properties.

Breaking a Vicious Cycle

1. On the Win95 desktop, right-click on the Recycle Bin, then choose Properties from the shortcut menu.

   Displays the Recycle Bin Properties menu.

2. On the Global tab, click on the Use one setting for all drives radio button.

   Instructs Win95 to use the same settings for all drives.

3. Click on the Do not move files to the Recycle Bin… check box.

   Files are now actually deleted when you delete them (see fig. 1.20).

4. Click on Apply, then click on OK.

   Confirms your changes; closes the Recycle Bin Properties dialog box.

Again, if you need a "waystation" for files on their way off your system, you shouldn't perform the previous exercise. However, the responsibility is yours to "take out the trash" regularly, to ensure that the specified hard disk(s) don't become too congested with files marked for deletion.

You'll notice that if the Recycle Bin is active, the dialog box you see when you delete a file says that Win95 is moving files to the Recycle Bin; this is true whether you drag-and-drop files directly into the Bin, click on the "x" button on a folder window menu with a file highlighted, or press the Delete key with a file, or several files, selected. Additionally, the Recycle Bin icon changes when it's active—you'll see little crumpled papers at the top of the wastebasket picture.

If you keep the Bin active, a natural question arises: how much stuff can I toss in the Recycle Bin? By default, each hard disk's Recycle Bin takes up 10% of the free space. It's not a good idea to change this setting, although Win95 offers you the opportunity. The amount and the quality of free hard disk space changes during the course of an average work session: files are deleted, new ones are added, and files become fragmented as they are written to different sectors of your hard disk's platters. If you allocate, say, 50% of the free space on a hard disk to Recycle Bin contents, your programs will run sluggishly because they can't freely access disk space to write temp files. You might also run *out* of free disk space; it's far better to practice your own file management than to let the Recycle Bin become your foremost application!

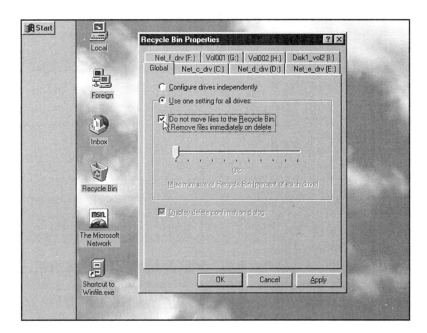

Figure 1.20
You can make the deletion of a file a permanent one by turning off the Recycle Bin.

Working with Associations and Open with Commands

The Windows 3.1x Registry and its editor, REGEDIT.EXE, might have been familiar to a lot of users as a method of building and breaking associations with programs. Say, for example, that program X is installed, and that it works with TIF images. Part of program X's Setup routine, therefore, writes a line in the Registry, causing Program X to launch when you double-click on a file with a TIF extension.

Double-clicking on a file icon is a common way of indirectly launching a program and getting down to business, but Win95's program Registry is a lot harder to use when you want to link a substitute program to handle a particular file type. Fortunately, there are two easy, graphical ways of changing the association of a file type in Win95, and one very "quick fix" for determining which program opens a file.

Using the Open With and File Type Commands

The Open With command is your best choice for changing the type of file that launches a host program, but this is not the same as changing a file extension *association*. The distinction between the two is somewhat nebulous—the only discernible difference is the way the file icon is displayed in a folder.

A perfect example of an application that writes associations to every possible bitmap file type is PHOTO-PAINT! 6, which opens TIF, PCX, GIF, Targa, and a host of other bitmap image types. PHOTO-PAINT! 6 claims the honor for opening TIF, PCX, GIF, Targa, and a host of other bitmap image types. The reason for this is that Corel Corporation makes the presumption that the average user owns only PHOTO-PAINT as a bitmap editor, and therefore any PCX, TIF, and so on file type would be orphaned on your hard disk without the PHOTO-PAINT association. This generosity can sometimes get in your way, however. Suppose you want to quickly view a Targa (TGA) image without taking the time to load PHOTO-PAINT; you have a shareware utility such as PaintShop Pro installed and want to use it instead. And suppose you're accustomed to double-clicking on an icon to open an image.

In order to make a link to PaintShop Pro instead of PHOTO-PAINT when you double-click on a file icon, you can perform the steps in the following exercise.

Creating an Open-With Link

Because the method of creating a file-type link—shown in this exercise—launches the application you've chosen and displays the file, be sure to choose a small image.

1. Open a Folder window that contains TIF file types.

   The TIF extension is the example file type used here; however, you can substitute a file of your own choosing.

If your file icons don't display a file extension, choose **V**iew, **O**ptions from the folder window menu, click on the View tab, then uncheck the Hide MS-DOS file **e**xtensions… check box, click on **A**pply, then click on OK.

2. Shift+right-click on a file whose extension is *.TIF.

   Displays a special shortcut menu.

It is only when you hold the Shift key that the shortcut menu you display by right-clicking contains the Op**e**n With command.

3. Choose Op**e**n With.

Displays the Open With dialog box.

4. Scroll down the program window until you find a host application you want to use to open the TIF image, then click on it.

   Selects the program used to open the *.TIF image.

5. Click on the Always **u**se this program to open this type of file check box.

   Specifies that Win95 should always launch the chosen application to view a TIF file type.

If the host program you seek isn't in the program window, click on O**t**her, then browse your hard disk for the application you want.

6. Click on OK.

   The program you've specified will now open and display the TIF image you selected.

The actual launching of an application to view the TIF image is an inconvenience—the price you pay for creating a "down and dirty" link. The following exercise illustrates a more "correct" way to make and break associations in Win95.

The following exercise describes the way to make associations, remove others, specify the privileges a host program has over a file (such as Open, Save, Copy), and how to change the icon a user file displays.

Making File Associations

1. In an open folder window, click on a TIF image icon (or other file type of your choosing).

   Highlights the icon and selects the file.

2. Choose **V**iew, then **O**ptions from the folder window menu.

   Displays the Options tabbed menu.

3. Click on the File Types tab, scroll down until you see CorelPHOTO-PAINT 6.0 Image on the list, click on it, then click on Remove (see fig. 1.21).

   Displays an attention box telling you that committing to this action will prevent launching the associated application by double-clicking.

4. Click on OK.

   The file association between PHOTO-PAINT (or other application) is removed.

Figure 1.21
You can remove the
association between
an application and a
file type through the
File Types Options
menu.

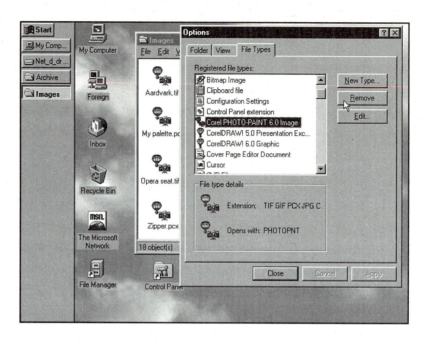

All you've done here is break a link between the application and a file type (or types). You haven't done anything to PHOTO-PAINT (or any other application). In this example, removing PHOTO-PAINT's association results in a number of different image formats being disassociated. To make an association between another application and this file type, follow these steps:

Making Associations

1. Click on New **T**ype, then type **TIF** in the **D**escription of File text field.

   This is the description of the file type that will appear in the file details list and on the File Type box in the future.

2. Type **TIF** in the Asso**c**iated Extension text field.

   This registers the type of file that will be associated with an application.

3. Click on **N**ew below the **A**ctions field.

   Displays the New Action dialog box.

4. Type **Open** in the **A**ction field.

   Specifies that the new association is limited to opening a file (but not deleting, or Saving As, for example).

5. Click on B**r**owse.

   Opens a file window for you to select the associated program.

In this example, we're associating PaintShop Pro with the TIF file type, but you can use any image editor or viewer you like. Choose one by clicking on it in the file window, then click on **O**pen.

6. Click on Change **I**con.

   Displays available Win95 icons.

7. Click **B**rowse, then select an icon from anywhere on your hard disk.

   You should choose from the following extensions: DLL, EXE, ICO. These are either icon (ICO) files, or icon resource files; collections of icons.

The preceding step determines whether your user files display a nice, large icon, or a tiny, 16×16 icon centered on page. If you don't select your own icon, Win95 builds one using the target programs icon resource file. And the icon will be small and hard to see in a file window.

8. Click on Open after you've selected an icon, or icon file, then click on OK.

   Returns you to the Add File Type dialog box.

9. Click on Close, then click on Close again.

   You're done, and back on Win95's desktop.

If you've added File Manager to your program folders, there's a more straightforward way to make associations. This third method for determining which program loads when you double-click on it is the Win3.1x way that works perfectly under Win95. Here's a refresher course.

Editing the Registry, the Windows 3.1x Way

1. Open File Manager, then choose a drive on the drive drop-down list where a Targa (TGA) image is located.

   Locates the file type with which you want to associate a program.

2. Choose **F**ile, **A**ssociate from File Manager's menu.

   Displays the Associate dialog box.

3. Scroll through the Associate With list until you find the application you want to associate with Targa images.

   Selects the program used to open the Targa image. (See figure 1.22.)

If the program is not listed in the Associate list, click on **B**rowse, locate the application, then click on OK.

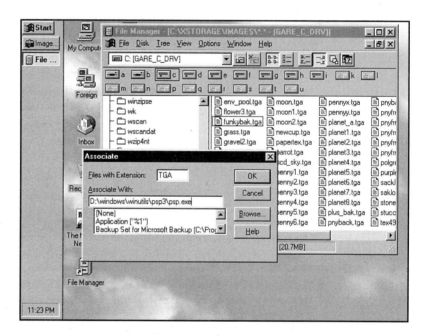

Figure 1.22
You can view and make new associations in File Manager.

4. Click on OK in the Associate dialog box, then close File Manager.

   You've made the association between the desired program and TGA file types.

5. Restart Win95 to make the changes take effect.

As you can see in figure 1.23, a folder that contains Targa images is now associated with PaintShop Pro, and not with PHOTO-PAINT. Double-clicking on any file icon in this folder will launch PaintShop Pro to view and edit the image.

There *are* clear advantages to an object-oriented operating system, and the applications that run under it; you'll see plenty of examples of CorelDRAW enhancements throughout this book. However, you don't have to give up the more straightforward ways of file transfer and management when you use Win95, as the preceding example illustrates.

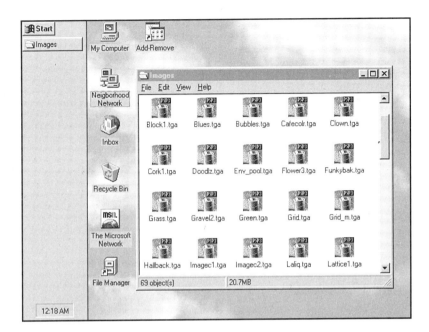

Figure 1.23
Files bearing the icon of a specific application can be launched within that application by double-clicking the file icon.

An Incomplete Shortcut List for Win95

This chapter is intended to be an essential guide for experienced Windows users to navigate Windows 95 with more confidence; it's not a *complete* documentation of Windows 95 features, but is instead designed to provide the CorelDRAW professional with some reference points in the new operating system under which CorelDRAW works. Think of this chapter as a condensation of the facts you need to know, so that you can get down to business—CorelDRAW! 6 business—more quickly.

This chapter would be incomplete, however, even at this break-neck pace, if it didn't include helpful shortcuts; some specific to Win95, and others that apply to CorelDRAW! 6, Win95, and even previous version of Windows. With Win95, you can use not only many of the accelerator keys and shortcuts you've memorized for Windows 3.1x, but also other shortcuts listed in table 1.1.

In table 1.1, you have a quick reference to commands that'll help navigating and managing files in Windows 95.

Table 1.1 Win95 Shortcuts

What You Do	What It Does
Ctrl+C	Copy.
Ctrl+V	Paste.
Ctrl+X	Cut.
Ctrl+Esc	Pops the Start menu over any running program.
Alt+Tab	Switches between running applications.
Backspace	Brings up previous folder window when you have two or more open. In single folder window, Backspace returns you to the previous (higher-level) folder).
Right-click	Displays a shortcut menu.
Shift+right-click	Displays additional Explorer options on shortcut menu.
Click-and-drag	Moves a Win95 object.
Ctrl+click-and-drag	Copies a Win95 object.
Ctrl+Shift+click-and-drag	Creates a shortcut to a Win95 object.
(When the Taskbar is foreground) Alt+M	Minimizes all open folders in the windows.
Shift+click on a folder	Closes folders open on current hard disk location.

For smooth sailing in Windows 95, just remember this simple maxim:

"Everything is an object in Win95, and you create an event by causing change to the object."

To conclude our adventures examining Win95, take a look at how you name files in this 32-bit operating system. How is it different from Win3.1x? For your information, this *sentence* is an acceptable file name under Win95!

Long File Names

Because Win95 uses an enhanced, 32-bit File Allocation Table (*vfat*), disk access is quicker, and you're no longer bound to the 8.3 naming convention for files. A file name can be up to 256 characters, including mixed-case text and spaces. The same characters that are prohibited for program folder names is in effect, however, so a file name containing say, a question mark, or the pipe symbol, is not legitimate.

What this means to the CorelDRAW! 6 user is an end to the cryptic file names you were typically forced to use under MS-DOS restrictions. Who could possibly remember that ACRT&HRS.CDR was an illustration of an apple cart and a horse?!

But Win95 ensures backward compatibility with file structures existing in DOS and previous versions of Windows, and that means that long file names become *short* file names when a Win95 user shares their work with users of older operating systems. The method that Win95 uses to *truncate* (to shorten) long file names for backward compatibility leaves the original six characters (without the upper/lower case enhancement), followed by a tilde (~), and then a single digit. Files opened by DOS or Windows 3.1x can read these files providing the content of the file doesn't use version-specific features. For example, a CorelDRAW! 6 design of my mom, entitled "Picture of My Mom.CDR", and saved as a CorelDRAW version 5 file could indeed be opened and edited in CorelDRAW! 5. The long file name doesn't matter; CorelDRAW! 5 views the file name as PICTUR~1.CDR.

However, if you saved the CorelDRAW! 6 design in the CorelDRAW! 6 file format, CorelDRAW! 5 couldn't open the file because there is version-specific information in the file. Also, if you do any editing to an image that has a long file name in the previous version, the previous version will truncate the saved file name, and your example file here would appear as PICTUR~1.CDR when opened next in CorelDRAW! 6.

There's a subtle danger in the way you name long files. Because of the backward-compatibility naming convention, you can wind up with a lot of files on your hard disk that have almost identical names! The very best way to use a long file name is to use a distinctive first six letters in it if you know a DOS or Windows 3.1x user will work with the file. For example, begin the long file name with a proper noun.

"Mary's Quarterly Report.doc" is a good long file name, because if it's truncated by Win3.1, the file will read "MARYSQ~1.DOC". Here's a graphic example of the perils of relaxed file-naming practices. In figure 1.24, two logos have been created. They're very different, and designed for entirely different people, but check out the file names...

In figure 1.25, you can see Windows 3.1's File Manager, and the truncated names for the saved files seen in figure 1.24.

File-naming conventions can be a boon or a curse in Win95, depending upon the name you choose for a file. Most users who have had years of experience with DOS and Windows might prefer to stick to the 8.3 convention for a while. If you decide to confine your file names to eight characters to enforce backward compatibility, you should remember one thing: Win95 long file names are also case-sensitive. So type your 8.3 name in all caps with no spaces to ensure that a previous operating system or program doesn't change the name. The author presently has a few goofy-looking user files in Win95, labeled "cArriAgE.CDr", and "mYsTUff.dOc"!

Figure 1.24
The first eight characters of each CDR file are identical.

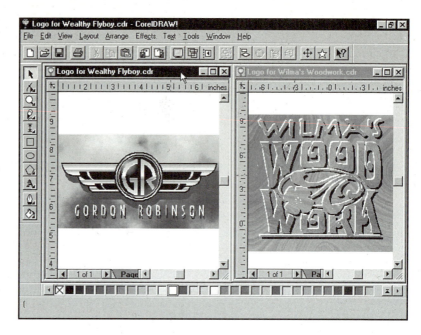

Figure 1.25
You're probably going to have to open both of these files to discern which is which!

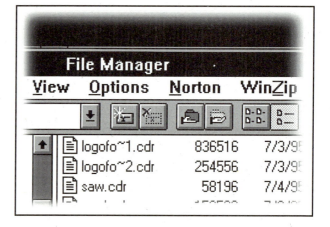

Moving to Customizing an Application

In Chapter 2, "Customizing CorelDRAW!," you'll make the logical migration from dealing with an object-oriented operating system to an object-oriented program. CorelDRAW! 6 is *not* the same "sit down and design" program you might have become used to. In fact, you're going to stand up and shout when you see what's hidden under tool icons, tucked away in dialog boxes, and generally rearranged to conform to new Win95 application standards. It's confusing stuff you're going to love, and Chapter 2 removes the confusion.

Customizing CorelDRAW!

The first time you open CorelDRAW! 6, you might be a little overwhelmed by the new interface. This is a natural reaction for users of previous versions because controls for tool settings and menu items are *not* in equivalent locations, and new tools fairly fill the workspace. With all these icons, you might feel that your style of design is being cramped!

However, Corel Corp. anticipated that the way you work in DRAW might be different from their style, and included in version 6 the ultimate in interface flexibility. You, the designer, have near-complete say over where toolboxes, toolbars, and even menu items are located. This chapter covers the how-tos that make the Drawing Window a more efficient, robust, and productive place.

Optimizing the Status Line and Tools

Corel Corp. followed Microsoft's recommendations for a standard Win95 application interface to the letter: tools have "persistent state" modes, Multiple Document Interface (MDI) is accomplished through the use of child windows, and status bars are located at the bottom of the screen. Figure 2.1 shows CorelDRAW's interface as you see it fresh out of the box with no customization. New toolbar items and tools are included; many of these items are moved to a better, more useful location later in this chapter.

Figure 2.1
The default configuration of DRAW's workspace complies with Microsoft's Win95 interface requirements.

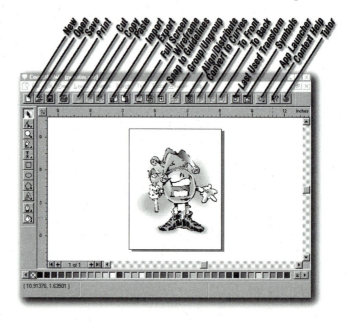

Corel Corp. acknowledges that the location of common menu items and other interface controls might be Microsoft-compliant, yet not to *your* individual taste. Therefore, this section examines how to customize some of the more basic elements within CorelDRAW's environment.

Configuring the Status Bar

In version 4 of CorelDRAW, the handy information area within the workspace became the Status Bar; in this version and subsequent versions, you have the capability of moving the Status Bar to the top or bottom of the screen. By default, the Status Bar appears at the bottom of the screen, in the larger of two sizes.

The first change most users make 30 seconds after installing CorelDRAW! 6 is to move the Status Bar to the top of the screen. Why? The Status Bar provides continuous updates on object information such as fills, outlines, font types, and relative position of objects on the printable page. At the bottom of the page, this information "fights" for attention with the color palette located next to it.

The Status Bar has been designed with the same flexibility as the rest of the interface elements in version 6; you can decide what information to display and where on the Status Bar. In the spirit of WordPerfect, Corel Corp. is anxious to make DRAW a place you almost never have to leave, from booting your computer 'til the 5 o'clock whistle. You have the freedom to assign different fields on the Status Bar the information you feel suits your work methodology the best. As an example, suppose you need to see the date and time in Corel's workspace. In the next set of steps, we'll walk through the customization of the Status Bar to provide this information.

Two key concepts apply to the arrangement of Status Bar elements, as well as every item you'll learn how to tweak in CorelDRAW's workspace:

✔ The right mouse button is your "spirit guide" to identifying and changing practically everything in CorelDRAW, other Win95-compliant programs, and Windows 95 itself. If you're lost, Property sheets can be accessed by right-clicking on a workspace object; a more complete representation of what you want to customize appears. Interface object properties are covered in detail.

✔ The resolution at which your video card displays Corel and the Win95 environment should be considered before customizing DRAW. The screen figures in this chapter were taken at 640×480 pixel screen resolution. If, like most users, you use 600×800 viewing resolution for Win95, you can cram more information and tools into CorelDRAW's workspace. We'll point out in this chapter where you have the opportunity to select large buttons for DRAW's workspace; large buttons are a must if you're running high screen resolutions, and they take up marginally more room than standard icons and buttons.

Here's how to include the information you want on the Status Bar while working in CorelDRAW! 6:

Customizing the Status Bar

1. In CorelDRAW, click-and-drag the Status Bar on the bottom of the screen to the top of the screen.

   Docks the Status Bar at the top of the screen, below the menu and above the toolbar. Alternatively, you can right-click on the Status Bar, and choose Place at **T**op from the shortcut menu.

Stop The S**m**all Status Bar option also can be found on the shortcut menu. Don't choose this, even if you're running 640×480 resolution, however. Doing this limits the number of fields in each region of the Status Bar to one.

2. Right-click in the right of the Status Bar, toward the top.

    Displays the shortcut menu for the Status Bar, and highlights one of two fields in this region of the Status Bar.

3. Click on **S**how, then choose **T**ime and Date from the fly-out on the shortcut menu.

    Automatically resizes the **L**arge Color Swatch to Sm**a**ll Color Swatch; adds time and date to upper field in region 3 of the Status Line (see fig. 2.2).

Figure 2.2

You can add two fields to each region of the Large Status Bar.

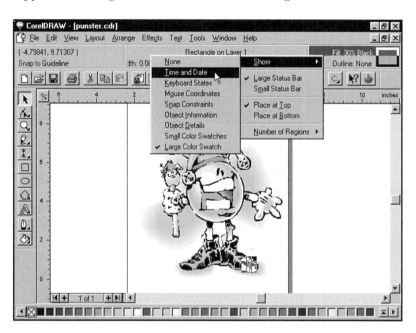

4. Click-and-drag the spacer between the first and second regions to the left, until the spacer almost touches the coordinates displayed in the first region.

    Allows more room for the Object Details field (the bottom of the two fields in the middle region) to display data. See figure 2.3.

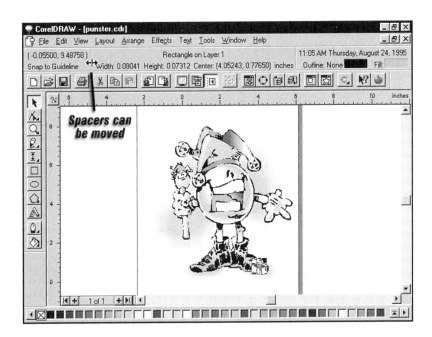

Figure 2.3
You can adjust the amount of space a region occupies by click-and-dragging a spacer.

You can have up to 6 regions on the Status Bar, and with the Large Status Bar option chosen, each region can have two fields. You'd need to run 1024×768 screen resolution to make all fields in all regions visible, and you'd also need a compelling reason to populate your Status Bar this way; there are only 9 possible data fields.

Unfortunately, CorelDRAW doesn't wrap data text, and the Object Details field cannot be adjusted to display less than 5 decimal places. Resizing the fields by using spacers is the smartest way to maximize field data on the Status Bar.

PHOTO-PAINT and a few of the other Corel modules offer flexible Status Bar and tool configurations, although their data differs from CorelDRAW. If you read this chapter thoroughly, you'll be well on your way to customizing all the Corel applications.

Using Object Properties to Customize Tools

Property sheets are a new feature in Windows 95 (usually found in the last slot on the right-click shortcut menus) that provide context-sensitive information about the object over which you've clicked.

Everything in Win95 applications is an object, and CorelDRAW's tools are no exception. You can extend the functionality of every tool to suit a specific design purpose. The following sections make recommendations and show you how to get the most out of your design tools.

Pick Tool Properties

The Pick tool—the primary selection tool for objects—can be changed to a cross hair cursor whose height and width span the Drawing Window. Although this option might make DRAW a more comfortable place for designers who came from a CAD background, cross hair cursors take longer to draw on-screen, and become irritating even after moments of use.

If you feel you must use the panoramic cross hair cursor as a metaphor for screen location targeting, you can select **A**pply All when in the Tool Properties dialog box. To access the Tool Properties dialog box, right-click on the Pick tool, choose Properties from the shortcut menu, and you're there. **A**pply All will turn the drawing and editing tools' cursors to cross hairs. If you do this by accident, the only way to defeat this feature is to choose Pick tool Properties again from the Tool Properties dialog box, and uncheck the option.

Other options for the Pick tool are Treat all objects as filled, and Draw objects when moving. Treat all objects as filled is a handy enhancement that is particularly useful in situations when a number of very small objects are on-screen with no fill properties. Ever try to select a 1-pixel wide outline? With Treat all objects as filled turned on, you can click in the center of a non-filled object and select it. Figure 2.4 shows the recommended options selected in the Tool Properties dialog box for the Pick tool.

Figure 2.4
The Treat all objects as filled option is the most useful property you can define for the Pick tool.

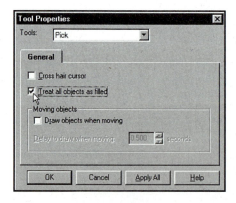

The Draw objects when moving option doesn't provide much better visual orientation of objects than the default of only displaying a bounding box while you move an object. With this feature turned on, you'll almost immediately be updated on the outline of a moved object, but you'll see no fill because you're asking so much of your video subsystem to constantly update additional screen information.

Shape Tool Properties

Although users of CorelDRAW have consistently referred to the Shape tool as the "Node Edit tool" (because of its primary use as a node editor), Corel Corp. has apparently adopted the popular nickname for the tool, at least in the Tool Properties dialog box. Don't look for Shape tool Properties after you right-click on the Shape tool and choose Properties from the shortcut menu; it's now called the Node Edit Properties!

The only option that can be changed for the Node Edit (Shape) tool is the method it uses to automatically reduce the number of nodes along a path. The Contour effect applied to an object, imported Adobe Illustrator files, Corel OCR-Trace files, and TrueType (that has been converted to curves) often contains a surplus of control points along their paths. Manually deleting each and every superfluous node is time-consuming, and can cause a path's outline to flux in a widely inaccurate way. The Auto-reduce feature is available in the Node Edit Roll-Up and makes right-click shortcut menus quick and precise.

However, the default value for the Auto-reduce feature is a minuscule 0.004". This means that if you marquee select an object with a surplus of nodes, then choose Auto-reduce, CorelDRAW will not delete any node if it means moving the curve of a path more than 4/1,000 of an inch. This usually means that the Shape tool's Auto-reduce feature will fail to remove *any* superfluous nodes from a path.

In figure 2.5, you can see the Node Edit (Shape) tool's properties for node reduction being bumped up to a more realistic two hundredths of an inch. This value is a comfortable mid-point between no node reduction and gross inaccuracy in curve design as a result of eliminating too many nodes. If you work on an 8.5 × 11" printable page most of the time, 0.02", (about a *point and a half* in typographic measurement) is the recommended value in the Auto-reduce box.

In figure 2.5 you can see that no matter which tool you right-click over, you can access *other* tool properties by selecting a tool from the Tools drop-down list. Therefore, you can remain in the Tool Properties dialog box and change the defaults for all tools.

The Zoom Tool Properties

To be compliant with Microsoft's "recommendations" for tool properties, the Zoom tool has undergone a change in version 6, which might be unpopular with experienced users. In previous versions of CorelDRAW, users could access a flyout menu from the Zoom tool, adjust views of the drawing window in a single step, then automatically return to the last-used tool.

Figure 2.5
Two hundredths of
an inch is an
acceptable degree of
change for a path
that contains an
excess of nodes.

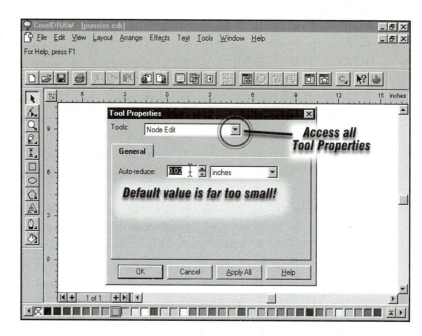

By default, DRAW now sports a *persistent state* Zoom tool: the Zoom tool remains chosen until you select a different tool. In addition there is no flyout from which you can choose different viewing resolutions. In figure 2.6, you can see a new way to access different zoom resolutions; you click on the Zoom tool, then right-click to choose resolutions from the shortcut menu. If you regularly need to zoom in and out without using a tool in between zooms (an impractical need), the persistent state configuration for the Zoom tool might be your ticket.

Fortunately for users of previous versions, the traditional Zoom tool can still be accessed and defined as the default method of adjusting screen views. In figure 2.7, you can see the Use traditional zoom flyout check box in the Zoom, Pan menu within Tool Properties.

For newcomers to CorelDRAW, figure 2.8 shows the traditional Zoom tool flyout. You choose a viewing resolution from the flyout (hover the cursor for a label of each button), and after selecting the view, the flyout retracts and you return to the tool you were using.

You also might consider assigning the Zoom out general Zoom Tool property for your secondary mouse button. Many programs, including PHOTO-PAINT, offer the left-click zoom in and right-click zoom out mouse settings. The Zoom out property is also a persistent state for the Zoom tool.

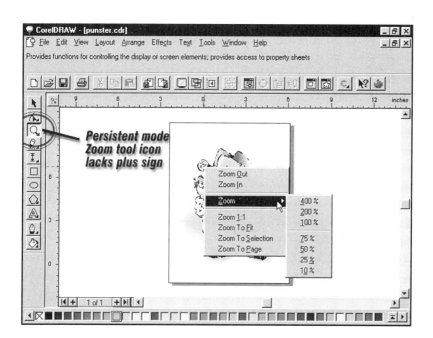

Figure 2.6
In its default configuration, the Zoom tool remains selected until you choose a different tool.

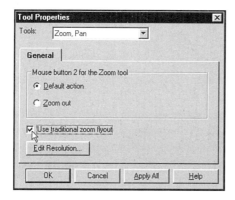

Figure 2.7
Experienced users will appreciate the traditional Zoom flyout as part of the complete CorelDRAW toolbox.

Zoom Problems

Because CorelDRAW! 6 takes advantage of 32-bit program architecture, measurements, including measurements pertaining to zooming, can now be carried out with fantastic precision. This also means that the "thumb"—the button in the middle of the scroll bars—should not be used in CorelDRAW.

Figure 2.8

The traditional Zoom tool flyout gets you back to designing after one step.

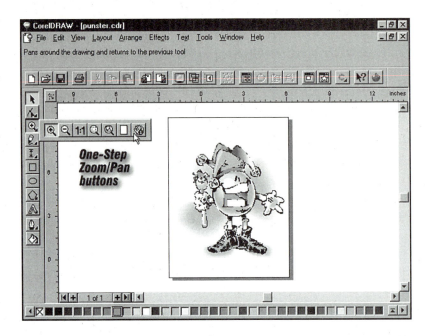

Stop   Even the slightest tap on CorelDRAW's scroll bar thumb can send your view to yards off the printable page.

You can overcome this inconvenience in two ways: tap the scroll *arrows* to move your view, or use the Pan tool to move your view. Unfortunately, if you choose the traditional Zoom flyout as the default tool, you have to repeatedly select the Pan tool to make more than one move to your view.

The author recommends that you use the traditional Zoom flyout, and use the scroll arrows in combination with the Zoom tool buttons to adjust your view. The View Manager (Ctrl+F2) in CorelDRAW! 6 can save various zoom resolutions and recall them, but you might find this implementation of zooming to be awkward, and three or more of DRAW's Roll-Ups can easily clutter your view of the Drawing Window.

Tip   Some, but not all of any panning woes might be auto-corrected by enabling the **T**ools, **O**ptions, Display, Auto-**p**anning feature. This option is on by default, so if you've accidentally turned it off, click on this check box on the display menu. Auto-panning automatically scrolls the window when you attempt to move objects outside of the document window. With a little practice, you can "force" CorelDRAW to follow your moves and provide the view of the document you need.

The Pencil Tool Properties

Properties for both the Bézier and Freehand mode of drawing can be changed by selecting the Curve, Bézier mode from the Tool Properties, Tools drop-down list, as shown in figure 2.9. Like the Zoom tool, you can access the Curve, Bézier Tool Properties by right-clicking on the Pencil tool on the toolbox. You may never need to change the default values (of 5) for curve drawing, but you should be aware of this tool's options:

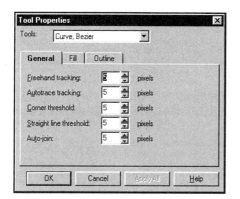

Figure 2.9
The Tool Properties dialog box.

✔ **Freehand Tracking.** Controls CorelDRAW's precision for rendering curves based upon mouse movement. The default value provides a good degree of tracking accuracy, but freehand drawing is not the most accurate method for designing in CorelDRAW anyway (double-clicking and Bézier techniques are shown throughout this book, and are the recommended styles of Pencil tool drawing).

✔ **Autotrace Tracking.** You might want to specify 1 pixel in this field if you use CorelDRAW's built-in feature to trace the curves found in imported bitmap images. Chapter 3, "Beating Nodes and Paths into Submission (The Easy Way)," shows the technique for automatically tracing the edge of contrasting colors in an imported TIFF, BMP, or other bitmap image. The lower the Autotrace Tracking value, the more accurately CorelDRAW will trace a bitmap, and the more nodes will be produced along the outline path. This contrasts with a higher pixel value in this field.

✔ **Corner Threshold.** Determines where cusp nodes are placed when autotracing or using the freehand mode of the Pencil tool as you would a physical pencil. The lower the value specified in this field, the more "corners"—nodes with the Cusp property—are produced around an outline path.

✔ **Straight Line Threshold.** The Autotracing and Freehand modes of the Pencil tool can be used to produce a combination of straight lines and curves. By specifying a high value in this field, more straight lines are produced with the tool, and lower values produce more curved path segments.

✔ **Autojoin.** Determines how close, in pixels, the endpoint needs to be to a path's starting point to allow CorelDRAW to close the path. Unless you're using a 45" monitor with resolution that's about 1 atom per pixel, you may never need to change the default value of 5 pixels.

Dimension Line Properties

The Dimension tools (which include the Callout tool)are not artistic tools; instead, they are used to tag specific distances, measurements, and titles to objects within a layout. Dimension tools are dynamic; distances marked using any of these tools are updated as you scale or move the control objects to which they are linked, a principle similar to Blend objects.

The options you can change for Dimension tools are the point size of the text (if you don't like AvantGarde 24 pt. wherever you use the tool), the fill of the text, and the outline attributes of a dimension object.

Rectangle and Ellipse Properties

Like the options for adjusting the Pencil tool, you may never need to change the Rectangle or Ellipse tool properties. The Rectangle tool Properties menu offers default fill and outline properties; you can also adjust the roundness of a rectangle's corners.

The default of 0.003" black outline and no fill allows users to see other objects which might be placed behind the rectangle. If you need to quickly draw 2,000 texture-filled rectangles, you might consider changing the property to reflect this need. Similarly, you can change the roundness of the corners (non-corners?) of the rectangle from 0 to 100 (no specific corner radius is available on the General tabbed menu). This feature can mess up your work in future sessions, particularly if you forget that you changed it. The author recommends that if you want to design rectangles with soft corners, use the Shape tool to modify the corner node of a sharp-cornered rectangle.

The Ellipse tool can be modified so that it produces filled ellipses with different outline properties, but like the Rectangle tool, the benefit of doing this might not outweigh the advantages to leaving Ellipse with its default settings.

You can also define an open or closed arc to be created every time you use the Ellipse tool by choosing from the General menu in Tool Properties for the Ellipse. However, as with the Rectangle tool, the Shape tool can be used to modify an ellipse to represent a pie wedge (click-and-drag on the ellipse's single node toward the inside of the ellipse), or an open arc (click-and-drag to the outside of the ellipse).

After an ellipse becomes a pie wedge or an arc, it is nearly impossible to shape the object back into a closed ellipse, so you'd be better off leaving these options alone.

Tip Although the Ellipse tool's Property dialog box provides the user with precise increments for making pie wedges and arcs, these effects can be created manually, with an equal amount of precision, by accessing the General tab of the **T**ools, **O**ptions menu.

By default, the **C**onstrain angle is 15°, which means that when you hold the Ctrl key in combination with drawing and editing tools, angles of drawing, movement, skewing, and rotation are constrained to 15° increments. If you specify, say, 1° in this field, you can then edit an ellipse to any of 359° of a pie shape.

Polygon Tool Properties

In addition to the Rectangle and Ellipse tools, the new Polygon tool produces closed paths that can be edited without converting the path to simpler curved segments.

The Polygon tool, by default, produces a pentagon. This can be changed to produce a star shape (Polygon as Star), and also a self-intersecting star shape (**S**tar). You can define the **N**umber of points a drawn polygon has, and determine the amount by which the Polygon as star shape bows inward or outward through the Sharpness slider in this property dialog box for both types of star polygons.

Tip Although you cannot define a default Sharpness for the **S**tar Polygon tool shape in the Tool Properties dialog box, you *can* increase a polygon object's sharpness *manually* after such a shape has been created.

With the Shape tool, click-and-drag one of the nodes at the inner, intersecting area of a Star polygon shape toward the center of the object.

One of the advantages to creating a polygon using the Polygon tool rather than dragging a shape from the Symbols palette is that a polygon can be dynamically reshaped. For example, a five-point star shape can be converted to a pentagon by click-and-dragging on a control point with the Shape tool; move an inner vertex away from the center, and you can turn the star inside-out.

Polygon shapes can also be edited across their symmetry by editing a single line or node. If you want to create a flower, begin with an eight-point star, then convert two converging line segments to curve property (use the Shape tool and Node Edit Roll-Up). Afterward, when you bow the curved segments outward, the other "petals" will automatically mimic these segments.

Figure 2.10 shows a star being created whose component lines bow outward. Without the Polygon tool, a star such as the one shown in the preview box would be almost impossible to find in a clip art collection, and near-impossible to design manually without a knowledge of 2nd year geometry!

Figure 2.10
The Polygon tool can create the basic elements you need to design spokes, petals, saw blades, and other symmetrical objects.

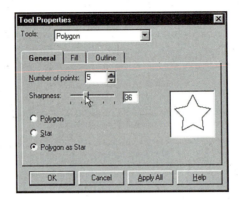

The purpose of the Polygon as Star option is still unclear with many users; on a PostScript printer a self-intersecting polygon generally prints as well as any self-intersecting shape (that is, not predictably; see Chapter 3). Corel Corp. has been known to incorporate whimsical features into past builds of CorelDRAW, and occasionally superfluous ones. Nevertheless, don't mistake the capability of the Polygon tool to shave hours off design assignments of machine parts and other symmetrical objects.

Properties for the Polygon, Spiral, and Grid tools can be accessed by double-clicking on the face of the tool; you don't need to right-click to access Properties.

The Spiral Tool

The Spiral tool does not produce objects with special properties; you cannot, for example, reduce the number of rotations in a spiral shape after it has been drawn. The only options for the Spiral tool under Tool Properties are Outline, Fill, and the **N**umber of Revolutions for objects created with this tool.

The fact that the Spiral tool creates open paths would seem to make the Fill option at least a puzzling one in Tool Properties. However, if you assign the Spiral tool a color fill, the moment you close the spiral path, the fill color becomes apparent within the object. You determine the start point and direction of a spiral by the direction in which you draw, and the size of the spiral depends upon how far you drag away from the starting point. Additionally, if you hold Ctrl while you click-and-drag, you can create a circular spiral shape.

The design uses for a spiral are somewhat limited when compared to rectangles, ellipses, and irregular freehand shapes. A closed spiral also doesn't always print correctly to a PostScript device because the shape contains a self-intersecting path (see Chapter 3 on the Winding Path rule). If you close a spiral, however, then use half of the object to trim a different object, the design possibilities suddenly expand.

In the next set of steps, you'll see how to create anything from an automobile emblem to a dish of spaghetti by using a modified spiral as an editing tool.

Creating a Geometric, Closed Spiral Path

1. Click and hold on the Polygon tool, then click on the Spiral tool on the flyout.

   Displays the tool flyout; chooses the Spiral tool.

2. Double-click on the Spiral tool.

   Displays the Tool Properties for the Spiral tool.

3. Type **12** in the **N**umber of revolutions field, then click on OK.

   Specifies that regardless of spiral size, the spiral shape created will always consist of 12 revolutions.

4. Click-and-drag from upper left to lower right of the document page, then release when the cursor has traveled about 2".

   Creates a counterclockwise spiral, with the endpoint on page right, about 2" in diameter. You can rotate the spiral, and use the Ctrl+click-and-drag technique on a middle selection handle of the spiral to change the endpoint location and direction of revolution. You can also change spiral node properties directly with the Shape tool; no Convert to Curves command is required (unlike polygons, rectangles, and ellipses).

5. With the Freehand Pencil tool, click on the endpoint of the spiral, then click on the beginning point, in the center.

   Closes the spiral. It can now be filled. See figure 2.11.

6. With the Rectangle tool, click-and-drag a shape much wider, and a little taller than the spiral, then click over the magenta swatch on the color palette.

   Creates a target object for trimming; fills the rectangle with a color so that the upcoming effect is more visible. Choose blue if you don't like magenta.

7. Press the spacebar, then click-and-drag the rectangle so that it's positioned on less than the top half of the spiral; don't let the bottom edge touch the line you drew to close the spiral.

   Puts rectangle in position to be trimmed by spiral.

Figure 2.11
A spiral shape has
no interior or
exterior until you
close it with a path
segment.

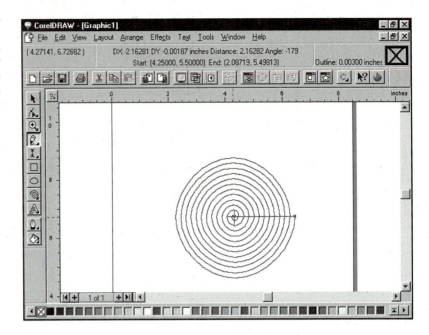

Figure 2.11
A spiral shape has
no interior or
exterior until you
close it with a path
segment.

8. Click on the To Back button on the toolbar.

   Sends rectangle to the back of the page. Both objects should be clearly visible now.

9. Choose **A**rrange, T**r**im.

   Displays the Trim Roll-Up.

10. Uncheck the Other Object(s) check box on the Roll-Up.

    Specifies that the object *other* than the object which is trimmed—the spiral shape in this example—will be deleted after the Trim operation.

11. With the Pick tool, click on the spiral.

    Defines the spiral as an "Other Object," not the Target Object in the Trim process.

12. Click on Trim, then point and click the huge arrow cursor at the magenta rectangle.

    Specifies the rectangle as the Target Object. See figure 2.12. Finalizes the Trim action; the spiral and original rectangle are deleted, and an intricate shape consisting of a rectangle shape minus the overlapping spiral areas is created (see fig. 2.13).

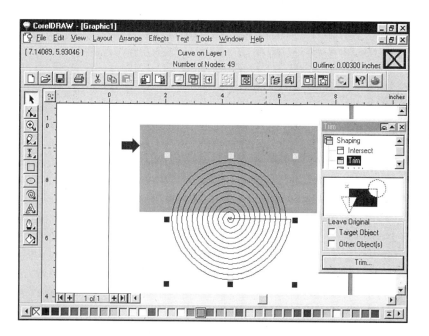

Figure 2.12
A closed spiral will remove a volume from another closed object; an open spiral, however, simply creates a weird target object.

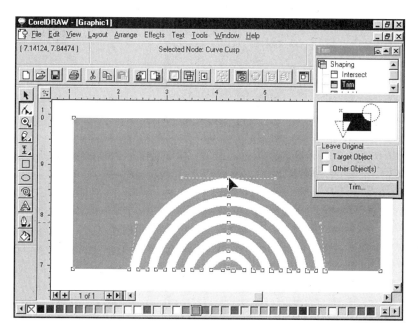

Figure 2.13
A closed spiral can be used to trim away different closed shapes, to create a weaving, complex pattern that's hard to create.

13. Press Ctrl+S (File, Save), then save the file as SPAGHETTI.CDR, but only if you really like the design.

Saves your work; author acknowledges that this might not be an award-winning design.

Stop Open spiral paths can create severe problems when used with other objects; let this be a warning for users of Corel 6.00.118 (version D2) and earlier releases. Paragraph text should not be wrapped around spirals or other open paths. We'll show you two methods, one of them fail-safe, for wrapping a block of text around shapes later in this chapter (see "Advanced Text Options").

You can have a lot of fun with *closed* spiral shapes, but attempting to trim a closed shape with an open one creates a "math problem" for DRAW. And attempting to define an open path such as a spiral as a text wrap object can ruin data on your hard disk. Call Corel Customer Support for updates to version 6 if you've experimented with the Spiral tool and are experiencing system problems.

In the previous example, the beautiful "spaghetti" design you just created does *not* contain curve connection properties identical to those in the spiral which created the curves. Trimming and other operations which add to, subtract from, and create other geometric objects (sometimes called *Boolean operations* for the "if, and, or" math statements which create geometric instances) can leave a cusp node where you'd normally expect a smooth or symmetric node. Check the connections of nodes in newly-created objects with the Shape tool, then use the Node Edit Roll-Up or the shortcut menu to correct node properties.

Grid Tool Properties

In this book, we'll occasionally refer to shapes produced by the Rectangle, Ellipse, and Polygon tools as *complex, high-ordered shapes.* Unlike the Spiral tool, the shapes produced by these other tools produce objects that cannot be node-edited in the conventional sense; you must use the Con**v**ert to Curves command (Ctrl+Q) to break the complex geometry into a simple path whose nodes you can directly manipulate.

The Grid tool creates complex, high-order objects. Although all the Grid tool does is produce grids, the resulting grids can be ungrouped to reveal nested rectangles (with properties similar to shapes produced with the Rectangle tool) of perfectly equal proportions and size.

The Tool Properties for the Grid tool contains the Fill and Outline tabbed menus, and also includes Number of cells **w**ide and Number of cells **h**igh fields, where you can specify how many rectangles make up a grid object.

Although grid cells are identical, you cannot constrain the proportional height or width of the cells when you create a grid object. If you need perfectly square cells, you must type an equal value in the cells wide and cells high fields in the Tools Properties dialog box, and use the Ctrl key to constrain click-and-dragging when creating a grid object.

The Grid tool comes in handy when you want to create a form such as a school report or a custom invoice. A grid object also transports perfectly from DRAW to other applications through the clipboard. And if you ungroup a grid, you can make a checker pattern fairly quickly by filling every other object in CorelDRAW.

Text Properties

Two different types of text can be added to a CorelDRAW design: Artistic Text, which can be modified by effects and other transformations, and Paragraph Text, which can be of much greater length than Artistic Text, but cannot be extruded, contoured, or otherwise transformed.

The Tool Properties dialog box offers complete control over how text appears in your document when you type with the Artistic or Paragraph tools. Unfortunately, you cannot define the point size and choice of font of an imported block of text as you import it; the styles associated with formatted text are generally retained when you use CorelDRAW's text import filters.

You can, however, easily change either imported Paragraph or Artistic Text by right-clicking on the text with either the Pick or Shape tool to bring up the shortcut menu. The shortcut menu is context-sensitive in Win95 and Win95-compliant applications, and Property sheets are assigned to *all* objects—screen elements and the graphics you create.

Artistic Text and Paragraph Text have near-identical Tool Properties menus. One minor difference is a frame option for Paragraph Text because this type of text is formatted in frames. Paragraph Text also has a **P**aragraph button on the General tabbed menu. The Paragraph dialog box offers controls for tabs, indents, spacing, and the use of special Symbols Roll-Up characters for bullets within the text block. Both Paragraph and Artistic Text Properties include **C**haracter formatting; you can specify choice of font, font size and style, and spacing between words, characters, and lines of text.

Therefore, when you choose Artistic and Paragraph characteristics, you must ask yourself, "What is the most common and easiest sort of text to work with?" AvantGarde 24 point is Corel's default for both Artistic and Paragraph Text. Artistic Text, which is usually used for headlines, is acceptable at 24-points, and as a font style, AvantGarde is unobtrusive...until you choose the font you really want to use. However, Paragraph Text is usually much smaller than the 24-point AvantGarde default; body copy in publications and advertisements generally follow the 11- to 12-point convention, and serif, roman fonts are easier to read in long blocks of text than the sans serif, gothic AvantGarde.

In figure 2.14, you can see that the user right-clicked on the Paragraph Text tool, and the Tool Properties for Paragraph Text can now be changed. 12-point Times New Roman has been specified: every time a new frame of Paragraph Text is defined (by marquee dragging with the Paragraph tool), Times New Roman in 12 point will be the font that appears.

Figure 2.14

Choose a font and a font size you're comfortable with for headlines (Artistic Text), and body copy (Paragraph Text).

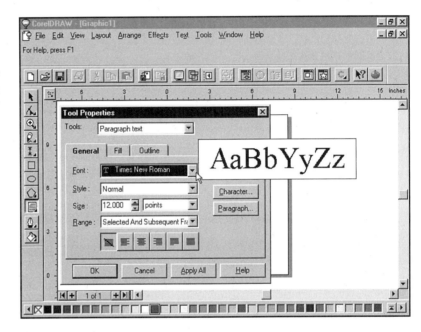

The Default Styles on the Styles Roll-Up (Ctrl+F5) change when you change the Text tool properties. If you've made changes to either the Paragraph or Artistic Text tools, these changes are automatically updated on the Styles Roll-Up.

The Fill and Outline tools can be customized, although these tools are actually menu flyouts that contain many subcategories. You can read about customizing these tools later in this chapter when you see how to create custom toolbars.

Customizing the Color Palette

The color palette at the bottom of the screen in CorelDRAW can display different saved palettes, such as the ones you'll learn to create in Chapter 4, "Mastering Color Models and the Fill Tool." You can also quickly change to a different color specification by choosing from the View, Color Palette command, which offers commercial color matching systems such as PANTONE.

Getting Up and Running

However, the physical configuration of the color palette, like everything else in CorelDRAW, is up to you. If you don't like a color on the default palette, you can delete it or move it.

Stop If you intend to modify the color arrangement on the Custom color palette, make certain you keep a backup copy of the CORELDRW.CPL file on your system. The default palette file is *not* write-protected, and if you accidentally close CorelDRAW without saving changes to the palette *as* a new palette (Save **A**s), the default colors you've deleted are gone forever.

The commercial color matching colors found in the Color Palette cannot be changed. You can append a copy of, say, the PANTONE color palette, but the **D**elete Color option on the shortcut menu will not change anything. To move colors on the default palette, click-and-drag, then drop the swatch on the position you want the color to occupy. You don't have to have an object selected to perform this maneuver; CorelDRAW will signal you with a system beep.

More important than color arrangement is the *location* of the color palette. With version 6's addition of 19 pixels of extra Status Bar and Rulers, you might feel as though the workspace is getting a little crowded for portrait-orientation work at 640×480 viewing resolution. Let's look at Corel's options, and your own, for clearing away a little space for the drawing window.

Figure 2.15 shows the Customize menu that appears when you right-click over the background area of the color palette.

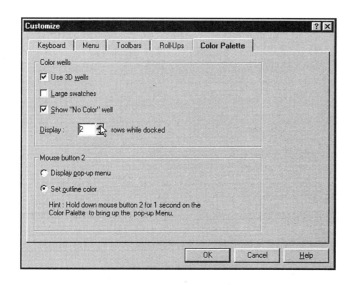

Figure 2.15

You can customize the appearance, and the location, of the color palette in CorelDRAW.

The Color wells configuration for the color palette is mostly a matter of personal aesthetics. By default, the Use 3D wells option is checked; the chiseled metal look of Win95 is endorsed by Microsoft for application manufacturers. The number of colors displayed on the first row of the color palette remains the same whether you choose 3D wells or something else.

The option to select Large swatches is beneficial to those running 1024×768 screen resolutions, but will cut the average user's visibility of the first row of swatches in half.

The Show "no color" well option is an absolute must-have item at the beginning of the color palette. Without it, you would have to define no fill and no outline for objects by making two separate trips to the Fill and Outline tools on the toolbox. Keep this option checked.

However, there is *no* real reason to choose the Display pop-up (shortcut) menu as the right-click function; click on the Set outline color radio button in this menu if it isn't already the selection. There are two ways to define a color for the outline of objects: by right-clicking on a color palette, or by right-clicking on the palette to display the shortcut menu, *then* selecting the Set Outline Color option. Ostensibly, Corel Corp. gives this option for users who have a hard time distinguishing between the color palette *edges*—the neutral, chiseled steel, background colored regions—and the actual color swatches on the palette. If you keep the default to Set outline color, you can still make the same choice from the shortcut menu.

The Display number of rows while docked option is helpful if you want to change the location of the color palette. You can "float" the color palette and position it anywhere in the drawing window, but this adds another element of clutter among all the Roll-Ups you might have in the workspace during an assignment. In figure 2.16, 2 was defined as the number of rows for the docked position of the color palette. If you choose this setup, then click-and-drag the color palette to the extreme right of the screen, you can display 40 colors at 640×480 viewing resolution. With this setting, you still have approximately as much space as you did in CorelDRAW! 5 for either portrait or landscape orientation work.

If you take a look back at figure 2.1 in this chapter, you'll see a wealth of shortcut buttons on the default toolbar. However, as you work more with this new version of DRAW, you might find that you've outgrown some of the buttons, and would really like to add some hard-to-find commands. No problem. That's what we'll cover in the next section.

Figure 2.16

You can average more screen real estate and more color palette colors by moving the palette and changing the default options.

Optimizing the Toolbar

If you've used Word for Windows for more than 6 months, you've probably dispensed with the menu buttons you never use, and populated the toolbar with your most-used commands. CorelDRAW is the first graphics application on the Windows platform to offer the same capabilities. In the following sections, you'll see how to remove toolbar buttons you never use, and dig into a treasure trove of new commands to add to the toolbar that aren't even listed as menu items.

Removing Redundant Commands

The concept behind the Windows 95 "look" for applications is that a user can feel at home immediately within a new program's workspace because there is a general consistency of features. However, many users have grown accustomed to *accelerator keys*—a combination of keystrokes such as Ctrl+C—that make several of the *common* command shortcut buttons on DRAW's toolbar simply take up precious screen space.

The following accelerator keys are supported not only be DRAW, but by most Windows 95 applications. If you memorize them (which isn't difficult after several years of Windows computing), you'll see that several buttons on DRAW's toolbar can be replaced with more useful commands.

Table 2.1   Common Windows Accelerator Keystrokes

Keyboard Shortcut	Menu Equivalent
Ctrl+O	File, Open
Ctrl+N	File, New
Ctrl+P	File, Print
Ctrl+C	Edit, Copy
Ctrl+V	Edit, Paste
Ctrl+X	Edit, Cut
Ctrl+Z	Edit, Undo

If you know these commands, you'll see that at least six default buttons on DRAW's toolbar serve no purpose. Although there is no hard and fast limit to the number of buttons you can place on the Standard (default) toolbar, the methodology we propose for customizing the toolbar requires that redundant buttons are removed before adding to the toolbar.

In the next set of steps, you'll read about recommendations for replacing buttons you might never use. The Standard toolbar can be reset to its default configuration at any time by choosing **R**eset from the Toolbars dialog box. If you're unhappy with your toolbar editing work, you can easily undo changes.

Clearing Away Space on the Standard Toolbar

1. Right-click over the toolbar, then choose Toolbars from the shortcut menu.

    Displays the Toolbars dialog box.

2. Click on **C**ustomize, then click-and-drag the Customize dialog box by the title bar, and move it away from the toolbar, partially off-screen if it provides a better view of the toolbar and drawing window.

    Displays the Customize dialog box. You won't be using any of the features in the customize dialog box; the Customize dialog box simply has to be on-screen to remove or add buttons to the toolbox.

3. Click-and-drag the New button (far left) from the toolbar into the drawing window.

    A bounding box appears around the button, the other buttons move to the left to create more space on the toolbar, and the button disappears after you release the mouse button.

4. Click-and-drag the Open button (now the far left) from the toolbar into the Drawing Window.

   Removes the Open button from the toolbar. See figure 2.17.

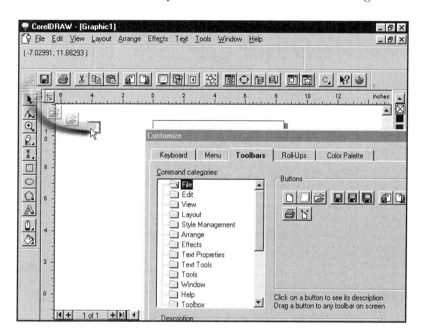

Figure 2.17
Buttons can be removed from the toolbar while the Customize dialog box is on-screen.

5. Perform step #4 with the Save, Print, Cut, Copy, and Paste buttons.

   Creates a substantial amount of room on the toolbar for adding buttons you use more often.

6. Optional: Click-and-drag the Last Selected Transform button, then the Application Launcher, the Context Help, and the Corel Tutor buttons off the toolbar, and into the drawing window.

   Removes these buttons from the toolbar. Although these buttons may not have easy-to-remember keyboard accelerator equivalents, experienced users will benefit very little form their presence on the toolbar. These and other buttons can be added to a custom toolbar, and the toolbar can then be displayed only when you need to access these shortcuts.

The Standard toolbar now has plenty of room for adding up to 11 buttons of your own choice, and all the buttons will be visible when the toolbar is in its docked position. In the next section, we'll examine the best replacements for the buttons you've removed.

Quick Access to Arrange Commands

On occasion, you may wonder why graphics applications have menu commands; menus make sense for word processors, but the menu commands you really need to edit or transform objects always seems to be nested in an inconvenient location, and require you to move your cursor far away from a design.

Although CorelDRAW has made consistent use of accelerator keys for frequently-used Arrange menu commands, practically speaking, there are only so many keyboard shortcuts you can *remember*! Given that many *other* graphics applications sport their own proprietary keyboard shortcuts, you might find it easier to add the Combine command to the toolbar than to try and remember Ctrl+L, which might serve a different function in another application.

In the next example, you'll see how to add frequently-used Arrange commands to the toolbar in a sensible order. In this chapter, we feature a drawing assignment that can be accomplished in about 30 seconds *if* you have the toolbar optimized for graphics design.

Here's how to populate the toolbar with Arrange menu commands you might find more useful than Cut, Copy, or Paste!

Adding Arrange Menu Commands

1. Click on the Arrange folder icon in the Command categories window.

   Displays the buttons in this menu category which you can add to the toolbar.

2. Click on the Combine button, then drag it to the right of the Convert to Curves button on the toolbar.

   Adds Combine to the toolbar, placing it next to another Arrange command button. Some of the buttons in the menu categories might have icons that are somewhat obscure. In figure 2.18, you can see that when you click on a button, a brief description of the command pops up in the Description field, and if you hover the cursor over a button, a pop-up title appears.

3. Click-and-drag the Separate, Intersect Target, Weld Target, and Trim Target buttons to the right of the Combine button on the toolbar. Finally, click on OK.

   Adds these commands to the toolbar, returns you to the workspace. Now you can access these commands with a single mouse click, instead of through their Roll-Ups.

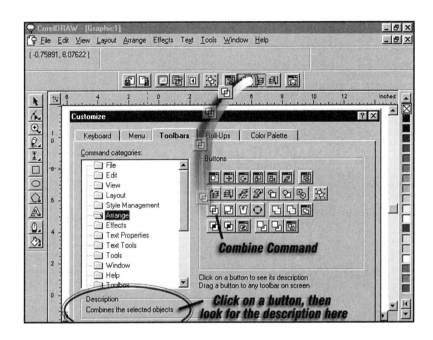

Figure 2.18
Add shortcut menu
command buttons to
the toolbar in an
arrangement that will
make sense later.

Getting Up and Running

Depending on how you build complex shapes in DRAW, the Separate command can be indispensable on the toolbar. Blend objects, text fitted to a path, and PowerLines all require separating the Control Object from the effect to more easily work with individual paths; with the Separate button "up front" in DRAW, you can edit your work much more quickly.

The selection arrow will appear when you click on the Trim, Intersect, and Weld buttons, and by clicking on the target, the command is performed. No longer is a Roll-Up left after the operation that must roll up or close to conserve screen real estate. By replacing the Trim, Intersect, and Weld Target commands with default menu selections, you've made DRAW a more convenient place to work.

It must be noted, however, that the Weld, Intersect, and Trim Target commands *use the Object check box settings* on the Trim/Intersect/Weld Roll-Up, whether the Roll-Up is on-screen or not. Therefore, you should open the Trim/Intersect/Weld Roll-Up before using these new toolbar buttons extensively, and make certain, for example, the Leave Original Other Object(s) check box is checked if you intend to re-use trimming objects in a design. Otherwise, objects will start disappearing on you when you use them in combination with the Trim Target button on the toolbar!

An Alternative to the Text Toolbar

In CorelDRAW! 6, the Text Roll-Up has been replaced with a Text toolbar that you can access by right-clicking on the Standard (default) toolbar, then choosing Text from the shortcut menu.

Two approaches are available for making Text formatting controls a single click away. If a particular assignment requires that several text edits be performed, you can display the Text toolbar, then reshape the toolbar to resemble a traditional palette. Few users willingly accept the addition of a docked toolbar for occasional use; toolbars eat up screen space in CorelDRAW! 6. To create a more compact, floating set of Text tools, simply click-and-drag on the toolbar window edges until you have a squarish palette. DRAW remembers the configurations for toolbars, and subsequent calls to the Text toolbar will display it in the shape you've created.

Another technique for quick access to font selection, size, placement, and alignment is to add the Character Attributes button to the toolbar. You can't change text styles (such as Paragraph default style) in the Character Attributes dialog box, but if you work with Artistic Text a lot, the Character button might be all you need in your workspace.

Giving the Toolbar Character

1. Right-click on the toolbar, choose Toolbars from the shortcut menu, then click on Customize. In the Customize dialog box, click on the Text Properties folder in the **C**ommand categories window.

   Displays all the text commands you can add to the toolbar.

2. Click-and-drag the "F" button to the left of the toolbar.

   Adds Character Attributes shortcut to the toolbar. See figure 2.19.

In the Text Properties field of the Customize dialog box, all sorts of text formatting buttons can be added to the toolbar. You can even add a Font list drop-down window to the toolbar, and then a font preview would appear as you select a font from the toolbar. However, the drop-down window would take up precious toolbar space, and you can always see a font preview while visiting the Character Attributes dialog box.

Although these buttons make speedy work of font changes, keep in mind that there has been a shortcut keyboard combination since version 4 of CorelDRAW for quickly changing font size, alignment, and other attributes. After you type a phrase using the Artistic Text tool, press Ctrl+spacebar to select the entire text object. Then press Ctrl+T to access the Character Attributes dialog box.

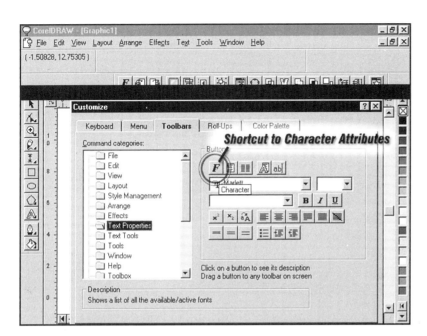

Figure 2.19

An easy way to access Character Attributes for Artistic Text is through the Character shortcut button.

The spacebar is usually the toggle key to switch between the Pick tool and the current tool, *except* when text enters the picture: you must press Ctrl+spacebar to perform the toggle. You must either select a text object with the Pick tool, or highlight an entire text string with the Artistic Text tool to apply font changes to an object. Many experienced users (including the author) forget about this keyboard exception when attempting to redefine a character format. Character Attribute changes do not take place unless one of the conditions for selecting the text objects is met.

▶ Tip   To add spacing between groups of buttons on the toolbar, you must first display the customize dialog box, then click-and-drag a button until it's halfway on top of its neighboring button. A space will then be created on the opposing side of the button you're moving when you release the button.

Make Room for Effects!

If you've followed the steps so far, you now have a more robust, artistically useful toolbar, with a little room on the right for one or two more buttons (unless you've already added some personal favorites). What other tools would complement your working set of buttons at this point? You can add Roll-Ups to the toolbar—the Extrude or Lens Roll-Ups are useful. If your work involves these effects, you should add them. In figure 2.20, you can see the Effects folder opened in the **C**ommand categories window, and the highlighted Perspective and Envelope effects buttons.

Figure 2.20

If you still have room on the toolbar, add one or two of the most frequently used effects.

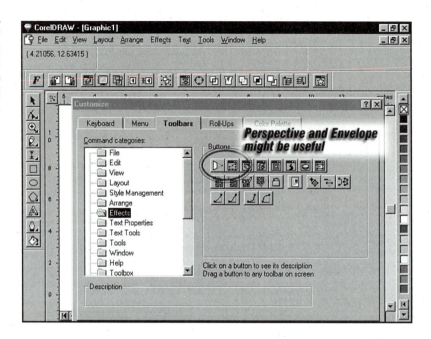

These buttons (Perspective and Envelope) are the author's personal choices for addition to the toolbar because:

✔ The Perspective Effect command has no Roll-Up, and therefore no options offered by a Roll-Up. Now you can access all the functionality of the Perspective command with a simple click instead of accessing a menu item.

✔ The Envelope Roll-Up is phenomenally useful for applying effects to both text and graphics. Desktop Publishing documents, Web page graphics, and advertisements can benefit from the attention-getting quality of an enveloped graphic or headline. Although you can specify your own hot key for displaying the Envelope Roll-Up (the default is Ctrl+F7, which is a tad hard to memorize), it's much easier to put the Envelope, or any other effect's command on the toolbar.

Thoughts on the Portability of Your Custom Workspace

We've taken you through the customization of the Standard toolbar to give you a feel for the techniques used to make this screen element a more valuable one in your work. And we've used the Standard toolbar as our experimental target because it can be returned to default values with a simple mouse click in the customize box.

But suppose that you're called out of town on an important CorelDRAW design assignment, and don't want to take the time to customize the host system where you'll work. The configuration for the toolbar, the toolbox, and other workspace parameters you've tweaked can be found in the DRAW folder on your hard disk in a file called CDRBARS.CFG. You can copy this file, and load it on another user's machine, but before you do this, read a little further.

It's always a better idea to customize a toolbar that will "travel" with you by first creating a unique, user-defined toolbar, rather than modifying an existing one. Why? Because standard toolbars can be reset to their original state; if someone inadvertently clicks on the Reset button in the Customize dialog box, your changes are gone forever.

The following section creates a new toolbox to replace the default one. You cannot rename the default toolbox, but you can substitute your own toolbox file to speed up your work.

Trimming Down and Beefing Up the Toolbox

The new look and design of CorelDRAW's interface might present some stumbling blocks to experienced CorelDRAW designers because of "conditioning." For example, the Dimension and Callout tools now have their own unique location in the toolbox; in versions 4 and 5, Dimension tools were neatly tucked in the Pencil tool flyout. If you're the type of user who is so accustomed to tool location that you merely point at the screen to access something, version 6 might have some design "surprises" for you!

You can configure your own toolbox to suit your working needs. In the next set of steps, you'll see how easily you can create Fred's toolbox, or Sarah's.

Customizing CorelDRAW!'s Tools

1. Right-click over the (horizontal) toolbar, then choose Toolbars from the shortcut menu.

   Displays the Toolbars dialog box.

2. Click on **N**ew.

   Creates a Toolbar 1 record in the **T**oolbars window.

3. Type a distinctive name in the highlighted text field in the **T**oolbars window.

   Names the toolbar (see fig. 2.21). The name and configuration will be stored on your system as CDRBARS.CFG. Although you have the option of specifying **S**mall, **M**edium, or **L**arge tool buttons in the Toolbars dialog box, these are global settings that affect all the buttons in DRAW. Don't change the default unless you're running high display resolutions.

Figure 2.21
Create a name for
your new toolbar to
ensure easy location
and identification.

4. Click on **C**ustomize, then click on the Toolbox folder in the Command categories window.

   A new, empty toolbar appears in the drawing window; displays the commands and buttons available for the toolbox.

5. The Pick tool seems like a natural for the beginning of your custom toolbox, so click-and-drag the Pick tool button to the custom toolbox.

   Adds the Pick tool to the custom toolbox.

6. Click-and-drag the Shape tool to the custom toolbox, then Rectangle, Ellipse, and Polygon tools from the customize dialog box to the custom toolbox.

   Adds these tools to your custom toolbox. Notice that the Dimension tool button is omitted from these selections. This is a personal preference; if you use Dimension lines a lot, by all means include this button.

Additionally, while the Customize dialog box is on-screen, you have the opportunity to rearrange the order of any and all tools on your custom toolbox by clicking and dragging them on top of one another, as you did with the toolbar buttons earlier.

7. Click-and-drag the Zoom tool from the default toolbox onto the custom toolbox.

   The Customize dialog box does not offer a flyout button for Zoom tools. However, dragging a default toolbox tool to a custom toolbox copies the flyout, or other tool. See figure 2.22.

8. Click-and-drag the Pencil tool flyout from the Customize dialog box to the custom toolbox.

   Adds Freehand and Bézier Pencil tools to the custom toolbox.

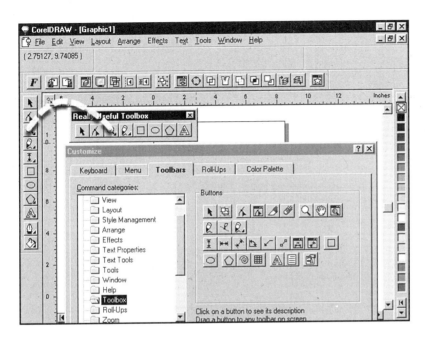

Figure 2.22
Add default tool configurations to a custom toolbox by dragging them from one toolbox to the other.

At this point, you have a neatly organized, custom toolbox, with only the tools you use regularly. The Fill and Outline flyouts on the default toolbox contain many carry-overs from previous versions that don't really enhance the layout of the current version. Specifically, why would you need default outline widths (which cannot be changed) and three Roll-Ups for outline attributes, when one Roll-Up can provide controls for all outline changes. As another example, the Fill flyout provides a valuable gateway to different types of special fills, but the Special Fill Roll-Up puts the options on-screen obscuring the Drawing Window, not in a dialog box. The following steps provide one of several possible customizations to access more quickly object fill and outline properties...

9. Click on the Outline folder in the **C**ommand categories window, then click-and-drag the Outline Pen button to the custom toolbox.

   Adds a single button to the toolbox, from which you can define outline width, connection type, color, arrowheads, and scale.

10. Click on the Fill folder in the **C**ommand categories window, then click-and-drag the Special Fill Roll-Up to the custom toolbox.

   Adds the button that will display a Roll-Up in the Drawing Window for accessing, copying, and modifying all types of object fill, except Uniform fill (see figure 2.23). If you don't use custom uniform fills very often, you can access solid fills from the color palette. If you need more flexibility, however, you can add the Uniform Fill button to the custom toolbox in addition to the Special Fills Roll-Up button.

Figure 2.23
Add the buttons to the custom toolbox that give you the quickest access to common editing and design features.

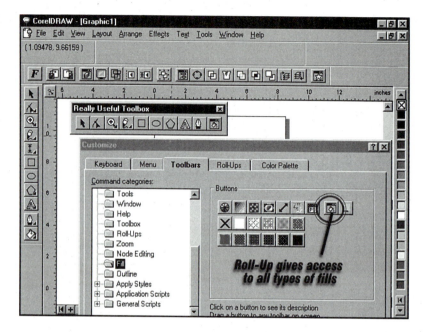

11. Click-and-drag the default toolbox away from its docked position, click on the close box on the toolbox, then click-and-drag the custom toolbox into the docked position on the left of the Drawing Window.

Replaces the default toolbox with your own. See figure 2.24.

Now you can take your custom workspace configuration for a test drive. In the next section, we'll show you some of the accessibility enhancements available if you followed the examples up to this point.

Creating Complex Shapes in a Custom Workspace Is a Snap

Corel's tools seem to be geared toward the construction of symmetrical, geometric primitives—shapes whose outlines represent the most basic of elements. The timeless task of computer graphics designers has been to combine primitives—rectangles, ellipses, and other symmetrical shapes—into more complex outline paths, to create illustrations audiences recognize.

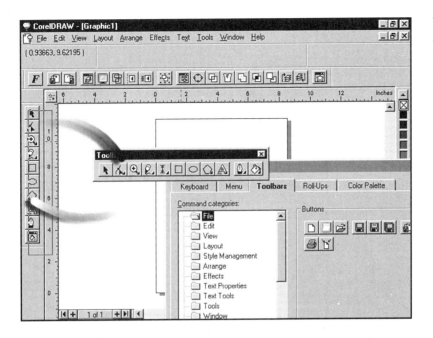

Figure 2.24
The default toolbox can always be restored or displayed by opening it from the toolbar shortcut menu.

In the following set of steps, you'll use several of the new buttons on your custom toolbar to better work with combinations of objects. However, don't forget that the Weld, Intersect, and Trim Target buttons are always defined by the options on the Weld/Intersect/Trim Roll-Up. Before starting the steps to follow, make sure that Leave Original Other Object(s) is checked on the Trim area of this Roll-Up; if it's not, the Trim Target trick won't work in the example.

Here's an example of some of the power you can immediately access because all the "good stuff" is now located within easy reach in DRAW:

Creating a Complex Outline Using Automated Features

1. With the Ellipse tool, Ctrl+click-and-drag a circle about 2 1/2" on the printable page of a new document.

   Ctrl key constrains Ellipse tool to creating equilateral ellipses—circles.

2. With the rectangle tool, click-and-drag a rectangle about 1 1/2" in width and 3" in length so that it intersects the circle and extends slightly above the circle.

   This object will becomes part of a complex object, and also serve as a Trim object to modify the circle.

3. Click on the Align and Distribute Roll-Up button on the toolbar. Press the spacebar, marquee select both objects, click on the Align vertical center button, then click on Apply.

Displays the Align and Distribute Roll-Up, toggles Rectangle to Pick tool, and aligns the circle and rectangle vertically. If you want to sneak a peek at figure 2.28 to see what's you're going to build, feel free. You're going to create the outline of a wrench. The rectangle will serve as the stem between the two crescent heads, but will also be used to trim away the top of the circle to create one of the "business ends" of the wrench.

4. Click on a blank area of the printable page. Click on the rectangle, then click on the Trim Target button on the toolbar.

Deselects the two objects and selects the rectangle; clicking on the Trim Target button turns the cursor into huge selection arrow.

5. Click the selection arrow on the circle.

Removes the overlapping rectangle area from the circle; retains the rectangle on the page because Leave Original Other Object(s) option was previously checked on the Weld/Intersect/Trim Roll-Up. See figure 2.25.

Figure 2.25
There is substantially less workspace clutter when you isolate the features you really need, and assign them toolbar buttons.

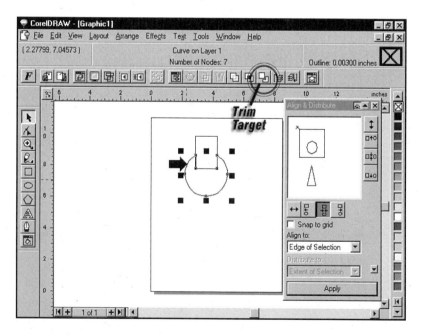

6. Select the rectangle, then click-and-drag the top, middle selection handle downward by about 8".

   Mirrors the rectangle, and scales the y dimension so the rectangle becomes the stem of the wrench. See figure 2.26.

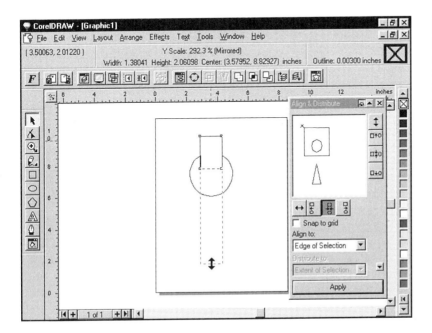

Figure 2.26
By disproportion-ately scaling a selected object, you can maintain alignment with its original position.

7. Click on the rectangle's top, middle selection handle, then drag the top side down into the circle shape.

   You'll use the Weld Target command on the objects to create the wrench; by dragging the rectangle's top side into the circle shape there will be no unwanted overlapping areas when you weld.

8. Click on the circle shape, then hold Ctrl while you click-and-drag downward on the circle's top, middle selection handle; right-click before releasing the left mouse button.

   Creates a vertically mirrored duplicate of the circle shape. This will be the other end of the wrench. See figure 2.27.

9. Ctrl+click-and-drag the duplicate circle to the end of the rectangle, stopping when the circle overlaps only the bottom side of the rectangle.

Figure 2.27
Create mirrored
duplicates of objects
by Ctrl+click-and-
dragging middle
selection handles,
and right-clicking
before releasing.

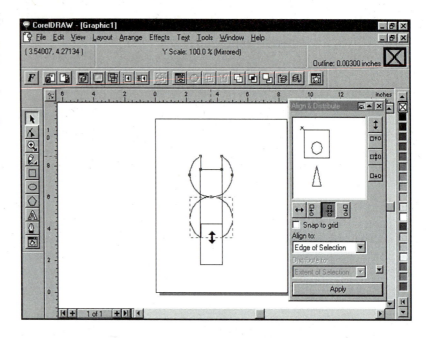

Places the circle in position for welding to the other objects. Ctrl constrains movement of the circle to the direction in which you first click-and-drag (which is vertical). Alternatively, you can drag the circle to its bottom position without holding the Ctrl key, then use the Align and Distribute Roll-Up to align the center of the circle with the rectangle.

10. Marquee select all three objects, then click on the Weld Target button.

    Cursor turns into huge selection arrow.

11. Point the arrow at any of the objects, then click.

    Welds objects, removes interior path, and completes the assignment. See figure 2.28.

Think about the time saved and precision gained by combining primitive shapes to achieve your design goal. In figure 2.29, you can see other tools have been created using the same techniques. The handle to the screwdriver was created by trimming a large circle with eight small circles. The objects were extruded and shaded using techniques covered in Chapter 11, "Special Effects for Web Pages."

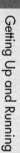

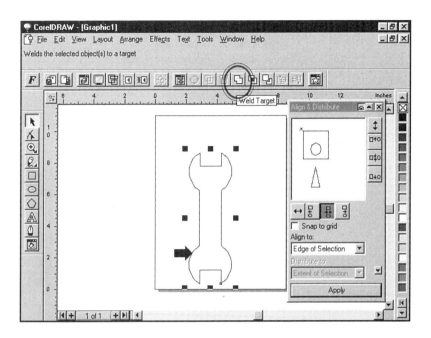

Figure 2.28
Precise alignment and speed are qualities you pick up when you're familiar with Corel's tools and their locations.

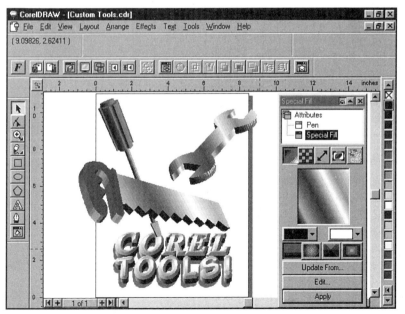

Figure 2.29
Use the information in this book with your custom tool sets to create anything you can imagine.

Admittedly, even the best organization of Corel's tools won't help you finish a design if you don't first visualize the potential for combinations of primitive shapes. It's been the author's experience that the Trim, Intersect, and Weld tools have been the greatest enhancement Corel Corp. has made to the application. Before version 5, users were obliged to separate curved segments manually to make a complex object, with no reassurance that curve fidelity would remain in the finished composition. Given a small investment of time, you might find yourself designing more frequently with rectangles and polygons in combination with your new tool commands, than using the Pencil tool to achieve similar results.

Advanced Text Options

Screen elements, such as tools and buttons, and objects you *create* using tools are considered the same class of items within CorelDRAW and Windows 95. Objects, by convention in Win95, have property sheets attached that allow you to see, and usually modify, the object's properties.

Although DRAW would not be the best choice of applications to use for a document as text-intensive as a magazine, the Paragraph Text-handling features in version 6 can be used to produce a quick, professional-looking full-page advertisement. One of the visual *hooks* professional advertising folks use to integrate elements in an ad is the "wrap around" text feature. Users who are familiar with Adobe (formerly Aldus) PageMaker know how easy it is to create a barrier between text and graphics to make text flow around the periphery of a graphic, or even another block of text.

CorelDRAW's features provide two ways to create the text wrap look, one of which can be accomplished by changing a Paragraph Text object's properties. Because this chapter is dedicated to changing the look of DRAW, and bending the rules, the examples to follow show how to wrap text using both techniques.

Creating a Custom Advertisement

1. Open the GAMBLE.CDR document from the EXAMPLES.CHAP02 folder of the *CorelDRAW! 6 Expert's Edition Bonus CD.*

   Opens the page layout you'll use to create flowing, wrap-around body copy.

2. Click on the Import button on the toolbox, then choose GREEKING.DOC from the EXAMPLES.CHAP02 folder of the *CorelDRAW! 6 Expert's Edition Bonus CD.*

   This is a text file containing nonsense words, (usually Latin words), which designers use as a placeholder until the copywriter finally comes through with some text. If you didn't install the Word for Windows 2.0 import filter when you ran CorelDRAW setup, you really should run setup again to add this filter. But for the purposes of this example, you can open GREEKING.DOC in Windows 95 WordPad, copy the contents to the clipboard, marquee drag a Paragraph text area on the workspace (using the Paragraph Text tool) then paste the text into the frame as unformatted text.

3. With the Pick tool, click-and-drag the Paragraph Text frame off to the paste-board area of the Drawing Window.

   Clears room on the printable page for creating the text wrap effect. See figure 2.30.

Figure 2.30
The frame that holds Paragraph Text is an object; it has properties you can modify.

4. *Ignore this step and step 5 if you used the Import filter to bring in the greeking.* With the Pick tool, right-click on the Paragraph Text, then choose **P**roperties from the shortcut menu.

   Displays the Object Properties dialog box. Clipboard text doesn't often transfer with the originating application's styles, so the text you've pasted into the frame could be Courier, or the default style for DRAW's Paragraph text.

5. Choose Times New Roman from the **F**ont drop-down list, type **18** in the Si**z**e field, then click on OK.

   Formats the text as Times New Roman, 18 points.

Note You can change the properties of *any* object in CorelDRAW using this technique. It's usually a quicker technique than selecting and redefining an object using the tools, because Object Properties dialog boxes contain tabbed menus of many different aspects you can change in a single session.

6. With the (Freehand) Pencil tool, create a straight line border around the dice on the page, about 1/4 inch outside the edges of the dice.

   Creates an object that will be used as the Wrap Paragraph text object. You have no control over the amount of padding surrounding objects that repel Paragraph text. Therefore, you need to manually build an additional object that serves the design purpose. If you're not familiar with the double-click technique for building closed shapes, check out Chapter 3 for instructions.

7. Press the spacebar, then right-click over the path you created, and choose **P**roperties.

   Toggles current tool to the Pick tool; displays the Properties dialog box for the object you selected.

8. On the General tabbed menu, click on the **W**rap paragraph text check box, then click on OK.

   The irregular border you created around the dice will now repel Paragraph text (see fig. 2.31).

Figure 2.31
Use the Wrap paragraph text option with rectangles, freeform shapes, and other closed path objects.

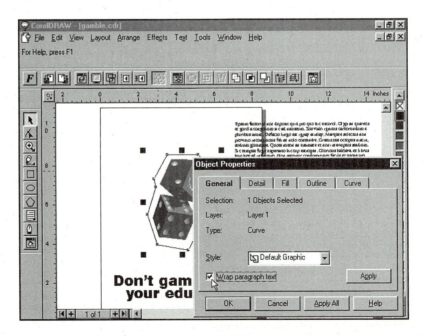

Stop Again, it should be stressed that DRAW will allow you to assign a text wrap property to spiral and other open path shapes, but you can wreck your system, or at very least crash the CorelDRAW session by doing so. *Use* closed objects only *with the **W**rap paragraph text options!*

9. Click-and-drag the Paragraph Text frame onto the printable page, then release it and deselect it when the dotted bounding box is centered on the page.

   Text wraps around the path and around the dice.

10. Click on the irregular shape you drew, then right-click on the white color swatch on the color palette.

   Selects a color that blends into the paper white background of the design. You're done! See figure 2.32.

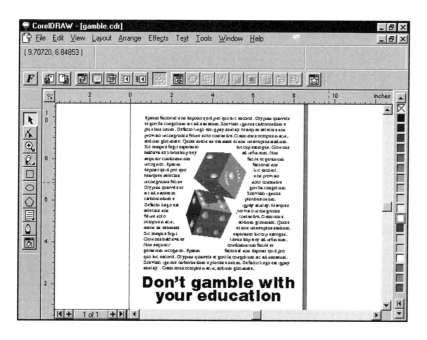

Figure 2.32
Create an advertisement quicker than someone can come up with a concept by using DRAW's advanced text-handling properties.

Although the Envelope Roll-Up cannot accept a template for transformations of text that contain a subpath, you can still do some pretty amazing text-wrapping design work with Paragraph Text *frames*. Unlike Artistic Text, which is completely subject to CorelDRAW's effects, Paragraph Text lies inside a container—a Paragraph Text frame. You can distort the frame, but not the Paragraph Text.

This limitation leads to the second method of wrapping text:

Enveloping Paragraph Text Frames

1. Click-and-drag the Paragraph Text frame off the printable page.

   The Paragraph text reshapes to original dimensions.

2. Click on the Wireframe/Preview toggling button on the toolbar, then click on the irregular text wrap outline on the page, and press Delete.

   Deletes the outline you hid on the page in the previous example. You should toggle back to preview display mode now.

3. With the Pick tool, click-and-drag the dice object to above the word "with" on the ad layout.

   Repositions the dice for a different layout design. The dice objects are grouped; don't worry about accidentally repositioning a component of the group.

4. With the (Freehand) Pencil tool, double-click a border which will define the Paragraph Text space within the ad; allow some space around the dice. Look ahead to figure 2.33 to see what the optimal design of this closed path should be. If you want to keep the straight lines of the path absolutely parallel to the page borders, hold Ctrl while you click points defining the straight path segments.

   Creates the shape with which the Envelope Roll-Up will pattern an envelope for the Paragraph text.

5. Click on the Envelope Roll-Up on your custom toolbar (or press Ctrl+F7—Effects, Envelope—if you didn't add the Roll-Up to the toolbar).

6. With the Pick tool, click on the Paragraph Text, click on the Create From button on the Roll-Up, then click on the path you designed on the page. See fig 2.33.

   Selects the Paragraph Text, adds a dotted line border around the text to indicate the proposed envelope effect for the text. A freeform envelope, the type created when the far right button is selected on the Envelope Roll-Up (which is the default setting), allows you to modify an envelope outline after the effect has been applied. Notice the nodes on the Envelope dotted outline; they have the same properties as the source object you based the Envelope upon, and the nodes and dotted lines can be modified using the Shape tool at any time. However, you must always click on Apply to affect the changes to the Envelope outline.

7. Click on Apply.

   Reshapes the Paragraph Text frame to mimic the path you drew on the page.

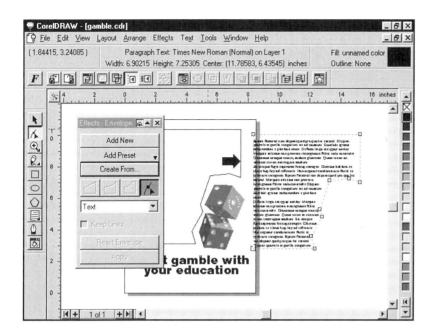

Figure 2.33
Create a shape that
the Envelope effect
will use as a
template for
reshaping the frame
of the Paragraph
text.

Getting Up and Running

8. With the Pick tool, click-and-drag the Paragraph Text so that it lies aligned with the path you drew on the printable page.

   Places the text in position for the layout.

9. Press the Tab key repeatedly (and slowly) until the Status line says that a Curve on Layer 1, with no fill, has been selected, then press Delete.

   Tab key toggles between objects in the drawing window. This is a useful feature when you have an object of equal size and dimensions on top of the object you wish to move or delete. See figure 2.34 for the finished layout.

It might be hard to believe but there are several more areas with feature sets you can customize in DRAW. The following sections briefly describe minor alterations you can make to access commands you use most.

Creating Keyboard Shortcuts

Many graphics applications use common keyboard accelerator commands to perform the same function. For example, Ctrl+A is the shortcut for selecting all items in Adobe PageMaker, Word for Windows, Photoshop, and Fractal Design Painter. However, Corel Corp. has assigned this popular and accepted command to display the Align and Distribute Roll-Up, which is by default, located as a button on the default toolbar.

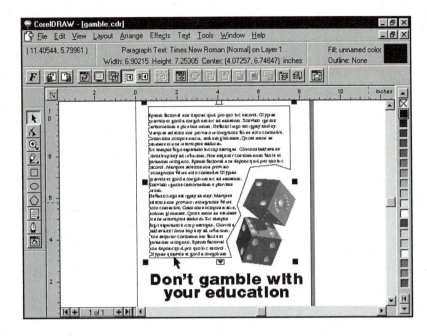

Figure 2.34
Paragraph Text
wrapping can be
accomplished
through object
properties, or by a
technique with the
Envelope Roll-Up.

If you'd like to change Ctrl+A to select all, or create keyboard shortcuts to other commands, here's the basic recipe:

Creating Custom Keyboard Shortcuts

1. Choose **T**ools, **C**ustomize.

   This is an another way to display the Customize dialog box.

2. Click on the Keyboard tabbed menu.

   Displays options for assigning keyboard combinations to menu actions.

3. Click on the **G**o to conflict on assign check box.

   Displays an alert when you want to overwrite an existing, default keyboard command. You already know what the conflict will be in this example, but make this step a practice when you alter other default settings.

4. Double-click on the Edit folder in the **C**ommands categories window.

   Expands the Edit tree to display individual commands.

5. Click on the Select All icon, then place your cursor in the Press new shortcut key field, and press **Ctrl** and **A** on your keyboard.

Registers the keys pressed in the field. Also displays the conflict in the Current shortcut keys field.

6. Click on Assign, then click on **S**ave As.

    Displays Save As dialog box.

7. Type MY-KEYS.ACL in the File **n**ame field, then click on Save.

    You've appended the default keyboard accelerator list. All the other keyboard commands are still listed in the new file along with the custom command. Click on OK now to leave the customize dialog box.

If you followed the previous example, but now want to restore the default keyboard commands, choose R**e**set All in the Keyboard menu.

Tip   CorelDRAW has had a "hidden" shortcut for the **E**dit, Select **A**ll command since version 4, and you might prefer to use it instead of a keyboard shortcut. Double-click on the Pick tool. This action selects all objects in the Drawing Window.

Changing Menu Commands

It is doubtful that designers would have much need for rearranging the order and structure of DRAW's menus, but you can customize menu commands in version 6, just as you did with tools and toolbar buttons.

Be aware that you can create incredible disorder in the menu structure if you decide that, for example, Paste would make a good Text menu entry. Nevertheless, if you'd like to place all your commands under one roof, here's an example of how to create a new menu group, and how to copy menu items to this new location:

Creating a Custom Menu Item

1. Choose **T**ools, C**u**stomize.

    Displays the Customize tabbed menu.

2. Click on the Menu tabbed menu.

    Displays all the commands available in CorelDRAW. Adding an ampersand before a letter in a word is the method used for assigning a hot key to the letter following the ampersand in a menu item.

3. In the Me**n**u window, click on the Help icon, then click on the Add **M**enu button.

Adds the Menu menu to the position directly after the Help menu. The title for the menu is highlighted now.

4. Type **Private Stock** in the highlighted menu text.

Creates a menu item after Help called "Private Stock" with the P underscored for use as a hot key.

5. In the **C**ommands window, click on the +key to the left of the Tools folder.

Performs the same action as double-clicking on a folder; the folder expands to show all menu commands.

6. Click on Options, then click on **A**dd.

Adds the Options command to the Private Stock menu.

7. Click on OK.

Completes the menu editing; you can now access CorelDRAW's Options dialog box from the Private Stock menu.

Because you added the Options command to the Private Stock menu without removing it from the Tools menu, you now have identical commands under two different menus. Does this potential silliness cause problems in CorelDRAW? No, but you can reset all the menu items quickly by choosing the R**e**set All command in the Menu menu after the novelty of creating custom menus has worn off!

The Corel Classic: The Preferences Menu

Version 6 has done away with the Tools, Preferences menu and instead we now have an Options menu which contains some of the options for display, nudging, and specifying the number of bands DRAW displays in a fountain filled object.

The following section is a rundown of highlights found in the Options dialog box. Many of the options you'll never need to fine-tune; others require attention, and can help speed along your work.

The General Options Menu

On this menu, you'll find options for placing a duplicate object. The shortcut for the **E**dit, **D**uplicate command is Ctrl+D, or you can press the + key; a duplicate is automatically created over the original. You probably will never need to respecify the offset value for Place Duplicates and clones; many alternate schemes are shown throughout this book for positioning duplicate and original objects.

Also on the General menu is the Nudge value, a handy keyboard property you might want to access when aligning objects manually. The arrow keys nudge selected objects, and it is in this menu where you specify the amount of nudging.

The General menu also contains the option to reinstall Corel 6's Welcome screen. You might feel as though the Welcome screen outgrows its charm after the fifth time you see it. If you want to *restore* the welcome screen, the Application start-up area is the only place you can re-install this feature.

The Display Menu

This menu enables you to change the number of steps a fountain fill object appears with on-screen. If you take a screen capture to instantly convert a CorelDRAW design into a bitmap, you'll want to turn the value of Preview fountain steps up to 100 or more. The more steps you specify, however, the longer the screen redraws will take to display the object.

Also on the Display menu is the option to turn off Tooltips—the sometimes helpful pop-up labels that indicate the name of a tool or feature when you hover your cursor.

Occasionally, your video subsystem will have a quarrel with CorelDRAW, and the video subsystem will lose. When this happens, you get "screen artifacts" (that is, *screen trash*) on your display. When this happens, you can manually refresh the screen by pressing Ctrl+W. If you, by chance, check the **M**anual Refresh option here, the screen will not update your work until you press Ctrl+W. Do not be misled by the title of this option. Except in extremely rare situations (the author can think of none), you'll always want an instant update to the drawing Window. In other words, don't check the **M**anual Refresh button.

The Advanced Menu

In the Backup field of the Advanced menu, you might want to choose a different backup directory location for files that CorelDRAW creates when it detects system inactivity. CorelDRAW and other applications today demand more and more hard disk space. DRAW's auto-backup might fail someday because the hard disk appointed to hold the backup files has become full.

Stop The other Advanced options are fairly self-explanatory, except the Enable-**m**ultitasking option. *Do not, under any circumstances*, check the Enable-**m**ultitasking check box; not with build D2 (600.118) of CorelDRAW! 6, and perhaps not *ever* until Corel Corporation has notified users that this specific feature works correctly with a specific updated build of the program.

The Tools, Options, Advanced, Enable-**m**ultitasking feature was originally intended to allow users to control the amount of resources used by CorelDRAW to carry out different tasks simultaneously; printing and drawing at the same time for example. However, this is an *unsound implementation* of multitasking in the current version of CorelDRAW. Version 6.00.118 (also known as version D2 to Corel Customer Service) will thrash your hard disk, then make sushi out of hard disk information, and quite possibly cause *permanent hardware damage* if you check this box.

So in this sense, it's okay if you don't consider yourself an "Advanced" user.

Tweaks, Hacks, and Backdoors

Because practically every square pixel of CorelDRAW's interface can be customized, you'd think there would be no reason to poke around in a configuration file looking for additional enhancements. However, if you'd like to customize the way the Outline menu creates dotted lines, or change the order in which import and export filters display in the dialog box, this is the only place to do it because DRAW doesn't offer direct controls. The following sections offer the only methods for tweaking some of DRAW's more obscure options.

Moving Export File Types to the Top of the List

Many users frequently need to import specific file types. For example, if you like adding text to PhotoCD images, you probably import TIFF images regularly. Perhaps you want to export Windows MetaFile images (WFMs) for a customer who still uses Windows 3.1 and WinWord version 2.

CorelDRAW's import and export filters appear in the Files of t**y**pe section of the Import and Export dialog boxes in a rather scattered fashion; bitmap and vector types of files seem to be intertwined in no particular order. In figure 2.35, you can see the author, who is frantically trying to meet an assignment due date, looking in a folder for Adobe illustrator files that will be imported and converted to CorelDRAW format. Notice that JPEG, GIF, and Windows Icon Resource files top the list; Illustrator AI format is somewhere in the middle of a ponderously long list.

Changes to the import and export filters list require the use of a plain text editor—not a word processor that codes character styles into a document, thus ruining the program file. TextPad, a 32-bit shareware plain text editor designed for use in Windows 95 and Windows NT, is a perfect application for editing program files and composing Internet and other online communication.

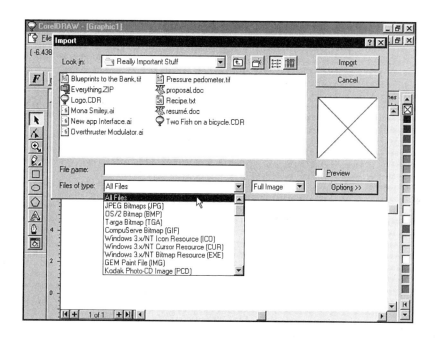

Figure 2.35
Wouldn't it be nice if you could change the order in which import and export filters appear in the Files of type field?

A shareware version of TextPad can be found on the *CorelDRAW! 6 Expert's Edition Bonus CD*. If you'd like to install this working version before continuing with the example steps to follow, now's as good a time as any. (You can also perform the edit shown in the following steps with Windows NotePad.)

Here's how to change the order of the filters listed in DRAW's import and export filters area:

Hacking an INI File

1. Make certain CorelDRAW is not running.

   This step deserves no explanation!

2. In TextPad (or other text editor), open CORELFLT.INI from the CONFIG folder within the CorelDRAW! 6 folder on your system.

3. Save the file as CORELFLT.NEW.

   Saves the original file so that you can load it in case you make a mistake in this file.

This file contains a list of filters in the order they appear in the Files of type drop-down list in CorelDRAW.

4. Scroll down to the section header in the file marked **[Corel DRAW 6.0]**.

   This is the first of two areas in the INI file you need to change. The changes will affect both the Corel applications that use some (or all) of the import/export filters, and CorelDRAW-specific filters listed in the Import and Export dialog boxes, so you'll need to duplicate the editing work you do in the first section of the INI file to a second section.

Suppose you want to make the Adobe Illustrator (AI) filter appear at the top of the Import and Export drop-down lists. *Substitute a filter of your own choice if you like as we go along.*

5. Scroll down to the **FilterNo##** line; the two numbers after FilterNo correspond to the AI filter (or filter of your choice). Highlight the entire line, then press Ctrl+C (Edit, Copy).

   Copies the line to the clipboard. Filter numbers are relatively attributed; if you installed only a few filters during Corel setup, the AI filter might be number 8; the author's AI filter was assigned the number 36 slot. See figure 2.36.

Figure 2.36

Do not perform these edits to the original INI file; make a backup of the file before you begin editing.

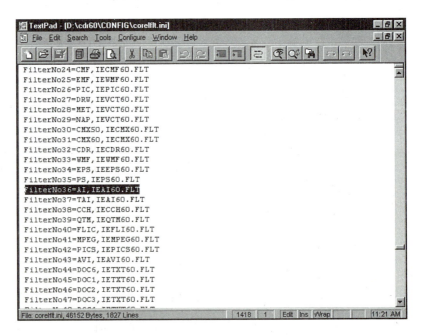

6. Scroll to the top of the **[Corel DRAW 6.0]** section, place your cursor to the right of the first filter entry, press the spacebar, then press Ctrl+V (**E**dit, **P**aste).

   Pastes the line after the first entry, leaving a space so you can clearly see where the original line ends.

7. Highlight the first line, beginning directly after the first equal sign, and ending directly after the second equal sign.

   Selects the text you will now copy to the original AI line in the INI file. The **FilterNo** information will not be used in the finished edit of this file; you're copying it to simply check to be sure that the text you'll now cut is copied to the correct location.

8. Press Ctrl+X (**E**dit, Cu**t**).

   Removes the first filter's information in the list, and the filter number of the place in the INI file where you'll paste the text.

9. Scroll down to the Filter number of the line you copied to the top of the section, type a space after the filter's last character, then press Ctrl+V (**E**dit, **P**aste).

   Pastes the original first position filter's name to the slot where you copied the AI filter name.

10. Remove the duplicate FilterNo characters from the line; make sure there is no space between the equal sign and the filter name.

    You've successfully transposed two filter positions in the first half of two INI sections that need changing.

11. Repeat steps 5-10 with other filters you want "bumped" to the top of the drop-down list.

    Creates a drop-down import and export filter list that you can work with more easily in CorelDRAW. In figure 2.37, you can see the editing process in action; the next step that this figure illustrates is to cut the OS2 filter name, and move it to the original position of the Tiff import/export filter.

12. When you have your "top ten" filters at the top of the list, highlight the entire list—from the F in FilterNo1, to the last character in the last line before the [**CorelDRAW**] section, then press Ctrl+C.

    Copies the contents of the section to the clipboard.

13. Highlight the entire contents of the [**CorelDRAW**] section (after the [**Corel DRAW 6.0**] section you've edited), then press Ctrl+V (**E**dit, **P**aste). Be *very careful* not to highlight into the section that comes after [**CorelDRAW**].

    Finalizes the editing work on the INI file.

14. Choose **F**ile, **S**ave, exit the text editor, then move CORELFLT.INI to a safe location, and name the file you edited CORELFLT.INI.

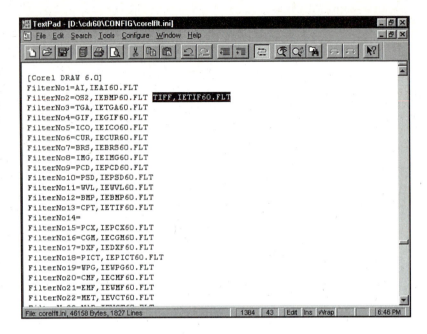

Figure 2.37
Filter numbers (the text preceding the equal sign) must appear in sequential order, but the *names* of the filters can be rearranged.

Makes the edited file the new filter INI file for CorelDRAW. The new file must be located in the CONFIG folder for it to work.

The next time you need to export or import a file, you'll be pleasantly surprised with your cyber-surgery. In figure 2.38, the author followed the preceding steps, and Illustrator files pop right up in the folder window when the first File of **t**ype (after All Files) is selected from the drop-down list.

Creating New Dotted Outlines

In the CorelDRAW version 2's Technical Reference volume, page 79, there was an absolute gem of a hack one could perform to the Outline Pen dialog box by editing the CORELDRW.DOT file. The purpose of CORELDRW.DOT isn't currently documented in the version 6 manual, so we thought we'd share a really neat trick with you to conclude our adventures in customizing. By default CorelDRAW's Outline Pen dialog box offers 27 styles of dotted lines, but can accommodate a total of 40 styles. To some users, 27 might seem like enough, but what if you want to define your own custom style? You can if you own a text editor and know where to find the CORELDRW.DOT file!

If you need a specific space between dotted lines—a coupon, for example—and a specific amount of space between dots in the line, here's the safest hack you can perform to version 6:

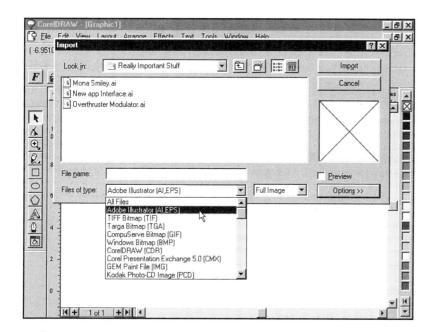

Figure 2.38
Copy important files
before you edit. You
can then manually
change a wealth of
CorelDRAW options.

Creating a Custom Dotted Line

1. With CorelDRAW closed, launch a plain text editor, then load the
   CORELDRW.DOT file, located in the CUSTOM folder of the CorelDRAW
   folder on your hard disk.

   This is a carefully annotated file that is fairly self-explanatory. Nevertheless, let's
   walk through the creation of a dotted line whose line segments alternate between black lines of 4 pixels in width by spaces of 4 pixels in width.

2. Place the cursor after the word **styles** in the line of remarked-out comments
   (lines preceded with a colon), press the down arrow keyboard key, then press
   Enter.

   Positions your cursor in the left character column; places a hard return and
   opens a line preceding the number values.

3. Type **2**.

   Specifies that the unique dotted line you're creating consists of two elements (a
   line and a space).

4. Press the spacebar once, then type **4**.

Specifies that the first of the two elements (the line, or "dot") will be 4 pixels in length (the width of a dotted line is specified in the Outline Pen dialog box).

5. Press the spacebar once, then type **4**.

Specifies that the second element in the dotted line, the space, will be 4 pixels long. See figure 2.39.

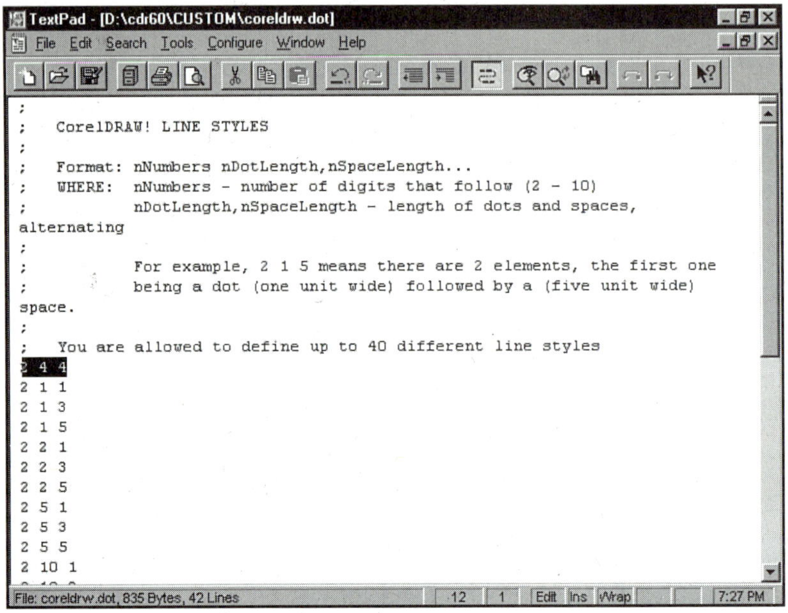

Figure 2.39

You can have a total of 40 dotted line styles in the Outline Pen dialog box. You can remove, edit, or add ones of your own.

6. Save the file, exit the text editor, and launch CorelDRAW.

You've added a custom dotted line to the first of the selections in the Style drop-down list.

As you can see in figure 2.40, the Outline Pen dialog box is open after editing the CORELDRW.DOT file. Sure enough, a four-pixel dot followed by a four pixel space is the very first entry. You can get more creative with exotic dotted line combinations, but sometimes you only need one specific dotted line type.

In figure 2.41, you can see that a combination of 0.05" **W**idth used with the custom dotted line style attracts attention in the clutter of *other* newspaper coupons on a tabloid page. Additionally, you can add the scissors icon to coupons simply by clicking and dragging symbol numbers 33 through 35 in the Dingbats font from the Symbols palette onto the page. See Chapter 8, "Creating Your Own Fonts" for more information on symbol (*pi*) fonts, and how you can create and use custom fonts.

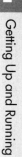

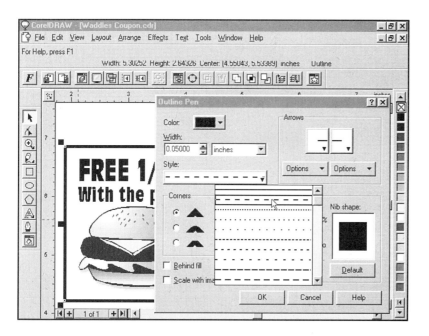

Figure 2.40
Dotted lines are important for coupon designs, maps, and paper airplane construction guides.

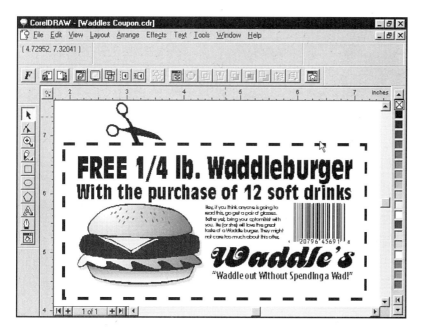

Figure 2.41
Dress up a border to a design with a dotted line style you've created yourself.

> **➤ Tip** If you're not happy with the rectangular "dots" that the Outline Pen Style drop-down list offers, you can create *true* dotted lines by using 2, (space), 0, (space), 3 as a style value in CORELDRW.DOT. Follow the directions in the preceding example, then when you change an object's outline properties in your next session of CorelDRAW, the second Style preview in the Outline Pen dialog box (the style beneath the solid line Style) will show a blank preview.

All is well; what you've done is to attribute a zero pixel length to your custom line Style in the CORELDRW.DOT file (2 elements, 0 dot length, 3 pixel space between lines). Click on the rounded Line Caps radio button in the Outline Pen dialog box, specify a **W**idth such as .08 in the spin box, then click on OK. The result is a dotted line composed of circular dots, because you specified that the zero pixel length segment between spaces in the dotted line should have rounded end caps. With rounded line caps, but zero line length, perfect, circular dots along the outline you've drawn is the result.

The Upward "Path" to Higher CorelDRAW! Skills

Now that you've learned some of the secrets for optimizing CorelDRAW's workspace, it's time to optimize the paths you draw *within* the workspace. Path construction is easy in DRAW, but correct path construction can mean the difference between award-winning artwork, and art that won't print!

Chapter 3, "Beating Nodes and Paths into Submission (The Easy Way)," is a tour of the conventional—and not so conventional methods for producing elegant, complex, awe-inspiring paths and subpaths in less time than you can imagine. With Corel's new tools at your disposal, all you need is a guide.

Beating Nodes and Paths into Submission (The Easy Way)

E very time you pick up the Pencil tool in CorelDRAW, you're doing something
fantastic. When you design an arc, you're actually telling DRAW to plot a curve
based on control points relative to the page. A bitmap representation is then
quickly displayed by the monitor. When the design is saved, it's stored as a series of
mathematical equations—nothing as straightforward as the pixel-by-pixel color values
in a bitmap image file.

CorelDRAW insulates the graphics designer from most of the calculations that go into a
vector drawing. Because you're dealing with on-screen bitmap *representations*, however,
you can sometimes create a curve that breaks the rules that allow the underlying math
equation to print—and sometimes to display—the way you envision it.

Instead of breaking math rules, it might be time for users of previous versions of
CorelDRAW to break some habits, beginning with this new, enhanced version of the
program. If you've ever had a design that failed to output to an imagesetter, or
wouldn't display properly when you copied it to another application, this chapter is for
you. You'll examine artwork drawn in Corel from the ground up to reveal the slickest,
smartest way to approach vector design work using the host of new features and options
version 6 offers. It all begins with the humble node and path segment—the building

blocks of complex vector designs. When you understand the properties of nodes, you can build artwork that looks handsome on-screen, exports to other formats with ease, and will print without a hitch.

Your Smooth Connection to Advanced Design

Anyone who comes from a traditional art background immediately appreciates the advantages of working with vector-based drawing tools. For example, if you've used technical pens and French curves, you already know the perils of stopping the pen in the middle of a curve—the ink spreads on the drawing surface, and you're obliged to spend time whiting-out the connection between two path segments.

Fortunately, when you design a curve using math equations instead of a technical pen, you can correct mistakes invisibly and make connecting path segments flawlessly smooth. "Smooth" is the whole point to working with the CorelDRAW type of computer graphics. If your style of expression consists of rough, imprecise, uneven strokes; all you need is a bitmap-based program, such as Microsoft Paint.

Curves, Splines, and Paths

There are several terms in vector drawing programs that have come to mean the same thing, either due to their misuse, or due to the reality that some aspects of computer graphics have no traditional art equivalent. A *curve* is sometimes qualified as being a *Bézier curve*; you'll also hear the term *spline* thrown out in discussions of vector graphics, and Corel has its own terms for parts of *path segments*. Technically, every curve you draw in CorelDRAW is a spline—a mathematical definition of a curve based on how the curve passes through, or comes close to (approximates), a set of control points. *How* the curve is defined by the control points, how *many* control points are used, and how connections are made from one curved segment to the next determine the curve's proper mathematical name. For example, a Bézier curve (named after Pierre Bézier, a French engineer) is a spline that always has four control points—two points that lie directly upon the curve (which are the *endpoints*; CorelDRAW's term for them are *nodes*), and two control points that the curve may not necessarily pass through.

Figure 3.1 is a diagram of a curve, as drawn in Corel using the Pencil tool in Bézier mode. The *control handles*, as they're called in Corel, lie off the curve, and the distance between them and the curve's endpoints determine the "slope" (the *inertia*) of the curve. If you connect the points that describe the curve (as shown by the light gray lines in fig. 3.1), you can see that this curve fits the ABCD bounding polygon fairly closely; the control handles AC and BD are the *tangents*, the directions of the path. In CorelDRAW, tangents to a curve are represented by the control handles, which are moved by dragging on control points. For the designer, this means that you can design curves with great flexibility and accuracy.

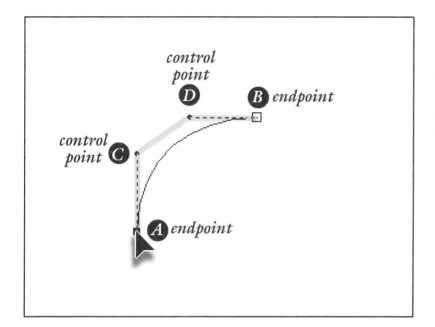

Figure 3.1
A path segment you draw in CorelDRAW consists of at least two control points that lie on the curve at the beginning and end.

Another quality of Bézier curves is that a smooth connection (a smooth *node*) is used to create the transition from one segment of a complete path to the next. CorelDRAW uses Bézier curve math when you create a design, but also offers three different types of connections when different types of curves make up a path. *Cusp* nodes (*connections*) determine the angle at which a straight line segment meets a curve. You also can attach a line to a curved segment with a Smooth property node, but you might find that the control handles of a node with such properties are difficult to manipulate. This is because it's the wrong type of connection for the two path segments, although CorelDRAW allows such a connection to be made. A *Smooth* property node is the type used to connect two curve path segments, and the control handles for a Smooth node always oppose one another at 180 degrees, although each control point at the end of the control handles can be at a unique distance from the Smooth node. *Symmetrical* nodes create the same type of connection between two curved path segments, but the distance from the control points on each control handle is always an equal distance from the node.

Although you can use all of these types of connections in a CorelDRAW design, using an inappropriate kind of connection for a specific path can cause printing problems when printing to high-resolution PostScript printers. You can avoid headaches by developing a drawing methodology that always keeps the underlying math correct and appropriate for expressing a path.

Conventions for the Placement of Nodes

It's almost impossible to create a single vector path (curve) that's constructed wrong mathematically, but most designs that earn significant money feature more than one path segment! The type of work you've probably become accustomed to executing in CorelDRAW consists of several open or closed paths. These paths may be composed of *subpaths* (closed paths that create a "hole" in another closed path). All of the paths and subpaths consist of curves (segments connected by *nodes*—also called control points).

CorelDRAW is a very obliging program in that it allows the creation of nodes on paths in any fashion the designer wants. But there *are* rules for defining vector shapes, and ignoring them can often result in a saved file that simply won't print. The following list describes path properties that should exist in any CorelDRAW design. Don't think of this as a list of "thou shalts"; just use it as a set of guidelines for creating accurate, printer-digestible work. If you follow these conventions, you'll find that they really aren't artistically confining. Rather, they will guide you to valuable insights about how the basic elements of computer graphics design can work for you.

1. **There should be nodes at extremes in a path.** On a smooth path, such as an ellipse, an extreme (the farthest point from the center of an object) is located about every 90 degrees. Therefore, a well-constructed ellipse has four nodes (on-curve control points), evenly spaced. An ellipse constructed with less than four nodes might look the same on-screen, but the math information that makes up the curve isn't adequate to describe the path of the ellipse to a printer. A node that's forced to portray more than 90 degrees of arc will have off-curve control handles that are exceedingly distant from the curve itself. The artistic disadvantage to this scenario is that manipulating the direction of the curve becomes somewhat like paddling a boat with a 50-foot long oar. And the resulting hard copy of an ill-constructed ellipse might contain errors such as a "bump" in the path, because the printer can't handle the vector-to-bitmap translations when they are so far "off the curve."

2. **Use points of inflection when a shape needs a sharp corner.** When a path takes a sharp change in direction, the spot where the change takes place is a *point of inflection*. When a curved path is connected to a straight line, the connection at the point of inflection should be a *cusp* connection. Smooth connections don't accurately describe a sudden change in the direction of a path. As you might have already experienced while working in CorelDRAW, trying to manipulate a smooth point of inflection between straight and curved paths is next to impossible. You simply can't change the direction of the control point associated with the curve!

3. **Use only as many nodes as are necessary to create a path.** Excessive, unnecessary numbers of nodes along a path are often the creation of bitmap-to-vector conversion utilities (such as Corel OCR-Trace). Your design

instincts might be to place a node at regularly-spaced intervals along a shape, but you're designing with *math*, not actual lines in a vector drawing program. Follow guidelines 1 and 2, and then use the Shape tool to delete superfluous nodes—those that aren't relevant to the architecture of the design—on paths in a design. Unnecessary nodes (or too few nodes) often produce curves that are overly complex. In these situations, "complexity" does *not* mean "elaborate" or "intricate"; overly complex paths mean that the math required to describe a curve is too complex for the output device.

Most high-end imagesetters use a PostScript language RIP (raster-image processor) as a means for describing a graphics page before a file is converted to machine code. Each PostScript device is capable of rendering (calculating) only a certain amount of curve complexity. This amount, which varies from device to device, is called *the threshold of curve complexity*. If your design contains curves whose complexity exceeds the threshold of curve complexity of your intended output device, your design will fail to output correctly.

Determining the complexity of a curve is not as simple as counting nodes. A curve can become too complex for any of the following reasons:

✔ Too few nodes are used to describe a path's curves.

✔ Too many nodes are used.

✔ Some nodes have the wrong connection property.

✔ Any combination of the factors above.

A poorly made connection between path segments can cause a PostScript print job to fail even though there might be only 10 or 20 nodes along the path. Conversely, a path with more than 400 perfectly constructed nodes (connections) might also fail to be described to the printer through the use of PostScript language. All of this is compounded by the fact that what is too complex for one PostScript device may not be so for another device.

 Tip   As a rule of thumb, the higher the resolution of the PostScript device, the more likely it is that an ill-made curve will exceed the threshold of curve complexity of the device.

In figure 3.2, you can see a path whose segments are connected in different ways. The middle of the path features an example of a correct smooth connection, one whose control points (its node and associated control handles) lie along a straight line—they are *collinear*. Toward the end of the path, the author got a little cavalier with the path construction, and failed to place a node at a path extreme. It's okay if your design displays dramatic transitions along a path, but it's *not* okay if the connections between nodes—math components of your design—have corresponding drama!

Figure 3.2
Nodes along a path should have smooth transitions, with nodes only at points of inflection and at extremes in curves.

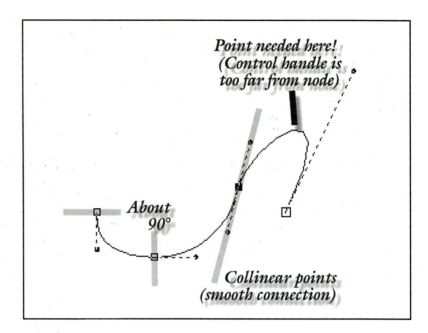

The preceding section has detailed the conventions for how a single path, and a series of connected paths, should be constructed so that the equations for the designs you build can be properly expressed. There are other conventions, those that have to do with building more complex shapes, that we'll get into next.

Font Architecture and Paths

On-the-fly, scaleable typefaces are part of every computer designer's set of graphics tools, and whether they're TrueType or Adobe Type 1, digital fonts are made up of path and subpaths. The following discussion briefly covers some of the truths you should be aware of when converting a string of Artistic Text in CorelDRAW to curves, why and when you should, and what to watch out for so that your textual design will print.

How CorelDRAW! "Looks At" a Font

Chapter 8, "Creating Your Own Fonts," takes you into a more detailed exploration of digital typefaces and their use with CorelDRAW, but for the moment, let's examine what happens when you type a character on DRAW's printable page and convert the character to curves. Type 1 and TrueType fonts are constructed from the same "vector material"—splines and connecting nodes—as anything you might build manually using CorelDRAW's tools. However, Type 1 and TrueType fonts use a different, but closely related, kind of math to produce the spline curves that make up a fonts paths and subpaths. The difference caused by dissimilar math is not immediately evident to the eye, but becomes apparent when a font character (or string of text) is converted and filtered by CorelDRAW.

TrueType was created by Microsoft and the Apple Computer Company as an alternative to Adobe System's Type 1 PostScript fonts. There are two differences between these font technologies that a graphics designer should be aware of.

Comparing Type 1 to TrueType

Type 1 fonts are built around a strict set of coding rules that belong to the PostScript page descriptor *language*. Yes, PostScript is an actual computer language, whose vocabulary can accurately describe the graphical and typographic contents of anything you put on a digital page within a program such as CorelDRAW. The PostScript language is also *device-independent*. As long as a printer, imagesetter, or "print-to-file" utility (such as Corel's EPS export filter or Adobe Acrobat Distiller) can read and write PostScript, the device itself doesn't affect the accuracy of the output, and the device doesn't care about the program used to generate the PostScript code.

The Truth about TrueType

On the other hand, TrueType is a font technology, but not a true *language*. This technology, unlike the PostScript language, has no facility for describing page size to a printer, for generating camera-ready halftones, and cannot recognize bitmap-type graphics contained within a computer file. CorelDRAW offers the option to convert TrueType information into Type 1 information (at the price of output speed) when you print to a PostScript device; otherwise, TrueType is sent to a PostScript printer as pure graphics information, and special font information is ignored. *Hinting*—the capability of a font to adjust typeface character component widths to achieve better output printing at low resolutions—is an example of font information within a digital typeface that you don't usually see, but notice when it's missing.

TrueType uses Quadratic B-spline curve construction, as opposed to Type 1's Bézier curve formula. B-splines create very elegant and smooth curves, but Corel converts B-splines to Bézier curves when a font character is simplified to curve structure. B-splines generally *approximate* a curved path segment; the control points are close to, but don't actually fall on, the curve. Corel's method of handling this possible incompatibility with the different curve math is to filter (convert) the outline description of a TrueType font to the closest match to the original outline shape created with Bézier curves. Doing this creates an excess of nodes along the converted font outline path; typically, you'll see a node every 45 degrees along the curve of a converted TrueType character.

In your professional design career, there may be times when you need to combine font characters to create a logo or similar textual ornament, and this means reducing a complex font structure to curves. Using Type 1 fonts instead of TrueType is best when text is converted to curves, because paths will contain fewer unnecessary nodes you'll have to edit. In figure 3.3, the letter *Q* from the VivaldiD font (from one of the CorelDRAW! 6 CDs) has been converted to curves using the Convert to Curves command (Ctrl+Q). On the left is a converted Type 1 character, and on the right is the equivalent TrueType character.

Figure 3.3

A TrueType character converted to a graphic will contain more nodes along a curve than the equivalent Type 1 character.

For a single character, a PostScript printer probably would render the converted TrueType character just fine, except there might be some minor irregularities where the course of the path is slightly altered by excess nodes. You should note, though, that a long string of TrueType text converted to curves could easily exceed 1,500 nodes per path, a CorelDRAW PostScript printer option and typical PostScript descriptor limit you'd be unwise to exceed. All 1,000 or so of the typefaces on the CorelDRAW CD #2 are Type 1 copies of the 1,000 TrueType fonts on the setup CD, so as long as you have Adobe Type Manager installed, you're not limited to TrueType in your selection of fonts. Save yourself some serious graphics-editing time by sticking with Type 1 fonts if you intend to convert text to curves. If you're printing to a PostScript printer or other PostScript-based output device, *always* use Postscript Type 1 fonts.

Note   Often Type 1 fonts are referred to as Adobe Type 1 fonts. This is because Adobe Systems invented Type 1, and until Adobe released the complete specifications, they were the only company that produced "genuine" Type 1s with special hinting characteristics and optimized printing code. Today, you will find a wide variety of high-quality Type 1 fonts from a number of vendors, and you can even create them yourself. No matter who designed the font, if they were made to "spec," they *are* Type 1 fonts and will work as well as (and occasionally better than) genuine Adobe Type 1 fonts—sometimes even the standard-setter breaks the rules.

Folks at commercial printing houses have been known to kick up a fuss if you use fonts from foundries other than Adobe. That is usually because they have a large collection of Adobe Type 1 fonts and they like to use what they have. They also get nervous if you mention that the fonts you've used are from Corel. This is because Corel released many fonts in version 3 that were not up to spec and caused output problems. These fonts have for the most part been redone or replaced with compliant fonts, but unfortunately a few remain. If you have a problem outputting a file that contains a certain Corel font, check the date of the PFB file; 1992 was a good, but not perfect, year for Corel's Type 1 offerings. If you *must* use off-spec fonts in a design, you should convert them to curves and correct them using the techniques described in Chapter 8.

Working with Subpaths

A subpath is part of a complete shape that can be either within the main shape, like the *counter*—the subpath that creates the hole—within the letter *O*. Also, two subpaths can be combined in such a way that they're geographically isolated, such as the dot and the stem in the character *i*. Regardless of the physical locations of subpaths in a combined shape, their connection must observe the *Winding Path Rule* if the combined subpaths are to print correctly.

The Winding Path Rule states that:

If you were to walk along any closed path, or subpath of a combined shape, the filled area of the shape must be to your left.

This is not a frilly poetic allusion; PostScript language needs to define a start place for a closed path, and the Winding Path Rule is the built-in convention. There are many Type 1 fonts available whose creators didn't observe this rule. While the on-the-fly on-screen display of such a font might look fine, an *O* could fail to print with the appropriate hole punched through it. In figure 3.4, you can see a frilly *graphical* illusion that describes the Winding Path Rule...

If you dust off your high school geometry books, most of them describe a *vector* as having spatial coordinates and a direction traveled between them. It makes sense, then, that a filled, closed path with a combined subpath inside the main path should travel in the opposite direction to create a *negative* fill—a hole.

For the most part, CorelDRAW takes care of this Winding Path Rule automatically; when you combine two paths, it makes no difference whether any of the components were created in a clockwise or counterclockwise direction—Corel adjusts the path direction so that a combined shape prints or exports correctly. Because of CorelDRAW's "auto-directing" feature, the Winding Path Rule might not appear on the surface to be all that relevant to your design assignments, except if you want to use a really cool-looking, but poorly designed, font. Your solution, in this case, is to load the font, convert the character(s) that have filled-in counters (subpaths) to curves, break the character apart then recombine it, then export the character to the proper font register using either CorelDRAW's TTF or PFB Export filters.

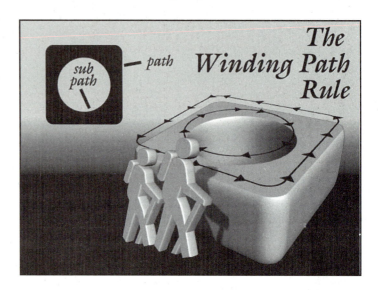

Figure 3.4
The filled part of a shape should always be to the left of the direction in which a path travels.

Combining Subpaths

As mentioned in the last section, a subpath in a combined shape doesn't necessarily have to lie inside another closed subpath. Most of the shapes on the Symbols Roll-Up, in fact, consist of *non-contiguous* (non-touching) combined subpaths.

However, when you take a font, or other shape in CorelDRAW that has a special, complex geometric construction (those that the Rectangle, Text, Ellipse, and Polygon tools create), and combine it with another shape, the properties of the path nodes *change*. And this is something to watch out for when creating the perfect design to print.

A CorelDRAW ellipse that's simplified to connected path segments through more conventional approaches (such as the Convert to Curves command) retains symmetrical node properties at each beginning/end point. However, the Eraser tool, Weld, Intersection, and other editing features will convert smooth path segment connections to cusp properties, something you probably don't intend. In figure 3.5, the shape on the right was constructed by using the Ellipse tool to draw a circle, then the Eraser tool was dragged through the center of the circle's center to create two combined, non-contiguous subpaths. In its present state, the figure on the right will print poorly, if at all, and have bumps where the Eraser tool placed cusp connections when it simplified the ellipse. The shape on the left, a copy of the one on the right, has been edited using the Node Edit Roll-Up to change the cusp nodes into smooth connecting nodes. Unlike the misshapen shape, the left shape will print correctly because the curves are smooth.

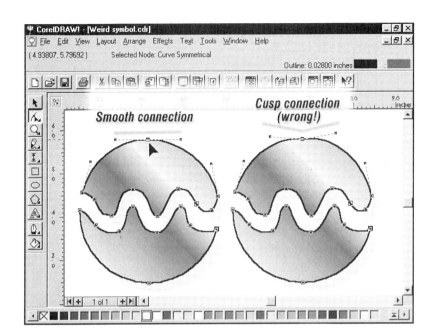

Figure 3.5
Combining and splitting apart complex geometry can change the properties associated with nodes.

Note *Complex geometry* is a term frequently used in this book to describe special classes of vector objects. Ellipses, rectangles, text, and polygons, created by their respective tools, are not mathematically built from the same class of curves as those produced with the Freehand and Bézier Pencil tools.

These objects have an internal structure that provides special effects when you click-and-drag on what appears to be a node on the curves to these objects. In order to edit a complex geometric object, you must either simplify its structure or combine the complex object and another object. To simplify the structure of the complex object, choose **A**rrange, Con**v**ert to Curves from the menu bar, or click on the Convert to Curves Toolbar icon. To combine the complex object and another object use Corel's Trim, Weld, Intersect features, the Combine command, or the Eraser tool.

To further understand how we, and CorelDRAW, look at paths, let's examine the process of bringing a vector design into the real world—the printed hard copy of a design. Accurately drawn paths become accurate instructions for an output device's *rasterization*. Rasterizing is the process by which vector information is plotted onto an imaginary grid that corresponds in size to an *imaging surface*; in the case of physical output, the grid lies on the surface we know as the printable page. This grid is sometimes called a *pixel grid*. The rasterizing process determines which squares in the grid should be filled to produce a printed image that closely approximates the shape defined by the vector curves you draw.

Figure 3.6 is part fact, part fiction. On the left is a representation of how a printer interprets the math equations that you build by connecting and filling vector paths.

On the right is a gridwork of pixels (*picture elements*) that are either filled or unfilled, depending upon the path that is superimposed on the grid at a size that a user defines at printing time. The fictitious part of figure 3.6 is that a pixel grid contains many more pixels than an artist's drawing could represent!

Figure 3.6
A printer plots (maps) coordinates of a design defined by paths onto a pixel grid, which determines areas of a page to be filled.

Note Besides "fill" and "no fill" properties, vector shapes also have *stroke* properties. In CorelDRAW, stroke properties are set by designating Outline Pen properties such as color, width, and end cap shapes. High-quality imagesetters are particularly sensitive to the design of a path when you've defined a weight to the stroke of an unfilled path. Unless path connections are precise and correctly chosen (cusp, smooth, symmetrical), any defects can become painfully obvious on the printed page.

You can do amazing things with combined paths in your CorelDRAW work. The next section covers the proper and improper creation of an inverted color design piece.

When Paths Collide

Self-intersection might sound painful, and the sport of a limited few contortionists, but it's also a near-impossibility for a combined path. Yes, you can indeed draw a "figure 8" using a single path that intersects itself and fill it in CorelDRAW, but doing so can yield a winding number error and potentially cause a print job to fail when you output your design to a PostScript device. Subpaths should be discrete within an image, and this means a negative space should not be physically related to the space defined by the main path.

Printers that use a technology other than PostScript (such as Hewlett-Packard's PCL language) don't grouse nearly as much as a PostScript printer when handed a design that contains a self-intersecting shape. This is because PCL and other language printers are frequently "dumb" in that they are given explicit, total direction on printing from the host application's print engine. PostScript printers, on the other hand, actually are *active participants* in the process of how the images you send it are rasterized and printed. PostScript printers can modify the instructions they are sent to produce the best results achievable on that device. But participation also means that the PostScript printer must be fed "legal" information that it can work with; otherwise, the printing process falls apart.

Does this mean that you can only print a self-intersecting design to a low-resolution, non-PostScript printer? Not at all. The illusion of a graphic that makes a transition from black-on-white to white-on-black is an attractive design hook, and the example coming up contains the steps for making a striking graphic that only looks as though a combined path intersects itself.

MESSENGR.CDR is found in the CHAP03 folder (formerly "subdirectory" under Win3.1!) of the *CorelDRAW! 6 Expert's Edition Bonus CD*. Open MESSENGER.CDR and follow along in this experiment involving the creation of a "half moon" sort of graphic. As you can see in figure 3.7, the "live" elements in this design are an unfilled rectangle half the width of a border frame, one side positioned exactly in the middle of the graphic, and a combined, stencil shape of a messenger.

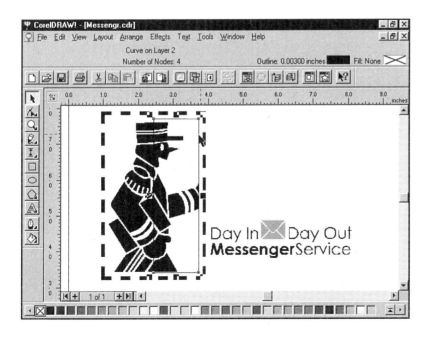

Figure 3.7
MESSENGR.CDR contains all the objects you need to create a half-inverted style of graphic.

Tip   The text object in MESSENGER.CDR is locked on Layer 1, and was converted to curves in case you don't have the same font currently loaded on your system. Many sample designs on the *CorelDRAW! 6 Expert's Edition Bonus CD* have converted text on locked layers where it's important that a design feature a certain font, but the font itself isn't edited as an example step.

Converting *short* strings of Artistic Text is a perfectly acceptable practice when you need to send a design out to a service bureau. Doing this ensures that the character of a font is output exactly the way you intended it, without the bother or legal stickiness of shlepping a disk of fonts to your service bureau. If you have a design that includes *massive* amounts of text, you should seriously consider using only the fonts included on the Corel CD, leaving the text as editable text (don't convert to curves), and choosing a service bureau that also has CorelDRAW version(s) 5 or 6. Almost all font licenses clearly state that you purchase the right to use a font either on your computer or on an attached printer, but that you do *not* have the right to distribute copies of the font as the need arises.

Before the "right way" example in this section, let's walk through the "wrong way" of creating a "day/night" scene from a single combined path. You should sit this one out, and let the author do something self-effacing and idiotic. In figure 3.8, the stencil object and the unfilled rectangle have been both selected, and the **A**rrange, **C**ombine (Ctrl+L) command was chosen. Because the unfilled rectangle overlaps the stencil shape, the image reverses colors at the horizontal halfway point because the "outside" of the single combined path folds inward to become the *inside* in areas where the rectangle doesn't overlap.

Figure 3.8

CorelDRAW enables you to create complex objects that can be visually interesting, but are incapable of being printed to PostScript output.

This effect is fast, striking, and absolutely headache-inducing to the folks at the service bureau! The following example shows you how to create the same effect without generating PostScript errors, in only a few more steps than described in the previous method.

Using the Intersect and Trim Commands

1. Open MESSENGR.CDR from the CHAP03 folder of the *CorelDRAW! 6 Expert's Edition Bonus CD*.

   This is the image you'll convert to a special effects image.

2. Click on the Zoom tool on the toolbox, then marquee around the design leaving about 1/2 screen inch around the top and bottom drawing window edges.

   This is a comfortable viewing resolution for your editing work.

3. Choose **A**rrange, **I**ntersection.

   Displays the Weld, Intersect, and Trim Roll-Up menu.

4. Press spacebar, then click on the unfilled rectangle in MESSENGR.CDR.

   Spacebar toggles the Zoom tool to the Pick tool; selecting the rectangle makes it the source object—Other Object(s) on the Intersect Roll-Up—awaiting your choice of target objects with which to create an intersecting object.

5. Make sure both the Target Object and Other Object(s) check boxes are checked (click inside them if they're not checked).

   Specifies that the rectangle and the target object you choose are not deleted after performing the Intersection operation.

These new option check boxes can get you into trouble, although they were provided in this version to retain objects you might want a copy of after the originals have been trimmed, welded, or intersected. Until you grow more accustomed to this new feature, you might want to always check both boxes before performing an operation.

6. Click on the Intersect With button.

   Your cursor turns into a gigantic arrow, indicating that this is now a cursor used to select the object to be intersected with the selected object (the unfilled rectangle).

7. Click on the stencil of the messenger.

CorelDRAW creates a new object, based on areas of the messenger that overlap the rectangle (see fig. 3.9).

Because the new intersection shape's fill is based on the target object's fill (that of the messenger stencil), you might not easily see the new object, although the status line indicates that the selected shape has 105 nodes as opposed to the messenger stencil's 199. If you like, click on a bright color on the color palette with this new intersection shape selected to see your handiwork.

Figure 3.9

The Intersect command is perfect for creating a copy of a portion of one or more overlapping objects.

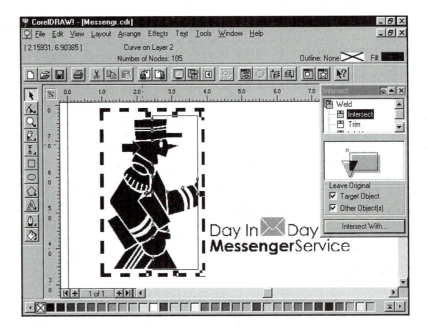

8. Scroll down in the Intersect Roll-Up's list of commands, then click on Trim.

   The Roll-Up now offers options for trimming a target shape with a source shape.

9. Click on the rectangle shape.

   Selects the shape as the Other Object(s) for the Trim operation.

10. Uncheck the Target Object check box.

    Specifies that the original target object (the messenger shape in this example) will be deleted after the Trim operation.

11. Click on the Trim button, then click the gigantic arrow over the left of the messenger stencil (see fig. 3.10).

Deletes the right half of the messenger stencil, starting at the left side of the unfilled rectangle.

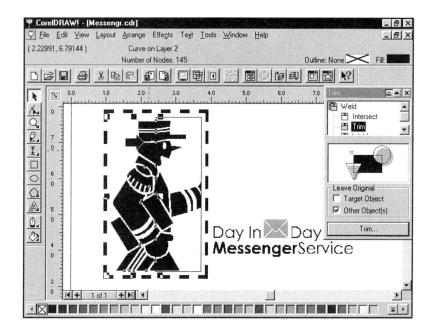

Figure 3.10
The Trim command removes the area of an object that is overlapped by the source object.

12. Click on the messenger stencil intersect object (it appears to be the right side of the original messenger), then left-click on the white swatch on the color palette.

    Makes the intersect object white. It should appear to be invisible now against the white printable page.

13. Click on the unfilled rectangle, then click on the To Back button on the toolbar (or press Shift+PageDown).

    Sends the rectangle to the back of the stack of objects in the MESSENGER design.

14. Left-click on the black swatch on the color palette, then right click on the "X" on the color palette.

    Makes the rectangle black with no outline, and you've accomplished the inverted design effect (see fig. 3.11).

Figure 3.11
The design appears
to reverse itself, but
is actually composed
of two perfectly
aligned halves with
contrasting color
schemes.

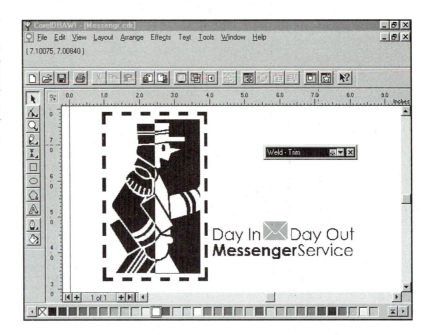

To experienced CorelDRAW users, the preceding example might seem primitive, or the "long way" to do things. It's true that you can recreate this effect by placing the rectangle on top of the right half of the messenger, then filling it and assigning it the Invert Lens (Roll-Up) property. Lens objects will travel through the clipboard to other applications, but they become terrifically complex in terms of the number of nodes used to represent an effect such as the one you've created manually. Many special effects objects are filtered for Clipboard use, creating a multiplicity of nodes along paths. This means slower printing time, and you cannot easily edit a Lens object export with other applications that lack drawing tools.

Additionally, the Lens method cannot be used to produce a graphic that's a candidate for inclusion in a symbol font. The preceding example produced a design that, if you selected all objects and then combined them, would indeed contain subpath information that would qualify as a TrueType or Type 1 character.

"Simplicity" is the key to designing graphics that look good and also print well. CorelDRAW offers at least two different ways to accomplish a design effect, but it's up to you, the designer, to decide on the best route to a specific goal. When it's high-quality imaging, you need to stick to techniques that are accepted in the printer's language.

I

Getting Up and Running

The New Look of the Node Edit Roll-Up

Like most on-screen graphical elements that have experienced a renaissance under the Win95 operating system, the Node Edit Roll-Up, the set of tools for modifying node and control point properties, has been augmented and sports a new look. Gone are the chicklets that had text commands written on them; clean, obscure pictures now hint at the node operation you can perform by selecting nodes and clicking on an icon.

Chances are that a design assignment that crosses your desk cannot be completed by using only the complex shape toolbox tools and the Arrange commands. Therefore, it's a good idea to familiarize yourself with what these Node Edit icons mean and what the new functions offer, and get re-acquainted with node editing.

To display the Node Edit Roll-Up, you double-click on the Shape tool. Figure 3.12 is an enlargement of the Node Edit Roll-Up, with callouts that this section explains in detail next.

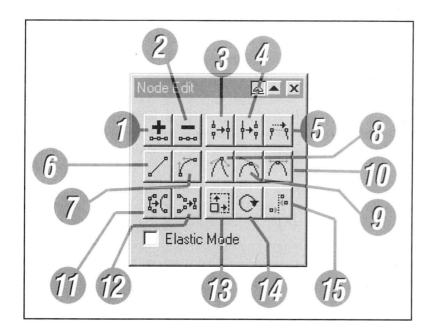

Figure 3.12
The Node Edit Roll-Up in CorelDRAW! 6.

1. **Add Node.** As the plus sign on the button suggests, clicking a point on a curve (or straight path segment) then clicking on this button adds a node to the segment. Repeated clicking on the Add Node button doubles the previous number of nodes you add, so you can very quickly create a path that has plenty of nodes that you can then manipulate to make instant, intricate outlines. Nodes created by clicking the Add Node button repeatedly are created along the path in a direction *opposing* the direction of the path, for example: if you draw a path from left to right, successive nodes added will appear from right to left.

The shortcut to adding nodes, with or without the Node Edit Roll-Up present is to press the + key on the keypad section of your keyboard.

2. **Remove node.** The inverse function of the Add Node function. Deleting nodes often changes the shape of a path, so you should not use this tool indiscriminately.

   Alternative methods for removing nodes are to select one and press the keypad − key or the Delete key, or to marquee-select multiple nodes with the Shape tool, and press the − or the Delete key. You also can select multiple nodes you want to delete by holding down the Shift key and clicking on the nodes you want to add to the current selection. By using the Shift-click technique, non-adjacent nodes can be selected *anywhere* on the object's path.

3. **Join.** Two nodes that are part of the same subpath can be fused together to create a single node by marquee-selecting the nodes, then clicking on the Join button. If you have two, separate, open paths, you can use the Join function by first selecting both segments, then choosing **A**rrange, **C**ombine (Ctrl+L), then marquee-selecting the endpoints of the paths you want to make into a single path.

   It's usually a good practice when using the Join command to position the endpoints of the path to be fused as closely together as possible. When joining two end nodes that are a great distance from one another, the resulting single node will be positioned exactly equidistant from the two nodes' original location.

4. **Break Apart.** This is the inverse of the Join function, and typically requires the Join function to restore a path you've broken apart. The Break Apart function isn't confined to breaking apart nodes; you can break a path segment anywhere you choose. This function is particularly useful when you want to insert a second path along the curve of the main path on which you're working. For example, you've drawn a perfect duck head, and want to attach a beak that's an open path. You'd use the Break Apart command on the appropriate areas of the duck's head, use the **C**ombine command (Ctrl+L) to make both paths into one non-contiguous path, then use the Join function on the end nodes of the component paths to make a closed path you can then fill in.

➤Tip   When you use Break Apart on a closed path with a solid fill, the fill disappears, as the path no longer defines a closed shape. However, when you join the endpoints in the open path, the path will once more take on the foreground color you've assigned to it.

An open path can be reassigned a fill while it's open, and a path that wasn't ever closed can also be reassigned a fill value. The moment you close the path by using the Join command, the paths will blossom into the foreground color you've selected.

5. **Connect with Straight Line.** Perhaps this function's moniker is why Corel gave up labeling the Node Edit Roll-Up buttons! Actually, this is a handy new feature in version 6 that accomplishes two things at once. The Connect with Straight Line closes an open path without repositioning the endpoint nodes you've targeted for joining. A segment with straight line characteristics links the two end nodes; the line property of the segment can then be modified with other node edit functions to suit a specific design need.

6. **To Line.** This function converts a path segment to an inflexible segment between two nodes. Control handles for the nodes associated with the converted segment are lost.

> **Note**   It is important in the effort to design a path that's easy to manipulate (and a legitimate one to print) that a line segment's associated nodes have *cusp* properties. Curves that share a common node with straight line segments cannot meet at a flexible tangent if the node property is Smooth or Symmetrical. Try to rotate the control point of a Smooth node that connects a line with a curve; you can change the *distance* of the control point from the node, but cannot change the control point's *orientation* to the node. In English: if a control handle is not budging when you attempt to reposition it, the node connection is most likely incorrect. After you've converted a curve segment to a line, you should check the end nodes to make sure they're Cusp nodes. If the Cusp button (callout #8) is dimmed on the Node Edit Roll-Up when you click on a line segment's endpoint, the node is correctly attributed. If not, you should click on the Cusp button.

7. **To Curve.** Before a straight line segment can take on cusp, smooth, or symmetrical end node properties, it must first become a curve. The To Curve function is an excellent resource for converting simplified polygons and other line-only shapes into malleable paths. The To Curve function can turn multiple nodes into cusp nodes if you first marquee-select several nodes with the Shape tool.

> **Tip**   When you turn a line into a curve by using the To Curve function, the control points associated with the curve lie directly on the line. This is called the control point's *launch point*, and you'll need to click-and-drag directly on the converted line, away from the center of the new curved segment, to expose the control points.

8. **Cusp.** Assigning this property to a node enables the two control points associated with a curve to be moved independently of one another. In contrast, a Smooth connection offers control points that always move in opposite directions, although the distance from each control point to the node can be unequal.

> **➤ Tip** A Cusp attribute for a node is the ideal connection between a curve segment to a straight line segment, but you should think carefully about the role a cusp node plays in connecting two curves. Yes, you can do this, but consider the construction of the path segment connections. A cusp node connecting two curves can result in an infinitely sharp point of inflection; one that some imagesetters may be unable to properly resolve. Additionally, a symbol font you might create in CorelDRAW for use in CorelMOTION or CorelDREAM may fail to extrude properly in these programs because a cusp node in a character is too extreme in its angle.

9. **Smooth.** The Smooth node attribute is the best choice for making a perfectly seamless transition between two curves. You cannot create a smooth connection with two connected lines without converting the connection to Cusp first, but you can convert a smooth segments directly to lines.

   Smooth node control points are always 180 degrees opposite from one another. The control handles may have different lengths; however, by click-and-dragging a control point away from the associated node, a greater slope (inertia) can be set for only one of the two curves connected with a smooth node.

   If you want to precisely adjust the slope of a curve connected by a smooth node, you can hold the Ctrl key to constrain control point movement to the number of degrees specified in the **C**onstrain angle field in **T**ools, **O**ptions menu. Alternatively, you can use an Angular guideline placed at the same position and angle as the control handle, then turn on the snap-to guidelines option, then click-and-drag the control point.

10. **Symmetrical.** This type of node connection is similar to the Smooth function, except the distance between control points and the associated node remains constant. When you drag a symmetrical control handle away from a node, the opposing control point moves in 180 degree opposition, at exactly a 180 degree opposing angle.

    Symmetrical node connections are useful for building ellipses from freehand shapes. A curve drawn with the Bézier mode of Freehand tool displays Symmetrical connections.

11. **Auto-reduce.** This function decreases the number of nodes along a path when you marquee-select part or all of the nodes in an object using the Shape tool. Do not expect a dramatic reduction of nodes along the path of an autotraced outline, such as you'd create by using Corel OCR-Trace on a bitmap image. Nodes that are placed by an application along a path tend to be seen by Corel as all necessary connections. However, Auto-reduce can detect superfluous nodes in a design you've created and reduce the number of connections to more or less the minimum number. CGM and WMF format objects you've imported into DRAW can also benefit from some auto-reduction. To accurately import these types of vector graphics, Corel must filter (translate) a lot of curve information,

and in the process create outline nodes every few degrees of an arc. As a CorelDRAW object, however, these excess nodes can and should be deleted, and Auto-reduce is a very quick way.

Like the Remove Node function, Auto-reduce can change the shape of an outline path while it eliminates nodes. If you intend to use this function frequently on filtered imports, you might want to place the original on a locked layer, then reduce the nodes in the copy on a new layer above the original. See how the reduced node copy compares to the original, then make path adjustments where necessary.

To specify how many or how few nodes are eliminated when you use the Auto-reduce feature, right-click on the Shape tool, then choose Properties. Lower fractions in the Auto-reduce spin box means that less node reduction is performed, and higher fractional amounts—those fractions approaching 1—will result in more nodes being deleted, and a path that resembles its unedited appearance less closely. See Chapter 2, "Customizing CorelDRAW!," for more information on Tool Properties.

12. **Extract Subpath.** This function operates a lot like the **A**rrange, **B**reak Apart command (Ctrl+K), except you have the choice of whether to break out all subpaths from a main path, or only one. Suppose you have converted the character "B" to curves, and now want to remove the upper counter in the character, but want the bottom counter in the "B" to remain. You'd select only the nodes that make up the counter in the upper half of the "B," then click on the Extract Subpath button. The selected subpath immediately becomes its own path, and the "B" is deselected.

13. **Stretch.** You can do some wonderfully bizarre things by selecting a few nodes on path, then clicking on the Stretch button. This function treats connected path segments as though they are a discrete shape. The selection bounding points around the selected nodes are treated like the selection points around a selected object. You can proportionately or disproportionately scale path segments while leaving the deselected nodes and paths unchanged. You can even *mirror* the selected segments (by holding Ctrl while click-and-dragging a side handle to the opposing side of the selection points).

14. **Rotate.** All selected nodes and the path segments they govern will rotate around a center of your choosing when you apply the Rotate function to them. This can create the effect of a bent object without using the Envelope Roll-Up. For example, you can create a rectangle, press Ctrl+Q to simplify the rectangle, marquee-select the nodes and convert them to curves (callout #7), then select the top nodes and click on the Rotate button. You can make an apparently straight-edged path swoop and sway, and you can also click-and-drag the center point of the rotation bounding box to create off-center rotation.

15. **Align Nodes.** This function works only with two nodes at a time. Suppose you've created a freehand, four-sided shape that you now decide you'd like as a rectangle. Marquee-select the bottom two nodes, then click on the Align nodes button. The dialog box offers you the choice of Align **H**orizontal, Align **V**ertical, or Align **C**ontrol Points (which places the selected nodes directly on top of each other). This is not the most straightforward of dialog boxes, because if you want to align two nodes horizontally, you *un*check the Align **V**ertical check box, and the reverse.

Finally, the Elastic Mode check box enables you to move a group of selected nodes different distances. The aesthetics of the Elastic Mode makes moving two or three selected nodes result in a smoother curve transition between selected and deselected segments. With elastic mode turned off, selected nodes and paths move an equal distance, and can sometimes result in a visible "lump" where a selected path meets a deselected one. If you need precise control over curve placement, it's best to leave the elastic Mode check box unchecked. However, if you want to create a truly freeform, yet overall smooth, shape, Elastic mode can assist you.

The Many Ways to Begin a Drawing

The term "tracing" has earned unsavory connotations in professional circles; "cheating," "copying," and "unoriginal" are, unfortunately, right up there as synonyms to "tracing." However, if you've come to CorelDRAW from a traditional art background of using physical tools on a stylus or drafting table, your most productive time in CorelDRAW might be spent with a "template" of what you envision a final design to be. By using, for example, a bitmap "rough" of a design beneath your Pencil tool work, you can quickly block in geometric shapes, then refine the work as you move along.

Although CorelDRAW features many digital equivalents to physical design tools, it is folly to believe that one can comfortably port traditional skills to those used in electronic media without some human invention. Corel's Pencil tool is *not* an actual pencil, and therefore your methodology needs to change somewhat when designing with vectors. Also, if you're experienced with other drawing applications such as Freehand or Designer, Corel's Pencil tool doesn't operate the same way.

In the following sections, you'll explore four different techniques you can adopt to quickly and precisely create paths in CorelDRAW, using the Freehand and Bézier modes of the Pencil tool in combination with the Node Edit Roll-Up's features.

CorelDRAWing Method #1: Beginning with Autotracing

There's a feature right in CorelDRAW's workspace that operates like a mini-Corel OCR-Trace; the Pencil tool can autotrace an imported bitmap by simply clicking on an area of high contrast within the bitmap image. Although this feature is not intended as a replacement for OCR-Trace, and the accuracy of the paths produced by autotracing ranges from fair to inspired guesswork, autotracing nonetheless creates a closed path that you can reshape to fit the bitmap template in no time.

You can set Autotrace to create an outline that matches the edge of contrasting colors in a bitmap tightly (producing many nodes along the path), or loosely (producing a less accurate path with fewer nodes). To change the autotrace setting, double-click on the Pencil tool, and then in the Tool Properties menu, use the Autotrace Tracking spin box to set the tolerance of drawn path closeness to the bitmap area you want traced. The quality of the picture you use to autotrace plays a role in the autotrace path precision, as well. If you need a tree as part of a design, for example, a high-contrast, almost posterized image would be the best to autotrace, with clearly defined areas where a tone begins and ends. Also, it would be a good idea to take the photo of such a tree on a cloudless day, to keep the tree clearly profiled against a solid tone.

Here's an example of how you can save some steps in CorelDRAW by using a bitmap image as a source of a design element along with the autotrace feature.

Autotracing a Bitmap Image

1. In CorelDRAW, choose File, New, Document (or press Ctrl+N).

   Opens a new document window.

2. Choose File, Import (or click on the Import button on the toolbar), choose your CD-ROM drive from the Look in drop-down list, double-click on the CHAP03 folder, click on the DIMBULB.TIF file, then click on Import.

   Imports the bitmap image, and it's the currently selected object on the printable page (see fig. 3.13).

3. Click on the Pencil tool, then position the special cursor so that its right edge (the dotted line) meets the edge of the contrasting lightbulb and background, then click.

   Creates an outline path that approximates the shape of lightbulb (see fig. 3.14).

Figure 3.13

You can import many different types of computer graphics and text without specifying the extension in the Files of type list.

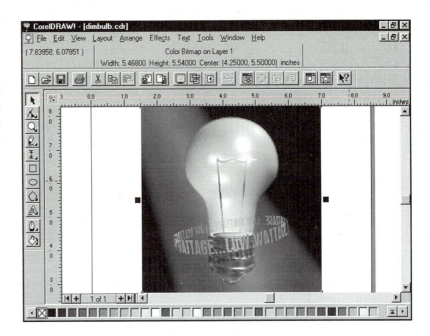

Figure 3.14

A closed path, with nodes at points of inflection, is created by clicking on the bitmap with the autotrace cursor.

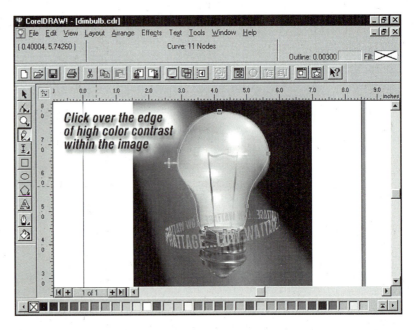

Because autotrace doesn't replace artistic talent, you'll probably find that this is a good, working, rough path around the lightbulb, but it doesn't describe the bulb's shape flawlessly. Now that you have a good beginning shape, it's time to "work over" the composition by moving from general details to more specific ones…

4. With the autotrace path selected, right-click over the bright green swatch on the color palette.

   Changes the outline of the path from default to bright green, so you can visually separate the path from the color bitmap beneath it.

5. Click on the Zoom tool, then marquee-zoom into the top third of the lightbulb.

   Provides you with a comfortable view in which to edit nodes.

6. Double-click on the Shape tool.

   Changes tools and displays the Node Edit Roll-up.

7. Click-and-drag the top node so that is it exactly on the edge of the bulb and its background.

   Repositions the node to accurately pass through the outline of the bulb that was autotraced.

8. Click on the top node of the outline path, then click on the Smooth button on the Node Edit Roll-Up.

   Converts the node to Smooth property (see fig. 3.15).

If the autotrace you performed didn't produce a node toward the top of the outline, follow the next step…

9. Click on the top of the outline, then press the + key on the keypad.

   Creates a smooth node at the top of the path.

Note Smooth nodes are created along curves by default when you add them to a path. This is because Corel assumes that when you add a node to a curve, you don't want the "flow" of the curve interrupted with a cusp property, which is true most of the time.

When adding nodes to straight line paths, however, the resulting node connection has straight properties. This is done to create continuity among path segments; if no other path segment has off-curve control points, adding a node will not produce off-curve control points.

10. Repeat the steps of repositioning and attributing nodes a Smooth quality to the other nodes along the path.

    You are duplicating the shape of the lightbulb in the image.

Figure 3.15
You need to manually adjust node properties in an autotraced object to reflect the type of shape you design.

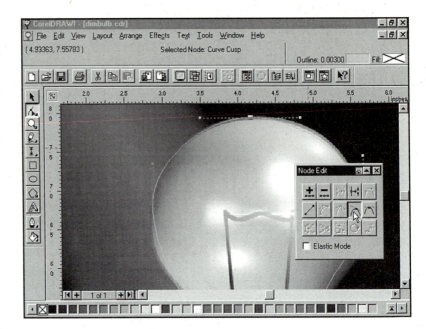

11. When you're happy with the outline, choose **F**ile **S**ave (Ctrl+S), then save the design as BULB1.CDR to your hard disk.

Saves the work for use in the next example.

There are plenty of approaches for filling the outline you created in the preceding example to make this a finished illustration; there are several creative suggestions for custom blends and fills in Chapter 4, "Mastering Color Models and the Fill Tool." But a finished illustration isn't the point of this section—a solid working methodology needs to be developed with CorelDRAW to make your design work an inspired task instead of simply a task. And it's always best to peruse your options for creating the rough framework of a design.

It's also important to use a bitmap image source as an option, but not to rely on it too heavily. With so much digital stock photography available today, it's not hard to inadvertently create a piece that infringes on copyrighted work. Let a bitmap template be a guide to the flow of a composition, but don't trace something to represent the main thrust of a piece. Besides photography, modeling applications are an excellent starting point for generating bitmap templates. CorelDREAM 3D comes with several preset shapes that you can pose and render, then bring the rendered bitmap into CorelDRAW as template material. In fact, DIMBULB.TIF is a rendered model, and a lot of the clip art on the Corel CD began as physical pen-and-ink work that was scanned, then manually converted to vector format using some of the same techniques you're reading about right now.

CorelDRAWing Method #2: Double-Clicking to Design Paths

Many applications that have path tools follow a convention of single-clicking to produce progressive, connected straight lines, and a path is closed with a double-click. If you're familiar with this feature set from another application, these steps are exactly the opposite of how you draw connected path segments in CorelDRAW—double-clicking connects and produces a straight path segment, and a single click on the start point closes a path.

Sometimes it's easier to manually create a path than to autotrace around areas of a bitmap image. Because most drawing tasks require using a combination of the Pencil and Shape tools, it's a good idea to keep node editing tools close at hand. This next example demonstrates how you can use the double-clicking method of drawing to define a shape, and how the straight line properties of path segments can instantly be converted to curves that can be refined. *Points of Inflection*, as described earlier, should be used as a guide as to where the nodes should go in a manual tracing—every 90 degrees between path segments, and at points along the curve where the path takes a markedly different direction.

Double-Clicking a Manually Created Path

1. Open BULB1.CDR from your hard disk, delete the autotrace path, then choose File, Save As, and save this file to hard disk as BULB2.CDR.

   Saves having to import DIMBULB.TIF again to a new document. This file contains the bitmap you'll manually trace.

If you don't have a BULB1.CDR file because you didn't walk through the preceding example, follow the first two steps in the preceding example to import DIMBULB.TIF.

2. Click on the Zoom tool, then right-click over the drawing window, and choose Zoom to Fit from the shortcut menu.

   Zooms the bitmap image to fill the drawing window vertically. If you've chosen to customize the Zoom tool to operate in the Traditional mode, or right-click Zoom-out mode, use the custom settings to zoom to a close-up of the bitmap image.

3. Click on the (Freehand, default) Pencil tool, then click on the left edge where the bulb meets the base.

   This is the starting point for the path you'll draw.

4. Double-click about an inch above the bulb, on its edge, where the bulb begins to curve outward.

   Creates a straight line between the first and second node; second node will be a point of inflection.

5. Right-click on the white swatch on the color palette.

   Makes the outline you're creating white, which is easier to see and work with.

6. Continue double-clicking clockwise around the edge of the bulb, placing a node about every 90 degrees around the top, and where the edge of the bulb changes direction. Stop at the right edge where the bulb meets the base.

   Creates a rough outline of the bulb. See figure 3.16 for recommended locations for double-clicking.

Figure 3.16

Approximate the shape of the lightbulb by drawing straight lines between extremes (points of inflection) along the bulb's outline.

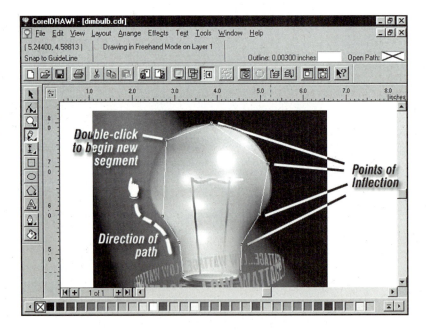

7. Single-click at the start point of the path.

   Closes the path.

8. Double-click on the Shape tool.

   Changes tools; displays the Node Edit Roll-Up.

9. With the path selected, marquee-select all the nodes in the path, click on the To Curve button, then click on the Smooth button.

Creates a more accurate outline around the lightbulb shape (see fig. 3.17).

> **Note** Holding Ctrl+Shift and clicking on a node in a selected path automatically selects all nodes.

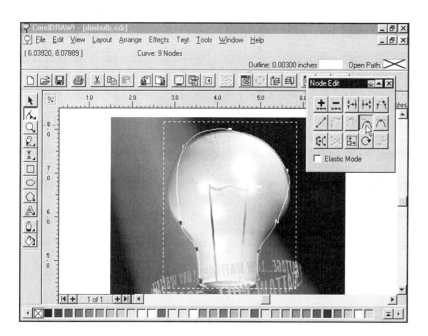

Figure 3.17
Smooth connecting nodes accurately describe the shape of the lightbulb.

> **Note** Converting straight lines to curves doesn't change the shape of a path, but as you've seen, converting cusp curves to smooth ones does. Procedurally, a straight line must always be converted to a curve before the connecting node can take on a Smooth quality, and the curve initially has to have a cusp quality. The functions on the Node Edit Roll-Up are dimmed for those node characteristics that don't apply or are unavailable for a selected node.

However, a Smooth, Cusp, and Symmetrical path segment can be converted directly to a straight line.

Unlike the experiment with the autotrace path, the path you've manually created around the bulb has all nodes lying directly on the edge of the bitmap bulb image. Therefore, to conclude this assignment, you have two options for further node editing; to shape the steepness (*inertia*) of the curves, or to specify the direction of the curves. Let's continue…

10. Click on the center of a path, then slowly click-and-drag it away from the center of the path.

    Changes the direction and steepness of the path segment; also affects the direction of the path segment that precedes it (see fig. 3.18).

Figure 3.18
You can directly manipulate a curved path, but a smooth connection always means you change the curve of the connecting path segment.

The direct manipulation method works sometimes for correcting a path's curvature, but it's not the most precise way to fit a curve to an edge. Here are the other methods…

11. Click-and-drag a node's control point away from the node.

    Creates a steeper arc to the curve.

12. Click on a control point, then drag it in a revolving direction around the node *without* changing the control handle's length.

    Makes the curve "point" in a different direction (see fig. 3.19).

Once you've fine-tuned a curve by changing the control point's orientation and distance from the node, and the resulting curved segment closely matches the curve of the lightbulb image, tweak the rest of the nodes in the path, until the path shape conforms to the lightbulb's edge.

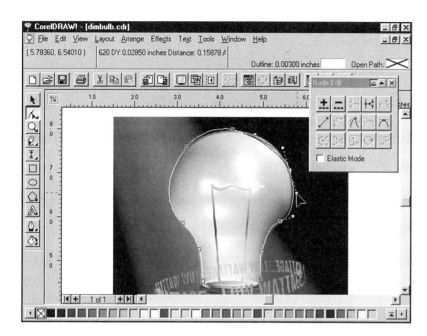

Figure 3.19
You're actually setting a new tangent for a curve when you change the angle between a node and a control point; you "direct" the curve.

CorelDRAWing Method #3: Freehand Drawing

There is another way to use the Freehand mode Pencil tool to manually create an outline around a template, and this is where the Freehand mode gets its name. You can simply click-and-drag the cursor around to create a shape, as you would use a paint program's brush tool. However, the resulting curve would be irregularly shaped, and you'd be obliged to slow the cursor down at the closing of a freehand path to ensure that the path closes at its beginning point, which is *not* a natural design inclination. Also, "freeform" Freehand mode drawing requires extensive node editing to correct path segment inaccuracies, node connection properties, node positions, and the occasional need to add and delete nodes.

➤ Tip Generally speaking, owners of digitizing tablets can make the best use of the Freehand mode Pencil tool, because the digitizing tablet's stylus can be guided more like a physical pencil and the resulting lines are more flowing, precise, and natural-looking.

The Guide to Perfect Paths

Here's a checklist for you to follow that sums up the sequential procedures for creating curved paths regardless of any technique you choose to use with the Pencil tool. The emphasis is on nodes, not paths, because nodes govern the appearance of a CorelDRAW design.

✔ **Accurate node position.** Do a node's XY coordinates on the printable page properly express where a curve passes through? If not, use the Shape tool to reposition the node.

✔ **Correct Node Property.** Is the connection between path segments the right one to express a shape? If a straight line connects to a curve, the node should be a cusp node; when two curves meet, the connection should usually be smooth. In isolated incidences, where the distance between two nodes is very small, it's okay to place a cusp node between two curved segments. Imagesetters can properly interpret and output small sharp, curved corners, but you should not create a large arc that abruptly changes direction and continues as a curved segment without placing smooth, intermediate nodes as "braces" close to and on each side of the cusp node.

✔ **Control point distance from node.** The distance between a control point and a node can be measured by the control point's handle. The distance determines the severity of the associated curved path segment—how much of a slope the path takes from its connecting nodes. In general, if a control point handle appears longer than half the distance of the path segment it controls, you should either shorten the distance and reduce the curvature of the path, or add a node to the middle of the curve.

✔ **Control Point Aspect to a node.** Control Points can be rotated relative to the node they control, and rotation affects the direction of the associated curved path. If a control point is actually located on a path, you don't need this control point, and the path probably should be a straight line (the node should be a cusp).

CorelDRAWing Method #4: The Bézier Mode of Drawing

Bézier curves can be used to describe most every object you can imagine, but their creation is not the easiest to grasp intellectually. This is partially due to the implementation of Bézier design tools. Most every program, including CorelDRAW, uses the graphical metaphor of a pencil tool that produces curves *after* you've click-and-dragged, and then only displays a guideline of the *tangent* you're supposed to set between the last curve, and the curve you're *about* to create!

Nevertheless, CAD folks have been using Bézier drawing tools since the beginning of CAD. If you can "think" Bézier, you'll enhance your creative talent, and create complex curved shapes quicker than any method described so far in this chapter. If you have a lot of weaving elements in a design—ocean waves, fashion design plates, "coily" telephone cords—definitely check out the following example of how to make the Bézier mode Freehand tool work for you. At the same time, let's dig a little deeper into Corel features that can speed up production of complicated design work; there are some tricks in the next set of steps that you'll want to add to your CorelDRAW repertoire.

Here's how to set up a tracing template for this section on Bézier drawing, that you might find works for *all* types of design work in CorelDRAW...

Setting Up a Locked Template Layer

1. Choose File, New, Document (Ctrl+N).

   Opens a new drawing window.

2. Choose File, Import, choose your CD-ROM drive from the Look in drop-down list, double-click on EXERCISE, double-click on CHAP03, click on BIGTOP-P.TIF, then click on Import.

   Imports BIGTOP-P.TIF, a monochrome (black and white, 1 bit per pixel) image to be used as a template.

3. With BIGTOP-P selected, right-click over the 30% Black swatch on the color palette.

   Turns the foreground pixels in BIGTOP-P to a light gray.

The bitmap graphics type that consists of only one bit of color information per pixel can be colorized in CorelDRAW; left-clicking over a swatch on the color palette changed a selected monochrome bitmap's background color. This makes tracing with CorelDRAW's default color of black outline easier to see against the bitmap image. This trick does *not* work with bitmap images of higher color capability.

4. Choose Layout, Layers Manager (Ctrl+F3), then right-click over the list area of the Layers Roll-Up, and select New.

   Displays the Layers Roll-Up; creates a new layer with the default name highlighted (see fig. 3.20).

5. Type **Tracing** in the Layer 2 highlighted text box.

   Makes the layer you'll trace on easier to reference in the future.

Users of previous versions of CorelDRAW have grown accustomed to clicking on the Roll-Up pop-up menu button, the triangle that's now beneath the Close button, to access options for a Roll-Up. But because CorelDRAW! 6 is completely Win95-compliant, almost every object you see on-screen has a shortcut menu, including the Layers list. The preceding step—where you added the new Tracing layer—shows that there are now two routes to a common destination.

Because each new layer you create has its default name highlighted, you can quickly rename a new layer; it's then easy to see which layer you're working on by referring to the status line, which continually updates drawing window information.

New to CorelDRAW! 6 is a toggle that you can set to work across layers. By default, **E**dit Across Layers, the option on the pop-up shortcut menu, is on. You can "lock" Layer 1, the layer that presently holds the monochrome bitmap, in one of two ways: You can uncheck the **E**dit Across Layers option on the shortcut menu, or...

Figure 3.20

Create a new layer on which to work; let a bitmap template remain on a separate layer.

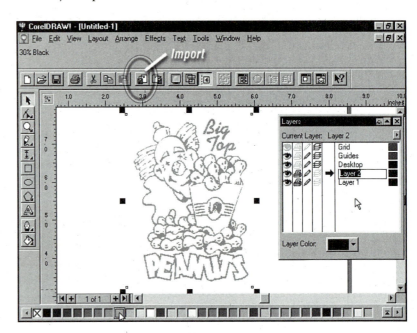

6. Click on the pencil icon to the left of the Layer 1 title on the Layers list.

    Locks Layer 1's contents from editing or selecting.

7. Choose **F**ile, **S**ave, then save the new document as BIGTOP.CDR to your hard disk.

    This is the file in which you'll create a Bézier curve tracing.

Now that the template for Bézier drawing has been set up, it's time to get more familiar with the mode of Pencil tool that produces Bézier curves. You'll notice that the BIGTOP-P imported bitmap's visual content lends itself to the type of smooth curves that Bézier curves define; the peanuts and ruffles around the clown's neckpiece consist of very few "hard" direction changes in a path that would describe these areas. And when an abrupt change *does* take place along a traced path, the following example shows how to address the issue.

The Layers Roll-Up has undergone some changes in this new CorelDRAW version, and the Options dialog box is gone. All the printing, viewing, locking, and other options are "up front" on the Layers list. The column that features the large arrow indicates the current editing layer. Make certain that this arrow now points to the Tracing layer title; if not, click in the arrow column next to the Tracing layer to move the selection arrow. Once this has been done, you can close the Layers Roll-Up (by clicking on the Close button) to conserve screen real estate.

Here's a simple "road test" to get a feel for designing with the Bézier mode Pencil tool.

Designing Bézier Curves

1. With the BIGTOP-P.CDR open, choose the Zoom tool, then marquee-select a small area around the peanuts above the letters "PE" in the bitmap template.

   This is the target area for beginning a Bézier curve.

2. Click+hold on the Pencil tool; while holding, move your cursor to the Bézier button, then release.

   Chooses the Bézier mode Freehand tool for drawing.

3. Click, hold, and drag the Bézier tool at a point of inflection (middle of a curve) on one of the peanuts in the bitmap image

   Creates a starting point for a path; first node sprouts control points and handles.

4. Move the cursor around until the control handles make a tangent line to the curve in the bitmap pointing to the next point you'll make to create a curve.

   You're shaping the beginning of a curve yet to be completed by clicking a second node.

This is the part of making a Bézier curve that frustrates users accustomed to drawing a path, then shaping it later using the Shape tool. With the Bézier mode tool, every subsequent "drag" after clicking is actually an *editing* move. Your cursor switches functions immediately after clicking a point; the cursor becomes an editing tool, and by dragging, you set the length of both control handles on the node, and set the direction of the curve. In a way, when you single-click points, then drag, the Bézier mode alternates between a drawing tool and a shape tool. One click-and-drag sets half the curve you'll create, and a second click-and-drag completes the curved path, and sets the slope and angle of the other half of the curve.

5. Find another point along the outline of the peanuts template where the outline changes direction, then click a point and drag the cursor.

Completes a path segment; dragging the cursor shapes the path to conform to the peanuts template.

6. Click-and-drag on the next point along the peanuts template curve where you see a point of inflection along the outline.

Sets the node connecting previous and future path segment; shapes last half of previous curve, sets direction for future curve (see fig. 3.21).

Figure 3.21
The tangent line created by a node's control handles determines the slope and direction of curves that connect at the node.

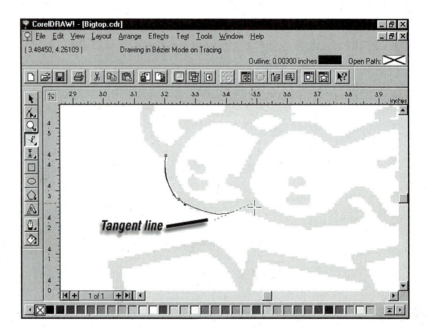

When you come to a connection point that should be a cusp (all Bézier curve connections are symmetrical), draw a curve with a point of inflection on the spot where the node *should* be a cusp, then place one node *beyond* this cusp point by click-and-dragging (see fig. 3.22).

An endpoint on a Bézier curve cannot be changed from Smooth property because the Smooth property refers to the connection between two path segments; without continuing the path, you'd *have* no connection to correct. In the next steps, you'll see how to change the symmetrical connection with a minimum of interruptions to your design work...

7. After you've click-and-dragged a point *beyond* the node that should be a cusp on the path, press F10.

Switches the Pencil tool to the Shape tool.

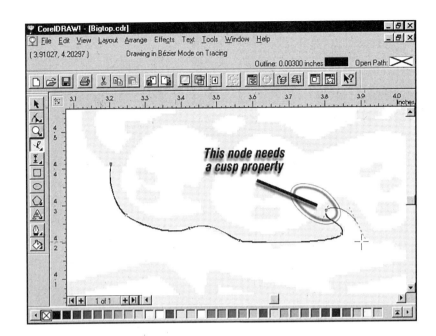

Getting Up and Running

Figure 3.22
Although the node property might be wrong for a node, draw beyond the node, then return to fix the connection (and the connecting paths).

8. Click on the node you want to convert to cusp property, then right-click on the node.

   Displays a context-sensitive shortcut menu for node properties.

9. Choose Cusp from the shortcut menu.

   Converts the Smooth connecting node to Cusp property (see fig. 3.23).

10. Click-and-drag the control points on the curved path so that the path segment fits the peanuts template.

    Cusp node control points can be manipulated independently of one another; you can shape one segment without changing the connecting segment (see fig. 3.24).

As mentioned earlier, cusp nodes between curves can fail to be interpreted correctly by a high-end printer, so to buy some insurance that the path, overall, has a smooth set of segment transitions...

11. Click a point between the Bézier curve endpoint and the cusp node, then click on the + keypad key.

    Adds a smooth node to the Bézier path (see fig 3.25).

Figure 3.23
To use the Node Edit Roll-Up functions from a shortcut menu, select a node or path, then right-click.

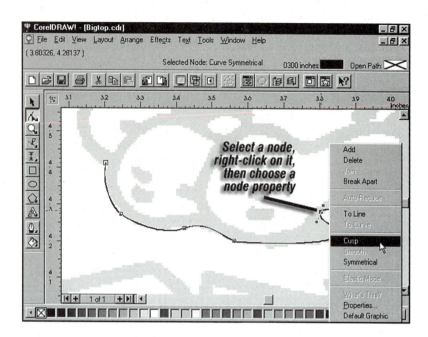

Figure 3.24
Cusp node properties allow individual manipulation of control points around a node.

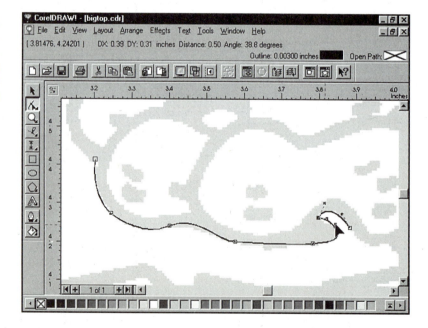

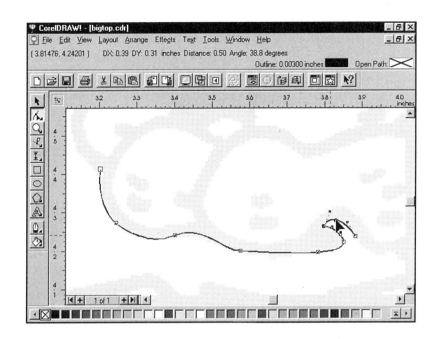

Figure 3.25
Points added to a curved segment become nodes with the smooth property.

12. To continue tracing the Bézier curve, press F5.

    F5 is the toolbox shortcut for the Last Used Curve tool (the Bézier mode Pencil tool).

13. Click on the endpoint, then drag.

    Resumes the Bézier path; makes the endpoint a Smooth, not Symmetrical connection.

14. Continue click-and-dragging to create nodes at points of inflection along the peanuts template until you're comfortable with the way the Bézier mode works.

    You've mastered the workings of the Bézier mode Pencil tool.

Note Stopping to edit a Bézier curve's node while designing might be a distracting technique, and you can certainly complete a closed path, then select nodes and paths to refine. But the technique shown in the preceding example ensures that a designer doesn't forget to finesse an incorrect node connection. On occasion, you'll want to use a combination of Bézier and Freehand modes to complete a shape. Alternating between node editing and drawing also helps reduce the repetitive motions caused by creating complex designs.

Earlier in the preceding example, it was mentioned that you cannot click on an end-point to change node property. You can, however, click on a path segment and set cusp, smooth, and other properties, but doing so might create a path that's "in conflict" with the property of the node that connects the segment with the *following* segment.

✔ A line connected to a line requires a line property node.

✔ A line connected to a curve requires a cusp property node.

✔ A curve connected to a curve requires a smooth (or symmetrical) property node, unless a cusp node is absolutely required to express a shape.

The only real distinction between a smooth and a symmetrical connection between curves is that a symmetrical connection ensures that the direction and amount of curve of both segments that the node connects is equal.

The final section of this chapter travels a little off the beaten path, and focuses on a new feature in CorelDRAW's node editing tools: the Eraser tool. You can use the Eraser tool to remove large sections of closed paths to produce paths with irregularly shaped edges. As you'll discover in Chapter 5, "Complex Fills and Blend Shading," the better you understand how to manipulate path segments, the more easily you can make compound objects that can express exactly what you intend.

Erasing as a Method of Path Manipulating

The Eraser tool uses algorithms (a set of mathematical procedures) similar to the Contour Effect, which is discussed in detail in Chapter 8. But instead of only broadening the outline of a single drawn path, it goes a step beyond and trims the object that you dragged the Eraser through. As a final cleanup step, it deletes the path made by the stroke of the Eraser. Corel has refined the math behind the Contour algorithms in version 6 to produce Eraser strokes and Contours that contain far fewer extraneous nodes along the target path, which makes both features in CorelDRAW! 6 more of a pleasure to work with.

Erasing Your Way to High Art

The Eraser tool doesn't exactly erase; if you want to remove a Pencil tool line, you're better off deleting it, or pressing Shift while you backtrack the line's path with your cursor. The Eraser tool's intended purpose is to remove areas from a closed path, freehand fashion, while leaving the target filled shape as one or more closed paths.

In the following example, you'll see one of the creative uses for the Eraser tool; to create an irregular edge on a drawing of a sheet of paper. If you don't use a digitizing tablet with CorelDRAW, you'll find that the Eraser tool can be a wonderfully expressive device for producing naturalistic bends and curves along a closed path. It's also a very quick way to create two or more non-contiguous subpaths from a single closed path.

Here's how to take a design of a clean sheet of paper and quickly turn it into a slightly *tattered* sheet of paper:

Creative Uses for the Eraser Tool

1. Open the TEAR-OFF.CDR file from the CHAP03 folder in the EXERCISE folder of the *CorelDRAW! 6 Expert's Edition Bonus CD*, then save the file as TEAR-OFF.CDR to your hard disk.

   This is the sample file you'll work with in this example.

If you examine this design, you'll notice that the pushpin and shadow are grouped objects; as such, they cannot be used with the Eraser tool. This experiment involves only the sheet of paper that the pushpin is poking through.

2. Click on the Zoom tool, then marquee-zoom into the design leaving about 1/2" space on the top, and 1" space on the bottom.

   Zooms to a comfortable view of the design; leaves room for editing on the bottom of the design.

3. Click+hold on the Shape tool, then click on the Eraser tool.

   Chooses the Eraser tool.

4. Double-click on the Eraser tool.

   Displays the Tool Settings menu; the Eraser tool is displayed on the drop-down list as the active tool.

5. Highlight the value in the Thickness field, then type **.4**.

   Sets the width of the Eraser tool.

6. Make certain that the Auto-reduce nodes of resulting objects check box is checked, then click on OK.

Figure 3.26
Check CorelDRAW's rulers before you set the Eraser tool Thickness; the Thickness should scale to the objects to be erased.

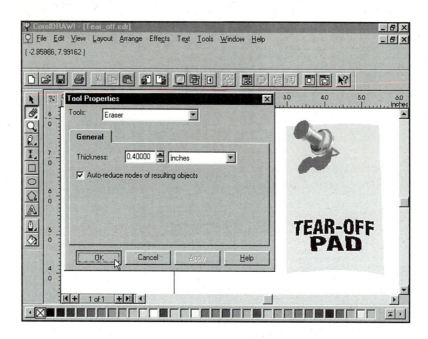

Ensures that objects resulting from the Eraser tool's use contain only nodes at points where the Eraser tool creates a change of path direction (see fig. 3.26).

7. Press the spacebar, click on the sheet object to select it, then press the spacebar again.

   Toggles Eraser to the Pick tool; pressing spacebar again returns to the last-selected tool.

8. Pretend that someone is bumping your elbow as you try to draw a straight line across the bottom of the paper sheet object. Click an inch to the left of the sheet, then drag and release an inch to the right of the object.

   Produces a "torn look" edge to the paper object (see fig. 3.27, and see Note that follows).

10. Choose **F**ile, **S**ave (Ctrl+S).

    Saves your work up to this point.

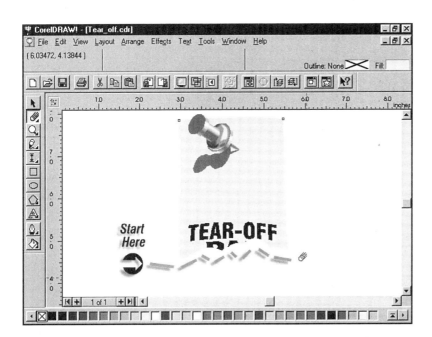

Figure 3.27
The Eraser tool changes the path segments of an object you click-and-drag through; areas directly beneath the tool are deleted.

Note The Contour and Eraser tools still have a "problem" in version 6. The algorithm that creates the shape outside of a path "flutes" the beginning and endpoints; the path bows outward at these points.

This phenomenon sometimes produces unexpected results in your artwork. The workaround for creating a uniform Eraser tool path is to begin erasing outside an object, and conclude the stroke outside the object.

Corel Corporation is aware of this oddity, and plans to correct it in future updates of the program. However, you might speed up the future patch by contacting Corel Corporation directly at 613/728-8200, or leaving CompuServe e-mail in the Customer Service section of the CorelAPPS forum.

You'll notice that although the sheet object looks torn now, the lettering (text converted to curves) was untouched by the Eraser tool. The Eraser tool works on only one selected object at a time, and will not erase grouped objects, which leaves this masterpiece a little unfinished. The key to this problem—and the solution—is in the next section.

Repeating an Eraser Stroke

Because the random path you drew through the sheet object in the last example doesn't remain after an erasure, it's unlikely that you can exactly duplicate the last Eraser tool stroke on the lettering still atop the sheet object. However, once a path has been made, it can be duplicated in CorelDRAW for other uses. If you recall the messenger example earlier in this chapter, you can use the same Trim command technique to create a *template* of the Eraser stroke, and apply it to the lettering object to match the erasure.

Here's how to create an identical path as that left by the Eraser tool, and remove some of the lettering object.

Creating an Eraser Template

1. Click on the Rectangle tool, then marquee-drag a shape that encompasses the bottom third of the sheet object.

   This is the basic shape from which you'll create a template of the Eraser tool's work (see fig. 3.28).

Figure 3.28
Include most of the lettering object in the rectangle you design; the lettering will be partially "erased" using the template.

2. Choose **A**rrange, **T**rim.

   Displays the Trim, Intersect, Weld grouped palettes.

3. With the Pick tool, select the paper object, uncheck the Target Object check box on the Trim Roll-Up, check the Other Object(s) check box, then click on Trim.

   Paper object will trim the target object (destroying original target). Paper object will remain; cursor becomes giant arrow prompting you to select Target Object with it.

4. Click on the rectangle.

   Removes the portion of rectangle that the sheet of paper object overlaps (see fig. 3.29).

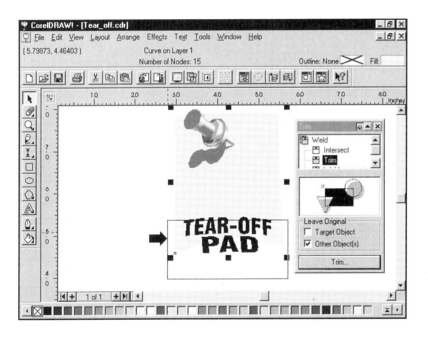

Figure 3.29
The rectangle becomes an irregular path, the inverse shape of the bottom of the paper object; perfect for trimming the lettering.

5. With the Pick tool, click on the trimmed rectangle.

   Chooses the rectangle as the "other object" (the Trimming object) for another Trim maneuver.

6. Uncheck the Other Object(s) check box.

   Specifies that after the trimmed rectangle trims another shape, it will be deleted.

7. Click on Trim, then with the arrow cursor, click on the lettering object (see fig. 3.30).

Trims the lettering exactly the same way as the paper was erased; deletes trimmed rectangle from the workspace.

Figure 3.30
The inverted template of the erasure path duplicates the erasure effect on the lettering.

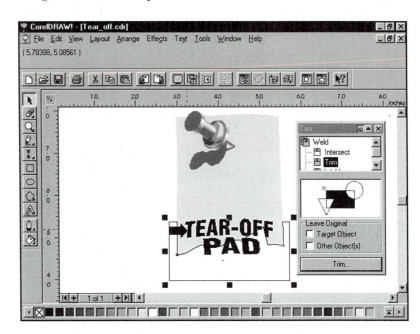

8. Press Ctrl+S (**F**ile, **S**ave).

Saves your work up to this point.

There's only one thing missing from this piece of artwork. If you notice, the pushpin casts a shadow on the torn sheet of paper. But to make this piece truly dimensional, it would be nice if the *paper* casts a shadow on the background—the white printable page of the document!

This is easily accomplished in the next section, which shows how and why CorelDRAW's tools and effects work best when used in concert.

Creating Instant Drop Shadows

In Chapter 5, you'll see how to create a semi-transparent shadow that looks as real as a photographic one, but right now in this assignment, you'll see an effective "cheap trick" that simulates a drop shadow.

It's important to understand as an artist how light reacts to surfaces. An understanding of light direction, light properties, and surface response to light allows you to better simulate realistic textures. This in turn, makes more realistic art, and helps non-artists visualize a concept that's executed graphically.

The simple study in geometry and lighting in this section requires one or two steps to make it a more believable scene of a torn piece of paper tacked against a surface. The viewer shouldn't care what the surface is, but only that the main attraction, the piece of paper, has opacity, and *casts a shadow at the same angle as the pushpin.*

 Note The illustration of the pushpin is a group of simple shapes. What makes the pushpin lifelike in appearance is the shading—groups of blended objects and fountain fills.

The pushpin was traced from a template of a *model* (as in CorelDREAM 3D) of a pushpin. See Chapter 9, "Working between CorelDRAW! and CorelDREAM 3D," for the scoop on building your own virtual reality.

Here's how to add a little dimension to the TEAR-OFF.CDR illustration.

Adding a Drop Shadow to an Object

1. With the Pick tool, click-and-drag the paper object down and to the left of its original position by about 1/4", then right-click before releasing both mouse buttons.

   Copies the selected paper object, and moves it the distance you dragged it. The paper copy is now selected, and is on top of the original.

2. Click on the To Back button (see fig. 3.31) on the toolbar (or press Shift+PageDown).

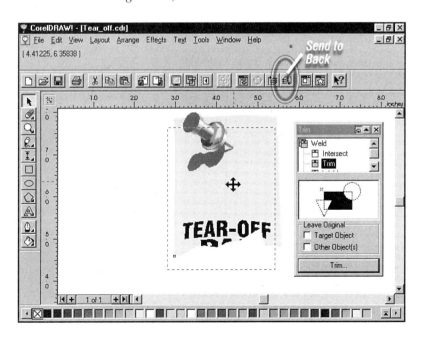

Figure 3.31

Use the toolbar to quickly move the order of selected objects.

Moves the copy of the paper to the back of the order of objects in the illustration.

3. Click on the 40% Black swatch on the color palette, then press Ctrl+S (File, Save).

Fills the copy with a shade of gray to represent a drop shadow.

End of line! In figure 3.32, you can see the finished TEAR-OFF.CDR image. Admittedly, the last example provided little in the way of node editing, but it did demonstrate how CorelDRAW's tools work together. As part of your work methodology, you should regularly evaluate during the course of an assignment which CorelDRAW features can be best used to complete it.

Figure 3.32
The TEAR-OFF design is a happy blend of crisp, clean lines, and a natural, realistic flow. Opposites within art create interest.

Take some of the techniques you've learned in this chapter into the next chapter, and see how working with complex shapes—polygons, rectangles, ellipses, and freehand paths—can all be used to complete a thought. The *inspired use* of a tool is the best approach for making the most of CorelDRAW's fantastic collection of features. And the best way to get inspired is by understanding the potential for each tool.

Mastering Color
Models and the Fill Tool

A *model* is something you build to work with whatever the model represents. A flight simulator is a model of the workings of an aircraft (or spacecraft) that lets trainees better understand what it's like to navigate such a craft—without the perils of inexperience.

Similarly, *color models* are used in computer graphics to represent the physical behavior of light. Computer monitors working with an application such as CorelDRAW can simulate the color of a certain pigment on canvas or printed ink on glossy paper. CorelDRAW offers several different views of color arrangement, each model designed for a specific purpose. If you intend to print a design, have a 35mm slide made from it, or plan to include your CorelDRAW work in a multimedia presentation, you can ensure color reproduction that's faithful to what you see on-screen by understanding how different color models work.

Visible Color and Its Subsets: Monitor Color

The monitor of your PC is a window to the much larger world of the visible light spectrum. Monitors create the colors you see on-screen by combining red, green, and blue light. Because a computer monitor and video card are confined to expressing all possible colors as combinations of red, green, and blue brightness values on a scale of 0 to 255, a monitor's color space is confined to 16.7 million unique colors. A total of 16.7 million colors gives the user an acceptably large color palette for expressing most graphical concepts.

Groups of red, green, and blue phosphors on your monitor are charged by a series of voltage signals sent by your PC to display the colors in the *RGB* color model. RGB color is a *subset* of the visible spectrum because it can't express *all* colors the human eye can perceive. Unlike the human eye, digital color must be *quantized*—broken into discrete, whole number values—before a digital color image can be written to a digital media such as your hard disk. The gaps that digital color fails to display in the same way as the color receptors in your eyes do is negligible, and your PC video subsystem's shortcomings shouldn't leave you restless at night.

In fact, RGB color was created for computer video as the closest electronic mimicry possible to the human eye's red, green, and blue light receptors. But the RGB color space, expressed as a color model, is *not* the most intuitive to grasp or work with, primarily because artists have been educated to get colors by mixing light-reflecting pigments together, not by adding different amounts of colored light together. It's sometimes difficult for artists to adapt to the PC method of mixing colors, using light's additive principles instead of pigments' subtractive principles.

Although RGB is the physical model used by your monitor to display color, the final output of your design probably is not to a computer monitor. Most likely, your finished design work will be printed on something that uses subtractive pigments or dyes to recreate the colors you've chosen. Other color models, such as CMYK (cyan, magenta, yellow, and black; process printing colors), and color matching systems such as Pantone, have been developed to make it easier for a computer artist to choose colors that will print as expected. CorelDRAW offers many different color models and color matching systems that you can use to "spec" color. In this chapter, you'll see how working with the appropriate color model for the job makes your work faster and more efficient.

Color Gamut and Overlapping Color Models

Not every color can be expressed by the RGB color model, or any other color model used to describe color relationships and color space. The computer's inability to offer all visible spectrum colors mimics the real-world experience where every color cannot be created by mixing dyes and pigments together. The method and materials used to print a color determine the number of colors that can be expressed.

As an example, the four process color inks that a commercial printing press typically uses to print "full color" produce a different set of colors than those produced by a digital printer that uses toner, wax, or dye. The range of color that can be produced by a color model or an output device is called the color *gamut*. A color gamut is always a smaller set of colors, or a *subset* of the visible color range.

In figure 4.1, you can see a model of the visible spectrum with subsets of computer color inside of it. Outside the tongue-shaped, visible spectrum color space, a color wheel includes the names that describe primary and secondary colors. The traditional color wheel is an imprecise convention used to describe color *relationships*; as our eyes perceive color, the visible spectrum color space is disproportionately skewed toward greens and away from blues. This skew is because more of the receptors in the human eye are sensitive to the energy wavelength that we see as green, and fewer are devoted to wavelengths associated with blue.

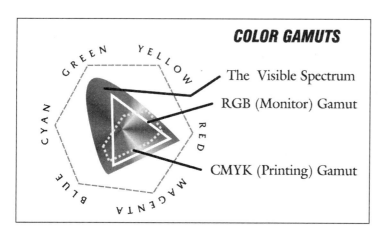

Figure 4.1
The visible spectrum is the largest color space, within which other color models for video and printing exist.

If you consider the final output of most design tasks, you see that commercial printing and on-screen display are the two most important areas in which color accuracy comes into play. For example, if you design a teal-colored pattern for a company logo, have a copy printed that looks more like turquoise, then submit it to the client, you've failed to communicate your design. This sort of miscommunication usually occurs because someone doesn't understand that monitor color (expressed in the RGB color model) does not correspond exactly to the process colors that make up a printed image (expressed in the CMYK color model). If you look back at figure 4.1, you'll see that the CMYK color model and the RGB color model occupy different areas of the visible spectrum, and there's a narrow area in which they overlap.

This overlapping area of the RGB and CMYK color models might seem like a confining workspace, but most of the glorious color content you see in magazines and coffee table books use the CMYK color model to express the creator's concept. The following sections cover the color models and spaces that CorelDRAW offers users, and the best way to approach designing. Those sections ensure that what you design on-screen is accurately communicated through media that uses other color models and that has different color gamuts.

Working with Corel's CMYK Color Model

Process color is a combination of three primary pigments—cyan, magenta, and yellow—plus a fourth pigment, black, to express a full-color image. Because primary color pigments often contain impurities, a *key* process color plate of black has been used to ensure that black areas of a full color picture are actually represented as black. Although there's little direct correspondence between the three primary pigments and the primary light components found in the RGB color model, a CMYK representation can be created in CorelDRAW to give the designer a ballpark estimate of how a color design will actually print.

In figure 4.2, you can see CorelDRAW's color model for CMYK definition. By default, it's the CMYK color model that's offered when you click on the Uniform Fill button on the Fill Tool fly-out menu, because Corel presumes that your intended final output of a design will be commercial printing.

Figure 4.2
CorelDRAW's CMYK color space offers users the selection of all colors that fall within the CMYK color gamut for printing.

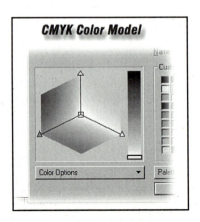

I

The CORELDRW.CPL file, the color palette that displays at the bottom of CorelDRAW's drawing window, consists of CMYK color values. At a glance, it seems that CorelDRAW artists have their work cut out for them when designing a color "legal" piece—a design that contains only colors that fit within the CMYK gamut. However, there are two important reasons why you *shouldn't* trust your eyes when designing a piece for CMYK output:

✔ RGB monitor colors don't, by default, represent similar colors based around the CMYK color model. CorelDRAW and other graphics applications must perform on-the-fly calculations to display CMYK values, and because this is a processor-intensive task, CorelDRAW and other applications remain in RGB mode unless you explicitly request a converted color display. More on this later.

✔ CMYK values displayed on-screen are approximations. Even when you choose CMYK display for CorelDRAW, you're telling a program that uses an internal RGB model to display a different color model to a monitor that uses red, green, and blue phosphors, not cyan, magenta, and yellow. Therefore, there's an inherent discrepancy between the colors you need for printing and the colors the computer uses to mix a specific color.

It can be a strain on the eyes to switch between Win95's and other application's RGB color mode to CorelDRAW CMYK display. View, Color Correction, None (RGB setting) is the default setting for CorelDRAW's display. Color Correction's CMYK display mode is designed for occasionally taking a peek at how a composition is coming together, color-wise.

The best way to work quickly on a design, *and* keep colors you use within legal commercial printing gamut, is to begin by calibrating your monitor.

Your next step is to create a profile for your printer if one hasn't been defined already by running the Color Wizard. Choose Tools, Color Manager, Select Color Profile in CorelDRAW, then select the profile to which your design will ultimately be sent for output.

Finally, at regular intervals, choose View, Color Correction, Accurate, and select the Simulate Printer menu option. This turns on the CMYK preview, which helps you determine whether the screen colors you've chosen will print as you intend. The Color Correction option can be turned off after you've evaluated the colors you've used, and reassigned values based on the Color Correction display to create CMYK-legal colors in your composition.

To assist you in finding objects within a composition that fall outside of the CMYK legal color model, choose View, Color Correction, Gamut Alarm, when Fast or Accurate color correction is turned on. The Gamut Alarm feature changes the display color of objects whose fill (or outline) color falls outside of CMYK gamut.

The Gamut Alarm feature isn't useful if the color for the Gamut Alarm display is similar to the colors you use in the composition. To set a unique color for the Gamut Alarm, choose **T**ools, **O**ptions, then click on the Advanced tab. Click on the Gamut Alarm Color swatch, then choose a color that contrasts with most of the colors used in the composition, then exit the Options menu.

Defining Custom CMYK Colors

CorelDRAW's default color palette displays 101 colors, most of which display on-screen as they'll print. Corel's color offerings on the default palette should in no way be mistaken for all available CMYK colors, however. You can append colors to Corel's default CMYK palette, or even start a new palette based on color specifications requested by a client. The following example takes you through the process used to create a custom CMYK color palette based upon Corel's default palette. There's no "right" or "wrong" way to perform the next example; it's simply an exploration of the Uniform Fill dialog box and CMYK color specification, and there is no perfect end result to the exploration.

Creating a Custom CMYK Palette

1. In CorelDRAW, open a new document window, then choose the Rectangle tool and draw a box on the page.

   To define a new color for a palette, you need to create a closed object first.

   If you don't have an object selected in a document window before you click on the Fill tool, Corel presumes that you want every object you create to be filled with the color you define or choose next. Without a selected object, a dialog box pops up asking whether all future graphics, Paragraph Text, or Artistic Text should be created with the color you're about to select. Because it's not your intention to edit default fill settings, it's best to begin creating a custom palette by selecting an object in the document window.

2. Click on the Fill tool, then click on the Uniform Fill button (the color wheel icon on the fly-out).

   Displays the Uniform Fill dialog box (see fig. 4.3).

3. Click on an area of the CMYK color space.

   Moves the wireframe color selector across two dimensions to specify a CMYK color composed of two primary colors.

4. Click-and-drag the color selector handle from the center outward.

   Adds a third primary component value to the color you're defining.

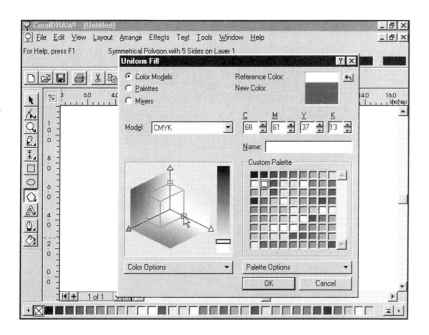

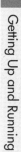

Figure 4.3

The Uniform Fill dialog box has features for choosing different color models, palettes, and for creating and editing palettes.

5. Click-and-drag the opposing color selector handles, one at a time, closer to the center of the CMYK color space.

   You're removing pigment from the specified color; the color becomes lighter.

6. Click-and-drag the black slider toward the top.

   Adds black to the primary pigments; makes the result color, seen in the New Color preview box, darker and less colorful.

Because the CMYK color model is composed of only legal colors, any colors specified within this dialog box will be CMYK "legal," and displays fairly accurately on-screen if you preview using the Color Correction options.

However, the CMYK color model is fairly user-*un*friendly; you'll notice that it's hard to define a specific shade because adding component colors makes the result color muddy and dark. Let's remove the key color, black, from the color model, and try specifying a color using only the C, M, and Y components....

7. Click on the Mod**e**l drop-down list, then choose CMY.

   The model doesn't appear to change, but the number entry field for K (**K**ey, or Black) disappears.

8. Click-and-drag the black slider toward the top.

   Equal amounts of C, M, and Y are used to create shades of gray (percentages of black); all three color sliders move equally outward from the center of the color space.

9. Click-and-drag any of the color selector handles within the model toward the center of the model.

   Result color in the New Color box gets lighter; the Printable Color preview box appears when the New Color falls out of printable gamut.

10. Click on the bent arrow next to the Printable Color box.

    Changes the specified color to different component colors that meet the criteria for legal CMYK values.

11. Take a good look at the number entry fields for the New Color, then choose CMYK from the Model drop-down list.

    New Color box remains the same color, but C, M, and Y values change with the addition of K.

12. Click on the Color Options drop-down list, then choose **A**dd Color to Palette.

    Adds the new color to Corel's default palette.

13. Click on the Palette Options drop-down list, then choose Save **A**s, and name the palette CMYK.CPL.

    Saves the appended palette to a unique name; doesn't alter the default palette.

14. Click on OK.

    Returns you to the workspace; the object is now filled with new color. The color palette at bottom of drawing window now contains new color at end of palette.

Besides defining a new color and creating a custom palette, the preceding example shows how different color models sometimes, but not always, contain the same values. The CMY color model is a "fictitious" one; a good commercial printer would never run a process color design without using a Key plate, but it's a little easier for a designer to specify an exact shade of color with three components to manipulate instead of four. Nevertheless, you saw that component values changed drastically when converting a color between models, and that a new color can be created within a CMY color space, but not be CMYK legal.

Additionally, the CMYK255 color model is available in the Models drop-down list, which offers the same color space within which to define colors, but measures the C, M, Y, and K components colors in brightness increments—from 0 to 255—instead of the traditional 0 to 100 percentages of C, M, Y, and K inks.

> **Tip**   The CMYK color model is the only model in the Uniform Fill dialog box that offers a slider, one that works independently of the primary color selection handles within the wheel portion of the model. When working with the CMYK color model, you should define a color first within the color wheel, then add black to the CMYK components only when your eyes tell you the black contribution is needed.

The Printable Color feature that chooses the closest legal color to the illegal color you've specified, is new to CorelDRAW! 6 and offers an "easy out" for refining a new color so that it fits the CMYK color gamut. But Corel's choice of closest color match might not always be what you want. In the next section, you'll see how to work with other available color models, and how to manually edit a color so it's both CMYK legal *and* matches your own aesthetics.

RGB and HSB Color Models

Manipulating primary color components within a color model doesn't necessarily get you to the color definition you seek—be it navy blue or pale ochre—as quickly as some of the other color models CorelDRAW offers. In figure 4.4, you can see the RGB color space in the Uniform Fill dialog box. It looks like an "inverted" CMYK color model hexagon, with RGB colors replacing CMY colors, and black at the center of the hexagon instead of white.

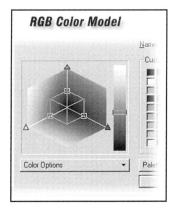

Figure 4.4
The RGB color model in the Uniform Fill dialog box.

Because the model for light, RGB, is based on additive principles instead of CMYK's subtractive, pigment-based model, lower brightness values for RGB component colors result in a color approaching black. Unlike the CMYK color model, moving the slider next to the color-wheel portion of the RGB model moves all the primary color values in one direction—toward lighter or darker shades of a color you specify.

The quality that the RGB and CMYK color model share in common is that they're empirical, math-oriented models by which engineers and programmers benefit the most, and designers benefit the least. It's important to understand the relationship between primary color values in color models, but to work quickly to define a color you want to use, the HSB (or Hue/Saturation/Brightness) color model is probably the best to use.

In 1978, Dr. Alvy Smith saw a need for traditional artists to describe color when working with computer graphics, and developed the Hue-Saturation-Value color model (HSV) that engenders RGB color space, but offers a more palette-like organizational structure that's easy to use. At about the same time, Gerald Murch at Tektronix created the HLS, or Hue-Lightness-Saturation, color model, and there have been several other models subsequently created that describe computer color in user-friendly terms.

CorelDRAW uses the HSB (Brightness instead of Value) and HLS color models to define RGB color space; they're an absolute picnic to work with. But you should be aware that the HSB and HLS color spaces have a different color gamut than that of the CMYK color model, which means that it's easy to specify colors that are not legal CMYK colors. If your intended output is to a film recorder rather than a print press (which requires the use of the CMYK color model)—or for a presentation played to a monitor—CMYK color specs are irrelevant; you can freely design without color space gamut constraints.

HSV, HSB, and HSL become only so many cryptic acronyms unless you understand what the color components mean. The following is a definition for color qualities that help you describe a specific color in the Uniform Fill dialog box:

✔ **Hue.** Hue is what we perceive as the primary distinguishable quality of a viewed color. Dark blue, pastel blue, periwinkle blue all belong to the hue in the visible spectrum that is primarily made up of wavelengths that produce blue. What affects the shade or tint of a hue is how much black or white is added to the color.

✔ **Saturation.** Saturation is the measure of relative strength of a wavelength of light. A blue piece of candy, for example, looks rich in the color reflected toward the viewer, because blue is being reflected while other wavelengths of light in the visible spectrum are being almost completely absorbed by the candy. A scene that's low in saturation, like a grayscale photograph, has no predominant hue, and all frequencies of light wavelengths are reflected from the photo in equal amounts.

✔ **Brightness, Lightness, Value.** These three terms have become synonymous with respect to computer colors, basically because these color qualities describe how physical light (not light generated by a monitor) strikes a surface, or how physical pigments interact. *Brightness* is the measurement of how strongly a light reflects (or passes through) a surface.

Lightness is a combination of color saturation and brightness. Lightness is a more accurate description of the real world phenomenon of color, but the HLS model in its accuracy is harder for artists to work with. Value is the relative measure of how much pure black or white is added to a color to produce a *shade* (color mixed with black) or a *tint* (color mixed with white).

CorelDRAW! 6 has a new color model to represent the HSB components, and if you've been accepting the CMYK model as your default for color specing, you owe it to yourself to check the HSB model out. The following exercise shows how to work with the model to define a color in the HSB color model that's also legal in the CMYK color space.

Color Spec(k)ing with the HSB Model

1. Create a closed object in a document window in CorelDRAW.

    You need a target object selected to access the Uniform Fill box without resetting default graphics and text attributes.

2. Click on the Fill tool on the toolbox, then click on the Uniform Fill button on the fly-out menu.

    Displays the Uniform Fill dialog box.

3. Choose HSB from the Mod**el** drop-down list.

    Displays the model for defining colors using Hue, Saturation, and Brightness.

4. Click-and-drag the "x" around the periphery of the color ring in the color model.

    Sets the Hue of the color you want to define.

5. Click-and-drag the square in the color triangle to the bottom left.

    Specifies that the Hue for the color is 100 percent saturated; the Hue is completely predominant over other lightwave frequencies that might be present if the color was viewed on an actual, physical surface.

6. Click-and-drag the square to the midway point on the right side of the color triangle.

Removes saturation from color; all light frequencies are equally present; color is neutral, medium gray.

To achieve tints of a color, click-and-drag the square toward the left of the triangle, then upward toward the white corner. To shade a color, drag to the bottom and right of the color triangle.

7. Click-and-drag the square in the color triangle until the Printable Color preview appears in the upper right of the dialog box.

   Tells you that the color you've selected can't be reproduced with process color inks.

8. Click-and-drag the square in an arc, toward either brightness extreme in the triangle.

   Changes the color to one that's CMYK legal (see fig. 4.5).

Figure 4.5
Corel can automatically choose a CMYK-legal alternative color from the HSB model, or you can choose one manually.

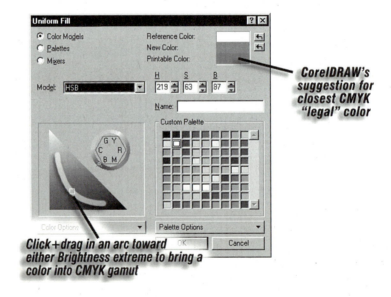

CorelDRAW's suggestion for closest CMYK "legal" color

Click+drag in an arc toward either Brightness extreme to bring a color into CMYK gamut

9. Click on OK.

   Returns you to the drawing window; fills the object with the color you've selected.

The key to defining colors that are artistically useful and CMYK legal is to make manual adjustments to a color you've decided upon to bring it back into CMYK gamut. Don't leave it to CorelDRAW to decide on a close CMYK color match. CorelDRAW is an application, and it doesn't get paid for creating design work! Instead, move the square inside the saturation/brightness color triangle in an arc, moving toward more saturation (lower-left triangle corner) as you reach the midpoint of the triangle. If you decrease saturation as you move the square toward the extremes of the brightness edge—the right side of the triangle—the Printable color legend and the bent arrow will eventually disappear; that means that the color directly beneath the square is legal within the CMYK gamut.

Color models are invaluable for helping artists visualize the relationship between color components, but palettes that you can select colors from are even more useful. The next section gets into the application of color theory, how it has a direct impact on your work, and how you can customize a palette to serve a specific design need.

Using Color Palettes for Color Specifications

After you have a structure for color specification such as a color model provides, it's only natural that a *sampling* of colors within a given color gamut speeds up the creation of a design in CorelDRAW. In the same way that color models were invented to describe color, *color matching systems* were invented to organize colors, and make it possible for design firms across continents to use exactly the same colors to fulfill an assignment. The following sections describe how color houses and designers can share and organize custom colors using CorelDRAW.

PANTONE, DuPont, FOCOLTONE, TRUMATCH, and Other Palettes

There are several color specification standards that designers and companies can choose from to ensure that a medium tan and deep maroon logo, for example, always appears the same on a package in Poughkeepsie as it does in Albuquerque.

When you accept a corporate identity assignment, it's always a good idea to ask what the color specs are for the logo, packaging materials, or any other place where a design might be used. It's also prudent to ask which color-matching standard the company's commercial presses use, then to go to an art store and buy the swatch book that corresponds to the color specification system. Color matching is an art and a science, and you can remove a lot of the guesswork from your design work if you have samples of physical ink printed on paper in front of you as you pour through digital simulations Corel has purchased in the form of palettes.

PANTONE is the most widely used color-specification standard; you'll be hard-pressed to find a commercial printer who didn't buy or license PANTONE inks. Other color-matching systems aren't quite as universally accepted, but if you have a client in Japan (hint: use the Toyo palette), or if you want a wide assortment of CMYK colors arranged in tint percentages (use TRUMATCH), you can use their corresponding video palettes in CorelDRAW.

PANTONE Color Matching System colors come in many different configurations, but the two types you'll use the most and that are supported in CorelDRAW are *process color* specifications and *spot color* specifications. The difference between spot and process color used with CorelDRAW, in a nutshell, can be defined as follows:

✔ *Process color* is created by sequentially applying Cyan, Magenta, Yellow, and Black inked plates to the printed page to create the illusion of full color. PANTONE process colors use a specific value for CMYK inks, and the inks are mixed to specifications established by PANTONE, Inc. You'll notice that when you select PANTONE (or other color-matching system) in the **P**alettes drop-down list, the CMYK fields in the Uniform Fill dialog box are dimmed. This is because if you change the percentages of PANTONE inks, you'd be specifying a non-PANTONE color. Conversely, copying the CMYK values found in the numerical fields of a PANTONE to create a color using the CMYK color model, the color displayed on-screen wouldn't match physical output because PANTONE colors are a unique formula that take into account not only the formulation of the ink, but also the basic paper type (coated or uncoated).

✔ A *spot color* is a pre-mixed ink that's applied in one step to an indicated area of a design. Unlike process color, a spot color doesn't have to be created by sequential passes of its component colors. A spot color can be the second color on a black and white print, or spot colors can be additional printing plates that are added to a four-color process printing. Spot colors are typically used to highlight a design area—for example, fluorescent or metallic inks are sometimes used as spot colors to call attention to the product name on a cereal or detergent box.

Although CorelDRAW offers a handsome collection of PANTONE Spot Colors in the **P**alettes, Typ**e** drop-down list, reserve your use of them for assignments where a special color is needed *in addition to* CMYK process colors. Corel Corp. has experienced an annual nightmare with the World Design Contest, because artists sometimes submit work that contains spot color specifications. The result? When CorelDRAW's print engine spools separation information to an imagesetter, any color designated as a spot color generates a piece of film. Imagine a design composed of 500 objects, each filled with a different spot color!

Unlike a custom palette or Corel's default palette, color-matching palettes can be accessed at the bottom of the drawing window with a mouse click or two. Choose **V**iew,

Color Palette, then choose the matching system you need for an assignment. When you want to return to the familiar Corel default palette, choose **C**ustom Colors from the Color Palette list.

> **Tip** To quickly search for a PANTONE color in the Uniform Fill dialog box, place the text cursor inside the Searc**h** field, then type the number of the color you want. The Search field only appears when you have a matching system chosen (click on the **P**alettes radio button), and you can type alphabetical suffixes for a color-matching name where applicable. For example, a search for SpectraMaster Color BS104 is made by typing **BS104** in the Searc**h** field. However, because PANTONE Process Colors are all prefixed with an S, typing 122 would display PANTONE Process color S12-2.

Sampling Colors to Create a Custom Palette

When you need to match a CorelDRAW color to exact specifications, the Uniform Fill **P**alettes feature can be invaluable. Additionally, colors that don't belong to a matching system can be conveyed to business partners by providing the numeric values for a color.

But how do you *create* a color you envision? Specifying a particular flesh tone, for example, isn't as easy as it might seem. Although we depend upon our eyes for accurate color evaluation, our minds often influence our choice of colors. If you simply start clicking and dragging in a color model to arrive at what you perceive to be a usable flesh tone, you might be surprised when you compare the color you've settled on with a swatch of flesh tone color from a photograph.

People are inherently drawn to bright, saturated colors, and this can affect our color evaluation capabilities. Fortunately, CorelDRAW has a color-mixer feature built into the Uniform Fill dialog box, which makes it easy to sample digital samples of photographs. You can build an entire palette of flesh tones, forest greens, or other combinations of real-life colors for use on a design that requires realistic color schemes.

In the following example, you'll see how to create a color palette in less than 5 minutes that can then be used to fill a composition whose objects make up a stylized image of a hand. By choosing colors found in a scanned image of a person, you can ensure that the colors you work with in a design that requires flesh tones is perceived by the viewer as lifelike and authentic.

Creating a Flesh Tone Color Palette

1. Open a new document window, then create a closed shape by using the Rectangle, Ellipse, or Polygon tool.

Creates an unfilled object that lets you access the Uniform Fill dialog box without changing default fill values.

2. Click on the Fill Tool, then click on Uniform Fill.

Displays the Uniform Fill dialog box.

3. Click on the Palette Options drop-down list, then choose **N**ew Palette.

Displays the New Palette dialog box, in which you provide a name for the new palette.

4. Type **FLESHTONE.CPL** in the File **n**ame field, then click on OK.

You're returned to the Uniform Fill dialog box, with a blank Custom Palette field to fill with new colors.

5. Click the Mi**x**ers radio button, then choose Mixing Area from the Mod**e** drop-down list.

Displays a sample palette for mixing color samples.

6. Click on the Color Options button, then select **L**oad Bitmap from the drop-down list.

Displays the Load Mixing Area File dialog box.

7. Make sure the *CorelDRAW! 6 Expert's Edition Bonus CD* is in your CD-ROM drive, then select it from the Look **i**n drop-down list.

You're looking for a file created especially for this example.

8. Double-click on the EXAMPLES folder, then double-click on the CHAP04 folder.

Displays the files created for this chapter's examples.

9. Click on SWATCH.BMP, then click on **O**pen.

Loads the bitmap SWATCH.BMP into the paint-mixing area.

10. With the eyedropper tool, click on a part of the face in the bitmap image.

Displays a New color in the upper right of the Uniform Fill dialog box.

11. Click on Color Options, then click on Choose **A**dd Color to Palette.

    A swatch appears in the Custom Palette area.

12. Click on a different area of the face, then choose **A**dd Color to Palette.

    Adds this color to the Custom Palette.

13. Click on the Paintbrush icon, then make a few strokes in the empty area to the right of the face image.

    Paints the current color onto the empty area.

14. Click on the first color swatch in the Custom Palette field, then click-and-drag the paintbrush through the strokes you created on the empty area in the last step.

    Blends the first strokes with the current selected color.

By default, the contribution of paintbrush color to existing colors in the mixing area is 50 percent. If you want less of the selected color blended into the existing color, click-and-drag the Blend slider, which is only active when the paintbrush icon is chosen.

Additionally, if you'd like a different shape for the paintbrush tip, choose Brush Type or **B**rush Size from the Color Options drop-down list. You can also tweak a sampled color by choosing from different color models in the Color Options drop-down list, then change the numeric values for CMYK, RGB, or HSB color models.

15. Click on the eyedropper tool, then click over the blend of the first and second paintbrush strokes.

    Samples the color blend you created.

16. Choose **A**dd Color to Palette.

    Adds the Blend color to the Custom Palette swatches.

17. Continue sampling and blending new colors, and add them to the Custom Palette swatches until you have about 30 unique shades of flesh tone.

    Creates a color palette you can use for special design needs. (See figure 4.6.)

18. Click on Palette Options, then click on **S**ave Palette.

    Saves the changes you've made to the custom flesh tone palette.

Figure 4.6
Save a digitized
image as a BMP,
then load it into the
Color Mixer area to
sample the colors for
use in CorelDRAW.

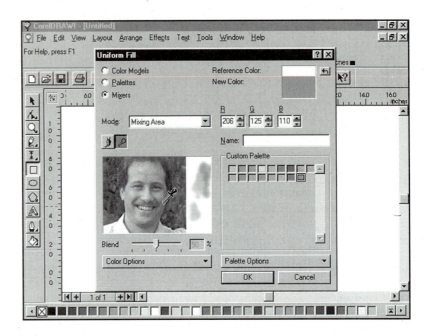

19. Click on OK.

Returns you to the drawing window, with the custom palette at the bottom of the
drawing window.

If you want to size or crop an image of your own for use as a color sampling image, the
mixing area is 177 by 122 pixels. Bitmap images can be resized through CorelPHOTO-
PAINT or other image-editing software. If you load an image that's larger than 177×122
pixels, CorelDRAW dynamically resizes the image to fit in the mixing area. Sample
images can be 24 bits per pixel, and it's usually best to crop tightly around an area in an
image that you want to sample from because you can't zoom into the mixing area to
precisely select a color. The only other qualification a sample image must have for
candidacy in the mixing area is that the image must be saved in the BMP image format.

Until now, you've been asked to draw a simple closed shape, then fill it with colors
taken from the various color models, palettes, and sample images. Because actual
design work usually consists of more intricate objects than rectangles and ellipses,
PALM.CDR can be found in the CHAP04 folder in the EXERCISE folder on the
CorelDRAW! 6 Expert's Edition Bonus CD. PALM.CDR is an unfinished symphony; the
design is yours to complete using the Flesh tones palette you created in the previous
example. If you didn't create the custom-color palette, SKINTONE.CPL is also in the
CHAP04 folder, and it was created using the methods found in the previous example. If
you'd like to finish the composition, here's a brief list of steps to follow:

Using a Custom Color Palette

1. Open the PALM.CDR file from the EXERCISE.CHAP04 folder of the *CorelDRAW! 6 Expert's Edition Bonus CD.*

   This is an unfinished design whose color areas were filled using the SKINTONE.CPL color palette.

2. Click on an unfilled object using the Pick Tool.

   Selects the object.

3. Click on the Fill Tool, then click on the Uniform Color button.

   Displays the Uniform Fill dialog box.

4. Choose **O**pen Palette from the Palette Options drop-down list, then choose SKINTONE.CPL from the EXERCISE.CHAP04 folder of the *CorelDRAW! 6 Expert's Edition Bonus CD.*

   Loads the custom-color palette.

5. Move the dialog box out of the way of the document window by clicking and dragging the title bar.

   Gives you an unobstructed view of PALM.CDR design.

Evaluate which color would best suit the object you've clicked on. Bear in mind that the hand design suggests a light source directly from the top of the page. Therefore, the objects closest to the bottom of the page should be filled with darker tones, those closest to the beginning of the SKINTONE color palette.

6. Move the Uniform Fill dialog box back on-screen, click on a custom palette color, then click on OK.

   Fills the object with the selected color; exits the dialog box. The color palette at the bottom of the Drawing Window is replaced with the colors from the SKINTONE.CPL (see fig. 4.7).

7. Right-click over the X on the color palette at the bottom of the screen.

   Removes the black outline from the filled object.

8. Select a different, unfilled object with the Pick Tool, then click on a swatch on the color palette you think is appropriate for the object.

   Fills the selected object.

Figure 4.7

Choose—or create—
a color palette for
the bottom of the
drawing window
whose colors match
the theme of your
design.

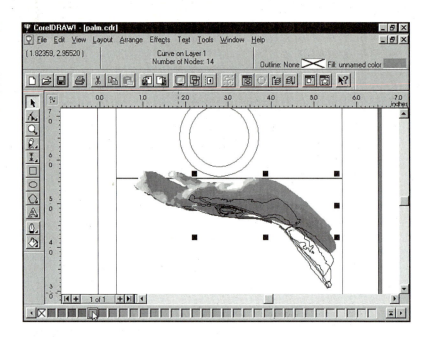

9. Repeat the last two steps until all the objects that make up the hand are filled with no outline attribute.

   Completes the hand design.

10. Choose **File**, Save **As**, then save the file as PALMTONE.CDR to your hard disk.

   Saves the design at this intermediate stage of completion. (You'll use it again in the next section.)

When you're finished with a custom color palette, it's a good idea to right-click over the border of the color palette (not a swatch, the neutral colored edge), choose **O**pen from the shortcut menu, and select CORELDRW.CPL from the COREL60.CUSTOM folder. This restores the color palette at the bottom of the drawing window.

Other fills that are available in CorelDRAW depend upon the color palette you've selected in the Uniform Fill dialog box for available component colors. For example, if you choose a Fountain Fill for an illustration of your own at this point, your selection of beginning and endpoint fountain colors is confined to flesh tones.

In the next section, you begin to explore the other fills found in the Fill Tool fly-out, and get into completing the PALM composition and other designs using some atypical object fills.

Moving into Complex Color Fills

Although vector art consists of only fills and outlines to describe shapes, there are a multitude of different *kinds* of fills that can be used to create realistic, exotic, and even surrealistic graphical concepts. CorelDRAW's Fill Tool offers advanced users almost every facility for design as one would find in robust bitmap editing programs such as Corel PHOTO-PAINT and Adobe Photoshop. In the next sections, you'll see how to integrate some of CorelDRAW's design features to make object fills the "star" of a composition, and also how to establish a work methodology for filling objects that can lead you to extremely complex, attention-getting design work.

Working with the Bitmap Pattern Editor

Detail work in artwork is important; a glint on a glass vase makes it look more dimensional, and the suggestion of leaf outlines on a design of tree make it look more, well...*tree*-like. However, vector designs—those you produce in CorelDRAW—are made of discrete objects, and to draw each and every leaf on a tree becomes a problematic chore. Unless there's an award to be won somewhere for Most Diligent Artist, pure and simple vector art is the wrong mode of artistic expression for designing a composition that features sand on a beach, or a thousand leaves on a tree. A much better set of design tools for such images would be a bitmap editor, where a few leaves could be detailed, and the rest of the tree could be "faked"—washes of color could suggest the rest of the leaves.

When you approach the detail work in a CorelDRAW design, you have several alternatives—most of them having to do with object fill properties—that can help you avoid a ponderously complex, labor and time-intensive, object-filled printable page. One such feature is the Two-Color Bitmap Editor, a Fill tool feature that creates an endless pattern within a closed object.

In the PALM.CDR design, the background has been locked and given a color override of blue to allow you to better concentrate on the foreground element, the upturned hand. However, in the next set of steps, you'll see how to unlock the layer, add it to the composition, then sprinkle some stars against the night-like sky without resorting to drawing each individual star as an object.

It's a simple, neat, effective trick for adding a suggestion of background detail to your artwork. Here's how to include bitmap information in a vector drawing:

Using the Two-Color Bitmap Editor

1. Open the PALMDONE.CDR image from your hard disk, or open PALM.CDR from the *CorelDRAW! 6 Expert's Edition Bonus CD* if you didn't follow the previous example.

This is the design to which you'll add a bitmap-filled object.

2. Choose **L**ayout, **L**ayers Manager (Ctrl+F3).

Displays the Layers Roll-Up.

3. Right-click over the Layer 1 title, then choose **S**ettings from the shortcut menu.

Displays properties for the selected Layer 1.

4. Deselect the Override **f**ull color view check box, then click on OK.

The background layer changes from colored wireframe to full-color preview.

5. Click-and-drag the arrow on the Layers Roll-Up from Layer 2 to Layer 1.

Specifies the layer you want to edit.

Alternatively, you can right-click on the Layer 1 title and select the **E**dit Across Layers option. This option *should* be the default setting for layered designs, but selecting this option doesn't hurt.

6. Click on the (Freehand) Pencil tool, then create a four-sided object to the right of the fountain-filled ball on Layer 1.

You can use the double-click, straight-line method described in Chapter 3, "Beating Nodes and Paths into Submission (The Easy Way)."

7. Click on the Fill tool, then click on the Two-Color Bitmap Pattern button (the checkerboard on the second row of option buttons).

Displays the options for the Two-Color Bitmap Pattern fill.

8. Click on Cre**a**te.

Displays the Two-Color bitmap Editor.

9. Click on the **3**2 ×32 Bitmap size radio button, then click on the 1×1 Pen Size radio button.

Specifies that the grid for the bitmap pattern is 32×32 pixels, and the pen used to create the pattern is single pixel in height and width.

10. Click in various, random places on the bitmap grid.

Defines places where foreground color will be located within the pattern (see fig. 4.8).

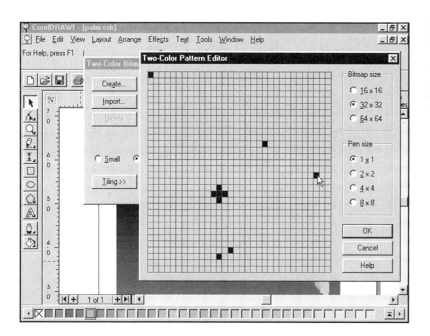

Figure 4.8
You can set the size of the bitmap canvas and the pen size within the Two-Color Pattern Editor.

If you draw a dot by mistake, right-clicking on the pixel will change its attributes to those of background color. "Sparseness" is a key concept when designing a pattern to be filled with stars. Remember that this pattern will repeat within the selected shape in the PALM.CDR design, so you don't need many foreground pixels.

11. Click on OK.

    Returns you to the Two-Color Bitmap Pattern dialog box.

12. Click on the Back color button, and choose a light purple from the color palette, then click on the Front color button, and choose Black.

    Sets the colors used in the two-color bitmap fill.

Bitmap images usually feature a dark foreground color against a light background color. But because this starry sky design uses inverted color values (dark background, light foreground), you need to pick fore/background colors that are the inverse of what appears to be correct in the color selection boxes.

13. Click on the **M**edium radio button.

    Makes the pattern you created repeat more frequently within the selected object.

14. Click on OK.

Returns you to the drawing window; the object you created is now filled with a tiling pattern of stars.

Patterns become obvious when they're placed inside symmetrical shapes. However, you can disguise the bitmap pattern property of the fill by creating an irregularly shaped object.

15. With the bitmap pattern object selected, click on the Zoom tool, then right-click, choose Zoom to selection, right-click again, then choose Zoom Out from the shortcut menu.

    Zooms you to a tight view of the bitmap-filled object, then zooms out to offer a little more space around the object so you can edit more freely.

16. Choose the Shape tool (press F10), then click-and-drag one (or more) nodes away from the center of the bitmap-filled object.

    Creates an irregular shape; makes the bitmap pattern appear more random (see fig. 4.9).

Figure 4.9

The path surrounding a bitmap fill is a window to the pattern; you can hide parts of the pattern by changing the path's shape.

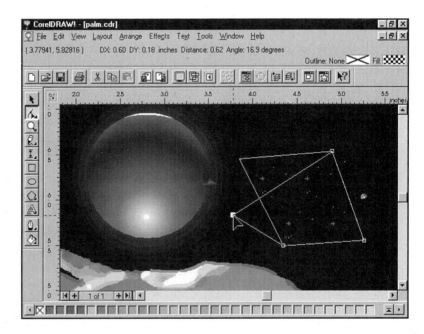

17. Choose **F**ile, **S**ave (Ctrl+S), then save the finished piece as PALMDONE.CDR to your hard disk.

    Saves the completed composition.

In figure 4.10, you can see the finished PALM illustration. We'll get into how the glowing ball was created in Chapter 5, "Complex Fills and Blend Shading," but for now, a valuable observation can be made about objects in CorelDRAW that are filled with bitmaps:

 Tip   Bitmaps within objects are oriented and exist within their own space. Changing the path of the outline object does not change the visual content of the bitmap fill.

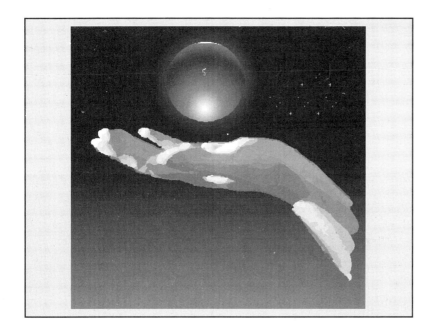

Figure 4.10
Designs that require several simple, similarly shaped objects can be better expressed through the use of a pattern.

In addition to creating a Two-Color bitmap pattern, you can select from the presets that ship with CorelDRAW by clicking on the down arrow in the preview box. You can also import a monochrome (1 bit per pixel) bitmap image created in a bitmap editing program; such a bitmap can be in any number of file formats, but the color capability must be 1 bit per pixel.

Our excursions into the different kind of fills CorelDRAW offers wouldn't be complete without an examination of Grayscale fills, the type most commonly used in graphics destined for black and white output. Let's backtrack in the next section, and revisit the Uniform Fill dialog box to work with grayscale designs.

Grayscale Designs, Black and White Printing

Color fills and CMYK legal colors have been emphasized in this chapter, primarily because the world is in color, and color printing has become available at lower costs in recent years. However, black and white printing still fuels the bulk of business graphics needs, and this section addresses this need.

It's been emphasized in this book that you should always consider your final output before picking up the Pencil tool. Certainly, you can print a color design to a black and white laser printer, but you lose control over the tones rendered to paper. Computer colors, as you've seen in this chapter, contain components of primary values, and a color design printed to black and white output occasionally suffers because there might be hidden black content to any given color that makes it print darker or lighter than you anticipate.

To avoid tonally mismatched output, and to make CorelDRAW an environment suited for black and white printing, you can build a grayscale palette for the bottom of the drawing window, or better still, use the one provided on the *CorelDRAW! 6 Expert's Edition Bonus CD*.

Here's how to fill a design with values appropriate for black and white printing, create a custom grayscale palette, and preserve the design so that it's easy to create an additional color copy:

Working with Grayscale Values

1. Open the OUTPUT.CDR design from the EXERCISE.CHAP04 folder of the *CorelDRAW! 6 Expert's Edition Bonus CD*.

   This is the design you'll color using grayscale values.

The OUTPUT design's elements are on locked Layer 1, and the current editing layer should be the layer labeled Fill. If it's not, click-and-drag the arrow on the Layers Roll-Up so it points to Fill. You'll be editing Layer 1 a little later, so it will need to be unlocked eventually.

2. With the (Freehand) Pencil tool, use the double-click technique to create a closed shape that leaves a small empty space to the left of the top of the printer cartoon.

   Defines the area to be filled in the OUTPUT design (see fig. 4.11).

By *not* completely defining the top of the printer cartoon, you're creating lighting within the design; the unfilled left area appears as white when printed, creating a design highlight, suggesting that light is coming from the upper left of the design.

The additional "perk" to filling shapes on the layer beneath the main design elements is that you don't have to be terribly precise with the fill objects. The black shapes that portray the outline of the cartoon printer on Layer 1 disguise the outline of the fill objects on the Fill layer, and you have a little "play" to the fill outline because the Layer 1 objects cover the fill outline.

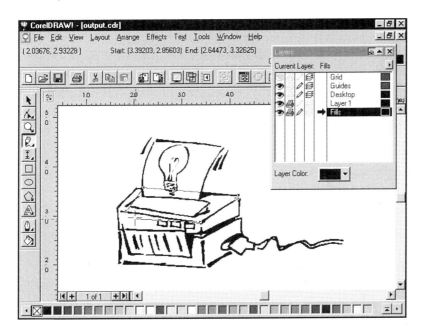

Figure 4.11
You can fill design elements by creating and filling an outline on a layer beneath the main composition.

3. Click on the Fill Tool, then select Uniform Fill.

   Displays the Uniform Fill dialog box.

4. Click on the Palette options, then choose **O**pen Palette.

   Displays the Uniform Fill dialog box.

5. Choose GRAY32.CPL from the EXERCISE.CHAP04 folder of the *CorelDRAW! 6 Expert's Edition Bonus CD*, then click on **O**pen.

   Loads a color palette designed around 32 black values, with a red location marker at the 50 percent point.

6. Click on the 17% Black color swatch.

   Selects 17% Black as the fill for the object you created in the OUTPUT document (see fig. 4.12).

You have the opportunity to name a shade you've defined by typing a name in the **N**ame field directly after choosing a new color from any color model. This is how you can easily retrieve a color by name, and this is how the small grayscale palette was created—by changing the amount of Black in the CMYK color model, then changing the value by one increment to get each new shade.

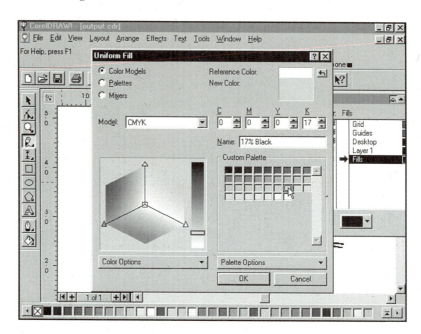

Figure 4.12
Colors that have been added to a palette can have a name that will appear on CorelDRAW's status bar when you hover your cursor over the swatch.

7. Click on OK.

   Returns you to the design; loads the GRAY32.CPL color palette at the bottom of the drawing window (see fig. 4.13).

You're really not limited to the number of swatches you add to a custom palette; system RAM is basically the limitation here (the TRUMATCH color system has 2,000 entries). So, why only 32 shades of black on the GRAY32.CPL palette? Because there are a limited number of slots available without extending the color palette (by clicking the up arrow on the palette), or by scrolling the palette. With 32 grayscale shades at hand, you can quickly access a wider ranges of neutral tones than the 10 available on the default color palette.

8. Create an outline of the paper coming out of the cartoon printer with the (Freehand) Pencil tool.

   This is the next area to be filled using the GRAY32 custom palette.

Straight lines won't accurately define the paper object because the outline on the Layer 1 suggests a curve. To define a fill object, double-click a straight line outline around the paper shape, then select the Shape tool, click on a line that needs to be curved, then right-click and select To Curve from the shortcut menu. Then click-and-drag the converted line until it matches the curvature of the paper shape.

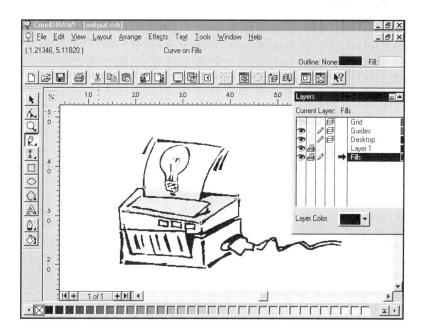

Figure 4.13

A sample of only grayscale values on the color palette is ideal for working on images whose intended output is black and white.

9. Click on the 5% Black swatch on the color palette.

Fills the shape behind the paper shape with 5% black (see fig. 4.14).

Although this is a handsome collection of grayscale shades, suppose you want a color not found on the GRAY32.CPL palette, like 32% Black? Follow these steps:

10. Create a shape behind the front of the printer cartoon.

This is the area you'll fill next.

11. Click on the Fill Tool, then click on the Uniform Fill.

Displays the Uniform Fill dialog box.

12. Click on the 30% Black swatch, then click on the up elevator button on the K spin box twice.

Increases the value of a new color to 32% black.

13. Type **32% Black** in the **N**ame field, click on Color Options, then click on **A**dd color to Palette.

Adds color to GRAY32 palette, at the end of the samples.

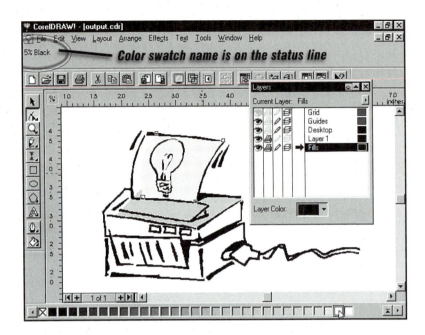

Figure 4.14
By naming a color in the Uniform Fill dialog box, you can easily reference it by hovering the cursor above the swatch.

14. Click on, then drag and drop the 32% gray swatch on top of the 30% gray swatch on the Custom Color area.

    Repositions the swatch so that it's in the sequence of shades.

15. Click on the Palette Options drop-down list, then click on Save **A**s, and save the palette as GRAY32.CPL to your hard disk.

    Saves the palette with changes to your hard disk; CD-ROM files cannot be edited!

16. Click on OK.

    Fills the path with 32% black.

17. Choose **F**ile, Save **A**s, then save the design as OUTPUT.CDR to your hard disk.

    Saves the design to your hard disk.

To complete the cartoon printer design, two things need to be done. The first is to create fill objects behind the as-of-yet uncolored areas of the cartoon. Pay attention to lighting. Because you've established an upper-left light source, you should continue the lighting effect by filling shapes to the lower left of the design with darker shades of black, and leave blank areas in upper-left design areas to suggest a brilliant highlight.

The second thing needed to complete this design is to reassign black filled shapes on the locked Layer 1. The next section poses some interesting design possibilities when you begin with a black and white design on one layer, and add fills to a layer beneath.

Using Objects as Highlight Elements

When you conceptualize a CorelDRAW design as having shades of grayscale for colors, and begin the piece as black and white only , there's an opportunity down the design road to integrate the black and white elements with the shading. Visual content in a design comes from two places: the outline (or basic shape) of an object, and the fill, the pattern, surface reflectance, or other *texture* that goes into the shape.

Unlike bitmap and modeling/rendering applications, vector drawing programs have the capability to transpose the qualities of fill and outline; in the printer cartoon, what you see as a black-and-white outline drawing is actually composed of filled objects with no outline properties. And there's no reason a component of the cartoon printer's "shape" can't be turned into shading, thus softening the composition and making it less stark-looking by changing the color of some of the objects that make up the black and white design.

In the next set of steps, you'll see a technique for shading objects in a design that were intended to represent the cartoon printer's outline. It's important to choose *non-critical* objects—those whose existence doesn't interfere with the recognizability of the design as a printer. The objects that represent the edges of the cartoon printer, for example, are objects that don't contribute to the viewer seeing the cartoon as that of a printer. Let's unlock Layer 1 and see how shading portions of a design intended as outline objects can enhance the piece.

Shading Object Outlines

With OUTPUT.CDR as the active document window in CorelDRAW...

1. Press Ctrl+F3 (or choose **L**ayout, **L**ayers Manager).

2. Click on the pencil icon next to Layer 1.

   The icon changes to black, indicating that Layer 1 can now be edited (see fig. 4.15).

Figure 4.15

Unlike previous versions of CorelDRAW, locking—and unlocking—layers is now an attribute you set by simply clicking on the pencil icon.

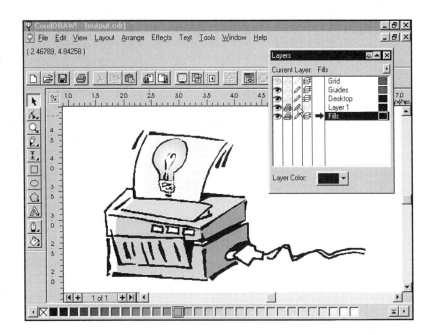

Make sure the <u>E</u>dit Across Layers option is active by right-clicking anywhere in the Layers Roll-Up title field, seeing that this option has a check mark next to it in the shortcut menu. Alternatively, you can click-and-drag the arrow in the title field to point at Layer 1; either way, Layer 1 is now unlocked, and can be edited.

3. Click on the black edge shape that divides the front from the side of the cartoon printer, then click on 25% Black on the color palette.

   Adds a grayscale fill to the object.

4. Click on the black edge object that divides the right of the cartoon printer from the top of the printer, then click on 40% Black on the color palette.

   Makes the edge appear lighter, suggests edge lighting.

5. Click on the black edge object that divides the front from the top of the cartoon printer, then click on the 5% Black swatch on the color palette.

   Lightens the object; creates the impression that the printer has slightly soft edges (see fig. 4.16).

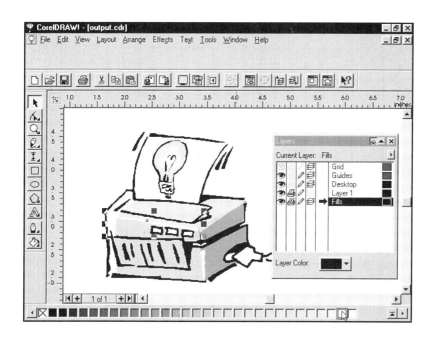

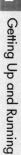

Figure 4.16
Using a light shading to describe a compositional element's edges helps make the element softer and more dimensional.

6. Choose **File**, **Save** (Ctrl+S).

Saves the completed INPUT.CDR design.

You'll notice that there many more black objects that define the cartoon printer that can be shaded different colors without destroying the cartoon's "outline." In figure 4.17, you can see the finished piece continues to bear a resemblance to the original OUTPUT.CDR design. However, the cartoon printer has a more refined quality now, and the design will print as you see it on-screen, because it's composed of only shades of black with no color influence from primary hues.

The printer cartoon was created using Corel OCR-TRACE, a scanner, and a pen-and-ink drawing. To learn more about this method of working with converted physical artwork in CorelDRAW, read Chapter 7, "Corel OCR-Trace: Converting Bitmaps to Vectors."

It should be apparent that the texture of a filled object can be as important to a design's content as the shape the object describes. *Texture* has an interesting definition when describing computer graphics; colors, surface detail, reflectivity, and other characteristics all fall under one roof, because they're all qualities that fill an outline shape. In the next section, you'll see an experiment that has to do with increasing the visual richness of a shape through the use of fountain fills—geometric bands of color that can simulate a variety of real-world textures.

Figure 4.17
A simple drawing
that's carefully
shaded can take on
the appearance of a
more complex
design.

Creating and Sharing Fountain Fills

Fountain fills have different names, depending on the application you use. *Gradient fills* and *ramp fills* are synonymous with Corel's Fountain Fills, and Corel's Fill tool offers many variations on the transition within a fill from one color to another.

Fountain fills can often replace the use of color blends (see Chapter 5) to create a gradual transition from one color to another—thus saving several steps and precious moments creating a realistically shaded composition. Although Corel Corp. has provided some exquisite controls for defining fountain fills from not two but up to 100 unique colors, there has never been the built-in facility in CorelDRAW to save a custom fountain fill in a file users could share. Part of the following section covers a method for distributing fountain fills you've created, saving a sampled fountain fill for future use, and how to create a custom fountain fill.

Copying and Saving a Custom Fountain Fill

In the following example, FILLS.CDR in the EXERCISE.CHAP04 folder of the *CorelDRAW! 6 Expert's Edition Bonus CD* is a "swatch book" of exotic, funny, and visually arresting fountain fills, shown in figure 4.18, that were created in the fountain fill and texture fill dialog boxes.

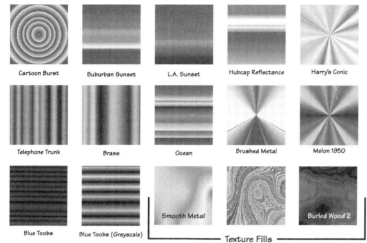

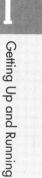

Figure 4.18
These samples can be added to your preset collect to use later in your own assignments.

The example image is for a mock hardware store that commissioned a competent, yet uninspired CorelDRAW artist to make an ad. The ad features the creative use of the Polygon tool and the Extrude Roll-Up (see Chapter 11, "Special Effects for Web Pages," for the lowdown on the Extrude Roll-Up), but you'll see that the ad is missing something. That something is called texture, and here's how to copy a sample of an appropriate texture and use it to complete the ad.

Adding to a Fountain Fill Collection

1. Open the S&P.CDR design from the EXERCISE.CHAP04 folder of the *CorelDRAW! 6 Expert's Edition Bonus CD*.

   This is the design that needs some fountain fill help.

As you can see in figure 4.19, the S&P.CDR graphic is well laid out, but it appears flat, even though the saw blade looks 3D. Flat colors and dimensional objects fight each other in a composition. The text layer has been converted to curves and is locked (on the layer entitled Locked); Layer 1 contains the only elements you'll work with in this example.

2. Open the FILLS.CDR file from the EXERCISE.CHAP04 folder of the *CorelDRAW! 6 Expert's Edition Bonus CD*, then choose **W**indow, Tile **V**ertically.

   Tiles the two files to fill the drawing window.

Figure 4.19
A "flat" composition depends on compositional elements, not shading, to direct the viewer's attention. Boring!

3. Click on the S&P.CDR document window, then marquee zoom around the saw blade.

   This is the object that will be filled with a custom fountain fill.

4. Click on the FILLS.CDR title bar, click on the Zoom tool, then marquee around the swatch entitled "Brushed Metal."

   This is the fill you'll add to your personal preset collection, and use to shade the saw blade.

5. With the Pick tool, click on the fountain fill swatch, click on the Fill tool, then choose the Fountain Fill button (the icon with the linear fountain fill on it; see fig. 4.20).

   Displays the Fountain Fill dialog box, with the custom fill you selected displayed.

6. Type **Brushed Metal** in the Presets text field, then click on the + button.

   Adds the custom fill to your collection of presets, and can be used in a design of your own anytime in the future (see fig. 4.21).

7. Click on Cancel, then click on the Close box on the FILLS.CDR document window.

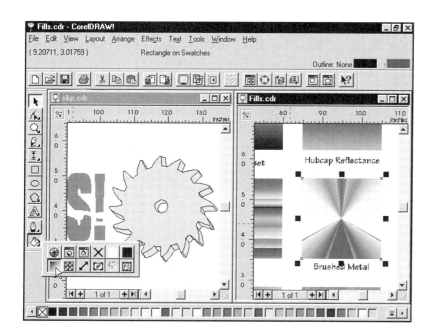

Figure 4.20
You can see how a custom fountain fill was created by selecting it, and then choosing the Fountain Fill dialog box.

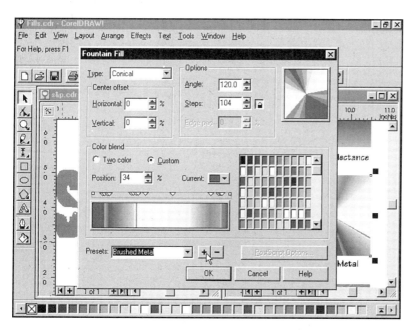

Figure 4.21
You can create, or copy, as many custom fountain fills to the preset list as you want, to be applied to different objects.

You've sampled the custom fill without reapplying it to a read-only file (CorelDRAW complains about this when you do!).

The techniques for creating a fountain fill such as the one you copied to your Presets list in the preceding example are covered in the next section. The important point to remember, always, when sampling colors or texture fills is to cancel out of the dialog box after sampling. If you click on OK, CorelDRAW reapplies the fill you only want to sample, and tells you (when you attempt to close the file) that the image has changed (when you're certain you did nothing to change it!). We all get a little panicky when this occurs.

How a Custom Fill Is Created

The Fountain Fill dialog box has undergone minor improvements since version 5. Gone is the Rainbow option, although you can still create chromatic spectrum fills. This is now performed by selecting beginning and end colors that lie on opposite sides of the color spectrum in the From and To color-selection boxes. Although **C**ustom fountain fills are not a new feature to CorelDRAW, users occasionally overlook this option because the controls for defining a custom fill are hidden. The following list describes the step-by-step procedures for creating a custom fill; it's not in the traditional example format because it's more useful to provide a generic "recipe" here, so you can create any type of custom fill you need for an assignment:

1. You might want to load (or create) a custom (Uniform) color palette before opening the fountain Fill dialog box. The shades of metallic color that make up the Brushed Metal fill you copied in the preceding section were actually sampled from a digitized photo of some industrial piping.

   The current color palette is the one presented for you to choose from in both the texture fill and fountain fill dialog boxes. You can select colors outside of the default palette, but you have to wade through an additional dialog box to get to other solid fills when you are in the fountain or Texture Fill dialog boxes.

2. Choose the pattern (the geometric type of transition for the custom fill you want to create). CorelDRAW offers Linear, Radial, Conic, and Square Fountain Fill transitions (in the **T**ype drop-down list). The type of transition should, ideally, have some compositional harmony with the object you intend to fill with the custom fill. For example, the saw blade is round, so Conic type was chosen when designing the fill. Radial would be another candidate for a saw blade fill, especially for a radial saw.

3. A custom fill is created by beginning with a series of intermediate colors. Click on the **C**ustom radio button, and by default, a fountain fill appears in both the Options preview window, and as the *Color Blend* area in the lower part of the dialog box. It's the color Blend area where you set colors; the Options preview window is where you set the amount of transition, direction, and qualities unique to the type of fountain fill.

4. Double-click on either a point within the Color Blend area, or just above the Color Blend Area. A marker within a band above the Color Blend area appears. This indicates an intermediate step in the transition between the From and To colors.

5. If you're unhappy with the location of the intermediate step, click-and-drag it to the left or right, or precisely reposition the marker by typing a value in the Position field after you've selected the marker by clicking on it. You then can set the color of this transitional blend point by clicking on a swatch on the current color palette to the right of the color Blend area.

6. For Conical fills such as the type specified for the Brushed metal example, it's useful to set the From and To colors to exactly the same shade. Do this by clicking on the tiny white dot at either end of the marker band, then select an identical color for both from the current color palette. Doing this prevents the conic fill from abruptly beginning a new color cycle at the endpoints.

7. The preview window is where you set the direction for Linear fills, and the location of the custom fill's center relative to the center of the object you fill. In most cases, a custom fill won't look correct when applied to an object—the center of the fill will look off-centered because it's tough to see the exact center of a solid or unfilled object. You can make after-the-fact corrections to the center of a custom filled object by clicking on OK in the Fountain Fill dialog box, then displaying the Special Fill Roll-Up in the Drawing Window (the icon in the Fill Tool fly-out with the tiny paint bucket inside a menu). The Special Fill Roll-Up can sample a fill of an object within a document; then, you can make minor changes to the fill and reapply it without a return trip to the Fountain fill dialog box.

8. Before clicking on OK to exit the dialog box, however, check the Edge Pad value for the custom fill. Edge Pad amount increases the rate of transition between intermediate colors. For example, if you've designed some tubes using the fountain fill dialog box's controls, you can make them small or wide tubes by adjusting the Edge Pad value. The Options preview window displays a low-res view of the effect of Edge Pad settings.

9. Also consider the number of **S**teps in a custom fill. By default, the number is set to 50. Corel Corp. did this to spare users redraw time, and to eliminate unnecessary fill steps at printing time. A higher **S**teps value results in smoother custom fills (less visible banding), but be aware that the PostScript language is limited to describing 256 unique colors in a fountain fill. This means that this is the maximum number allowed in the **S**teps field, and it's possible to create a custom blend that exceeds this limit. And this means that you'll get banding *and* slower printing if you increase the Steps value. So go ahead and get fancy with your custom fills, but remember that there's a limitation in what you can output.

Also check the **T**ools, **O**ptions, Display menu if you can't achieve a smooth custom blend on-screen. By default, CorelDRAW displays 50 bands of color to represent a fill. It's possible to max out the number of Steps in the Fountain Fill dialog box and still see crummy fills on-screen because this option wasn't set to a higher value.

10. Finally, save anything you like, or you even *think* you like that you've created, as a Preset entry, because if you don't save the object you fill, a custom fill is gone forever. Press the + button to save a custom fill, and press the − button to delete one.

There are one or two more tricks to making Fountain Fills work for you in CorelDRAW. In the next example, you'll touch up the Sanders and Primers advertisement, and work with a new feature in the Fountain fills dialog box.

Adding Custom and (Not-So) Standard Fills

1. Click on the saw blade image in the S&P document.

   Selects the shape so it can be filled.

2. Click on the Fill tool, then click on the Fountain fill button.

   Displays the Fountain Fill dialog box.

3. Click on the down arrow on the Presets field, then type **B.**

   Moves you to the "B" section of the Presets list.

CorelDRAW ships with a lot of different presets, and the best ways to retrieve/find your own are to prefix a name with an exclamation point (!) to drive it to the top of the Preset list, to weed out the factory presets you don't use or care for, and to hot key your way to a section of the alphabet (as you just did).

4. Find "Brushed Metal" and click on it.

   Selects the preset you copied in the previous example.

The degree of rotation of the Brushed Metal Preset might not be to your liking for this assignment. To make the fountain fill's darker areas appear more to the bottom right of the saw blade ....

5. Click-and-drag the **A**ngle spin box control up or down.

   Changes the degree at which the beginning and endpoint appear in the filled shape.

6. Click on OK.

Changes have not been made to the custom fountain fill preset; fill is applied to the saw blade object (see fig. 4.22).

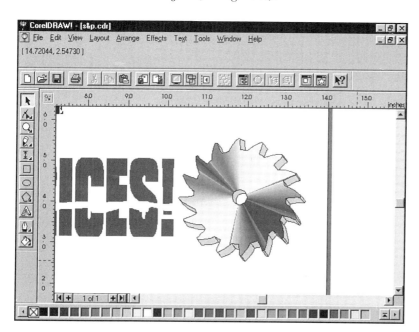

Figure 4.22
You can customize a custom fountain fill preset by adjusting its properties to suit a specific design need.

7. Choose **F**ile, **S**ave, then save the design as S&P.CDR to your hard disk.

Saves your work up to this point.

New to version 6 is the Mid-point control, available only when you specify a t**w**o-color fountain fill. The Mid-point control allows you to specify where the midpoint is between the From and To colors. This option lets you "prefer" more of one transitional color than the other in a standard fountain fill. If you look at the edges of the extruded saw blade, you'll notice that they're not filled with the custom fountain fill, because they're separate, grouped objects. The extrusion is broken apart and simplified for this example; fountain filling an extrusion created by CorelDRAW ties up even a fast Pentium for minutes while CorelDRAW calculates and redraws the object.

A simple fountain fill fits the bill here in terms of adding shading to the sides of the saw blade; it's a compromise between elegant shading that'll take forever to redraw and print, and the plain uniform fill presently on the side of the saw.

Here's how to shade the sides of the saw blade:

Fleshing Out a Design with Fills

1. Click on any object other than the front of the saw blade.

   Chooses the grouped objects that make up the side of the saw blade.

2. Click on the Fill Tool, then choose the Fountain Fill button.

   Displays the Fountain Fill dialog box.

By default, a new fountain fill is Linear Type, from white to black. This is fine for our purposes. The shading applied equally to all the grouped objects won't automatically create accurate, lifelike shading, but that's okay. A linear fill applied to dozens of small objects gives the feeling of light striking a surface from a number of different directions, and this is what the teeth to a saw blade would look like in real life. The secret here is to keep the shading within the selected object fluid and moving to simulate the appearance of brushed metal. The front of the saw, with its elegant fill is the main attraction, "carries" the composition.

3. Click-and-drag within the preview window until the **A**ngle field reads about 120°.

   Sets the angle for the Linear fill so that the saw blade appears to be lit from the upper-left of the composition.

4. Click-and-drag the Mid-point slider to about **22.**

   White will predominate in the fountain fill, with slight amounts of darker tones and black.

5. Click-and-drag between the elevator buttons on the **E**dge pad spin box until the value is about 25%.

   Increases the rate of transition between white and black (metal displays sharp transitions between shadows and highlights).

6. Click on OK.

   Applies the fountain fill to the selected, grouped objects (see fig. 4.23).

7. Press Ctrl+S (**F**ile, **S**ave).

   Saves the completed composition.

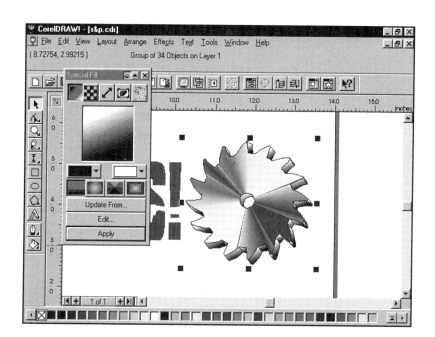

Figure 4.23
Shading doesn't
necessarily have to
be accurate within
all filled shapes to
create realism and
attract attention.

In the preceding example, accuracy and realism were apparently tossed to the four winds by adding a fountain fill to the grouped objects that make up the side of the saw blade. Indeed, accuracy and realism were discounted; however, there's a good reason for recommending this. It's called "saving time," and this is one of the reasons artists come to CorelDRAW for graphics solutions. Background details can be finessed until everything is technically accurate, but time is a luxury many professional designers cannot afford. The sides of the saw blade are minor details; they're not the prime focus of the composition, and whether each tooth on the saw is accurately shaded becomes a secondary consideration—a detail that will be lost on most viewers of this advertisement.

The point is that accuracy is a powerful artistic tool that computing brings to us, but so is artistic judgment and the wisdom to decide when you have to "let go" of a commercial piece. When you exercise good artistic sensibilities and can weigh the investment of additional time against the constraint of deadlines, you have nothing to apologize for as a professional and you've overcome a great hurdle that computer technology poses to artists: that of knowing how to fix something to the greater audience's satisfaction, and to know when a design is completed.

Beyond Automated Fills

As mentioned earlier, fountain fills are a quick method for shading objects, but they're by no means the only method you'll want to use on assignments. What happens when you have an ellipse-shaped object you want to shade? There isn't an elliptical fountain fill type! And what about the other Fill tool features? Chapter 5 is an extension of this chapter that gets you working with shapes *as* fills, not simply as containers for a preset. In the next chapter, you'll learn how to get the best of both bitmap and vector drawing tools from within one workspace—CorelDRAW's.

Complex Fills and Blend Shading

What's the first thing you remember about the chair you walked past a few minutes ago? Was the chair wooden? Was it a Breuer chair—with shiny chrome tubing and fake caning? The point is that your capability to quickly discern real world objects depends upon two object qualities: the underlying *shape* of an object, and the *shading*—the texture—that fills the shape.

The texture of an object most often plays the primary role in an audience's recognition of that object. Accordingly, an artist who's a successful visual communicator spends a great deal of time finessing the lighting, surface reflectance, bumpiness, and other aspects of a composition that constitute what something is made of.

In Chapter 4, "Mastering Color Models and the Fill Tool," color specification was discussed as a foundation for creating work that's expressive and outputs as you'd expect it to. Uniform color fills have a limited niche in advanced computer graphics, however, because flat shades of color portray the world in an extremely stylized and abstract way. Audiences have high expectations of realism, photorealism, and even surrealism when viewing a computer-generated piece. Realism is the key—the emotional hook—that draws the viewer into a composition.

Fortunately, you have two tools close at hand to assist you in giving your artistic expression a more appealing, provoking, attractive look through the elegant shading of objects: CorelDRAW! 6, and this chapter. *Integration* of bitmap and vector formats of computer graphics is key to attaining the most flexibility in designing what you imagine, and this chapter shows you how to accomplish this goal using the Corel suite of applications.

How CorelDRAW! Handles Bitmaps

Although CorelDRAW's tools can be used to create and edit *vector* information—the type of fill and stroke a path can have—*bitmap* graphics can also be used as an integral part of a CorelDRAW composition. Besides the capability to import a bitmap image, CorelDRAW also has *internal* bitmap generators that can be used to fill a shape.

This happy coexistence of bitmap and vector information within a single CorelDRAW document brings powerful imaging possibilities to the computer designer. There are some limitations as to how extensively you can manipulate bitmaps within a CorelDRAW document, however. Whenever you specify a bitmap type fill for a closed path, the bitmap extends to the horizontal and vertical extremes of the shape—even though the vector path shape might not completely fill the horizontal and vertical measurements. For example, you can never see the upper right pixel in a bitmap fill whose parent shape is an oval; the oval's shape simply doesn't extend to where the bitmap begins. It helps to think of a vector shape filled with bitmap information as a *portal* (a limited view, of the total bitmap's visual information).

You can accomplish several effects with bitmap fills that would be time-consuming or impossible to achieve without CorelDRAW's facility to handle different types of computer graphics. We'll begin the exploration of exotic fills and realistic shading with the Texture Fill feature, a repository of almost unlimited variations of fractal designs.

Working with Fractal Textures: Using Texture Fills

The term *fractal* is used mostly in computer-design applications to indicate a specific type of math equation whose appearance is remarkably similar to textures you'd find in nature. Fractal Design Corp.'s Fractal Design Painter, and HSC Software's KPT Texture and Fractal Explorer tap into the same sort of fractal algorithms that CorelDRAW and PHOTO-PAINT use to create textures that look like a photographic close-up of something, usually an unspecified "thing"!

An *algorithm* is a declared set of procedures within an equation; for example, if you specify a palette of colors, then specify that this palette is used to fill an area by distributing colors using a random value, you have the basis for a fractal fill. Is creating a fractal math equation this simple? No, but fortunately, designers don't have to dig into the math to modify a fractal equation, and can produce a wide variety of different textures from a single fractal algorithm.

In the following steps, you'll see how to put CorelDRAW's Texture Fill dialog box to some innovative use by creating a wood texture from one of the fractal algorithms Corel supplies. You'll begin by specifying a *seed number*—one of 32,767 different permutations of a fractal algorithm...a "preset"—then use the controls in the Texture Fill dialog box to modify the texture to suit a design purpose. The Texture Fill dialog box controls represent graphical handles for manipulating parts of the underlying math; basically, you're specifying that colors in the resulting texture fill be *modulated*—the HSB or RGB values are changed—according to a mathematical value within the algorithm.

To demonstrate the power of fractal texture fills in a CorelDRAW design assignment, you'll use an emboss technique commonly used by filters in bitmap programs. Most plug-in filters achieve an emboss effect by copying the information about the shape to be embossed, offsetting the copies behind the original, then assigning the copies lighter and darker shades to suggest highlights and shadows along the sides of the embossed shape. The best types of shapes to use for creating an emboss effect are stencils— silhouettes of shapes—with plenty of outline detail, with little or no visual business occurring within the outline path of the objects. Here's how to create textured high- lights and shadows to create a sign for a fictitious chess organization. The woodcut shingle look can be used in a variety of professional situations in which you need to replicate the shop signs commonly found in New England from the 1600s to about 15 minutes ago.

Creating a Custom Texture

1. In CorelDRAW, open the CHESCLUB.CDR. document from the EXAMPLES.CHAP05 folder of the *CorelDRAW! 6 Expert's Edition Bonus CD*.

   This document contains the basic shapes you'll use to create the woodcut emboss design. (See figure 5.1).

2. With the Pick tool, click on the black Chess Club lettering.

   Selects the lettering.

Note that the chess piece and the lettering are one combined object; you'll add texture to all of the foreground objects. The reason the objects are combined is because you need a contiguous texture—one that spans the entire foreground design—to make the design look as though it's carved out of a single piece of wood. If the objects are grouped or otherwise left uncombined, each receives a discrete fill pattern, and the overall design looks as though several different pieces of wood are used.

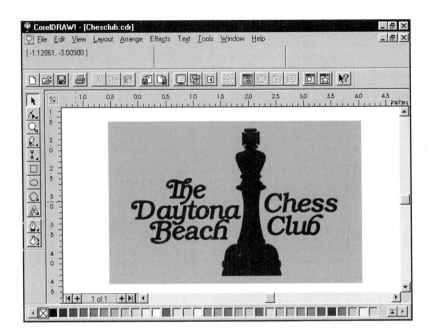

Figure 5.1

Begin an emboss
design by creating
silhouette objects.
Copies of the shapes
will be offset and
filled with different
textures.

3. Click on the Fill tool, then click on the Texture Fill button (the cloudy-looking icon to the left of the PostScript "PS" icon).

   Displays the Texture Fill dialog box.

4. Choose Styles from the Texture library drop-down list.

   Displays the "master" fractal textures in the Texture list.

5. Scroll in the Texture list box until you find "Mineral.Cloudy 2 Colors," then click on it.

   Specifies the type of fractal algorithm you'll modify to create a wood appearance.

6. Type **23694** in the Texture # field.

   Specifies a preset configuration for the fractal texture.

The values used in this example are of the author's choosing, and they happen to work; but if you find a more interesting combination of values that you feel look more like wood, use them! Also feel free to use any color model CorelDRAW offers for specifying texture colors; colors are suggested in this exercise in RGB format, but you can also work with the HSB or CMYK models.

7. Click on the 1st mineral color drop-down box, click on Others at the bottom of the color drop-down box, then choose R:217, G:168, and B:99 from the RGB color model; click on OK.

   Specifies one of the component colors in this fractal texture.

8. Click on the 2nd mineral color drop-down box, click on Others, then choose R:173, G:130, and B:46 from the RGB color model; click on OK.

   Specifies the other component color in this fractal texture.

9. Type **73** in the Softness % spin box (or click-and-drag between the elevator buttons to change the spin box values).

   Specifies that the fractal pattern is composed more of waves than random "splotches" of color pattern (produced by entering low Softness % values).

10. Type **27** in the Grain % spin box.

    Increases the contrast between color "waves" in the fractal pattern; creates a more wood-like appearance.

11. Type **3** in the Rainbow grain % spin box; then click on **P**review.

    Introduces a mild amount of random color values in the fractal pattern. (See figure 5.2.)

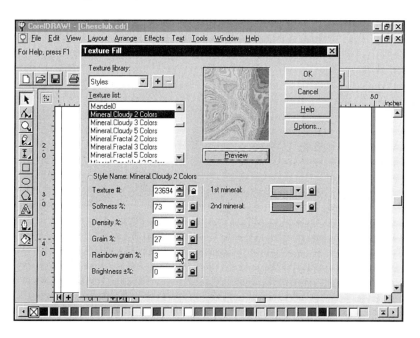

Figure 5.2

By changing values within a texture's math equation, you can create an entirely different look.

Whenever you like a texture preset variation, it's very important to save it by naming it to a collection of textures. Because there are so many different parameter variations, you're unlikely to be able to re-create a texture variation later that you didn't save.

12. Click on the + button to the right of the Texture library drop-down list.

    Displays the Save Texture As dialog box.

13. Type **Chesswood** in the **T**exture name box, type **Natural** in the library name box, then click on OK.

    Adds Chesswood to the Natural library; creating a new library (Natural) separates Corel's presets from custom textures you've created.

In figure 5.3, you can see that the **O**ptions for fractal textures has been selected. You might never need to change these values, but they relate to how many pixels per inch a texture contains within an object you fill. The subject of bitmap image resolution is covered following this example.

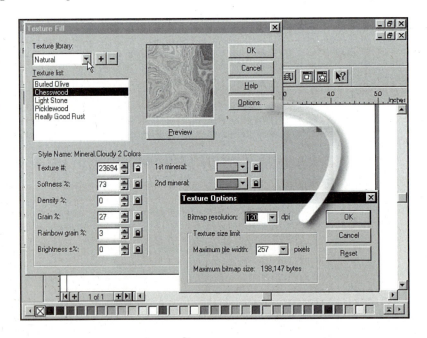

Figure 5.3

You have the option to save a texture setting, and to specify the resolution of any texture fill in the Texture Fill dialog box.

14. Click on OK, then choose File, Save **A**s, and save the composition as CHESCLUB.CDR to your hard drive.

    Fills the lettering and the chess piece in the design (it's a combined object); saves the composition at this intermediate stage of completion. (See figure 5.4.)

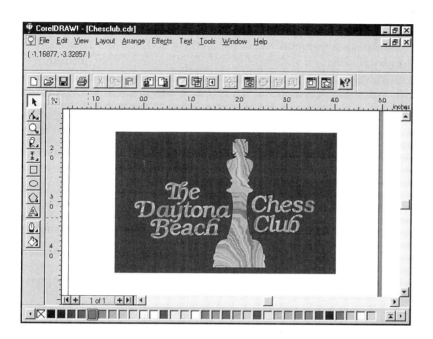

Figure 5.4
The Chesswood texture fills the selected object with a pattern, measuring from the upper left to bottom right object extreme.

As you explore and modify texture presets other than Minerals.Cloudy 2 colors, you'll find different controls offered as spin boxes that relate to the specific fractal. Although the names on the controls are fairly straightforward and occasionally whimsical, each spin box varies a component in the underlying math equation to produce a different pattern. The Texture Fill's Options dialog box doesn't change the appearance of a fractal texture, but it does affect how the texture displays and prints, because bitmap fractal texture fills have a fixed *resolution* at file saving and printing time. This is the subject of the next section.

Understanding Resolution Dependence

Before continuing with the embossed sign example, take a moment to concentrate on the limitations and uniqueness of a bitmap fill within a vector object. Although vector objects and bitmap graphics use entirely different calculations to represent a shape, they're both mapped to the screen and to an output device as *resolution dependent* entities; monitors have a finite number of pixels that can be drawn upon, and printers have a maximum capability to express an image in toner dots per inch.

Because vector images are resolution independent, however, it's easy to smoothly scale a vector design up or down without loss of detail within the design. A vector object only becomes of a fixed resolution—a finite number of screen pixels or toner dots—as you view the design (from moment to moment), or decide to print it.

Bitmap fills (such as the fractal texture we're working with here) need to have each *bit* of visual information *map*ped to a location within a coordinate system that exists within the filled object. If you were to increase the size of the chess piece lettering right now, the appearance of the outline of the lettering would display and print smoothly, because all you've changed about the original design is the distance between the nodes that make up the path. However, the texture fill would look distorted and unaesthetic, because you've instructed CorelDRAW to use the same number of pixels to portray an object much larger in physical dimension. CorelDRAW does not dynamically resize bitmap fills.

It is always best, then, to decide upon the final dimensions of an object you intend to fill with a fractal or other bitmap fill, before you fill the object. You should also consider the output of your design: what is the screen frequency of the output device? If you're using a PCL printer, Corel's Print dialog box is dimmed in the Print Options, Options tabbed menu for **S**creen frequency; this means that the non-PostScript, PCL printer cannot generate an accurate line screen, and you're best off leaving the Texture Options Bitmap **r**esolution and Maximum **t**ile width at their default values.

However, if your design is to be output to a PostScript printer (or imagesetter), check the Print Options, Options Screen frequency value (measured in lpi), then remember this value, because you'll need it to specify the best texture resolution in the set of steps to follow.

Here's how to specify the best bitmap resolution for any design that uses fractal, texture fills:

Defining Resolution for a Texture-Filled Object

1. Make a mental note of the object's size in inches before doing anything.

   The largest side of an object's bounding area determines the resolution you need to use for the texture fill to print correctly.

2. Select the object, click on the Fill tool, click on the Texture Fill button on the Fill tool menu flyout, choose the fractal fill you want from the **T**exture list, then click on **O**ptions.

   Chooses a texture preset; displays the Texture Options dialog box.

3. Set the dpi in the Bitmap **r**esolution for twice the screen frequency of the line screen used for output. If in doubt, choose 266 dpi from the drop-down list (half of 266 is 133, which is a common screen line per inch frequency for 2,540 dot per inch and higher imagesetters).

   Specifies the resolution you'll use for a specific output device.

4. Multiply the dpi value by the largest dimension of the object you intend to fill in the design. For example, if the largest dimension of the object is 3 inches, multiply 3×266; this yields the value of 798 pixels. Hang onto this number for the next step.

   Creates a value for you to plug into the Maximum tile width box.

5. From the Maximum tile width drop-down list, choose the first value that meets or exceeds 798 pixels. In this example, you'd choose 1,025 from the Maximum tile width drop-down list, which results in a 3.15 MB bitmap fill.

   Specifies a size for the texture to tile within the object you're filling. 3.15 MB is a large fill, and will plump your saved file size, but if you want the best output, resolution-dependent bitmaps within a CorelDRAW file demand large file sizes.

6. Click on OK, then click on OK in the Texture Fill dialog box.

   Returns you to the design in your document; fills the selected object.

"Dots per inch" is a Corel misnomer here; you're actually specifying *pixels* per inch resolution for the texture fill, which is not equivalent to the dots per inch measurement of printed, hard copy resolution. The default of 120 dpi in the Texture Options dialog box is adequate for printing to a personal 300 to 600 dpi laser printer, but you might want to increase the texture's resolution if your CorelDRAW document is destined for high-resolution imagesetting.

For more information on output, see Chapter 12, "Outputting Your Input" on the Bonus CD.

Resizing a texture-filled object within your document does not change the Texture Options dialog box values. If you've disproportionately resized a texture filled object—you've dragged a middle selection handle away or toward an object's center—the fill will distort accordingly. If this is not your intention, there's a quick restore procedure that doesn't require resolution calculations: Choose the Special Fill Roll-Up from the Fill tool's menu flyout, click on Update From, then click on the distorted object's fill. With the object selected, click on Apply. Doing this re-applies the texture fill to reflect the new shape of the object. This trick also works with proportionately resized objects, but you cannot respecify a bitmap resolution using the Special Fills Roll-Up.

You can squash a texture within an object as you resize it, but you can't rotate or perform envelopes, extrusions, or perspectives as modifications to the original texture's visual content. You'll learn about workarounds for shaping the shading as well as the shape of an object later in this chapter.

Adding Shading to a Textured Emboss

Color is the one quality about texture fills that CorelDRAW users can safely change without worrying about resolution or distortion of the bitmap's grid of information. Because colors are selected independently of a texture fill's brightness, smoothness, or other parameters, you can easily create a duplicate of the chess lettering now, reassign color values to suggest shaded wood, and reposition the copy so it appears to be a drop shadow of the original.

This exercise shows you how to complete the chess club sign using variations of the original Chesswood texture you created in the last example:

Creating an Emboss Effect

1. In the CHESCLUB.CDR document, click on the wood-filled lettering, then right-click over the "x" on the color palette.

   Assigns no color/zero stroke width to outline path of object.

2. Click on the background rectangle in CHESCLUB.CDR, then choose **E**dit, Copy Properties **F**rom.

   The Copy Properties dialog box appears.

3. Click on the **F**ill check box, click on OK, then click on the gigantic arrow cursor over the wood-filled text.

   Copies the Chesswood texture to the rectangle.

4. Right-click on the "x" on the color palette.

   Assigns no color/zero stroke width to the rectangle outline.

Okay, it's a little difficult to proceed with this tryout assignment if the foreground and background objects are filled with the same texture. The solution lies in a new feature in CorelDRAW! 6, the **W**indow menu. Because CorelDRAW is fully multiple document interface (MDI)-compliant, you can open a second view of CHESCLUB, and assign it a wireframe view. This way, you can watch the composition come together, and accurately select objects as you create them.

5. Choose **W**indow, **N**ew Window, then choose **W**indow, Tile **V**ertically.

   Opens a second window, entitled CHESCLUB.CDR:2.

6. Click on the CHESCLUB.CDR:1 window's title bar, then click on the Wireframe toggle button on the toolbar (or press Shift+F9).

Toggles your view in the original CHESCLUB window to wireframe view.

7. Choose **T**ools, **O**ptions, type **0.2** in the Nu**d**ge spin box on the General tab, then click on OK.

Sets the nudge value for selected objects in the document.

8. In the wireframe view window, click on the lettering with the Pick tool.

Selects the wood-filled lettering.

9. Press the keypad + key, then press the down arrow and the right keyboard arrows once.

Duplicates the selected lettering object; nudges the selection .2" right and down. (See figure 5.5.)

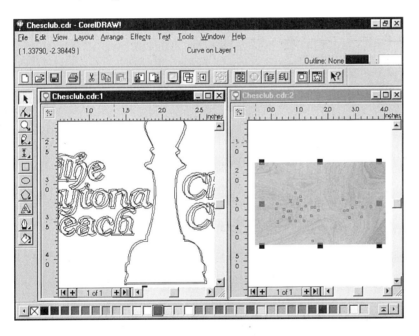

Figure 5.5
Duplicate a selected object, then nudge it an infinitesimal amount by using the keyboard arrow keys.

10. Press Ctrl+PageDown.

Moves the offset duplicate of the lettering one object down in the object stack; it's directly behind the original.

11. Click on the Fill tool, then click on the Texture Fill button.

Displays the Texture Fill dialog box.

Getting Up and Running

12. Click on the 1st mineral drop-down color palette, click on Others, then click-and-drag the composite color slider (to the right of the RGB color model) downwards until the New Color Swatch appears noticeably darker than the Reference Color swatch.

    Creates a darker 1st mineral color with little change in the hue of the original color.

13. Click on OK.

    Returns you to the Texture Fill dialog box.

14. Click on the 2nd mineral drop-down color palette, then click on the first column, fifth row brown on the drop-down palette.

    Selects a new, darker 2nd mineral color. See figure 5.6.

The 2nd mineral color selection was made from the drop-down list instead of a Uniform color model because it happens to work in this example; you're creating a textured drop-shadow fill whose primary value should approach, but not be entirely black. In your own assignments, you might want to carefully select shades from a CMYK or HSB color model for all colors in a texture fill, or load a custom uniform color palette for assignments where specific texture colors are critical.

Figure 5.6
Choose darker shades of brown to represent shaded areas of the embossed chess club sign.

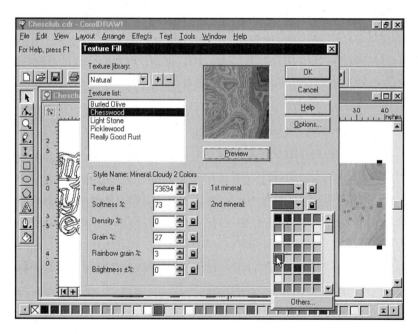

15. Click on OK.

Adds a textured fill with darker color values to the copy of the lettering.

If you want to minimize the wireframe window, and maximize the full-color preview window, you can zoom into the piece at this point to examine the difference a texture makes when creating a drop-shadow—the first of two elements that will make the emboss effect. In figure 5.7, you can see that the darker copy of the lettering isn't a simple, uniform shade, but is composed of the same patterns of colors that make up the Chesswood custom texture. This is the way actual wood behaves when shaded by sunlight; some, but not a lot of object surface characteristics show through.

Figure 5.7

The right amount of texture added to supporting objects in a composition can highlight a design and accentuate a "look."

In the previous steps, the darker texture fill was not saved, and therefore, will not appear as a Texture Fill preset if you have a new or different document open.

> **Tip** An alternate, slightly risky way of storing presets is to copy them—when needed—from a document that contains many different fractal textures you need to access. This is not a smart working methodology, because if you lose the file, you lose the presets, but a texture's specific values and colors are embedded in a document, and you can retrieve them and copy them if you're in a bind. This is how the FILLS.CDR piece was created in Chapter 4's examples, and you can add FILLS.CDR's textures to your own collection by simply selecting them, going to the Texture Fills dialog box, then clicking on the + button.

In the next exercise, you'll finish the composition by adding a textured highlight object:

Adding a Highlight to the Textured Design

1. With the Pick tool, click on the original lettering object, press the + keypad key, then press Ctrl+PageDown.

   Creates a duplicate of the original lettering object and fractal fill; moves the copy behind the original.

2. Press the left keyboard arrow once, then press the up arrow.

   Nudges the copy .20" left and .20" up.

3. Click on the Fill tool, then click on the Texture Fill button.

   Displays the Texture Fill dialog box.

4. Click-and-drag between the elevator buttons of the Brightness (+/−)% spin box until the field reads 17, then click on **P**review.

   Increase the brightness value of the Chesswood colors (see fig. 5.8).

Figure 5.8
Regardless of the type of texture preset you choose, all fractal textures have a Brightness spin box.

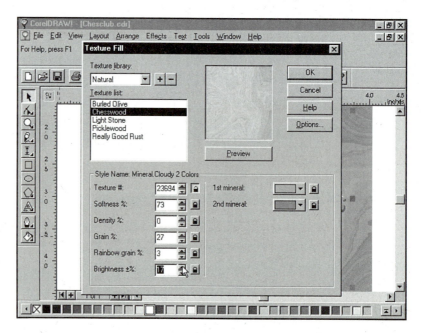

5. Click on OK, then press Ctrl+S (**F**ile, **S**ave).

Completes the composition; saves the piece to hard disk.

There's a qualitative difference between adjusting the Brightness value for a texture preset, and specifying different colors used. Many of the presets change to unexpected, sometimes downright ugly, color combinations when the Brightness value is changed to an extreme amount. So, it's helpful to have different alternatives when you want to change the tonal qualities, but not the pattern of a fractal texture. In figure 5.9, you can see the finished chess club sign. It's a happy balance of shape—the outlines that contribute geometric form—and shading, the quality that viewers look for in a design piece to give the design substance.

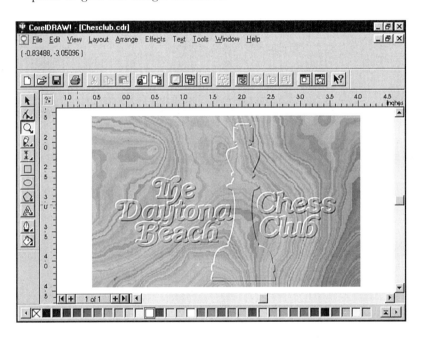

Figure 5.9

Using the techniques described in this section, you can create an embossed design from any Texture Fill.

You can also use some of Corel's presets, with no modifications, along with the emboss steps to create marble, metal, and other textured signage. Additionally, preset variations you create in CorelDRAW are saved to a common Corel preset extension. So, the Chesswood and Natural categories in the preceding example will also appear in Corel PHOTO-PAINT, and vice versa.

Note It's important to note that in the preceding example, the emboss effect you created is not a true representation of a shape stamped out of another shape. A real, physical emboss displays an even outline around the shape, with highlight areas gradually blending into shaded areas. The "offset emboss" trick fails to display this blending of the embossed object's sides—the highlight and shadow objects simply disappear behind the original object at a certain point—but the viewer's eye tends to dismiss this fact; it appears mostly correct, and the offset emboss trick is an effective art technique.

To achieve a true, photographic emboss effect, check out The Boss plug-in filter in CorelPHOTO-PAINT 6, or check out the new 32-bit version 2.0 filters from Alien Skin Software (see the Resource Guide on the *CorelDRAW! 6 Expert's Edition Bonus CD* for details).

PostScript Texture Options

Unlike bitmap fills accessed in the Fill tool menu flyout, PostScript Textures are resolution independent—sort of. PostScript is an output device language that directs a printer, film recorder, and other device how a computer graphics scene is rendered (rasterized).

PostScript Textures in CorelDRAW can be added to an object, and a PostScript-filled object prints as previewed even if you don't own a PostScript printer. CorelDRAW has an interpreting engine that converts PostScript code to non-PostScript in the event that you want to output to a PCL-based laser printer. However, because PostScript code isn't normally intended to be viewed on a monitor, you cannot preview a PostScript fill within the context of a composition in a CorelDRAW document; you must click on **P**review in the PostScript Texture dialog box, or output a file to hard copy to see a PostScript fill.

So what's the big attraction of PostScript Textures if you can't work with them as "normal" object fills? A PostScript-filled object can be scaled up or down to suit any design need; Corel's implementation of a PS fill contains vector patterns and fractal-type algorithms, not pixel colors of a fixed resolution bitmap image. Also, the PostScript Texture dialog box gives you several parameters for each PostScript preset that you can change in the same way you modify a fractal texture preset.

In figure 5.10, you see the PostScript Texture dialog box, and the Landscape preset. Depending upon the preset, you can change the grayscale values, the size of the tiles, line widths, and random seed number for the more organic-looking fills.

Because PostScript code is device independent, you can even print a design to Adobe Acrobat Distiller and the resulting PDF file can be viewed on-screen with the PostScript texture intact. However, there are few graphical descriptions contained within each preset parcel of PostScript Texture that cannot be created manually or with other CorelDRAW fill types. And compositionally, it's hard to visualize a PostScript Texture because the on-screen display consists of tiny "PS" bitmap placeholders, not the preview image.

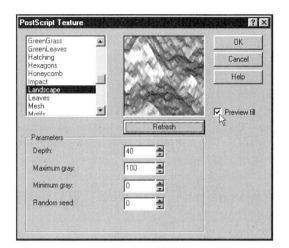

Figure 5.10
PostScript fills come in a variety of presets that you can edit and print to PostScript, and even non-PostScript, devices.

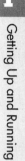

⚑ Stop   Make certain that you have a compelling reason to click on the Preview fill button in the PostScript Texture dialog box. Even with a fast Pentium processor, CorelDRAW's rasterizing engine can take up to 15 seconds to interpret and preview a PostScript Texture.

Again, PostScript was not originally intended to be viewed on a monitor from within an application, but as a compact, platform and device independent method of describing a page to be printed. If you're designing an Internet web page screen, or a multimedia show, PostScript Textures simply don't fit the media. CMYK screen colors, the ability to fill an object of unspecified dimensions, and the capability to share a file that contains PostScript code with Macintosh and Unix users make the PostScript Texture fill a good choice for desktop publishing and other physical output.

Conquering the Limitations of Automated Fills

Make no mistake: fountain fills, color bitmap fills, and all the others you can use in the Fill tool's menu flyout serve the bulk of design purposes more than adequately. For example, if you need a linear fountain fill for 100 different objects on a page, many other drawing applications oblige you to create the effect using blended objects. This creates an unnecessarily large file, and also outputs a lot slower than if a single gradient, fountain fill is used.

But fountain fills—actually, all the Special Effects fills in CorelDRAW—suffer from the "view through a window" syndrome; the container object can be manipulated to suggest perspective, and the nodes can be edited, but one's view of the fill through the shape of the container object remains constant. The reason for this unchanging behavior is because vector objects *are* actually "evaluation windows" for a preset pattern; you can alter the container, but actions don't affect the orientation of the fill. Fill tool patterns begin and end at the vertical and horizontal extremes of an object—regardless of whether the object's dimensions occupy all of the fill space.

In the following example, two patterns have been provided in NEON.CDR that look similar; one of them has been created using a series of blends, and the other is a custom fountain fill. Ordinarily, it would be time-intensive and unwise to build a fountain fill from overlapping blend objects, but this is no ordinary situation. Suppose you need to wrap a fountain fill around a 3D object. You cannot achieve dimensional texture—a gradient of colors that appear to bend around the corner of a perspective plane—through the use of fountain fills.

The next set of steps might seem like a classic television commercial, a "torture test" of Brand X—a custom fountain fill—and our hero, the "synthetic fountain fill" blend. You can sit out the first half of the test if you like (the "wrong" method), but be sure to check out how plastic and dimensional the blend in NEON.CDR is and how you can use blends in a multitude of special design assignments.

Note   The NEON.CDR document is multi-layered, so don't be alarmed if there are certain objects that can't be moved with the Pick tool when you try out the example. The text has been converted to curves, and a dimensional outline of a cube stroked with light blue are both locked on Layer 1, and you can work with the fill objects located on Layer 2.

Here's the wrong—and the right—way to add dimensional shading to a group of objects that display 3D perspective:

Creating 3D Surfaces

1. Open the NEON.CDR file from the EXAMPLES.CHAP05 folder of the *CorelDRAW! 6 Expert's Edition Bonus CD*.

   This is the document containing two different objects that appear identical.

2. Choose **L**ayout, Snap to **O**bjects.

   Creates environment in Drawing Window where objects and nodes are attracted to objects and nodes of other shapes.

3. With the Pick tool, click-and-drag the object marked "Fountain Fill" toward the cube outline, then right-click before you release the cursor.

   Leaves a copy of the fountain fill object where you dropped it; the original remains in the same location on the page.

4. Click on the Shape tool (or press F10), then click-and-drag the fountain fill's upper left corner so it snaps to the upper left corner of the cube outline.

You're shaping the fountain fill so that it conforms to the left facet shape of the cube outline.

5. Repeat the last step with the other three corners of the fountain fill (see fig. 5.11).

The left facet of the outline cube is filled with a fountain fill.

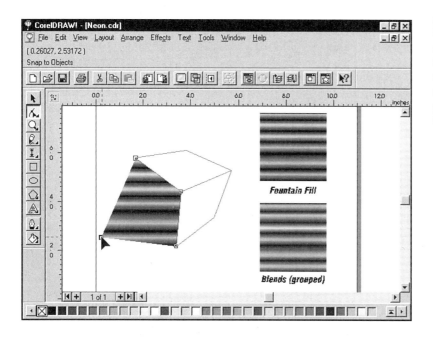

Figure 5.11

A fountain fill can be shaped to conform to different geometric designs, but the pattern maintains its orientation.

6. Press the spacebar, then click-and-drag the original fountain fill toward the top of the cube outline, then right-click before releasing the cursor.

Toggles the Shape tool to the Pick tool; leaves a 2nd copy of the fountain fill next to the cube outline.

7. Press spacebar, then repeat the previous steps used to make the fountain fill conform to the top facet of the cube outline.

Toggles the Pick tool to the Shape tool; fills the second side of the cube outline.

8. Repeat the last two steps, then choose **F**ile Save **A**s, and save the file as NEON.CDR to your hard disk.

Completes filling the cube outline; saves your work up to this point (see fig. 5.12).

Figure 5.12
The visual detail of the fountain filled object does not correspond to the dimensional outlines the shape suggests.

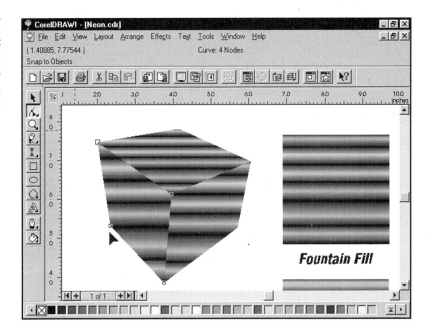

Fountain fills contain no information about perspective or the shape of the object they fill; this is why fountain fills are a poor choice for realistic objects that appear to recede into space, or are rotated. A fountain fill only contains information about a start and finish color, the angle of the fountain fill transition, and any Edge Pad or Offset property you've assigned to it.

You can, to some extent, cope with a fountain fill's lack of "direction" by changing the **A**ngle of the fill (click-and-drag in the preview box), but this doesn't solve the inherent problem of a special fill's rectangular property; fountain, 2 color, full color, and other special fills will always create a pattern within a rectangular area that *encompasses* the target shape. So it's unlikely that you can precisely fill an un-rectangular object with a pattern precisely.

In the following exercise, the blend object in NEON.CDR is manipulated in a similar way as the fountain fill, but entirely different results are achieved. The dimensional, angular effect is created using a blend, because each object in the blend has an orientation that can be changed, and each component of the blend has the same properties as any other object you'd create in CorelDRAW—you can distort and rotate objects in a grouped blend. This leads to some wonderful design possibilities, but because the blend objects are grouped, you can't manipulate the collection of objects with the Shape tool. Instead, you'll use the Envelope command, which works similarly to direct editing of an object's nodes with the Shape tool—except editing can be performed with many grouped objects at once. Here's how to make a dimensionally filled cube:

Filling an Object with a Collection of Other Objects

1. If you completed the previous exercise, choose the Pick tool, marquee select the three distorted fountain fills above the cube outline, then press Delete before beginning this example.

2. Select the Pick tool. In the NEON.CDR document, click-and-drag the objects labeled "Blends (Grouped)" to above the left facet of the cube outline, then right-click before releasing the cursor.

   Drops a copy of the grouped blends on top of the left cube facet.

3. Choose Effects, Add Perspective.

   A dotted bounding box appears around the grouped blend objects; the Shape tool is automatically selected.

4. Click-and-drag the upper left corner of the grouped objects to the upper left corner of the left facet of the cube outline.

   Corner snaps to the corner of the left cube facet.

5. Repeat the last step with the other three corresponding blend object corners.

   Completes filling the left cube facet (see fig. 5.13).

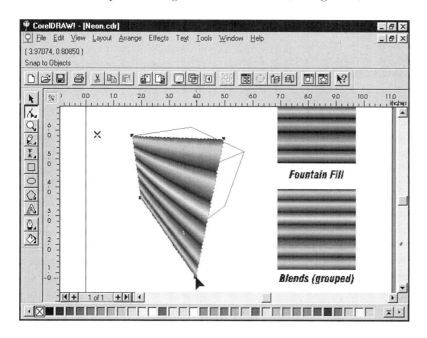

Figure 5.13

A collection of discrete objects can be distorted in a way that Special Fills cannot.

Feel free at this point to play with the blend objects a little. You'll notice that the effect of a custom fountain fill can be changed in many of the same ways as a single CorelDRAW object.

6. Repeat the previous four steps with the right and top sides of the cube outline.

    Completes the cube design.

7. Press Ctrl+S (**F**ile, **S**ave).

    Saves the finished piece to hard disk.

8. Choose **L**ayout, then uncheck the Snap to **O**bjects command.

    Eliminates the snap-to state from your future CorelDRAW work; prevents future Drawing Window behavior you might think of as strange!

In figure 5.14, you can see the result of the preceding example; the cube looks like it has been upholstered in tuck 'n' roll vinyl, but most importantly, the texture follows the lines of perspective of the cube.

Figure 5.14
A fill must suggest the same viewpoint as an object; blended objects help integrate the shape with the shading.

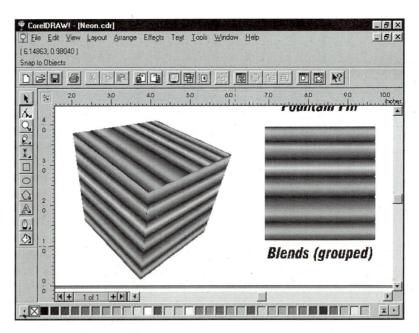

In the next section, a combination of fountain fills and blended objects are used to show how a boring geometric composition can spring to life through the use of accurate shading.

Using Combinations of Manual and Automated Shading

Integration is the key concept behind using CorelDRAW's feature set, and even other applications to create a composition. As you'll see toward the end of this chapter, fills for objects can come from many different places; CorelPHOTO-PAINT images can enhance a design and even play a central role in a composition.

Your choice of fill types for a design is necessarily governed by the shape—the geometric outline—of the design's elements, as you saw in the previous section. Now it's time to integrate grouped blend objects with fills to create shading in a design that requires both techniques of filling a space. In the example that follows, a poster for an animation festival features a bouncing ball illustrated in steps, shown in figure 5.15.

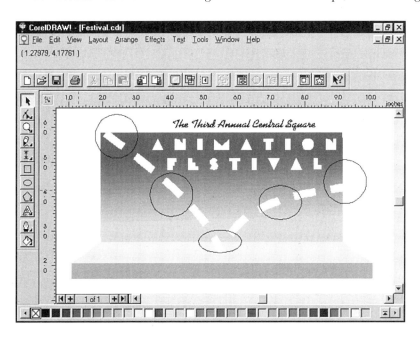

Figure 5.15

Different types of fills are required to realistically shade different types of outline shapes.

Getting Up and Running

At points along the ball's path, the ball becomes distorted as it hits the stage floor. Perfectly spherical shapes are ideally shaded with the Radial fountain fills, because this type of fountain fill begins with a color circle that emanates outward in concentric, perfectly circular bands of color. However, a Radial fountain fill cannot imitate real-life shading of a distorted circle because it always maintains the circular shading property.

In the next steps, you'll create shading fills for the round versions of the ball in the festival poster, then in later steps, you'll create complex blends to fill the flattened ball shapes. To heighten the sense of dimension for the bouncing ball, you'll use a custom

Radial fountain fill—one made up of beginning, end, *and* intermediate fill steps. The effect produces a highlight on the ball, shading, and also a *kick light*—a secondary light source in a scene frequently used to define an edge of an object whose outline might be lost in shaded areas of a scene.

Note   The FESTIVAL.CDR document contains unfilled ellipses on Layer 1; the Background layer and Locked layer contain other parts of the scene, and they are locked. Additionally, text elements have been converted to curves to ensure that you can see the composition as intended without having the same fonts installed on your system.

All you need to do to complete the example composition is to work with the objects on Layer 1, but feel free to unlock the other layers to see how the other scene elements were created.

Here's how to create a custom fountain fill that can be used for many different round objects in your CorelDRAW work.

Creating a 3D Sphere Fill

1. Open the FESTIVAL.CDR document from the EXAMPLES.CHAP05 folder of the *CorelDRAW! 6 Expert's Edition Bonus CD.*

   This is the composition to which you'll add shading.

2. Choose the Zoom tool, right-click over the document window, and choose Zoom To Fit from the shortcut menu.

   Zooms you into a comfortable editing view of the design. If you don't have the **D**efault action specified for the Zoom tool's properties (see Chapter 2, "Customizing CorelDRAW!"), and have Zoom out or Use **t**raditional zoom flyout specified as your Zoom tool's properties, simply marquee-drag around the design using the Zoom in tool.

3. Choose the Pick tool, click on the left ellipse outline, click on the Fill tool, then click on the fountain fill button.

   Displays the Fountain Fill dialog box.

4. Choose Radial from the **T**ype drop-down list, then click-and-drag in the preview box so that the center of the fill is in the upper left of the box.

   Selects the appropriate type of shading for the ellipse; establishes a direction of light source for the design.

From this moment on, anything you add to FESTIVAL.CDR should display lighting qualities that match the direction of the highlight for the ball that you've just specified.

In other words, light will be cast from the upper left of the composition; therefore, shading should occur on the lower right of all future objects.

5. Click on the **C**ustom radio button, then double-click above the Color Blend area about a third of the way from the left of the Color Blend.

    Creates an intermediate step in the Radial fountain fill; by default, the beginning color, black, is assigned to the intermediate step.

6. Click-and-drag the Color Blend marker to the right until the Position spin box reads 33.

    Accurately positions the intermediate fill step.

7. Click on the 80% black swatch on the color palette.

    Assigns 80% black to the selected intermediate color step in the fill.

8. Click on the left color marker on the color Blend area, then click on 10% black on the color palette.

    Makes the fountain fill move from 10% black to 80% black, to the default finish color of white.

9. Type **10** in the **E**dge Pad spin box (or use the elevator buttons).

    Increases the transition rate between the component colors in the fountain fill (see fig. 5.16).

You'll notice that increasing the **E**dge Pad value unaligns the Color Blend area markers. This is okay, and you shouldn't reset the marker you created. The Edge Pad value operates independently of the intermediate fountain fill steps to increase the rate of change in a fill; this is why changing the Edge Pad setting for a custom fill should be the last step in creating such a fill. Now, you should save the fill you've created:

10. Type **3D Ball** in the Presets field, then click on the + button to the right of the Presets field.

    Adds the fountain fill you've designed to the list of presets.

11. Click on OK.

    Returns you to FESTIVAL.CDR, with the left-most ellipse filled.

12. Right-click over the "x" on the color palette.

    Assigns no outline to the ellipse.

Figure 5.16

You can create a second source of lighting within a fountain fill by adding intermediate steps to the Color blend area.

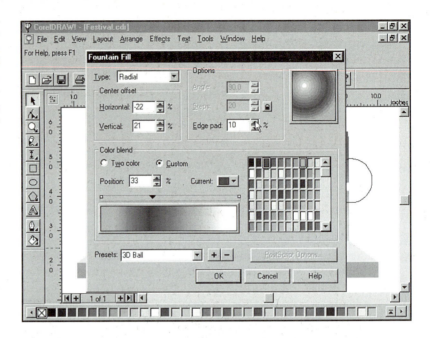

13. Choose File, Save **A**s, then save the composition as FESTIVAL.CDR to your hard disk.

    Saves your work at this intermediate stage.

As you can see in figure 5.17, the bouncing ball steals the show; the dimensional fountain fill shading is similar in pattern to the outline shape of the object. Whenever you need to light an object so it appears in 3D, choose the sort of shading that matches the shape of the thing the fill is supposed to shade.

Two other balls in FESTIVAL are identical to the ball you've shaded. To fill them, you can select them and return to the fountain fill dialog box, but it's much quicker to copy the outline color and width (which are none) and the fill of the existing 3D ball. To do this, select the two unfilled ellipses (numbers 2 and 5 in the left to right sequence), choose **E**dit, Copy Properties **F**rom, click in the Outline **P**en, Outline **C**olor, and **F**ill boxes to check them, click on OK, then point the large arrow cursor at the ball you've already shaded and click, as shown in figure 5.18.

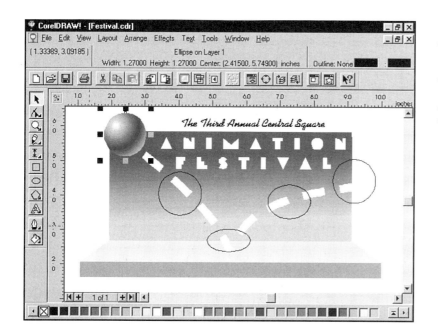

Figure 5.17
The play of light colors against darker ones in a fountain fill imitates the shading of objects in the real world.

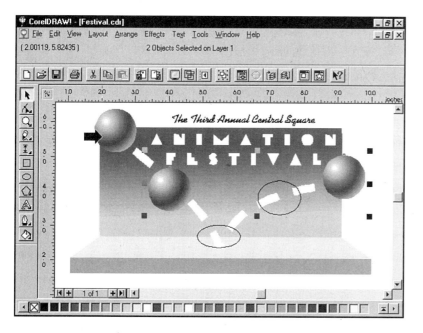

Figure 5.18
You can copy the properties of an object to other objects by using the Edit, Copy Properties From command.

Tip   The default number of Steps in a fountain fill is 50, because Corel Corp. presumes that you want optimal screen redraw time. This value of 50 was fine for the preceding example image, but if you want to output the image to a high-end imagesetter, increase the number of **S**teps by unlocking the **S**teps spin box in the Fountain Fill dialog box, then increasing the number.

The optimal amount of fountain fill steps can be calculated by CorelDRAW at printing time, or you can manually adjust the **S**teps value to suit a particular need. However, don't increase the Steps value if you only want to preview more fountain fills; the Display menu in the **T**ools\O**p**tions command is your ticket for viewing higher fountain fill step values.

Creating a Synthetic Fountain Fill

In the NEON example, you saw that a CorelDRAW blend of objects successfully imitates a custom fountain fill, but has the advantages of being able to present the same shading information when distorted or rotated. The ellipses in the FESTIVAL design that have yet to be filled require a similar blend fill because they aren't perfectly round; a Radial fountain fill would look phony because its pattern of banded fills doesn't correspond to a distorted ellipse.

Therefore, it's time to create a two-step color blend that uses the same color values as you defined for the custom fill in the last example. Because blends are dynamic, the three objects you'll create to portray intermediate color transitions can be changed—repositioned—after the Blend effect is applied, so that a fill that appears to be identical to the custom fountain fill is easily achieved. Here's how to create a blend that's harmonious with the custom fountain fill shading.

Creating a Manual Fountain Fill Shading

1. With the Zoom tool, marquee around the middle (#3) ellipse in the FESTIVAL design.

   Provides a close-up view of the target object for editing.

2. With the Pick tool, click on the outline of the ellipse, then click on the 10% black swatch on the color palette.

   Selects the object and fills it.

3. Press +, then click on the 80% black swatch on the color palette.

   Copies the selected ellipse; fills it with 80% black.

4. Click on the middle, right selection handle of the 80% black ellipse, then click-and-drag to the left until the status line reads X Scale: 80%.

Disproportionally scales the horizontal dimension of the ellipse.

5. Click on the bottom, middle selection handle of the 80% black filled ellipse, then drag upwards until the status line says that the Y scale is about 90%, then release the cursor.

Disproportionately scales the vertical dimension of the ellipse (see fig. 5.19).

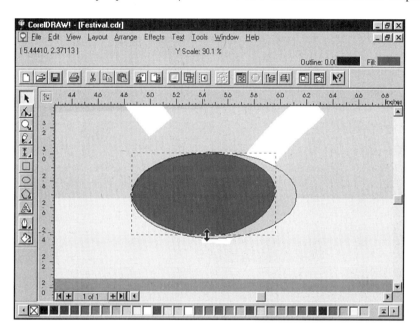

Figure 5.19

Create a copy of the original object, then scale it to match a color transition area of the custom fountain fill you created.

What you've done in the last step is to create an area of color transition for the distorted ball that corresponds to a color shaded area in the fountain fill the three other balls are presently filled with. Now you'll create the *transition* between the two objects.

6. Marquee select both ellipses, then choose Effe**c**ts, **B**lend (Ctrl+B).

Displays the Blend Roll-Up.

Consider output for a moment before you create a blend. If you print the finished piece to an ordinary 300 dpi laser printer, the maximum number of unique grayscale shades this image can render to is about 49. That's from white to 100% coverage (usually black). Additionally, the ball isn't very large; it's only about an inch in diameter, and the area of transition is even smaller. You'll only see about 1/8th of an inch of blended objects between the beginning and end object. Also, the color transition the Blend effect creates through in-between objects travels from 10% to 80%, so it won't require 49 possible shades of printer halftones.

You should try a Blend Steps amount of *less* than the default 20; 14 is an arbitrary number (it happens to work effectively), and helps limit the number of objects on the page, thus improving rendering and screen redraw time.

7. Type **14** in the Steps spin box, then click on Apply (see fig. 5.20).

Create 14 intermediate steps (objects) of transitional values in between the 80% black and 10% black ellipses.

Figure 5.20

Evaluate the number of blend steps for a design element based upon the size of the transitional blend and printer capability.

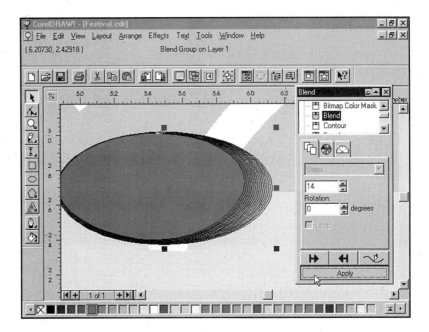

8. Right-click over the "x" on the color palette.

Removes the outline from the Blend and control ellipses.

9. Click on the background of FESTIVAL.CDR, then click on the 80% black ellipse.

Deselects the Blend group, then selects the 80% black ellipse.

Ordinarily, you'd accidentally select the background object(s) by clicking over them in an attempt to deselect the Blend group. However, the background objects are on a locked layer in FESTIVAL.CDR; CorelDRAW won't acknowledge objects on a locked layer, so the last step worked.

10. Press +, then click on the white swatch on the color palette.

Creates a copy of the 80% black control ellipse; fills it with white.

11. Click-and-drag the white ellipse's middle selection handles until the ellipse is basically circular (less distorted), then click-and-drag the lower right selection handle until the white circle is about 1/15th the size of the 80% black ellipse (check the status line as you do this).

You've created the "finish step" for this compound Blend.

12. Click-and-drag the white circle until it's repositioned within the upper left of the 80% black ellipse.

Resizing objects tends to also reposition them.

13. With the white circle selected, Shift+click on the 80% black ellipse, type **20** in the Steps field of the Blend Roll-Up, then click on Apply.

Applies a blend between the 80% black and the white ellipse.

14. Press F3 (or zoom out with the Zoom tool).

Zooms you out to a view that includes the compound blend and at least one of the fountain filled.

If the compound blend ball looks similarly shaded to the fountain filled balls, you're in business. If the shading appears off-center or otherwise dissimilar to the fountain filled balls, select one of the control ellipses with the Pick tool and move it. The Blend objects will readjust to compensate for any changes made to control objects because Blends are dynamically linked to "parent" objects. Additionally, you might want to reset the **N**udge value in the General **O**ptions dialog box to about .007" and try nudging instead of directly manipulating a control object.

15. Press Ctrl+S (**F**ile, **S**ave).

Saves your work at this intermediate stage.

In figure 5.21, you can see the result of the preceding steps.

Corel Corp. can't anticipate your personal design needs, and therefore can't accommodate them with an elliptical fountain fill, a trapezoidal fountain fill, a flying toaster-shaped fountain fill, and so on. However, you've now learned how to manually create a smooth color transition between intermediate control objects, and you can use this technique in almost any design situation that calls for soft, airbrush-like effects.

The #4 ball remains to be filled, but you don't have to repeat the previous example steps. As you saw in the NEON example, a grouped blend can be reshaped, and its

Figure 5.21

You can create your own photo-realistic lighting effects when you use Blend objects in combination with fountain fills.

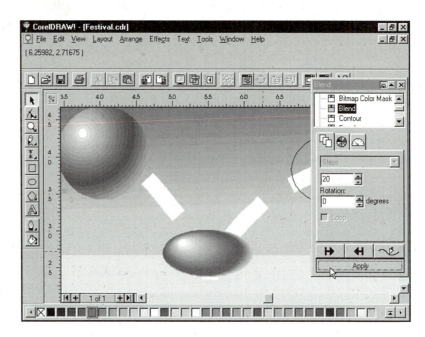

internal pattern proportionately adjusted to reflect changes. To shade ball #4, follow these steps:

1. Marquee select all the Component blend objects with the Pick tool. Make certain that the status line says that a Compound Object of five Elements is the current selection. If you mistakenly select a control object instead of all the components, you'll distort the compound blend, but not move it in the next step.

2. Click, hold, and drag the objects to the bottom of the #4 ellipse, then right-click to drop a copy onto the #4 ellipse while the original bunch of blends remains where you created it.

3. Click-and-drag the top, middle selection handle of the Compound object upwards until the preview (dotted blue) outline meets the top of the #4 ellipse, then release. (See figure 5.22.)

4. Delete the #4 outline, then press Ctrl+S to save your work.

When you want to create dimensional objects, here's a tip that's sometimes overlooked by even the best professional designers. If a 3D shape has a highlight (hint: the balls in this scene do), it's reflecting light; that means that the object is opaque. Therefore, some source light is *not* passing through the object. This means that the 3D surface that suggests a stage floor in FESTIVAL.CDR is missing something (like the shadows you'll learn to build in the next section)!

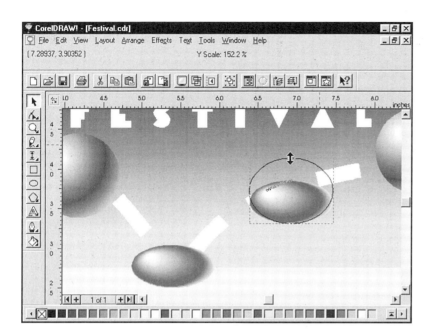

Figure 5.22
You can distort a Compound Blend to accommodate a different sized area.

Using the Right Fills and Distortions with Shadows

A *shadow* serves many design purposes beyond heightening the realistic quality of lighting in a scene. A shadow can help define the edge of an object, and it can add overall contrast to a scene composed of soft, pastel colors. A shadow can also redirect attention within a composition.

Shadows also have different texture properties. Their edge can be soft or hard depending upon how close the light source is to an object, and shadows can vary in their degree of opacity. All of these considerations for shadows would typically be ascribed to work created in a bitmap editing program, but if you know a few tricks to working with shading and blends, you can create the appearance of very lifelike, subtle shadows right within any CorelDRAW design.

Adding Shadows to the FESTIVAL Scene

If we examine the dimensional object within the FESTIVAL design, it's apparent that the strobing ball is bouncing off the object we perceive to be the floor. Therefore, a corresponding shadow for each "version" of the bouncing ball should be beneath each ball, with a little extra shading to the right of each shadow, because the source of light in the scene (the direction reflecting each ball's highlight) is from the upper left.

Because the stage floor apparently comes toward the viewer at a steep angle, the shape of each shadow should be that of an extreme ellipse. This makes it unfeasible to use a fountain fill to create the shadows, but you've already learned how to "fake" a fountain fill by using blend objects.

Before starting the following example, it's important to note that the beginning and end blend objects for the shadow should not be centered; the "core" of the shadow should be to the left of the shadow's weakest point, to suggest a shadow cast onto a surface from an object that is lit at an angle—not from above. Also, the floor object— although it's on a locked layer and not easily accessed—is a 10% black fill. You need this information to build shadows because, ideally, a shadow should fade from a dark shade to the exact shade of the surface it's casting upon at the edge of the shadow.

Here's how to give this 3D scene a little more substance:

Creating Shadow Blends

1. With the Ellipse tool (press F7), click-and-drag a narrow ellipse beneath the first ball, within the dimensions of the top and bottom of the stage floor shape.

   Creates the outside object for the first shadow element.

2. Click on the 10% black swatch on the color palette.

   Fills the ellipse with 10% black.

3. Click-and-drag a second ellipse, about 1/3 the size of the first, inside of the first ellipse; click on the 40% black swatch on the color palette.

   Creates the "core" of the shadow element.

4. Press spacebar, then click-and-drag the 40% black ellipse so it's a little toward the upper right of the larger ellipse.

   Offsets the second ellipse; the blend will be off-center.

5. Shift+click on the larger 10% ellipse.

   Adds the second ellipse to your selection (of the 40% black ellipse).

6. Type **12** in the Steps field on the Blend Roll-Up, then click on Apply.

   Creates the shadow for ball #1 (see fig. 5.23).

7. Marquee select the shadow blend objects (or *carefully* select the blend, not either Control Object), then click-and-drag the blend objects so the "core" object is beneath ball #1, and half the shadow is to the right of the ball.

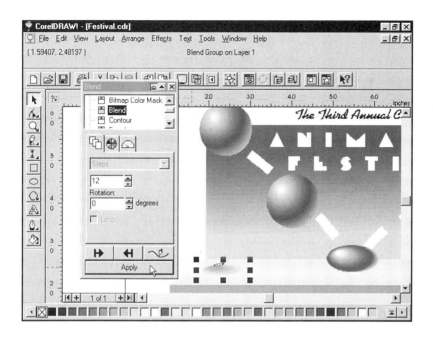

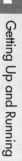
Figure 5.23
A soft-edge shadow can be created from different colored control objects of very different sizes.

Positions the shadow to accurately suggest that the ball is casting it.

8. Click-and-drag the blend objects to beneath ball #2, then right-click, and release the cursor.

    Drops a copy of the original shadow beneath ball #2.

9. Repeat the last step for balls #3, 4, and 5.

    Creates shadows for the rest of the bouncing balls.

10. Press Ctrl+S (**F**ile, **S**ave).

    Saves your work at this intermediate stage.

You can perform a number of artistic tweaks to the composition right now that'll enhance the dimensional look of the design. First, ball #3 actually touches the floor object, and therefore the shadow might overlap and obscure the ball. Shadows almost never do this in real life, so click on the blend, then press Shift+PageDown to send the shadow blend to the back of the object "stack" on Layer 1 (or click on the To Back button on the toolbar).

Also, shadows become more dense, and their edges a little better defined when an object is close to a shadow. To imitate this phenomenon, you can make shadow #3's core—the 40% black control ellipse—darker, say 70% black, and you can make the ellipse a little larger. Scaling the ellipse will dynamically adjust the blend to occupy less visible space in the shadow element, and make the transition between beginning and ending control ellipse in less space, thus sharpening the edge of the shadow.

A final point on your shadow-making adventure: the shadow #5 looks a little goofy dangling off the edge of the stage floor object, doesn't it? There are a number of solutions for chopping off the shadow area that extends beyond the stage floor object—most of them labor-intensive. You can rebuild the blend by Trimming the original ellipses, but this means you'd have to separate and delete the blend group; Trim functions don't work on linked or grouped objects.

Here's the expeditious method for hiding, not eliminating, the portion of the shadow that extends off the stage floor object:

Hiding an Unwanted Part of a Design

1. Choose **L**ayout, Snap to **O**bjects of.

   Turns on the "attractive" property nodes and objects within the active image window.

2. Zoom into the right side of the stage floor.

   This is where you'll perform editing.

3. Choose the Pencil tool (or press F5), then click on the top right corner of the stage floor object.

   Creates the first point in an object; the point "sticks" to the vertex of the floor object.

4. Double-click, clockwise, around the offending area of shadow #5, then single-click at the beginning of the path.

   You've created a closed path which describes the area where shadow #5 shouldn't be visible (see fig. 5.24).

5. Click on the white swatch on the color palette, then right-click on the "x" on the color palette.

   Assigns the new object a white fill and no outline.

6. Press Ctrl+S (**F**ile, **S**ave) then press F9.

   Saves the completed image, and displays a full-screen preview (see fig. 5.25).

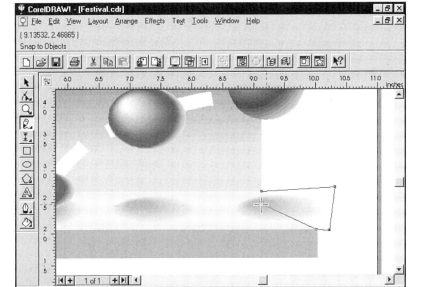

Figure 5.24
Snap-to properties ensure that objects you draw are precisely aligned to other objects.

Figure 5.25
The completed design. Central Square doesn't really have an Animation Festival, but it's a nice Upstate NY place to visit.

Getting Up and Running

7. Press F9, then choose **L**ayout, and uncheck the Snap to **O**bjects command.

Returns you to the workspace; frees objects from stickiness.

The preceding exercise demonstrates the creative use of an object filled with the same color as the document page color. Virtual correction fluid should be used sparingly, however. If you need to extensively edit a design, it's usually best to conserve file size and complexity by directly editing objects you're unhappy with, rather than "stickering" over them, as you've just done.

Creating Different Types of Shadows

One of the easiest tricks you can perform to make an object appear as though it's floating above a page is the "drop shadow" technique. To create a drop shadow in CorelDRAW, follow these steps:

1. Begin with a simple object—ideally one that contains no subpaths—and make sure it's filled with a color or texture that's substantially darker than the page color.

2. Press + to copy the object, then click-and-drag it to offset it from the original.

Usually, classically, drop shadows are made to the lower right of an original, but you can offset the copy in any direction in which your artistic inclinations lean.

3. Fill the copy object with a 20% or 30% black fill, then send the copy behind the original (press Ctrl or Shift+PageDown). Presto, instant drop shadow effect!

The reason a drop shadow original should contain no subpaths is because the shadow peeks through the holes in the object; this can sometimes create an interesting design, however.

In addition to drop shadows, you're more likely to see a second sort of shadow—a *cast shadow*—beneath strongly illuminated real objects. In figure 5.26, you can see a visual example of the two types of shadows that express common, single source lighting results in the real world. A drop shadow gives the impression that an object is lifted off the page, while a *cast* shadow suggests that you're looking *into* a page, and that the page has depth. The cast shadow recedes along a perspective line into the distance.

The reason different types of shadows enter the discussion now is because the next section shows how to use a photographic image as a fill for a CorelDRAW object, and you'll need to know how to *integrate* a bitmap image with other CorelDRAW objects. Shadows pull off the illusion as a binding element quite nicely. And cast shadows are almost as easy to create as drop shadows if you understand lighting effects.

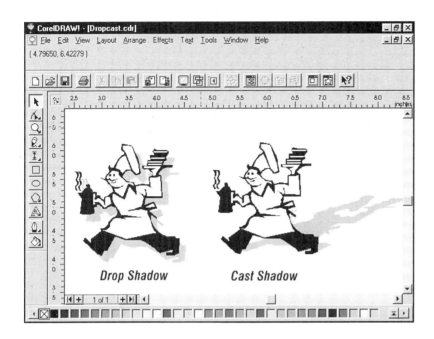

Figure 5.26
Drop and Cast shadows both give the illusion of depth to a flat illustration.

Using the PowerClip Feature

PowerClips aren't exactly a member of the Fill tool features, but PowerClips operate in the same graphical way as a Texture or Fountain Fill. A *PowerClip* is an object whose fill is composed of anything you can create or import into CorelDRAW; vector objects, bitmaps, and even text can be "masked" through a PowerClip object's shape to only allow a view of the interior of the PowerClip object. In this sense, the "windowed" view of a fill is the same as the limited view through a PowerClip object to see its contents.

Here's the methodology and the specifics of the following assignment that works with PowerClips and the Full-color Bitmap Pattern feature:

The Modern Café (most likely located in Central Square) needs a color poster to hang outside. Elements of vector and bitmap graphics are in order here; the poster needs text and graphics, and text usually renders cleaner in vector format. A bitmap image of a coffee cup and some coffee beans are provided, and it's up to you to create the scene.

Some of the design issues have been eliminated, such as composition and choice of fonts—the CAFE.CDR image on the *CorelDRAW! 6 Expert's Edition Bonus CD* contains these elements on a hidden layer—all you need to do is experiment for a while. In the process, you'll discover some of the unique capabilities of CorelDRAW! 6, and how you can integrate shading, bitmaps, and vector artwork into a seamless composition.

Before beginning this assignment, it's important that you have CorelPHOTO-PAINT installed on your system; we'll be using this program to finesse the MOD-CAFE.TIF image and the CAFEBEAN.TIF images used in this example. The assignment begins in PHOTO-PAINT, because you need to crop the MOD-CAFE image. PowerClips hide image areas outside of the PowerClip's edges, but PowerClips don't eliminate the "clipped" area of an imported bitmap. Therefore, to conserve the saved file size of this assignment, it's best to only import the areas of a bitmap image that will be seen in the interior of a PowerClip.

PowerClipping a Bitmap Image

1. In CorelPHOTO-PAINT, open the MOD-CAFE.TIF image from the EXAMPLES.CHAP05 folder of the *CorelDRAW! 6 Expert's Edition Bonus CD.*

   This is the "fill" image for a PowerClip object yet to be created.

2. Choose the Crop tool from the toolbox, then click-and-drag a rectangle that fits around the coffee cup and saucer tightly (don't crop into the edges, though).

   Creates a bounding box with eight selection handles around the boundary.

3. Click-and-drag on the middle selection handles to adjust the crop box.

   Refines the selection of the coffee cup and saucer (see fig. 5.27).

Figure 5.27
You can precisely refine an initial crop box by click-and-dragging on a crop box selection handle.

4. Double-click inside of the bounding box.

   Executes the crop; the image file size and image are smaller now.

5. Choose **F**ile, Save **A**s, then save the image as MOD-CAFE.TIF to your hard disk.

   Saves the cropped image for future use.

Stop If your system is equipped with less than 12 MB of RAM, you're skating on thin ice and shouldn't have more than one application open at a time under Win95. Even with preemptive multitasking, the author recommends that when your business is finished in one program, you should close it before opening another application.

We have a good rule for estimating the amount of RAM your system *really* requires to run a Windows application with any degree of speed or stability: Whatever the software box recommends, multiply the amount by 2, and then you have the *minimum* system RAM requirements.

6. Click on the close box on the MOD-CAFE document window, click on the close box on PHOTO-PAINT's application window, then launch CorelDRAW from Explorer.

   Closes PHOTO-PAINT; starts CorelDRAW.

7. Open the CAFE.CDR document from the EXAMPLES.CHAP05 folder of the *CorelDRAW! 6 Expert's Edition Bonus CD*.

   This document contains the additional elements you'll need to complete the design; they're hidden on a locked layer.

8. Click on the Import button on the toolbar (or choose **F**ile, **I**mport).

   Displays the Import dialog box.

9. Choose MOD-CAFE.TIF from your hard disk (*not* the Bonus CD location in the Look **i**n drop-down list), then click on Imp**o**rt.

   Imports the cropped image you saved to hard disk.

10. Press F4 (the shortcut for Zoom To Fit), or click-and-drag the Zoom tool to create a close-up view of the imported TIFF image.

    Zooms you to a comfortable viewing resolution for editing.

11. Click on an empty area of the printable page. Choose the (Freehand) Pencil tool (press F5), then click on a point at the top edge of the coffee cup.

    Deselects the TIFF image; begins a path.

12. Double-click in a clockwise direction at changes in the outline direction around the edge of the cup and saucer, then single-click at the first point you clicked.

Creates a closed, straight line path around the cup (see fig. 5.28).

Figure 5.28
Double-click to create a node at points of inflection—extremes of an outline's shape—to create a rough outline path.

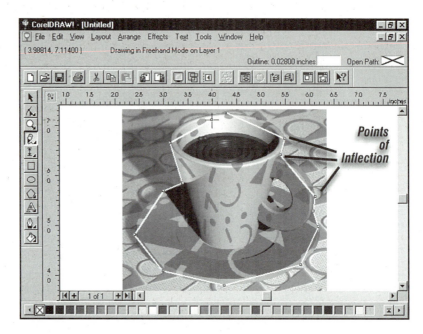

13. Choose **F**ile, Save **A**s, then save your work as MOD-CAFE.CDR to your hard disk.

Saves your work at this intermediate stage.

> **Note** The path seen in the figures has been exaggerated to more clearly illustrate the path you should create around the cup and saucer. You can accurately create an outline using the default width of .003" for the Pencil tool (the figures show a .28" line), but you might want to shade the path a brilliant primary or white color to more easily separate it from the cup/saucer image's background pattern.

In the following set of steps, you'll finalize the path construction that describes the cup shape in the TIFF image; the handle requires a subpath, and you need to refine the path so that it reflects the cup and saucer outline more accurately.

As mentioned in Chapter 3, "Beating Nodes and Paths into Submission (The Easy Way)," Bezier curves were examined as an alternative to creating, then modifying straight line paths to describe a shape. The straight line method is used in this example because there are a combination of straight and curved segments that describe the outline of the cup and saucer, and it's faster to accurately convert and shape a straight segment into a curve than to correct both the node and segment of a Bezier curve to create a straight line segment.

Here's how to conclude the outline that you'll use as a PowerClip for the cup image:

Finishing the Outline

1. Click at the top point where the handle meets the cup.

   You're beginning a second path which describes the interior of the cup's handle.

2. Double-click around the inside of the cup handle in a clockwise direction, then single-click at the start point.

   You've created a closed path.

3. Press spacebar, then Shift+click on the outline of the cup and saucer.

   Switches to the Pick tool; selects both objects.

4. Choose **A**rrange, **C**ombine (Ctrl+L).

   Combines the two paths; the combined path has a "negative space" inside of the cup's handle area.

5. Press F10 (or click on the Shape tool), marquee select all the nodes along the path, then right-click over a node and choose To Curve from the shortcut menu.

   Converts all the segments to curves; all the nodes now have the Cusp property (see fig. 5.29).

6. Carefully, click, then click-and-drag on line segments to make the curves fit the edge of the cup and saucer image.

   Effectively changes the control handles associated with nodes at either end of the segment; reshapes the curved segment. (See figure 5.30.)

The term "carefully" was emphasized in the preceding step because direct manipulation of a curve often yields unexpected results; the curve can suddenly bow steeply out of window view unless you first click on a segment to select it, then slowly click-and-drag the curved segment away or toward the object from the *middle* of the segment. Dragging the midpoint on a segment ensures that you're moving the control points at either end of the curved segment in an equal amount, and usually in a complementary direction.

Figure 5.29
The shortcut (pop-up) menu is context-sensitive; you must click on a node to redefine node properties.

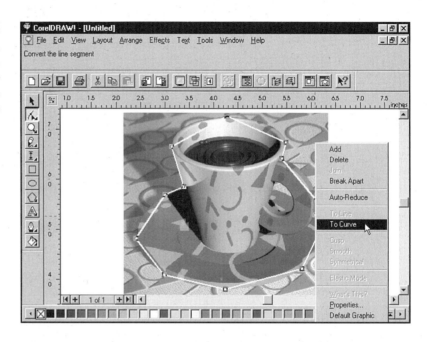

Figure 5.30
Directly manipulating a curve can save time selecting, then changing, the curve's two control handles.

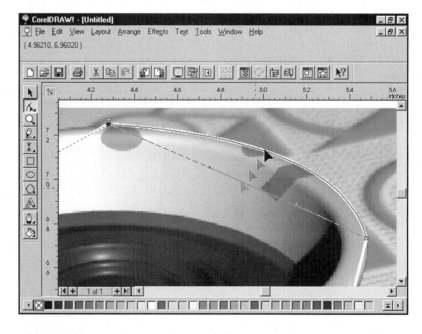

As you refine the curve to better match the outline of the coffee cup and saucer, you'll want to convert connecting nodes along the top of the cup and the bottom of the saucer to smooth connections. Do this by selecting the node, then right-clicking to access the Node Edit Roll-Up's shortcut options. Additionally, the sides of the cup edge are straight, and you'll want to click on these segments and change them back to straight lines. The connection between a curve and a straight segment should be Cusp; you can change node properties by clicking on them and selecting the appropriate connection type from the shortcut menu.

For quick, minor editing assignments, you really don't need the Node Edit Roll-Up cluttering the workspace; however, if you feel more comfortable using the Node Edit Roll-Up for editing, double-clicking on the Shape tool still displays the Roll-Up as it did in version 5.

7. Press Ctrl+C (**E**dit, **C**opy).

   Copies the path to the Clipboard. You'll need a copy of the path shortly.

8. Choose **T**ools, **O**ptions, and make sure the automatically c**e**nter new PowerClip contents is not checked; click on OK when the box is unchecked.

   Ensures that the TIFF import will become the PowerClip contents in the same relative location to the path you've created, and doesn't automatically become centered. The center of the image is not the center of the PowerClip path, you'll almost never have a need for the auto-center option, and it's best to leave this Tools, Option off.

9. Press the spacebar, click on the bitmap image, then choose Effe**c**ts, Po**w**erClip, **P**lace Inside Container (see fig. 5.31).

   Cursor turns into a large arrow.

10. Click on the outline path you created.

    CorelDRAW places the bitmap inside of the path you created (see fig. 5.32).

11. Right-click over the "x" on the color palette.

    Removes outline attributes from the path that contains the bitmap; image looks more plausible now.

12. Press Ctrl+V (**E**dit, **P**aste), then press Ctrl+PageDown.

    Pastes the unfilled path copy on top of the PowerClip object; moves the unfilled path behind the PowerClip object.

13. Press Ctrl+S (**F**ile, **S**ave).

    Saves your work up to this point.

Figure 5.31
The PowerClip command requires that the object to be placed inside a different object is selected prior to the command.

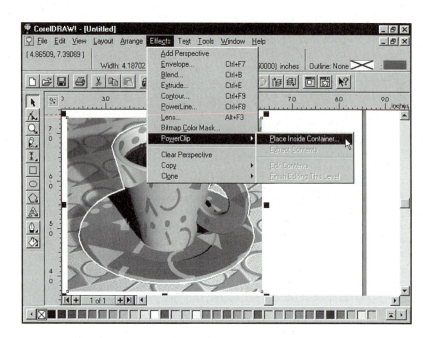

Figure 5.32
The Container object is actually a mask—the contents *outside* of the Container object are hidden and cannot be selected.

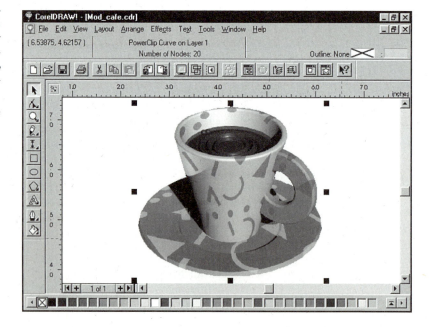

As with most edits that you want to perform in CorelDRAW, there are several ways to accomplish a task. For example, you'll need a copy of the outline of the cup and saucer to create a shadow; the Clipboard copy maneuver was only one end to a means. You could also have duplicated the path before making it a PowerClip, but doing this would have added an unnecessary page element.

Similarly, you could have opened a new document window and dragged the copy to a temporary storage site, but it's not as quick as sending a copy to the Clipboard.

Note There are only two things to be remembered about Windows 95's clipboard that are both carryovers from Windows 3.1x: you can only copy one object at a time to the Clipboard (the most current copy removes previous copies), and large objects on the Clipboard steal from application performance by taking up system resources.

Creating Variations on Shadows

One of the most powerful design perks that comes with PowerClip objects is the capability to place other objects in front of, or *behind*, the PowerClip. Before version 5, users were forced to use an accurate outline of a bitmap shape as a mask; the outline is combined with a larger shape to create a "window" through which you can see the bitmap image. The drawback to masking bitmap images is that there is no way to place additional objects behind the bitmap; very elegant, time-consuming workarounds were cooked up by CorelDRAW artists, but PowerClips provide the solution to creating an irregular outline to an imported bitmap.

Because you can now place any object behind the cup and saucer, let's begin experimenting with adding a vector shadow to make the cup appear to sit within the page, rather than on top of it. The direction of the shadow is clearly suggested within the PowerClip's contents: there's a remainder of a shadow in the saucer, and even if there isn't, highlights are toward the left and bottom of the cup—requiring that shading occurs to the right and top of the design.

There are a few methods for creating different types of shadows, but they all begin with a copy of the silhouette of the PowerClip's contents. Here's how to create a cast shadow for the Modern Café poster:

Creating a Solid Cast Shadow

1. With the outline copy selected in MOD-CAFE.CDR, click on the copy.

   The selection handles change, and the selected outline is now in skew/rotate mode.

2. Click-and-drag on the top, middle handle to the left until the status line says about 30°.

Skews the selected object (see fig. 5.33).

Figure 5.33

An object, or selected group of objects, can be put into skew/rotate mode by clicking on the object(s).

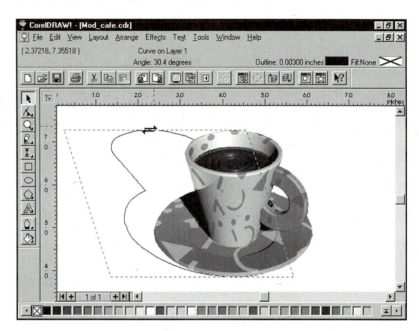

Some brief observations before continuing: 30° is not a "magic number" for creating a cast shadow from a copy of an object. 30° was the choice for this example through trial and error—mostly error. The shadow within the saucer, cast by the cup, was the "study" for this cast shadow; if you can match the angle of a natural shadow within an image, you can convincingly replicate it. Naturally, this can only be accomplished if the image already contains part of a shadow. You can also measure the angle of a diagonal edge by using the Angular Dimension line tool, if an outline must precisely match an edge in a bitmap image. If the cup casts no shadow on the saucer, you can create a cast shadow by skewing a copy of the outline by 20° or even 40°, and the resulting skewed shape would look correct when added to the scene.

3. Click on the black swatch on the color palette, then right-click on the "x" on the color palette.

Fills the skewed outline with black; removes outline properties (see fig. 5.34).

4. Press Ctrl+S (**F**ile, **S**ave).

Saves your work up to this point.

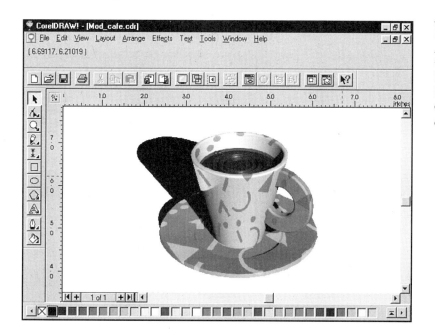

Figure 5.34

A good example of the integration of bitmap and vector information within a CorelDRAW document.

You should now have a perfunctory cast shadow "behind" the PowerClip object that indicates that the cup and saucer are perched on a white, hard surface. The cast shadow has hard edges; they abruptly disappear—surfaces consisting of hard material don't scatter light as it's reflected.

To tone down the harshness of the shadow, you can do one or more things. A lighter color for the shadow would suggest that light doesn't miss the shadow area completely, but instead, light is diffused by a coarser surface, and some of the light spreads into the shadow.

A second technique is to soften the edge of the shadow. In the FESTIVAL design, the ball shadows are composed of a number of blend steps, and if you use the same technique with two shadow-shaped objects in the Modern Café poster, you'll achieve a softer, more photo-realistic shadow. Here's how to make a shadow that looks every byte as real as shadows found in digitized photographs:

Creating Photorealistic Shading

1. Click on the black filled object behind the PowerClip, then click on the 50% black swatch on the color palette.

   Changes the object color to 50% black.

2. Press the + keypad key, then press Ctrl+PageDown.

   Creates a copy of the object, and sends it to a position beneath the original.

3. Click on the 10% black swatch on the palette.

   Fills the selected copy with 10% color black; makes it easier to distinguish from the 50% black object while editing.

4. Press F10 (or choose the Shape tool), then click-and-drag a few of the nodes of the selected copy outward from the object by about 1/8".

   The copy will be used as a beginning control object for blending; it needs to be larger than its duplicate in order to create the blend effect.

5. Continue click-and-dragging the 10% black copy's nodes away from the original object until you've created an object that's 1/8" uniformly larger object.

   This object will be the outermost edge of the soft shadow blend (see fig. 5.35).

Figure 5.35
A soft-edge shadow can be created using two objects of slightly different size and color.

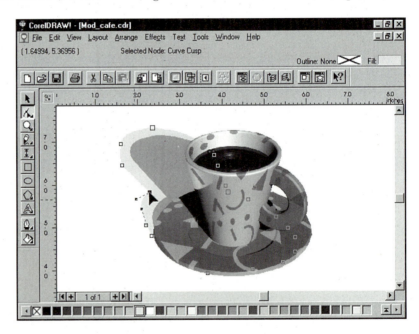

6. Press spacebar, then Shift+click on the original 50% black object.

   Selects both objects.

7. Press Ctrl+B (Effe<u>c</u>ts, **B**lend).

Displays the Blend Roll-Up.

8. Click on Apply.

Applies a (default) 20 step Blend to the two objects.

If you are not pleased with the 10% black to background white transition, blends are dynamically updated by simply changing one or both control (parent) object's attributes. For example, in figure 5.36, you can see that the 10% black object has been changed to white, and the Blend shadow fades seamlessly into the background. Additionally, the shape of the shadow might not be quite perfect. You can change the overall Blend by editing nodes in either control object.

Figure 5.36
You can change the overall color or shape of a Blend shadow by editing control objects after the blend has been created.

9. Press Ctrl+S (**F**ile, **S**ave).

Saves your work at this intermediate stage of completion.

▶Tip Besides changing the shape and/or color of a Blend, you can also, at any time, respecify *how many* blend objects are created between control objects.

For example, if you were to open MOD-CAFE.CDR a month from now, and decide that 20 blend steps are too much for low-resolution printing, all you'd do is click on the Blend Group (not either control object), open the Blend Roll-Up, type in a new Steps value, then click on Apply.

For whatever reason, if you ever decide to break the dynamic link between blends and control objects, your only option is to click on the blends, then choose **A**rrange, **S**eparate. This command is also used to break the link between objects in extrusions and other multiple-object effects.

As mentioned earlier in this section, the Modern Café poster is composed of several objects, one of which is a background of coffee beans. The preceding example was a study in the different types of shading you can manually create to integrate different types of objects in CorelDRAW. In the next section, you'll continue to explore object integration within a design, but you move from Blends-as-fills, to the Full-Color Bitmap Pattern feature in CorelDRAW.

Manual Seamless Tiles

Did you ever try out one of the "seamless tiling" engines in the more popular design programs? For the most part, the title "seamless tiling" is overpromise. At best, programs usually soften the edges of a single image tile, then mix some of the left image edge colors with the right image edge; the same technique is performed to the top and bottom edges. CorelDRAW isn't an exception to this overpromise, and perhaps it's time to clarify what seamless tiling means, or *should* mean, to the computer graphics designer.

The key phrase left out of seamless tiling is *pattern*. It's visible *patterning*, usually left at the edge of a tiled image, that stands out like a sore thumb in design work. This chapter has concentrated upon the integration of shading objects, and this section is a brief excursion into a method for creating an image that can be imported through CorelDRAW's Full-color Bitmap Pattern feature that is seamless when it tiles, and doesn't call attention to a repeating pattern. For example, an image of a brick wall is fairly useless if it tiles in such a fashion that you can clearly see regular intervals where one or more bricks are suddenly clipped and a new brick begins. In the example to follow, we visit CorelPHOTO-PAINT once again to show how a small image of coffee beans can be cloned in certain areas to create yards and yards of coffee beans that *do not* appear to repeat as they tile across a large object.

The advantage to creating a personal collection of special endlessly tiling images is that you can use them as design assignment resources without keeping megabytes of image files on your hard disk. There are several custom, seamless tile patterns on the *CorelDRAW! 6 Expert's Edition Bonus CD*, and the following example shows how they can be created.

Creating a Custom Tile Pattern

1. Close CorelDRAW, then launch CorelPHOTO-PAINT from Explorer.

   PHOTO-PAINT is where you'll create a seamless pattern.

2. Open the CAFEBEAN.TIF image.

   This is the target image for some editing work.

3. Choose Effects, 2D Effects, Offset.

   Displays the Offset dialog box.

4. Type **50** in both the **H**orizontal and **V**ertical Shift boxes; check the **S**hift value as % of dimensions check box.

   You instruct PHOTO-PAINT to Begin the CAFEBEAN image at the center of the image window.

5. Click on Pre**v**iew.

   Confirms values you set. The image is definitely turned inside-out (see fig. 5.37).

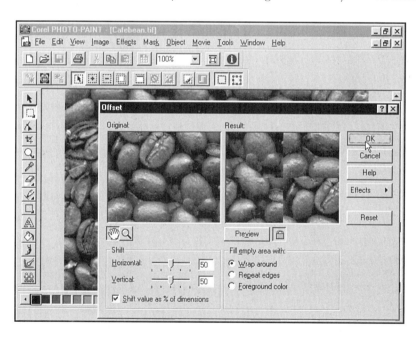

Figure 5.37
One way to disguise an image tile's edges is to place the edges in the center of an image using the Offset effect.

This will all make sense in a moment! The edges of the CAFEBEAN.TIF image—the top, bottom, left, and right—will now seamlessly butt up against copies of the tile, because edge information is copied from a continuous texture originally located at the center of the image. All of which makes the inside of the image somewhat of a mess right now, but because a pile of coffee beans display random detail, it's not hard to use PHOTO-PAINT's Clone tool to copy over the hard edges in the image's center with coffee beans from other image areas. Here goes:

6. Click on OK in the Offset dialog box. Double-click on the Clone tool (at the bottom of the toolbox).

   Applies the Offset effect; selects the Clone tool and displays the Tool Settings Roll-Up, with options for cloning.

7. On the Tool Settings Roll-Up, click on the 10 pixel diameter soft brush tip located in the drop-down box to the left of the **S**ize spin box (or type **10** in the **S**ize spin box, and **80** in the Soft **e**dge field).

   Sets the Clone tool's tip to a small size for precise work, and with a soft edge to hide brush strokes within the image you'll edit.

8. Type **100** in the Zoom level box.

   Sets a comfortable view of the image for performing precision cloning.

9. Shift+click in the center of a coffee bean that's unspoiled by an edge running through it.

   This sets the sampling point for the Clone tool.

10. Slowly click-and-drag across the horizontal edge of the CAFEBEAN image; keep an eye on the traveling sampling cursor and stop dragging when you reach the edge of the sampled coffee bean.

    Copies the sample coffee bean to cover the edge within the image; hiding it.

The last two steps represent the sum total of the secret to creating a seamless tiling pattern. You sample a coffee bean by Shift+clicking, then paint over the visible edges in the image. Try to pick a bean, or several, that look similar to coffee beans on or near the visible edges in the image. Be careful not to create an obvious repeat pattern as you clone; scatter a few clone copies of beans in areas that *don't* need the edges hidden. You might also want to use the Effect tool (the Q-Tip icon) set to Thick Smear to blend darker areas that contain an edge. Detail is important to make this image a successful seamless tile, but areas that don't have much detail (except a crease!) within the image don't deserve hours of attention. As you can see in figure 5.38, the cloning process is about halfway completed.

Spend about 15 minutes on this task, and if you're unhappy with the results, use BEANTILE.TIF (in the CHAP05 folder of the Bonus CD) to complete this section's assignment. BEANTILE.TIF is the finished image created by the author. When you think you've removed all traces of edges from the image:

11. Choose **F**ile, Save **A**s, then save the image as BEANTILE.TIF to your hard disk.

    Saves the image for use in the MOD-CAFE.CDR design. (See figure 5.39.)

Figure 5.38
Hide the edges you created with the Offset effect by cloning samples of other beans at unobvious locations.

Figure 5.39
Replace the edges with cloned samples of whole coffee beans, and you've created a pattern that will not display a tiling effect.

12. Close CorelPHOTO-PAINT, then launch CorelDRAW from Windows Start menu.

You're finished creating the tile, it's time to apply it to the MOD-CAFE design.

As you accept work from a wide variety of clients, you'll find more and more uses for seamless tiles. For example, a new Netscape browser enhancement now allows Web pages to be constructed with tiling bitmap images. You can create a seamless tile of paperclips for a stationery store that wishes to advertise on the Internet using the same technique as described in the last section. A small bitmap pattern can become a large backdrop for text, or other graphical objects, as you'll see shortly.

Note If you decide to create a custom pattern image using the techniques found in the previous section, you might want to bear one or two things in mind before creating or scanning the raw target image: CAFEBEAN.TIF measures 500×500 pixels (or 4×4", and it's 125 pixels per inch, which yields a 733K image written to disk (or approximately 75,000 fresh-brewed cups of coffee).

This is a large bitmap to use as a tiling fill, but it also guarantees good output to imagesetters capable of more than 1,500 dots per inch. The coffee cup bitmap is of similar resolution in MOD-CAFE.CDR.

Plan the scale and size of a bitmap you use in a CorelDRAW design by considering final output first. And bitmap images that are to be tiled are a lot easier to scale and calculate when the dimensions and/or resolution are of whole, even integers. This spares the need to stop your work and to go fish for a pocket calculator!

Using the Full-Color Bitmap Pattern Fill

With version 6 of CorelDRAW, the Full-Color fill has been broken into two separate features: The Vector Fill and the Full-color Bitmap Pattern Fill are now independent Fill Tool functions. I'll cover the Vector tool in Chapter 6, "Bitmaps and Vector Designs," because the creation of vector fills is very similar to creating custom symbols, another important aspect of creating a publication.

Full-Color Patterns are the exclusive province of bitmap type graphics in version 6, and although CorelDRAW ships with a handsome collection of bitmap presets, the objective here is to use the fill feature to express an idea that might not be offered as a preset.

In the next exercise, you'll use the empty rectangle that surrounds the coffee cup PowerClip in MOD-CAFE.CDR as the target object for a ton of coffee beans. Here's how to complement a PowerClip image with a background texture that's as photographic and detailed as a foreground TIF image.

Working with the Full-Color Bitmap Pattern Feature

1. After Launching CorelDRAW, open the MOD-CAFE.CDR document you last saved to your hard disk.

This is the design you'll now complete.

Chances are that the document is still listed on the last-four used area at the bottom of the **F**ile menu.

2. Click on the top control object in the shadow blend, then press Ctrl+C.

   Copies the top control object to the Clipboard.

3. Click on the Blend objects, then press Delete.

   Removes the blend shadow from MOD-CAFE.CDR, because these objects aren't required in this example.

Now's a good time to choose **F**ile, Save **A**s, and rename the current file if you want to hang on to the blend shadow you created last. The PowerClip and the shadow outline on the clipboard will be used in the final composition, however.

4. Press Ctrl+V, then press Shift+PageDown.

   Pastes the Clipboard copy of the original 50% black shadow into the document; Shift+PageDown sends the object to the back of the Layer 1 stack of objects.

The Clipboard copy is not a control object, because it's not linked to a Blend. Because it's now located at the back of Layer 1, consider it safely tucked away while you experiment with the rectangle and the Full-Color Bitmap Pattern feature. When the rectangle is filled, it will obscure your view of the clipboard copy shadow, but this is okay. You'll only use the object toward the end of this assignment.

5. Click on the rectangle surrounding the coffee cup PowerClip, click on the Fill tool, then click on the Full-color Bitmap Pattern button (the picture frame icon to the left of the Texture Fill button).

   Displays the Full-Color Bitmap Pattern dialog box.

6. Click on **I**mport, then track down and select BEANTILE.TIF from either your own hard disk (if you completed the previous example), or from the EXAMPLES.CHAP05 folder of the *CorelDRAW! 6 Expert's Edition Bonus CD* (if you didn't do the previous example).

   Selects the bitmap image you want to fill the selected rectangle in the MOD-CAFE.CDR design.

7. Click on OK.

   Returns you to the Full-color Bitmap Pattern dialog box. The bean image appears in the preview box.

8. Click on **T**iling.

   Extends the dialog box to offer more tiling options.

The dimensions of the selected rectangle are approximately 6 1/2 " wide by 9" tall. As mentioned in the previous NOTE, the BEANTILE image is 4" square. To make the beans a prominent design element, it would be good, then, to tile the pattern only a few times to maximize the size of the image.

9. Click on the Scale pattern with object check box, then type **50** in the **W**idth and **H**eight boxes.

   The Scale Pattern…option changes the measurement fields to relative percentages from absolute increments such as inches. (See figure 5.40.)

Figure 5.40
You can choose absolute measurements for a bitmap tile, or choose to make relative, scaling factor specifications.

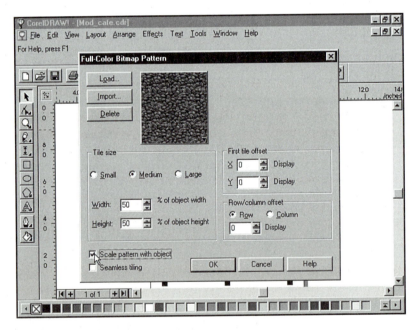

The preceding step ensures that if you want to resize the finished design, the beans shrink proportionately with the image. If you always want a Full-Color fill to display elements of a constant size, leave this box unchecked. Be aware, though, that if you scale an object containing a bitmap fill so that it's larger than the original bitmap image, CorelDRAW reduces the resolution of the bitmap—the number of pixels per inch—and your printed output might look a little coarse.

10. Click on OK.

The remaining options, those of offsetting the bitmap tile, are unwanted in this example. You are returned to the composition, with coffee beans filling the rectangle. Smell the aroma and see figure 5.41.

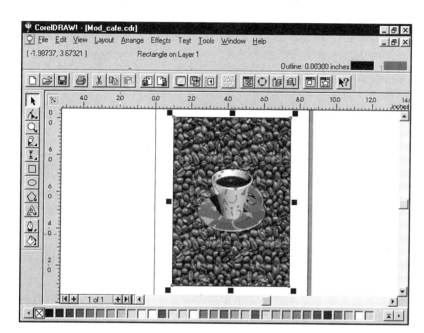

Figure 5.41

Because the BEANTILE image was carefully retouched, there is no trace of tiling in the background fill.

11. Press Ctrl+S (File, Save).

Saves your work at this intermediate stage.

In the next section, you'll complete the poster design, with a little help from the hidden objects on a locked layer within the document, and with the assistance of CorelDRAW's Lens Roll-Up.

Melding Vector and Bitmap Elements into a Composition

It would be a simple matter to drop some fancy text on top of the Modern Café poster right now and call it quits. However, there's a certain something missing from the poster—shading—that thwarts the interaction between the coffee cup and the tiled bean background. So how do you add shadows to a pattern as complex as a bunch of beans? The answer lies in the Lens Roll-Up.

It is the software engineers' intention at Corel Corp. to provide near-equal imaging capabilities in CorelDRAW that the user has in PHOTO-PAINT. This statement is ambitious, to say the least: how can a vector-based drawing application hope to match the tools and effects found in a bitmap editor? You've seen in this chapter how airbrush-quality blends can work harmoniously with bitmap fills, and the Modern Café poster is almost entirely composed of bitmaps, and not vector designs. This chapter is intended to make "drawing type" computer graphics artists feel more at home with different types of graphics, and to prove that realistic shading is not solely the territory of bitmap editing programs.

The Lens Roll-Up is sort of a vector drawing program's equivalent to a collection of plug-in filters, the 3rd-party special effects modules such as Kai's Power Tools that can be accessed from bitmap editing programs which accept Adobe Systems specifications for plug-in architecture. With the Lens Roll-Up, you can assign a shape a Lens property, then achieve some wonderful tints and distortions to objects you place beneath the Lens object. Lens objects affect bitmaps *and* vector designs, so the final example in this chapter shows how to cast a shadow from the coffee cup (and additional lettering) onto the bean background to create realistic, semi-transparent shading.

A Small Example of the Transparency Lens

1. Click on the bean-filled rectangle, then press Shift+PageDown.

   Sends the rectangle to the back of the object stack on Layer 1. The 50% black object you copied to the back of the stack should be visible now.

2. Press F4.

   Zooms you into the Zoom to Fit (page) viewing resolution.

3. Click on the 50% black object, then click on the (100%) black swatch on the color palette.

   Fills the object with black.

If you haven't rearranged any of the objects within the composition, the black object should presently be slightly above and to the left of the PowerClip object. If it isn't, click-and-drag it to the location where you created the Blend shadow earlier in this chapter.

4. Choose Effe**c**ts, **L**ens (Alt+F3).

   Displays the Lens Roll-Up.

5. Choose Transparency from the Lens drop-down list, then click-and-drag between the spin box elevator buttons until the Amount is 45.

Specifies that the black object will be a little less than half opaque when it becomes a Lens object.

As with most values suggested in this book, they are suggestions. A black object that is a little less than 50% transparent, when covering mostly dark beans in a bitmap, creates a shadow that's dense, but you can still discern the visual detail of the underlying beans. If you use a different bitmap, for example, such as a tile of oranges, you might want to pick a higher transparency value, and specify a shade of brown instead of black, to create a more appealing shadow Lens object.

6. Click on Apply.

    Applies the Lens property to the selected shadow object (see figure 5.42).

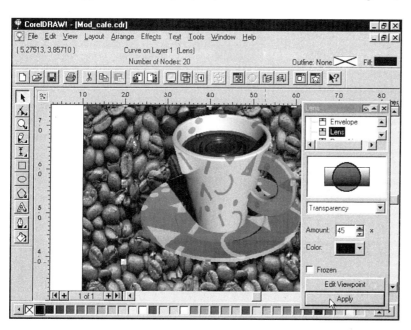

Figure 5.42
Shading of visually complex areas in a design can be accomplished quickly by creating a Lens object.

7. Choose **L**ayout, **L**ayers Manager (Ctrl+F3).

    Displays the Layers Roll-Up.

8. Click on the eye icon to the left of the Layer 2 title.

    Makes the objects locked on Layer 2 visible and the composition leaps to completion.

9. Press Ctrl+S (**F**ile, **S**ave).

    Saves the completed design to hard disk.

You should take the time now to unlock Layer 2 and examine the elements that were created to complete the design (click on the pencil icon to the left of the Layer 2 title). Every technique that went into the creation of Layer 2 has been covered in this chapter; the lettering is simply Artistic Text converted to curves (the typeface is not part of the Corel collection), and the Lens objects that create the drop shadows for the lettering are also black with a 45% Transparent Lens property. In figure 5.43, you can see the completed design, except it's smaller and in black and white.

Figure 5.43
The Modern Café poster combines elements of vector and bitmap graphics, and a special effects Lens.

Take what you've learned in this chapter about vector and bitmap graphics types, accurate shading, and the extraordinary capability to integrate different media into a solid, exciting composition, and mix this wisdom with some of the examples in other chapters. Shading is only a component in the sum total of your CorelDRAW design tools, and as you progress through other examples, you'll see how the most important tool is your own capability to select the right effect, tool, or feature to express your own ideas.

Part II

Document-Centricity: Using CorelDRAW! as the Design Hub for Assignments

Bitmaps and Vector Designs

Designs created in CorelDRAW offer the artistic flexibility of smooth resizing, and the capability to break apart and combine component shapes without leaving a trace of editing. But *vector* computer graphics—the type CorelDRAW produces—cannot represent foreground focus, reflections, and other photo-realistic qualities without investing a great amount of skill and time. Conversely, an image editor such as CorelPHOTO-PAINT doesn't offer all the editing flexibility one finds with vector shapes because *bitmap* computer graphics are created with an entirely different digital structure.

If you limit your thoughts to an "either/or" scope, a virtual chasm exists for the designer when you want to combine vector and bitmap design elements within a single composition. This chapter features two different approaches to similar assignments: to show how vector art can be integrated with bitmap images, and vice versa. If your client requires a finished piece in vector or bitmap format, the following sections show you how to make artwork that suits visual content and file-format needs.

Retouching Bitmap Images with CorelDRAW!

Package design is handled by manufacturers in two separate divisions: a design group that creates prototype packages, and the graphics group, which works on color schemes, an identifying logo, and supporting label embellishments. In this chapter's first assignment, you play the design group, and your group's charge is to create the Timeless Perfume bottle label.

The package design for Timeless Perfume has already been created, and a prototype has been photographed. Now, concerned parties need some visualization help as to how the label will look on the package. To complicate things, the perfume bottle image needs to be distributed in-house and to potential buyers as a bitmap image; a CorelDRAW file can't be used in this situation because the audience might not own CorelDRAW.

Therefore, this assignment is a two-parter: create a label for the perfume, and integrate the design in a bitmap format so that the label appears to have been on the package when it was photographed.

Creating a Design Template

The first step in creating a label for an image that has already been photographed is to convert a copy of the original image to a low-resolution one that can be used in CorelDRAW as a template. High-quality RGB bitmap images used in commerce are typically 4 to 30 MB in file size, and it's ridiculous to import such an image to trace over in CorelDRAW, because redraw times would be slow and the saved file would be larger than necessary. PERFUME.TIF is the packaging image you'll use in this example as the target for a label. The image is a small one for the purposes of example; it's smaller than 1 MB, which doesn't yield a professional-quality print but suits our *conceptual* work perfectly.

In the following steps, you'll see how to use CorelPHOTO-PAINT to convert a copy of PERFUME.TIF for use as a template in CorelDRAW.

Working with CorelPHOTO-PAINT! Color Modes

1. Launch CorelPHOTO-PAINT from the Explorer, then open the PERFUME.TIF image from the EXAMPLES.CHAP06 folder of the *CorelDRAW! 6 Expert's Edition Bonus CD*.

   Opens the image you will work with in this example.

2. Choose **I**mage, **S**plit Channels To, then choose **H**SB.

   CorelPHOTO-PAINT creates three image files based on the component values of the PERFUME.TIF original. In figure 6.1, you can see the original PERFUME.TIF image, and on the right, three individual images windows; the one in front is an image based upon brightness values (B-0).

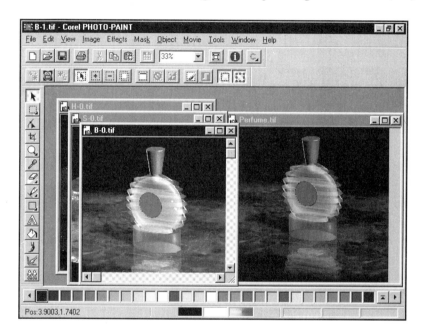

Figure 6.1

Individual grayscale images representing amounts of Hue, Saturation, and Brightness can be copied from an original image.

Document-Centricity

3. Click on the B-0.TIF title bar, then choose **F**ile, **S**ave (Ctrl+S) and save the image as PERFUME-G.TIF to your hard disk.

   Saves the Brightness grayscale image to hard disk for use later.

4. Close CorelPHOTO-PAINT, do not save the H-0 or S-0 images, then launch CorelDRAW.

   Exits the program; launches CorelDRAW.

5. Choose **F**ile, **I**mport (Ctrl+I; or click on the Import button on the toolbar).

   Displays the Import dialog box.

6. Choose PERFUME-G.TIF from your hard disk, then click on Imp**o**rt.

   Imports a copy of the grayscale image you saved to hard disk.

7. Choose Layout, Layers Manager (Ctrl+F3).

Displays the Layers Roll-Up.

8. Click on the pencil icon to the left of the Layer 1 title.

Locks the layer containing the perfume bottle image from editing.

9. Right-click on the layers titles, and choose New from the shortcut menu.

Creates a new layer on top of Layer 1.

10. Type **Logo** into the highlighted text on the Layers Roll-Up.

Assigns a name to Layer 2 for easy future reference (see fig. 6.2).

Figure 6.2
Lock the layer that
contains the image
template, then create
a new layer upon
which you'll create
the logo.

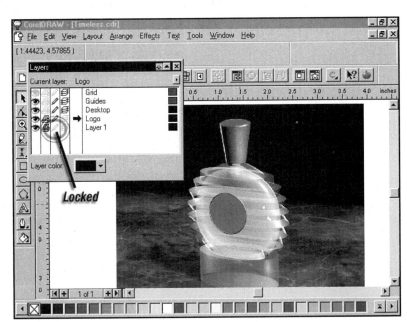

11. Choose File, Save (Ctrl+S), then save the file as TIMELESS.CDR to your hard disk.

"Timeless" will be the name of the perfume.

Although this chapter is goal-oriented, you need to back up a little in the next section and find out some answers to a few questions. Why were you asked to perform a seemingly fanciful maneuver to a copy of the PERFUME.TIF image in the last example? What not create a grayscale image by switching image modes? What's an image channel? Bitmap images have fundamentally different file structures than vector designs, and understanding how bits of information are mapped to a file format can help you create better work of your own in less time.

Image Modes and Color Mapping

Most of the bitmap images you'll encounter in professional work will fall into two different categories: *indexed color* and *channel color,* and each of these types of bitmap is saved to disk within a special file format used for expressing color values in a unique way. Unlike vector drawings—ones you produce in CorelDRAW—all bitmap images display both image content and color values through an arrangement of pixels (*picture elements*). In other words, pixels represent the color fill of a photograph of a ball, but pixels also represent the outline of the ball and the highlight and shading of it.

Because bitmap, or *raster* images, depend entirely on rectangular building blocks— pixels—for both shape and shading of image content, we often turn to the color capability and arrangement of pixels in a file format for qualitative descriptions of a bitmap image. The term *bitmap* was first invented to describe a single bit of information mapped to an invisible grid that defines the dimensions of an image. A single bit of digital information, however, can only express an on or an off state for a pixel— resulting in a bitmap image with a color capability of 2 (black and white are usually used).

As the calculating capability of the personal computer grew, more information could be stored in a pixel, and the term bitmap today is somewhat of a legacy phrase, because *bytes* of information can now be used to express a wider range of color values. RGB images have a color capability of 16.7 million possible unique values within a saved bitmap image format, because RGB images have 24 bits of information per color pixel (or 2 to the 24th power). Grayscale images, such as the one you saved in the previous example, have a color capability of eight bits (a *byte*) of information per pixel.

Design applications use encoding schemes to organize color information into a file format that's easy to retrieve and is platform-independent. Although users have their choice of the bitmap file *type* (BMP, PCX, TIFF, and so on) in which to save an image, the format of bitmap graphics can be broken into two distinct categories, as you'll see in the following sections.

Indexed Color Images

Indexed color images typically have a maximum color capability of 8 bits per pixel, resulting in bitmap images that contain 256 unique color values. The way an indexed color image is stored is through a design application saving a color table (also called a *lookup table* or *color palette*) as part of the header information for an indexed color file. This index of specific color values is then read by an application before loading a file saved in this format.

Obviously, the full gamut of visible colors can't be faithfully saved to indexed color format, and programs such as CorelPHOTO-PAINT perform *color reduction* to eliminate colors in the creation of indexed color images. You'll often see *dithering*, the scattering of random color pixels, throughout an indexed image, as a result of an image editing program's attempt to "fake" colors that can't exist within an indexed image's limited color palette.

The indexed color format is not an ideal choice for performing editing. Most of CorelPHOTO-PAINT's plug-ins won't work or produce unacceptable results. However, indexed color images offer a compact file structure used with the GIF format (for Web Page graphics), and other formats of files used in electronic presentations.

Channel Color Images

Channel color images offer the widest spectrum of available colors because unlike indexed images, color information stored as relative strengths of color components. Most TIF, Targa, and CPT (CorelPHOTO-PAINT's proprietary bitmap format) images use three discrete channels of color to express a composite color image; these three color channels are presented to the user as 8-bit, grayscale channels whose relative brightness constitute a contribution of the color channel to the overall picture.

As an example, if you view the blue channel of an image of a blue chair in CorelPHOTO-PAINT, the channel displays a lot of white areas, because the blue channel's contribution to the overall RGB image is high. You'd most likely see fairly dark grayscale representations of the green and red color channels for such an image, because red and green don't contribute a lot of pixel information about a blue chair.

Color channel images generally don't load as quickly into an image-editing application as indexed color images do because the application doesn't read a header for color information. Instead, *explicit brightness values* for red, green, and blue color information are blended together to present the *composite* (the RGB view) of a channel color image.

Although grayscale images are confined to 256 unique tones, they can be thought of as a single-color channel image. It's true that an indexed color palette can be used to create a grayscale image, but images that are scanned in grayscale mode, or color-reduced to grayscale from RGB format, retain the format arrangement of channel color. It is this color channel format that you'll use throughout this chapter for bitmap images, because color channel images, even grayscale, look better when output to printed media, and can contain more unique color values than indexed images.

The channel format of bitmap images presents graphic designers with some wonderful and flexible possibilities. In the preceding example, you told CorelPHOTO-PAINT to split the channels of PERFUME.TIF to an arrangement of separate Hue, Saturation, and Brightness channels. Although PERFUME.TIF was originally designed around the Red, Green, and Blue channel arrangement, this feat was possible because there's a direct relationship between RGB and HSB color spaces. Color spaces that are defined as color component strengths, and not as indexed, preset values, can be mapped to suit a number of design purposes (as you just participated in).

The Brightness channel CorelPHOTO-PAINT created from the RGB PERFUME image contains only the tones of the original image—without information about the original hues, or the amount of *predominant hue* (called *saturation*) within the original. This trick is particularly useful when converting a color image to grayscale, because straight conversions between color modes frequently results in a dull image. Try photocopying a color image; the result is usually dull because the photocopier's imaging device reads the relative strengths of colors *in addition to* the *tonal*—the neutral grayscale—information contained within an image. Reds come out darker than you expect, and blues appear faint when RGB color is transformed directly to grayscale mode.

However, the HSB channel conversion trick avoids the pitfall of including color information in color reduction. The saturation and hue channels are generally worthless as a byproduct of splitting channels; the information is unintelligible by the human eye, and this is why we discarded them in the last example.

The TIMELESS.CDR file contains one-third of the complete PERFUME.TIF information, and therefore one-third of the total file size of the image. You can work quickly with this template file to design a logo, even on a system whose amount of RAM is modest.

Creating the Timeless Clockface Logo

Whenever you analyze a design need, it's best to look for obvious visual "hooks" that immediately convey to the viewer whatever you're trying to communicate. In this example, because the perfume is called Timeless, and the blank shape on the bottle is round, a clock face design visually reinforces the name brand.

The example to follow makes use of CorelDRAW's Blend feature to construct roman numerals rotated around a circle. One's first instinct when given a similar assignment is to use the Te**x**t, Fit **T**ext to Path command. However, this is the wrong feature to use. The Fit Text to Path Roll-Up is terrific for short sentences, but individual numbers need to be precisely placed at regular intervals around a circle in this assignment. Unfortunately, the correct selection of CorelDRAW features, the Blend Roll-Up, cannot retain blend objects' text properties—text becomes curves along a blend, so unique numbers along a Blend path cannot be created. However, there's a simple manual editing technique that can be used *after* using the Blend Roll-Up, that achieves the intended goal here. After this example, you'll see how to edit the Blend group of Roman numerals to represent a traditional clock face.

Here's how to create the basic logo design:

Blending a Clock Face

1. Open the TIMELESS.CDR document CorelDRAW.

2. Press PageDown.

   Displays the Insert Page dialog box.

3. Press Enter (or click on OK).

   Adds the default number of pages (1) to TIMELESS.CDR, and you're moved to page 2 view. This step lets you work without displaying the locked image on page 1. You're in the same document, but you'll work more quickly at this preliminary stage without the encumbrance of displaying a 300K bitmap in the document.

4. Choose the Ellipse tool (or press F7), then Ctrl+click-and-drag a circle about 2" in diameter starting from the upper left, and finished at the lower right of the page.

   Holding Ctrl constrains an ellipse to a circle; this is the shape of the perfume logo. The direction in which you click-and-drag a circle has an impact upon how a Blend group is arranged around the path represented by the circle; draw the ellipse from left to right and then top to bottom of the page to create a circle whose outline path is a *clockwise* one.

5. Press F8 (or click on the Artistic Text tool), click on the page, then type **XII**.

   You've created the first Roman numeral for the clock face.

6. Press Ctrl+spacebar, then press Ctrl+T (Te**x**t, **C**haracter).

   Toggles to the Pick tool; displays the Character Attributes dialog box.

7. Choose a classic font, click on the Alignment tab, click on the Center radio button, then click on OK.

   Selects the typeface used for the logo design.

Some of the designs you'll create using the Blend Roll-Up need to be replaced in a later example. For reasons you'll see shortly, the Artistic Text number needs to have a Center alignment property.

Optima is the font selection used in this example, for a few good design reasons. First, Optima is legible at small point sizes, which many product graphics require. Optima is stylish, but more conservative than most fonts CorelDRAW ships with, and a "timeless" perfume would be ill-served by using a "fad" font. Also, at small point sizes, serifs tend to get lost, particularly when vector art is converted to bitmap format, as you'll do in this chapter. So Optima is a "clean" choice, but feel free to substitute if you have a strong preference.

8. Press Alt+F9 (**A**rrange, **T**ransform, **S**cale and Mirror).

   Displays the Scale and Mirror Roll-Up.

9. Click on the circle with the Pick tool, type **80** in the H and V Scale spin boxes, then click on Apply to Duplicate.

   Creates a smaller circle within the original (see fig. 6.3).

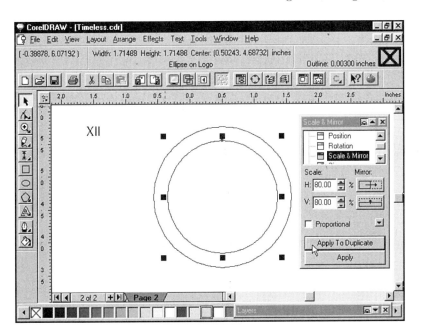

Figure 6.3

The Scale and Mirror feature can help create concentric circles inside or outside an original.

10. Click on the "XII" text, drag it about 2" to the right of the original position, then right-click before releasing it.

    Drops a duplicate of the XII to the right of the original.

11. Marquee select both Roman numerals with the Pick tool, then choose Effe**c**ts, **B**lend (Ctrl+B).

    Displays the Blend Roll-Up.

12. Type **10** in the Steps spin box, then click on Apply.

    Blends 10 intermediate objects between the Roman numerals.

13. Click on the path button on the Blend Roll-Up, choose <u>N</u>ew Path, then click the cursor on the duplicate, smaller circle on the page.

Defines the circle as the path the blended numerals will conform to.

14. Check the Full Path check box, then click on Apply.

Applies the effect (see fig. 6.4).

Figure 6.4
You can blend a number of objects along a path by specifying an object within the document.

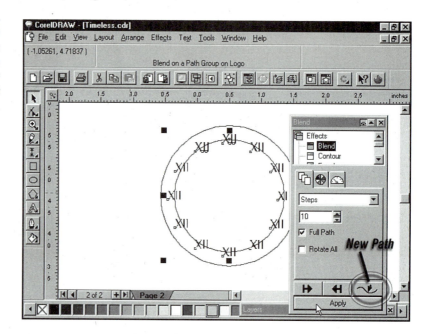

15. Press Ctrl+S (<u>F</u>ile, <u>S</u>ave).

Saves your work at this intermediate phase.

In the next section, you'll see how to break a Blend object dynamic link, and fix the numerical values you've created.

Using the Align and Distribute Feature

Now it's time for the manual portion of the logo-creation process. A clock face with 12 identical XII symbols is terrific for a cartoon, but doesn't serve this particular design purpose. The Blend group currently consists of two control objects—the original and duplicate Optima XIIs—and a subgroup of 10 objects that appear to be text, but are actually curves.

In the next set of steps, you'll replace the collection of objects with copies of the Artistic text within the design, then retype the Artistic text to represent the corresponding hour on the clock face. There's a rhythm to this editing technique, and if you understand the steps, you can quickly replace any sequence of objects in your own work:

Substituting Blended Text

1. Click anywhere on the blend group of objects (not the control objects at 12 and 1 o'clock), then choose **A**rrange, **S**eparate.

   Separates the group into two individual Artistic text objects and a group of ten objects.

2. Click on the group of 10 objects, then click on a light color on the color palette (cyan is good).

   Changes the color of the whole group of objects. Recoloring the former Blend objects while they're still grouped is a good, fast method for making them clearly distinguishable from the replacement text you'll create.

3. Press Ctrl+U (**A**rrange, **U**ngroup; or click on the ungroup button on the toolbar).

   Ungroups the 10 objects.

4. Click on the Align and Distribute button on the toolbar.

   Displays the Align and Distribute Roll-Up.

5. Click on the 12 o'clock XII Artistic text object, then press + on the numeric keypad.

   Duplicates the XII.

6. Shift+click on the cyan object at 2 o'clock around the circle, click on the center horizontal and vertical buttons on the align and Distribute Roll-Up, then click on Apply.

   Aligns the XII Artistic Text to the 2 o'clock cyan object (see fig. 6.5).

7. Press spacebar, then backspace three times and type **II**.

   Toggles to the last used tool (the Artistic Text tool); replaces the XII with a number more appropriate for the two o'clock position on a clock face. *This* is why we recommended that the original XII Artistic Text should have a Center alignment character attribute. As you can see, the "II" is still perfectly centered about the cyan object.

Figure 6.5

You can align replacement objects within a design by using the Align and Distribute Roll-Up.

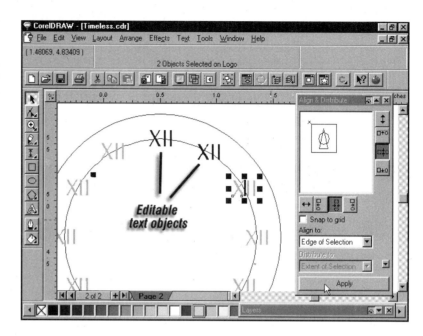

8. Repeat the previous three steps with the other cyan objects around the circle, typing the correct number after aligning a duplicate Artistic Text object.

   Completes the number element of the clock face logo.

9. Select the other Artistic text XII and type **I**.

   Completes the clock face.

10. Press Ctrl+S (**F**ile, **S**ave).

   Saves your work at this intermediate stage.

You should delete the placeholders—the cyan objects—after replacing the Roman numerals. Basically, you've got the shape and most of the graphic completed for the perfume label. In figure 6.6, you can see the Scale and Mirror Roll-Up used to create smaller duplicates of the original circle. Two inner circles have been combined, and all the component objects have been assigned a white or black fill.

In the next section, you see how to add text to the logo. The choice of white text and Roman numerals is important because, after the logo is exported to bitmap format for use in the TIMELESS.TIF image, a special merge mode—which drops out white—composites the logo to the TIF image.

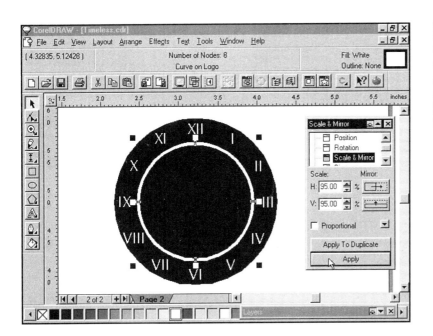

II

Document-Centricity

Figure 6.6

Create auto-aligned circles for the logo design by creating duplicates with the Scale and Mirror Roll-Up.

Modifying Artistic Text Strings

Almost every book written about scalable computer fonts includes the warning that you should confine yourself to two or three fonts per document. The reason for this warning is to prevent the "ransom note" effect—users who suddenly own over 1,000 high-quality Corel fonts often feel the urge to use them all in a single design.

Although a text-based document can indeed take on the appearance of criminal-inspired newspaper clippings, package design often calls for the use of a handful of different typefaces to complete a certain look. If you understand font weights, serif characteristics, and have an artistic flair for mixing fonts, you can create attractive logos.

In the next exercise, you'll see how Shelley Allegro, copperplate, and Futura can be used to complete the Timeless logo design. If these fonts aren't already installed on your system, you can install them by loading Corel CD number 1 and choosing them. The TrueType format is acceptable in this instance, because the fonts are converted to bitmaps through the course of this example, and as a bitmap, PostScript interpretation isn't used. If the graphic is to remain in CorelDRAW and the text is to remain as editable text, Type 1 font format is recommended. See Chapter 8, "Creating Your Own Fonts," for advice and information on working with digital font formats.

Here's how to create a text design for the perfume logo:

Mixing and Matching Typefaces

1. Press F8 (or choose the Artistic Text tool), click an insertion point in the center of the logo design, then type **Timeless.**

   Adds "Timeless" to the logo in Corel's default font.

2. Press Ctrl+Spacebar, then press Ctrl+T (Te<u>x</u>t, <u>C</u>haracter).

   Toggles to the Pick tool; displays the Character Attributes dialog box.

3. Choose Copperplate from the <u>F</u>onts list, then click on OK.

   Converts the default font to Copperplate; returns you to the document.

4. Click-and-drag a corner selection handle around Timeless toward the text object's center, until it fits inside of the area defined by the Roman numerals.

   Scales the text down to the correct proportion for the design. Unless you have a specific font size in mind for an assignment, it's usually easier to scale text using the Pick tool than entering a size in the Character Attributes dialog box. You'll notice that the text is quite small—it should only be about five points—because the template you created from the original TIF image is small. On assignments of your own, you could expect to work with 8 to 12 points or so for similar package design elements.

5. Click on an empty document area, press spacebar, then click an insertion point beneath "Timeless" and type **"PERFUME"**.

   Adds a second text element to the design.

6. Press Ctrl+spacebar, then press Ctrl+T.

   Toggles to the Pick tool; displays then Character Attributes dialog box.

7. Click on Futura in the <u>F</u>onts list, then click on OK.

   Changes the text to the Futura font.

8. Click-and-drag the corner selection handle of PERFUME toward its center until the status line tells you the font is about four points.

   Scales the text down to fit the logo design.

9. Click on the Shape tool, then click-and-drag the right text selection handle to the right until there are spaces of about three or four character widths between characters.

The Shape tool creates wider inter-character spacing for the PERFUME Artistic Text. This preceding step is a creative "look" that desktop publishing folks have been using in recent years to make text more of a design element. With the Shape tool, this is an easy embellishment, but you can also create it by specifying 400% Character Spacing on the Character Attribute's Alignment menu.

10. Click on the "Timeless" text, then click on the first text-selection node.

   Selects the text, then selects the first "T" character only.

11. Press Ctrl+T.

   Displays the Character Attributes dialog box.

12. Choose Shelley Allegro from the **F**onts list, type **14** in the Si**z**e field, then click on OK.

   Changes only the "T" to Shelley Allegro (see fig. 6.7).

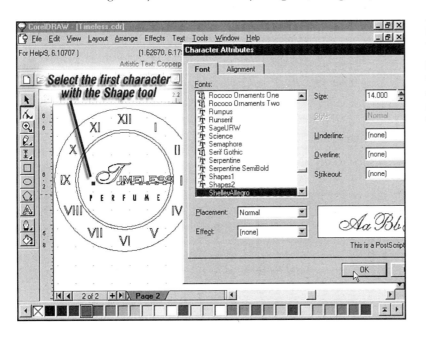

Figure 6.7
You can change the position, font, size, and other attributes of a single character by selecting it with the Shape tool.

13. Click-and-drag the text selection node to create better composition between the T and the smaller Copperplate text.

   Moves only the Shelley Allegro character relative to the rest of the "Timeless" word.

14. With the Pick tool, click- and-drag Timeless and PERFUME until they're centered within the logo design.

    Finalizes the logo. Alternatively, you can nudge small objects by using the keyboard arrow keys to precisely place them. Set the Nudge amount on the **T**ools, **O**ptions, General tab.

15. Press Ctrl+S (**F**ile, **S**ave).

    Saves your work at this intermediate stage.

At this point, the logo might be ready for press, but it's not ready to represent a photographic element in TIMELESS.TIF. As you can see on page 1 of the CorelDRAW document, the product was photographed at an angle, and the area destined to get the label isn't circular. This minor hurdle is addressed in the next section.

Distorting a Group of Objects

TIMELESS.TIF's vacant, logo-absent area is an ellipse—specifically an ellipse distorted toward the viewer at a superior camera angle. This means that to portray the logo with matching distortion, it needs to skew downwards (the opposite of the camera angle)and needs to condense slightly across the horizontal measurement.

In the next exercise, you'll copy the logo to page 1 of the TIMELESS.CDR document (never use an original when distorting things), and use the manual rotate/skew feature to adjust the logo so that it appears to be placed on the perfume bottle. The new slanted guidelines feature proves to be an immense help with chores such as these.

Skewing the Logo

1. Double-click on the Pick tool, then click on the Group/Ungroup button on the toolbar.

   Selects all objects in the Drawing Window; groups them.

2. Click-and-drag the grouped logo design off the printable page to the left, then right-click before releasing.

   Places a duplicate of the logo on the pasteboard portion of the Drawing Window. The pasteboard area is great for leaving scraps of objects, but it's also a "commons" area between pages of a multi-page document. This makes it an easy matter to copy the logo to page 1, which contains the bitmap image, without using Windows' Clipboard.

3. Press PageUp.

   Moves you to page 1 of the TIMELESS.CDR document.

4. Click-and-drag the logo onto the printable page.

   Moves the copy of the original logo to page one, remaining on the Logo layer (see fig. 6.8).

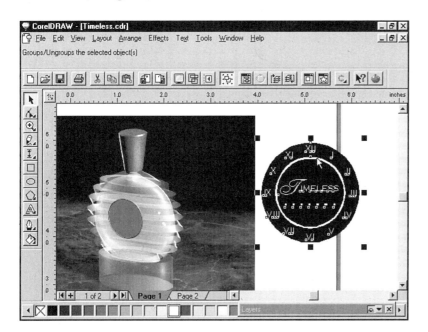

Figure 6.8

Windows' Clipboard uses system resources. Conserve resources by using Corel's internal duplicating commands and the pasteboard.

Document-Centricity

5. Click-and-drag a guideline out of the horizontal ruler, and position it on the bottom third of the perfume image.

   This guideline will be used to determine the amount of skewing you apply to the logo design.

6. Click-and-drag the left guideline handle so the guideline runs parallel to the horizontal indentations on the perfume bottle.

   Makes the guideline parallel to the angle of inclination within the bitmap image. 7° is about the right angle for the guideline; you can check this figure by double-clicking on the guideline, then checking the Slanted Guidelines Setup menu.

7. With the Pick tool, click-and-drag the logo so it's over the distorted circle area on the image, then click-and-drag a corner selection handle toward the center of the object until you can see the edges of the bitmap image's distorted circle.

Positions and resizes the logo design. The logo is smaller than its final size, but you need to see the edges of the bitmap target area.

8. Click on the selected logo.

   Changes selection handles to skew/rotate handles.

9. Click-and-drag the right skew handle to the logo (see fig. 6.9).

   Applies the correct amount of skew until the logo's bottom bounding box edge is parallel to the slanted guideline.

Figure 6.9

Use a slanted guideline to help sync the amount of distortion seen in an image to the distort you apply to an object.

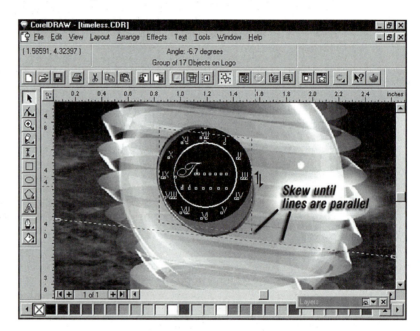

A minor amount of tugging and pulling is now required to make the logo fit perfectly inside the corresponding area on the bottle.

10. Click on the grouped logo object.

    Returns selection handles to normal resizing function.

11. Click on the top side selection handle and drag away from the object group.

    Disproportionately resizes the vertical measure of the group.

12. Click-and-drag the right side selection handle away from the object.

    Disproportionately resizes the horizontal measure of the group.

13. Press Ctrl+S (**F**ile, **S**ave).

   Saves your work at this stage.

Preparing to Export the Logo

As mentioned earlier in this chapter, the logo best serves this design example if the lettering and Roman numerals are white. Many programs have the capability to "ignore" certain colors. GIF graphics used for World Wide Web pages, for example, can feature a drop-out color; and, as you saw in Chapter 9, "Working between CorelDRAW! and CorelDREAM 3D," DREAM 3D can assign white in an imported image to a transparent status.

In this section, you'll see how to export the vector logo design, then import the design as a bitmap in CorelPHOTO-PAINT. You should leave some blank space around a selection you export, however—it makes cropping a selected area easier in the host application. Therefore, if you know in advance that white will be dropped out of this logo design, by placing a white rectangle behind the logo, it, too, will be dropped out when the final image is assembled.

Additionally, because this logo will be transformed by CorelDRAW into bitmap format, the resolution of the exported bitmap is critical. TIMELESS.TIF is 150 pixels per inch; therefore, under normal circumstances, if the vector design perfectly fits an area in an imported bitmap, it will perfectly fit the image when imported to the same resolution and size. However, anti-aliasing should be performed upon the exported logo if it is to maintain smooth edges like the rest of TIMELESS.TIF. So what is anti-aliasing?

Anti-aliasing is the placement of similar shades of color around a bitmap image area to provide a smooth transition between one color area and another within the image. *Aliasing* occurs in the conversion of vector information to bitmap because computers are very precise and literal. Vector images need to be *resolved* to pixel level (broken into whole color units) because bitmaps contain a finite number of pixels, whereas vector designs contain any number of picture elements when you display to screen or print. Without the assistance of anti-aliasing, most applications "see" an abrupt color change from pixel to pixel instead of a smooth transition, because vector art contains no information about pixel color transition—as vector art, it doesn't *need* to.

Although CorelPHOTO-PAINT makes the claim to importing and exporting anti-aliased images (and a check box is visible in the Import/Export dialog boxes), the *quality* of the anti-aliasing leaves much to be desired in version 6.00.118 of PHOTO-PAINT. PHOTO-PAINT'S anti-aliasing filter places an unacceptably low number of anti-alias pixels at color contrast edges in an imported vector graphic, when the Anti-aliased check box is marked in the Import into Bitmap dialog box. Check with Corel Customer Support to get the latest version of the Corel suite, and perhaps the Anti-aliased feature will work better in later builds.

Manually performing anti-aliasing isn't that complicated, however, if you understand how it's accomplished. To ensure that the logo is placed in the finished bitmap composition with a minimum of tell-tale, stair-stepped (*aliased*) edges, edge pixel colors need to be defined by using different resolution copies of the vector information. Many applications generate anti-aliased images by sampling a bitmap at several resolutions, then averaging the pixel colors for the finished image. This is often called *subsampling*. If you export the design at 300, not 150 pixels per inch, you can then use CorelPHOTO-PAINT's Resample command to *create* soft, anti-aliased edges in the imported bitmap logo.

By taking a little time to understand why programs do what they do to create an effect, you become not only less dependent on the feature set of a specific application, but also a more accomplished craftsperson.

Here's how to translate the logo you've created for the perfume into a format that CorelPHOTO-PAINT can import:

Exporting to a Vector File to PHOTO-PAINT

1. Press F6 (or choose the Rectangle tool, then click-and-drag a rectangle that encompasses the grouped logo.

   Creates the outside dimensions of the image CorelPHOTO-PAINT will import.

2. Press Shift+PageDown (or click on the toolbar's To Back button).

   Sends the rectangle to the back of the stack of objects on the Logo layer.

3. Left-click on the white swatch on the color palette, then right-click on the "x" on the color palette.

   Assigns the rectangle white fill and no outline attributes (see fig. 6.10).

In figure 6.11, we've created an enhancement for the finished image in this assignment; a mirrored logo has been created and placed upon the mirror image area in the bitmap. To do this yourself, copy the logo from page 2 of the document, mirror it horizontally by pressing Ctrl+click-and-dragging the top selection handle downwards, then apply a skew in the opposite direction as the first logo. You can then move the mirrored logo as close as you like to the first logo for export. You'd be selecting the imported logos individually for placement, and importing both logos with a huge space between them would result in an unnecessarily large bitmap image.

Figure 6.10
White areas of the exported design will be dropped out in the finished bitmap image in CorelPHOTO-PAINT.

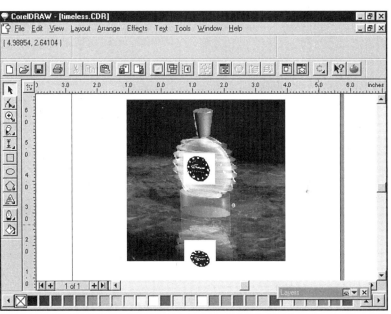

Figure 6.11
Apply a skew to a mirrored copy of the original log to create a perfume label for the reflected image in TIMELESS.TIF.

4. Choose **F**ile, **E**xport (Ctrl+H; or click on the Export button on the toolbar).

Displays the Export dialog box.

5. Choose Corel Presentation Exchange 6.0 (CMX) from the Save as type drop-down list, name the file TIMELESS.CMX, click on the Selected only check box, choose a convenient hard disk location in the Save in list, then click on Export.

   Exports the selected logo. Because vector file formats such as CMX are resolution-independent, you aren't queried by CorelDRAW as to the resulting file resolution.

6. Close CorelDRAW.

   Quits the application so that you can launch PHOTO-PAINT in the next set of steps without creating an unnecessary resource overhead on your system.

Now that the logo for the perfume bottle has been exported to the correct dimensions for editing and placement work in PHOTO-PAINT, let's continue the assignment in Corel's bitmap editing program.

Importing and Retouching the Label Design

1. Launch CorelPHOTO-PAINT from Win95's Start menu.

   This is the application in which you'll import the CMX file.

2. Open PERFUME.TIF from the CHAP06 folder of the Bonus CD.

   This is the image that will be retouched.

3. Choose File, Open (Ctrl+O), then choose TIMELESS.CMX from your hard disk.

   Displays the Import into Bitmap dialog box.

4. Choose 256 Shades of Gray from the Color drop-down list, Size: 1 to 1, check the Identical Values, do *not* check the Anti-aliasing check boxes, type **300** in the Horizontal DPI spin box, then click inside the Vertical DPI spin box.

   Sets the resolution and color mode for the CMX imported graphic (see fig. 6.12)

Anti-aliasing should be performed only once on bitmap images; two applications of anti-aliasing tend to blur the image details. The Anti-aliasing import filter in the Import into Bitmap check box would provide too little anti-aliasing to create a smooth bitmap import, but just enough to blur the label if it was applied in addition to the steps to follow.

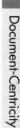

Figure 6.12

Exported CorelDRAW graphics have no fixed size or resolution until you define them as bitmap graphics imports.

5. Click on OK.

A bitmap version of TIMELESS.CMX appears in a new document window.

6. Choose **I**mage, R**e**sample.

Displays the Resample dialog box.

7. Leave Image Size **W**idth and **H**eight at their default of 100%, choose Anti-alias from the **P**rocess drop-down box, check **M**aintain aspect ratio and *un*check Maintain original **s**ize Type **150** in the H**o**rizontal Resolution spin box, place the cursor in the **V**ertical spin box, then click (**M**aintain aspect ratio automatically changes the **V**ertical resolution to match H**o**rizontal resolution).

Specifies that TIMELESS.CMX will be sampled down to half its original imported size (see fig. 6.13).

Although the anti-aliasing feature in PHOTO-PAINT's Import into bitmap dialog box doesn't create an adequate amount of anti-aliasing, resampling the resolution *after* the logo has been imported creates a more photographic logo. The Anti-aliasing process in the Resample box works because you've commanded CorelPHOTO-PAINT to reassign pixels within the TIMELESS.CMX image to represent a different sized image, and to do this, CorelPHOTO-PAINT analyzes and averages original image content to create the change.

Figure 6.13
Resampling the
imported logo design
will bring it to the
correct size for the
perfume bottle, and
smooth image edges
through Anti-
aliasing.

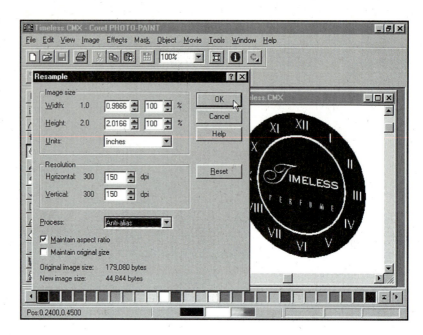

8. Click on OK, then choose **F**ile, Save **A**s, then save the image as LOGO.TIF to your hard disk.

   Saves the imported copy of the logo to your hard disk.

At a one-to-one viewing resolution, the new bitmap logo displays similar photographic qualities as the perfume bottle. Digitized images almost never display hard edges. If you zoom into a PhotoCD image, for example, you'll see that even the clearest, sharpest of edges around an object is made up of a band of pixels whose colors blend into the background colors.

Image resolution—the number of pixels per height or width measurement—is inversely proportional to the dimensions of a bitmap image. In the preceding example, the Maintain original **s**ize check box was unchecked, because with the option enabled, reducing the resolution to one-half the original size would have increased TIMELESS.CMX's width and height by 200 percent. In this case, no anti-aliasing and no actual change to the image would have occurred.

Because the Timeless perfume assignment is a small example designed to show editing and file-conversion principles, you might notice that the lettering on the logo image isn't very detailed. That's because small bitmap images have a limited number of pixels with which to represent overall detail. In assignments of your own, achieving adequate resolution for an imported logo is accomplished by choosing a large (4MB or more) host image, then sizing the CorelDRAW logo correspondingly. High resolution *or* large image dimensions will provide an ample number of pixels to create logo typography.

Using CorelPHOTO-PAINT!'s Objects Merge Modes

CorelPHOTO-PAINT has the capability to float an area of a copied bitmap above a different bitmap image; repositioning and editing the bitmap object is an action performed independently of the background areas of an image. However, an object-oriented bitmap image is *not* a standard graphics format—it's one provided to facilitate image editing, and objects must be *merged* with the background image if the bitmap is to be saved to a common file format.

Our interest here in bitmap objects lies in CorelPHOTO-PAINT's options for how a floating object should be merged with the background. In this section, you'll make the logo a floating object above the PERFUME.TIF image. Sixteen different modes of merging can be performed as an object becomes a unified part of a bitmap image background. Merge modes offer a way for the designer to specify which pixels in a floating object will replace the underlying pixels on the background.

The merge mode you'll be working on in this assignment is Multiply—Multiply combines the color density of the object pixels with those the object floats above. Therefore, the white areas of the logo disappear when merged with the perfume image because white is lighter than the underlying background of the perfume image, and the black areas of the logo remain black, and darken the lighter areas of the perfume bottle. This exercise shows you how to add the logo to the perfume image:

Creating a Bitmap Image Object

1. With LOGO.TIF as the active image window, choose the Freehand Mask tool from the Mask tool fly-out menu (the dotted, freeform outline icon).

   This is the tool for creating irregular selection areas in an image.

2. Click-and-drag a loose border around the logo, then double-click where the selection marquee begins.

   Closes the selection border; marquee lines indicate selected area.

3. Press Ctrl+F7 (**V**iew, Roll-**U**ps, **O**bjects).

   Displays the Objects Roll-Up.

4. Arrange the windows in CorelPHOTO-PAINT so that you have a clear view of both PERFUME.TIF and LOGO.TIF.

II

Document-Centricity

You need to see both windows: to copy the selection from one window to the other.

5. With LOGO.TIF as the active document window, click on the Convert to Object button on the Objects Roll-Up.

   Changes the selected logo to create a floating object in LOGO.TIF; Freehand Mask tool toggles to Object Picker tool.

6. Ctrl+click-and-drag the object into the PERFUME.TIF image window.

   Copies the logo to PERFUME.TIF (see fig. 6.14).

Figure 6.14
Copy objects between image windows by Ctrl+click-and-dragging them.

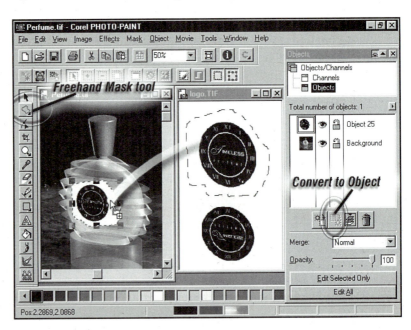

7. Choose Multiply from the Objects Roll-Up's Merge drop-down list.

   Drops white out of the logo object; you can now see only the logo and the perfume image background (see fig. 6.15).

Floating objects aren't merged automatically when you copy them; instead, you can preview the merge mode effect on objects by selecting them, and switching modes.

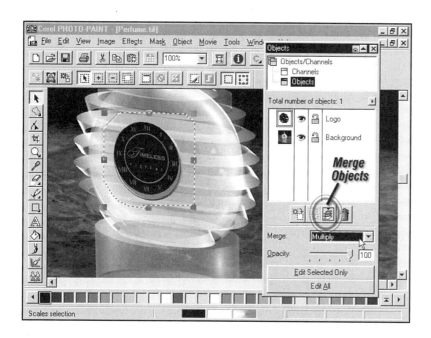

Figure 6.15
Merge modes offer
different ways to
replace—or
combine—floating
object pixels with
those of the
background image.

8. Click-and-drag the logo object until it fits within the circular label area of the perfume bottle.

   The default nudge value in PHOTO-PAINT is one pixel per arrow keystroke; use the arrow keys for precise placement.

This is the end of the merge mode example, but do *not* choose Save right now. See explanation following.

You're almost finished editing the PERFUME image to add the logo, but in the interest of conserving hard disk space (and saving some confusion), you shouldn't save the PERFUME image yet.

Note   Objects in bitmap images are a proprietary arrangement of digital image structure. You cannot save an image containing an object to TIF, Targa, BMP, or other commonly used file formats, because these formats don't acknowledge objects.

If you really need to interrupt an image-editing session, your only alternative to preserve this work at this stage is to save the image as a CPT file, CorelPHOTO-PAINT's proprietary format that *can* save object information. If you have a moment to spare to complete the assignment, however, don't save the PERFUME.TIF image as a CPT file—you'd be creating an extra 1 MB file on your hard disk. Instead, move to the next section to cover one or two CorelPHOTO-PAINT enhancement techniques that will make this product image really stand out on the shelf.

> **→Tip** If you find that the marquee lines in an image are distracting, two icons on CorelPHOTO-PAINT's Mask/Object toolbar can help. The two far-right icons are the Show/Hide Mask Marquee and the Show/Hide Object Marquee buttons. By toggling them on or off, you can remove the visible marquees of a selected area, or an object, without merging the object or deselecting an image area.

Applying Contrast Controls to the Background

If you chose to put a little extra time into the CorelDRAW work in this section, you'll have a second, mirrored logo to place in the PERFUME.TIF image as an object. You should follow the steps in the previous example to accomplish this before we get into some minor image enhancements in this section.

Objects in CorelPHOTO-PAINT images are mutually exclusive items; you can colorize, distort, and otherwise edit an object without altering another, or even the background to an image. In PERFUME.TIF, you'll notice that the transparent areas of the logo allow a view of the dark tan label area on the bottle, but the contrast between the black logo areas and the label is poor. To correct this problem, you'll brighten the areas, creating a highlight that will make the Roman numerals on the logo more legible.

Here's how to use the Effects tool to apply the corrections to only a small area of the overall PERFUME image:

Using the Effects Tool

1. Click on the lock icon to the right of the logo icon on the Objects Roll-Up.

   Prevents accidental editing of the logo object.

You'll notice that the Merge drop-down list becomes dimmed when you lock an object. This is a visual confirmation that you are not about to edit objects, but instead, the remaining background area in PERFUME.TIF.

2. Double-click on the Effects tool (the Q-Tip icon) on the toolbox.

   Selects the tool and displays the Tool Settings Roll-Up.

3. Scroll up on the icon list on the Tool Settings Roll-Up, then click on Brighten icon (it should be the third from the left on the top row of the scrolling icon area on Tool Settings).

   Chooses the type of Effects tool that will Brighten areas you click-and-drag over.

4. Click-and-drag the cursor over the Roman numeral area of the image (see fig. 6.16).

Brightens the background label area without affecting the logo object.

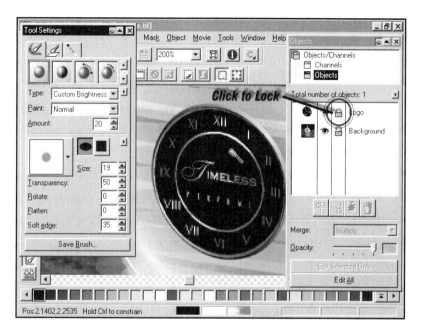

Figure 6.16

By locking objects, you can apply effects "through" the objects to only affect the background image areas.

5. When the lettering is legible, click on the lock icon, then click on the Combine icon (to the left of the trash icon) on the Objects Roll-Up.

Unlocks the logo object; merges the object to background to create standard, non-proprietary bitmap image.

6. Choose **F**ile, Save **A**s, then save the image as TIMELESS.TIF to your hard disk.

Saves the completed image.

There is an ulterior motive to this chapter's assignments; that is, to make CorelDRAW users a little less leery of CorelPHOTO-PAINT's features. Both applications contain tools that the graphics professional should become familiar with. Commerce doesn't limit itself to a single computer graphics file format!

The completed image, as shown in figure 6.17, is the result of knowing how to combine graphics file formats, but you also achieve platform-independence when you know how to move CorelDRAW elements to bitmap format. The TIMELESS.TIF image can be used by professionals who don't own CorelDRAW, CorelPHOTO-PAINT; those running Macintosh and UNIX systems can also read the image.

Document-Centricity

Figure 6.17
When a design is of a format best used in CorelPHOTO-PAINT, but the editing tools are in CorelDRAW, use *both* programs.

Adding Vector Enhancements to an Image

The flexibility of working between vector and bitmap types of graphics is frequently overlooked by designers. That's because editing tools for each type of art is often located in two different applications.

If you have a stock art collection on PhotoCD, for example, you might need a traffic sign in an assignment. But the sign has to say 30% off instead of STOP. You can labor away for hours in CorelPHOTO-PAINT on such an image, but it might prove to be the wrong application for the task. CorelDRAW handles text much more elegantly then CorelPHOTO-PAINT, but CorelPHOTO-PAINT *seems* like the ideal application because it offers bitmap editing tools—as opposed to vector tools. If you want text that suggests dimension, or if you want to apply a decal to a rendered model, the quickest solution often lies in importing the bitmap into CorelDRAW and finishing the composition as a hybrid of bitmap and vector graphics.

In this section, you'll see how to integrate the text-handling and special-effects capabilities of CorelDRAW with a bitmap image that's missing a certain artistic something.

Preparing a Bitmap Image for CorelDRAW! Output

Chapter 4, "Mastering Color Models and the Fill Tool," provides a sound basis for understanding and working with digital color models, but a brief recap here provides a reason why you often need to convert an image's color structure.

As mentioned earlier in this chapter, most high-quality bitmap images are saved in a file format according to the relative contributions of red, green, and blue colors expressed as brightness in color channels. RGB image types have been organized this way because your monitor uses red, green, and blue phosphors to display an image, and the human eye has red, green, and blue photo-receptors. Red, green, and blue are added together to create the gamut of visible color in the RGB color model.

Printed material is based around a different color model—the reflective (subtractive) cyan, magenta, yellow, and black pigments. CMYK images are not equivalent to RGB images of identical subjects, and the CMYK gamut is narrower than the RGB gamut. CorelDRAW performs on-the-fly conversions of RGB images you import and print to CMYK format, but you have no control over how the component inks are separated, and no way to correct out-of-gamut colors with an imported RGB bitmap.

Although your monitor is designed around the RGB color model, CorelPHOTO-PAINT and CorelDRAW can *simulate* the CMYK color space on-screen, and present you with a fairly accurate representation of how an image will print. Additionally, CorelPHOTO-PAINT can detect and allow you to correct areas within an RGB image that have no CMYK equivalent—the *out-of-gamut* colors. In this section's assignment, you'll add text to a bitmap image of a book, showing editing techniques *and* how to get the most out of your work when you know in advance that a finished composition will be saved in the CorelDRAW file format.

In the following set of steps, you'll convert 9PM.TIF (from the CHAP06 folder of the Bonus CD) to CMYK format, then check and correct any out-of-gamut colors. The book in the image needs some text to complete the composition, but you need to translate the image to a different color model before creating the text element. When CorelDRAW imports a CMYK bitmap image, it does not perform color model translations (because the image has already been converted), and you can be assured that what you see on-screen prints as faithfully as possible to the original. The following exercise shows how to convert a bitmap for printing, and solve out-of-gamut problems:

II

Document-Centricity

Changing Color Gamut and Format

1. In CorelPHOTO-PAINT, open the 9PM.TIF image from the EXAMPLES.CHAP06 folder of the *CorelDRAW! 6 Expert's Edition Bonus CD*.

   This is the image you'll work with in this assignment.

2. Choose **T**ools, **O**ptions, then click on the Advanced tab.

   Displays a menu of Advanced CorelPHOTO-PAINT options.

3. Click on the **G**amut Alarm color drop-down list, then choose brilliant green.

Chooses a color not found in 9PM.TIF; makes out of gamut areas easier to spot (see fig. 6.18).

Figure 6.18
Choose a color for the Gamut Alarm that is distinctly different than predominant colors in a bitmap image.

Gamut Alarm displays "problem" areas in an image in the color of your choice. This Gamut Alarm color is *not* part of the image; it rests above the image on a display layer the same way a cursor does.

4. Click on OK, choose **V**iew, **C**olor Correction, **A**ccurate, then choose **V**iew, **C**olor Correction, **G**amut Alarm.

Changes display in CorelPHOTO-PAINT to simulate printed inks; out-of-gamut color areas turn brilliant green.

This book's figures are in black and white, so you can't really see the effect of the Gamut Alarm feature. However, if you perform this step, you'll see brilliant green in the clouds, the lamp base, and the yo-yo in 9PM.TIF. Here, you need to make a judgment call based on your artistic needs and your time. CorelPHOTO-PAINT can automatically bring most, but not all, out-of-gamut colors back into printable range.

Mostly, colors have saturation removed through color-model conversion, and in a dimly lit picture such as 9PM.TIF, there will be no significant difference in image quality when CorelPHOTO-PAINT does so. Every photograph has its own unique color range and associated out-of-gamut problems, but for the purposes of example, let's let CorelPHOTO-PAINT perform an RGB to CMYK color reduction to see how well colors are brought into printable range.

5. Choose **I**mage, Con**v**ert To, then choose **C**MYK Color (32-bit).

    9PM.TIF changes slightly in color range, most Gamut Alarm overlay color disappears.

6. Double-click on the Effects tool, then choose Sponge from the Tool Settings icon list.

    Displays the Toll Settings Roll-Up; chooses the tool that removes saturation from areas of an image.

7. Type **–7** in the **A**mount spin box, type **1** in the **S**ize spin box, and type **40** in the Soft **e**dge spin box.

    Specifies a brush nib that can be used to remove saturation from a very small part of the image; the –7 Amount setting specifies that a minor amount of color will be removed.

8. Zoom into a 200% view of the yo-yo, then click-and-drag, carefully, over the image (see fig. 6.19).

    The green disappears, indicating that sufficient color has been removed to fall within printable range.

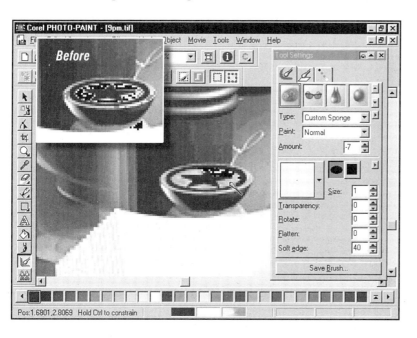

Figure 6.19

When the Gamut Alarm color disappears from the image, you've brought pixel colors into CMYK printable range.

9. Choose <u>F</u>ile, Save <u>A</u>s, then save the image as 9PM-CMYK.TIF to your hard disk.

Saves the CMYK image for future use.

 In RGB mode, you can also bring image areas back into printable range by replacing colors, or simply reducing the color component in areas, as you did in the previous example.

CMYK images are called *32-bit images* for an unobvious reason. Although it's true that a CMYK digital image consists of four color channels, made up of 8 bits per pixel color information, don't believe that a CMYK image is of higher color quality than 24 bit per pixel RGB images.

Although the number of possible colors in a CMYK image is greater, its overall range of expressible, unique color values is limited in comparison to RGB color. Colors you see on a monitor are *quantized*—that is, they have to have a fixed numerical value assigned to them to be saved to digital format. Because the CMYK image structure contains more integers does not mean that the range of expressible colors is higher than RGB color structure, nor does a CMYK color have higher color capability.

Think of it this way: at better pizza take-out places, you have the option to have pizzas cut into 6 or 8 pieces. Does a medium pizza cut into 8 slices contain more pizza information than a large pizza cut into 6 pieces?

CorelPHOTO-PAINT performs color reduction when it performs the translation between color models, and because of this, you should make certain that you don't convert CMYK images back to RGB. You can undo a color conversion from CorelPHOTO-PAINT's <u>E</u>dit, Undo List, but it's far better to manually edit a CMYK image to color compliance, and always keep an RGB original of an image at hand for further tweaking. CMYK colors don't spring back to life when you convert back to RGB mode; filtering processes with bitmap images *progressively* diminish image quality.

CorelDRAW! as the Media Blender

The CMYK copy of the 9PM image is only one component of this mixed media composition. BROWNING.DOC is in the CHAP06 folder of the Bonus CD, and this document contains text saved in Word for Windows 2.0 format. CorelDRAW can import a formatted document with choice of fonts and alignments preserved, but we're going for a special effect in this assignment, and this means using Artistic, not Paragraph Text in CorelDRAW.

By default, text imported into CorelDRAW becomes Paragraph text. Paragraph Text, which has a much higher character capability than Artistic Text (up to 32,000 characters per paragraph), is used for brochure and page-layout creation, but you can't perform special effects with Paragraph text. Artistic text has a limit of approximately

32,000 characters, period—depending mostly upon the complexity of the chosen font—but this number is acceptable for the composition's content. Additionally, you can use all of CorelDRAW's Effects features with Artistic Text—the next set of steps shows you how to add text and the 9PM-CMYK image to a CorelDRAW document.

Gathering Compositional Elements

1. Launch CorelDRAW from Windows Explorer, then in a new document, click on the Import button on the toolbar (**F**ile, **I**mport; Ctrl+I).

   Displays the Import dialog box.

2. Choose 9PM-CMYK.TIF from your hard disk, then click on Imp**o**rt.

   Imports the CMYK image to the center of the [Graphic 1] document.

3. Press Ctrl+F3 (**L**ayout, **L**ayers Manager), then click on the pencil icon to the left of the Layer 1 title.

   Locks the 9PM image on Layer 1. It cannot be accidentally moved now.

4. Right-click on the Layers Roll-Up list, choose **N**ew from the shortcut menu, then type **Text** in the highlighted new layer title.

   Creates new, editable layer on top of Layer 1; names it for easy future reference (see fig. 6.20).

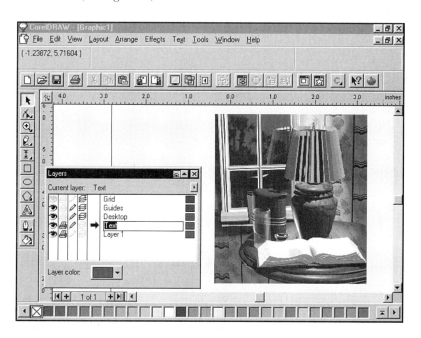

Figure 6.20

Months from now, you'll be able to tell at a glance why the imported bitmap won't move when you try to select it!

5. Click in the document window, press PageDown, then press Enter.

   Changes DRAW's focus from the Layers Roll-Up to the document; displays the Insert Page dialog box; accepts the defaults to add one page after page 1; you're moved to the page 2 view of the document.

6. Click on the Import button on the toolbar(Ctrl+I; File, Import), click on BROWNING.DOC in the EXAMPLES.CHAP06 folder of the Bonus CD), then click on Import.

   Displays the Import dialog box; imports the WinWord document as Paragraph text.

7. Choose Text, Convert to Artistic Text (see fig. 6.21).

   Converts the Paragraph Text to Artistic Text; you can now manipulate the text using CorelDRAW's effects.

Figure 6.21
You can convert inflexible Paragraph Text to Artistic Text with the new Text command in CorelDRAW.

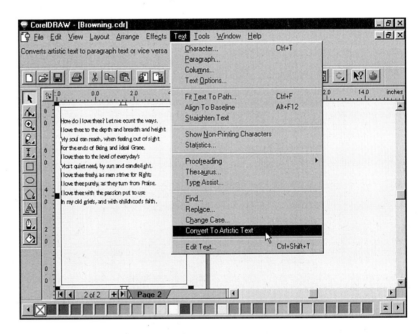

8. Press Ctrl+S (File, Save), then save the document as BROWNING.CDR to your hard disk.

   Saves the document at this intermediate stage.

Artistic Text can also be converted to Paragraph Text, but the text must be selected with the Pick tool, not the Text tool. But if you choose to break a block of Paragraph text, you can't convert linked paragraph blocks to Artistic text. Additionally, text imported to CorelDRAW retains formatting, but loses the formatting if you convert between Paragraph Text and Artistic. It's usually a good idea, then, to remember the font you used when creating a word processor document.

The book in the 9PM image is face open, and it would be nice if both facing pages contained the classic lines from Elizabeth Browning's sonnet. In the next section, you'll see how to define borders for the text that you'll flow into image areas, and will look as though the scene originally contained the sonnet.

Creating Envelope Templates

The secret to making 2D text appear dimensional in a CorelDRAW composition lies in knowing how to use the Envelope Roll-Up. Although the Envelope Roll-Up's capability to bend Artistic text is limited to the character limit for Artistic text, the truncated version of "How Do I Love Thee" consists of a mere 364 characters; it will be easy to manipulate, and if you get more ambitious in your own assignments, you can try longer text passages.

Note The Envelope Roll-Up can use any closed path you create as a template for distorting objects. Part of the trick here is to keep the definition of the envelope template as simple as possible; use nodes to trace the outline of the book pages only where needed. The Envelope Roll-Up calculates envelopes based not only on the shape of a template path, but also the direction and number of nodes along a path.

Here's the way to create a template that will be used to flow the text into the composition:

Creating Paths for Bending Text

1. Press PageUp, then zoom into the book area of the 9PM image, and press F5 (or click on the Freehand Pencil tool).

   Moves your view to page 1; chooses the Pencil tool.

2. Click on a corner of the left book page, then double-click to the right, where the book page curves downward.

   Creates a path segment ending at a point of path inflection.

3. Continue double-clicking at points of sharp direction change along the book page's outline, then single-click at the beginning of the path.

Creates a rough path around the left book page (see fig. 6.22).

Figure 6.22

Create a straight line path with node connections at points where the book page outline shows a change in direction.

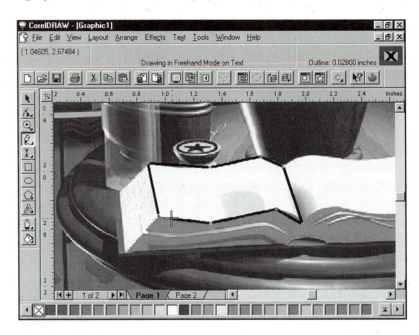

4. Press F10 (or click on the Shape tool), marquee select all the nodes on the path, right-click, then choose To **C**urve from the shortcut menu.

   Converts the straight path segments to curves.

The left and right sides of the page outline need to be straight; although it would be fastidious to convert each path segment that required it to a curve, you can often accomplish node editing in fewer steps if you convert a whole collection of nodes to curve property, then backtrack to correct one or two.

5. Click on the left side of the path, then right-click and choose To **L**ine from the shortcut menu; repeat this with the right side of the path.

   Converts the left and right path segments to straight lines.

6. Marquee select the upper and lower side nodes, then right-click and choose **S**mooth from the shortcut menu.

   Creates a smooth curve transition on the top and bottom sides to match the book page's curves.

7. If necessary, click-and-drag on individual node handles to refine the shape of the path.

   Creates a path that can be used to create an envelope with the imported text (see fig. 6.23).

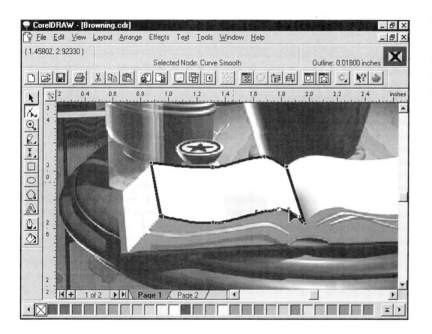

Don't forget that this path serves as a good book page description, but what about margins for the text? Unlike word processors, Artistic text on a CorelDRAW page contains no margins, so unless you want the text to look like it's escaping from the book page, you now need to move the edges of the path inward. Fortunately, when you select multiple nodes in a path, they move in synch, so the flow of the path edge remains the same.

8. Marquee select the bottom nodes along the path, then click-and-drag them about 1/10 " upwards.

   Creates a bottom margin on the left page.

9. Repeat the last steps with the left, right, and top sides of the path.

   Creates an ideal envelope within which the text will flow (see fig. 6.24).

Figure 6.24
Books contain text
margins; take
margins into account
when creating text
envelope templates.

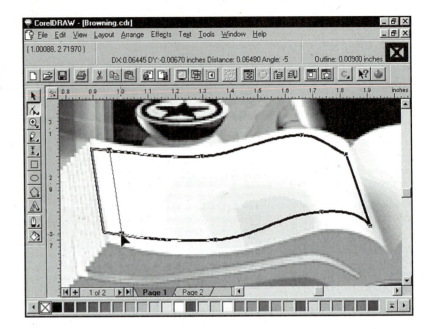

10. Using the same steps as described in this section, create a template for the right page of the book.

    Completes the template creation for this composition.

Text Formatting and Sizing

As mentioned earlier, text attributes assigned to a document in a word processor are retained when CorelDRAW imports the text, but the document reverts to Corel's default font style when converting between Artistic and Paragraph text. That gives you an opportunity here to choose an appropriate font for the book, and also to demonstrate a feature new to this version of CorelDRAW.

If you don't have Lydian BT installed from Corel's type collection, you might want to consider it; Lydian is a classic font that's used to set religious publications and timeless documents, yet has a clean, legible, Roman sans serif feel, which is perfect here due to the small size the text needs to be on the book. Lydiann.pfb is the Type 1 font name in the B Type 1 folder of the Corel CD; we recommend Type 1, not TrueType in this example, because the text—unlike the perfume bottle's—would be printed as text to an imagesetter, and imagesetters use the PostScript Type 1 font standard.

Here's how to prepare the text for the Envelope effect:

Sizing and Specing Type

1. Double-click on the Pick tool of BROWNING.CDR.

   Selects all (unlocked) objects on page 1.

2. Press Ctrl+C, press PageDown, then press Ctrl+V.

   Copies the envelope templates to page 2; moves your view to page 2.

3. Click on the Artistic text, then press Ctrl+T.

   Displays the Character Attributes dialog box.

4. Choose Lydian BT from the **F**onts list, then click on OK.

   Changes the Artistic text from the default font to Lydian BT.

5. With the Pick tool, click-and-drag the lower right selection handle toward the center of the text until the marquee bounding box appears to fit the width of one of the page templates.

   Scales the text to fit within the envelope template (see fig. 6.25).

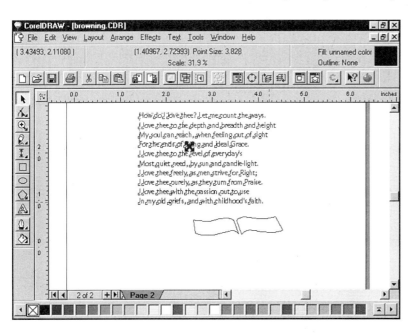

Figure 6.25

Repositioning and resizing the text before enveloping it means that the Envelope effect will proceed more quickly.

II

Document-Centricity

In general, it's best to do everything you can to get text, or other objects, in a state that requires the least Envelop effect calculations. By scaling the text so the Envelope effect doesn't have to, you save editing time.

6. Press Ctrl+K (**A**rrange, **B**reak Apart).

Whoa! New Corel feature that breaks Artistic text into individual lines.

7. Marquee select the top 5 lines of text, then press Ctrl+L (**A**rrange, **C**ombine).

Combines the 5 lines of text into a single Artistic Text block.

8. Marquee select the bottom five lines of text, then press Ctrl+L.

Combines the other 5 lines into one Artistic Text block (see fig. 6.26).

Figure 6.26

Artistic text does *not* lose its editable property when you use the Combine and Break Apart commands.

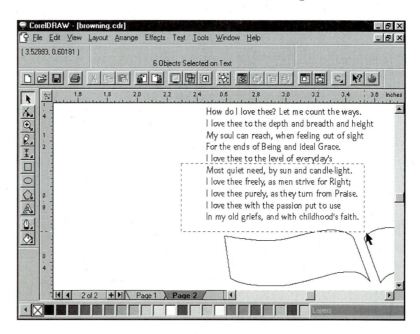

9. Press Ctrl+S (**F**ile, **S**ave).

Saves your work at this intermediate point.

This new text handling feature in CorelDRAW has extended capabilities as well. If you take a single line of Artistic text and choose the Break Apart command, individual words can be selected. The reverse process works too by using the Combine command, but you'll get unexpected results if you attempt to combine words whose position on the page is out of sequence. ***It look might like this!*** Also, if you rotate a line of text that's the last (top object) item added to the page, then combine it with unrotated text, the combined Artistic Text is rotated.

The Envelope, Please

To conclude the example and this composition, it's time to bring out the Envelope Roll-Up. The Envelope Roll-Up offers many modes of Envelope distortion, but the most flexible is the Putty mode, where an editable path is created around the target object. With the text elements, you want to reshape them to conform to the templates you created of the book pages. The Putty envelope creates an envelope path with identical nodes as the path templates, and the envelope nodes and path segments have identical properties to the original path templates. Here's how to pour the text blocks into the book templates:

Enveloping Artistic Text

1. With the Pick tool, click on the first text block.

    Selects the text.

2. Press Ctrl+F7 (Effects, **E**nvelope).

    Displays the Envelope Roll-Up.

3. Click on Create From.

    Cursor turns into a huge arrow.

4. Click on the left page template, then click on Apply (see fig. 6.27).

    Applies the left page shape to the text; toggles current tool to the Shape tool.

You'll notice that the text will remain stationary after the effect is applied. You'll have to move the enveloped text to its correct position by marquee selecting all the envelope nodes with the Shape tool, then repositioning the text, then clicking on Apply, or switching to the Pick tool and simply clicking on and dragging the text. An envelope is a "live object" on the workspace, and if you change it by reshaping it *or* moving it, you must execute the edit by clicking on Apply on the Envelope Roll-Up.

5. Click on the second, undistorted text block (with either the Shape or the Pick tool), then click on Create from on the Envelope Roll-Up.

    Cursor turns to big arrow.

6. Click on the remaining path template, then click on Apply.

    Applies the template shape to the text block.

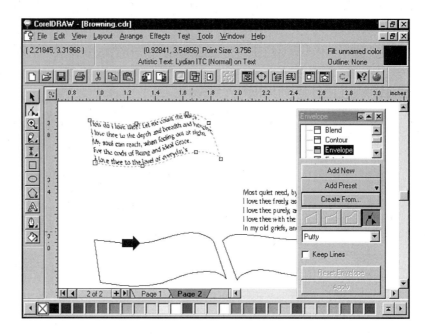

Figure 6.27

Select a target path for the Envelope Roll-Up to apply the effect to the currently selected object.

7. Press the spacebar, then click-and-drag each enveloped text block to the corresponding path template.

   Toggles to Pick tool; aligns the text relative to the template shapes (see fig. 6.28).

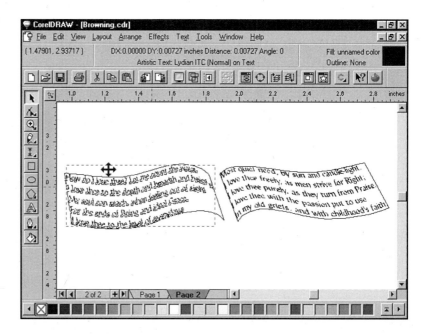

Figure 6.28

You can place the text on page 2 in the same relative position as their destination on page 1 by aligning them to the template paths.

8. Shift+click on the other text block, then press Ctrl+C.

   Selects the remaining text block in addition to the current one; copies both to the clipboard.

9. Press PageUp, then press Ctrl+V.

   Moves your view to page 1; pastes a copy of the enveloped text blocks on top of the 9PM image.

10. Press Ctrl+S (**F**ile, **S**ave).

    Saves your work at this intermediate stage.

Objects that you copy to the clipboard, or duplicate by pressing +, retain their orientation to the original object when they appear. Because the envelope template paths were not moved when they were copied to page 2, the enveloped text plops perfectly into position above the bitmap image.

In figure 6.29, you can see some last-minute touch-up work being performed on a text block. The Envelope effect is perfect in its calculations, but it sometimes produces an effect other than precisely what you intend. For example, the arc of the bottom left corner of text in figure 6.29 needs to be a little sharper.

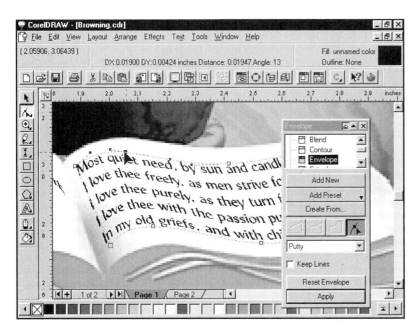

Figure 6.29
Although an envelope can be made visible by clicking on it with the Shape tool, the Roll-Up is required to Apply editing steps.

Tip   You can also access the same commands you'd use with the Node Edit Roll-Up by right-clicking, then holding over an envelope node or envelope path segment with the Shape tool. Doing this displays the shortcut menu, with context-sensitive commands relating to node and path properties.

You can clean up this document now by deleting page 2 (**L**ayout, **D**elete Page), and the original template paths aren't necessary on page 1. The document will print splendidly to separations for commercial printing, and the black text will be automatically added to the K (Black, or Key) plate.

The Envelope Roll-Up is not offered in CorelPHOTO-PAINT, and hopefully you've found a compelling reason to use CorelDRAW as a home base for mixed-media compositions. CorelDRAW is the only drawing application at present—PC or Macintosh—that offers complete, user-defined envelope control over objects—text or other types. You can use the fluid property of the Envelope effect to "get into" an image, not simply lay text over an imported image.

In figure 6.30, you can see the completed composition. A floral symbol was grouped with the text block to add a flourish to the page; you can include non-text objects in an envelope to create mini-DTP layouts within similar compositions, or wrap a logo around the side of a photo of a coffee cup (this is how the design on the MOD-CAFE coffee cup was created in Chapter 5, "Complex Fills and Blend Shading").

Figure 6.30
Image retouching is not the sole province of bitmap editors. You can change reality using CorelDRAW's feature set.

The sample images in this chapter were created in a modeling/rendering application, but they could have been photographic and the same editing techniques used. The next time you need to enhance a PhotoCD image, or a DREAM 3D creation, consider using the best of bitmap and vector editing worlds. The tools are in different applications, but they're all yours to use.

Corel OCR-Trace: Converting Bitmaps to Vectors

T he vector format of design presents CorelDRAW users with several advantages. Even an intricate CorelDRAW masterpiece is compact with respect to saved file size, and usually fits on a floppy disk. Vector designs can be scaled to fit on a pinhead or an outdoor display and never lose compositional detail, because vectors are resolution-independent.

The medium of computer *bitmap* (raster) graphics, however, as discussed in Chapter 5, "Complex Fills and Blend Shading," is essential for creating photographic images. Bitmap editing tools are more closely related to physical, traditional design tools. When a traditional artist chooses a pencil or paintbrush tool in an application, the result is generally what one would expect from a physical equivalent.

Because the personal computer has a wonderful faculty for translating data formats, it doesn't matter very much in which electronic media you begin a piece of artwork. Filters are available within CorelDRAW for creating a bitmap copy of a vector design, and when you want a bitmap image to offer the flexibility and resolution independence of a vector image, all you need to do is understand a little about Corel OCR-Trace. Version 6, unlike previous versions of the program, has been reworked and enhanced by Corel's programmers to present even more design opportunities for the graphics professional and business user.

Understanding How OCR and Tracing Works

Corel OCR-Trace has the following two discrete functions:

✔ Optical Character Recognition (OCR)

✔ *Tracing*—using vector shapes to outline contrast areas in bitmap images

Although this chapter emphasizes the artistic possibilities of OCR-Trace—the tracing capability—you might occasionally need to use the OCR capability to convert a physical sheet of text to electronic word processor format. Therefore, you should know how OCR works and how to get the most out of this capability. The following section covers the methods and settings used to get the best results from Optical Character Recognition.

Before You Launch OCR-Trace

Although the process of character recognition is a speedy method of converting printed text to electronic, a little time spent optimizing the scanning hardware and source document can make the experience a more productive one. The following list provides information that you should address before launching OCR-Trace, for character recognition *or* the auto-tracing of a graphic.

✔ If you only intend to scan text or simple, high-contrast graphics, your choice of scanning hardware is easy. A 256-shade grayscale scanner suits printed text, black-and-white photographs, and pen-and-ink drawings adequately, and OCR-Trace accepts images scanned in grayscale mode.

✔ If you have more than three full 8.5" by 11" of text that you want OCR to convert to a text file, your best bet is a flatbed scanner. Prices have dropped in recent years for grayscale and color flatbed scanners. You now can purchase a bare-bones flatbed for the same price that hand-held scanners were initially priced at—less than $300.

 Although graphics can be scanned satisfactorily with a hand-held scanner, a hand-held grayscale scanner is unacceptable for OCR work for two reasons.

✔ The inherent jitter created by dragging a scanning surface across a document can lead to numerous errors in OCR-Trace's recognition process. You might find it quicker and more accurate to manually re-enter printed text in a word processor.

✔ Hand-held scanners typically offer a scanning surface of about 4". Many hand-helds include an auto-stitch utility that aligns multiple passes of scanning and creates a wider scanned page, but this feature is sometimes inaccurate and usually time-consuming.

✔ Make certain that the scanner you use is TWAIN-compliant to ensure that you can scan a document directly into OCR-Trace, thus saving the extra step of acquiring and saving a scanned image from a separate program. TWAIN, a standard created by a consortium of hardware/software manufacturers, enables applications to "shake hands" with future and present hardware peripherals (such as digital cameras and scanners), to provide a common interface that can be accessed from within an application. A meeting of the "twain." More and more manufacturers are adopting the TWAIN convention of working with other manufacturer's programs. Corel Corp. has even written TWAIN-compliant interfaces for the more popular scanner models.

If you didn't choose from the list of supported scanning hardware when you ran Corel Setup, you can make a selection from the list by running Setup again.

When adding scanning hardware to a Windows 95 operating system, keep in mind that 32-bit operating systems and applications require a 32-bit TWAIN module; or the 32-bit application should have built-in 16-bit compatibility features. Don't expect the 16-bit scanning driver software that came with the scanner you purchased in 1994 to automatically work with Windows 95 programs. You might need to reinstall the software drivers, or check the manufacturer's BBS or online site for the most recent drivers for a particular manufacturer's hardware.

✔ Even moderately priced scanners are more sensitive than you might think to stains, lint, dust, and other particles. If you have a borderline document (one whose text is in marginally legible condition due to abuse or age), you should keep the scanner in tip-top shape with periodic cleaning of the user-accessible parts (such as the scanning surface). The less dust that OCR-Trace has to read through, the more accurate the optical recognition.

✔ Placing the edge of a printed page so that it's flush with the edges of the scanning surface might seem like a nit-picky routine, but text that is skewed—at an angle to the horizontal scanning surface—creates OCR accuracy problems. If someone gives you a dozen scanned images that are all crooked, your recourse is to use the OCR-Trace, OCR Settings, Source menu's Deskew feature to correct the document before performing OCR. This option only appears when you've loaded an image to be scanned. The Deskew feature should be considered a desperate measure, however, and one that's unnecessary if someone takes the time to align the document before scanning.

Document-Centricity

✔ Most scanners support multiple sampling rates, usually specified in dots or pixels per inch. OCR-Trace prefers a 300 pixel per inch sampling rate for scanned text documents (although electronic fax files are only sent at 200 pixels per inch). If you specify a file whose resolution is less than 300 pixels per inch, OCR-Trace will notify you of this in a dialog box, and ask whether you want to attempt an OCR session anyway. In general, you should give OCR-Trace the document resolution it needs when you're performing the scan yourself. If a bitmap file comes to you with less resolution, your best bet is to try character recognition anyway. Given a clean, legible typeface in the original scanned image, you might get the results you need with less image resolution.

✔ "Garbage In, Garbage Out" has been the maxim of computer programmers for more than a decade, and it especially applies to original documents you want to scan. OCR-Trace is a program, not a mind-reader, and cursive, hand-lettered text, ornate fonts (such as Fette Fractur), or text the size of warning labels on aspirin bottles are unlikely candidates for character recognition. Your best chances for successful conversion of printed text to electronic is to acquire from a printed page of monospaced type (Courier is a perennial favorite), type no smaller than 10 points, with minimal formatting. OCR-Trace can recognize and format multi-column text, and even tables within a document, but you introduce the possibility of more OCR error when a document has complex composition.

✔ A scanned file of a document should have the minimum of color capability. 1 bit per pixel is the file structure preferred by OCR-Trace; only black or white text pixels are evaluated by the program. Therefore, if the original document looks a little smudged or dense, you might want to use PHOTO-PAINT to clean up the scan before performing character recognition. Most scanners have manual brightness and contrast controls; consider using them before scanning to keep the interior of characters, such as "d" and "o," looking white. Blocked-in characters cause a recognition error, and there's no feature to "train" OCR-Trace to correct these mistakes; multiple pages with the same defective character(s) need to be corrected manually or edited after the OCR session.

If a page is scanned at sufficient resolution, the document's edges are flush with the scanning surface, and the text within the document is clear and legible, you'll find very few necessary corrections to an OCR-Traced file.

How OCR-Trace Recognizes Text

Several commercial software applications are available whose purpose is to help business users convert physical archived documents to electronic format. If you have only an occasional need to convert printed text, however, Corel OCR-Trace just might be your best bet. The accuracy of optical character recognition depends a great deal on the quality of your input.

OCR-Trace performs character and pattern matching when it creates text based on the appearance of a scanned page. As an example, the typed letter O is evaluated by OCR-Trace as having similar properties to the shape of an O that's stored within the OCR-Trace program. Think of a physical stencil of the letter O. If you were to lay this stencil over a printed O of similar size, most (or all) of the printed O would be visible. Although Corel OCR-Trace is more complex and sophisticated, this example is the physical equivalent of what Corel OCR-Trace performs to a selected area of a scanned page.

If you have a magazine article that you need to quickly send across the world through an online service (such as CompuServe or America Online), or if you want to preserve a thesis paper you wrote 20 years ago, let OCR-Trace do the typing.

The following set of steps shows you how to use Corel OCR-Trace's character-recognition capability. For this exercise, you'll use the RECTANGL.TIF image from the CHAP07.EXAMPLES folder on the Bonus CD. The TIF image contains a short paragraph of text, scanned at 250 pixels per inch (less than Corel's recommended 300), at a color capability of 1 bit per pixel.

Using Optical Character Recognition

1. In Corel OCR-Trace, press Ctrl+O (**F**ile, **O**pen) then choose RECTANGL.TIF from the CHAP07.EXAMPLES folder of the *CorelDRAW! 6 Expert's Edition Bonus CD*.

   This is a sample document that uses optical character recognition.

2. Choose **O**CR-Trace, O**C**R **S**ettings.

   Displays a tabbed menu of OCR options.

3. On the Language tab, make certain that English is chosen from the **L**anguage drop-down list, select **C**heck Spelling, and click-and-drag the C**o**nfidence slider to about 70.

   Specifies that spell checking is performed in the language used in document; spelling engine will display a dialog box after conversion; low Confidence slows OCR performance speed, but ensures that you are always prompted for questionable characters after OCR.

4. Click on the Content tab, then check the **S**ingle column text check box.

   The RECTANGL.TIF image is a scan of a single column of text.

In your own OCR sessions, you should check the areas that apply to the scanned image. The settings recommended here only apply to RECTANGL.TIF's contents. On the Source tab, there are options for types of electronic bitmap source images. For example, if you received an electronic fax file, you select fax from the **S**ource drop-down list; you'd also specify paper orientation and any skewing function if the original document was scanned poorly.

5. Click on the Formatting tab.

    Displays the formatting options.

Formatting options can make life easier if you have a complex document of indents, different column widths, or special fonts. The RECTANGL.TIF image has no special qualities, so the only reason for clicking on this tab in the last step is to become familiar with these options for your own future work.

6. Click on OK.

    Returns you to the document window.

7. Choose **O**CR-Trace, Perform **O**CR.

    OCR-Trace recognizes the image for text elements. When it's through, the Verification dialog box appears.

Okay, there's a fictitious word in the RECTANGL.TIF file: GeometryLand. OCR-Trace's Verification module flags you on this, because it recognized the text, but not the word.

8. Click on **I**gnore.

    Verification box closes, document has been converted to editable, electronic text.

9. With the cursor, highlight the text in the Text view window, then type **12** in the text size spin box on the toolbar, then press Enter.

    Scales the text down to a size more appropriate for a document.

Because scanned type has no direct correlation to font size (it's actually a graphic that OCR converts), you might find somewhat laughable text sizes after an OCR session. You can correct font sizes, or even the font choice within an OCR document, by using the features on the Text toolbar.

10. Choose **F**ile, **S**ave, **T**ext.

    Displays the Save Text dialog box.

11. Save the document in a format of word processor you own.

    Saves the text to a format that a word processor can open.

12. Close OCR-Trace without saving the RECTANGL.TIF image.

    Exits program.

If your OCR needs are only occasional, OCR-Trace version 6 is essentially free when you upgrade or purchase CorelDRAW, so it's a prize in the package. For more intensive document conversion, several products are available that range from $200-$700, which can handle formatting, proofing, and learning repeat errors in scanned text. Repeat errors are the recurring inability of an OCR engine to accurately detect a specific character, or group of characters, because the source material is not legible to the OCR reading engine. For example, a typewriter might have an inked-up "o" character. OCR-Trace might see the typed "o" as an "e," and do this consistently, and you cannot "educate" OCR-Trace to see this typed "o" as an "e" within the specific scanned document. But OCR-Trace *is* flexible; you can highlight text in the Text view window and copy it to the Clipboard, and manually correct misspellings within the Text view before you save to a file type.

Document-Centricity

Moving Artwork from the Easel to CorelDRAW!

The Trace part of Corel OCR-Trace operates in an identical manner as optical character recognition, except there is no character matching involved. Instead, OCR-Trace "sees" a line wherever there is a sharp change in color transition in a bitmap image, and creates a path. The definition of *path* is a loose one here; OCR-Trace can create filled outlines, centerlines, woodcut shapes, and even 3-D pyramids from a simple scanned image.

The capability of OCR-Trace to convert bitmap images to vector outlines provides exciting possibilities for the traditional artist, as well as photographers. You can preserve the bulk of compositional content within a digitized photo, a paint program design, even a pen and ink sketch, when you allow OCR-Trace to evaluate outline areas in a bitmap and then create the vector equivalent of the artwork.

The following artistic use of OCR-Trace covered in this chapter shows how to take a simple cartoon, let OCR-Trace convert a copy to a computer format CorelDRAW can work with, then you see the techniques for embellishing the cartoon with fountain fills and blends. It's possible to begin with only the sketchiest of graphical details on paper and wind up with a handsome, unique piece of artwork if you know some of the techniques for porting physical artwork to electronic format.

Scanning into PHOTO-PAINT

Unless you've created a pixel painting using PHOTO-PAINT, Fractal Design Painter, or other paint program, scanning an image is the first step in creating, or re-creating, a digital equivalent. ANT-SCAN.TIF, a bitmap image on the *CorelDRAW! 6 Expert's Edition Bonus CD*, was created as an example image, and was scanned at 150 pixels per inch using a flatbed scanner in grayscale mode.

Before you even flick on the scanner's power switch, some conceptual considerations need to be discussed about working between the physical and electronic media to create artwork.

Don't Use Shading in Your Physical Design

To begin with, you should always omit characteristics of shading from a pen and ink drawing if you know beforehand that shading is a characteristic you'll create using CorelDRAW. For example, the ANT-SCAN.TIF image has only a suggestion of shading; there are a few dark areas that represent shadows in the illustration, but cross-hatching, stippling, or other line art attributes were deliberately left out when the image was inked. This might seem like a subtle point, but you should learn to leave a piece "unfin-ished," because you create extra work for yourself later when original art shading needs to be removed or replaced.

Also, because of the way OCR-Trace performs its magic, it's a good idea to add a short, broken style of line drawing to your artistic repertoire. It's harder for OCR-Trace to create accurate paths that describe long lines than short ones, and closed ink lines will result in an additional path created by OCR-Trace. Keep your physical ink strokes a little on the short side, and occasionally unconnected; you can use CorelDRAW to close paths based on short lines later.

Select Physical Art Materials That Scan Well

Your choice of art materials is your own; the author prefers common 20 lb. laser paper, occasionally bond "all purpose" pads, a #2 pencil from the stationery store, and the felt-tip pen that has two hearts on the pocket clip. Your selection of art materials might shift (and perhaps downgrade!) when you realize that your final output will be from a digital source, and that physical artwork is only an intermediate step in art production. Liquid inks take too long to dry before scanning, and to a scanner, the only quality of an ink that is important is that it covers an area that can be sampled as a solid color.

In the following exercise, you'll take a walk through the acquisition phase of a pen and ink drawing. The sampling session takes place within CorelPHOTO-PAINT, because most physical artwork needs to be retouched before OCR-Trace is used for converting graphics format. If you're following this example with one of your own pen and ink drawings, set your scanner for grayscale acquisition mode (explained later in this

"Astrotext"

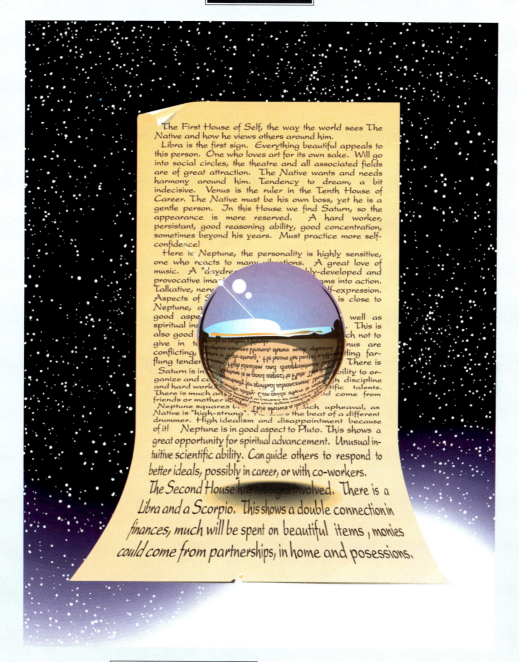

Ingredients: CorelDRAW! v2.01.

Finalist in the Third Annual CorelDRAW! World Design Contest

CorelDRAW 6! Expert's Edition

"Palm"

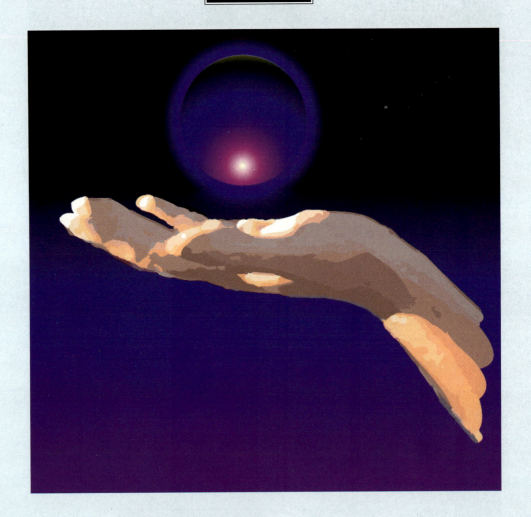

Ingredients: CorelDRAW! 6

CHAPTER 4 "Mastering Color Models and the Fill Tool"

CorelDRAW 6! Expert's Edition

"Homework"

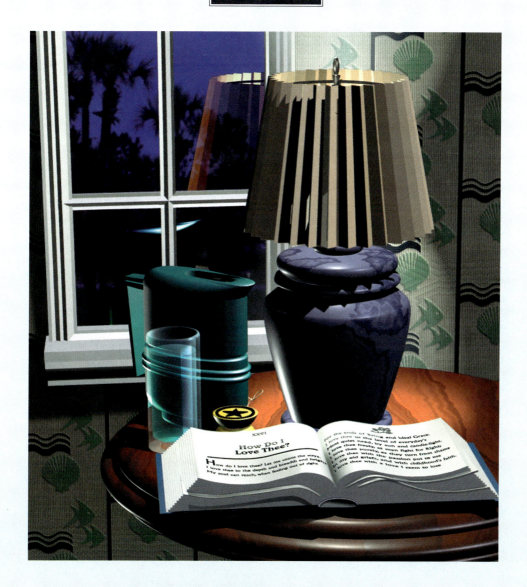

Ingredients: CorelDRAW! 6, MacroModel, PIXAR RenderMan, Fractal Design Painter, Adobe Photoshop.

CHAPTER 6 "Bitmaps and Vector Designs"

"Filmstrip"

Ingredients: CorelMOTION 3D, CorelDRAW, MacroModel, PIXAR RenderMan, Fractal Design Painter, Adobe Photoshop.

CHAPTER 8 "Creating Your Own Fonts"

CorelDRAW 6! Expert's Edition

"Attitude"

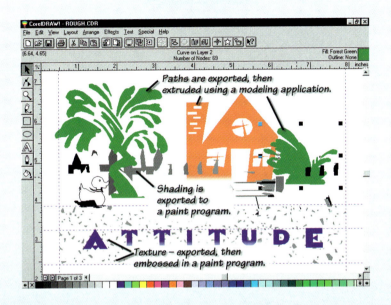

Ingredients: CorelDRAW, Renderize Live, Fractal Design Painter. Assembled in Adobe Photoshop.

"Surprise!"

"The Smirks"

YA GOTTA LOVE 'EM

Ingredients: CorelDRAW

Scanned pen & ink drawing.

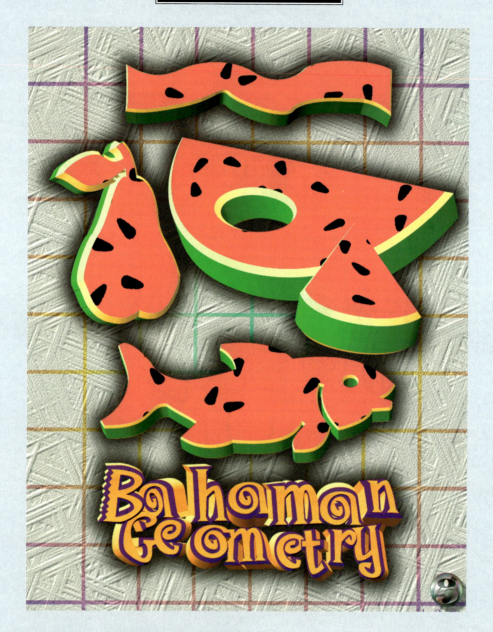

CoreDRAW 6! Expert's Edition

"Duck Chart"

Ingredients: CorelDRAW

"Cactus Todd's"

Ingredients: CorelDRAW, CorelMOTION 3D.

CHAPTER 10 "Adding DEPTH and MOTION"

"DOCUMENT EXCHANGE"

Ingredients: CorelDRAW,
Scanned pen & ink drawing, Fractal Design Painter. Assembled in Adobe Photoshop.

CorelDRAW 6! Expert's Edition

"Plus/Null/Minus"

Ingredients: CorelDRAW.

CorelDRAW 6! Expert's Edition

"Modern Cafe"

Ingredients: CorelDRAW,
Fractal Design Painter, MacroModel, PIXAR RenderMan.

CHAPTER 5 "Complex Fills and Blend Shading"

"Big Top"

Ingredients: CorelDRAW, Renderize Live, MacroModel, Fractal Design Painter.

CHAPTER 3 "Beating Nodes and Paths into Submission (The Easy Way)"

Custom Fountain and Texture Fills

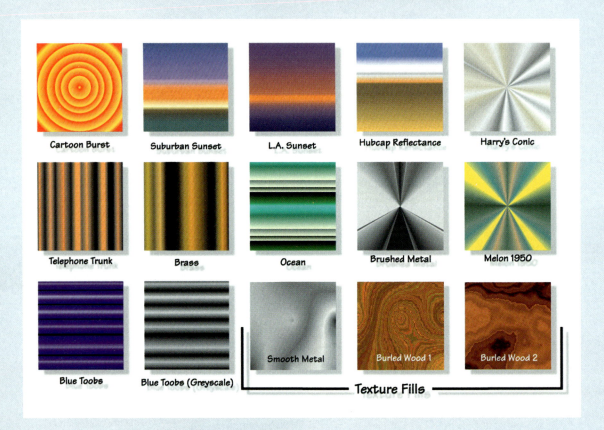

Cartoon Burst

Suburban Sunset

L.A. Sunset

Hubcap Reflectance

Harry's Conic

Telephone Trunk

Brass

Ocean

Brushed Metal

Melon 1950

Blue Toobs

Blue Toobs (Greyscale)

Smooth Metal

Burled Wood 1

Burled Wood 2

Texture Fills

Ingredients: CorelDRAW

CHAPTER 4 "Mastering Color Models and the Fill Tool"

*CorelDRAW! 6
Experts Edition—*
Special Styles
palette for
CorelDEPTH!

Ingredients: CorelDRAW,
CorelDEPTH.

CHAPTER 10 "Adding DEPTH and MOTION"

"Timeless"

Ingredients: CorelDRAW, MacroModel, PIXAR RenderMan. Assembled in Adobe Photoshop.

CHAPTER 6 "Bitmaps and Vector Designs"

section), and scan at a resolution of no less than 100 pixels per inch, but not more than 200. Because of the way OCR-Trace looks at a digitized design, an excessive number of samples per inch can slow down the path-tracing feature, and resulting paths can actually become harsh-looking and stair-stepped in appearance if too much data is presented to OCR-Trace.

Sampling Pen and Ink Work

If you don't choose to use the ANT-SCAN.TIF image for this example, make certain that your scanner is hooked up, turned on, and you have a piece of artwork on the scanning surface before launching CorelPHOTO-PAINT.

1. In PHOTO-PAINT, choose **F**ile, Acq**u**ire Image, then **A**cquire.

   Displays the TWAIN interface specific to your make and model of scanner.

2. Use the native features specific to your scanner to crop the artwork, adjust the tone, sample size (in inches), color depth, and resolution (in pixels per inch or dpi).

   Creates conditions for the most accurate scan with best detail for use with OCR-Trace.

In figure 7.1, you can see the TWAIN interface for a Microtek color flatbed scanner. Your TWAIN interface will most likely look different due to manufacturer's specifications, but there should be equivalents for image resolution, color scanning mode, cropping, and brightness/contrast. Try to leave a little border around the scan area, but do not scan an entire page when the target image takes up a fraction of it! Doing this places an unnecessary burden on your computer's system resources, and results in a much larger file than is required by OCR-Trace.

3. Click on OK (or Scan).

   Launches the digitizing process; depending on your scanner, you might be switched to PHOTO-PAINT after the scan. Otherwise, you might need to click on a Close or OK button to return to PHOTO-PAINT.

4. Choose **F**ile, Save **A**s, then save the image to your hard disk.

   Saves the bitmap image.

The scanning process is not intellectually demanding, but you can't proceed with the OCR-Trace conversion process unless you take some care in sampling the image you work with.

II

Document-Centricity

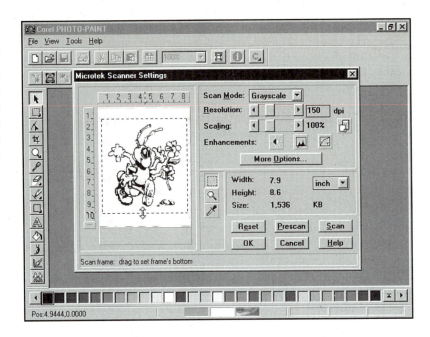

Figure 7.1
Try to use the
TWAIN controls to
correct a target
image as much as
possible; you'll save
post-scanning
retouching time in
PHOTO-PAINT.

Color capability is an elusive quality when it comes to accurately sampling a pen and ink image. OCR-Trace provides the best results (the most accurate path), when presented with a bitmap of 1 bit per pixel color depth, and, ostensibly, a black and white pen and ink drawing should be accurately reflected in a 1 bit per pixel sampling of the original. However, grayscale is a better mode of *acquisition* of black and white work, because an 8 bit per pixel (grayscale, 256 shade) digitized image has more information to work with, and PHOTO-PAINT's tool set offers more features when the target image is grayscale. For example, the Paint tool offers smooth, feathered edges for correcting a place you might have gone off-course while inking your illustration, but only when the target image is Grayscale or higher color mode. In Black and White, 1 bit per pixel mode, the Paint tool is dimmed and you cannot use it in PHOTO-PAINT.

It's only natural that your target image might contain a line you're not entirely pleased with. Or, perhaps you weren't thorough enough erasing pencil lines, and you currently have smudges in the scanned image. Scanner options might not correct all the flaws contained in an original pen and ink drawing, and this is why PHOTO-PAINT is discussed in this chapter. In the next section, you'll see how easily a scanned image can be retouched so that OCR-Trace can convert it to vector format.

Retouching and PHOTO-PAINT

Forget about non-bleed white paints and correction fluid when your pen and ink work is destined to become a digital design. As mentioned earlier in this chapter, a pen and ink design is merely a guideline for OCR-Trace to pattern a collection of vector paths

CorelDRAW will accept. You have filters and digital "paint" that's dry on contact in PHOTO-PAINT to assist in minor clean-up work after scanning.

In figure 7.2, you can see that the author was tidy—but not obsessive—about removing pencil marks from ANT-SCAN.TIF. They're minor, but clearly visible impedances to OCR-Trace's capability to accurately trace the outlines; unless they're removed, OCR-Trace includes them in the resulting converted file. ANT-SCAN.TIF is not an exaggerated example; scanners are quite sensitive to any and all material you use, and the only way to ensure against unwanted marks in a scan is to manually ink a pencil design on a clean sheet of paper placed on top of the pencil sketch.

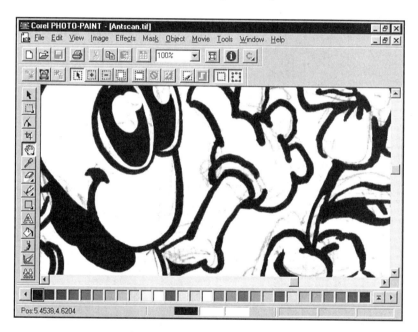

Figure 7.2

Depending on your art materials, pencil marks can persist; PHOTO-PAINT's filters and tools can correct these errors.

Document-Centricity

Fortunately, even dense pencil marks can be filtered out of a scanned image, and grayscale images allow soft-nib PHOTO-PAINT tools to adjust the visual content of a bitmap image. Here's how to clean up ANT-SCAN.TIF, or an image of your own that you'd like to use in the OCR-Trace adventure:

Cleaning Up a Digitized Image

1. In PHOTO-PAINT, open ANT-SCAN.TIF from the EXAMPLES.CHAP07 folder of the *CorelDRAW! 6 Expert's Edition Bonus CD*.

   This is an image used in this chapter's example of converting/enhancing artwork.

2. Choose Effe**c**ts, Color Adjust, Brightness-Contrast-Intensity.

   Displays Brightness-Contrast-Intensity dialog box.

3. Click-and-drag the **I**ntensity slider to about 36, then click on Pre**v**iew.

   Brightens and increases contrast in only lighter shade pixels in image; tends to drop out pencil marks without changing black tones (see fig. 7.3).

Figure 7.3

Intensity increases brightness and contrast simultaneously, removing lighter shades in an original grayscale image.

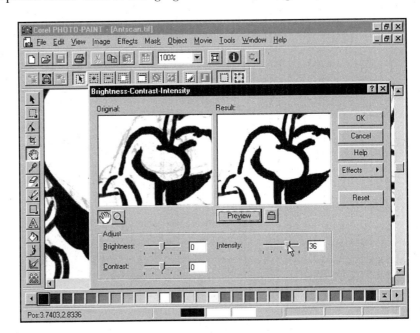

4. Click on OK.

   Returns you to image, with most, or all of the pencil marks gone.

There are a number of different filters you can use for removing parts of an image based on a narrow range of tonal value; the Color Adjust submenu's Gamma and Tone Map commands can also remove "in between" shades from an image without disturbing ink lines. However, Intensity is the quickest method for removing most upper tones from a grayscale composition. To remove *all* defects from ANT-SCAN.TIF, use these steps:

5. Double-click on the Paint tool, then set the Custom Art Brush to: **P**aint: Normal, **S**ize: **10**, **T**ransparency, **R**otate, and **F**latten: **0**, and Soft **e**dge: **80**.

   Chooses the Paint tool and displays Tool Settings Roll-Up. Creates a small, soft nib for tool.

You've created a special eraser tool in the last step. Unfortunately, PHOTO-PAINT's selection of Eraser tool nibs are confined to 1 bit per pixel, which are unsuitable for editing a grayscale image due to the harsh edge they leave.

6. Click on the white swatch on the color palette.

   Sets foreground color to white for the Paint tool.

7. Type **200** in the Zoom level field on the toolbar, then scroll the window until you find an area where pencil lines are still apparent.

   Zooms picture in for precision editing; finds target area(s) for retouching.

8. Click-and-drag the Paint tool around areas of pencil marks in the image.

   Retouches away the pencil marks. (See figure 7.4.)

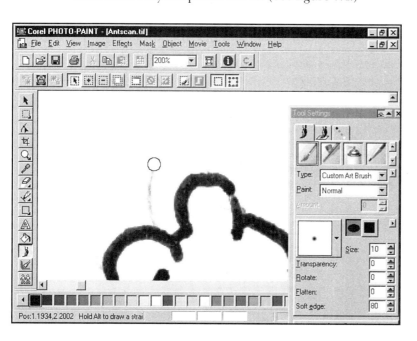

Figure 7.4
Use the Brush tool as a soft-edge eraser for retouching unwanted areas in the illustration.

Document-Centricity

If you make a mistake, press Ctrl+Z to **E**dit, **U**ndo your last action. Continue retouching areas that need pencil lines removed, then when you're finished:

9. Choose **F**ile, Save **A**s, then save the image as ANTCLEAN.TIF to hard disk.

   Saves your retouching work.

Tip If you feel that the default cursors in PHOTO-PAINT interfere with your view of editing or painting work, you can specify an accurate shape cursor instead, like those shown in the figures in this section. Choose **T**ools, **O**ptions, then select the Use shape **c**ursor check box.

As mentioned earlier, shorter pen strokes with occasional breaks in lines in original artwork can make OCR-Trace's conversion of the art to vector format go quicker. Also, the resulting collection of paths will be easier to work with in CorelDRAW. However, if short strokes don't fit your artistic style, there's a trick in PHOTO-PAINT to edit the scanned illustration; this trick is covered in the following section.

How OCR-Trace "Sees" an Image

Whether it's color or black and white artwork, OCR-Trace evaluates bitmap image areas the same way when it creates vector paths; the program "looks for" areas of high contrast, then creates a path at the edge of the contrast. Because of this method, closed paths are drawn *on top of* paths to represent an original design. For example, an illustration of a ball with a fat outline—OCR-Trace begins with a white background, creates a black-filled path, then a smaller white-filled path to represent the ball. In figure 7.5, two different artistic approaches have been used to draw a ball—broken pen lines will generate several filled paths with no image "interior" shape, while solid original lines are OCR-Traced as a collection of shapes on top of one another.

Figure 7.5
OCR-Trace views an illustration having closed shapes as a layered stack of closed, filled paths.

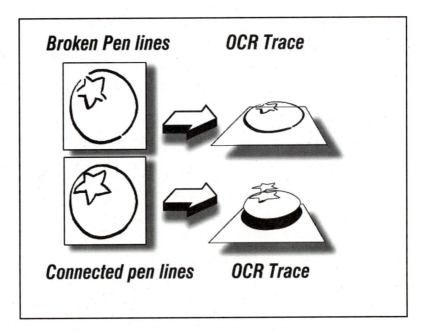

OCR-Trace cannot combine paths to create "open" objects whose interior can be filled, and this reality leads to two different approaches to manually creating "holes" in vector art that you can fill later in CorelDRAW. The first method is to simply let OCR-Trace create paths based on color areas in bitmap artwork, then use the Combine command in CorelDRAW with two or more objects to create subpaths ("holes"). Let's call the combining technique "The Post-Production Approach"; we'll use this technique later in this chapter after the OCR-Trace file has been imported to CorelDRAW.

For right now, however, let's consider an alternative to post-production path "surgery," and look at a way to optimize the bitmap image for OCR-Trace *before* the tracing occurs; the "Pre-Production Approach" can save you grief in the long run; less node editing required in CorelDRAW can mean you have more time to shade and refine the illustration. This method of optimizing a bitmap image before using OCR-Trace is one we discuss in the following set of steps; however, the steps outlined for CorelDRAW editing of OCR-Trace images later in this chapter use "Post-Production" editing techniques.

If you examine the ANT-SCAN.TIF image carefully, you'll find that the outline of the ant is actually a continuous pen stroke—the upper body is connected to the hands, and you can visually trace a rather long outline around the ant. If the final design—the vector copy imported and enhanced in CorelDRAW—were to be sent to an imagesetter with the long, complex path outline unbroken, the design might not print. This means that you should perform some Pre-Production work in PHOTO-PAINT to make smaller shapes from the continuous outline, or use methods described later in this chapter to use CorelDRAW to break the path that OCR-Trace produced from the original pen outline.

In figure 7.6, you can see a small break created in one of the ant's forearms. Doing this allows OCR-Trace to view the arm as a separate shape to be outlined, and the main body of the ant is represented as a vector object consisting of several less nodes.

Your choice of editing tools for breaking a continuous bitmap line should be the Paint tool, set to a hard edge (see fig. 7.6 for settings), and you should plan breaks in a bitmap line in places that are easy to mend using CorelDRAW's tools. In the example in figure 7.6, the breaks in the arm can easily be connected by creating small objects with CorelDRAW's Pencil tool; the objects are then filled with black, and the printed piece never reveals that the ant outline is composed of several objects.

You don't have to perform the preceding editing steps with the ant example, however—the technique is mentioned only as one you can use in your own work when there are an enormous amount of connected lines in the scanned image. The ant image is not of sufficient complexity to resort to bitmap editing before OCR-Tracing, and we'll do all the editing work in CorelDRAW to make the correct path combinations as a "Post-Production" technique with the vector information about the ant image in this example.

II

Document-Centricity

Figure 7.6

Create a break in a continuous line within a bitmap image to allow OCR-Trace to create smaller, more numerous paths.

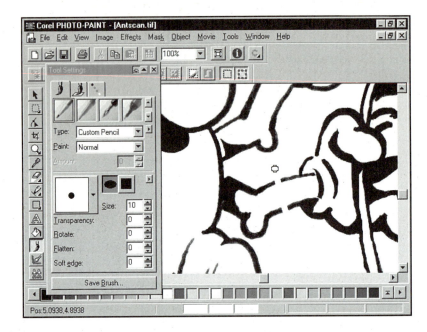

Setting Options in Corel OCR-Trace

ANTCLEAN.TIF is provided on the *CorelDRAW! 6 Expert's Edition Bonus CD* (in the EXAMPLES.CHAP07 folder); it's a version of the original scanned cartoon that has been cleaned up for use in OCR-Trace. The following example is a walk-through of the steps and options for converting the ant cartoon, or a scanned image of your own, to vector format.

Achieving the Best Vector Conversion

1. Launch Corel OCR-Trace from Win95's Start menu.

   Loads the application used to convert the scanned image.

2. Press Ctrl+O (**F**ile, **O**pen), choose ANTCLEAN.TIF from the EXAMPLES.CHAP07 folder of the *CorelDRAW! 6 Expert's Edition Bonus CD*, then click on **O**pen.

   Loads the ANTCLEAN.TIF image into the Bitmap view window.

3. Choose **I**mage, Conver**t** to Black and White.

   Displays the Convert to Black and White dialog box.

> **Note**   Although you might go through great pains to retouch a grayscale mode image, it's usually best to convert a copy of it to black and white (1 bit per pixel mode) in OCR-Trace, to ensure that the trace doesn't detect any bitmap values *other* than black or white. Because OCR-Trace is capable of detecting edges between colors, a grayscale image might generate several unwanted paths around areas of near-black or near-white, slowing processing and resulting in an overly complex vector design.

4. Check the Preview check box, place the cursor between the elevator buttons on the Threshold spin box, then increase the value to about 195.

   Increases the "break point" at which OCR-Trace views gray pixels in the scanned image as black. (See figure 7.7.)

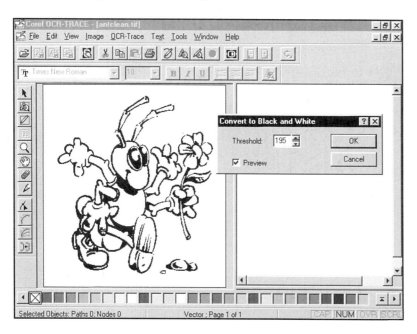

Figure 7.7
The Convert to Black and White dialog box allows you to specify whether shades of grays in a scan are converted to black, or to white.

The Threshold feature is terrific for "fattening up" lines in a scanned illustration. A high Threshold value, in this example, creates more substantial black areas in the ANTCLEAN image, and OCR-Trace will create paths that are more well-defined and easier to work with. However, if your illustration already features heavy lines, you might want to reduce the Threshold value; a value of 128 means that pixels above 50% black will turn to white, and pixels darker than 50% black will become black.

5. Click on OK.

   Reduces the ANTCLEAN image to black or white areas.

Before executing the trace of the illustration, let's take a brief detour to graphically demonstrate what your options are for vector tracing. In figure 7.8, you can see a faint "O" shape, constructed of bitmap pixels. When OCR-Trace evaluates the tonal areas in such an "o," it first places a circular object around an averaged sample of the color bitmap pixels; the resulting vector shape contains nodes at points of inflection (change of path), and it's smooth in appearance because OCR-Trace's interpretation of the bitmap outline is an approximation—it averages sharp pixel edges into smooth paths. Additionally, OCR-Trace creates a second object on top of the first to make the counter in the "O." A white filled shape on top of a black shape is the result.

Figure 7.8
OCR-Trace averages the shape constructed by hard-edged pixels to produce smooth, rounded vector objects.

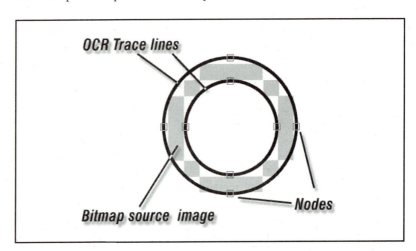

Noise, in computer graphics, is a term used to describe random pixels around the edge of color contrast in an image. In figure 7.9, you can see a "noisy" 1 bit per pixel curve that's the product of gray pixels being converted to black or white. It's a time-consuming process to manually remove noise from an image, but fortunately OCR-Trace has a feature for ignoring noise around color edges, which we'll get to next.

6. Choose **O**CR-Trace, Trace **S**ettings.

   Displays the Trace Settings dialog box. By default, the menu tab pertaining to the Outline method of tracing, the one used in this example, is displayed.

7. Click-and-drag the N**o**de Reduction to about 70.

   Specifies that the resulting trace slider will feature less nodes (and a slightly less accurate tracing).

8. Click-and-drag the **C**olor tolerance to 0.

   Specifies that you want OCR-Trace to follow color edges in the illustration very closely.

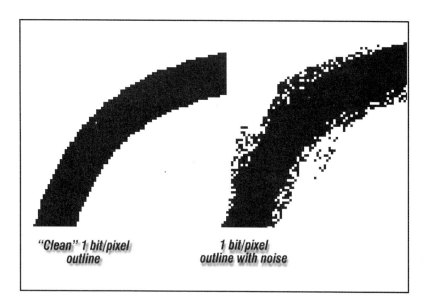

Figure 7.9
Occasionally, a grayscale image converted to Black and White produces noise around image edges.

Color tolerance is generally used to specify how closely vector paths are created based on color difference OCR-Trace finds in the source image. However, there is only black or white in ANTCLEAN.TIF, so the result of setting the Color tolerance to 0 here is that OCR-Trace will fit vector curves to the path it "sees" in ANTCLEAN.TIF with a good degree of accuracy.

9. Enter **14** in the **N**oise reduction spin box (or use the elevator buttons). (See fig. 7.10.)

   Specifies that pixels that are up to 14 pixels away from a substantial number of pixels in the illustration are considered part of the resulting vector shape.

10. Click on OK.

    Returns you to OCR-Trace's workspace.

11. Choose **O**CR-Trace, Perform **T**race, then choose by **O**utline.

    OCR-Trace creates a number of vector objects to describe the drawn lines in ANTCLEAN.TIF.

Depending on the complexity of a source image and the speed and memory of your computer, the tracing process can take anywhere from five seconds to several minutes. In figure 7.11, to better show you OCR-Trace's handiwork, **V**iew, O**b**jects, Wir**e** Frame has been chosen. You can clearly see that the ant cartoon is now fairly well represented as a collection of overlapping vector objects.

Figure 7.10
The complexity (number of nodes) in a Traced curve, and the fidelity to the bitmap drawing are specified in the Trace Settings dialog box.

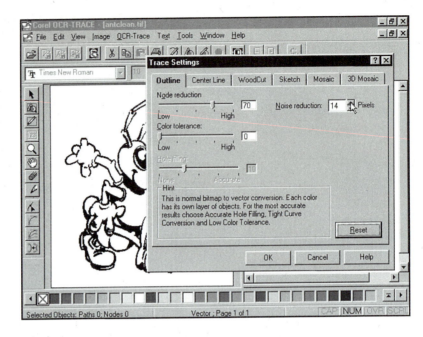

Figure 7.11
OCR-Trace creates a copy of the color information in a bitmap image as a collection of overlapping vector paths.

12. Choose **F**ile, **S**ave, **V**ector.

    Displays the Save Vector dialog box.

13. Click on the Save as **t**ype drop-down list, and choose Corel Presentation Exchange 6.0 (CMX).

    Specifies a vector format for the OCR-Trace work that's compatible with CorelDRAW.

14. Name the file MARCHANT.CMX, and save it to your hard disk.

    Saves the vector tracing to your hard disk.

15. Close OCR-Trace; do not save changes to the ANTCLEAN.TIF image.

    You don't need a black and white converted illustration cluttering your hard disk.

The Corel Presentation Exchange format is a limited subset of the CorelDRAW file format; it can contain vector information, but not information about links and control objects such as you produce with blends, extrudes, and dimension lines. However, OCR-Trace doesn't generate dynamically linked objects, so the format is okay for importing into CorelDRAW. Alternatively, the AI (Adobe Illustrator) and Windows Metafile (WMF) formats can successfully describe the vector shapes created by OCR-Trace in a format organization that CorelDRAW can import.

Working with Imported Vector Files

After OCR-Trace creates a vector version of an illustration, it's time to embellish the artwork; the following sections describe how to break apart objects, add fills, and generally finish a scanned drawing in a "color by number" fashion. Because this section concentrates on how to work with the objects produced by OCR-Trace, we're going to eliminate color considerations from the design, and simply work in grayscale. All the steps you'll learn in this section *could* add color to the design; feel free to experiment with color while enhancing the design.

In the following example, we chose not to edit the bitmap image in the "Pre-Production" technique explained earlier in this chapter, to give us a chance to work with bitmap-to-vector conversions in a "Post-Production" style within CorelDRAW. Let's see how an overly complex path can be manually edited using CorelDRAW tools. MARCHANT.CMX is in the EXAMPLES.CHAP07 folder of the *CorelDRAW! 6 Expert's Edition Bonus CD*; you can use this OCR-Trace of the ant cartoon if you didn't perform the previous example. Here's how to import and edit the OCR-Trace image file:

Importing and Editing an OCR-Trace Image

1. Launch CorelDRAW, then click on the Import button on the toolbar (or chose **F**ile, Import; Ctrl+I).

   Displays the Import dialog box.

2. Choose MARCHANT.CMX from the EXAMPLES.CHAP07 folder of the *CorelDRAW! 6 Expert's Edition Bonus CD*, then click on Imp**o**rt.

   Imports the trace OCR-Trace created (see fig. 7.12).

Figure 7.12

Objects created in OCR-Trace are always imported as a grouped collection of objects.

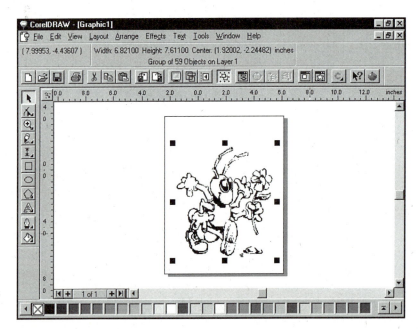

Occasionally, an imported group of vectors don't automatically center to CorelDRAW's design page. If this happens, you can click-and-drag the group to the center of the page, or if precision is called for in an assignment, click on the align and Distribute button on the toolbar (or press Ctrl+A), click on the horizontal and vertical align to center buttons, then choose Center of Page from the Align to drop-down list.

3. Choose the Zoom tool, then marquee zoom into the area where the ant's hand is holding the flower.

   This is the area you'll edit first.

4. Press spacebar, then click on the Ungroup button on the toolbar (or choose **A**rrange, **U**ngroup; Ctrl+U).

Toggles to the Pick tool; Ungroups the imported design; the status line should say 48 objects selected.

5. Click anywhere outside of the ant cartoon, press F10, then click on the outside of the black edge around the ant's arm.

   Deselects the 48 objects; toggles to the Shape tool, displays all the nodes that make up the outside vector path (see fig. 7.13).

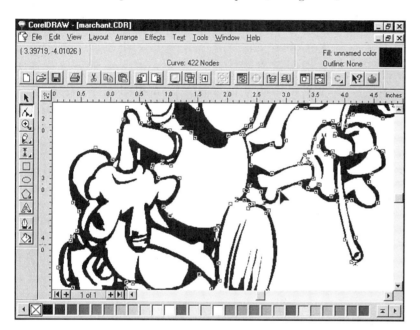

Figure 7.13
An unbroken bitmap line can produce several hundred vector nodes along a path.

Depending on the exact Node Reduction settings you used in OCR-Trace, this ant outline could be composed of anywhere from 300 to 400 nodes. This is an unacceptably large number of control points for a single vector shape—in its present state, the design might fail to print to an imagesetter. To correct this problem, use these steps:

6. Press spacebar, press Ctrl+C (**E**dit, **C**opy), then press PageDown.

   Toggles to the Pick tool, copies the selected object to the Clipboard, opens the Insert Page dialog box.

7. Press Enter, then press Ctrl+V (**E**dit, **P**aste).

   Confirms the default settings (to add a single page after page 1); pastes a copy of the selected shape into page 2.

There are a number of ways to isolate an object on a page for editing, but copying it to a new page is perhaps the quickest. CorelDRAW pastes the copy of the overly complex path in exactly the same relative position to its original on page 1, so it's no problem to insert your edited work back into the design when you're finished.

8. Press spacebar, click on the lower part of the ant's arm, then right-click and choose **B**reak Apart from the shortcut menu.

   Makes the overly complex path an open path (see fig. 7.14).

Figure 7.14

A path that contains too many nodes can be broken into two or more paths.

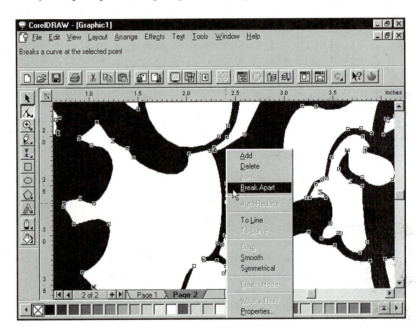

When a filled path is broken, it loses its fill. For this reason, you must switch to wireframe view to continue editing, because the object is now invisible in preview mode!

9. Click on the Wireframe toggle button on the toolbar (or press Shift+F9).

   Switches the active document window to wireframe view.

10. Click on the other side of the ant's arm, then right-click and choose **B**reak Apart from the shortcut menu.

    You now have a single path, with two breaks in it.

11. Press Ctrl+K (**A**rrange, **B**reak Apart).

    Breaks the single path into two open paths at the points where you create breaks in the path; Shape tool is replaced by the Pick tool.

> **Tip** There's a difference between creating a break in a path, and breaking an object apart. A broken path is still a single path, with combined subpath elements. This is why you need to use the **A**rrange, **B**reak Apart command to split the overly complex object into separate objects.

12. Click outside of the path.

   Deselects the 2 selected paths.

13. Choose **L**ayout, Snap to **O**bjects.

   New and existing objects are now attracted to objects and nodes you create or edit.

14. Click on the arm part of the path.

   Selects the path; the status line should say you've selected a curve with a little more than 100 nodes, and that the path has no outline or fill.

15. Press F5 (or choose the Pencil tool), click on a visible node, then click at the other visible node.

   Connects and closes the path for the ant's arm (see fig. 7.15).

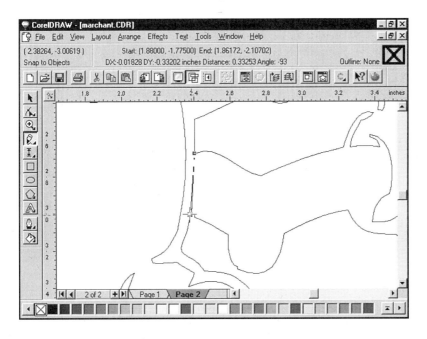

Figure 7.15
The Snap to Objects command makes it easy to precisely close a path using the Pencil tool.

Document-Centricity

16. Press spacebar, click on the body part of the path, press spacebar, then repeat the preceding step.

    Selects the remaining open path; toggles back to the Pencil tool, closes the path.

If you're ambitious at this point, you might want to try creating breaks in the path in other areas, such as the ant's right arm(s). Use the Arrange, Break Apart command to create additional open paths, then close them with the Pencil tool, as seen in figure 7.16.

Figure 7.16
Simpler filled paths can be more easily printed to high-end imagesetters.

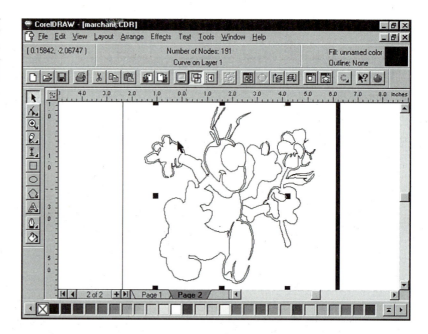

Because the Snap to Objects feature attracts your Pencil tool cursor, you can be assured that the objects created by breaking apart this overly complex path are perfectly aligned, and that breaks won't show when you print the design. When you're finished editing, follow these steps:

17. Double-click on the Pick tool, then press Ctrl+C.

    Selects all the objects on page; copies objects to Clipboard.

18. Press PageUp.

    Moves you to page 1 of the document.

19. With the Pick tool, click on the original, overly complex object, then press Delete.

    Deletes the original object.

20. Press Ctrl+V (Edit, Paste), then press Shift+PageDown.

    Pastes the collection of Clipboard objects into Page 1; Shift+PageDown moves the objects to the back of the object "stack."

21. Press Ctrl+S (**F**ile, **S**ave), then save the file as MARCHANT.CDR to your hard disk.

    Saves your work at this intermediate stage.

You can delete page 2 from the MARCHANT.CDR document at any point now by choosing **L**ayout, **D**elete Page; specify page 2 in the **D**elete page spin box, then click on OK. You should also uncheck the **L**ayout, Snap to **O**bjects feature immediately after you're through with the feature (like right now!); Snap to Objects is an unwelcome feature when you want to edit, draw, and move shapes in an unrestricted fashion.

Filling Vector "Holes" with Fills

There are several areas in the MARCHANT design where original, pen-drawn lines were unconnected; therefore, an empty space exists within the design. These spaces can be filled with CorelDRAW objects. This is the gist of turning a black and white drawing into a magnificent, tonal illustration.

Because the objects that make up the design aren't grouped right now—nor should they be, to allow free access to an individual object—it would be difficult to work around the piece without first creating a new layer for the additional objects.

We'll begin slowly in the MARCHANT composition in the next set of steps, as you'll see how to build a work methodology as you also build a more complex composition. Here's how to organize and work within the imported vector design:

Organizing and Filling the Design

1. Choose **L**ayout, **L**ayers Manager (or press Ctrl+F3).

    Displays the Layers Roll-Up.

2. Right-click over the Layer (Black and White) title on the Layers list area, then choose **D**elete from the shortcut menu.

    Deletes a superfluous layer that contains no information about the ant design. OCR-Trace exports in the CMX format produce this layer when a CMX file is imported to CorelDRAW, and Corel Corp. has no explanation for the curious, yet harmless phenomenon.

3. Right-click over the Layers list area, and select **N**ew from the shortcut menu.

   A new layer appears on the list, entitled Layer 2.

4. Type **Fills.**

   The highlighted Layer 2 text changes to Fills.

5. Click outside the Fills title, then click-and-drag the Fills title to the Layer 1 title.

   Closes the text editing mode for the Fills title; changes its order beneath the page so that it's underneath Layer 1.

6. Click-and-drag the layer selection pointer to the Fills layer title.

   Specifies that all additional drawn objects in the composition will be created on the Fills layer (see fig. 7.17).

Figure 7.17
Editing can be performed to all layers in the image, but object *creation* is limited to the currently selected layer.

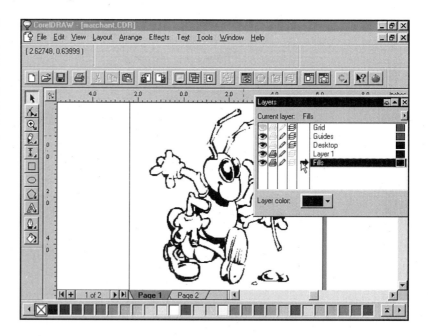

7. With the Zoom tool, marquee zoom into the ant's hand that's holding the flower.

   This is the first area to which you'll apply shading.

8. With the Pick tool, click on the first two fingers of the ant's hand.

The status line states that the filled path is a closed path containing an unnamed color (it's white) on Layer 1. Unless a closed path is filled with a color from Corel's own default color palette, the color will appear as "unnamed" on the Status Bar. However, if you check out the RGB values for the object, using the Uniform Fill dialog box, you'll see that the object is R: 255, G: 255, and B: 255 in component color values. In other words, the fill is white.

Occasionally, "poking around" an imported vector design to see which areas are the printable page, and which areas contain white fill, is an easy, quick method for determining which areas can be recolored, and which areas need a closed, filled path created behind them to add shading to the composition. Because the fingers are a closed shape on Layer 1, all you need to do to color them is decide on a fill. Here's a suggested approach that will make the design look more dimensional and airbrush-like:

9. Click on the Fill tool, then click on the Fountain Fill button.

   Displays the Fountain Fill dialog box.

10. Click-and-drag the direction in the preview box to the right, until the linear fill makes a left-to-right, black to white transition.

    The ant cartoon's fingers have a shadow beneath and to the left of them. This suggests that the light source is from the upper right in the drawing, so the direction of the fountain fill should be similar.

11. Click on the black From: color box in the Color blend field, then click on the 30% black swatch.

    Makes the shading less intense; medium gray will not compete for attention quite as much against the black objects in the design.

12. Click on OK.

    The ant fingers are filled.

Let's face it; going to the Fountain Fill box—through the Fill tool—is a tedious process for shading an entire illustration. You *can* customize the toolbar to add the Fountain Fill dialog box to it for handy access (see Chapter 2, "Customizing CorelDRAW!"), but you also have two invaluable features in CorelDRAW that can be used as a method for copying and speeding up the shading process. Here's one method:

13. Click on the bottom white finger of the ant.

    Status line indicates that this object is already filled, so it's cool to copy a fill for it.

14. Choose **E**dit, Copy Properties **F**rom.

    Displays the Copy Attributes (Properties) dialog box (see fig. 7.18).

Figure 7.18
Use the Copy
Properties From
command to quickly
assign the same fill
to several objects.

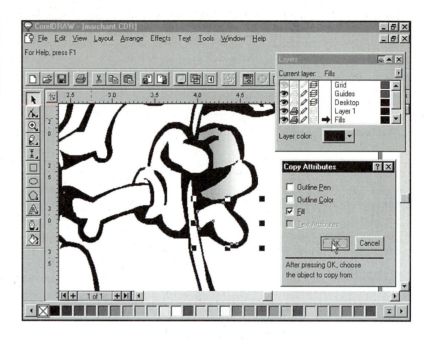

15. Click on **F**ill, then click on OK.

    Cursor turns into a huge arrow, which you're supposed to click over the source object.

16. Click over the Fountain Filled fingers.

    Copies the fill to the second finger shape.

17. Press Ctrl+S (**F**ile, **S**ave).

    Saves your work up to this point.

One of the advantages to working with a vector trace of your design, as opposed to creating something you envision with CorelDRAW's native tools, is that there is a quality of humanity about the shapes that represent the outline of a pen and ink drawing. You'll notice, as you zoom in, that subtle nuances of uneven pen strokes—and control over the flow of an angle or curve—are visible and obvious. You can't achieve the same "feel" as a natural pen and ink drawing with Corel's tools, but Corel's features can convert pen and inks to a format that, as you can see, become a pleasant, even exciting collage of electronic and traditional artistic methods.

Additionally, because the objects that represent the outlines of a pen and ink sketch are wider than Corel's default Pencil lines, you can now hide a fairly crudely drawn outline behind these objects to fill in areas of the design. You'll see how a quick, unusual technique can be used for completing the design in the next section.

Everything in a Design Can Be a Fill

A filled object with no outline attribute can easily replace an outline attribute for a closed path, and by using paths as outlines, you can tap into many design advantages. A closed, filled path *playing the visual role* of an outline can be scaled without adjusting any outline width. If you think about it, there are really only two attributes to a vector object: outline and fill. Certainly, a cartoon such as this ant could be constructed with a minimum of paths, and a heavy, angled outline could be assigned to the objects as a substitute for the many objects in the MARCHANT.CDR design, which represent the original pen and ink lines. However, the expressiveness of the objects that portray outlines in this design simply can't be imitated with Outline properties; the unevenness of the "outline" objects contribute to the overall design, and you should keep this fact in mind when designing.

There are presently areas in the MARCHANT design which are actually unfilled and display the paper color, as opposed to object filled with white. To color them in, you'll use the Fills layer you created in the last example. Although the objects that make up the outline of the cartoon ant suggest curves in many areas, the following example demonstrates that straight, short path segments can be used very effectively for creating a closed fill object.

Filling in an Open Design Area

1. Press F3.

   Returns your view of the document to the last Zoomed state.

2. Press F5 (or click on the Pencil tool).

   Selects the Pencil tool.

If you look closely at the area where the ant's hand meets its arm, there's a gap between objects representing the outline of the ant on Layer 1. You could also click on this area with the Pick tool to discover that this is an unfilled area, but the point is that the empty area needs to be filled.

3. Click on the point where the cartoon hand's cuff meets the hand.

   You've begun a path with the Pencil tool.

4. Double-click on the first knuckle of the thumb, then continue double-clicking, clockwise, at points where the hand's outline takes a sudden change in direction.

   You're creating a path to fill on Fill layer behind layer 1.

Make sure that the path segments stay within the objects on Layer 1. In figure 7.19, you can see the path needed to create a fill object.

Figure 7.19

Use straight line segments, and keep the path outline concealed behind the objects on Layer 1.

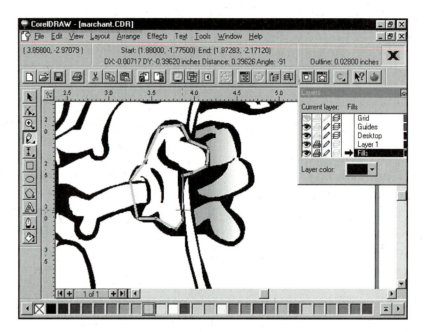

The preceding figure is exaggerated to emphasize the path—it's wider than default lines created by the Pencil tool, and because the path is drawn beneath the objects on Layer 1, you probably will only see reverse video preview lines as you create the path.

If you find areas of the path you've created fall inside of the hand objects on Layer 1, these areas won't be filled. To remedy this, you can add nodes to the path (click on a path with the Shape tool, then press +), or:

5. Press F10, click on a line segment then right-click and choose To **C**urve, from the shortcut menu.

   Converts a straight path segment to a curved one (see fig. 7.20).

6. Click on the Fill Tool, then click on the Special Fill Roll-Up button on the menu flyout.

   Displays the Special Fill Roll-Up.

7. Click on Update From, then click on the finger fills.

   Preview on the Special Fills Roll-Up changes to the fountain fill you clicked on.

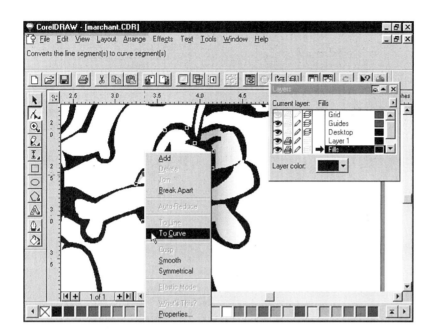

Figure 7.20
Except for specialized operations such as Align, the shortcut menu is a good alternative to the Node Edit Roll-Up.

II

Document-Centricity

8. Click-and-drag in the Special fill preview so that the 30% black fill color is to the right, and white is on the left.

   Reverses the direction of the fountain fill.

9. Make sure the path you created is still selected, then click on Apply.

   Applies the reversed fountain fill to the path beneath the hand shape (see figure 7.21).

10. Right-click on the "x" on the color palette.

    Removes the outline property from the object.

11. Press Ctrl+S (**F**ile, **S**ave).

    Saves your work up to this point.

In the last two examples, you've seen how to make quick work of filling in the cartoon by beginning with only one fountain fill. Copying and editing a fountain fill not only saves time, but also insures a certain tonal consistency within a design.

Figure 7.21
You can copy, and alter, fill properties when you use the Special Fill Roll-Up.

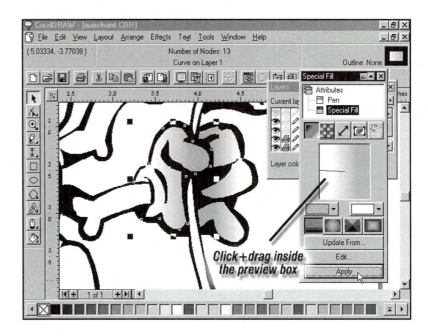

> **Tip** An object drawn using straight path lines is inherently less complex than an object composed of curved segments. Straight line vector shapes also take up less saved file space than curved-line compositions.

In the preceding example, and in your own work, you can be a little more indulgent with adding nodes to a straight-line object. Complex fills, such as fountain fills, are more likely to print when they fill an area defined by a straight-line path. A straight-line only object is much easier to describe in PostScript language, and you shouldn't usually have problems printing this sort of shape, as long as the number of nodes doesn't exceed 1,500 for a single path.

Although you can't change the Mid-point, the Edge pad, or the number of steps in a fountain fill directly from the Roll-Up, the Special Fills Roll-Up can see you through most of a design assignment. It's more convenient for accessing a wide range of texture, fountain, and other fills than constantly clicking on the Fill tool, and you can roll it up without closing it when screen real estate is at a premium.

In figure 7.22, the original fountain fill has been modified once again, this time to a darker beginning color, and you can see that the tone and direction makes it a perfect fill for another of the white objects on Layer 1.

> **Note** You can create a steeper transition between fountain fill colors, and move the mid-point of such a fill through the Fountain Fill dialog box, but the *linearity*—the way a color makes a transition to the next—always remains constant.

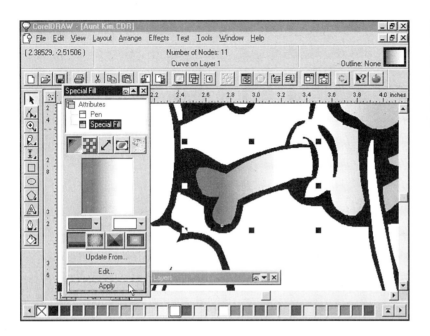

Figure 7.22

You can change the From and To colors of a sampled fill, then apply it to a new object with the special Fill Roll-Up.

To create the *appearance* that a fountain fill "stays" at the From color for a while, then makes the color transition in a non-linear fashion, try breaking an object into two separate objects as described in the first ant cartoon example. Then, fill one object with a uniform color that's the same as the fountain fill's From color, and then fill the other object with the fountain fill. If you check out MARCHANT.CDR, the finished assignment in the GALLERY folder of the CHAP07 folder, you'll see that this is how some "steep," non-linear shading was accomplished in the ant's arms.

Irregular Objects Require Blend Steps

In Chapter 5, "Complex Fills and Blend Shading," the use of the Blends feature was used to fill a bouncing ball with what appears to be a fountain fill. Blends—the auto-creation of intermediate objects and colors between two control objects—can be a life-saver when an irregularly shaped object needs a smoothly shaded fill.

The ant's head is just such an irregularly shaped object. In the next example, you'll create a path on the Fill layer (the ant's head is an open shape on Layer 1), modify the path to fit between the line objects on Layer 1, then use a compound Blend fill to give the ant head the same "look" as the hands.

Creating Compound Blend Shading

1. Use the arrows on the scroll bars to move your view to the ant's head.

   This is the area you'll fill next.

2. Press F5.

   Switches cursor to the Pencil tool.

3. Double-click around the ant's head until you've created a closed path.

   You shouldn't need more than about 10 subpaths (10 nodes).

4. Press F10, then marquee select all the nodes, click on a single node, right-click and choose To **C**urve from the shortcut menu, then right-click and choose **S**mooth.

   Switches to the Shape tool; converts all object nodes to Smooth; all straight path segments are curved (see fig. 7.23).

Figure 7.23
You can quickly make a rounded object by changing straight line segments to curved, then to Smooth node property.

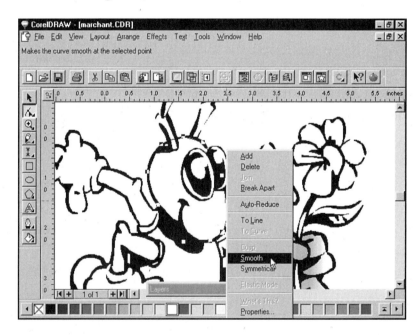

You might need to use the Shape tool now to adjust a few of the nodes to hide all parts of the path segments behind the black outline objects on Layer 1. Having done that, use these steps:

5. Press spacebar, click on 10% black on the color palette, then press +.

    Toggles to the Pick tool; fills the object with 10% black; duplicates object, and duplicate is now selected.

6. Click on the 50% black swatch on the color palette, then click-and-drag on the lower left selection handle in an up and right direction.

    Changes the fill of the duplicate, resizes the shape and moves it toward the upper right of its original position.

7. Click-and-drag the duplicate object to inside of the original shape.

    Keep it to the upper left Inside of the original. This duplicate object will be used as a control object for blending.

8. Shift+click on the 10% black original, then press Ctrl+B.

    Adds the original to the current selection, displays the Blend Roll-Up.

9. Type **14** in the Steps spin box, click on Apply, then right-click on the "x" on the color palette.

    Adds 14 intermediate shapes between the selected objects; fill of the blend shapes makes transition between selected object (*control object*) shapes; removes the outline property from all the component Blend object paths (see fig. 7.24).

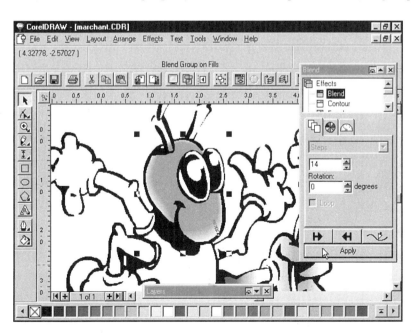

Figure 7.24

Blend objects can make a smooth transition from beginning to end color in objects whose shapes are not symmetrical.

10. Click outside of the Blend objects, then click on the 50% black shape.

    Deselects the Blend group; selects only the 50% black control object.

11. Press +, then click-and-drag the shape's lower left selection handle up and to the right until the shape is about 1/4" in width or height.

    Copies, resizes, and repositions the third object.

12. Click-and-drag the smallest object inside of the second object's border so that it is to the upper left inside the 50% black object.

    Places the object in a position where it can represent a highlight on the ant's forehead.

13. Click on white on the color palette.

    Turns the smallest object white.

14. Shift and click on the 50% black object.

    The small white and 50% black object are now selected.

15. Click on the Apply button on the Blend Roll-Up.

    Creates 14 blend objects between the 50% and the white object; removes outline attributes from all objects (see fig. 7.25).

Figure 7.25

Reverse transitions of shading can be accomplished by the use of two different Blends in the same design area.

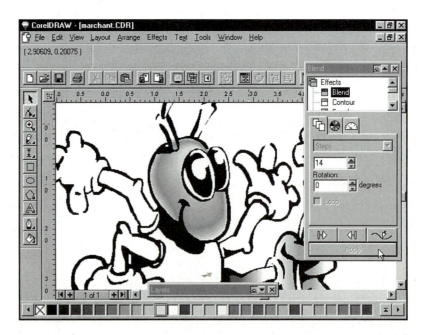

16. Press Ctrl+S (**F**ile, **S**ave).

> Saves your work at this intermediate stage.

You now have two rather substantial tricks rolled up your sleeve for shading a black and white illustration. As you progress with this image, it's important to take a look at a shape in the composition, consider how light would reflect off of it in real life, and then create the appropriate highlight and shading. Through blends and fountain fills, shading should appear to be a result of the same lighting source.

So what happens when an area in the cartoon is filled with a white object, and the shape cannot be filled with a type of fountain fill that suggests dimension? In the next section, we tackle this with a new editing technique.

Combining OCR-Traced Objects

Earlier in this chapter, it was recommended that you break complex objects into a number of objects that, naturally, contain fewer nodes as a Pre-Production editing step. The reason for this is primarily output considerations; there isn't a fixed limit to curve complexity, but a 700 node object with a fountain fill isn't likely to print to a PostScript imagesetter. Unfortunately, there isn't a "magic number" for curve complexity because PostScript's description of a curve depends on a combination of factors: imagesetter memory, curve description, type of fill, and so on. Additionally, if Windows 95 has had some memory resources "stolen" by an ill-written application, an overly complex object won't copy to the Clipboard properly either.

There's a secondary "perk" to breaking up complex shapes, and that is you have an opportunity to use the Combine command on simpler shapes to create holes (*counters*, *subpaths*) by using other shapes. A good example of an occasion where you need to combine objects is in the ant cartoon—the ant's upper right arm is filled with an OCR-Trace object, and you're not going to easily find a type of fountain fill that can realistically shade this object. No sweat; you learned how to use Blends to create simulated fountain fills in the last section. Here's a set of steps that shows how easily you can combine the arm object with the outline to create a "see through" area that exposes the Fill layer.

Combining Objects/Blending a Custom Fill

1. With the Pick tool, click on the right arm of the ant.

> Selects the object on Layer 1 that you'll combine with the ant's outline object (see fig. 7.26).

2. Shift+click on the black object that represents the edge of the ant's arm.

Figure 7.26

If you want to create a hole (a subpath) in a design, remove the foreground object by combining it with the background object.

You now have two objects selected; Shift adds to the current selection.

3. Press Ctrl+L (**A**rrange, **C**ombine).

   The white object disappears, and there is now a white object-shaped hole in the black background object.

4. Press F5 (or click on the Pencil tool); then click-and-drag the status arrow on the Layers Manager's list to the Fill title.

   Selects the last used tool (the Pencil tool); moves your editing work to the Fills layer, beneath Layer 1.

5. Click a point at a corner of the ant's arm, double-click around the border of the empty area, then single-click at the beginning point.

   Creates a path on the Fill layer that describes the area to be filled.

6. Press spacebar, then press +.

   Toggles to the Pick tool; duplicates the path.

7. Press F10, then click-and-drag the middle nodes in this long-shaped path toward the center of the path (see figure 7.27).

   The copy will be the ending control object in a Blend.

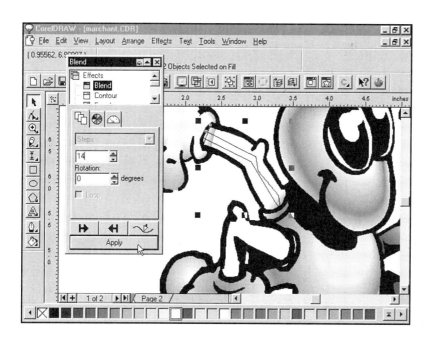

Figure 7.27
A Blend between these two shapes results in a "tube" shading of the ant's arm; dimensional and harmonious with other shading.

8. Press spacebar, click on the white swatch on the color palette, press tab, then click on the 40% black swatch on the color palette.

   Fills the top object; Tab key toggles to select next object in the stack of objects on the Fill layer, larger object is filled with 40% black.

9. Shift+click on the white object, then click on Apply on the Blend Roll-Up.

   Creates 14 objects that blend in shape and color from the front to the back object.

In figure 7.28, you can see the Shape tool being used to bend a line in the path that has been changed to a curve. Basically, you have all the editing steps in this chapter to completely shade the ant cartoon.

10. With all the Blend objects selected, right-click over the "x" on the color palette.

    Removes outline attributes for all the selected objects.

11. Press Ctrl+S (**F**ile, **S**ave).

    Saves your work.

II

Document-Centricity

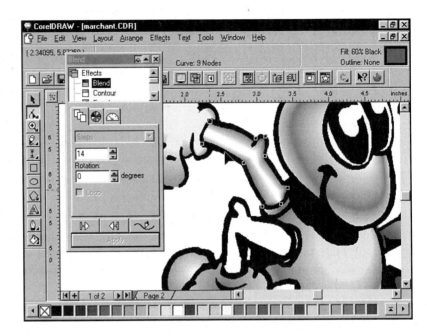

Figure 7.28
It's often easier to
refine a control
object after a Blend
has been made;
editing changes are
then made to the
entire linked Blend.

There have been a number of techniques in the past few examples that you might want
to adopt in your own CorelDRAW illustration work.

✔ **Leave default outlines around Blend component objects until
you're finished editing.** It's much easier to remove outline attributes as a
last step in creating blends. The reason for this suggestion is that it's easy to
spot and node edit an object that has an outline; you can switch to wireframe
mode where all objects are outlined, but this step takes you away from your
prime concern and you eventually have to switch back to Preview mode—so it's
sort of a redundant effort.

✔ **Default values on CorelDRAW Roll-Ups are suggestions, not mandates.** I've used fewer than 20 Blend steps on several illustrations, and they've
output quite nicely. Limiting the number of Blends reduces redraw time,
reduces overall file complexity, and reduces file size. Try "leaning down" the
number of blend steps in a Blend, and see if the design images okay to your
printer. For small areas (like less than a page inch), and for color transitions
between, say, 10% black and 40% black, you might be able to get away with less
than 20 blend steps.

✔ **It's easier than you might imagine to use the straight-line, double-
click technique to begin a rough shape.** By converting the resulting
polygon to curves, then to Smooth curves, you usually arrive at a rounded
object that's very close to a fill object you had in mind. If you have an accurate

eye for where points of inflection (nodes at a sudden vector direction change) should be placed, only minor node editing is required to complete the object you need. Bézier drawing produces smooth curves from the very beginning of a design, but they are a little harder to manipulate than freehand Pencil-generated path segments.

Creating Instant Backgrounds

Compositionally, the ant is the "star" of this design; few people are going to gasp in awe of the two pebbles at the ant's feet! However, something is missing with this dimensional ant, and it might be that there's no background. Whenever you design, particularly with CorelDRAW, it's easy to forget that a viewer needs a point of reference, at least a 2D plane, behind a drawing to help one's eye with orientation within the composition.

This does *not* mean, though, that an intricately detailed background is required in MARCHANT.CDR. Too much detail work in the background, even a tree or something, would compete and most likely overshadow the importance of our foreground hero here.

For decades, a *wash* has been used by cartoonists and advertising illustrators to push a foreground element even further into the viewer's face, without introducing a competing design element. An artistic wash is simply a vague, abstract color design that fades into the paper color at the wash's edges. Historically, washes have been created using watercolors or pastels (*soft chalks*, if you're under 30), but as you've seen, Blend objects can imitate anything from a fountain fill to an airbrush rendering.

Here's an example of how a wash behind the ant design can help round out the composition:

Creating a Digital Wash

1. Press F4, then press F3.

    Zooms you into a view that includes all page objects, then zooms you out a field. This is a comfortable viewing resolution for creating the wash.

2. Right-click on the Layers Roll-Ups list, then choose New from the shortcut menu.

    Creates a new layer.

3. Type **Background**, click on the Background Layer list title, then drag the title beneath the Fills Layer title.

Names the new layer; places it behind the Fills layer.

4. Click in the document window, press F5 (or click on the Pencil tool), then create an abstract background, like that shown in figure 7.29, by using the double-click method of drawing.

Clicking in the document window moves CorelDRAW's focus from the Layers Manager to the document; creates a rough shape you'll refine using the Shape tool.

Figure 7.29

Backgrounds don't have to "say" anything to a viewer; sometimes, a background is needed to support the foreground.

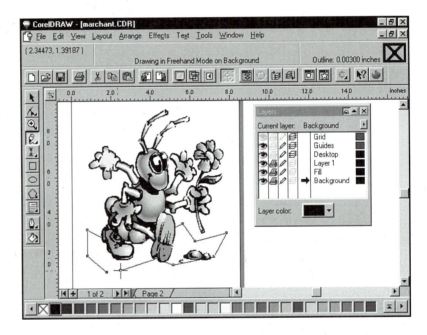

Now that the rough background shape has been created, it's not necessary to display the ant or Fills layer on-screen. CorelDRAW takes time to redraw objects, and all the fountain fills and blends might be slowing your work.

5. Click on the eye icons on the Layer Roll-Up list next to Layer 1 and Fill.

Makes these layers invisible.

6. Click on the white color palette swatch, press spacebar, then press +.

Toggles to the Pick tool; creates a press duplicate of the shape you drew.

7. Click on the 30% black color swatch on the color palette.

Makes the duplicate (top) object 30% black.

When you duplicate an object, the most recently created object is always on the top of a stack of objects on a layer. This is why the last step worked for filling the duplicate, not the previously selected original object.

8. Press F10 (or choose the Shape tool), then click-and-drag the duplicate object's edges toward the inside of the original shape.

   Creates an "end" control object for a group of Blends. (see fig. 7.30).

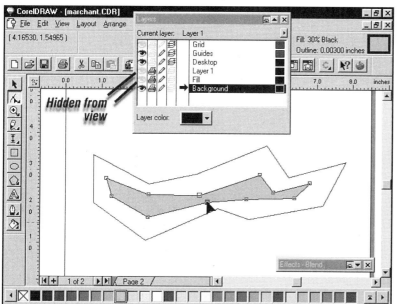

Figure 7.30
Begin a digital "wash" background by defining an area with straight path segments, then duplicate the object and recolor it.

II

Document-Centricity

9. Select both objects with the Pick tool, type **25** in the Blend Roll-Up's spin box, click on Apply, then right-click on the "x" on the color palette.

   Makes 25 transitional objects between the white object and the 30% Steps black object; removes the outline property for the Blend group of objects (see fig. 7.31).

10. Click on the eye icons on the Layers Roll-Up for the Layer 1 and Fills titles.

    Restores these layers to view.

11. Press Ctrl+S (**F**ile, **S**ave).

    Saves the finished work to hard disk.

Figure 7.31
A high number of Blend steps creates an extremely diffuse wash of tone, perfect for highlighting foreground elements.

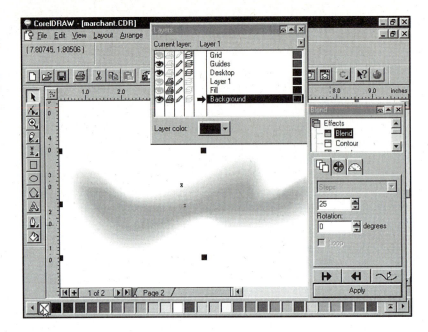

Although it was suggested that a low number of Blend steps can usually work for shading interiors of a foreground design, a high number was specified in the preceding example because the transition area—the distance between the outer and inner control objects—is a lot greater than interior areas of the cartoon ant. The greater the page distance, the greater the number of Blend steps you'll want to use. Additionally, a good way to ensure that the foreground character visually separates from the background wash is to use a dissimilar fill. The ant fills use a greater tonal difference between beginning and ending control objects, and their appearance is a little coarser than the 25 step background wash.

Figure 7.32 is the finished composition, which can also be viewed on-screen by loading the MARCHANT.CDR image from the GALLERY folder in the CHAP07 folder of the *CorelDRAW! 6 Expert's Edition Bonus CD*. Why not load it, view it, and perhaps take it apart, to see how the elements were built?

We need to backtrack in the next section, because there are some artistic features in OCR-Trace that have been neglected. If you want to create a vector "woodcut" pattern, OCR-Trace can assist you 90% of the way.

Figure 7.32
A simple concept can be embellished to a state of "High Art" when you convert the art, and use CorelDRAW's feature set.

Creating Stylized OCR-Trace Artwork

The closest thing you'll find to an "Instant Art Machine" exists within OCR-Trace. All you need is an idea, a rough sketch, and some familiarity with OCR-Trace's options, and you can generate icons, drop caps, or simple filler for a magazine in the blink of an eye.

Creating a Woodcut Vector Design

Corel engineers seem on the verge of obsession with "really neat tricks" they invent to stick in Corel's modules. OCR-Trace, for example, would be a perfectly adequate bitmap-to-vector conversion filter if it only offered the Outline method of tracing. But no: Outline, Sketch, Mosaic, 3D Mosaic, and Woodcut are also available, and although the techniques for converting scanned artwork to these exotic types is embarrassingly simple, the critical considerations for producing interesting art have almost everything to do with the *content* of your scanned image.

Therefore, I'm not going to dwell on example steps in this section. Instead, I'll concentrate on what type of art will make the best woodcut, 3-D pyramid mosaic, and so on.

Basically, the Center Line method of tracing is useful if you want to refine a scanned road map, or schematic drawing, where line thickness is unimportant, and connected, filled paths are not the objective. Center Line is the only non-effects filter for OCR-Trace, and can also be useful for engraving professionals or signmakers who need center line data whose path width is defined by a steel nib, stylus, or physical pen. The best scanned artwork to use with the CenterLine setting is pen and ink work, although large filled, enclosed areas will take up processing time, and the resulting vector file will not display any filled areas. Additionally, because the paths in a CenterLine OCR-Trace are not connected, this option is a poor choice for cartoons and line illustrations.

The Mosaic and 3D Mosaic produce a "fly's eye" view of an original scan—visual detail is reduced to a coarse pattern of large dots. You can generally achieve this effect using PHOTO-PAINT's Pixelate filter, or Adobe's Gallery Effects' Halftone plug-in, and you have more artistic control over the results by using a bitmap editor. Black and white scanned images produce less stunning results than color images, but you should choose your scanned original very carefully. Simple, large, primitive objects with a lot of color contrast produce the most appealing results with the Mosaic style of OCR-Trace.

The 3D Mosaic produces a collection of neighboring 3D enlarged pixels, viewing from an aerial perspective, in your choice of pyramid, brick, or fan (venetian blind) styles. The original visual content of the scanned image is almost completely lost in the 3D Mosaic trace; the artistic content actually lies in the rendering style of the trace. Although the 3D Mosaic style is of extremely limited usefulness for a talented designer, you should check out the brick style of 3D Mosaic for use in creating interface icons or for embellishing other extremely simple shapes.

Sketch and Woodcut are very similar procedures in OCR-Trace, which produce a series of unevenly shaped lines, sort of like a mezzotint of a photograph. Both Sketch and Woodcut can be used effectively with simple, stencil-style bitmap designs to produce an intricate vector variation of the original's visual content.

In the following example, FRUIT.TIF, is the target for the Woodcut style of tracing. FRUIT.TIF can be found in the CHAP07.EXAMPLES folder of the *CorelDRAW! 6 Expert's Edition Bonus CD*; it's a 1 bit per pixel pen and ink drawing of the traditional still life/fruit composition. Notice how the dense black areas of the composition play nicely to the Woodcut's taper setting. If you have a bold, simple typeface character, a simple black and white logo idea, or similar composition that uses a lot of black played against white, here's how to make the composition a little more ornamental-looking:

Using the Woodcut Style of Tracing

1. In Corel OCR-Trace, open the FRUIT.TIF image from the EXAMPLES.CHAP07 folder of the *CorelDRAW! 6 Expert's Edition Bonus CD*.

This is the target image for the Woodcut trace.

2. Choose **O**CR-Trace, then Trace **S**ettings box.

   Displays the OCR-Trace settings dialog.

3. Click on the Woodcut tab, then click-and-drag the N**o**de Reduction slider to about 70.

   Ensures that the resulting trace contains as few nodes as needed to describe the scene.

4. Set the **T**hreshold slider at 128.

   Specifies that the resulting trace contains the same proportion of dark and light areas as the original scanned image.

5. Click on the Ta**p**ered Ends check box.

   Tapered Ends provides the most dramatic woodcut trace, with thick lines tapering to thin ones at areas of image contrast (scanned image color edges).

6. Type **45** in the **A**ngle of cut spin box.

   Specifies that OCR-Trace creates woodcut vector lines at a 45° angle to the page.

If you want to convert a logo to woodcut vector shapes, you might want to consider changing the angle to 90° to make the resulting lines run horizontally, imitating speed lines or electronic mezzotints.

7. Type **10** in the Sa**m**ple width spin box.

   Specifies that the maximum width of tapered lines is 10 pixels. The minimum width of the taper cannot be defined in OCR-Trace.

8. Click on OK, then click on the Trace button on the toolbar (the pencil drawing the circle icon).

   Launches the trace. (See fig. 7.33.)

9. Choose **F**ile, **S**ave, **V**ector, then save the file in the CMX format to your hard disk.

   Saves the trace to a format which can be imported by CorelDRAW.

II

Document-Centricity

Figure 7.33

The Woodcut style of OCR-Trace can stylize a scanned image. Take care not to make a design illegible with a style that's too intense, though.

The style settings in OCR-Trace are *filters*, although the software trade commonly calls a graphics filter a *plug-in* these days. By definition, filters translate data. With computer graphics technology, filtering a poor piece of artwork and passing it off as a digital masterpiece is easier than ever. But as a designer, you always owe it to yourself to ask a magic question: "Does an audience *really* mean it when they say a piece of art is "interesting"?

At their worst, filters can turn an uninspired design into a *stylized*, uninspired design. The best use for a filter is to help push an incomplete creative piece of artwork toward completion. For example, if you have a digitized photo that really needs to look as though it's curling off the image window, you'd be best served by using the KPT Page Curl Effect found in PHOTO-PAINT. Your alternative for such an effect would be to create it manually—a tedious, unnecessary task.

Read on, and you'll learn how even CorelDRAW-phobics can produce beautiful graphics with a camera, OCR-Trace, and the right composition.

Beyond Drawing and OCR-Trace

Up to this point in this chapter, we've dwelt upon the conversion of physical artwork to vector format, making the presumption that you're experienced with traditional drawing tools. However, CorelDRAW has attracted talented individuals from all kinds of creative backgrounds, and many business designers today *began* their careers with the personal computer as a drawing tool.

Let's suppose that before you adopted the PC as a tool, you had extensive experience in photography. OCR-Trace and CorelDRAW also provide valuable enhancements and features for translating photographic information into a format that can be manipulated as vectors. In the next section, we'll take a look at how the art form of photography can be ported to a unique type of digital format.

The Digital Approach to Posterizing Photography

Hopefully, this chapter has provided an insight or two on how you can work between Corel applications to arrive at a finished piece. Even if you feel you're "CorelDRAW-centric" and can't find an artistic niche within PHOTO-PAINT or the other modules, you've seen that important, specific tools are sometimes located outside of DRAW's workspace.

This section's example is centered around a black and white photo of an architectural ornament. Content-wise, it's a good, clean image of a piper dressed in 12th century apparel. Non-trademarked objects that can be seen from public right-of-ways are fair game to include in a composition without royalties or releases, so the piper is a good subject for an adventure here in transforming artwork.

As mentioned earlier, it's usually a good idea to reduce the number of unique colors in an image before using OCR-Trace to create vector art based on an image. However, the black and white image of the piper contains many more shades than black or white; it's a grayscale mode image, and as such, contains up to 256 unique intensities of black.

It would be folly to import the piper image in its original state to OCR-Trace. With Color tolerance set to the minimum, OCR-Trace will process for moment upon moment, trying to separate unique grayscale tones and create hundreds of vector outlines to represent the image. Although there is no hard and fast limitation to the number of objects OCR-Trace can generate from a bitmap image, Corel's Import/Export filters have a definite limitation. Additionally, even if you could export a thousand objects in the AI, EPS, CMX, or WMF format, you might not find the experience of manipulating so many component objects of a design to be a worthwhile one in CorelDRAW. Conversely, OCR-Trace's maximum Color tolerance value would produce only a few objects based on a narrow range of grayscale image tones, and the resulting trace would look inaccurate and somewhat like a photocopy of the original image.

Using PHOTO-PAINT to Color Reduce a Photograph

The solution to converting photographs to vector objects is to filter the photo before bringing it into OCR-Trace. PHOTO-PAINT has a Posterize effect that can reduce the number of unique tones or colors in an image to a specified amount. Depending on the visual content in an image, you can generally filter substantial amounts of image information from a picture and still retain a recognizable composition. Images become stylized when you reduce and adjust image information, but by using PHOTO-PAINT before OCR-Trace, it is you, the creative talent, who plays the deciding role in what information is used or discarded.

Here's how to use the Posterize effect in PHOTO-PAINT to limit the amount of visual detail OCR-Trace has to convert:

Posterizing an Image

1. In CorelPHOTO-PAINT, open the PIPER.TIF image from the EXAMPLES.CHAP07 folder of the *CorelDRAW! 6 Expert's Edition Bonus CD.*

   This is the image you'll convert to vector format.

2. Choose Effe**c**ts, Color Transform, Posterize.

   Displays the Posterize dialog box.

3. Click-and-drag the **L**evel slider to 6, then click on the Pre**v**iew button.

   Displays a posterized preview of the piper image. (See fig. 7.34.)

Figure 7.34
The Posterize effect can reduce the number of unique colors in an image to anywhere between 2 and 32 tones.

This example uses the number 6, because through trial and error, it seems to be the minimum number of unique tones that adequately describe the visual content within PIPER.TIF. The key here is to see how few posterized tones describe your target image.

The facts that the piper is made of stone and the lighting in the scene is a little harsh both help to limit the number of grayscale tones that make the image recognized as that of a piper. Choose your target images similarly, and experiment with how few levels of posterization can successfully convey the composition you have in mind.

4. Click on OK.

   Returns you to the workspace and posterizes the image.

5. Choose **F**ile, Save **A**s, then save the posterized image as PIPER.TIF to your hard disk.

   Saves the image for future use in OCR-Trace.

6. Press Alt+F4 (**F**ile, E**x**it).

   Closes PHOTO-PAINT.

You might also try making adjustments in the Brightness-Contrast-Intensity dialog box (under Effe**c**ts, Color Adjust) prior to posterizing an image of your own. Posterized shades are averaged areas of original color (or tonal) values, and you can "push" a shade so it becomes a more predominant posterized tone by changing the original image tonal values. Try adjusting the tones, previewing the Posterize effect, then canceling and readjusting the tonal values until you find a Posterize preview you like.

➤ **Tip** New to version 6 of PHOTO-PAINT is the Undo **L**ist, accessed through the **E**dit menu. Choose this command, and you can see all the actions you've performed in a PHOTO-PAINT session. You can choose to undo one or more effects, filters, or editing steps you've performed, and the number of undo steps is basically limited to your system memory and hard disk space.

So take your time comparing and revising edits to an image you want to Posterize; anything you do to an image can be Undone!

Posterized Images and OCR-Trace

If you followed along in previous sections of this chapter, you already know that the color tolerance feature in OCR-Trace determines how accurately the program evaluates the edge between two different color or tonal values in the source bitmap image. We "force" OCR-Trace to evaluate only 6 tones in the PIPER.TIF image by posterizing it prior to importing it into OCR-Trace; therefore, we limit the number of unique tone areas the program has to trace into vector objects. This is why it's important that you take your time with images of your own that you want to posterize—make sure they are the way you want them in PHOTO-PAINT, because OCR-Trace will make a faithful vector conversion of the visual information you see.

The following set of steps are used in OCR-Trace to create 6 grouped layers of closed, filled paths that represent the visual information in PIPER.TIF.

Converting a Grayscale Bitmap Image

1. Launch Corel OCR-Trace from Windows Explorer, then choose **F**ile, **O**pen, and select PIPER.TIF from your hard disk.

   Loads the PIPER image into the bitmap view window.

2. Choose **O**CR-Trace, Trace **S**ettings.

   Displays the Trace Settings dialog box.

3. Click on the Outline tab, then make the following settings: N**o**de Reduction: 85, **C**olor tolerance: 5, **H**ole Filling: 0, and **N**oise Reduction: 18.

   These settings will produce a fairly accurate group of objects, with a minimum of nodes in object paths. See "Colorizing from within OCR-Trace" after the example for details.

4. Click on OK, then choose **O**CR-Trace, Perform **T**race, By **O**utline (see fig. 7.35).

   OCR-Trace traces all the areas of color contrast in the PIPER image.

Figure 7.35
The calculations for converting a complex image to vector format are immense; expect that this trace will take a few minutes.

Figure 7.35 shows the resulting trace in Wireframe view, but you have the option of viewing the colored, filled groups of objects by choosing <u>V</u>iew, Ob<u>j</u>ects, Show all <u>O</u>bjects. Check this option now to see how closely OCR-Trace converted the image information to vector format.

This is the end of the steps used to convert the image, but we aren't through with the OCR-Trace options for *colorizing* the vector objects. Read on through the next section, and don't close OCR-Trace or save the vector objects yet!

Colorizing from within OCR-Trace

Because a grayscale, posterized image is not exactly an exciting one, you'll see how to *colorize* the posterized image from within OCR-Trace next; CorelDRAW can import any color set that you create within an OCR-Traced file.

Let's review a little about how OCR-Trace works with objects before getting into the colorizing phase. Unique colors in a bitmap image are converted in OCR-Trace to a group of objects which OCR-Trace assigns to a layer, similar to the capability you find in CorelDRAW for stacking different groups of objects on layers. However, layer information in OCR-Trace *does not* export in any vector format to CorelDRAW in a way that allows CorelDRAW to accept OCR-Traced layers as CorelDRAW layers—we'll show you how to manually arrange an OCR-Trace import into CorelDRAW in layers shortly.

Note   As of this writing, Corel Corp. is aware that it would be more convenient if OCR-Trace saved discrete layer information, and that an imported trace should contain individual object layers. This capability would spare users the manual labor of separating and assigning object groups their own layer, as you were obliged to do in the preceding example.

Check with Corel Corp. periodically for the availability of patch disks for version 6. They have historically been free of charge (all registered users need to do is call and ask), and might contain this enhancement for OCR-Trace in the near future.

So what good are OCR-Trace layers? OCR-Trace layers allow you to assign different colors to every object in a color group of objects. This means that the black objects in the PIPER trace can be changed to dark olive, and the lighter tones can all be changed to deep mustard in one fell swoop without messing up the dark olive objects. If you performed the previous exercise, you now have an incredible number of objects in OCR-Trace, and it only makes sense for OCR-Trace to group them in order to work with them in any organized sense.

The Hole Filling function, which we skipped over in the previous exercise is an interesting implementation Corel Corp. has for disguising "holes" between objects. Vector traces are not precise, in that a vector curves generated for, say, all the 30% black areas in the original image might not abut perfectly with the neighboring curve that represents all the 50% black original image areas. The result is a gap, which exposes the bottom layer of the vector file, which is usually a contrasting color. To correct this appearance, OCR-Trace can create a bottom layer composed of many rectangles, each filled with an average of the color samples that correspond to areas in the original image. Hole Filling needlessly complicates the resulting vector image, however; it's an inventive workaround for fixing holes, but it adds substantially to the file's complexity and number of objects. We don't recommend that you use the Hole Filling option in OCR-Trace for this reason.

Here's the game plan for manually correcting the gaps between groups of different colored objects. First, you'll decide upon a custom palette of colors for the piper image—you're free to specify your own shades, but to get us started, you can use the following substitution table for each layer of grayscale objects:

Table 7.1 Color Scheme for the Piper Image

Original Object Color	New Object Color
Black	R:0, G:51, B:0 (dark olive)
Dark Gray	R:102, G:0, B:0 (maroon)
Medium Gray	R:122, G:56, B:0 (neutral brown)
Light Gray	R:255, G:153, B:0 (gold)
Near white	R:255, G:255, B:102 (cream)
White	R:255, G:255, B:255 (white)

It's important to actually create and save this palette while you colorize each layer; the palette will be used in CorelDRAW to define outline colors. By outlining the objects on a layer, you can close the gaps invisibly, with exact color values that match each object fill.

After you get the hang of the process, it will be easy for you to choose your own color schemes, and colorize your own OCR-Traced designs. So, by example…

Colorizing Object Layers/Saving Color Palettes

1. Choose **T**ools, **L**ayer Manager menu.

   Displays the Document Information tabbed.

2. Click on the Layers tab.

   Displays the color of each layer, along with the number of objects on each layer.

3. Right-click over the second-to-bottom layer title (darkest grayscale tones, not the Empty Layer title), then choose Change Layer color from the shortcut list (see fig. 7.36).

Displays the Uniform Fill dialog box.

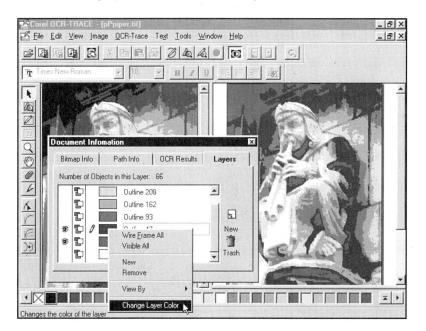

Figure 7.36

Access custom colors, and create a custom palette, by right-clicking over a layer color swatch on the Layers Manager's list.

4. Click on the Mod**e**l drop-down list, then select RGB.

Displays the RGB color model.

5. Enter the following values in the R, G, and B spin boxes: R:**0**, G:**51**, B:**0.**

Specifies a dark olive to replace all dark gray fills on the selected object layer.

6. Click on Palette Options, then click on New Palette.

Displays the New Palette dialog box.

7. Type PIPER.CPL in the File **n**ame field, then click on **S**ave box.

Saves a new (empty palette); returns you to the Uniform fill dialog.

8. Click on Color Options, then choose **A**dd Color to Palette.

Adds the dark olive to the PIPER.CPL palette.

9. Click on OK.

    Returns you to the workspace; all the dark gray areas are now dark olive.

10. Repeat the last 6 steps; right-click on the other grayscale tones on the Layers Manager list, add new colors to the PIPER.CPL palette as you define them.

    Use the RGB color values from Table 7.1 for specifying the other colors.

If you'd like to colorize the OCR-Trace, but don't have the time to create PIPER.CPL, you can load it from the EXAMPLES.CHAP07 folder of the *CorelDRAW! 6 Expert's Edition Bonus CD*. Use the Palette Options, **O**pen Palette command in the Uniform color dialog box to do this.

If you're the ambitious sort, and want to create the palette in this example, you must do the following after adding the last color to the palette…

11. In the Uniform color dialog box, click on Palette Options, **S**ave Palette.

    Saves the most recent changes you've made to the palette.

12. Click on OK, then choose **F**ile, **S**ave, **V**ector, then save the trace as PIPER.CMX to your hard disk.

    Saves the composition in a format that CorelDRAW can import.

13. Press Alt+F4 (**F**ile, E**x**it) and choose No to saving the PIPER.TIF image.

    Closes OCR-Trace.

There is a less complicated way to create a colorized, posterized photograph (you select the image areas in PHOTO-PAINT and apply color), but what you've achieved in the preceding example is to take a resolution-dependent design, and make it resolution-*in*dependent. Bitmap images, such as PIPER.TIF, cannot be scaled to be larger without sacrificing quality of image detail because a finite number of samples (pixels) make up the image. In the CMX format, all the objects that make up the piper design can be smoothly scaled to fit a postage stamp, a poster, or a T-shirt, without loss of a single curve or object shape, because vectors, not pixels, make up the design.

Finalizing the Piper Design

To complete the piper design, you need to do something about node complexity, and handle the fissures between color layers. As you may recall, Chapter 3, "Beating Nodes and Paths into Submission (The Hard Way)," emphasized that incorrect node connections can cause imagesetter failure at printing time, and that there's clearly a "right" and "wrong" way to connect path segments. This chapter, however, does not emphasize correct node connections—smooth, cusp, or symmetrical control point properties— because OCR-Trace handles quite satisfactorily the connections of nodes it creates when it traces.

Although a connection you'd prefer to be a Smooth connection is often an OCR-Trace Cusp connection, some of the fundamental errors made with connections are taken care of in Trace. Specifically, cusp connections can be made between curved path segments, and the outcome is a sharp, yet PostScript-acceptable connection. OCR-Trace does *not* create smooth connections, period, so there will be no problems with a straight line segment connecting to a curve with a smooth node. You can spend hours, or no time at all, editing connections in an imported OCR-Trace design—it's a matter of how much time you're willing to invest in editing, and how unhappy you are with OCR-Trace's work. It's the *number* of nodes, not necessarily the node connections in an OCR-Trace piece, that will make the image too complex to print.

But the whole reason why you'd use OCR-Trace to create a posterized image hinges on image detail, the *quality* of the posterized collection of objects. Do the groups suggest a naturalistic flow of lines? Does the unevenness of the edges contribute to an appealing composition? Half the trick to creating attractive computer art is to use every feature and capability of applications to defeat the stereotype, sterile, pixelated look typically ascribed to computer-generated art. By using a combination of features in different programs, you work in a way similar to that of a traditional artist who mixes media. When you arrive at a happy blend of techniques and graphics types, you've usually defeated the obvious mechanics of the PC, which produces lifeless, cookie-cutter-type artwork.

Importing and Organizing the Piper Import

Using the following steps, you'll import the PIPER.CMX file. Following this set of steps, you'll ungroup the imported vector file, and examine the composition for problem spots.

Importing the Piper Design

1. Launch CorelDRAW from Windows Explorer, then choose **F**ile, **I**mport (or click on the import button on the toolbox).

   Displays the Import dialog box.

2. Choose PIPER.CMX from your hard disk, then click on **I**mport.

   CorelDRAW imports the PIPER.CMX file.

If you'd like to work in CorelDRAW with the imported piper design, but didn't convert the image in OCR-Trace, PIPER.CMX, the finished trace, is located in the EXAMPLES.CHAP07 folder of the Bonus CD.

CorelDRAW's status line will tell you that there is a group of 6 objects on Layer 1. OCR-Trace grouped all the objects into 6 discrete color groups, and CorelDRAW's import filter nests the groups into one imported object. This is sort of like picking apart an artichoke, and some care should be taken when you ungroup the import to keep groups on separate layers.

3. Click on the Ungroup button on the toolbar (or press Ctrl+U; **A**rrange, **U**ngroup).

    Ungroups the grouped layers; all six groups are selected.

4. Choose **L**ayout, **L**ayers Manager (Ctrl+F3).

    Displays the Layers Roll-Up.

5. Right-click on the Layers list, and choose **N**ew.

    A new layer appears on the Layers list (see figure 7.37).

Figure 7.37
Create a new layer
for each of the six
groups of objects.

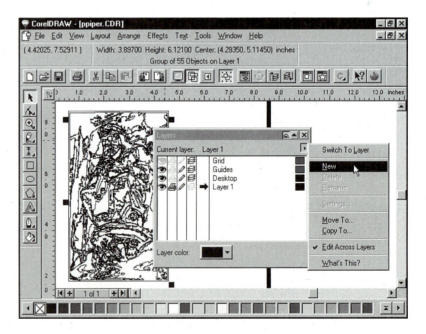

6. Type **Olive**, then right-click and choose **N**ew.

    Names the layer you created; creates a new layer.

You need to create five layers in the new CorelDRAW document; the sixth color, white, can remain on the bottom, default page layer as Layer 1.

7. Repeat the last two steps until you have six layers on the page.

   These layers will contain the six groups of colored objects.

8. Click on the Dark Olive group of objects, click on the menu flyout button on the Layers Roll-Up, and choose **M**ove To.

   An arrow appears with the word "To?" on it.

9. Click the arrow on the Olive title on the Layers Roll-Up.

   Moves the grouped objects to the Olive layer in the document.

10. Repeat the last step for the other grouped objects.

    Assigns each group a unique layer in the document.

As you can see in figure 7.38, the process of assigning each group of objects a separate layer is not hard; the process goes quickly, and the benefit of separating groups of objects is that you can now edit a group without messing up other groups.

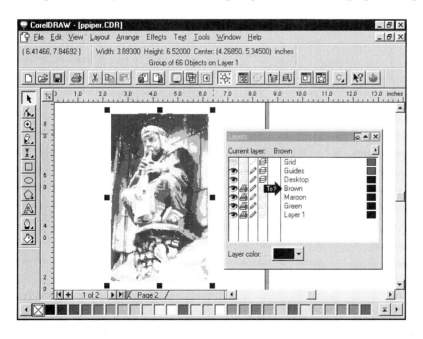

Figure 7.38

Keep objects in separate layers, to confine your editing work to a specific design area.

11. Choose **F**ile, Save **A**s, then save your work as PIPER.CDR to your hard drive.

    Saves your work at this intermediate stage of completion.

Due to the reality that Corel version 6 is continually being updated by Corel Corp., you might or might not have imported layers bearing the title of "Empty Layer" to CorelDRAW, and this title might initially appear on the Layers Manager's list. In version 6.00.118 of CorelDRAW, if this happens, delete the Layer title from the Layers Manager by right-clicking on the title, then choosing **D**elete from the shortcut menu. There's noting on the Empty Layer in OCR-Trace imports, and you're doing yourself a favor by eliminating confusion in the future when you reopen the file.

Now that the design has been saved, and the layers are organized according to object color, we have two working techniques to cover to finalize the piper composition.

Simplifying Complicated Objects

OCR-Trace was designed to assist you in creating intricate curves, but it is not the responsibility of the program to create exactly the right number of objects, or nodes within objects, that will successfully output to a printer or film recorder. The price one pays for a marvelously intricate poster design is an excess of path nodes. However, this problem can be solved using the same technique as described in "Working with Imported Vector Files," earlier in this chapter.

Follow this list to optimize the objects in PIPER.CDR for printing:

1. First, you'll want to copy a layer to a separate page in the document. Select the grouped objects on the layer, press Ctrl+C to copy the objects, press PageDown then press Enter to add a page 2 to the PIPER.CDR document, then press Ctrl+V to paste the copy onto page 2.

2. Press Ctrl+U to **A**rrange, **U**ngroup the grouped objects (or click on the Ungroup toggle button on the toolbar).

3. Use the Tab key to toggle the active selection to the separate objects on page two, and stop when the status line tells you that a selected object contains more than 300 nodes. This is a "problem" object, and needs to be broken into two or more objects.

4. Use the Shape tool to break the path in the same way as you did the ant outline in this chapter, then use the **A**rrange, **B**reak Apart (Ctrl+K) command to split a path into subpaths. Then select a subpath and connect the first and last nodes using the Pencil tool. The **L**ayout, Snap to Objects command is great for auto-aligning the Pencil tool cursor with the first and last nodes.

5. Once the complex objects on a layer have been broken into smaller objects containing fewer than 300 nodes each, select all the objects (double-click on the Pick tool), then regroup the objects, copy them to the clipboard, press PageUp to return to Page 1, delete the original objects on the layer, then press Ctrl+V to

paste the new objects onto the layer. Make certain that the target layer is the same as the one you copied the objects from! The current layer is designated by the arrow next to the layer title on the Layers Roll-Up list. Click-and-drag the arrow to a new target layer as soon as you've completed editing a layer.

The 300 nodes figure was created based on the author's experience with a service bureau, and attempting to export objects to the EPS (Encapsulated PostScript) format from CorelDRAW. The EPS format is a "flavor" of PostScript language, and its implementation as a file format is not identical to the PostScript language used by imagesetters. This is not a hard-and-fast number, but 300 to 400 nodes in a single, *fairly* intricate object seems to be the upper threshold of PS language that is understood by imagesetter interpreters and software conversion filters. You might try to get away with more nodes in an object, but you're safer at production time with less than 300 nodes per object.

Filling In Object Gaps

The following is a "down and dirty" trick, which like most tricks, happens to work for a specific design need. If you have PIPER.CDR open in CorelDRAW right now, you'll see the gaps that OCR-Trace left between different colored objects. The absolutely, by the book, correct, masochistic method of correcting this design problem is to set aside a few days, and reposition the nodes in each object so that they align with neighboring objects. This solution is assisted by the Snap to Objects feature in CorelDRAW, and perhaps the thought of taking a long vacation after the editing session.

However, if you want to finish the composition, so it prints well and looks perfect on-screen, and accomplish this within 5 minutes, here's a short outline of the "down and dirty," pragmatic, realistic steps to take:

1. The Olive Layer (and all layers) needs to be visible but the selection arrow doesn't need to be pointing to it on the Roll-Up. Click on the group of objects on the Olive layer, click on the Outline tool on the toolbox, then choose the Outline Pen tool (the fountain pen icon) on the menu flyout.

2. Type **.014** in the **W**idth spin box, and check **B**ehind fill and **S**cale with image check boxes. Doing this ensures that the outline width will fall behind the selected objects, and that if you scale the finished piece, the width of the outlines will adjust accordingly. 0.014 inches is an arbitrary value—you might want to choose a greater value for filling in the "holes" in the design, but don't use a value higher than you really need.

3. Click on the **D**efault calligraphy button. Doing this ensures that the outline around each object is uniform in shape.

4. Click on the Color button in the Outline Pen dialog box, click on Others, click on Palette Options, then choose **O**pen Palette. If you didn't create a custom palette in this chapter for the piper, you can select PIPER.CPL from the CHAP07 folder on the Bonus CD. Click on **O**pen to return to the Outline color dialog box.

5. Click on the dark olive swatch, then click on OK to return to the drawing window and the composition.

6. Once the color palette has been "primed" with the selection of the custom palette for the first outline color in the composition, PIPER.CPL remains as the CorelDRAW color palette at the bottom of the drawing window. You can now click on the maroon group of objects, choose **E**dit, Copy Properties **F**rom, click on the **O**utline Pen check box in the Copy Attributes dialog box, then click on the Dark Olive group of objects. Doing this copies the outline width, nib shape, and scaling attributes.

7. Right-click on the maroon swatch on the colors palette to make the outline for the grouped objects the same maroon as you filled the objects with in OCR-Trace.

8. Repeat these steps with the objects on the other layers.

9. Astound anyone you can drag over to your monitor now!

One of the nice features of CorelDRAW objects is that you can copy and assign attributes to *grouped* objects. This spares the necessity of ungrouping and regrouping, and in this example, performing individual edits to hundreds of shapes. In figure 7.39, you can see the finished piper design.

If you've taken a crack at all the examples in this chapter, you deserve a hearty congratulations, and perhaps even the author's apology! But what you've learned through hands-on experience here has also saved you possible months of "problem/solution" mental gymnastics. The fact is, that Corel has a wonderful, not absolutely straightforward collection of features scattered throughout the various modules that hold design answers if you ask the right questions.

There have been some high hurdles in this chapter, but if you crossed them, you've learned several methods for creating *significant* design work, the kind that gets you recognized as both a creative type and as a problem-solver. Ask yourself what sort of price this commands in the business market today.

Figure 7.39
Photographic images
can be translated,
and even have
artistic qualities
enhanced, through
the use of Corel's
suite of applications.

Document-Centricity

Creating Your Own Fonts

The field of publishing has never been as varied and exciting as right now; desktop publishing, online publishing, and CD-ROM-based interactive documents have all but redefined the term "publishing." However, the *content* of a published document, regardless of its form, still relies on pictures and words to convey a message. Although most of this book concentrates on the techniques used to create fantastic pictures using the Corel suite of applications, this chapter concentrates on the building block of text: the not-so-humble *font*.

Since CorelDRAW! 3, Corel has provided users with the capability to create, edit, and enhance digital typeface programs and fonts. Because Win95 handles fonts differently from previous versions of Windows, and because some of the Corel applications have specific font requirements, learning the ins and outs of font creation and export is a must. By the end of this chapter, you'll understand the relevance of specific font types in different applications, how to create a text font, and how symbol fonts can be used in a number of design implementations.

The Anatomy of a Font

Like many traditional, physical business tools, typefaces in a computer system arrived at their measurements, component nomenclature, and other specifications from physical typesetting equipment that goes back to the first Guttenberg press. To be able to create a font using CorelDRAW, it's necessary first to understand and adopt some of the conventions and terms typesetters have used, and continue to use in the age of electronic publishing.

Understanding Digital Font Programs

The term *font* was originally used by typesetters who worked with metal slugs of typeface characters to describe a specific size and type of typeface. Times Roman 12 point is a font, for example. However, Microsoft and Adobe Systems have blurred the distinction between a typeface and a font, due to the capability of digital font programs to smoothly scale text to almost any size. Therefore, we use the term *font* in our discussions of CorelDRAW and other programs that can use digital type, regardless of the point size of a particular typeface.

The term *digital font program* is used on occasion in this chapter to reinforce the idea that Type 1 PFB and PFM files, and TrueType's TTF files are actually programs stored in hard disk cache. These programs are called on the fly when you use the specific fonts. Adobe Type Manager, for example, is a rasterization utility for font programs; ATM treats the monitor screen as though it's a printer, and displays a bitmap preview of the font program you use within a document. The most relevant part of a font program for designers, however, is the description of the outline of the font's characters. This chapter focuses primarily on two areas: how cleanly fonts appear and print, and how consistent characters in a font family are.

Choosing a Font Technology

In professional publishing circles, a popular discussion topic is the preferred format of digital fonts. Microsoft and Apple Computers created the TrueType structure for fonts as an alternative to Adobe System's Type 1 standard. The characters within a TrueType and Type 1 font can be identical, but it is the digital format of the font itself that can create a difference in your printed piece, and the way you work with a typeface.

For "text as text" assignments—those designs where a font is used for body text and headlines, it is almost universally accepted that Type 1 fonts are the standard. Type 1 fonts are more than a digital technology; they are an implementation of PostScript, the page descriptor language that high-resolution imagesetters use. Because of Adobe PostScript's predominant use in the publishing field, and the need for designers and commercial printers to be able to "speak" the same digital typeface language, Type 1 fonts became the standard.

However, the *general* market for fonts apparently has room for two digital typeface standards. TrueType, the second, is frequently used in enterprise computing for correspondence and memos. The reason for TrueType's acceptance in business is primarily due to financial and cosmetic considerations. TrueType prints cleanly to low-resolution laser printers, and TrueType fonts are easy to install on a system. Additionally, because this font technology is supported by most font creation programs (including CorelDRAW), almost anyone can create legitimate TrueType font designs, which has resulted in a flood of TrueType fonts, driving the overall price of digital typefaces to a pittance.

In Chapter 3, "Beating Nodes and Paths into Submission (The Easy Way)," the structural advantages to saving font characters in the Type 1 format are discussed. To recap, Bézier math—the type of information Type 1 fonts use to describe character outline paths—is inherently less complicated than the B-spline structure of TrueType characters. Simpler math goes into a font manager's cache more quickly; Type 1 fonts download the math equations of a font in a structure that PostScript devices (imagesetters, EPS rasterization filters in applications, film recorders, Acrobat Distiller) can quickly understand.

However, on some occasions the use of a Type 1 font is not possible. CorelDEPTH and DREAM 3D do not acknowledge the presence of Type 1 fonts in Win95. Fortunately, all the fonts available on the Corel CD-ROM are in both Type 1 and TrueType formats; you don't have to compromise a design because identical font designs can be used in either format.

Interestingly, TrueType doesn't actually remain an editable font in DEPTH and DREAM 3D. Like PHOTO-PAINT, fonts become rasterized—the outline information is converted to pixel-based format—in the final rendering within these programs. As a graphic, DEPTH and DREAM 3D designs that incorporated TrueType font information don't affect a PostScript imagesetter because the graphic contains no font program information; the TrueType text is converted to curved paths.

As mentioned earlier, CorelDRAW doesn't care whether you choose the PFB or TTF format for exporting characters of a digital font. This chapter shows you how to create a character outline for both TrueType and Type 1 formats.

Strong Recommendations for Accessing Fonts

Regardless of whether you use your own fonts, the fonts on the Corel CD, or some other source, keep in mind a few serious recommendations.

> ✔ If you want to keep that cordial relationship with your service bureau or commercial printer, make sure the editable text in your CorelDRAW documents and other documents uses Type 1 fonts. Where possible, use genuine Adobe Type 1 fonts, if for the only reason that most well-established publishing

II

Document-Centricity

services already own the same fonts. This is a reality, and not a promotion of Adobe's product in this book.

✔ If you need to use CorelDRAW's fonts, or the ones you'll learn to create in this chapter, make certain that your service bureau or commercial printer can use these fonts. Check the license carefully accompanying fonts you've purchased to see whether you may bring copies of the fonts used in a document to an outside service. Legal language is vague on the subject of using fonts you've purchased on multiple systems, and although your service bureau might be stumped on rendering your piece without the font you've used, violating a *software program* license is a matter you alone must decide. Happily, many service bureaus and commercial printers also own a version of CorelDRAW, so the ramifications of copying fonts often become moot.

✔ Confine the use of TrueType in your design work to programs that render the font characters to a graphic. Bitmap editing programs and modeling applications such as DREAM 3D never contain font information in the finished image. With these programs, it's okay to send a design with TrueType as a finished *bitmap* image to printers and service bureaus. TrueType is met with hostility and loathing at service bureaus because it frequently halts imagesetting devices; even when sent to an imagesetter as a graphic, TrueType takes longer to render than Type 1 because of its structural complexity.

Tip If you have a one-of-a-kind, must-have TrueType font you absolutely must use in a CorelDRAW design, try breaking the text into curves (**A**rrange, Con**v**ert to Curves, Ctrl+Q). If the lettering object then contains more than, say 350 nodes, use the **A**rrange, **B**reak Apart (Ctrl+K) command to separate the subpaths from the overall lettering object, then recombine objects (Ctrl+L) you've marquee selected, so that each collection of subjects combined together contains less than 200–300 nodes.

PostScript language complexity has its upper thresholds, and even imagesetters with adequate amounts of RAM can sometimes fail to decipher PostScript code for highly complex objects.

In Windows 95, you can "hot swap" TrueType fonts, moving them easily in and out of the system by click-and-dragging the TTF folder to, or from, the Fonts folder nested within the Windows 95 folder. (You don't actually need the Fonts utility in the System folder to add and delete TrueType fonts.) Should you choose to adopt this "hot swapping" practice, however, make certain the application in which you want to use the TrueType font is not currently running. And be aware that swapping a TrueType in and out of system is not a good idea if the TrueType font is used in an application in which text is always editable. If you've removed a font used in a document, then open the document in the application used to create the document, you might end up with a missing font at press time. See Chapter 12, "Outputting Your Input" (on the Bonus CD), for suggested workarounds to the "Missing Font" problem.

Different Classes of Fonts

The art of creating display (or *headline*) fonts and body text fonts would require a book or two, not a chapter, to document. The following brief discussion of the *styles* of fonts included on the Corel CD helps illustrate how you would create these classes of fonts. Typefaces, both digital and traditional, can be divided into the following two categories, each of which branches into other unique descriptors:

- ✔ *Roman* typefaces contain character components of different widths. You'll notice that the horizontal and vertical stems of roman typeface characters are typically different; the crossbar on a roman *H* is not as wide as the horizontal stems that make up the remainder of the character.

- ✔ *Gothic* typefaces use a uniform width to describe a character. Although Futura, Helvetica, and Olive Antique don't have exactly the same stem width within component characters, they are commonly referred to as gothic-style fonts. Avante Garde and Century Gothic are better examples of gothic font architecture, although they are less frequently used.

A modification of a basic typeface, called a *serif*, predates the printing press, and as early as the Roman times, slight artistic irregularities to the stems of a character were created to add legibility to stone-cut faces and hand-inked text. Font serifs became both an artistic embellishment and a means for controlling ink spread in centuries to come, and serifs also make a font appear more legible when a serif font is rendered at small point sizes. Serifs also seem to create more of a clean, professional edge on characters printed with ink on porous paper. We don't honestly need serifs today when text is rendered using dry laser toner, or when text is imaged to film, but serifs continue to maintain the quality of legibility in modern publications, and add an ornamental quality to the printed word.

Although almost every tradition of "good" typographic use has been somewhat abandoned since digital fonts became available to everyone, professional designers still lean toward the use of gothic fonts for headlines, and roman fonts for body text. This preference remains because gothic fonts tend to "shout" a message; when used as body text, these fonts cause some eyestrain.

The introduction of the gothic, serif letterform into typography presents an interesting compromise between gothic and roman font attributes—roman characters generally use serifs. Many would agree that Courier is an awful artistic font because of its coarse, gothic characteristics, but makes a wonderful substitute for System, Terminal, and MS-Sans Serif screen fonts because of Courier's serifs.

Conversely, roman fonts, with their soft, flowing construction, tend to lead the reader's eye through columns and columns of text, but fail to create visual "punch" when used in a headline at 24 points or more. As an attempt to make a bolder type of roman font, sans serif versions of popular typefaces were created.

II

Document-Centricity

In figure 8.1, you can see four examples of the basic types of fonts, in serif and sans serif styles.

Figure 8.1
Roman and Gothic
typefaces can have
serif or sans serif
styles.

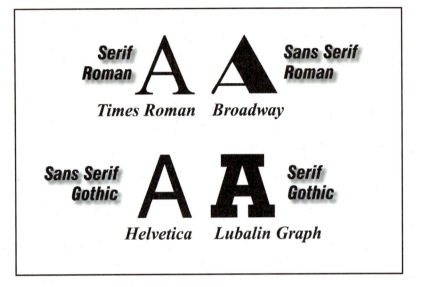

Why Bother Creating Fonts? Corel's CD Has 1,000 of Them!

Three compelling reasons lure graphic designers into the font-creation business, and entice them to experiment with some of the research mapped out in this chapter:

✔ You love how the expressiveness of a font's design can enhance, and sometimes replace, the content of the printed word. Vivaldi, Zapf Chancery, and Cataneo, to name but a few Corel fonts, are more than digital programs. These fonts speak eloquently of their creators, and are miniature pieces of artwork.

If you have some experience with a calligraphic pen, imagine the possibilities of your script after it's been digitized. See Chapter 7, "Corel OCR-Trace: Converting Bitmaps to Vectors," on techniques for bringing a pen and ink drawing into CorelDRAW. After your quill work has been converted to vector format, this chapter shows you how to organize the objects so that they can be exported as a digital font.

✔ You've grown tired of copying and pasting the same corporate logo into a half dozen ongoing design assignments. If you place the logo into an existing (or an original) font, you, or anyone else in your firm, can access the logo simply by typing the character it replaces.

✔ Your hard disk is as poorly organized as the author's, and you want quick access to basic shapes to be extruded or lathed in DREAM 3D, DEPTH, or MOTION 3D. Quite literally, digital fonts are only a collection of geometric paths organized according to the systems' scan code—the electronic signals sent by the keyboard. Therefore, a symbol font can be used effectively for creating borders and other repeat or constantly re-used shapes. More discussions about symbols fonts and DRAW's Symbols Roll-Up are in this chapter.

Begin by tackling the first of these compelling reasons in the next section, by creating a template for almost any kind of text font.

The "Rules" for Creating a Font Program

Some physical and procedural guidelines need to be followed to create a digital font worth posting online, using in your own work, or selling. Fonts you create in CorelDRAW are your own property; they are as much your own creation as a CorelDRAW drawing.

Let's begin with some suggestions and guidelines to make a font you or others will actually want to use:

✔ **Keep characters consistent.** The letterforms (characters) in your font should have the same vertical and horizontal stems across all characters. If, for example, the horizontal stem on your font's *H* is not the same as the *A*, your font will look like cartoon lettering when long lines of text are typed using the font.

Many methods can be used to address the issue of cross-character consistency. In an example that follows this section, you'll see how to use the template provided on the *CorelDRAW! 6 Expert's Edition Bonus CD*, and you will understand the typographic purpose for all the intricate guidelines in the template.

✔ **Create Succinct Characters.** Let Chapter 3 be your personal resource for the proper construction of curves in paths that make up your font's characters. The Trim, Weld, Intersect, and Combine functions in CorelDRAW are quite useful in maintaining character consistency, but they often produce an excess of nodes and incorrect path connections. In some applications, the way a font is designed is not important; and TrueType specifications for outline properties are more lax than those of Type 1. If careful inspection of a character you've created reveals redundant or unnecessary nodes, however, you should delete these nodes and edit the curve if the deletion changes the curve.

Create the best outline character, using the fewest nodes, and set your sights for the Type 1 format of fonts. If you need TrueType, CorelDRAW automatically adds nodes to the exported character (not your original in DRAW's drawing window) to make the underlying spline math correct for TrueType specifications.

✔ **Horizontals and Verticals are Absolutes.** Thanks to hours of trial and error, the author has created only a few fonts whose component paths aren't precisely on the horizontal and vertical axis of the page. Certain mistakes were unavoidable in previous 16-bit versions of CorelDRAW, which don't have the computational power to measure paths down to microns. With CorelDRAW! 6, you now have the power to zoom as closely as you like to the intersecting node on a path, and make certain that it's aligned with an adjacent node. A font with even a fraction of a degree tilt on a character stem will result in unaesthetic display on-screen at small point sizes, and will print with the error more apparent than you might think possible.

Tip The Snap To Guidelines feature in DRAW is excellent for keeping freehand Pencil tool lines perfectly vertical and horizontal. Also, use the Align feature on the Node Edit Roll-Up to ensure that a path segment in a character is on the up-and-up when designing font characters.

✔ **Make Correct node connections.** The construction of a path is important to ensure correct high-res output; this especially applies to font characters, whose format is usually PostScript (Type 1). Incorrect node connections might print fine to a 300 dpi laser printer, but modeling applications using font information are exceptionally picky about font construction. An ill-conceived font outline can result in a missing backface on a 3D text object. Read Chapter 3 on the finer points of creating paths with off-path control points that lie in a tangent to one another. Chapter 3 also shows how cusp connections should be used when a curve segment meets a straight line segment.

Guidelines for Fonts

In the same way that you'd design a machine part or advertising layout with CorelDRAW's guidelines, you can also build fonts using guidelines. But where does one begin to create a template for a font?

Traditionally, typeface designers would make a physical drawing of a font character on a piece of paper or vellum. The font is drawn to larger-than-life proportions to ensure that at finished reproduction size, any hand-drawn errors would be minimal or unseen. The traditional font designer would then play with the pieces of paper to see how the characters interact. Sometimes a character design needs to be modified because a serif smashes into another character, or the baseline of the font needs to be dropped to accommodate a special character.

Like traditional designers, it's still a good idea to design fonts much larger than the size at which they will be used, but you now have the option of skipping the rendering and scanning process and working directly in a CorelDRAW document.

If you're new to CorelDRAW's font export capability, you should design characters at 720 points to coincide with CorelDRAW's default Design size value for exported fonts. Where does 720 points come from? There are 72 points to an inch; 10 times this amount allows possible outline errors to be minimized. However, a 720 point character doesn't take up 720 points of printable page space; this is where *character space*—and the definitions and reasons behind font architecture—need to be examined.

Figure 8.2 is a schematic of the components of Times New Roman and where they lie within the font information of a Type 1 or TrueType file. Even if you never intend to re-create Times New Roman, understanding where the guidelines should go to create a font is a key lesson. Definitions of the guideline labels follow this figure:

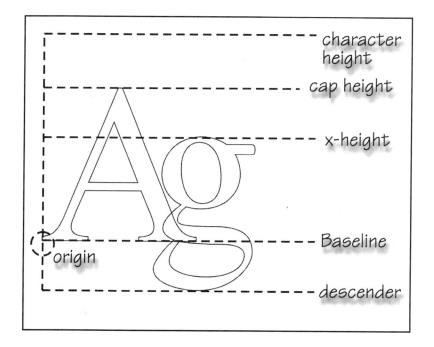

Figure 8.2
Characters in a font have components; use these guidelines to ensure font consistency.

✔ **Character height.** The mathematical coordinates within a digital font that represent the complete "live" area of a font when it is rendered to the screen or printed page. Character height is not the same as *cap height*; characters frequently have accents that *overshoot* cap heights. Character height is the maximum definition of one dimension of *character space* (explained when we get to exporting a character from DRAW in "Exporting a Font," later in this chapter).

✔ **Cap Height.** The typical height of a capital letter within the font. If you begin with a definition of character height as 720 points, it's not unusual to find a cap height in commercial fonts of only about 500 to 600 points. As a designer, you have the freedom to choose any cap height you like (within the character height), but by keeping the cap height reasonable within the character space, you can add accents to capital characters without having to rescale the entire character set down the road.

✔ **x-height.** The typical height of a lowercase character; folks usually measure the *x* in a font to determine the lowercase height because the *x* is flat, not rounded, on top and bottom and it has no descender. The distance between the x-height and the cap height is usually called the *ascender height*—a phrase used to describe, for example, the upper portion of the horizontal stem of a lowercase *h.*

You can have a lot of fun designing a font whose cap height is *consistently* lower or higher than a well-proportioned font such as Times New Roman. Parisian, Dolmen, and many fonts created by Lucian Bernhard (such as Modern and Fashion) are examples of fonts with deliberately low cap heights, creating an Art Deco look.

✔ **Baseline.** This is the most important guideline when exporting characters to a font format. The baseline determines the bottom of upper and lowercase characters that do not have descenders. Exported characters *must* be located on the same baseline in CorelDRAW, or the font in use will look like the "golfball" in an ancient IBM Selectric that wasn't seated properly.

✔ **Descender.** The measurement of the lower extreme of certain characters such as a lowercase *g* or *y.* Foreign characters containing slashes and underscore characters reach into the descender zone of a font's character space, but these special characters never reach the descender line.

✔ **The Origin.** Represents the bottom left of a typical character in a font. "Typical" is stressed because some character elements, such as the descender of a lowercase *y,* can extend below and to the right of the origin. This is okay, though; the origin is a convention for the program that uses the font to establish a relative baseline when the font is used to typeset words.

If you intend to create your own font template, the zero origin for the printable page *must* meet the lower left corner of the letterform's character space, for this is the origin point for the fonts you export using CorelDRAW. Click-and-drag on the zero origin box (the box at the intersection of the rulers) to change the zero origin of the printable page.

A brief explanation is necessary at this point because the information that follows may seem to contradict "good font" guidelines mentioned earlier. It is *more* than possible to create a consistent font—one whose character measurements abide by the guidelines—that still "looks" wrong on-screen and on paper. The reason for this is that *optical* centering of a character within character space is just as important as linear centering. In other words, if something is correct when you measure it, but looks wrong, then it *is* wrong. Trust CorelDRAW's rulers, but also trust your eyes. A good example of an optically centered character is the Times New Roman capital *O*. The *O* extends below the baseline, and above the cap height. And yet the *O* looks fine in the context of a typeset paragraph.

✔ **Overshoot.** The measurement above the cap height, above the x-height, and below the baseline, to accommodate characters—usually with rounded tops. An acceptable measurement for overshoot distance is between 5 and 10 percent of the overall character height.

✔ **Next Character origin.** Typically defines the end of the previous character's character space. We'll get into an unorthodox use of next character origin later in this chapter. For the time being, the right side of a character's space usually defines the next character origin.

✔ **Maximum character width.** It's usually a good idea to reverse-engineer a font; that is, create the widest character first, even though it's not the first letter you might export. See how an *M* looks on your font design template, then gauge the width of your other characters accordingly. Again, it's a pain to have to rescale all the characters because you didn't leave enough room for the widest character in a font. The horizontal width of the widest character (such as a capital *M* or *W*) should not overlap the origin of the next character. Fortunately, CorelDRAW enables you to fine-tune the right side of the character space before you export a character.

✔ **Sidebearings.** Measurements to the left and right extremes of a character that offer "padding," or virtual insurance that adjacent characters don't collide when used in programs that don't implement font tracking. A sidebearing is part of the character space, but you cannot set this value in CorelDRAW without seeing how two characters "fit" next to one another. You might need to fine-tune a completed font in an additional program to achieve optimal character spacing between characters. Some characters in a well-proportioned, well-spaced font, will extend *beyond* the character space, to create a more coherent look in a block of text.

Given all these considerations for font characteristics and measurements, it's time to take the show on the road in the next section, get your virtual feet wet, and begin designing and exporting a font.

CorelDRAW! as Your Font Toolkit

Many commercial applications, such as Macromedia Fontographer, provide a rich set of tools you can use to draw, kern, customize, and create a working digital font. Nevertheless, if you've ever downloaded a shareware font from an online service and inspected the header information for the PFB or TTF file, you'll often see "Copyright Corel Corporation." The font passed through CorelDRAW's doors. What this says is that although DRAW doesn't have all the specific tools you need for defining font *parameters*, it's still the most commonly used font *design* application because of its precise tools and ease of use.

The following section should be entitled "Where Shall I Begin?"; it's difficult to conceptualize a collection of font characters and how they work together. Actually drawing and exporting the first character is a great ice-breaker and introduction to the procedure, and we have some detailed steps lined up for you to follow.

Working with a Template and Reusable Font Parts

The trick to setting up a template for a font you want to create lies a good deal in pre-planning. To this end, we've created the CHARSPEC.CDT document, a CorelDRAW template file you can pop into Corel's Templates folder, and use for the express purpose of proportioning your own font. The exercise that follows is an excursion into the tools CorelDRAW offers for creating font components, and how to get the most from the guidelines in CHARSPEC.CDT.

Everything on pages one and two of CHARSPEC.CDT is locked; if you would like an unobstructed view while you work, use the eye icon toggle on the Layers Manager to make the Specifications and Desktop layers invisible. Because of the many uses for a single horizontal and vertical stem in CorelDRAW! 6, and thanks to the program's Boolean features for welding and intersecting objects, the process of creating a font in which the dimensions are consistent for all characters is easier than you might expect.

Here's how to create a capital *A* with a look similar to Bremen, the popular Bitstream font included on the Corel CD:

Using Boolean Features to Create a Font

1. In CorelDRAW, choose **N**ew, **F**rom Template, then choose CHARSPEC.CDT from the CHAP08 folder of the EXAMPLES folder on the *CorelDRAW! 6 Expert's Edition Bonus CD*. Check the **W**ith Contents check box, then click on **O**pen.

   Creates a GRAPHIC1 file in the drawing window, complete with annotations and guidelines, ready for designing a character.

2. Click on the Zoom tool, then marquee zoom around the capital *A* on the template page.

   Zooms you into a comfortable viewing resolution, where you can view the annotations and create components for the font you'll create.

3. Click on the Snap To Guidelines button on the toolbar.

   Although the Guidelines layer is locked, the guidelines will still snap any object you draw on the template page or move near the guidelines. This makes precise font component alignment...a snap!

4. Press F6 (or click on the Rectangle tool), then click-and-drag a rectangle on the page from the baseline guideline to the overshoot guideline.

   You've drawn one of the vertical stems for the capital *A*, imitating the construction of the Times New Roman character within the template for placement of your character's top at the overshoot guideline. Although this stem will eventually be a diagonal component of the "teepee" that shapes the letterform *A*, when a character stem is more vertically than horizontally oriented, it is considered to be vertical, both in terminology and in PostScript language.

5. Press the spacebar, then click-and-drag the left or right selection handles on the rectangle away from or toward the center of the rectangle.

   Toggles to the Pick tool, resizes the horizontal measurement of the rectangle, then makes the vertical stem thinner or thicker. This is an artistic call; make sure you're happy with the width of the right stem of the *A* before proceeding.

6. Click-and-drag the vertical stem off the page, right-clicking before releasing the left mouse button.

   Drops a copy of the vertical stem on the pasteboard section of the drawing window. You'll reuse this stem to create other characters of the font. If you have the Layers Manager open (Ctrl+F3), you'll also notice that the rectangle duplicate is on Layer 1; the Desktop layer where the pasteboard is usually located is locked.

7. Click twice on the rectangle on the template.

   Selects the rectangle, then puts the rectangle in Rotate/Skew mode.

8. Click-and-drag the top selection handle of the rectangle to the right until its right side matches the angle of inclination of the Times New Roman guideline cap on the page.

Creates an angled stem that will be used to represent the right side of the capital *A*. You might want to drag and drop a copy of this stem to the pasteboard, too, as we've done in figure 8.3. *W, M,* and other characters have angled vertical stems.

Figure 8.3

Decide on a width for vertical stems in a font, then duplicate the component whenever you need this part of a character.

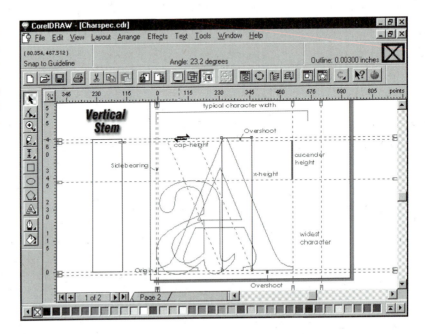

9. Create a more slender rectangle of equal height to the first rectangle, then drag and drop a copy of the rectangle onto the pasteboard area of the drawing window.

   This is the second component of the *A*; you can use it later for components of similar width in other characters.

10. Select the more slender rectangle, position it on the baseline to the left of the first rectangle, then click on it and skew it to the right, so that it appears to be the same angle as the vertical stem on the left of the Times New Roman *A* template.

    Creates the left side of the capital *A*. If the two skewed rectangles don't intersect toward the top of the design, click-and-drag them so they lie on top of the Times New Roman capital *A*.

11. Click-and-drag to create a slender rectangle that intersects both skewed rectangles midway up the objects.

    Creates the crossbar for the letterform.

12. By clicking and dragging on the crossbar's selection handles, make certain that areas overlap the two skewed rectangles only on the interior of the shape.

    You'll use the Weld command next to make a single text object, and eliminate overlapping rectangle areas. You don't want any crossbar areas outside of the future letterform.

13. With the Pick tool, marquee select all three objects.

    Selects all the objects for welding.

14. Click on the black swatch on the color palette.

    Fills all selected objects with black, making editing a little easier to see.

15. Choose **A**rrange, **W**eld.

    Displays the Weld Roll-Up.

16. Click on Weld to, then click on any of the three objects selected.

    Welds the objects together. By selecting all the objects to be welded before executing the command, it doesn't make any difference which object you point to with the Weld pointer. See figure 8.4.

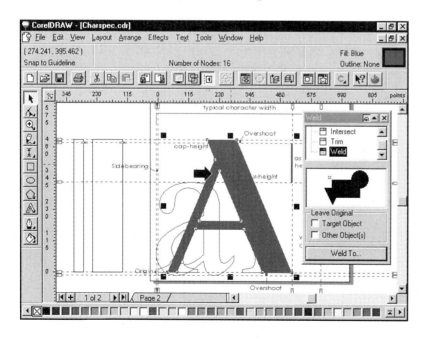

Figure 8.4
The Weld command fuses objects together, removing internal, overlapping path segments.

17. Press Ctrl+N (or choose **F**ile, Save **A**s), then save the document as MY-SANS.CDR to your hard disk.

   Saves the file at this intermediate phase of completion.

18. Click on the Snap To Guidelines button on the toolbar.

   Toggles the feature to its off position. Snap To Guidelines is a hindrance when you no longer need the feature.

There is no "right" or "wrong" design to your font; there might be internal structure problems, but if you have a capital *A* that looks a little different from the one shown in these figures, it's quite all right. This example is like a test with no grades passed out at the end!

Pre-Flight Tips for Exporting Fonts

The Weld command is only one of many automated routines that can shave minutes if not hours of design work from the creation of the rough outlines of characters. Yes, the last sentence strongly indicated that the character *A* in "My Sans Roman" is not yet ready for exporting as the first character in a font.

Note As a rule, it's not a good idea to start exporting characters that will make up a digital font until 1/2 hour after you're absolutely certain you will make no further changes, and you have the character set neatly laid out on multiple pages within a document. CorelDRAW sets the grid size for a font by the dimensions of the first character exported; you'll find nothing but grief down the road if you have to resize a font's character set because of a change in character size.

This chapter is not intended as a complete guide to creating letterforms—the complete character set to "My Sans Roman" depends on your instincts and ingenuity. The important thing to do now is address the structure of the letterform you've created. There are several extraneous nodes along the path of the capital *A* (the Weld and Intersect commands create these where paths slightly overlap) and the Boolean functions of Weld, Combine, Trim, and so on often change the node connection properties.

If you're going to create a functional, utilitarian font, you must thoroughly examine its content. You pay for understanding the techniques of digital font creation up front, or you pay for it later with a font that's flawed. Treat fonts you create like the rest of your artwork; finesse them until you're sure you're happy with your work.

In the next example, you'll perform some minor fixes around the path of the capital *A*, and make changes so that only the essential information about the path describes the font character. The fewer the nodes used to describe a shape, the better the font will work.

Refining a Typeface Character's Outline

1. With the Zoom tool, click-and-drag a marquee around one of the vertices of the letterform.

   Zooms into an area where an excess of nodes generated by the Weld command could exist. The top of the A has been chosen in the following figures, but you should examine *all* areas where the overlapping rectangles intersected.

2. Press F10 (or choose the Shape tool), then click on the outline of the letterform.

   Selects the letterform, and displays the nodes.

3. Marquee select the extraneous nodes, then press Delete.

   Deletes the nodes, and also changes the line segment's property from line to curve. See figure 8.5.

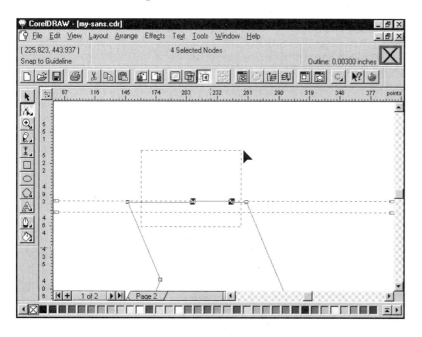

Figure 8.5
A straight line in a path segment requires only two points to define it. If you have more, delete them with the Shape tool.

4. Marquee select the two nodes that should define a straight line, then right-click on one node and click on To **L**ine if the option is available.

   Ensures that a straight line is actually a straight line. Some of the procedures in this exercise are detective work, and might not require an action. Deleting nodes often causes CorelDRAW to reposition nodes to accommodate the segment's new shape, and this means nodes that are horizontally aligned might have become unaligned. If you suspect this...

5. Double-click on a node, then marquee select the two nodes that define the segment.

   Displays the Node Edit Roll-Up; selects the nodes and path in question.

6. Click on the lower right button on the Node Edit Roll-Up.

   Displays the Node Align dialog box.

7. Uncheck the Align **V**ertical check box, then click on OK.

   Aligns the nodes horizontally. If the nodes don't quite touch the overshoot guideline on the template page, you can turn on the Snap To Guidelines feature, and drag both nodes to the guideline.

8. Marquee select all the nodes in the letterform's path.

   Reveals the connections' properties. As shown in figure 8.6, the To Line button on the Node Edit Roll-Up is dimmed, which means that all path segments are straight lines, which is cool and proper for this letterform. You're finished with the inspection routine for this font when the other areas of intersection have been checked to see whether any unwanted nodes exist.

9. Press Ctrl+S (**F**ile, **S**ave).

   Saves your work up to this point.

Figure 8.6

When a property button on the Node Edit Roll-Up is dimmed, the property already applies to the segment or node selected.

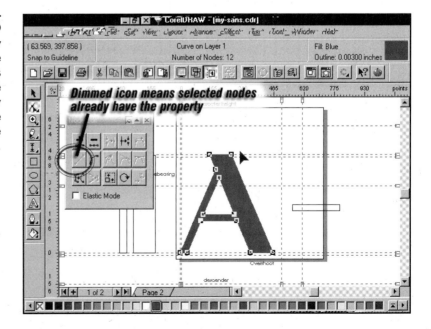

Serifs and Other Character Embellishments

Precisely designed fonts don't happen overnight; the author has designed fonts using CorelDRAW that are moderately complex. The process of creating over 100 characters for a font, from beginning to end, takes roughly two to three days; this includes testing the font on hard copy. The design work I do does not call for extended foreign characters, and I tend not to include them in many fonts. If you're designing symbol (or Pi) fonts, you might not need to fill even 50 typeface character registers. A *register* is the position a character is assigned within a font so that the corresponding keyboard key specifies that the character is used in a document.

Unlike characters in a font whose components are entirely straight segments, extended foreign characters and plain roman characters usually include a curve or two, and serifs can be either straight or curved. The best way to ensure consistency of stem strokes for curved fonts is to design a master template of the curves you intend to use for all the characters, then either accurately trace over it, or weld or trim the template into the character requiring a curved segment.

In figure 8.7, you can see page two of the CHARSPEC.CDT template. On this page, serifs have been created. The serifs don't belong to any particular font. However, if you need to add a serif to the stem of an *M*, an *F*, or an *A*, these serifs are ready and waiting. Try creating a series of serifs, with partial stems extending, and consistent stub height for the edge of the serif. Then use the Weld command on a duplicate of a serif to make the serif part of a character you've designed.

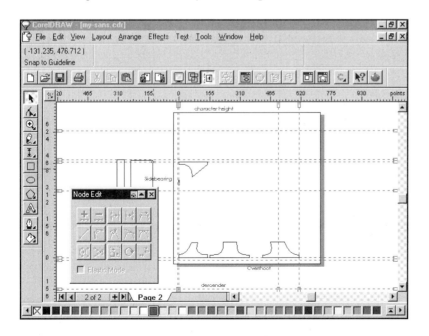

Figure 8.7
Design serifs with some form of consistency so that you can apply them to all letterforms requiring a serif.

Document-Centricity

After welding serifs to your letterforms, go back to the intersection point and make certain—you guessed it—there are no extraneous nodes and connections have the proper attributes.

Note If you remember the days of dry-transfer lettering, you'll recall what many designers did when they ran out of an important character. For example, if you ran out of *P*s (and no one was looking), you'd transfer the top and left of a *B* to the page, then clean up the edges with an exacto knife.

A similar procedure can be used to create curved letterforms. Try creating the bowls for the letterform *B* by creating two differently sized ellipses, use the Transform Roll-Up to align them, then use the **C**ombine command (Ctrl+L) to create a subpath drilled through the larger ellipse. When you have the bowl shape right, duplicate the shape and then weld it to the vertical stem of the B. Clean up the letterform with the Shape tool using the steps described in the last example, then re-use the bowl "template" to create the bowl of the letterform *P*.

Positioning Duplicate Elements

Procedurally, you've had perhaps the greatest assistant in font creation within CorelDRAW at your disposal since version 4. Although the new multiple document interface (MDI) feature is great for copying between documents, the multi-page format for Corel documents can make accurate positioning of duplicate elements a breeze. To take advantage of CorelDRAW's multi-page format, a CorelDRAW document that you'll use to create a font should be set up as a 100 page file. You don't need to do this right when you start working on that first character; more pages in a document can slow processing a little, so only add them as you need them. Also, make it a practice to press Ctrl+S at regular intervals; it would be heartbreaking to accidentally lose a hundred page document.

Let each page be a template for an individual letterform; you can proceed through the alphabet on each sequential page. This arrangement helps you keep track of which character you're currently exporting—DRAW auto-advances the export to the next ASCII character within a single CorelDRAW session.

The greatest advantage to creating a multi-page home for your font is that you can copy and paste into *exactly the same relative position* between pages. Therefore, if you want to compare the stem widths or other properties of a *W* with the *N* you created earlier (or want to copy a component of the character), select the character, press Ctrl+C (**E**dit, **C**opy), click on the Go To Page field on the bottom left of the drawing window, type in the page number, then click on OK and press Ctrl+V (**E**dit, **P**aste).

Consistency within a font isn't hard if you create a good curve, then copy it where appropriate to other characters.

What Makes a Letterform Perfect for Export?

CorelDRAW can create elegant fractal and fountain fills, and path line styles that are non-uniform in width. Because of these capabilities, a natural question at this point is, "What sort of fill and stroke should my letterform have to make it export correctly?" There are a few mandates for successfully exporting an object as a typeface character:

✔ The character must be a closed path. The object *can* have subpaths (use the Combine command to make a collection of paths a single path).

✔ It is best to assign the character you want to export no outline property (right click on the *x* on the color palette with a filled object selected). Corel's PFB and TTF export filters don't use outline property information. Although you can successfully export a character that contains a solid outline width, this practice can get you into trouble down the font-creation road.

A custom, dotted outline, for example, is not legitimate export data for PFB or TTF formats; CorelDRAW will tell you in a dialog box that the selected object contains "too many objects to export."

✔ Complex fill (fountain fill, texture, and so on) cannot be used; if used, the letterform will fail to export. Although certain figures in this chapter contain outlined characters, or characters filled with a uniform color other than black, they were created this way to illustrate a principle—not as examples for you to follow.

CorelDRAW exports characters with no outline attribute and black fill; this is the way you'll see the export preview whether the selected letterform is purple with a .28" outline width, or black with no outline. Make the export process for fonts an easy one; stick with "no frills" object properties.

Exporting the Character

In the following section, you'll walk through steps for calling CorelDRAW's PFB export filter, naming the font, setting the character width and spacebar width, and creating a digital font program that's ready to be loaded in Adobe Type Manager.

The wonderful thing about books is that they provide information that can be used in a non-linear timeline. If you'd like to hold off exporting a font so that you can create more than one character, this chapter will still be waiting when you come back. If you want immediate gratification of seeing how a single character font can appear in all your applications, here are the steps.

Exporting a Font

1. With the Pick tool, click on the (first) letterform you created, then click on the Export button on the toolbar.

   Selects the letter; displays the Export dialog box.

2. Choose Adobe Type 1 font from the Save as <u>t</u>ype drop down list. In the File <u>n</u>ame field, type **my-sans.pfb**, choose a hard disk location where you want the font created, check the Selected <u>o</u>nly check box, then click on E<u>x</u>port.

   Selects the font structure of the exported letterform, names the export file, and displays the Options dialog box.

3. Type **My Roman Sans** (or anything you like) in the <u>F</u>amily Name field on the Options dialog box.

   This is the user name for the font you export; the name displayed in the font list of applications that use Type 1 fonts. You can mix the name's case, use spaces, and exceed 8 characters. However, try to keep a font name short when you export it. Many applications offer a font drop-down list of fixed size, and long user names for fonts are often clipped, making the specific font name hard to discern.

4. Check the Symb<u>o</u>l font check box.

   Assigns the font the status of *Pi* (picture) font. This is actually a property of a font, and the property is saved in the header information in the PFB or TTF file. Many applications can do special things with a font designated as a symbol font. As you'll see in this chapter, the Symbol property for a font enables the font to be displayed on the Symbols Roll-Up in DRAW, and checking this box doesn't make the font size larger, or affect it in other negative ways. Also, when you check the Symb<u>o</u>l font, no font family properties (<u>S</u>tyle) are assigned to the font; the Style field is dimmed. That is good in this case, because there *are* no italic, bold, or bold-italic versions of My Roman Sans. If you're creating a complete font family—that is, at least four related typeface collections—you'd want to add <u>S</u>tyle information to the exported font, and wouldn't want to check the Symb<u>o</u>l font check box.

5. Type **375** in the Spa<u>c</u>e width field.

   Sets the amount of space assigned to the spacebar key, as shown in figure 8.8. There are no hard and fast rules for the amount of width you assign for inter-word space in a font. The default value in the Options box is generally too wide for the space key, however. You can play with this amount after you've exported several characters and played with the font in a word processing program or

CorelDRAW. See the TIP that follows this example for the specifics on fine-tuning the space character.

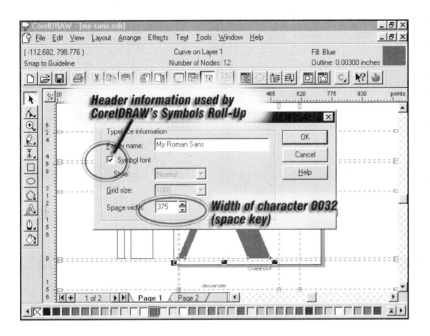

Figure 8.8
You can assign the spacebar key amount and the Style for a font in the Export Options dialog box.

Document-Centricity

6. Click on OK.

   Displays the Export Adobe Type 1 dialog box.

7. Scroll down the character box until you find the capital letter *A*, then click on it, then click on OK.

   Assigns the selected letterform to the keyboard scan code for a capital *A*, as shown in figure 8.9. It's worth noting here that the right sidebearing for the character space can be manually adjusted in the preview window. If you feel too much space is allotted to the character with the **A**uto box checked, uncheck the box, then click-and-drag the right sidebearing in the preview window to the left. The Auto option will remain unchecked, however, in a single export session from within CorelDRAW, so don't forget to check this option again before exporting the subsequent characters.

8. Press Ctrl+S (**F**ile, **S**ave).

   Saves your work up to this point.

Figure 8.9

You can assign an exported character to any keyboard scan code value; it's usually best to assign the obvious values, however!

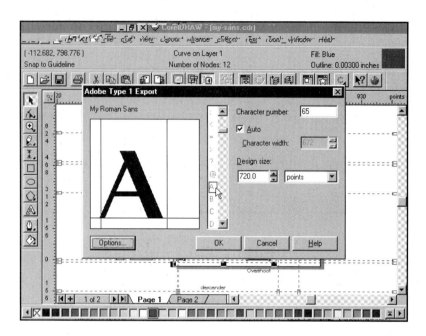

Although the preceding example showed you how to export a single character to a font, chances are that you'll create an entire alphabet for export that you or someone else will use in an assignment. If the space key space within the font is too wide, export an additional character to the PFB or TTF file. You won't actually export anything, and you don't need the original template files open in CorelDRAW to do this; you simply need to access the Options box. The only way to change the space is to open the font information within the file.

> **Tip** To modify the value of the space character within a font, you need to start a session in CorelDRAW. First, you select a character (or any legit object, no fancy fills or outline), click on the Export button on the Toolbar, choose the PFB file type, click on the MYFONT.PFB file in the folders window, check the Selected **o**nly check box, then click on E**x**port.

Whenever you export a character to an existing font, you get an attention box that asks you whether you really want to replace the selected file. You do, so click on **Y**es. In the Export dialog box, click on Options, then change the Spa**c**e width value. Click on OK, then click on **Y**es in the query box that asks whether you want to save this information to a file.

Finally, Cancel out of the Export box, and leave CorelDRAW. Your PFB or TTF file now has a new space key value. Don't forget to uninstall the original font through the same utility by which you installed the font—either ATM or Win95's Fonts utility, then load the edited version in Adobe Type Manager or Windows Control Panel Fonts utility.

Subsequent characters you might add to the example font in this chapter, or fonts of your own, will cause CorelDRAW to flash you an attention box, informing you that if you click on **Y**es, you'll replace the existing PFB or TTF file. This isn't exactly true; you're *appending* the existing file, and previously saved characters in the existing file will not be removed through the addition of a character.

Here are some important points to remember when "fleshing out" a font by exporting characters:

✔ Make sure the zero origin for the page is close to, or even touching, the lower left of the selected character you're exporting. If you use the CHARSPEC template for your font designs, you can't go wrong—the zero origin is correctly placed in this template. If you overshoot, sidebearings might make a character fail to actually touch the origin point. The origin point should be for the *character space*, not the selected object.

✔ Always check the Selected **o**nly check box after clicking on the Export button on CorelDRAW's toolbar. Naturally, you must have something selected on the printable page before doing this.

✔ Make sure you're only exporting a single path, and not a group of paths. If multiple items are selected—even ones outside the pasteboard in the drawing window—DRAW presumes that all the objects are part of the character. Uncombined objects cannot be exported as a font character, and you'll fail to export the intended object without the Selected **o**nly check box checked.

✔ Make sure the correct character is chosen on the scrolling strip in the Export dialog box. CorelDRAW auto-advances the default character on this strip with every subsequent export after the first one you selected. If you're not exporting characters in ASCII sequence, pay attention to the suggested export character; if it's not correct, find the correct corresponding character and click on it.

✔ In general, leave the **A**uto character spacing option checked. If you uncheck it to manually define the right sidebearing for a character, subsequent exports will have the **A**uto box unchecked, and the right sidebearing in the preview window will fail to appear. If this happens, the right sidebearing for the character will be located a few miles away from the character. Use of the font in an application would provide humorous results.

Check out the preceding TIP for information on defining the space key character width. Many word processing programs cannot compensate for a broader-than-average space width.

Grid and Design Size Options: Forget 'em!

If you followed the previous exercise, you might have noticed that the Type 1 export box contains a Grid Size field, and the set of steps made no mention of this option. You may never need to change the Grid Size; nevertheless, an explanation of Grid Size is in order.

Adobe's specifications for character space—the character outline *and* the "white space" that surrounds it—is based around an imaginary grid. The grid is used as a relational coordinate system; 1,000 grid units equal one user unit. The units don't have labels, such as points or inches, however. The grid is simply a coordinate system for defining character space. You can't change this option after a font file has been created and is populated with characters.

There is no relationship between the 720 point master characters you export and the 1,000 unit grid. CorelDRAW uses the grid coordinate information internally when it exports fonts, and you'd need a compelling, unusual reason to change it. Although the Grid size spin box values for the TrueType format differ from Type 1 values (the default TrueType value is 2048), the underlying reason for the grid is the same as for Type1 fonts. The **D**esign size of a font can be set to any value you please from within the Export dialog box, but as with the grid size option, if you use the CHARSPEC template to design your fonts, you have very little reason to ever change the **D**esign size option.

Problems with Path Tangents

As described in Chapter 3, control points (*handles*) that have a smooth property and are located off the curve create a collinear relationship between their location and the location of the control point (*node*) located on the curve. CorelDRAW treats off-curve control points as part of the overall path when it is selected; when off-curve handles aren't flush with the horizontal or vertical axis of an object, you'll notice selection handles located far away from the object when you move the overall path.

This problem becomes particularly troublesome when attempting to align a character to the zero origin. It's easy to correct and can be avoided if you make certain that control points are collinear and exactly parallel to axes when you export the character. In figure 8.10, you can see the proper and improper configurations for the control points along a curve. The illustration on the right is an exaggerated one, but as you can see, a control handle located far off and to the left of the character's outline makes aligning this character to the origin (or any other font guideline) an impossible task in DRAW.

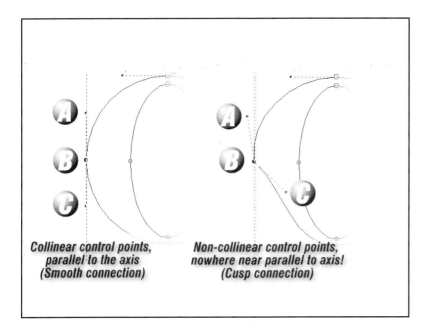

Figure 8.10
Make sure the tangents created by control points are lined up (collinear), and that a smooth curve has a Smooth property node.

Creating a Logotype Font

It seems as though even the smallest company today wants a logo—a pictogram representing the corporate entity. Similarly, *logotypes*—typefaces such as "Kellogg's" and "IBM"—are identifiable graphics that are becoming more popular with small businesses.

In the following sections, you'll see how to create a logotype font—one that can be used in a multitude of design applications. You'll even read about some of the design possibilities for which a logotype font can be used in some of CorelDRAW's new modules.

"Borrowing" from Other Typeface Families

Before beginning, this section requires a disclaimer about the sticky subject of *font piracy*. It should go without saying that stealing a font design to sell as your own is illegal, and at least one type foundry has been prosecuted for this practice in recent years. Similarly, with programs such as CorelDRAW, Fontographer, and others, it's very easy to copy a commercial font, alter the copyright information in the font's header and attempt to pass it off as your own. It's just as easy to be sued, fined, or imprisoned for such a practice.

You're not going to copy a font in this section; instead, you'll modify certain characters of an existing font to create a unique logotype for the fictitious Googoltronics Corporation. It is indeed an accepted and legal practice to add embellishments to an existing font (this is how many logotypes are created), and then save the logotype as part of a digital font.

To begin any logo assignment, you first need to get a feel for the type of company, then select the appropriate "stock" font you'll customize into a logotype. Googoltronics is a technology company, and as such, needs a logotype that's aerodynamic—sleek and futuristic—and a little conservative. Fonts such as Stop (which is not a very legible typeface)and ITC Machine are overused: fonts *do* go in and out of fashion. Handel Gothic has a pleasant, easy-to-read outline, but it's perhaps a little too fragile along some of the character stems to make a logotype with impact. This makes it a perfect target for some modifications that follow in the next set of steps. If you'd like to load this font on your system right now (from the Corel CD-ROM), we'll show you some of the techniques used to modify the font to create a splendid logotype design:

Creating a Bold, Expanded Logotype

1. With Handel Gothic loaded on your system, open CorelDRAW, choose the Artistic Text tool, then type **GOOGOLTRONICS** on a blank, new document.

   Produces the characters that will be used within the logotype.

2. Press Ctrl+spacebar, then press Ctrl+T (Te**x**t, **C**haracter).

   Toggles to the Pick tool (the text is selected); displays the Character Attributes dialog box.

3. Choose Handel Gothic from the **F**onts list, type **50** in the Si**z**e spin box, then click on OK.

   Changes the selected text from the default font to Handel Gothic, increases its size so it can be modified with some precision, then returns you to the drawing window.

4. With the Pick tool, click-and-drag the top selection handle toward the center of the Artistic Text until the status line says that the y Scale is about 70%.

   Creates a more squat typeface. Before you finish, the logotype will look extended, not squat. The difference between elongating the x scale and reducing the y scale of an object is nil.

5. Press F10 (or click on the Shape tool), then click-and-drag the kerning handle (the honey-dipper shaped icon on the right of the text) until the status line indicates that you've changed the inter-character spacing to make the text about .1" wider overall.

Creates more spacing between characters. You'll make this typeface bolder shortly, so you need some "play" between characters for this purpose. See figure 8.11.

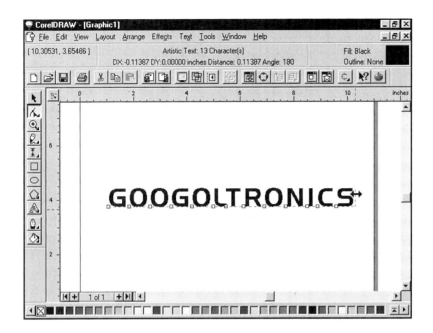

Figure 8.11
You can manually increase or decrease inter-character spacing by dragging on the kerning handle.

6. Choose Effe**c**ts, Co**n**tour from the menu (Ctrl+F9).

   Displays the Contour Roll-Up.

7. Click on the Outside radio button, type **0.025** in the Offset spin box, and type 1 in the Steps spin box.

   Defines the direction a contour shape will be created, how far from the original the contour will be created, and how many contours will be applied.

8. Click on Apply.

   Applies the Contour effect. The text also looks bolder now. See figure 8.12. The values suggested here are specific solutions for Handel Gothic at 50 points. Try different Offset values in your own experiments.

9. Choose **A**rrange, **S**eparate, then click on the grouped Contour object with the Pick tool, and drag it away from the original text.

   Separates the grouped Contour object from the dynamically linked Artistic Text, then moves it so that you can concentrate upon it, and not the original text.

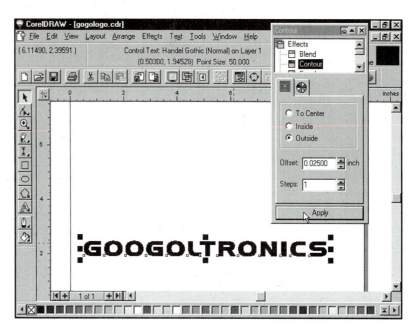

Figure 8.12
You can make a boldface font by applying a single Contour effect to the outside of the selection.

10. Click on the Group/Ungroup button on the toolbar.

    For some unknown reason, the Contour effect produces a grouped object, even though the group consists of only one object. By ungrouping it, you can now freely edit the nodes that make up the object's compound path.

11. Select the Handel Gothic text, then press Delete.

    Deletes the text. You can uninstall Handel Gothic from your system at any point after closing CorelDRAW without affecting this document in the future.

12. Choose File, Save (Ctrl+S), then save this document as GOGOLOGO.CDR to your hard disk.

    Saves your work at this intermediate stage of completion.

The logotype would look a little more striking and original if you customized a string of Artistic Text after applying the Contour effect. In the next section, you'll see one of the many ways you can combine a logo with text, to create logotypography.

Building a Logo within a Logotype

Practically no font used as a basis for a corporate logotype escapes transformations of some kind to serifs, font weight, and custom characters within the logotype signature. Perhaps you've seen a logotype for a restaurant, let's say "Sarah's Kitchen," where the *I* in "Kitchen" has been replaced with a spoon. It's a common design trick to bind the name of the product or service with a pictogram of a company's specialty.

Because Googoltronics is a technology firm, and because there is a proliferation of *O*s in their name, why not replace one of the *O*s with a high-tech looking piece of circuitry? Be careful when altering a letterform into a shape; you don't want to compromise the overall legibility of the logotype. In the next series of steps, you'll create a circuit design, then insert it into the logotype, thus creating a highly original corporate signature.

Modifying a Logotype Character

1. With the Ellipse tool, hold Ctrl and Shift, then click-and-drag a circle, starting from the center of one of the *O*s in "GOOGOLTRONICS." Release the cursor when the circle is slightly larger than the contoured *O* shape.

   Ctrl constrains the ellipse to a perfect circle; holding Shift begins the design of the circle from the object's center. You've created the size and shape of the circuit character you'll add to the logotype.

2. Press the spacebar, then click-and-drag the circle away from the logotype onto a clear area of the printable page.

   Moves the object so that you can work on it without visual clutter.

3. With the Zoom tool, right-click on the page and choose Zoom To _S_election from the shortcut menu.

   Zooms to a close-up of only the selected circle on the page. If you have the traditional tools option activated in CorelDRAW! 6, choose the Zoom To Selection button from the Zoom tool flyout.

4. Choose the Ellipse tool, then Ctrl+click-and-drag a circle about 1/8" in diameter inside the larger circle.

   Creates a circuit component within the circle.

5. Press the spacebar, click-and-drag the circle upward about 1/8", then right-click before releasing.

   Drops a copy of the circle above the original. Remember consistency when designing the components of a font character; copy elements whenever possible to accomplish this goal.

6. Add a slim rectangle or two to the inside of the circle to suggest wires connecting the circuits.

7. Copy the first rectangle you draw to maintain character consistency.

8. Draw a rectangle similar in size to the small circles, then with the Shape tool, click-and-drag on a corner of the rectangle until it looks like a capacitor or diode.

   Completes the electronic artifacts that will go inside the logotype character (see figure 8.13).

Figure 8.13
You might want to take the back off your Walkman, and duplicate some interesting circuitry work for the special logotype character.

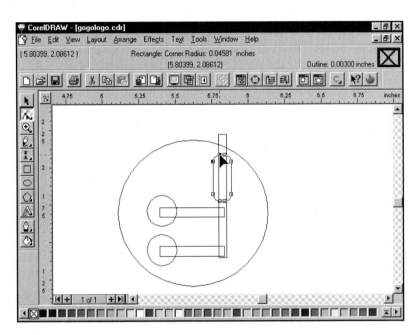

9. With the Pick tool, select all the interior objects within the circle, then choose **A**rrange, **W**eld from the menu.

   Displays the Weld Roll-Up.

10. Click on the Weld to button on the Roll-Up, then click the arrow cursor on any selected object.

    Welds objects together; eliminates intersecting paths in the interior of the resulting shape.

11. With the new, welded shape selected, choose Trim from the Group List window of the Trim Roll-Up.

    Changes the function of the Roll-Up to Trim features.

12. Click on Trim, uncheck the Other Object(s) check box, then click the arrow cursor on the large circle.

Removes the outline of the electronic circuit design from the circle and deletes the welded object. Figure 8.14 skips ahead and fills the resulting object with black so that you can see the result.

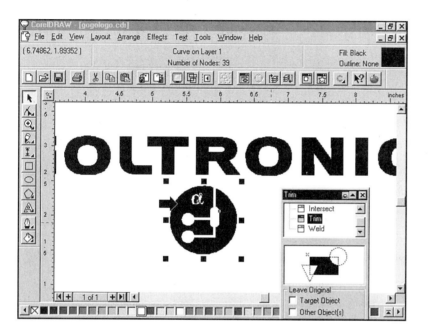

Figure 8.14
Use the Trim command on a path you want removed from the volume of a different object.

The alpha character from Win95's Symbols font was a design enhancement included in the Trim operation, as you'll see in future figures in this section. Don't be afraid to "mix and match" from other fonts to create a look.

13. Press Ctrl+S (**F**ile, **S**ave).

The next phase of logotype construction is to clean up the excess number of nodes currently located along the path of the contour shape. The logotype looks handsome and striking, but the Contour tool has a nasty tendency to create more nodes along a Contour path than are necessary for describing the shape. This issue needs to be addressed before adding the circuit character to the logotype.

Using the Shape Tool's Auto-Reduce Feature

Corel Corp. has moved many options for tools and features found in previous versions to other sites within the workspace. Although the Contour tool still has no curve complexity option in version 6, and it still produces an excess of nodes along a Contour path, the Shape tool can now be fine-tuned in CorelDRAW! 6 to summarily dismiss excess nodes along a path in one fell swoop.

In the next set of steps, you'll see how to perform fairly accurate node reduction automatically, and retain the general look of the contoured logotype.

Refining Outline Properties of the Logotype, Part I

1. Choose the Shape tool, then right-click on the tool and choose the Properties option from the pop-up menu.

   Displays the Tool Properties sheet for the Shape tool.

2. Type **0.002** in the Auto-Reduce spin box, then click on OK.

   Changes the distance by which the curve containing the selected nodes to be removed will change. Whenever you delete nodes from a path, the control handles on remaining nodes will shift to support the new structure for a curve segment. 0.002" is an acceptable amount of curve shift for the contour path, given its relative overall size. You'll manually refine the logotype path before exporting it, so curve fidelity is less important than removing nodes at this stage. Besides, the smaller the Auto-Reduce settings, the fewer nodes will be automatically deleted.

3. With the Shape tool, click on the contour logotype, marquee select a single character, click on one of the highlighted nodes, then right-click and choose Auto-Reduce from the shortcut menu.

   Dramatically reduces the number of nodes along one of the subpaths of the logotype (see fig 8.15). It's not necessary to select all the nodes in the logotype to perform node reduction all at once. In fact, this technique might lead to serious path construction distortions, due to the interaction of supporting nodes being removed at the same time. Curves produced by the Contour effect require the most attention; straight line segments such as the *I* will require no node reduction.

4. With the Shape tool, marquee select all the nodes in the *O* that precedes the *N* in GOOGOLTRONICS.

   Selects all the nodes.

5. Press Delete.

   Deletes the *O* shape; makes room for the addition of the circuitry shape you designed earlier.

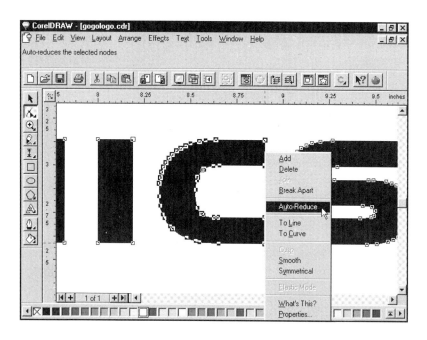

Figure 8.15
The Auto-Reduce feature produces the best results when the Shape tool's setting is equal to or higher than 0.002".

Document-Centricity

6. Press Ctrl+S (**F**ile, **S**ave).

Saves your work at this intermediate stage.

Two techniques are used for fitting the circuitry design into the logotype; you've begun working with one of them. The *O* in the last example could have been deleted by first using the **A**rrange, **B**reak Apart (Ctrl+K) command on the logotype. Both paths that comprise the *O* shape could then be deleted using the Pick tool. Breaking apart the subpaths, however, would also have broken apart the subpaths in the other *O*s in the logotype and the subpath in the *R*—all these objects would then require recombining before export. This technique might be more work than it's worth, when you understand the capabilities of the Shape tool.

Inter-Character Spacing and Character Additions

The goal of creating a logotype as a digital font has almost arrived; but first, consider how this logotype will export, and for what purpose, before finalizing the architecture of the design.

If Googoltronics really existed, chances are that the MIS Director of such a company would insist on the new logotype being a TrueType font rather than an Adobe Type 1 font. The reason: to avoid installing Adobe Type Manager on 4,000 machines. ATM is the graphics designer's utility of choice for high-quality font output, but many individuals don't bother with ATM when Windows natively supports TrueType, which is fine for inter-office quality communications.

Another compelling reason to export this font as TrueType is that Corel's 3D applications insist upon it; MOTION 3D and DEPTH only work with TrueType fonts.

Should you break the logotype down into individual characters for exporting to a TrueType file? Probably not; the font only contains 10 unique characters. As a whole, this logotype can be used to quickly type a letterhead on some correspondence; it might not be too popular if users are required to type 10 keystrokes every time they need the logotype.

However, you also don't want to make the logotype a *single* character; it would most likely exceed the character complexity for output to even a low resolution laser printer. The PostScript limit to character complexity is 200 control points; TrueType's threshold has never been officially recorded, but it is quite similar to Type 1 PostScript's.

Therefore, the next best solution is to break the logotype into two characters; asking a typist at Googoltronics to type *g*, then *t* isn't asking too much. Another advantage to breaking the logotype into two equal portions is that the narrower the exported character, the greater height you can give it. You cannot, as a responsible designer, violate the grid size that applies to all digital typefaces by exporting a 720 point character that's 5,000 points wide. Therefore, the "GOOGOL" and the "TRONICS" character will have to be of small cap height to fit a character space in a font. Users will have to grow accustomed to specifying a 200 point size for the logotype used in a word processor to make the logo compete with the point size of "normal" body text. Aside from exporting the logotype as clip art, there *is no* other legitimate way to add a logotype to a non-drawing application's document.

It's also not a bad idea to toss in the circuitry design as a separate character within the font, to make a font consisting of three characters in total. By doing this, you can create animations and 3D designs using a combination of the logotype and the design. In addition, this arrangement allows Googoltronics to decorate corporate documents with only the circuitry design.

Here's how to add the circuitry logo to the logotype, and evenly space the entire design so that it will look clean and polished when a user types the font:

Refining Outline Properties of the Logotype, Part II

1. With the Pick tool, click-and-drag the circuitry design so that it's centered within the logotype design. Make sure proportional space exists between it and the *R* character, then right-click before releasing the cursor.

   Drops a copy of the design in position for combining with the rest of the logotype. Don't worry if the circuitry design overlaps the *N* character. You'll fix this next. It's recommended that you fill the circuitry design with a color that contrasts with the logotype, to make editing work easier to see.

2. With the Shape tool, select all the nodes in the logotype from the *N* to the *S*.

   Selects characters that need to be moved to accommodate the circuitry design within the logotype.

3. Hold Ctrl, then click-and-drag one of the nodes to the right, until there is a character space between the *N* and the circuitry design equal to the rest of the character spaces.

   Ctrl constrains node movement to the direction from which you first click-and-drag, which should be a horizontal movement. See figure 8.16.

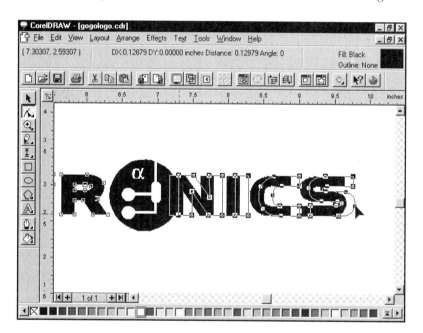

Figure 8.16
Use the Ctrl key to constrain the movement of the selected nodes. Ctrl keeps the baseline of the logotype straight.

II

Document-Centricity

4. Press the spacebar, select both the logotype and the circuitry design, then press Ctrl+L (**A**rrange, **C**ombine).

   Combines the two objects into a compound path.

5. Press +, click on a light blue on the color palette, then press F10.

   Duplicates the finished logo, fills it with a distinctive color, then selects the Shape tool.

6. Marquee select all the nodes in the light blue copy from the *T* to the *S* characters. If you accidentally select some of the overlapping nodes on the *L* character, Shift+click on the nodes to remove them from the current node selection. Then press Delete.

Creates the character "GOOGOL."

7. Press the spacebar and click on the black logotype lettering showing beneath the blue copy. Press the spacebar again, then marquee select all the nodes in the characters *G* through *L*. As in step 6, if there are unwanted nodes (like some on the *T* letterform) that are selected, Shift+click on each node to remove them from the current selection. Then press Delete.

   Toggles to the Pick tool, selects the black original logotype, then toggles back to the Shape tool. The lettering that *isn't* represented in the edited blue copy is selected, then deleted. See figure 8.17.

Figure 8.17

Create a two-character design by eliminating opposing halves of each of the two objects.

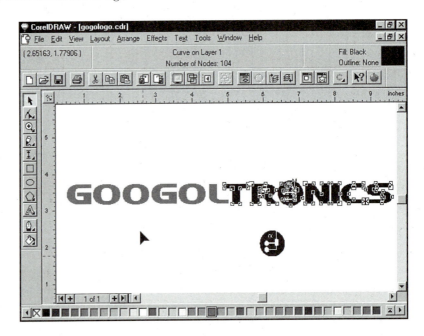

8. Press Ctrl+S (**F**ile, **S**ave).

   Saves your work at this intermediate stage.

Before continuing, check the "GOOGOL," the "TRONICS," and the standalone circuit design for correct placement of nodes, and correct node properties. Create additional nodes, if called for, to support a curve.

Exporting the Logotype

This section is where your knowledge of sidebearings and baselines pays off. To create two characters within a font that will "interleaf" correctly to create a single logo, you must export the "TRONICS" object with part of the *T* extending beyond the left side of the character origin. You do not have to pay special attention to the "GOOGOL" object when exporting it as a character, however. The two characters will, in theory, always be used in the same combination: the "TRONICS" character will always appear after the "GOOGOL" character.

Here's how to place the objects on a copy of the CHARSPEC template, and export them to create the Googltronics TrueType font:

Exporting a Logotype

1. Double-click on the Pick tool.

   Selects all three objects on the printable page.

2. Press Ctrl+C (**E**dit, **C**opy).

   Copies the objects to the clipboard.

3. Choose **F**ile, **N**ew, **F**rom Template, then choose the CHARSPEC.CPT file from the EXAMPLES.CHAP08 folder on the *CorelDRAW! 6 Expert's Edition Bonus CD*. Make sure the **W**ith Contents check box is checked before clicking on **O**pen.

   Opens a Graphic 1 document based on the CHARSPEC document.

4. Press Ctrl+V (**F**ile, **P**aste).

   Pastes the Clipboard copy of the Googoltronics logotype components on Layer 1 in the document.

5. Press Ctrl+F3 (**L**ayout, **L**ayers Manager), then click on the Specifications eye icon on the Layers-Roll-up.

   Hides the text on the Specifications layer of the template copy. You don't need the guideline labels hindering your work.

6. With the Zoom tool, marquee zoom closely around the area where the *L* and *T* letters meet.

   This is the area you need to examine to determine how far the "Tronics" object needs to exceed the origin on the page. It might help to place two guidelines at the points where the two characters overlap each other's character space. Make a mental note of the distance by which they overlap, or better still, draw a rectangle the exact width by which the two letters intrude upon each other. See figure 8.18.

Figure 8.18

The near points of the *L* and *T* letters mark the distance by which the "TRONICS" object must be to the left of the character origin.

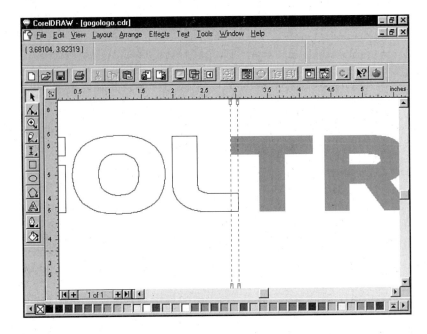

7. With the Pick tool, click-and-drag the "GOOGOL" object until a flat portion of the object's bottom (like the *L* shape) meets the guideline baseline, and the object's left extreme is flush with the vertical origin guideline.

   This puts the "GOOGOL" object in its correct character space position for export. Notice that the correct placement of the object allows the *O* parts of the object to descend slightly into the overshoot area, while the flat portions of the bottom of the lettering should touch the baseline guideline.

In figure 8.19, a deliberate boo-boo has been created to demonstrate a common problem. You'll notice that although the object rests flush with the baseline, the left edge doesn't meet the origin guideline because a control handle extends to the left of the object's extreme. If you have this problem, choose the Shape tool, straighten the control handles so that they are perfectly vertical, then align the object to the guideline.

8. With the Pick tool, click on the "TRONICS" object, Shift+click on the circuit object, Shift+click on the "GOOGOL" object, then click on the Align and Distribute button on the toolbar.

   The Align and Distribute Roll-Up will align the first and second selected objects to "GOOGOL," the last object that is selected.

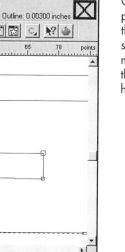

Figure 8.19
Control handles,
particularly those on
the left and bottom
sides of an object,
must be aligned with
the vertical or
horizontal axis.

9. Click on the align (vertical) left and (horizontal) middle buttons on the Align and Distribute Roll-Up, then click on Apply.

   Aligns the "TRONICS" and the circuit design to the horizontal middle and absolute left edge of the "GOOGOL" object, which is perfectly aligned to the origin of the character space. See figure 8.20.

10. With all three objects selected, click-and-drag the upper right corner selection handle away and up from the objects until the dotted bounding box reaches about 650 points on the horizontal ruler.

    Sizes all the objects proportionately, while the "GOOGOL" object remains flush against the origin and baseline. For characters that should be no more than 720 points, this vertical measurement is about the maximum you should allow the characters to become. Remember, we're concerned about character width; you can't add any more height to the characters without distorting them.

11. Click on the "TRONICS" and circuit design, then move them away from the "GOOGOL" object.

    Clears the way for exporting the first character. The figures in this section show the objects in different colors, and with outline attributes. This was done to illustrate the font exporting events, and you don't need to reassign objects different values. Go to wireframe view if you don't have a clear view of the objects.

Figure 8.20
Use the Align and
Distribute Roll-Up to
align the left sides of
the objects to the
object already
aligned to the origin
and baseline.

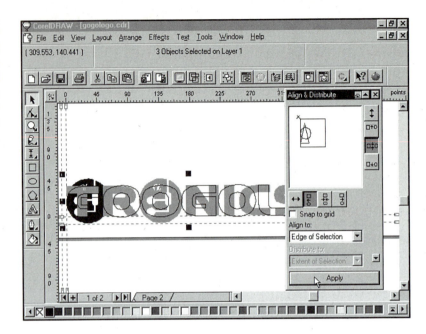

12. Click on the "GOOGOL" object, then click on the Export button on the toolbox.

    Displays the Export dialog box.

13. Choose TrueType font (TTF) from the Save as **t**ype drop-down list, type GOOGOL.TTF in the File **n**ame field, then select a convenient location on your hard disk from the folders window.

    Specifies the type of font you're going to export; names the file and location for the file.

14. Click on E**x**port.

    Displays the Options dialog box.

15. Type Googoltronics in the **F**amily name field, check the Symbol font check box, and don't touch the **G**rid size or Spa**c**e width fields, then click on OK.

    Displays the Export TrueType font Export query box. As with Type 1 fonts, the TrueType coordinate grid is of very little importance to the average designer. The default value indicates that there is a 2,048 to 1 relationship between font units of measurement and user units. This differs from the Type 1 default because the font formats are written to different specifications. You don't need to specify a Spa**c**e width value other than the default. For a 3-character font, you have no use for the space key when creating the logotype on a page.

16. Click on Yes to the query "Save changes to Font file."

   Displays the TrueType Export dialog box; the character you export will be saved to the TTF file format.

17. Choose the lowercase *g* from the character strip to the right of the preview box, leave the **A**uto (spacing) check box checked, and click on OK.

   The "GOOGOL" character exports to the lowercase *g* register of the GOOGOL.TTF file.

18. Press Ctrl+S, then save the file as GOGOLOGO.CDR to your hard disk. Click on Yes to confirm to CorelDRAW that you want to overwrite the previously saved GOGOLOGO file.

   Overwrites the saved version of this file. The current version has accurate guidelines, correctly scaled objects, and your original designs, so you don't need two copies of this file.

II

Document-Centricity

The Finer Points of Customizing a Font

The export of the "TRONICS" and circuit design are performed similarly, although the next set of steps has a twist. Instead of aligning the "TRONICS" object to the origin guideline, you'll extend the *T* portion of the object to the left of the origin guide. When the font is used later, this *negative kerning* value will cause the "TRONICS" character to fit nicely within the *L* portion of the "GOOGOL" character.

Here's how to complete the export of the Googoltronics TrueType character set:

Exporting the Rest of the Characters

1. Click-and-drag the GOOGOL lettering away from the baseline and origin guidelines. Now click-and-drag the TRONICS object into position so that the bottom of the *T* portion of the object is flush with the baseline, and the horizontal stem of the *T* extends beyond the origin guideline by the amount of space you measured in an earlier example.

   Places the object in the location where CorelDRAW will position it within the TrueType font's character space. Note that because the circuit is taller than the rest of the letters in the object, its lower portion descends beneath the baseline. This is correct. See figure 8.21.

Figure 8.21

Position the TRONICS object so that it is in relational space to the GOOGOL object you exported. The two characters will interleaf when typed.

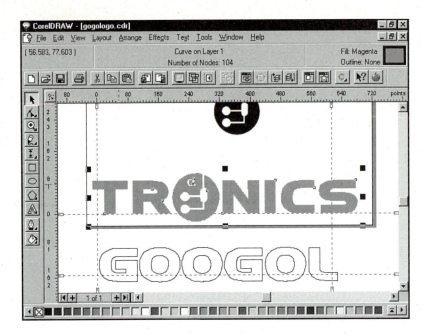

2. Click on the Export button on the toolbox, click on the Selected <u>o</u>nly check box, click on GOOGOL.TTF in the folder window, then click on E<u>x</u>port.

   The "replace existing file?" attention box pops up (remember this box when you were exporting a Type 1 font to an already existing file?). Click on <u>Y</u>es to proceed and ignore this erroneous message.

3. After you've clicked on <u>Y</u>es in the attention box, the TrueType Export dialog box appears, and the lowercase letter *h* is selected in the character strip. Scroll to lowercase *t*, click on the *t*, then click on OK.

   Exports the TRONICS object to the lowercase *t* register in the Googoltronics font. Notice in figure 8.22 that the horizontal stem to the *T* portion of the object extends beyond the origin guideline.

4. Export the circuit design using the same steps as those shown for the other characters. Remember that the circuit is a little larger than the lettering you originally created when you contoured the Handel Gothic text. Therefore, make sure that the circuit descends below the baseline guideline by the same amount

as the circuit portion of the TRONICS lettering. The left edge of the circuit design should be flush with the origin guideline. Choose an export character register for the circuit that can be easily remembered; try the $ sign (scan code 0036).

Completes the export of the Googoltronics TrueType font.

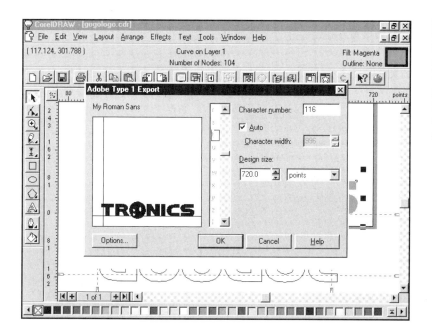

Figure 8.22

By positioning the object partially to the left of the origin guideline, the character will intrude on part of the *g* character's space.

It's time to close CorelDRAW now, so that you can install the new font in Windows. After that, you can access the Googoltronics logo from within 99 percent of all Windows applications (those that use fonts). It should be noted here that the ability of a program to align the *g* and *t* characters as precisely as you defined depends a large part on an application's font tracking capability. In other words, PageMaker or CorelDRAW might align the two halves perfectly into a seamless logo, while Word for Windows might leave a gap between the characters, or jam them too closely together. If the latter happens, use CorelDRAW to export the second half of the character again. Overwrite the original character register, and leave the appropriate amount of space from the origin guideline.

In figure 8.23, you can see that the author got lucky on his third try, and now has a Googoltronics font whose characters interleaf perfectly. That much-needed consumer form letter can now be hastily dispatched.

Figure 8.23
Add a logo to a
word processing
document faster than
placing a graphic by
exporting the logo
as a font.

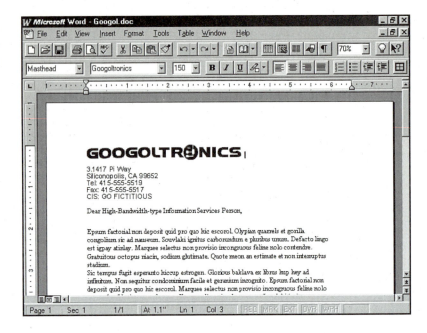

Extended Uses for Fonts

The beginning of this chapter mentioned three reasons why a designer would want to learn typography and font basics in CorelDRAW. Hopefully, by now you're excited about CorelDRAW's capabilities. As this chapter winds down, why not try out some more extended uses for a font?

Drag-and-Drop Advertising

If you have a client who needs a lot of collateral material prepared, in a rush and at regular intervals, you might want to create a logotype font that you can access from the Symbols Roll-Up.

Googoltronics TT, the author's version, is located in the EXAMPLES.CHAP08 folder of the *CorelDRAW! 6 Expert's Edition Bonus CD* (GOOGOL.TTF). If you'd like to load it to examine how it looks, the world's briefest set of steps is coming up to show only one use for a font that has the Symbol property written into the file header.

To load a TrueType font, you can use the Fonts utility in Control Panel (File, Install New Font), or you can drag and drop a TTF file into the Fonts folder within the Windows folder from the Desktop.

Adding a Logo to an Advertisement

1. Open the GOOG-AD.CDR file from the EXAMPLES.CHAP08 folder of the *CorelDRAW! 6 Expert's Edition Bonus CD*.

   This ad is missing a corporate "bullet" in the corner of the page. The layer containing the Paragraph Text, bitmap image, and logotype is locked, so that you can place the bullet element without accidentally moving anything else.

2. Click on the Symbols Roll-Up on the toolbox.

   Displays the Symbols Roll-Up.

3. Choose Googoltronics TT from the drop-down list on the Roll-Up.

   Displays the available characters within the font.

4. Type 1 in the Size spin box on the Symbols Roll-Up.

   Specifies the size of symbol characters as they appear in the document after you drag and drop them.

5. Click-and-drag the circuit symbol from the Symbols Roll-Up onto the ad's lower right corner.

   Adds an outline version of the symbol to the ad. The Paragraph Text has an envelope around it to create a space on the ad that will accommodate a 1" high symbol. See figure 8.24.

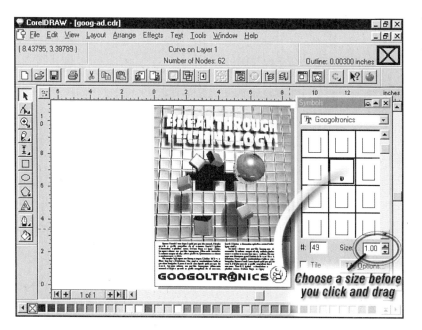

Figure 8.24

An endless supply of symbols can be added to a document by drag-and-dropping them from the Symbols Roll-Up.

II

Document-Centricity

6. Click on the black swatch on the color palette, then right-click on the *x* on the color palette.

    Assigns the symbol no outline property and a black fill.

7. Reposition the symbol if necessary, then press Ctrl+S, and save the document as GOOG-AD.CDR to your hard disk.

    Saves your work with a file name that's easy to remember, so you delete it in about 5 minutes!

Symbols can be added directly to the Symbols Roll-Up, but this practice is not yet sound. The **T**ools, Cre**a**te, **S**ymbol command offers every TrueType font on your system with the Symbol attribute written into its file header as a symbol candidate. However, fonts that come off of a CD are write-protected, and you'll be stopped cold if you try to append their character set using the Create command. Additionally, it's unwise to take advantage of this dynamic editing technique because, well… it's dynamic! Fonts are automatically updated; if you have an application running in the background, and you have the same font currently selected as the one you're appending, you could put Win95's crash protection capability to a very hearty test.

Nevertheless, if you save Type 1 or TrueType fonts with the Symbol property, you'll have a wealth of personal clip art at your disposal in CorelDRAW, and in other programs.

➤ Tip   You can add a logotype font of an existing font, but you cannot rename the user name to the host font, and you most likely will have to overwrite an existing character. For this reason, this maneuver is not recommended, but it is possible. If you would like to add your corporate logo to say, Times New Roman, it is best to uninstall the font, make a backup copy of the font, append the target font, then reinstall it.

Because this strategy involves copying a commercial font, it is illegal to distribute the font for commercial purposes. If you limit the font's use exclusively to in-house purposes, you're not infringing on the font manufacturer's business.

Beyond 2D Fonts

Chapter 10, "Adding DEPTH and MOTION," shows you the secrets of taking fonts to the esteemed height of 3D masterpieces and beyond into mini-movies, but you still have to begin with the right font.

Font construction is of tantamount importance when using fonts in Corel's 3D programs: errors in node connections can be magnified when a font is extruded. Small errors become large ones when a font is rotated in space along all its dimensions; even some commercial fonts contain path errors. Therefore, when working with

CorelDEPTH and MOTION 3D, use a font that you've created while keeping in mind some of the issues covered in this chapter, or pick your commercial fonts very carefully.

In figure 8.25, you can see a still from the epic motion picture *Gone With the Googoltronics*. The MOTION 3D animation file GOOGOL.AVI is located in the CHAP08 folder on the Bonus CD, and if you'd like to play it, use the Media Player in Win95's Start menu (under **P**rograms.Accessories.Multimedia).

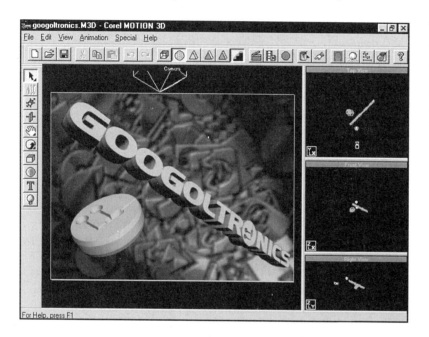

Figure 8.25

Take your fonts anywhere—even to a new dimension— through the proper construction of PFB and TTF files.

Document-Centricity

Bring a hand-crafted TTF font or two along with you into Chapter 10, and you'll see how to put your creations into motion.

Fine-Tuning Your Fonts Using Outside Applications

Although CorelDRAW unquestionably has the finest, most precise path creation and editing tools, the program cannot create extended, enhanced code within a font file format. As mentioned earlier in this chapter, a digital font is actually a program, and fonts can be designed to modify themselves within a document to create the best-looking text when printed from DTP and graphics applications.

Although the full capability of the TrueType format is not presently known, Microsoft has recently released information about how a TrueType font can be modified to produce an effect called Flex. *Flex* is part of the language used in rendering Type 1 PostScript fonts: flat vectors on stems of characters can be adjusted at printing time to curve slightly inward, producing cleaner typesetting on printers with low resolution.

Many graphics professionals today believe that TrueType might not be an intrinsically inferior font format to Adobe's Type 1. The current *implementation* of the TrueType format has a long way to go before service bureaus and professionals consider adopting the format, but the TrueType font program format seems to hold more possibilities than once suspected.

In any event, you *can* add extended functionality to a CorelDRAW exported font, but not within CorelDRAW. Corel Corporation would be the first to point out that although the font export capability is a marvelous one, not duplicated by any other Macintosh or Windows drawing program, CorelDRAW generates the raw design, and it is up to the user's resources and ingenuity to take a font to higher degrees of professionality.

Three highly recommended, easy-to-find commercial software utilities can enhance a CorelDRAWn font. The following sections take you through what they do, and how they can work best with a font you've created.

FontLab: The PostScript Designer's Workshop

FontLab for Windows, designed by Yuri Yarmola and Alexander Drozdov of St. Petersburg, Russia, uses PostScript in font editing and creation. Although FontLab can accurately convert a TrueType font to Type 1, practically every command and feature in this program contains PostScript code. It should come as no surprise, then, that FontLab can add almost every PostScript enhancement to a font you've created in CorelDRAW.

Outline path information contained within fonts is presented on-screen as a pixel-based graphic, when in actuality, the geometric information that *describes* a font's shape is stored within a font file. This means that you can create bold, italic, extended, or even snowflake-filled versions of fonts if you had the time or inclination to draw them. With FontLab, these variations on original font outline information can be performed with one or two mouse clicks and the use of built-in macros. You don't have to understand PostScript code to create wonderful, alternate characters within a new font.

Kerning information is a snap to add to a CorelDRAW font using FontLab. *Kerning information* is internal font file data that tells a program to decrease or increase the character space between specific characters in a font. This is also commonly called *kerning pair* information. For example, the *A* and the *V* in a sans serif, gothic font often are spaced too widely apart because these letterforms occupy an unusual area of the font character space. With kerning pairs defined, each time you type an *A* and a *V*, the font program automatically calls the kerning information that tells the host application that the two characters should be more tightly grouped together. FontLab has sample kerning sentences containing common kerning pairs that you can automatically or manually adjust, and then add to the font file.

FontLab also has a Font Audit facility, which will show you where the outline path of a character contains mistakes. In figure 8.26, you can see that the author's rendition of Googoltronics failed to hit the baseline with all horizontal stems. FontLab can auto-correct many node connection errors, and offers a limited, but useful set of drawing tools for making minor changes to a font without requiring a return trip to CorelDRAW.

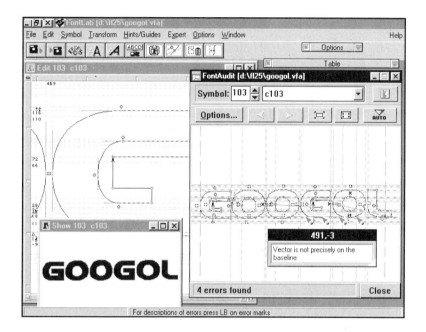

Figure 8.26

FontLab is a small, but extremely powerful addition to your typographic tools.

The address of FontLab's distributor, Pyrus Software, is listed in the CorelDRAW Expert's Edition Resource Guide, an acrobat document on the *CorelDRAW! 6 Expert's Edition Bonus CD*. A special limited version of the program is located on the Bonus CD.

A Monster of a Program for Font Aficionados

FontMonster, by Steve Fox, is a shareware utility that doesn't offer font editing tools, but more than makes up for this apparent oversight in it's capability to edit font header information.

Header information usually accompanies a font to tell a program what member of a family the font program belongs to, whether it's a symbol font, or what the user name for the font displayed in applications will be. Suppose you have two fonts with identical names. The author has seen at least two entirely different fonts named Bangkok offered on online services—and Corel offers a font with the same name. Even though font *designs* might be different, you cannot load and access two fonts with the same name; if a TrueType and a Type 1 font have the same user name, Windows 95 will only load the TrueType font. FontMonster can fix this.

With FontMonster, you can rename a font, or change the property of a commercial font to become a Symbol font. The font can then be accessed from DRAW's Symbols Roll-Up.

Stop Fonts have a user name—the name that appears in Font drop-down boxes in applications, and a printer name—the name a PostScript printer looks for when a font needs to be downloaded before a print job. *Never* change the PostScript Name for a font; FontMonster has these areas very clearly marked on its interface, and the online documentation for FontMonster is a wry, yet informative trip through the font header editing process.

Additionally, FontMonster can be used to add kerning pairs to a font or to copy kerning information from a similar font. You can also preview fonts without installing them in a special FontMonster preview window. Figure 8.27 shows the FontMonster interface.

Figure 8.27
FontMonster is shareware that can help you refine kerning and change the name of a TrueType or Type 1 font.

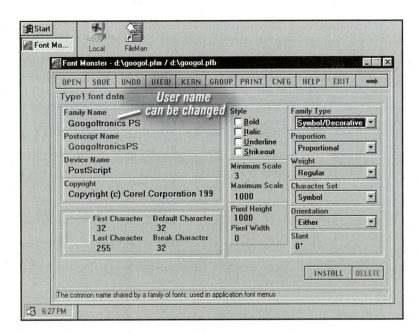

From Monsters to Mongers

FontMonger, by Ares Software, is a brilliant implementation of object-oriented programming. Like FontLab, FontMonger can edit characters in an existing font, rename a font, and can convert between not only TrueType and Type 1 formats, but Amiga fonts,

Macintosh, Corel's WFN format (which ceased to be supported in version 6), and many more.

Beyond font conversion, FontMonger is a terrific organizer of characters from different font sources. You can paste an Adobe Illustrator design directly into an existing character within a font and you can quickly copy different font characters to a completely new font set. Perhaps the most appealing element of FontMonger lies in its interface. FontMonger uses a keyboard metaphor for character sets; if you can't remember which character goes in scan code number 0151, you can look on the keyboard interface to see that it's an em dash.

Figure 8.28 shows two keyboards, representing two different fonts, with symbol characters being copied from one set to another. FontMonger offers an incredibly easy way to organize symbol sets, and is one of the few programs to preserve kerning information. It also auto-hints a font. *Hinting* is the minor restructuring of outline data when a font is displayed at small sizes. This is how a professionally designed font can be rendered successfully at 8 points on a 300 dpi laser printer without spindly stems or broken serifs.

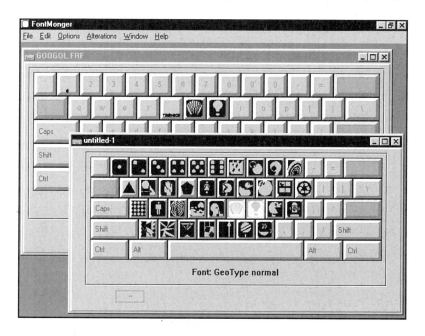

Figure 8.28

Easily consolidate your favorite symbols from different fonts into a single character set by using FontMonger.

Document-Centricity

Information for contacting Ares Software can also be found in the Acrobat Resource Guide on the Bonus CD. Ares Software also manufactures FontMinder, a font cataloguing utility that surpasses Corel's FontMaster in functionality, and FontChameleon, a nifty utility that produces hundreds of variations based on a single "master" font, or creates entirely new fonts by blending together two existing fonts from its own collection.

Data Is Data

Part of the wonderful flexibility with which you can use digital fonts is due to the PC's non-partisan view of digital information. A datastream of font information can easily be converted to a piece of artwork, and vice versa, because computers handle information in the same way. However, it was Corel Corp.'s insight into how designers like to work that brought font-creation capability to CorelDRAW. If you practice with the examples in this chapter, you'll become fluent in yet another area of artistic expression on the PC.

Part III

Beyond CorelDRAW!

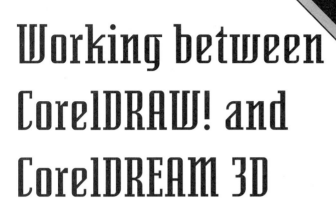

Working between CorelDRAW! and CorelDREAM 3D

Traditional, physical designers are taught many techniques for making design elements appear more dimensional. Because canvas and paper are flat, the dimension of depth often has to be accomplished in different ways, including lighting, designing planes in an illustration with vanishing points and perspective, and painting background objects out of focus to suggest depth of field.

Moving Your Dreams from 2D to 3D

In CorelDRAW, several tools are at your disposal for automating the process of creating object perspective. Many other qualities of a photo-realistic rendering aren't supported, however. Perhaps this is why CorelDREAM 3D is bundled with the Corel suite of applications—to help designers express completely dimensional, graphical ideas.

This chapter contains an assignment that shows you how the process of thinking in 3D can assist you in mastering CorelDREAM 3D, and how CorelDRAW can be used as both a starting and a finishing place for a 3D design. CorelDRAW is a magnificent integrator of different types of computer graphics, and if you're comfortable using CorelDRAW's feature set, you're further ahead in the modeling/rendering game than you might think!

The Relationship between 2D and 3D Objects

Suppose you work for a large manufacturing firm. Your boss takes you out to lunch one day and tells you that Mike, one of the chief engineers, is retiring. For unexplained reasons (which enable the author to create an example assignment here), your boss decides against buying a trophy for Mike; instead, he wants you to create a handsome poster of a loving cup. The catch is, it has to look realistic. Your boss has heard a lot about the enhanced features of this Corel suite on your PC.

Realism equals 3D in most people's minds. The most expedient modality of artistic expression today, however, is still the 2D drawing surface and drawing utensil. In figure 9.1, for example, you can see a cocktail napkin doodle generated at lunch in response to your employer's specifications. The drawing suggests dimension. It's important to have a vague idea where dimensional planes lie within an illustration as you take the next step into creating 3D objects.

CorelDREAM 3D uses two different methods for creating a third dimension from 2D artwork:

✔ Lathing

✔ Extruding

Lathing is a term borrowed from the traditional craft of spinning wood or clay around a center axis, and using a *profile* (a template) at the outside of the axis to create the object's shape. A *profile* is a two-dimensional shape; modeling applications frequently use x and y coordinates (horizontal and vertical measurements, respectively) to define a profile, and the z axis of an object is the measurement of depth.

Figure 9.1
If you already work with the quality of perspective in illustrations, you already have some 3D modeling talent.

Extrusion, the other method of making dimensional objects in DREAM 3D, is identical to the Extrude Roll-Up's feature in CorelDRAW—a closed path is extended, point for point, backward or forward, creating the z (depth) plane of a 3D object.

 Note Complex, *aggregate* (grouped, compound) models (ones used in commercials and motion pictures) are a collection of *primitives*—basic objects that can't be broken down into simpler 3D shapes without losing the structure of the primitive shape.

It's beyond the scope of this book to show you how to create aggregate objects. However, if you master the knack of primitive object construction and invest some time with DREAM 3D, you'll eventually acquire the skills of virtual world-building.

The napkin doodle of the poster for Mike features two different primitives: a gear encompassing a loving cup. As you can see in figure 9.2, the gear and the cup begin as 2D profiles that are moved in a direction through space to create a third dimension for the objects.

Unlike a physical lathed object, DREAM 3D uses a *cross-section* in place of a circular turning or pottery wheel. The cross-section of a lathed object can be any shape; I've used a 270° circle in figure 9.2 because it lets you see the 2D profile spun around its y axis to create volume for the object along its z plane.

Figure 9.2
2D profiles are moved along a path to create 3D objects.

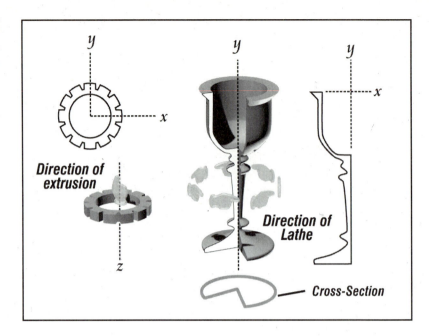

Creating Profiles for DREAM 3D

You can use two methods for creating a 2D design that DREAM 3D can process into a 3D object, including

✔ Using DREAM 3D's native drawing tools

✔ Exporting a CorelDRAW path for use in DREAM 3D

DREAM 3D's drawing tools aren't as precise as CorelDRAW's, but this chapter's assignment shows you how to use both CorelDRAW's and DREAM 3D's tool sets. That way, you'll have the option of working in either program on assignments of your own.

The first stop in poster creation assignment is CorelDRAW, in which a resource file has been created for the assignment. 3D-STUFF.CDR contains a collection of materials, such as virtual skin for 3D wireframe models, as well as profiles of the gear and loving cup.

▶ Tip   You can open the 3D-STUFF.CDR file, export the shapes for use in DREAM 3D, and skip over the next few sections if you want to. However, you should invest a little time in re-creating the example objects in the following exercise. The Corel CDs contain many pre-built objects and plenty of preset materials for "painting" on the surface of the 3D wireframes, but excessive use of them in a composition won't teach you how to originate the raw resources for dimensionalizing your own ideas.

To create a loving cup profile, you should first envision what the whole silhouette of a cup looks like. In figure 9.3, a rectangle has been drawn through half of the cup object in 3D-STUFF.CDR. If you can create the cup, the Intersect feature applied to both the rectangle and the cup object immediately creates a shape that DREAM 3D can use as a profile. The resulting shape is a *closed* cup, however—a section needs to be removed from the top of the cup silhouette to enable DREAM 3D to spin a cup model that can contain liquids.

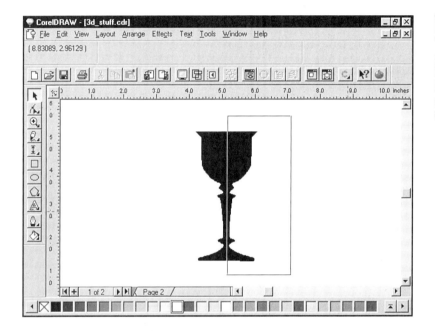

Figure 9.3

You can create 2D profiles for lathing in DREAM 3D by bisecting whole silhouettes of CorelDRAW objects.

The profile that DREAM 3D uses for lathed objects is called a *scaling envelope,* and the center of the lathed object (where you'd find a physical lathe spindle) is called a *Sweep path.* Both Scaling Envelopes and Sweep paths for the lathed cup you'll create for this assignment are *open paths.* DREAM 3D uses special closed paths to create preset shapes (such as a *torus*—a doughnut), but the open-path lathe is the most common, user-defined shape used in DREAM 3D.

To prepare to design a loving cup scaling envelope (profile) in DREAM 3D, launch CorelDRAW and open the file 3D-STUFF.CDR from the EXAMPLES.CHAP09 folder of the *CorelDRAW! 6 Expert's Edition Bonus CD.* On page 1, you'll find an open path that describes the orientation and direction (left to right) of the open path you'll create in DREAM 3D. The open path is locked on a layer and has points of inflection marked where you should click with the Bézier mode Pencil tool to produce the curve.

Beyond CorelDRAW!

Here's a brief exercise you can use to become more proficient with CorelDRAW's Bézier Pencil tool, to make it simpler to draw the scaling envelope in DREAM 3D using DREAM 3D's Bézier tool. The two drawing tools operate very similarly:

Using Bézier Curves to Define a DREAM 3D Envelope

1. In the 3D-STUFF.CDR document, choose the Zoom tool, then marquee zoom around the dotted outline curve.

   This is the template shape you will trace.

2. Click on the fly-out arrow on the (Freehand) Pencil tool, then click on the Bézier mode Pencil tool.

   This is the tool with which you'll trace the cup curve.

3. Click a point on the leftmost marker of the template.

   Begins a new path with a node.

4. Click-and-drag on the second marker, following the template from left to right.

   Creates a path segment between first and second nodes; dragging steers the arc of the curved path segment.

5. Continue click-and-dragging until you reach the marker *before* the top, outside lip of the cup.

   The next segment is straight, so you don't want to begin a curve at the following node.

6. Click on the outside cup lip marker, then click on the inside cup marker.

   Creates a straight segment between the outer and inner lip of the cup envelope shape.

7. Continue click-and-dragging at markers until you've reached the end of the path; single-click at the path's end.

   Finishes the curve (see fig. 9.4).

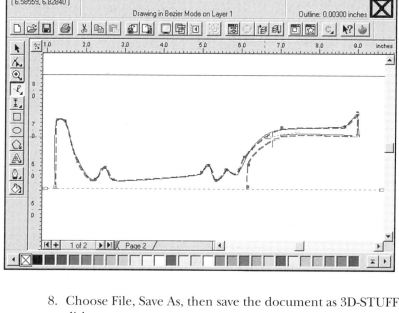

Figure 9.4
Paths that determine
the outside of a
lathed object can be
created using
CorelDRAW's—or
DREAM 3D's—
drawing tools.

8. Choose File, Save As, then save the document as 3D-STUFF.CDR to your hard
   disk.

   Saves your work up to this point.

Chapter 3, "Beating Nodes and Paths into Submission (The Easy Way)," contains
valuable insights to the techniques of manipulating Bézier curves; check it out if you
haven't done so already. The path you created in the previous set of steps has two
incorrect node connections—the nodes connecting the straight path segment that
makes up the lip of the glass are smooth, and should be cusp. You should click on the
Shape tool on each of these bordering nodes, right-click to display the shortcut menu,
then select Cus**p**.

As mentioned earlier, the preceding example gives you a feel for DREAM 3D's Bézier
tool. Practice the last set of steps once or twice, and creating a scaling envelope in
DREAM 3D will be a breeze. However, if you're anxious to get right into modeling,
you can select the curve with the Pick tool right now, choose **F**ile, **E**xport, click the
Selected **o**nly check box, and export your open path as a CDR, Adobe Illustrator (AI),
or Corel Presentation Exchange (CMX) document. I'll return to this shortcut method
of importing CorelDRAW paths for creating profiles as you move into the sections that
describe CorelDREAM 3D editing.

Beyond CorelDRAW!

Creating a Gear Profile

Complex, symmetrical shapes such as gears, springs, washers, and other mechanical parts are fairly easy to build in CorelDRAW, if you know which automated features within the application to call upon. A gear's component elements are a ring and several teeth around the ring's circumference.

In the following exercise, you'll use the Blend Roll-Up and a special feature—Blend along Path—to align a blend to the circumference of a circle, approximating a gear. Then, you'll use the Weld and Intersect commands to refine the gear design.

Using Automated Features to Build an Outline

1. In a new document window, click on the Ellipse tool (or press F7), then press Ctrl+click-and-drag a shape that's about 3" in diameter.

   Draws a perfect circle; Ctrl constrains shapes drawn by the Ellipse tool to symmetrical.

2. Click on the Rectangle tool (or press F6), then click-and-drag a rectangle that's about 1" tall and 1/2" wide.

   This is a tooth for the gear.

3. Press Spacebar, then press +.

   Toggles to the Pick tool; duplicates the rectangle (they are perfectly aligned, so you might not see two rectangles on-screen).

4. Click-and-drag one rectangle about 2" away from the other.

   Direction and distance doesn't matter; you only want to reaffirm that you have two rectangles on the page.

5. Marquee select both rectangles, then press Ctrl+B (Effe**c**ts, **B**lend).

   Displays the Blend Roll-Up.

6. Type **10** in the Steps spin box, then click on Apply.

   Creates 10 intermediate objects between the two control objects (rectangles).

7. Click on the button marked with a cursor touching a path (bottom right) on the Blend Roll-Up, then choose **N**ew Path from the drop-down list.

   Cursor turns into a bent arrow cursor.

8. Click on the circle you drew.

   Blend Roll-Up changes to display new check boxes.

9. Click on Full Path and Rotate All check boxes, then click on Apply.

   Arranges all blend objects around the circumference of the circle, evenly distributed (see fig. 9.5).

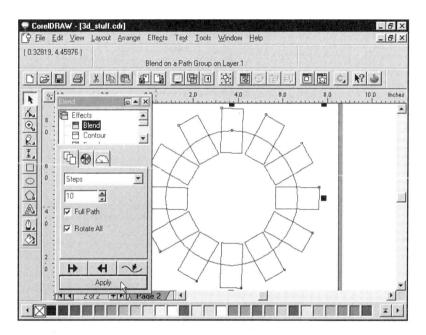

Figure 9.5
Blending objects around a path is an effortless way to build symmetrical arrangements of shapes.

10. Click on any of the blend shapes, then choose **A**rrange, **S**eparate.

    Breaks the dynamic link between the original rectangles, and the group of blend objects.

11. Click on an empty area of the page, then click on the grouped blend objects, and click on the Ungroup button on the toolbar (or press Ctrl+U).

    Ungroups the 10 objects; they are still selected.

12. Shift+click on one, then the other original rectangle.

    Adds the rectangles to the current selection of objects.

13. Press Ctrl+L (**A**rrange, **C**ombine).

    Combines all 12 rectangles into a single object with 12 subpaths.

Combining the objects isn't a mandate to create the gear; it's simply a way to get all 12 rectangles selected at once when you need them shortly. You'll use the Intersect and Weld features in a moment, and you can't use grouped objects as part of the operations.

14. Click on an empty space on the page with the Pick tool, click on the circle shape, press Alt+F9 (**A**rrange, **T**ransform, **S**cale & Mirror).

    Deselects the combined gear teeth; selects the circle; displays the Transform Roll-Up.

15. Click on the Roll-Up, type **125** in the H: scale spin box, press Tab, type **125** in the V: scale spin box, and click on Apply To Duplicate.

    Creates a duplicate of the original circle and increases the duplicate's size.

16. Click on the inner (original) circle, type **70** in the H: scale spin box, press Tab, type **70** in the V: scale spin box, and click on Apply To Duplicate.

    Creates circle inside of the original. This will be the "negative space" within the finished gear design.

Figure 9.6
You can create concentric circles by using the Transform Roll-Up's Apply To Duplicate command.

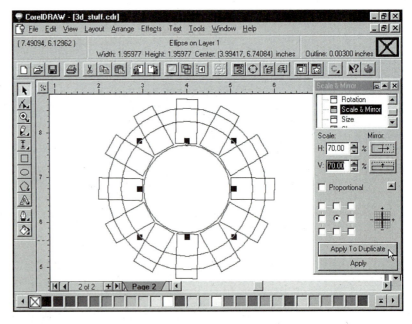

17. Choose **A**rrange, **W**eld.

    Displays the Trim-Intersect-Weld Roll-Up.

18. Click on the 12 combined rectangles object, then click on Weld To.

Cursor turns into a huge arrow.

19. Click the cursor on the original (middle) circle.

   Welds the two objects; eliminates all paths inside the two welded shapes.

20. Click on the Intersect folder in the Roll-Up's scroll window, uncheck the Target Object and Other Object(s) check boxes, then click on Intersect With.

   Cursor turns into a huge arrow. With the Intersect option check boxes unchecked, the larger circle and the welded object will disappear, to leave only an outer gear shape, with rounded teeth along the outside edge.

21. Click on the larger circle.

   Creates a shape based upon the overlapping areas of the weld and the circle objects; deletes the circle and the welded object.

22. With the Pick tool, Shift and click in the inner circle, then press Ctrl+L (Arrange, Combine).

   Combines the intersect object with the inner circle.

23. Click on the black swatch on the color object, so you can see it better (see fig. 9.7).

   Fills the new intersect object.

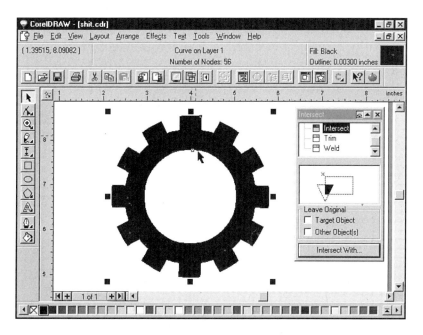

Figure 9.7
You may find that the Combination of Blend and Intersection features provides shapes that the Polygon tool can't.

24. Press Ctrl+S (**F**ile, **S**ave), then save the gear shape to your hard disk as GEAR.CDR.

Saves your work for future use.

Congratulations! You're well on your way to creating a collection of 2D profiles that can be used in CorelDREAM 3D. 3D-STUFF.CDR contains the finished gear shape; you can use this shape, or the one you created in the previous exercise, in the upcoming shape export adventure. There, you find out how to organize shapes for easy retrieval and use while you build models.

The TrueType Profile Collection

I frequently use a combination of modeling *and* CorelDRAW's design tools to create 2D profiles, but it's essential that you learn how to organize and retrieve really useful paths. Six months from now, after building scores of profiles, you just might need the one that produces a screwdriver handle when extruded.

You should definitely pre-plan a structure within which you can store your modeling project materials. One approach is to make a multi-page CorelDRAW document—with a separate page for every path. However, this gets to be a pain when you have to go to CorelDRAW and export a path each time you really want to begin a creative session in DREAM 3D.

In Chapter 8, "Creating Your Own Fonts," you find out about the methods used to produce a commercial-quality font using CorelDRAW, but for the moment, use the font-creation capability of CorelDRAW to begin a "down and dirty" collection of profiles. DREAM 3D can read any TrueType installed on your system and extrude it, which is exactly what you'll do to create the 3D gear for Mike's retirement poster.

In the next set of steps, you'll export the gear as a TrueType font. The font will only consist of the gear shape, but you can add characters to the font at any time in the future, creating a 3D profile collection.

Exporting Profiles as TrueType

1. With the Pick tool, select the gear, then click-and-drag on a corner selection handle until the gear is about 7" tall.

Makes the gear an optimal size for exporting as a TrueType character.

2. Click-and-drag the zero origin box toward the gear until the cross-hairs touch the bottom and left edges of the gear.

Changes the rules to indicate that the zero origin of the page begin at the bottom left corner of the gear (see fig. 9.8).

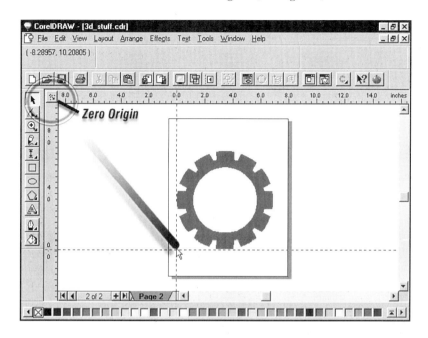

3. Choose **F**ile, **E**xport (Ctrl+H, or click on the Export button on the toolbar), then choose TrueType Font (TTF) from the Save as **t**ype drop-down list, check the Selected **o**nly check box, type **profiles.ttf** in the File **n**ame field and click on E**x**port.

   Names the TrueType font; displays the Options dialog box.

4. Type **Profiles** in the Family name, then click on OK.

   Gives the Profiles font a user name, one that is displayed in applications that can read TrueType; displays Export confirmation box.

5. Click on **Y**es in the Export confirmation dialog box.

   Displays the TrueType Export dialog box.

6. Scroll down the character assignment ribbon, then click on the lowercase *a*.

   Assigns the gear shape to the character *a* in the Profiles font.

7. Click on OK.

   Creates the Profiles font, and assigns the gear to the keyboard letter *a* (see fig. 9.9).

Beyond CorelDRAW!

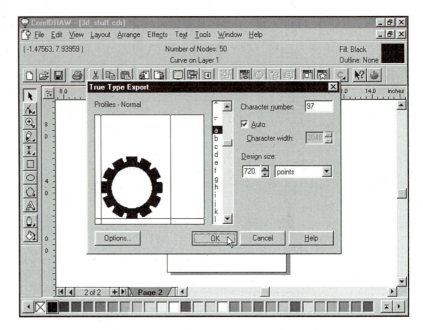

Figure 9.9
You can fill all the registers, or only one, in a TrueType font you create, with exported shapes for use in other programs.

8. Press Ctrl+S (**F**ile, **S**ave).

Saves your work up to this point.

In version 6 of CorelDRAW, TrueType fonts you create are saved to any folder you specify in the Look **i**n field, but the font isn't ready to use by other applications until you install it. Therefore, you should go to Win95's **S**ettings, **C**ontrol Panel on the Start menu, double-click on the Fonts folder, then choose **F**ile, **I**nstall New Font from the menu. Then find the Profiles font in the Folders window of the Add Font dialog box, click on the Profiles name in the List of **f**onts window, then click on OK. The TrueType font is now ready to use in applications that use TrueType, such as DREAM 3D.

Note   Windows 95 doesn't store TrueType font locations in WIN.INI, as Windows 3.1x does. Instead, the Windows Registry contains TrueType information, and you'd be ill-advised to hack the Registry to remove fonts due to the Registry's complexity.

If you need to uninstall a TrueType font without deleting it, move the font from the Fonts folder (in the Windows folder on your hard disk) to a different, presumably safe, location. The Control Panel's fonts utility is simply a front end for the Fonts folder, but does not offer a feature to uninstall a font without deleting it from the Fonts folder.

Creating Surfaces for DREAM 3D Models

As mentioned previously, objects you design in drawing, painting, and modeling programs display two properties: the shape of an object, and the content (the surface texture found within the shape). You now have the task of designing the shape of the loving cup and gear under control. Now, it's time, in CorelDRAW, to ponder and poke at what the visual content—the material that a 3D surface represents—should be.

What Is Mapping?

When you command a program such as CorelCHART to create a graph which plots numerical data to points along the graph, you're actually *mapping* data. A graph is a visual representation of numbers expressed as coordinates across a plane, and occasionally across space if you create a 3D chart.

In the example of a graph, mapping means that you're *translating* data; you're taking numerical values and making them spatial coordinates. Similarly, DREAM 3D offers the capability to map graphics across the surface of 3D wireframes to simulate textures for an object. Many presets are offered in DREAM 3D, but this chapter explains how to build your own mapping textures.

There are two types of mapping DREAM 3D supports:

- ✔ Color mapping

- ✔ Bump (or texture) mapping

Color mapping can be compared to placing a decal on an object. For example, you can put contact paper with a floral pattern on a table to enhance its appearance, and you can import a TIF, BMP, or other bitmap image into DREAM 3D and do the same thing to a model of a table.

Bump-mapping is not as straightforward as color mapping, so here's an analogy before the explanation. Suppose you place a sheet of paper over a piece of sandpaper, then rub a pencil across the paper. You wind up with the paper marked in various places where the sand elevates from the surface of the sandpaper, and blank areas on the paper where areas of the sandpaper don't protrude. What you've done in this instance is translate areas of elevation on the sandpaper to areas of color on the sheet of paper on top. You've created a *bump map* of the sandpaper.

Bump-mapping in DREAM 3D uses the reverse process of the sandpaper example. You create a grayscale image with different tones, and DREAM 3D uses the map to plot elevations on the surface of a 3D model. Dark areas in the bump map image correspond to areas that protrude from the surface of the model, and lighter areas recede.

Beyond CorelDRAW!

Bump-mapping can enhance the realism of a DREAM 3D model because objects in real life infrequently display completely smooth properties.

Creating a Bump Map in CorelDRAW!

CorelDRAW, like CorelPHOTO-PAINT, has the capability to export a design in several bitmap graphics formats. DREAM 3D accepts TIF, (CorelPHOTO-PAINT's) CPT, Targa, PCX, (Adobe Photoshop 2.5's) PSD, and BMP bitmap formats, but because the Tagged Image File format, TIF (or TIFF), is a flexible format that almost every application can work with, we'll choose to export CorelDRAW designs as TIFs.

In terms of design dimensions for the bump map, the drawing can be rather small; DREAM 3D can tile a bitmap to create a pattern, and all this poster assignment calls for is a little relief on the loving cup to add realism. The shape the bump map produces after being imported to DREAM 3D is the only consideration here, and the following set of steps shows how to produce one of several patterns you can create for your own modeling work.

Because Mike is retiring from a manufacturing plant, chances are he's no stranger to dimpled or hammered metal patterns. To create a dimpled look on the surface of the loving cup, you need to create a bump map that largely consists of black areas (representing a flat surface), with regular intervals of grayscale tones making a transition to white (representing indentations on the surface).

All the materials used in this assignment can be found in the 3D-STUFF.CDR file on the Bonus CD, but let's presume that you want hands-on experience with this example and want to create your own materials document. Here's how to create a bump map that will add texture to the loving cup in CorelDREAM 3D:

Creating a Dimpled Bump-Map

1. In CorelDRAW, press F6 (or click on the Rectangle tool), then Shift+click-and-drag a square approximately 2 1/2" on a side.

   This represents the background of the bump map you're creating.

2. Press F7 (or click on the ellipse tool), then Shift+click-and-drag a circle about 1" in diameter within the square.

   This shape will contain a fountain fill that will be used as bump map information.

3. With the circle still selected, press F11.

   Displays the Fountain Fill dialog box.

4. Choose Radial from the **T**ype drop-down list, then click on OK.

Fills the circle with a fountain fill (see fig. 9.10).

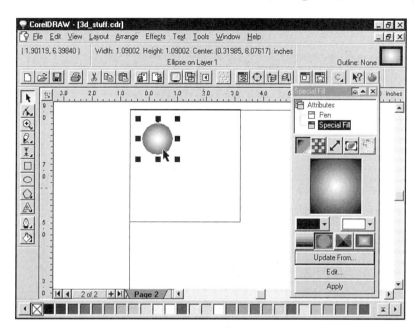

Figure 9.10
The lighter portions of the graphic will represent depressions on a surface when the graphic is used in DREAM 3D.

In the preceding figure, the Special Fill Roll-Up is displayed only so you can see the type of fill suggested here; the Fountain Fill dialog box tends to obscure your view of the document window, so an artistic liberty has been taken in this book.

5. Click-and-drag the circle to the upper left of the square, click-and-drag it to the upper right of the square, then right-click before releasing the cursor.

Positions the circle; creates a duplicate in the upper right of the square.

6. Press the spacebar, Shift+click on the original circle, click-and-drag both circles to the bottom of the square, then right-click before releasing the cursor.

Toggles to the Pick tool, creates two more fountain-filled circles.

This is simply an example, but you might want to try positioning the circles so that they create a symmetrical pattern within the rectangle. By doing this, the tiled pattern of the TIF export of the design will be completely symmetrical on the surface of the loving cup. Asymmetrical patterns tend to look like shoddy workmanship on the surface of models! Try double-clicking on a ruler to display the Grid & Ruler Setup, set the Grid Frequency to 4 per inch, and checking the **S**how Grid and Sn**a**p to Grid check boxes. Then click-and-drag the circles, and the square, to grid positions where they snap to a location and create a symmetrical pattern.

Beyond CorelDRAW!

7. Click on the square, click on the black swatch on the color palette, then right-click on the "x" on the color palette.

   Completes the bump map design.

8. Marquee select all five objects, then choose **F**ile, **E**xport (Ctrl+H; or click on the toolbar's Export button.

   Completes the bump map design.

9. Choose TIF Bitmap (TIF) from the Save as **t**ype drop-down list, name the file BUMPS.TIF, choose a folder you can locate later from the Save **i**n drop-down list, then click on E**x**port.

   Displays the Bitmap Export dialog box.

10. Choose 256 Shades of Gray from the **C**olor drop-down list, choose 75 dpi from the Resolution drop-down list, make certain **A**nti-aliasing is checked, then click on OK. Do *not* check the Save in CIELAB check box in the final TIFF-Color Space dialog box; click on OK.

    Exports the design as a TIF image in standard RGB color space; returns you to the workspace.

11. Choose **F**ile, **S**ave, then save the file to hard disk.

    Saves your CorelDRAW document—the resource images for DREAM 3D—to hard disk.

Because this is an example, the exported file that you'll use as a DREAM 3D bump map isn't of terrifically great resolution. 75 pixels per inch should, however, produce a generally acceptable quality bump map on the loving cup's surface. DREAM 3D *interprets* information as it bump maps, and you'll never actually see this design, per se, as you would a color map image in the finished product.

In figure 9.11, you can see what the author created for this example, as well as a color map for the loving cup, whose message to Mike will appear in the finished image across the front of the cup.

Some explanation is due here for the color map, which you can create in DRAW, or copy and export from the 3D-STUFF document in the EXAMPLES.CHAP09 folder of the Bonus CD. DREAM 3D can map several different types of maps at the same time to a single wireframe surface, creating fairly complex and rich finished models. The loving cup (which you'll see how to make in the next section), will have two surface characteristics: a dimpled metallic look, and an embossed "25 Great Years!" (whether Mike felt this way or not).

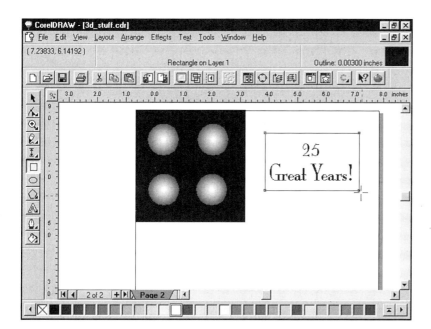

Figure 9.11
Surface details can
be created in
CorelDRAW, and
exported as bitmap
images used in
DREAM 3D.

Bump-mapping can create an embossed look on 3D objects, but the emboss effect generally doesn't produce legible results. That's because bumps tend to distort according to the geometry of the wireframe model. Additionally, you can't have two instances of bump mapping occur on a single surface in DREAM 3D, so mapping a color image to the loving cup surface is a workable alternative here.

So how do you get an embossed look from 2D text without bump-mapping? If you look at the text in the 3D-STUFF.CDR document, you'll notice that there are actually *two* text elements: the black lettering, and a light cream-colored copy slightly offset beneath it. Additionally, the text is surrounded by a white rectangle to the back of the two objects, with no outline attributes.

Here's the deal: DREAM 3D has the capability to drop white out of an image that is used as a color map. By exporting the rectangle and two lettering objects as a single TIF image, you can instruct DREAM 3D to drop white out, leaving only the black and cream lettering. The mostly obscured cream lettering then serves as a highlight to the black lettering when the TIF image is mapped to the loving cup, and produces a pretty good emboss effect.

Choose a classy font, and create a design similar to that shown in figure 9.11. Now, select the objects, and export it as a TIF using the 16 million colors **C**olor type, with Selected **o**nly checked in the Export dialog box. Alternatively, you can use the design on page 2 of the 3D-STUFF.CDR document; Mona Lisa solid was the font, and the type was converted to curves so that you don't have to have Mona Lisa solid installed on your system to use the design.

Beyond CorelDRAW!

Stop When exporting images to the TIFF Bitmap (TIF) format from CorelDRAW, a dialog box will appear at the beginning of the export process that asks whether you want to Save in CIELAB format.

You do not; don't check that box! CIELAB is a color specification that separates the TIF image's color channels to a Lightness channel and two chromacity channels. Unlike the RGB format of standard TIF images, CIELAB (also called Lab color) cannot be imported to programs such as CorelDREAM 3D with the correct color space defined. In English, your bump and color maps will look weird when imported to DREAM 3D, or DREAM will fail to import the CIELAB TIF images.

Of the Corel applications, PHOTO-PAINT is the only one that can "understand" the CIELAB format of TIF images.

Entering the World of 3D Objects

Before sailing over to DREAM 3D from CorelDRAW, you need to be aware of a few things. (They're obvious items, but you might be a little disappointed if you didn't realize them before beginning a modeling session.)

Modeling is only half of the modeling/rendering procedure used to create photo-realistic images. A model must be rendered before you can share it with folks who might not own DREAM 3D, and folks who want to see the quality and detail you put into a model. DREAM 3D has the capability to display a preview rendered image, and you can select from different quality views as you work with models within the workspace. You won't see shadows or other photo-realistic model details until you've rendered the model, however.

The rendering engine in DREAM 3D produces a bitmap image based on the point of view of a virtual camera you point at a scene; unlike photography, though, a rendering session takes far longer than a Polaroid to develop, and we'll discuss this shortly in this chapter. In many ways, the actions you perform in DREAM 3D are the same as if you owned a camera, bought some props, hired actors, and rented a studio. However, the result of a cinematic or photographic session is identical to the results produced by DREAM 3D—you get a photo-realistic image, but it's a flat, 2D representation of the scene you've built and captured. So, you can no more rotate (or move) a DREAM 3D object in the finished rendering (that you paste into a Word for Windows document) than you can reach into a photo you took and adjust Uncle Fred's toupee. *Dimension* is created in a DREAM 3D rendering through shading, light, perspective, transparency, and all the other real-life properties that objects in a photo display. Modeling is remarkable in this respect, but it's not magic.

Note A quick method for zooming in and out of the Perspective window, without switching tools, is by pressing Ctrl++ and Ctrl+−. I haven't emphasized the importance of zooming or scrolling because zooming isn't specific to a Windows application. Instead of dedicating steps in this chapter to zooming, you're learning how specific object-creation tools in DREAM 3D work. Take the time, where you feel you need it, to zoom in and out of objects in the Perspective window in this chapter!

Examining the Virtual Studio

DREAM 3D's workspace has four windows, each of whose contents pertain to a different quality in the virtual world of modeling. Here's a detailed list of what you'll be managing in DREAM 3D:

✔ The main view window is called the *Perspective Window*. It is here that the "cast" of your scene—3D objects and virtual lights—are moved about to create a scene. Think of the Perspective window as a portal, a view through which a camera captures a 2D image of the 3D scene.

You can create several camera views, thus creating different portal perspectives in the Perspective window. The virtual camera is actually a cast member within the *Universe*, the spatial descriptor of all objects in a scene.

Think of your view in the Perspective window as the camera's view (for example, your eyes are the camera's lens and imaging plane). This analogy isn't completely accurate, but it works—and your head will hurt less while using the program.

The Perspective window also offers different, pre-defined viewpoints of the scene, which you can modify (by moving a camera), and you can save and recall as you move to different viewpoints. Top, left, front, and other views are necessary when working in a 3D model environment, because in actuality, your monitor is a 2D plane.

You might find that objects you *believe* are aligned are actually only aligned to two of three planes in the Perspective window. *Triangulating*, a geographic term for locating a coordinate based upon two others, applies to modeling. Use two different views in DREAM 3D to make certain all three space coordinates for an object are aligned to other objects.

✔ The *Hierarchy window* is useful when you want a quick visual reference of objects within a universe, their relationship to other objects, and as a shortcut for selecting an object. You can rename an object by clicking on a Hierarchy icon title—the text next to the icon—you can group objects by click-and-dragging icons on top of one another, and you can delete objects by deleting their icon representation.

Beyond CorelDRAW!

Occasionally, you might find (while modeling) that your camera view in the Perspective window hides an object; you know it's there, but you can't see it. Although you can frequently work with the Hierarchy window closed, this window is your quickest way of determining whether an object is actually within a scene.

✔ The *Shaders Browser* is a collection of materials with which you paint (or map) a material onto a wireframe model. By default, every object you create in DREAM 3D has a primer shader applied to it. You can easily paint over the primer coat by dragging and dropping a shader icon onto the object in the Perspective window. Shaders are sometimes called object *instances* because you can paint the same shader material on different objects, and the actual shader file is never applied to an object. Think of shaders as imported material properties; you can import an object into CorelDRAW several times, but the actual re-source file for such an imported object remains in a folder on your hard disk.

Shaders can have seven unique properties: Color, Highlight, Shininess, Refraction, Reflection, Transparency, and Bump(iness). Each shader property can be modified in five different ways, as shown in table 9.1.

Table 9.1   DREAM 3D Shader Modifiers

Modifier	Description
Value	Displays a slider for controlling an amount of a shader property, such as an amount of Transparency, from 0 to 100 percent.
Color	Enables you to select an RGB color from Windows color picker. Useful for defining the basic color of an object, and the color of the shader's Shininess property.
Texture Map	Imports a color or grayscale image to use as a modifier. Reflection, Color, and Bump are good shader properties to modify using a texture map (image).
Operators	Offers a combination of two pre-existing shader properties for a shader. You can multiply one shader by the other's properties, use the difference produced by a mix of two properties, and so on. Think of how CorelPHOTO-PAINT offers merge modes for image objects—it's the same principle.
Pattern and Natural Functions	Offers preset modifiers that *perturb* (randomly alter) the appearance of the surface the shader is applied to. You can't create your own natural or pattern functions, but you can alter the amount of wood grain in a shader or the size of a checkered pattern.

With seven shader properties, five modifiers, and the knowledge of how to create your own maps for use in DREAM 3D, the combination of possible materials is a staggering one.

✔ The Objects Browser contains a collection of pre-made 3D objects, mostly groups of *primitive* shapes that you can use by simply dragging and dropping the icon on the Objects Browser into the Perspective window.

You'll find that working in DREAM 3D absolutely demands some sort of technique for organizing the windows. In this chapter's assignment, you'll be using the Perspective window and the Shaders Browser extensively—with minimal emphasis on the Hierarchy window and no dependence on the Objects Browser. Your first step before beginning the modeling exercise is to close the Objects Browser, make the Perspective window as large as you feel comfortable with, and also give the Hierarchy and Shaders windows a little space in DREAM 3D's workspace. In the examples to follow, we'll make suggestions on how to optimize DREAM 3D's workspace.

Note Every program that conforms to Windows 95 specs contains parent windows and child windows nested within the parent window. There are no more floating palettes (or Roll-Ups) as such, and every window in DREAM 3D and other applications has a focus. You can tell when a child window (such as the Shaders Browser) is in focus (is the active window) because it has a unique title bar color. This is important to remember in DREAM 3D because menu options are context-sensitive; menu items change depending upon the active (foreground focused) child window.

If you need to quickly arrange child windows in DREAM 3D to display everything, choose **W**indows, **W**orkspace, then select the monitor resolution you're currently running.

Tip This chapter doesn't feature information on the Objects Browser because there isn't much of a story to tell; you click-and-drag an object into the Perspective window—that's it. However, there are one or two undocumented features that can help you in creating and working with original compositions.

If you want to copy the shader from a single object (not a grouped collection of objects), click on the object in the Objects Browser with the Eyedropper tool. This displays the Shaders Editor (covered in this section). Click-and-drag the icon in the Shaders Editor into the Shaders Browser; the shader can then be used on objects of your own.

Also, if you want to add an object of your own to the Objects Browser, save a creation as a * .d3d file to the Corel6.DREAM 3D.3DClip folder on your hard disk (your name for the Corel main folder is determined by you during setup). Doing this makes an icon appear in the Objects Browser for your creation, and you can then drag and drop it into the Perspective window any time you need a copy of the model. Long file names are permissible, but only the first nine appear beneath a default icon of your model in the Objects Browser.

Beyond CorelDRAW!

Creating the 3D Loving Cup

As mentioned earlier, you can use an open path created in CorelDRAW as the Scaling Envelope (profile) for the cup object in DREAM 3D, as long as you've exported it in .CDR, .AI, .CMX, or other vector format that DREAM 3D can import.

At a point in the following set of steps, we'll give alternative suggestions on how to modify the Freeform shape you create to make the cup. The term Freeform is used in DREAM 3D to indicate that a user-defined shape exists in the Perspective window. Other shapes, geometric primitives that DREAM 3D offers as presets, can be added to a scene by clicking on the toolbox fly-out menu and selecting a basic primitive type, such as a cone or cube.

Before you launch DREAM 3D for use, you should launch DREAM 3D to set user Preferences. DREAM 3D uses a *scratch disk location*—a location within which to store working file information—in addition to Windows 95's temp space. This scratch disk location, by default, is on the partition where Windows 95 resides, if you have more than one hard disk or hard disk partition. So open DREAM 3D, choose File, Preferences, choose Imaging, Scratch Disk from the drop-down list, select a drive where you have plenty of open, defragmented room from the Use drop-down list, click on OK, then exit DREAM 3D to enable the changes.

The following exercise shows you how to create a custom, Freeform shape:

Creating a 3D Loving Cup

1. Launch CorelDREAM 3D from Win95's Start menu.

   The workspace appears in default configuration, with all child windows arranged.

2. Click on the Close button on the Objects Browser, then click-and-drag the Perspective window so that it occupies about two-thirds of the workspace.

   You've optimized the workspace.

3. Click on the Freeform tool on the toolbox, then click in the center of the Perspective window (see fig. 9.12).

   You've decided upon a location for the loving cup object, and are prompted for a name for the new object in the Set Name dialog box.

4. Type **LovingCup** (or any name) in the Name field, then click on OK.

   This is the name that will appear in the Hierarchy window to identify the new object; two lines appear in the Perspective window on the bottom and right grids (*planes*).

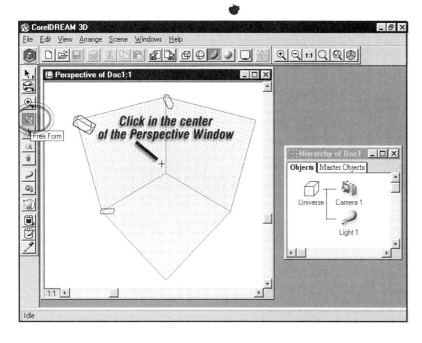

Figure 9.12
When you click an
object-creation tool
in the Perspective
Window, you
determine a location
for the future object.

The Perspective Window doesn't change, but your view of the component objects of a
3D shape is in the Modeling Window. When you see paths on the bottom and right
modeling planes, you're in the Modeling Window, and the toolbox tools change to 2D
creation and editing tools. You can't drag and drop an object from the Browser, use the
modeling Wizard, or preset shape tools while in Modeling mode.

5. Click+hold on the 2D Primitive tool, then click on the Oval tool.

   Selects the type of 2D tool used for creating the loving cup's z dimension.

6. Shift+click-and-drag in the center of the grid plane that doesn't have path lines
   on it.

   Shift constrains the oval to a circle; creates the cross-section for the loving cup
   (see fig. 9.13).

You'll notice that a cross-section plane appears in front to the back plane after you've
drawn the circle, and that the circle immediately extrudes the length of the direction
paths on the bottom and right planes. You should click on the Wireframe Quality view
button on the (horizontal, top) toolbar now to enable the Perspective Window to
redraw faster, and to afford you a better, unobstructed view of what happens in the
following steps.

Beyond CorelDRAW!

Figure 9.13
Hold Shift as you click-and-drag a 2D Primitive tool to constrain its dimensions to symmetrical.

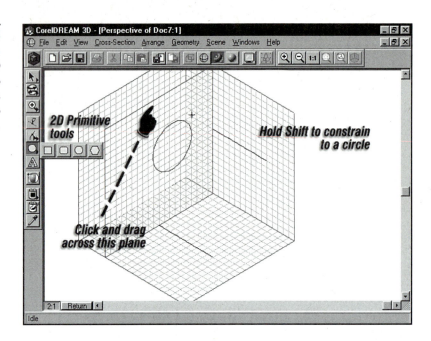

7. Right-click on the direction path on the right plane, then choose Extrusion Envelope, **S**ymmetrical from the shortcut menu.

   Creates two more lines on the bottom and right planes (see fig. 9.14).

Figure 9.14
A Scaling Envelope is a pair of lines on the outside of a Path Direction line that you can edit or replace to make a 3D object.

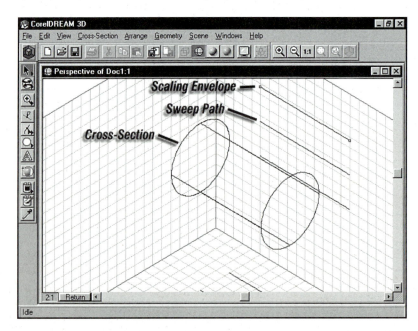

At this point, you have an extruded circle (called a *cross-section*), path direction lines on the bottom and right modeling planes, and Scaling Envelope paths surrounding each Path Direction line. Because you chose Symmetrical from the Extrusion Envelope shortcut command, each Scaling Envelope line responds in a mirror-like fashion to edits created to the opposing Scaling Envelope line. You can edit on the bottom plane's Scaling Envelope lines, or the right plane's; I use the right plane in this example. Because you've chosen Symmetrical, the bottom lines change when you edit a right plane Scaling line. To edit Scaling Envelope lines individually (and produce a very weird 3D shape), choose Symmetrical in **P**lane or **F**reeform (which allows four independent edits of each Scaling Envelope).

8. Click on the selection (Pick) tool, then, with any of the Scaling Envelope lines selected, choose **V**iew, **T**ype, **D**rawing Plane (or press Ctrl+F5).

   Moves your view in the Perspective Window to a 2D view of the selected Scaling Envelope.

At this point, if you've saved a CorelDRAW profile path in any of the vector formats DREAM 3D supports, you can import the path, and it will replace the highlighted Scaling Envelope. Use GOBLET.CDR, a file created from the 3D-STUFF.CDR file, in the CHAP09 folder of the Bonus CD if you'd like to see how the import is performed, but haven't created a profile in advance. See the following note after this example for special instructions on creating and saving a CorelDRAW profile.

9. Choose **F**ile, **I**mport, then select the type of file in the Import dialog box (and its location on hard disk). If you'd like to use the GOBLET.CDR file provided, for example, click on its name in the folders window, then click on Imp**o**rt.

   Displays the Import Artwork dialog box.

10. Click on the **E**nvelope radio button, then click on OK.

    The selected Scaling Envelope is replaced with the imported path. Depending upon where the CorelDRAW path "lands" on the Drawing Plane grid, you might need to click-and-drag the path closer to the center direction Path line, using the Selection tool. If you need to do this, be sure to click on a path segment, and not a node.

This is method number one for creating the loving cup. To get real working experience with DREAM 3D's Bézier tool, however, ignore the last two steps, and follow the next steps:

11. Click on the Bézier tool, then click (*don't* drag) a point close to (but *not* on) the area where the Scaling Envelope meets the cross section.

    Replaces Scaling Envelope with the curve you've begun (see fig. 9.15).

Figure 9.15
Clicking near the point where the cross section meets the Scaling Envelope replaces the Scaling Envelope and begins a new one you draw.

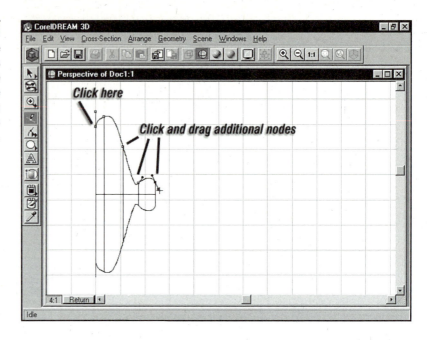

The trick in the last step is to click near, but not directly on, the node that represents the vertex of the cross-section circle you drew and the Scaling Envelope. It's a little hard to recognize the circle as a circle, because in this special view of the component paths, the circle's x and y coordinates lie on the z plane, which can't be viewed from this editing perspective. Simply trust that the line you see at either end connecting the Scaling Envelopes is the circle. If you by chance click on the vertex of the circle and Scaling Envelope, DREAM 3D won't see the curves you draw as a unique, new Scaling Envelope; instead, DREAM 3D sees the action as an attempt to augment the present Scaling Envelope—and makes a mess of your editing work. You might as well start over in this case!

Think of the first point you've clicked on as the base of the profile you saw and practiced with in the 3D-STUFF document in CorelDRAW.

12. Continue click-and-dragging the Bézier curve, clicking, but not dragging points at the top lip of the loving cup, then stop when you reach the end of the path at the edge of the Direction Path line.

    You create the loving cup profile, as rehearsed earlier in CorelDRAW (see fig. 9.16).

13. With the Selection tool, click-and-drag any nodes you feel are dislocated now, then click on the Return button on the Perspective window's bottom when you're done.

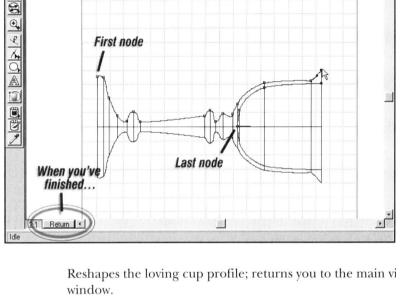

Figure 9.16
DREAM 3D creates
intermediate cross
sections for the
model, at nodes
you create with the
Bézier tool.

Reshapes the loving cup profile; returns you to the main view of the Perspective window.

14. Choose File, Save As, then save the document as LOVNCUP.RD3 (or *.D3D) to your hard disk.

    Saves your work at this intermediate point.

Because Corel Corp. licensed the technology of DREAM 3D from Ray Dream, Inc., there are two fairly identical file formats in which you can save work. Also, because DREAM 3D is a new Corel product, many tool, menu, and U-I (*user interface*) conventions have yet to make the transition to a Corel product. DREAM 3D has a Selection tool instead of a Pick tool, for example.

Note If you intend to create profiles in CorelDRAW for use in DREAM 3D, you should only have one path per CDR file; if you want to export multiple paths, you should only save one per CorelDRAW document. If you don't, DREAM 3D will only import the first (top) path in a collection of paths within a *.CDR file. Also, don't use a dotted line property on paths you intend to import to DREAM 3D; DREAM 3D sees dotted lines as a massive amount of individual, unconnected paths. Use solid outlines for paths you intend to import to DREAM 3D.

Additionally, you must check the Save Presentation Exchange Data check box when saving the CorelDRAW file, or DREAM 3D will not be able to import the path data for use as a profile.

If names for U-I objects seem a little inconsistent in this chapter, it's due to the newness of CorelDREAM 3D as a product, and this is the reason why this chapter requires a little more digestion than others. The steps you performed in the preceding exercise are called *jumping in* or *inspecting* an object—refining the paths that make up the vertices of a 3D model.

You will find a common, consistent behavior in how DREAM 3D and CorelDRAW objects are selected; objects, and component paths, are selected when you create them and continue to remain selected until you create a different object. You have to explicitly deselect an object by clicking on an empty space with the Selection tool; it's then that you can select a different object. This is an important point to remember as you continue with this assignment. The Add, Delete, and Convert Point tools are covered next, and none of them have the capability to select or deselect objects or paths.

Note   It's very easy to accidentally select the Direction Path for an object while working in the Drawing Plane view of the Perspective window, because the Scaling Envelope and Direction Path meet at two points on an object. If you do, by chance, select the Direction Path, use the Selection tool to change your selection; editing and drawing tools can be toggled to the Selection tool by pressing the spacebar. It is only when you're in the Reference view of the Perspective window, that you can use an alternative tool—such as the Virtual Trackball—to select objects.

In the next section, you'll learn a little more about object space and how DREAM 3D offers controls for navigating an object in virtual space.

Positioning and Copying Part of a 3D Object

If you completed the previous section, you now have a handsome 3D cup in the center of the Perspective window. By default, every new object created in DREAM 3D has a primer coat of red plastic material around it. Chances are, you'll want to reposition this cup by rotating it, and change camera angles to make it appear more dimensional in the final render.

You should resist the impulse to spin and move the loving cup in DREAM 3D's universe right now—for a couple of reasons. Other objects need to be created—and positioned—to complete the scene, and the easiest approach to aligning objects to the loving cup is to *leave the main object exactly where it is* until objects which need precise alignment to the loving cup have been created. Navigating 3D space using a 2D monitor as a reference isn't the most intuitive of sports, and it's a good idea right now to learn how objects are repositioned *before* you actually perform the repositioning.

Figure 9.17 is a view of the Perspective window that should be very similar to your own view of the assignment at this point; the exact position of the loving cup depends upon where on the grid you created the circle. DREAM 3D offers *projections*—the box-like silhouettes of objects—on the three Perspective window planes—as an alternative to directly manipulating an object. You can rotate these projections, and the object will rotate one axis at a time. When you've worked with projections for a little while, you'll find them indispensable. For example, when all three projections of an object align with the three projections of a different object, you can be assured that the objects are aligned—without the necessity of changing views in the Perspective window.

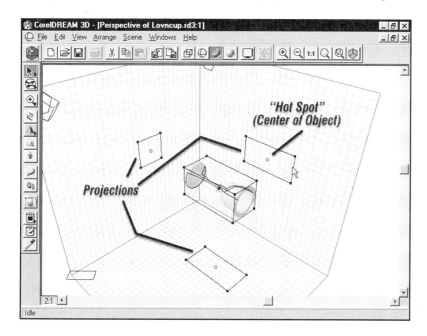

Figure 9.17

Every object in the Perspective window "throws" projections onto the grid planes; you can move projections to move an object across one plane.

Also in figure 9.17, *hot spots* have been called out. Hot spots are the center of an object; you have one within each projection, and one in the center of the object. The center hot spot can be moved so that you can rotate an object relative to a *different* center of rotation. The hot spot feature is useful when, for example, you've constructed a solar system using several spheres, with a sun in the center of the scene. The planets in this example might need to be rotated around the sun, but each planet's center of rotation is located in the center of the sun, not in its own center.

Additionally, you can resize an object within the Perspective window by dragging the bounding box selection handles in any direction. Although DREAM 3D makes it easy to resize an object this way, it will usually be important to *proportionately* resize objects—the x, y, and z dimensions should resize up or down in the same proportion. To do this, press and hold the Shift key while you click-and-drag a corner bounding box away from, or toward the center of, a projection or the object itself. Again, DREAM 3D does not follow all the conventions of its sister program CorelDRAW, where Ctrl, not Shift, is the key that constrains resizing and movement.

Beyond CorelDRAW!

In the next example, you'll add liquid to the loving cup. It makes sense, then, to reuse a portion of the loving cup's profile to serve as the outside Scaling Envelope for the liquid. Unfortunately, DREAM 3D has no facility for copying Scaling lines or Direction paths, so a workable alternative for creating liquid inside the cup is to duplicate the cup, then edit the duplicate's Scaling Envelope to arrive at the shape you need for the liquid.

The following editing technique shows you how to delete points on the Scaling Envelope and create a path for the Scaling Envelope that inverts; the inside dimensions of the cup will become the outside dimensions of the liquid.

Editing a Scaling Envelope

1. Choose the Selection tool from the toolbox, then right-click on the cup and choose **D**uplicate from the shortcut menu.

   Creates a duplicate of the cup occupying the same spatial coordinates.

2. Double-click on the cup.

   DREAM 3D pops up a message box informing you that the duplicate will become a separate object in the scene (a Master Object, not a clone or "instance" of the original), if you click on OK.

3. Click on OK.

   Changes view in window to Modeling window; Scaling Envelope lines can now be seen.

4. Click on a Scaling Envelope line, then choose **V**iew, **D**rawing plane (or press Ctrl+F5).

   Displays a profile view of the cup; nodes on Scaling Envelope are visible.

5. Click and hold on the Convert Point tool on the toolbox, then click on the Delete Point button on the fly-out menu.

   This is the tool for removing nodes along object paths.

6. Click, left to right, on the second, third, and following nodes along the Scaling Envelope path. Do *not* click on the first or last node, or before you reach the top outside lip of the cup profile.

   Removes intermediate nodes from Scaling Envelope; cup shape auto-simplifies (see fig. 9.18).

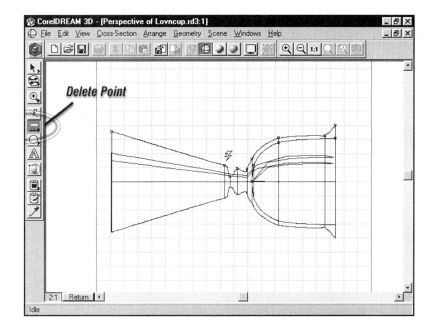

Figure 9.18
Remove the outside profile of the cup by clicking on nodes with the Delete Point tool.

What you're doing is simplifying the outer shape of the cup, so that you can invert the resulting shape by making the first node the last one along the Scaling Envelope path. It makes sense to make the liquid Scaling Envelope a little shorter than the top of the cup, because the liquid should not appear to be on the verge of overflowing.

7. Press the spacebar, marquee select the nodes surrounding the straight path at the right of the Scaling Envelope, then drag horizontally to the left by about one grid marker.

   Toggles to Selection tool; shortens the path horizontally (see fig. 9.19).

Remember that because the duplicate cup was created in the same relative space as the original, by dragging the nodes that represent the top of the cup toward the left, the finished liquid shape you're editing appears slightly inside the cup after you click on Return. (This is why it was important not to move either the cup or its duplicate before editing.)

8. Click on the outer, top lip node, and drag it to directly beneath the inner lip node.

   Makes the inner lip node the upper right outside point on the object.

9. Click-and-drag the beginning Scaling Envelope node to directly beneath the outer lip node, touching the center Direction Path line.

Beyond CorelDRAW!

Figure 9.19
Create a top to the duplicate object, which is shorter when measured against the relative height of the original cup object.

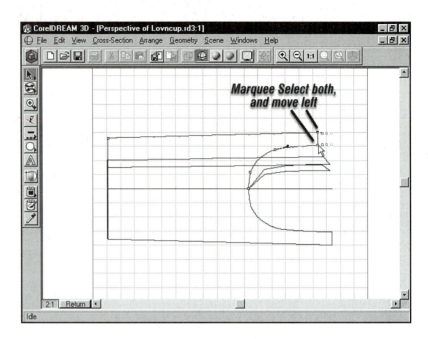

Inverts the duplicate cup's bowl, creating a volume inside the bowl instead of a negative space (see fig. 9.20).

Figure 9.20
Make the negative space within the object a positive space (a volume) by making the first node the last one.

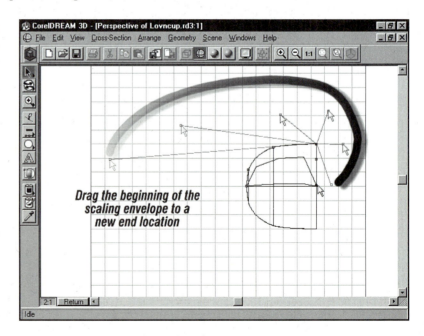

10. Zoom into the right side of the Scaling Envelope, choose the Add Point tool from the Convert Point fly-out menu, then click two or three points on the vertical (right side) portion of the scaling path.

    Adds nodes to the path.

11. Press the spacebar, then carefully click-and-drag the control handles on the new nodes to the left or right of their original position along the path.

    Creates ripples along the right of the path (see fig. 9.21).

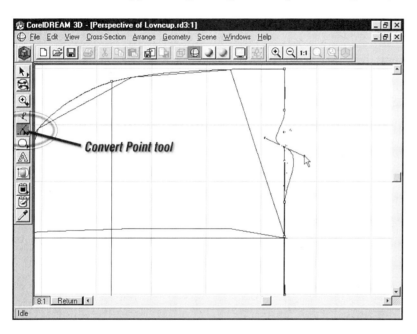

Convert Point tool

Figure 9.21
Add motion to the liquid object by making the line that represents the liquid's top a little more wavy.

The preceding step was an embellishment. The liquid could look motionless by leaving the right edge straight, and you'd have saved yourself an editing step. But it's a really good trick, and modelers who haven't read this book are going to wonder how you did this in the finished piece!

12. Click on Return on the Perspective window's bottom left, then press Ctrl+S.

    Returns you to the main view of the scene; saves your work up to this point.

You can now clearly see the advantages to leaving a model in a possibly awkward position and angle within the scene, so that a duplicate can be edited, and automatically aligns with the original. Next, you'll use the Hierarchy window to create a relationship between the cup and its liquid, so that the two objects stay aligned relative to each other when you move the loving cup.

III

Beyond CorelDRAW!

Understanding Hierarchical Relationships

There's a hierarchical order of objects within a DREAM 3D scene; the order describes the linking and relationship of objects to others.

Think about describing an arrangement of objects in a space shuttle for a moment. Weightless conditions are ideal for this example, because DREAM 3D objects have mass (usually described as volume), but no real weight. Within the shuttle is an astronaut holding a sandwich; the sandwich can be thought of as a child object—it moves in relational space as the astronaut—the *parent object*—moves about the space shuttle cabin. The space shuttle can also be thought of as a parent object, because as long as the astronaut stays indoors, the shuttle contains both the astronaut and the sandwich. However, the shuttle, as it orbits the earth, is also a child object, because it is linked in a way to the earth.

A similar structure to the astronaut scenario can be found in the Hierarchy window, which describes the LOVNCUP scene right now. If you open or restore the Hierarchy window (use the **W**indows command), you'll see that the default light and camera belong to the same hierarchy tree as the loving cup and liquid, and that all these objects are contained within to the universe. However, the liquid bears a relationship to the cup, but is not linked to the cup. This means that moving the cup would be an action independent of the liquid, and the liquid would become unaligned in space relative to the cup in doing so.

The following exercise shows how to use the Hierarchy window to create a more orderly, friendly DREAM 3D universe:

Creating a Child/Parent Object Link

1. Click on the LovingCup 1 title (beneath its icon) on the Hierarchy window.

   Pops up the Edit Object Name dialog box.

2. Type Liquid in the **O**bject name field, then click on OK.

   Assigns a unique name to the liquid object.

The preceding step is not necessary to link objects, but because the Hierarchy window icons are very similar, editing the name of an object which came into this universe as a duplicate of the loving cup helps you distinguish between objects you'll link.

3. Click-and-drag the Liquid icon (not the title) on top of the Loving Cup icon (see fig. 9.22).

   The liquid is now linked to the loving cup, and the parent object, the loving cup, can now be moved while always containing the liquid.

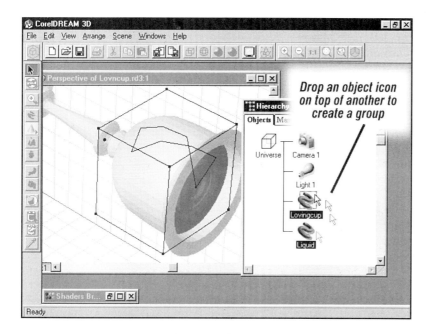

Figure 9.22
Child object icons move to the right of the parent icon after you drag and drop them to establish a link.

4. Zoom out of the scene, click on the Virtual Trackball tool, then click-and-drag on the loving cup until it appears upright.

Rotates both the cup and liquid in 3D space (see fig. 9.23).

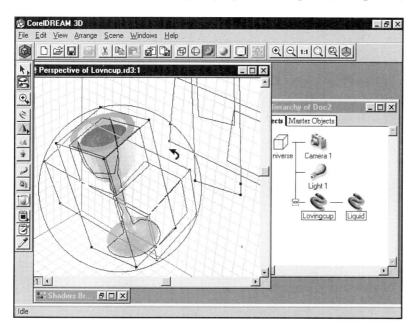

Figure 9.23
You can rotate an object and its contents, when you create a link between parent and child objects.

The exact degree of 3D rotation in this example is unimportant; use your own aesthetics to decide where in space the cup and its liquid should be posed for the final render. Remember that a gear needs to be added to the cup, so don't get *too* creative right now!

5. Press Ctrl+S.

    Saves your work up to this point.

Models that are a product of lathing (like the loving cup) can describe many real world objects, but you can generate most common objects with another method—simple extrusions of 2D paths. One aspect of this method—"cookie cutter" sweeping—is the topic of the next section, where you'll see how to use a CorelDRAW-created TrueType font to build a gear for the retirement poster.

Getting a Gear Aligned

You can jump to three subclasses of editing windows from the Perspective window, each for the type of objects you create: freeform, presets, and text objects. The Modeling window lets you edit paths in an Envelope object. Preset primitive shapes you might add to a scene can't be edited on a more basic level, and if you double-click on one, you can only rotate the object, not edit it. The third class of DREAM 3D objects are text objects. Because DREAM 3D text has a predefined property (that of a collection of scalable characters), you cannot simplify the shape of the characters. You can, however, specify different fonts at any time after a line of text has been extruded in DREAM 3D.

In this section, you'll use the Profiles TrueType font, created earlier in this chapter, and extrude a single character to make the 3D gear for the scene. The steps are obvious and self-explanatory, but I've deliberately created a challenge in the following set of steps. Because you were invited to rotate the cup and liquid in the preceding example, you'll be faced with the challenge of working with DREAM 3D projections to place the gear around the cup's stem. This is sort of a "virtual County Fair" example; you have to put the ring around the bottle!

If you didn't create the Profiles typeface earlier in this chapter, you can use the New Riders version of this TrueType font (located in the CHAP09 folder beneath EXAMPLES on the *CorelDRAW! 6 Expert's Edition Bonus CD*). Open the CHAP09 folder in a window in Windows Explorer, open the Windows.Fonts folder, then click-and-drag Profiles.TTF into the Fonts folder.

→**Tip**   You must exit DREAM 3D and restart the application to get DREAM 3D to recognize the font addition to your system.

Here's how to further embellish the design with the additional element of the gear:

Creating and Positioning the Gear

1. In the LOVNCUP.RD3 document, click on the Text tool, then click the cursor in the middle of the Perspective window.

   Opens the sub-window of the Perspective window that relates to Text objects.

2. (If you have more than 100 TrueType fonts installed), choose More fonts from the font drop-down list, choose Profiles, then click on OK.

   Specifies the font used in this example.

Consider for a moment how large the font should be and how deeply the font character should be extruded. Relative size of the gear is no problem here; you can shift+drag the gear's corner selection handle to proportionately resize it after it's created. We're talking depth to height ratio here. DREAM 3D has a bizarre method of measuring text height.

In other applications, 72 points is equivalent to one inch; however, if you divide the Font size value in the Font modeling window by 3, you'll arrive at the correct height of the resulting shape, in DREAM 3D "inches" space. Therefore, the default value of 72 will yield a 26" tall gear, and the default Depth value of 4 inches will suit our purposes here well.

3. Click in the Editing window, type **a**, then click on Return (see fig 9.24).

   Adds an extruded gear to the scene.

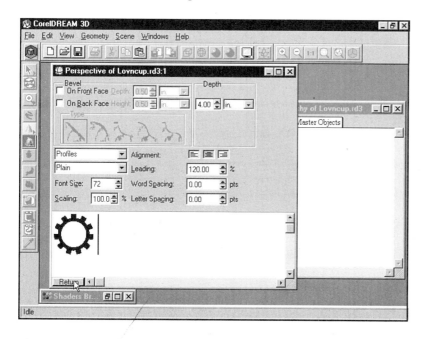

Figure 9.24

Use a symbol font in DREAM 3D to extrude a typeface character.

Beyond CorelDRAW!

4. With the Selection tool, click-and-drag the right projection of the gear to the vertical center of the cup projection, a little beneath the cup projection's horizontal center.

Aligns the gear to the cup in one of three dimensions.

5. Click-and-drag the gear's back plane projection so it aligns with the cup vertically, and slightly below the cup's midpoint horizontally.

Aligns the gear to the cup in the second of three dimensions.

Depending on where the gear appeared in the scene, it might not be necessary to align the third gear projection to the cup's projection. Click on the Preview Quality button on the toolbar and check out how the solid objects appear to be aligned. If they're okay, don't modify the bottom projection of the gear. If the gear appears to be penetrating the cup stem, click-and-drag the bottom projection of the gear so that it's centered within the cup projection.

The following step is an artistic call, one that you might choose not to follow. A completely symmetrical composition can be static and boring. To make the orbit of the gear around the cup stem more interesting, try this:

6. Click on the Virtual Trackball tool, then click-and-drag on the rear projection of the gear so that it appears to revolve around a "10 to 4 o'clock" angle around the cup stem.

Makes the composition more interesting (see fig. 9.25).

Figure 9.25

You can rotate an object along a single dimensional axis by using the Virtual Trackball tool on a projection.

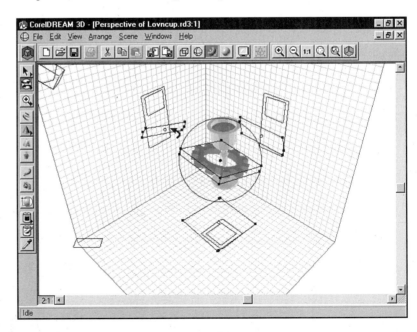

7. Press Ctrl+S (**F**ile, **S**ave).

   Saves your work to hard disk.

If you have the gear where you want it relative to the cup, there's no reason why you can't link the gear to the cup in the same way you linked the liquid. However, the camera and lighting angles are discussed next, and you might want to reserve the linking action until your final view of the composition is the way you want it.

 Tip   To unlink a child object, click-and-drag the child icon in the Hierarchy window away from the parent, then drop it on the main stem of the Hierarchy tree.

Refining the 3D Composition

I haven't discussed the preview modes in DREAM 3D until now because there hasn't been much to look at in the scene. You have your choice of bounding box, Wireframe, Preview, and Better Preview; you can access these preview modes by clicking on the icons on the toolbar. The toolbar preview modes apply to the entire scene, and if you have a 486DX 50MHz or better processor, you can work comfortably in the Preview mode most times. The Wireframe mode is good for selecting objects hidden behind other objects, and Better Preview mode provides high-quality images on-screen (at the price of processing speed).

The shortcut menu for objects you can click on with the Selection tool offers individual controls for preview rendering quality, and overrides the toolbar icon selections. As an example, if you want to hide the cup right now but leave the gear on-screen, you first click on the Preview Quality button on the toolbar, right-click on the cup, then choose Invisible from the shortcut menu. Great—so how do you return an invisible object to the Perspective window? You right-click over its icon on the Hierarchy window, and select a more visible state for the cup.

The following section covers other views of your scene and casts some light upon the assignment—in a virtual sense.

Lighting and Camera Angles

By default, the Reference view through the Perspective window (through the default camera) is an *axonometric* view—one that provides all three planes of view of a scene. While an axonometric view is interesting, it might not be what you envision for all your DREAM 3D modeling work. Therefore, let's take a breeze through the finer points of establishing a 3D composition—making it appear in final, rendered state, exactly the way you imagined it.

In the following set of steps, you'll edit and save a camera view, and angle the default light so it illuminates the scene rather than pointing into the Universe at an oblique, default angle.

Lighting and Setting Up a New View

1. Press Ctrl+E (**S**cene, **C**amera Settings).

   Displays the Camera Settings window.

2. Click on the Position drop-down list, and choose Front.

   Moves your view (the camera's view) of the Perspective window to the front of the Universe.

3. Choose Conical from the Type drop-down list.

   Provides you with Camera lens options; view becomes less "flat" in the Perspective window.

Isometric views of objects are flat projections—a 3D world without perspective—which can be quite useful for aligning objects without the distraction of different perspective convergences within a scene. However, an isometric view of the world is unrealistic, but hypothetical and mathematical in construction—not at all like the 3D scene you want for this composition. You'll notice that when you choose a specific plane for your Camera view, the other two grids vanish. To restore them, try this:

4. Click on the right rotation arrow twice on the Camera window, then click twice on the down rotation arrow.

   Moves the view through the Perspective window to the left and slightly above the objects.

5. Click on the unhighlighted floor and wall in the Display Planes tool in the upper left corner of the workspace, at the intersection of the toolbar and the toolbox.

   Restores the grid planes to view in the Perspective window.

6. Click in the Position drop-down list, then click on Save Position.

   Displays the Save Camera Position dialog box.

7. Type **MyCam1** (or whatever you like) in the Name field, then click on OK.

   Save your view of scene to be recalled at any future time.

8. Click on the Close button on the Camera window.

   Closes the window.

Because you've saved the camera setting, you're free now to display other views of the scene. Find, then move, and point the default light in the scene now.

9. Zoom out of the scene until you've located the camera.

   This is the object you'll pose next.

10. Choose <u>V</u>iew, <u>T</u>ype, then click on <u>T</u>op (Ctrl+8).

    Provides an aerial view of the scene.

11. With the selection tool, click-and-drag the light to a position toward the bottom left of the Perspective window (the front of the scene).

    Moves the light so that it will illuminate the scene from in front, slightly to the left.

12. Press Ctrl+1 (<u>V</u>iew, <u>T</u>ype, <u>F</u>ront).

    Moves your viewing angle to the front of the scene.

13. Click-and-drag the light to a position slightly above the cup.

    Changes the position of the light.

By performing the last two steps, the light is not pointed at the cup now, and will only be illuminated in the final render by ambient light (light from a non-specified direction). This would be a shame, because the cup is going to be dimpled shining gold in the finished scene. Here's how to change the angle of the light:

14. With the Selection tool, click on the light, then Shift+click on the cup.

    Selects both Universe objects.

15. Release the Shift key, then right-click and choose Point at from the shortcut menu.

    Points the light at the hot spot on the cup.

The Point at command is invaluable, because light bounding boxes don't indicate which side of the bounding box is the front of the light. Because the cup is not the center of *all* objects in the scene, the Point at command may have pointed the light a little too low. Point the light at the bowl of the cup, not its stem:

16. Click on the Virtual Trackball tool, then click-and-drag the back of the light downwards about one grid marker.

    Moves the front of the light upwards (see fig. 9.26).

Figure 9.26
Direct lighting
creates shadow and
highlights on objects;
a light must be
pointed at, not
around, an object to
produce shading.

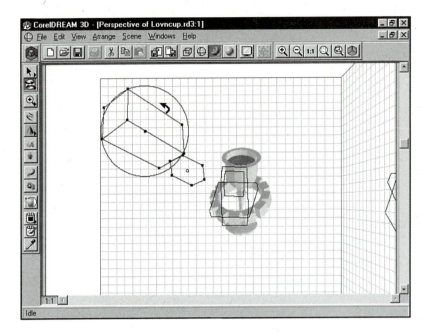

17. Press Ctrl+S (**F**ile, **S**ave).

    Saves your work up to this point.

In the preceding example, you clicked downward to move a light's target upward. The reason for the apparent discrepancy is that the light object is pointing away from you; therefore, you're adjusting it from the back. As you work more with DREAM 3D, you'll understand that object properties are like those found in real life, and that the 2D face of your monitor is like a window you can reach through to manipulate objects (a process called "thinking in 3D").

Finishing Touches for the Scene

The following set of steps aren't required for creating the entire poster, but they add a nice, almost humorous touch to the scene. To add more realism to the liquid in the cup, it would be nice if one or two splashes of liquid were exiting the cup. Liquids suspended in space are hard for photographers to capture, but in the weightless world of modeling applications, it's a snap.

The following steps don't include any new features—you already know them from previous examples—so the liquid splash embellishment to the scene is not listed as a set of example steps. In figure 9.27, you can see a Scaling Envelope line being converted to a curve using the Convert Point tool. This lathing object is created by clicking in the

Perspective window with the Free form tool, then Symmetrical Envelope is assigned to the object, and the Drawing Plane is displayed by choosing it from the **V**iew menu command.

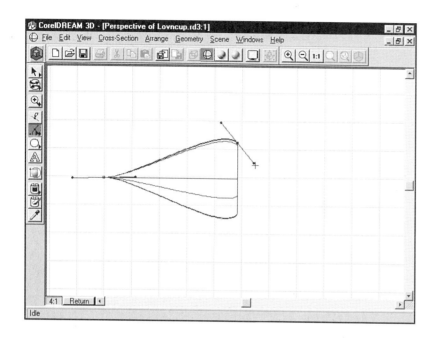

Figure 9.27
You can edit an existing Scaling Envelope with the Convert Point and Selection tools.

It's not always necessary to replace a Scaling Envelope line (as you did in building the loving cup) to make a custom contour for a lathed object. The Convert Point tool is different from the Shape tool in CorelDRAW in that it changes a node's properties by clicking and dragging on a node. The first time you click-and-drag on a node, a Smooth property is created. If you then click-and-drag on a control handle on the Smooth node, a Cusp property is made. A single click on a node converts lines controlled by the node to straight path segments.

  Tip   Adobe Photoshop isn't a Corel product, but the Change Direction Point tool on Photoshop's Paths palette operates identically to DREAM 3D's Convert Point tool. If you have experience with Photoshop, you're already experienced in reshaping envelope lines using the Convert Point tool.

After you've made the Scaling Envelope look like half a teardrop, you can click on Return and the splash droplet will appear as an object within the scene. You'll need to reposition it to the top of the cup to make the splash appear to be coming from the cup. After the splash has been positioned, choose Duplicate from the right-button shortcut menu, then click-and-drag the duplicate to a different location above the cup so that 2 drops are splashing out of this slightly tilted cup.

III

Beyond CorelDRAW!

Details are important to creating a realistic scene, and so is the intimation of action within a still frame. With little touches like the splashes, you can accomplish both.

Creating Custom Materials

Now that all the cast members are present and accounted for in the Perspective window, it's wardrobe call time—time to create custom textures for the objects using designs you created earlier in this chapter with CorelDRAW.

Making Dented Gold

The best, easiest way to create a custom material (shader) for objects, is to duplicate an existing shader that shipped with DREAM 3D. In the following set of steps, you'll see how to take the Polished Gold shader, add a bump map to it, and apply the shader to the loving cup.

Adding a Property to a Shader

1. In the Shaders Browser window, right-click on the Polished Gold icon, then choose Duplicate from the shortcut menu.

   Creates an identical icon in the window, with an identical title (see fig. 9.28).

Figure 9.28
The safest way to create a new shader is to duplicate one, and not modify an existing shader.

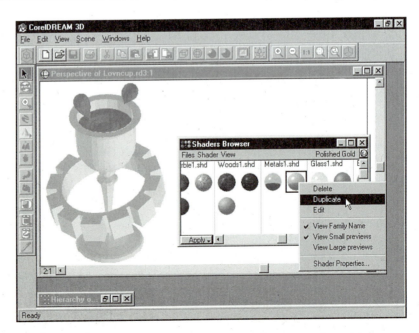

2. Double-click on the duplicated Polished Gold shader.

   Displays the Shader Editor window.

3. Click on the Bump tab in the Shader Editor, right-click in the control field of the Bump area, then choose Texture Map from the shortcut menu (see fig. 9.29).

   Displays the Open dialog box.

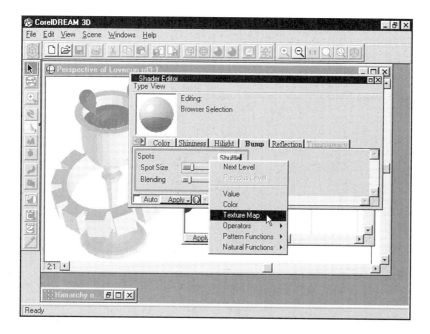

Figure 9.29

Every shader property tab contains an area in which you can specify a unique modifier—images, values, and others.

If you can't see the Bump tab when the Shader Editor window opens, expand the window by clicking and dragging on the edges, or use the arrow to move tabs to the left or right. The control area of a Shader property menu can be changed to any of the modifiers covered in table 9.1 (earlier in this chapter), and you can also click on the modifier controls. Then press Delete if you don't want a property to exist with a specific shader.

4. Choose BUMPS.TIF, which you exported earlier from CorelDRAW (or choose BUMPS.TIF from the CHAP09 folder on the Bonus CD), then click on **O**pen.

   Imports a copy of the bump map.

5. Click on the Better sampling check box, click on the Tile check box, then click-and-drag the Horizontal and Vertical sliders until they both read 9.

Beyond CorelDRAW!

Specifies that the Shader Editor should take a little time to produce an excellent bump map, and that the bump map shall repeat 9 times across the surface of the object you specify (see fig. 9.30).

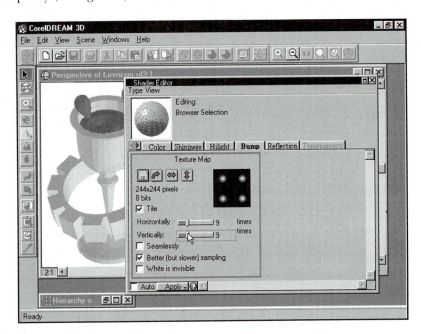

Figure 9.30

A bump map pattern can be used once, or repeated several times across the surface of an object.

6. Click on the close button on the Shader Editor window, then drag the icon for the dented gold shader to on top of the cup in the Perspective window.

   Applies the custom texture to the cup (see fig. 9.31).

7. Press Ctrl+S.

   Saves your work to hard disk.

Preview quality might not show the custom shader's bumpy properties, so why not click on the Better quality icon on the toolbar now? Additionally, you should give the shader a unique name: Duplicates have the same name as the originals in DREAM 3D. To do this, right-click on the shader icon, choose Shader Properties, then type **Bumpy Gold** in the Shader **N**ame field.

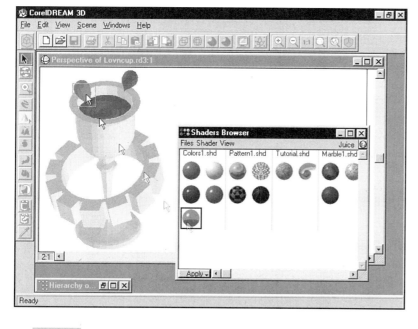

Figure 9.31
Applying a shader to
an object is as simple
as drag and drop.

▶Tip   3D objects have general shapes to which a color or bump map can conform. Because
maps are 2D images, they must have a beginning and an end point on a surface, and
an orientation. For the most part, DREAM 3D accurately evaluates and maps images to DREAM
3D-created objects. However, if you ever decide to change the default mapping, or if you import a
DXF file for use in DREAM 3D, right-click on the object to which you've already assigned a shader,
choose Shading Properties from the shortcut menu, then choose a Mapping Mode which fits the
general description of the object.

You can choose from Cylindrical Mapping, Spherical Mapping, Box Mapping, Parametric
Mapping (DREAM 3D's default mapping), and also choose the direction in which you want a
2D image mapped.

Color Mapping an Engraved Phrase

Color mapping is accomplished in an identical fashion to bump-mapping, except it's
the color property (not the Bump) of a shader that receives the 2D image. In the
following steps, you use the Paint Rectangular Shading Shape tool in combination with
another custom shader to put "25 Great Years!" on the bowl of the cup. The lettering
won't obscure the bumpy gold; color maps can contain drop-out colors to only display
foreground colors when applied to an object, or part of an object.

If you didn't export the lettering from CorelDRAW in the example at the beginning of this chapter, feel free to use 25GREAT.TIF, which can be found in the CHAP09 folder of the Bonus CD.

Partially Shading an Object

1. Right-click on the Sandstone shader icon in the Shaders Browser, then choose duplicate from the shortcut menu.

   Makes a duplicate of the shader.

Again, choosing a shader that already has many of the attributes you need for an assignment helps abbreviate your editing work. The Sandstone shader happens to be a color map-type shader, and you'll be able to replace the sandstone map with the 25GREAT.TIF image quite easily.

2. Double-click on the duplicated icon, click on the Shininess tab, then click on the slider and press Delete.

   Removes the Shininess channel property from the new shader you're creating.

3. Click on the Hilight tab, click on the slider, press Delete, then click on the Color tab.

   Deletes the Hilight property from your new shader properties; moves you to the Color channel for the custom shader you're designing.

4. Right-click over the controls area of the color menu, and choose Texture Map from the shortcut menu.

   Displays the Open dialog box.

5. Choose 25GREAT.TIF from your hard disk (or the Bonus CD), then click on **O**pen.

   Loads the color bitmap image.

6. Right-click on the icon window, then choose Flat Preview from the shortcut menu.

   Creates an icon that displays the color map on a flat surface, not a sphere.

The 25GREAT bitmap won't map correctly across the bowl of the cup because of its orientation. You created the cup on its side by lathing the Scaling Envelope path, and the orientation of the bitmap therefore needs to be 90° rotated. You can fix this stuff *after* you've created a unique shader and see that it's applied wrong to the object, but let's take care of it now:

7. Click on the Rotate button on the Color menu.

   Rotates the image 90°; the preview icon shows the change.

8. Select the White is invisible check box, then close the Shader Editor.

   You have a shader that will only display the foreground text (see fig. 9.32).
   Because the shader is the last chosen in the Shaders Browser window, it's the
   current shader.

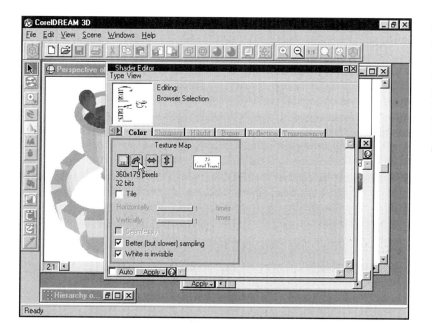

Figure 9.32
Color bitmaps that
are assigned to a
shaders color
property can display
white areas as
transparent when
mapped to an
object.

9. Click on the Paint Rectangular Shading Shape tool on the toolbox, then click-
   and-drag across the front of the bowl of the cup.

   Creates a rectangular painted area on the bowl (see fig. 9.33).

10. Choose **F**ile, **S**ave (Ctrl+S).

    Saves your work up to this point.

You only see the bounding box of a 3D painted-on shader while in Preview Quality
viewing mode, but if you click on Better Preview, you'll see an absolutely incredible
sight. It's fairly obvious when you paint with one of the 3D paint tools that you're
"painting in space." The tools follow a dimensional surface of the target object. It feels

Beyond CorelDRAW!

Figure 9.33

You can confine the painting of a shader onto the surface of an object by using the 3D paint tools.

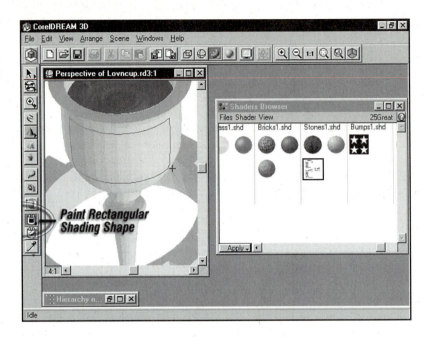

weird, but the effect is phenomenal. Think of how many partial surfaces you can cover with different shaders and the 3D paint tools. For freeform application of a shader, use the tool beneath the Paint Rectangular tool, the 3D Paint Brush. The flyout for the tool you used contains options for polygonal and oval surfaces, too.

Tip   If you've painted over an area with any of the 3D paint tools, and you feel the area is mispositioned, you can adjust a paint-shaded area by clicking and dragging it with the Paint Shape Selection tool in the Selection tool's flyout menu.

Also, with the Paint Selection tool, you can delete a painted area. Click on the area with the Paint Selection (not the regular Selection) tool, then press Delete.

Independent Study for Finishing the Composition

The step format of this chapter is abandoned in this section so you can complete the loving cup composition. If you've read this far, assigning new shaders to the rest of the objects should be a familiar procedure.

You'll want to add a shader to the gear. The gear probably shouldn't have the same bumpy property as the cup because there's a lot of innate detail to the shape of the gear, and bumpy texture would compete for attention. Therefore, click-and-drag the Polished Gold shader icon onto the gear, and the gear's all set.

With respect to the liquid and splashes, we have news that Mike doesn't drink, and grape juice would be a fitting beverage for his retirement toast. So you can modify a preset shader that has liquid properties to cast an appropriate color here. The Transparency shader at the right of the Shaders Browser is a good starting selection. Duplicate Trans1.shd, then double-click on the duplicate icon to jump into the Shaders Browser. On the Transparency menu, click-and-drag the slider from 90 to about 14 percent. Doing this creates a partially transparent shader, which—when applied to the liquid and splash objects—allows some of the cup detail to show through (like clear liquids often do in real life). Additionally, click on the Color property for the duplicate shader. You'll see that there is no color modifier set for this object, so right-clicking to produce the modifier menu won't work in this case. Instead, choose color from the Type menu in the Shader editor. This will display a color swatch in the controls area of the Color menu, and by double-clicking on the swatch, a fairly nonintuitive RGB color, slider window appears. If you then click on the color wheel icon, you'll move to Windows color picker, where you can choose a royal purple for the shader.

Click-and-drag the shader to the liquid, then repeat this step with the two splash objects.

You're done with the modeling part of 3D creation in DREAM 3D, and you're ready to render the scene.

Rendering Models

Rendered models are saved to your choice of file formats (TIF, BMP, and Targa being the most common). In this section, you'll select a file format, resolution, and size for the finished rendered cup scene, and pick up a few tricks to make the finished render one that you can work with in CorelDRAW and other applications more easily.

Taking Final Previews of the Scene

As stated earlier in this chapter, rendering a model is perhaps the most time-intensive part of the 3D creation process. Naturally, you don't want to wait a half an hour only to receive a "bum" render—one whose exposure is incorrect, or with objects clipped at the border of the image. A good working methodology to adopt when modeling is to check a high-quality preview of the scene, make adjustments to the file dimensions you want to render, check the scene one last time in high-quality preview, then let DREAM 3D render away. This methodology isn't unlike looking in the rearview mirror one last time before you make a turn into traffic.

Choose **S**cene, Camera **S**ettings now, then choose MyCam1 from the Position dropdown list. You might want to use the Zoom tool now to zoom in on the camera's field of view. Camera settings retain the position of the camera, but not the focal length, and manually zooming with the Zoom tool affects the final render, not simply the active view of a scene through the Perspective window.

In figure 9.34, the Render Area tool has been chosen and a marquee has been dragged around part of the cup. The render area tool is terrific, and in many respects is superior to clicking on the Render Preview button on the toolbar. You get to select an area, not the entire image, to perform a render within the Perspective window. In contrast, the Preview Render command renders the entire scene in a separate window, and can take three or four times as long as the Render Area tool's capability to accurately preview objects.

Figure 9.34
Use the Render Area tool instead of the Render Preview feature to see how parts of an image will render in the finished image.

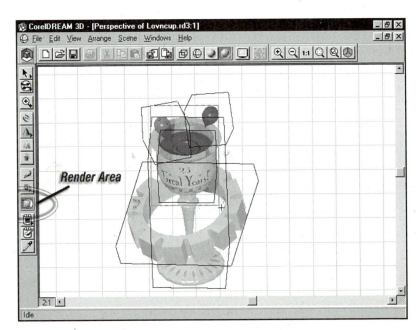

Choosing the Finished File Format and Dimensions

In the next set of steps, you'll see how to specify the measurements, file format, cropping, and time you want DREAM 3D to spend rendering the cup scene. Obviously, your own modeling work might not call for the same specifications, but play along here and you'll discover hidden options for making models turn out great.

Rendering Specifications

1. Choose **S**cene, **R**ender Setup, then **F**inal.

   The Artwork Settings dialog box appears.

2. Click on the O**t**her Resolution radio button, choose inches for both the Width and Height fields, enter 4 in both fields, make certain that in. (inches, not the default of pts.-points) is chosen in the drop-down box to the right of each number entry field, then enter 150 in the **R**esolution spin box.

Specifies that the image will be square, and of a resolution that will print well to a medium quality imagesetter (approximately 1,200 dpi).

3. Click on the **E**stimate Time button.

Tells you how much time DREAM 3D believes it will take to render the image to file (see fig. 9.35).

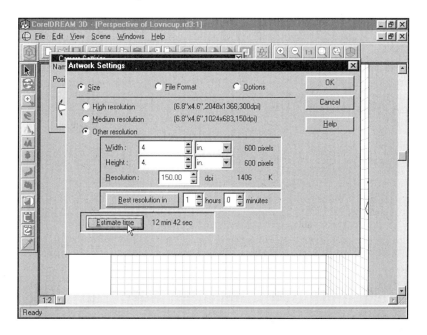

Figure 9.35

If the estimated time exceeds an hour, and you're in a rush, you might want to choose the Best Resolution (image) in option.

4. Click on the **F**ile Format radio button, then choose TIF from the Save Format drop-down list.

Chooses a format which can save a mask (explanation to follow).

5. Click on the **M**ask check box.

The rendered TIF image will now contain a mask, which helps separate the objects from empty scene areas (see fig. 9.36).

Figure 9.36
CorelPHOTO-PAINT can read DREAM 3D mask information; you'll use a mask to optimize the rendered image for use in CorelDRAW.

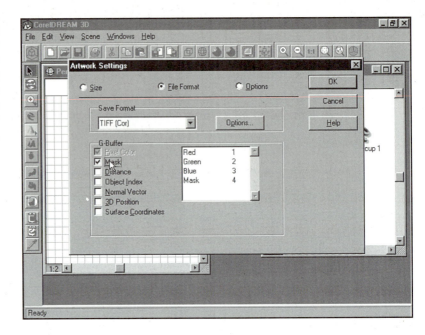

6. Click on OK, then click on **V**iew, Production **F**rame.

    Displays a rectangle in the Perspective window which represents the borders of the finished, rendered TIF image.

There's no need to save the file at the end of this example, but *don't close* the file. Important rendering options and information are in the following section.

We'll get into what a mask is and does in following sections, but for now, the Production Frame needs to be explained.

CorelDREAM 3D's Production Frame is the film behind the lens of a camera. Usually, you'll want to call the display of the Production Frame as a final step before rendering—modeling is nerve-wracking enough without worrying about the camera!

Adjusting the Production Frame

As in the real world, when you're concerned about what is being imaged on a roll or plate of film, you adjust the camera—not the objects in the scene. This is where modeling enthusiasts get into trouble; folks occasionally change the position of the model instead of the camera, or with DREAM 3D, the Production Frame. If you change a model, then you have to move the lighting, and your scene quickly becomes undone.

Think of the Production Frame *as* the film, the extent of the view of the finished scene as a bitmap image. Unlike the real world, a Production Frame can be of any dimension you choose—4" by 4" was recommended in the preceding example—because the scene is basically square, and DREAM 3D *will* take the time to process empty areas of a scene if this is what you choose.

The following set of steps takes you through the adjustment of the Production Frame and the final render of the composition.

Lights, Camera, Action

1. Choose <u>S</u>cene, <u>C</u>amera Settings (Ctrl+E).

    Displays the Camera Settings Window.

2. Click on the Position drop-down list, then choose **MyCam1.**

    Adjusts your view of the scene to a saved position.

Chances are that part of the cup or gear fall outside of the Production Frame, or you can't even see the Production Frame from your present level of zoom. Zoom out first so you can see both the scene and the Production Frame. Then,

3. Click on the Type drop-down list, and set the camera to Conical.

    Ensures that the image will be dimensional and not flat.

4. Click on the tiny ruler in the upper right of the Camera Settings window.

    Displays the Increments dialog box.

5. Type **4** in the <u>T</u>ranslation field, then click on OK.

    Specifies that clicking on a movement arrow in the Camera Settings window will change relative distance by 4 inches.

"Translation" here means the relative movement of the camera to the subject. This is how you position the scene in the Production Frame. For all intents and purposes, the Translation amount is a "nudge" factor, such as the Nudge amount in CorelDRAW's General Options menu.

6. In the Camera Settings Window, click on the left, right, in, out, up, or down arrows on the Translation (not the Rotation) controls, as needed, to make the composition appear as large in the Production frame as possible.

    Optimizes the view of the composition (see fig. 9.37).

Beyond CorelDRAW!

Figure 9.37
Your view through
the Production Frame
is exactly what
compositional
elements will appear
in the finished
render.

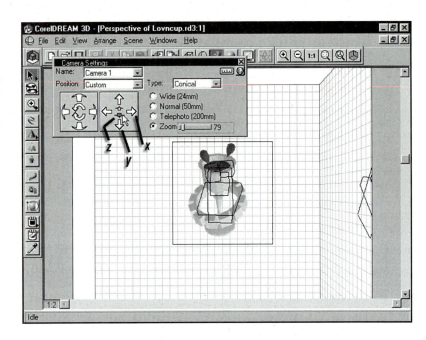

7. Choose **S**cene, Render, **F**inal.

    CorelDREAM 3D begins rendering the composition.

Your system will be tied up for however long DREAM 3D estimated the rendering time
to be. A new document window pops over the Perspective window, and you'll see
DREAM 3D's finished render appear in sampling patches— square areas that appear
sequentially in the render document window. Figure 9.38 shows the process in mid-
action.

8. With the rendering window as the foreground (in focus) child window, choose
    File, Save **A**s, then save the image to hard disk as LOVNCUP.TIF.

    Saves the finished render to hard disk.

If you're experienced with other graphics applications and modeling programs,
DREAM 3D's technique of rendering a finished file to screen first might come as a
shock. Do not, however, attempt to close the rendering window. Doing so (at the very
worst) closes your finished render without saving it to disk. At best, doing so pops up a
message box, which informs you that the Esc key is the method for stopping a render.

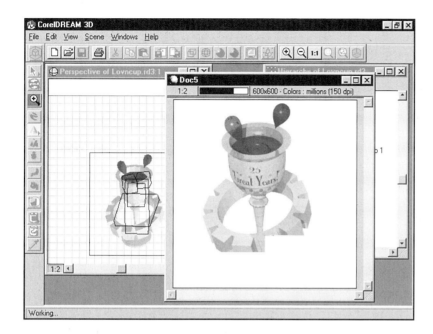

Figure 9.38
DREAM 3D renders
the finished
composition to
screen.

Using a Rendered Model in Other Corel Applications

You've seen in other chapters how easy it is to import a bitmap image for use in CorelDRAW. The following sections contain some surprises, as you learn about new Corel features specifically tailored for bitmap display, and how CorelPHOTO-PAINT can automatically separate backgrounds from rendered foreground objects.

CorelPHOTO-PAINT! and Image Masks

A bitmap image mask is an area within an image that is either protected from change or exposed for editing, depending on which areas are selected by the mask. The term *mask* is a misnomer, frequently used in computer graphics to mean two different things. In reality, when a digital mask exposes a foreground design, and protects the background, it's an artist's frisket—generally a sheet of vellum with a hole carved out of the center—that the digital simulation can best be compared to. When I refer to masking in DREAM 3D or CorelPHOTO-PAINT, we refer to protecting the background *or* foreground, but not both at once.

Beyond CorelDRAW!

Many image editing programs will write mask information to a separate channel of an RGB-type image, such as those produced by DREAM 3D. You might have noticed that the option for saving a mask in DREAM 3D in the BMP image format was not available. This is because it's only the TIF, Targa, and a few other proprietary image file formats that save bitmap information in red, green, and blue color channels, hence the term RGB image. The channel structure of color storage is unlike indexed color images, where each color value in an image is predefined, not stored as relative brightness strengths in color channels. For more information on channels and masks, refer to Chapter 6, "Bitmaps and Vector Designs."

CorelPHOTO-PAINT can save mask information, but not in the native CorelPHOTO-PAINT CPT format; instead, CorelPHOTO-PAINT can read mask channel information in TIF file formats. The TIF format is a mature, stable format which software engineers frequently adopt. CorelPHOTO-PAINT presents this unique mask channel view as an active selection marquee around objects DREAM 3D has rendered.

Your charge in this next set of steps is to use the selection (mask) information as displayed in CorelPHOTO-PAINT, to isolate the background of LOVNCUP.TIF, then paint it a flat, contrasting color to the foreground objects. By doing so, CorelDRAW can import the retouched file and drop-out the background paint color, in a similar fashion to how DREAM 3D can drop white out of an imported color map image.

Painting with a Mask

1. Close DREAM 3D after saving the LOVNCUP.RD3 file one last time, and launch CorelPHOTO-PAINT from Windows Explorer.

   This is the application in which you'll edit the rendered scene.

2. Choose File, Open, then open the LOVNCUP.TIF image from your hard disk.

   This is the target image for editing.

3. Click on the Invert button on the toolbar.

   Inverts the active marquee selection to encompass the background. The foreground cup and gear objects are now protected from editing (see fig. 9.39).

4. Double-click on the Fill tool. Choose the tool.

   Displays the Tool Settings Roll-Up.

5. Click on the Uniform Fill icon.

   Displays the Uniform Fill dialog then click on Edit box.

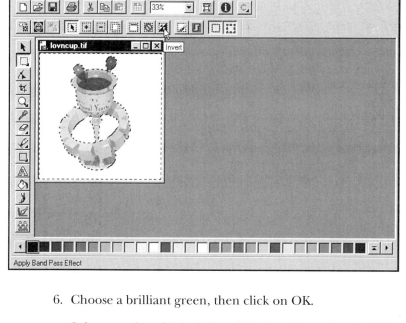

Figure 9.39
By default, DREAM 3D images that contain a mask channel appear with a selection marquee around the objects.

6. Choose a brilliant green, then click on OK.

   Selects a color which clashes with the other colors in LOVNCUP.TIF.

7. Set **T**ransparency to 0, check **A**nti-aliasing, and type **100** in the Tolerance spin box.

   Specifies that the selected green will completely cover the areas clicked upon in the image *not* protected by the mask selection marquee.

8. Click outside of the cup image on the background, then click the two other white areas in the LOVNCUP image.

   Fills the areas with bright green (see fig. 9.40).

9. With the Crop tool, marquee an area in the LOVNCUP image that includes the cup and gear, and eliminates excess green from the image, then double-click inside the crop selection.

   Crops excess image areas; reduces overall file size.

10. Click on the Remove Mask button on the toolbar (the international "circle-with-a-slash" icon).

Beyond CorelDRAW!

Figure 9.40

The selected uniform green fill will only affect areas encompassed by the selection marquee.

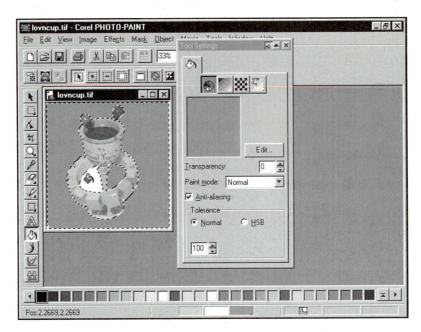

Removes the marquee selection, and the mask information will not be saved to TIF format. If you don't deselect the mask, CorelDRAW will read the mask information, and display a colored background with a *silhouette* of the cup within the image, but no 3D cup.

11. Choose File Save As, then save the image as LOVNMASK.TIF to your hard disk.

    Saves the image.

It's wise to crop a rendered image in an image editing program, and not in the modeling/rendering application. The Production Frame in DREAM 3D serves as a nice, loose cropping area, but you're going to drop out the green in the LOVNMASK image in CorelDRAW. Therefore, the smaller the image dimensions, the smaller the bitmap file size, and the quicker you'll be able to work with the image in CorelDRAW.

Note DREAM 3D has the capability to add a background color to a scene, but because DREAM uses *ray-tracing* (a photo-realistic procedure that creates shadows and reflections), you shouldn't use a background of clashing color in a finished render. Why? Because the ray-tracing process acknowledges the background color as a real part of the rendered image, and your foreground objects will display visible tinting of background color.

Think of how the flesh tones on a human model would look if you photographed them with a bright green seamless background, inches away from them. Some of the color would bounce into the model's face, making the photo look quite unattractive.

If you want a color background, or an imported image, to be included in DREAM 3D models' reflections and surface color, choose **S**cene, **B**ackground, then make your selections.

CorelDRAW!'s Bitmap Color Mask Tool

New to CorelDRAW 6 is a feature that makes it easier than ever to incorporate bitmap and vector art in a single composition. Now that a copy of the rendered loving cup image contains a unique background color—one not found in the cup, gear, or splashes—it's easy to use the Bitmap color Roll-Up to pinpoint the green in the imported image and essentially make it transparent. You can then create a background behind the cup, and integrate the cup and gear in a composition that simply wasn't possible before without the labor of creating a container PowerClip object.

Here's how to modify the LOVNMASK image for use as a compositional element in Mike's retirement poster:

Using the Bitmap Color Mask Feature

1. Close CorelPHOTO-PAINT, then launch CorelDRAW from Windows Explorer.

   CorelDRAW is where you'll finish the poster design.

2. Choose **F**ile, **I**mport (Ctrl+I; or click on the toolbar's Import button) choose LOVNMASK.TIF from your hard disk; click on Imp**o**rt.

   Brings a copy of LOVNMASK into the current document.

If you didn't create the LOVNMASK image, use LOVNMASK.TIF in the CHAP09 folder of the Bonus CD for this example.

3. Choose Eff**e**cts, Bitmap **C**olor Mask.

   Displays the Bitmap Color Mask Roll-Up.

4. Click on the eyedropper tool on the Roll-Up, then click over the green in LOVNMASK.

   Records one of ten possible colors you can hide in the image (see fig. 9.41).

5. Choose Hide Colors from the Roll-Up's drop-down list, set the Tolerance slider to about 25% on the Roll-Up, then click on Apply.

   The green in the bitmap image disappears.

Beyond CorelDRAW!

Figure 9.41
You select a value from a bitmap import with the eyedropper tool on the Color Bitmap Roll-Up to hide from view.

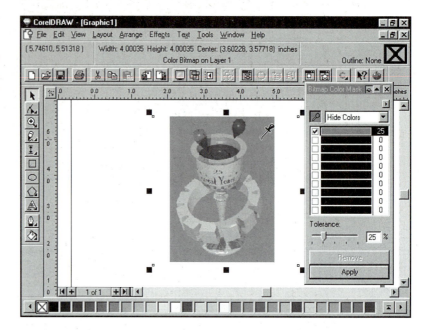

6. Choose **F**ile, Save **A**s, then save the current document as MISS-YOU.CDR to your hard disk.

The Color Tolerance is feature on the color Bitmap Roll-Up doesn't require much fine-tuning because you added a solid value of green to the LOVNMASK image in CorelPHOTO-PAINT. However, if you don't have the opportunity to retouch an image before Color Masking it in CorelDRAW, you might want to play with Tolerance settings for several different color samples.

As an example, if the background to LOVNMASK.TIF were a checkered pattern, you need to select two color areas on the Bitmap Color Mask Roll-Up, one for each checker value. Then set the Tolerance to isolate both these colors from any similar foreground object colors. This is why you should use a unique color value, one not found in foreground objects, as your background choice when using CorelDRAW's Bitmap Color Mask feature.

Adding a Vector Tiling Pattern

It would be nice if Mike's farewell poster has a background that doesn't attract too much attention, but is timely and compositionally attractive. To make quick work of a fancy background (as stipulated on the napkin in figure 9.1), you can use CorelDRAW's Symbols Roll-Up, and the Create Pattern feature. In Chapter 5, "Complex Fills and

Blend Shading," you explored Special Fills such as two-color bitmaps and fractal textures, but color vector fills are perhaps the easiest way to create a 2D pattern that can be scaled without sacrificing image quality.

In the next series of steps, you'll use the Household TrueType symbol font—in combination with the Create menu command—to add a custom Vector Pattern to your collection, and finish Mike's poster.

Dropping a Vector Background behind a Bitmap Import

1. With the Rectangle tool, Ctrl+click-and-drag a square about 1" on a side.

   This will be the pattern tile area.

2. Click on the Symbols Roll-Up button on the toolbar.

   Displays the Symbols Roll-Up.

3. Choose Household from the Symbols list, then scroll in the preview window, and find the alarm clock.

   This is the symbol with which you'll create a pattern.

4. Type **1** in the Size spin box.

   This specifies that symbols dragged out of the Roll-Up shall appear 1" in size, usually smaller (depending on how the symbol font was constructed).

5. Click-and-drag the alarm clock from the preview window to inside of the square you drew.

   Creates an outline object within the square (see fig. 9.42).

You've created an emboss effect with the alarm clock after filling the background square with black, and the alarm clock with 40 percent black. You can choose to skip the emboss effect, but do color in the square and clock shapes, and give them no outline attributes by selecting them and right-clicking over the "x" on the color palette. Embosses can be created by following the steps in Chapter 5. After the shapes are filled, use these steps:

6. Choose **T**ools, Cre**a**te, then choose **P**attern.

   Displays the Create pattern dialog box.

Beyond CorelDRAW!

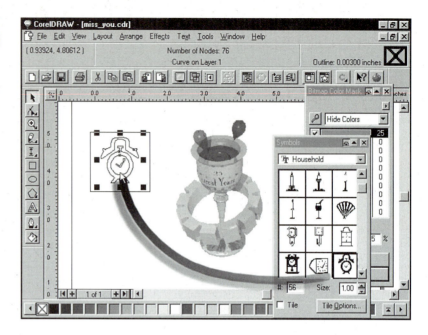

7. Click on **F**ull Color in the Type field, then click on OK.

   Cursor becomes a crosshair; you need to crop the target for the pattern image.

8. Click-and-drag the crosshair around the clock and square, keeping inside of the square.

   Defines the pattern area (see fig. 9.43).

9. Click on OK in the Create Pattern dialog box after you've cropped the pattern area.

   This confirms your targeted pattern and presents you with the Save Pattern dialog box.

10. In the File **n**ame field, type CLOCKS.PAT, then click on **S**ave.

    CLOCKS.PAT is immediately available for use as a Vector Fill; you return to the drawing window.

11. With the Rectangle tool, draw about a 6" wide by 9" tall rectangle around the cup image, then click on the To Back button on the toolbar.

    Creates a frame you'll fill with pattern; sends rectangle behind cup image.

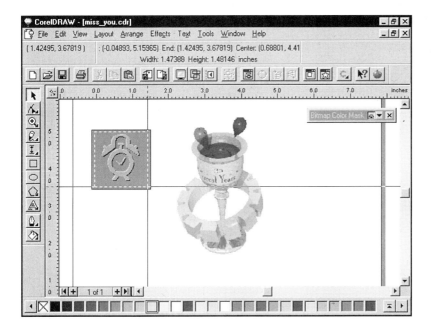

12. Click on the Fill tool, then click on the Vector Fill tool (the diagonal arrow button).

   The Vector Fill dialog box appears.

13. Click on the Preview window arrow, then scroll down to the clock pattern preview, and click on it.

   Provides a visual catalog of available vector patterns (see fig. 9.44).

14. Click on OK.

   You return to the document; tiny clocks pepper the background! See figure 9.45.

15. Choose **F**ile, Save **A**s, then save the finished piece as MISS-YOU.CDR to your hard disk.

   Saves the completed image.

Figure 9.44
All the vector patterns Corel provides, and custom patterns of your own, can be previewed and selected in the Vector Pattern dialog box.

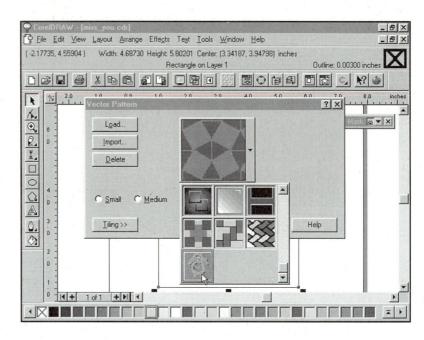

Figure 9.45
Tiling vector patterns can be scaled without losing detail; they're an ideal complement to an imported bitmap image.

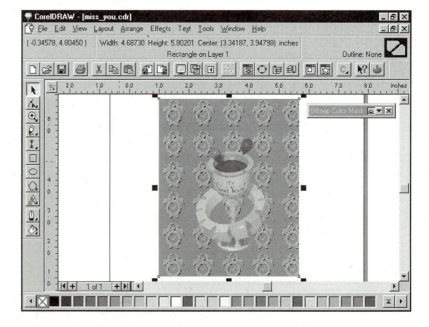

Note If for some reason, CorelDRAW doesn't offer the PATTERNS folder in the CUSTOM folder beneath the main CorelDRAW directory for a site for your custom vector patterns, specify the path for the Save in list to this location on your hard disk. By default, CorelDRAW always looks in this directory for available vector patterns.

Compositionally, the bitmap and the vector graphic play off one another handsomely. The viewer might never realize that two different types of computer graphics have been seamlessly integrated into a single piece.

In figure 9.46, we've added some text. Snell Black is available on the Corel CD; it's a script face that's bold and legible.

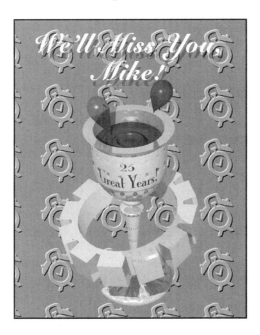

Figure 9.46
From napkin to modern masterpiece, you can take a concept in any direction with the features of different applications.

Although CorelDRAW contributed a minor graphical element to the finished piece, this poster is a good example of how CorelDRAW can integrate different media. Hopefully, your curiosity has been piqued with the introduction of another medium— that of modeling and rendering, and you'll spend some off-hour time investigating the feature set that's too large to thoroughly document in a single chapter.

You now have some excellent starting places with 3D imaging behind you. Think of variations you can perform on the steps contained in this chapter, and in no time you'll be rendering chairs, aircraft, spacecraft, and things that have yet to be imagined. Creating your own reality is the privilege of artists, and DREAM 3D makes your dreams that much more real.

III

Beyond CorelDRAW!

Adding DEPTH and MOTION

The most critical observation one might make about vector drawing programs is that the artwork produced within these applications lacks dimension—specifically that of depth. However, spline-based vector artwork can indeed display a "leap off the page" characteristic, especially when you familiarize yourself with two of the latest additions to the Corel bundle: CorelDEPTH and CorelMOTION 3D. Although the two programs use vector information to create different *types* of dimensional designs, these applications share a common property: DEPTH and MOTION both can use CorelDRAW paths as a basis for three-dimensional wireframe objects.

If you've read Chapter 9, "Working between CorelDRAW! and CorelDREAM 3D," many of the principles behind working with DEPTH and MOTION 3D objects will seem familiar. At a glance, DEPTH and MOTION 3D might seem like 3D text creation programs, but there are several undocumented features in both programs that can be used to create full-blown 3D masterpieces. Even if you have no experience with modeling and rendering programs, this chapter will take you through the steps needed to produce stunning designs in no time.

CorelDEPTH's Unique Approach to Modeling

Modeling is not a new computer capability; graphics workstations have been used for almost three decades to render a view of dimensional objects as seen through a portal (a monitor screen) of 3D space. The current *availability*, and subsequent popularity of modeling programs for the *personal* computer has been largely due to the exponential increase in processing chip power.

Traditionally, 3D computer graphics have been created by first defining coordinates in three-dimensional space for an object, defining a texture for the surface of the object, and finally rendering the object coordinates and the surface texture to a (2D) bitmap file. Generally, the finished image is from the same point of view as the user's view while he or she works on the 3D design; a *camera* is typically included in the definition of the world space of a 3D project. Enhancements to the finished image such as camera lens length, background, atmosphere, and lighting can also be specified during the modeling phase of the modeling/rendering work.

A model can usually be created in a matter of minutes; it has long been the lament of computer animators and designers that it is the *rendering* part of the 3D creation process that seems to take an eternity. Rendering involves the conversion of all the information within a scene captured from a virtual camera's point of view. Wireframe coordinates, reflection properties, surface textures, and so on must be calculated, pixel by pixel, to create a TIFF, BMP, Targa, or other type of bitmap image. Substantial amounts of processing power are required to render 3D model information, and because the finished image is bitmap format, if you've made a mistake in defining the 3D scene, you're obliged to render the scene once again.

Fortunately, CorelDEPTH breaks with tradition and departs from the bitmap format of 3D modeling; DEPTH is a *vector* 3D application, from the beginning of the process to finished image. Unlike conventional modeling and rendering applications such as CorelDREAM 3D, CorelDEPTH builds a scene on-screen in near-real time, composed of discrete *objects*. You can modify a DEPTH file as often as you like, and the scene can then be exported in a format that CorelDRAW and PHOTO-PAINT can import in a matter of moments.

Packing CorelDRAW! Provisions for the Trip to DEPTH

For experienced users of modeling and rendering applications, DEPTH might display some strange conventions, and create some mental and procedural hurdles in your quest for "instant" 3D graphics. The DEPTH example in this chapter is a lighthearted poster design, "Bahaman Geometry," whose design elements echo the flavor and feel of a Caribbean getaway. The author's first step to create the example design was to scout for an artistic font for use as a graphical element. As fate would have it, the ideal font, Copacabana Bold, is only available in Type 1 format; Unlike CorelDRAW, PHOTO-PAINT, MOTION 3D, and PRESENTS, CorelDEPTH only supports TrueType.

Don't you hate packing for an exciting adventure, only to find that your "currency" isn't accepted? This minor inconvenience can be overcome by making CorelDRAW your home base for DEPTH excursions. DEPTH accepts Adobe Illustrator (AI) and Windows Metafile (WMF) types of graphics, so the solution to adding text in this example is achieved by exporting the string of text from CorelDRAW as a graphic.

Here's how to create the first of two elements you need to bring along with you to DEPTH to complete the example design:

Exporting Text as a Graphic

1. In CorelDRAW, click on the Artistic Text tool (or press F8), click an insertion point in a new document window, then type **Bahaman,** press Return, then type **Geometry**.

   This is the textual content of the example design.

2. Press Ctrl+spacebar, then press Ctrl+T.

   Toggles to the Pick tool and selects the entire Artistic Text object; displays the Character Attributes dialog box.

3. On the Font tabbed menu, choose a font from the **F**onts list that suggests the tropics, and make the choice a Type 1 format font.

   Chooses the font you'll use. Because you'll be converting the text to curves, a TrueType font *could* be used in this example, but would fail to make the point here—DEPTH natively supports TrueType.

BAHATEXT.CDR, in the EXAMPLES.CHAP10 folder of the *CorelDRAW! 6 Expert's Edition Bonus CD* contains the converted text used to create the design in this example if you'd like to use it, but don't own La Bamba. Good alternative fonts, available on the Corel CD, are Croissant, Davida, Ad Lib, and Mr.Earl.

4. Click on the Alignment tabbed menu, click on the **C**enter Alignment radio button, then click on OK.

   Aligns the top and bottom row of Artistic Text; you're returned to the document window.

5. With the Pick tool, click-and-drag the text away from its original location, then right-click before releasing the cursor.

Beyond CorelDRAW!

Duplicates the Artistic Text object. It's good practice to create a copy of Artistic Text before converting it to curves. In this way, you still have a duplicate that can be edited as text.

6. With the duplicate object selected, press Ctrl+Q (**A**rrange, Con**v**ert to Curves).

   The text is no longer editable as text, but the resulting object can now be exported to DEPTH because it no longer contains Type 1 information.

7. Press Ctrl+K (**A**rrange, **B**reak Apart).

   Breaks the object into its component subpaths. The trick to successfully manipulating the "Bahaman Geometry" object as individual characters in DEPTH, is to export several paths, and not one object containing many subpaths.

8. If your group of letters contains a character that should be composed of more than one path (such as the letterform *B*), choose the Pick tool, marquee-select the components of the character, then press Ctrl+L (**A**rrange, **C**ombine).

   Combines the subpaths to create the character object.

9. With the Pick tool, marquee-select all the lettering objects, then click on the Export button on the toolbar (see fig. 10.1).

   Selects the objects; displays the Export dialog box.

Figure 10.1

By exporting a lettering object as individual characters, CorelDEPTH allows you to individually manipulate each object.

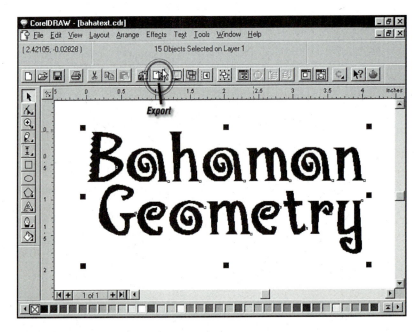

10. In the Save as type drop-down list, choose Adobe Illustrator (AI, EPS), type
    BAHATEXT.AI in the File name field, click on the Selected only check box,
    choose a location in the folders window that's easy to find for your export, then
    click on Export.

    Displays the Adobe Illustrator Export dialog box.

11. Click on the Adobe Illustrator **3**.0 radio button, then click on OK.

    Exports the selected objects as Adobe Illustrator paths, which CorelDEPTH can
    import. The Export Text as field in the Adobe Illustrator Export dialog box
    contains no option that is relevant to this example; as a collection of objects that
    have *already* been converted to curves, it makes no difference in this case which
    of the **C**urves or **T**ext radio buttons is selected in this dialog box.

12. Press Ctrl+S (File, Save), then save your work as BAHATEXT.CDR to your hard
    disk.

    Saves both the editable text, and the converted text for future use.

The Adobe Illustrator format is only one of the two types of file formats that
CorelDEPTH can import. The AI format is a better choice than Windows Metafile
(WMF) for exporting paths, because the initial release of CorelDRAW! 6 contains a few
errors in its import and export filters; the AI export filter works better than the WMF
export for exporting complex curves. See the following note that follows on the topic of
CorelDRAW! 6 import and export filters.

The "text as curves" object is the first of two CorelDRAW resources you'll create for use
in DEPTH. In the next section, you'll discover the secrets for creating a texture map
which can be used in CorelDEPTH as an embellishment for any 3D object you create,
or import into the application.

Note   CorelDRAW, version 6.00.118, also referred to by Corel Corp. as version D2,
contains import and export filters that don't always work as expected. For example,
subpaths exported in the Adobe Illustrator format don't always appear within the outside path
of an object when imported into CorelDEPTH, CorelDREAM 3D, or many of the other Corel
applications. As a result of this problem, you might find that a typeface character such as a P
when converted to curves and exported, will import to DEPTH or other programs with the subpath
filled in.

There are several workarounds for this problem, the simplest of them being to use CorelDRAW! 5
(if you still have this version on your system) for exporting objects until you receive an updated
copy of CorelDRAW. In CorelDRAW, click on **H**elp, **A**bout CorelDRAW for the version of the
program you currently have installed. CorelDRAW goes through one or two revisions with every
new version, but Corel Corp. has no way of knowing whether you have a current copy of the

Beyond CorelDRAW!

programs; there is no version information on your CorelDRAW registration card. You should contact Corel Corporation directly at 613/728-8200, or send CompuServe E-Mail to the Customer Service section of the CorelAPPS forum regarding the current version of Corel and how to get the update version.

Creating a Style for CorelDEPTH Objects

Most conventional modeling applications—such as CorelDREAM 3D—offer the feature of defining a bitmap image (BMP, TIFF, and others) as the "skin" with which you cover a 3D wireframe model. The *unconventional* CorelDEPTH, however, offers a similar feature to enhance the objects you import or create in DEPTH's workspace. True, three-dimensional objects have front, top, bottom, and side facets; in CorelDEPTH, you have the option of adding a custom image—a *decal*—to the front and back facets of any object you create.

CorelDEPTH offers a Style Browser—a collection of predefined decals, fountain fills, and color schemes—to quickly customize the appearance of 3D objects. The decal approach to creating a texture for 3D objects is perhaps the most interesting and offers the most creative expression in CorelDEPTH; for these reasons, we'll pursue the decal design route in this section—the less complex structures for DEPTH object Styles are easily discovered without the assistance of detailed documentation in this book.

So what should the decal look like, and what is the format for such a decal file? A file destined for use as a decal in DEPTH needs to contain vector graphics, because DEPTH is a vector-oriented application. This reality makes CorelDRAW, once again, the best site for CorelDEPTH decal creation. The visual *content* of a decal can be anything you like. In the EXAMPLE.CHAP10 folder of the *CorelDRAW! 6 Expert's Edition Bonus CD*, you'll find EXPERTS.ADS, a custom Style Browser containing 11 exotic, whimsical, and very useful decals created by the author for your continuing adventures in CorelDEPTH (you can see samples of the decals in the color plate section of this book). Use your imagination and inspiration to create your own custom decals.

The following is a list of steps used to create a watermelon texture for use in CorelDEPTH. This watermelon decal will play an important role in the creation of the Bahaman Geometry poster. PITS.CDR, located in the EXAMPLES.CHAP10 folder of the *CorelDRAW! 6 Expert's Edition Bonus CD* is the completed design, if you'd like to examine it, and use it for a guide to building your own decals.

Here's how to build a CorelDEPTH decal file:

Creating and Exporting CorelDEPTH Decals

1. In CorelDRAW, press F6 (or click on the Rectangle tool), then in a new document window, click-and-drag a rectangle that's approximately 2:1 in proportion, the width greater than the length.

   This is the background for the decal you'll create. There are no hard and fast rules for the dimensions of a CorelDEPTH decal—as vector information, the decal can be resized, proportionately or disproportionately, from within CorelDEPTH. However, if you intend to use the decal on a wider-than-tall 3D object, the decal's proportions should match your intended target object. Also, size is of no concern for the decal, because it's made of vector information. 2" by 1" will serve you well here.

2. Click on a pink swatch on the color palette, then right-click over the x on the color palette.

   Fills the rectangle with pink; removes the outline property of the rectangle.

3. Click and hold on the Pencil tool, then click on the Bézier mode tool on the Pencil tool flyout.

   Chooses the Bézier mode of drawing with the Pencil tool.

4. Click-and-drag to create watermelon seed shapes upon the pink rectangle. About 3 different shapes will suffice here.

   Creates the foreground pattern of the decal.

5. When you've closed a path for one of the seeds, click on the black swatch, then right click on the x on the color palette.

   Fills the seeds with black; removes the outlines.

6. Press spacebar, click-and-drag a seed to a different location on the pink background, then right-click before releasing both mouse buttons.

   Drops a duplicate of the seed where you released the buttons.

7. Click on the selected seed, then click-and-drag a (corner) rotation handle until the seed is rotated about 45°.

   Rotates the seed; creates more of an impression that this is a unique seed, and not merely a duplicate you've created. See figure 10.2.

Beyond CorelDRAW!

Figure 10.2
Duplicate objects
don't have to look
like duplicates, if you
rotate them after
copying them.

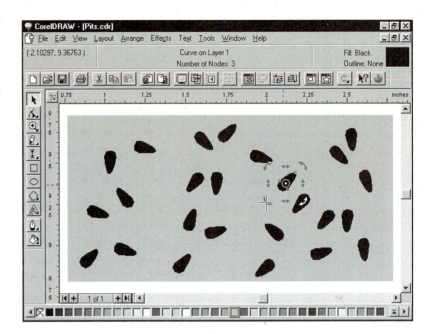

8. Create a number of unique-looking seeds for the decal, by copying, then rotating a few of the duplicates.

9. Save the file as PITS.CDR to your hard disk, double-click on the Pick tool, then click on the Export button on the toolbar.

   Saves your work; double-clicking on the Pick tool selects all objects in the document; displays the Export dialog box.

10. In the Save as type drop-down list in the Export dialog box, choose Adobe Illustrator (AI, EPS), type **PITS.AI** in the File name field, click on the Selected only check box, choose a location in the folders window that's easy to find for your export, then click on Export.

    Displays the Adobe Illustrator Export dialog box.

11. Click on the Adobe Illustrator **3**.0 radio button, then click on OK.

    Exports the watermelon decal as Adobe Illustrator paths, which CorelDEPTH can import.

12. Close CorelDRAW.

    Frees available system resources, so you can work more easily in CorelDEPTH.

We've concluded the gathering of resources for CorelDEPTH, and in the following sections, you'll see how to create a DEPTH composition. Again, it's important to note that Corel's import and export filters in version 6.00.118, are not flawless, and depending upon how ambitious you are with a decal resource file, the decal might import perfectly into CorelDEPTH, but won't be exported correctly to formats other than DEPTH's native *.DEP format. The next section takes a brief sidestep on the road to DEPTH to describe the workarounds necessary to make importing and exporting between DRAW and DEPTH a foolproof procedure.

Filter Problems in Version 118

This chapter outlines procedures for creating mini-masterpieces in DEPTH and MO-TION 3D, but occasional workaround techniques need to be mentioned because the first release of CorelDRAW! 6 contains import and export filters that do not always work as specified in Corel's documentation. Until the problems are corrected through an update, or *patch* CD distributed by Corel Corp., the workarounds mentioned in this chapter are the soundest advice for creating design work that's every byte as stunning as you can imagine.

Specific WMF and AI filter problems have to do with curve complexity and combined subpaths created in objects. For example, a concave path segment in a path that's part of an exported decal will display perfectly in DEPTH, but the resulting 3D image, when imported into DRAW as a WMF type file won't show the portion of the decal where a concave area was originally created. A crescent moon is a perfect example of a decal foreground shape that will import and display properly in DEPTH, but cannot be exported correctly as the front facet decal of a DEPTH object. The workaround here for creating a crescent is to create two circles on a background object, make the circles overlap to create the crescent shape, then fill the background and overlapping circle objects with the same color.

Additionally, CorelDRAW does not support the Adobe Illustrator *masking objects* feature in its AI import filter in version 6.00.118. The masking object feature is very similar to CorelDRAW's PowerClip feature, but the lack of filter information in this instance prevents CorelDRAW from reading an AI file exported from DEPTH correctly. Front facets on 3D objects exported in AI format that have decal or gradient fill properties may import to DRAW as separate objects *in front of*—instead of embedded within—an imported 3D shape.

This AI filter problem can be manually corrected by ungrouping the objects and changing their front-to-back order, but it's much simpler to import DEPTH objects in the WMF format, which will indeed import splendidly into CorelDRAW, but the decals for DEPTH shapes have to meet the construction requirements outlined in the preceding paragraphs.

Exploring DEPTH's Bézier Drawing Tool

When the product AddDepth—the original source code for CorelDEPTH—was created, its designers envisioned it as a utility for creating 3D text, but also felt obliged to make the application stand up on its own, without the need for CorelDRAW or other application assistance to complete a design. Therefore, you'll find drawing tools in CorelDEPTH that don't operate in the same way as DRAW's drawing tools. Nevertheless, if you practice a little with DEPTH's design tools, you might find that path creation can be accomplished entirely within DEPTH without the necessity to export a CorelDRAWn object.

The following example is intended to give you a feel for the DEPTH style of drawing, and at the same time create a 3D watermelon slice that's part of the "Bahaman Geometry" poster design. Here's how to get started...

Using DEPTH's 2D Design Tools, Part I

1. Launch CorelDEPTH from Win95's Start menu, then click on the Create a Blank **N**ew Document button on the Document Type dialog box.

   Creates a new page in the workspace. The Startup dialog box is terrific for novices, but can become quite annoying after a while (all the options can be accessed by clicking on the New button on the toolbar). To lose the Startup Dialog box, choose **F**ile, Pre**f**erences, then uncheck the **S**tartup Dialog check box. You might also want to change the Default Color **M**odel to RGB while in the Preferences dialog box if you have no intention to print from CorelDEPTH.

2. Click on the Bézier tool on the toolbox (refer to figure 10.3 for a callout of the tool), then click a point in the page window.

   Sets an anchor point for a straight line you'll draw.

3. Click a point to the right of the first point, about 10 grid markers to the right of the first point.

   A straight line is automatically drawn between the first and second points.

4. Click about 5 markers below the line segment (between the first two points), then drag to the left by about 5 grid markers, then release the cursor.

   Produces a Bézier curve between the second point and the point you last click-and-dragged. You'll notice a 50% black fill is automatically added to the interior of the three points you've made; DEPTH methods of path construction most closely resemble those used with CorelDRAW's Bézier mode Pencil tool, but the added benefit of auto-shading helps you visualize a shape *before* it becomes a closed path.

5. Click on your start point.

   Closes the path; creates a melon slice shape. See figure 10.3.

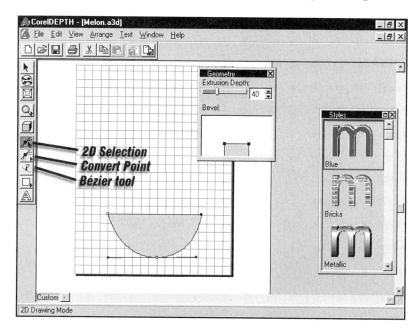

2D Selection
Convert Point
Bézier tool

Figure 10.3
Use the group of 2D selection and design tools to create a path that can then be extruded to make a 3D object.

6. Press Ctrl+S, then choose a hard disk location for your file in the folders window, name your design MELON.A3D, then click on **S**ave.

   Saves your work at this intermediate phase of completion.

You'll notice that the default extension for CorelDEPTH files is DEP. However, the A3D is offered in the Save as **type** drop-down list, and we recommend this extension for a special reason. The A3D extension refers to AddDepth, the original program for Windows and the Macintosh, from which CorelDEPTH was created by licensing the source code.

As a Corel user, you can share *.DEP files with other Corel version 6 users, but if you use the A3D file extension when saving, the DEPTH file can be used by Corel 6 users, *and* AddDepth users.

> **Tip** You can change the file extension of a *.DEP file to A3D at any time after a DEPTH file has been saved, to allow the file to be shared with AddDepth users. Additionally, AddDepth files can be loaded by CorelDEPTH.

III

Beyond CorelDRAW!

However, CorelDEPTH treats 3D text objects as editable objects. This means that if you've used DEPTH's Text tool to create a text object, if you want to share the file, you must also pass along the TrueType font you used. Because sharing fonts is a sticky legal issue, you might want to select TrueType text in your document with the 2D Selection tool, then choose **C**onvert to Curves from the **T**ext menu. But do this only with a copy of the file; converted text cannot be edited as text.

Editing a DEPTH 2D Object

Because Bézier drawing tools are harder to use than "freehand" vector drawing tools, your melon slice might call for a nip and tuck along its outline before you extrude it. DEPTH's editing tools—the 2D Selection and the Convert Point tools—operate in a very similar fashion to DREAM 3D's path tools; you can see the location of these tools in figure 10.3. The reason for this similarity—and their dissimilarity to DRAW's design tools—is that both DEPTH and DREAM 3D code were licensed by Corel Corp. from the same developers.

Before you click on another tool in DEPTH, it's important that you understand the difference between a 2D and a 3D Selection tool. The icon on the top of the toolbox might look like DRAW's familiar Pick tool, but in actuality, this 3D Selection tool is only used to resize and move 3D objects around in the document. Although the icon of the 2D Selection tool might *look* like a node editing tool, it's the tool you primarily use to edit nodes *and* select and reposition all 2D objects you create or import.

Ironically, the engineers of AddDepth chose to emulate the functionality of Adobe Photoshop's Convert Direction tool (on its Paths palette), not CorelDRAW's Shape tool, to create the Convert Point tool, the third of the 2D design tools found in DEPTH's workspace. If you're familiar with Photoshop, working with the Convert Point tool in DEPTH is a breeze. If not, here is a list of actions you can perform with the tool to change the path you created in the previous example:

✔ **Click-and-drag on a cusp node on a 2D path.** Converts the node to smooth properties, and produced control handles and control points which are at a 180° opposing direction from one another. Perform this action, then switch to the 2D Selection tool to further modify the control points, or the position of the node on the page. You begin by click-and-dragging on the node, but by dragging, you then are manipulating one of the node's *control handles*. Like CorelDRAWn Smooth nodes, each control point can be dragged from the node so that the control handles are of different lengths, but the *direction* of the control points always lies in 180° opposition.

✔ **Click-and-drag on a smooth node control handle.** This action changes the property of the node to cusp. Perform this action, then switch to the 2D Selection tool to further modify the control points, or the position of the node on the page. The control handles of cusp nodes, like CorelDRAWn nodes, can be rotated around the node, and each of the two control points can be a unique distance from the node (the control handles can be of different lengths).

Unlike CorelDRAW's Shape tool, the Convert Point tool cannot be used to reposition nodes, and its capability to reposition control points is confined to your initial click-and-drag. The Convert Point tool, as its name indicates, is only used to change the property of the node in question.

As with any new application, it helps to better understand a tool's capabilities by experimenting with it. If you'd like to design a lumpy watermelon slice by editing the path with DEPTH's 2D design tools, feel free. This is a fun poster assignment, and there are no "right" or "wrong" design concepts here!

Defining a DEPTH Style

As mentioned earlier, the Styles Browser in DEPTH's interface holds a collection of preset "looks" you can apply to a 3D object. You might get by for a few weeks with the default collection, and the Template Wizard (available on the Document Type dialog box when you choose **File**, **New**) can be of great help when you need design results, and are unfamiliar with the program. However, this chapter is devoted to the *custom* options that are mostly hidden from users in both DEPTH and MOTION 3D; therefore, the first item you'll see how to modify in this example is the Styles Browser. Here's the steps you need to take to add a Watermelon style to DEPTH's default Styles Browser:

Creating a Watermelon Decal Style

1. Click on any Style icon on the Styles Browser ("Blue" is a good choice), click on the menu button on the title bar of the Styles Browser, then click on Duplicate.

   Styles Browser changes to Edit Styles window; the Name Effect dialog box appears. Don't worry about DEPTH interface naming conventions; sometimes the engineers called a Style an Effect, and other times an effect is the color attribute of a 3D surface (Consistency of interface naming conventions is something Corel Corp. might address in future versions).

2. Type **Watermelon** in the Please Name the Effect Setting dialog box, then click on OK.

   A duplicate of the Blue Style (Effect) appears at the bottom of the Styles Browser's scrolling window. This effect is not visible, however—the default Styles Browser cannot be resized (regardless of the monitor resolution you're running), and you can only glimpse at three Styles at a time.

3. Scroll to the bottom of the Styles Browser, click on the icon marked "Watermelon," then click on Edit.

   Displays the Color Style window.

4. Click on the **F**ront Face radio button.

   Displays the present configuration for the properties of the front face of the Style you duplicated. Depending upon the preset style you duplicated to create the Watermelon style, it's likely that the Effect drop-down menu now has Shading highlighted.

5. Choose Decal from the Effect drop-down list, then click on the Choose Decal button.

   Displays the Open dialog box. By default, the Files of **t**ype drop-down list offers the WMF format. However, you exported the watermelon design as an Adobe Illustrator (AI) format.

6. Choose Illustrator (*.ai) from the Files of type drop-down list, find PITS.AI in the folder window, click on it, then click on **O**pen.

   DEPTH imports the image, and the CorelDRAWn watermelon design can now be seen superimposed over a lowercase *m* in the preview window. The lowercase *m* is the default preview object for displaying DEPTH styles, and you cannot change this.

7. The watermelon design might not "land" so that it covers the preview *m* perfectly. Click-and-drag a corner selection handle in the preview window so that the watermelon design covers the *m*.

   Redefines how the imported design will cover 3D objects you assign this Style to. See figure 10.4.

8. Click on the Front **B**evel radio button.

   Displays the current shading for the edge between the front and side surfaces for objects assigned this style.

9. Click on the C**u**stom Color radio button, then click in the color swatch beneath **C**ustom Color.

   Displays the Windows Color picker. Let's reflect on this one for a moment. To create an authentic watermelon slice, the front face should be pink with black seeds, and the rind should be dark green with a touch of pale cream color where the rind meets the edible portion of the melon (the *flesh*). Therefore, the bevel along the edge of the melon slice, the geometric area where the front face meets the side, should be cream colored. (This is the only CorelDRAW book to date which provides agricultural information.)

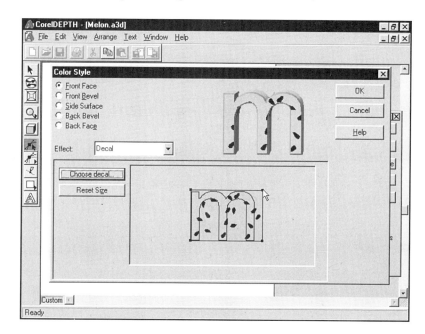

Figure 10.4
You can change the position of the imported decal object by moving it in the preview window, and you can resize it, too.

10. In the color dialog box, click on the top row, second color swatch, then click on OK.

    Defines a pale cream color for the Watermelon style's front bevel.

11. Click-and-drag the Shading slider to 75% of the way toward Black.

    Because DEPTH can add gradations of color on 3D object surfaces to simulate lighting conditions, you have control in this dialog box over how dramatic the change in color values vary across the surface of an object with a specific style. The further you click-and-drag the Shading slider to the right, the more variation from pale cream to black will appear along the front bevel of the watermelon slice.

12. Click-and-drag the Highlights slider about 30% of the way toward Main Color.

    Specifies that white, the opposing value on the slider, will not be used much in the gradations created to suggest highlights along the front bevel surface. A high White value for Highlights would create the appearance of a plastic watermelon slice, which would be interesting, but not very realistic.

Beyond CorelDRAW!

13. Click on the Side Surface radio button, choose Shading from the Effects drop-down list, then repeat steps 8-11, except choose a forest green in Windows color dialog box.

    Specifies a dark green edge for the object style, perfect to represent the outer rind of the watermelon slice.

14. Click on the Back Bevel radio button, then choose Invisible from the Effect drop-down list.

    You won't see a change in the preview window image, because the front face obscures your view, but you've eliminated a sizable number of component objects from the final version of any 3D object you assign the Watermelon style. See section that follows for a more detailed explanation of this step.

15. Click on the Back Face radio button, then choose Invisible from the Effect drop-down list.

    As with the Back Bevel property, the back face of any 3D object assigned the Watermelon style will be invisible. See figure 10.4.

Figure 10.5

You should assign a color, gradation, or decal property to only those sides of an object which will be visible in the finished design.

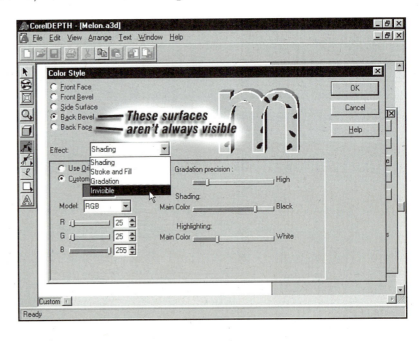

16. Click on OK, then click on the menu button on the title bar of the Styles Browser.

Returns you to the workspace; toggles the Edit Styles window back to the default Styles Browser. The two modes for this window might look similar, but you cannot apply a Style while in the Edit Styles window mode.

17. Click on the 3D Selection tool, click on the path you've drawn on the page, then click on the Watermelon icon on the Styles Browser.

    The object becomes 3D, acquires the default extrusion depth; applies the Watermelon style to the object.

18. Click-and-drag the left node in the Geometry palette upwards by about 1/8" and to the right by about 1/8".

    Specifies the height and width of the front bevel on the watermelon slice surface; you can now see the pale cream color. Front and back bevel surfaces "steal" from the surface sides of a 3D object; the front face always remains a constant size. The right node in the Geometry palette's preview is used to specify the amount of back bevel to an object, but because the Watermelon style has Invisible properties for the back bevel and back face, there's no reason to play with this option.

19. Click on the Virtual Track Ball tool (beneath the 3D Selection cursor on the toolbox), then click-and-drag the selected watermelon slice upwards and to the right.

    Repositions the watermelon slice in 3D space. See figure 10.6.

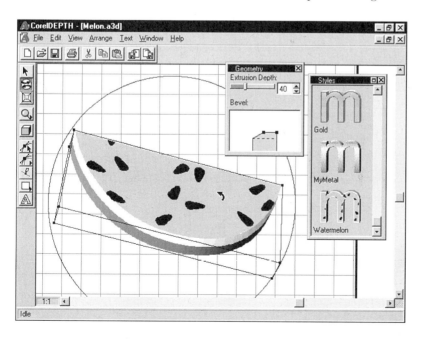

Figure 10.6
Use the top two toolbox tools to reposition and rotate 3D objects in page space.

Beyond CorelDRAW!

20. Press Ctrl+S (**F**ile, **S**ave).

Saves your work at this intermediate phase of completion.

Pretty stupendous, eh? Actually, CorelDEPTH operates in a very similar fashion to CorelDRAW! 6's Extrude Roll-Up; you cannot perform any modeling function other than extrusion in DEPTH, but front and back bevel sides cannot be created with DRAW's Extrude effect, and it's a time-consuming task to affix a decal to a DRAW extruded object. There's a quality of photo-realism to be had by shaping and reshaping designs in DEPTH, but as other chapters in this book stress, a good computer graphics designer should:

Always take into consideration the final output of a design before beginning.

...if you don't, it's possible that a DEPTH, DRAW, or other creation might never have a life outside of your computer!

▶Tip The Color Style dialog box offers Gradation in addition to the Decal property you can assign to the front and back faces of a 3D object. Gradation is an equivalent term to CorelDRAW's Fountain Fills, and when you select from the drop-down Effect list, you're presented with a diagram of a circle (the Gradation dial) in the Effects field of the Color Styles dialog box.

The Gradation dial is different in appearance to the preview box and custom Fountain Fill strip in CorelDRAW's Fountain Fill dialog box, but the Gradation dial serves an equivalent purpose in CorelDEPTH. You can click-and-drag the center point within the Gradation dial in any direction to specify the direction of the transition between foreground and background colors you choose for the Gradation. Click-and-drag the starting point within the dial toward the outer diameter of the dial to create a line within the dial, and make a slow transition in the gradation between colors. A short line between start and endpoints, where the endpoint on the line within the dial *doesn't* touch the outer diameter of the dial, creates a two-way gradation; for example, the gradation can be from black to green, then back to black again in the gradation.

Unfortunately, DEPTH's gradation can only consist of two colors. To create a multi-color surface for the front or back of an object, however, you can assign a solid color to the face of an object (Choose Stroke and Fill from the Effects drop-down, then choose **N**o Stroke, but specify a **C**ustom Fill of a uniform color). After you export the object to CorelDRAW, you can then ungroup the collection of shapes that make up the DEPTH object, and assign it a fountain fill.

Moving a DEPTH Object Out of DEPTH

DEPTH has its own printing engine, and although DEPTH doesn't use the Corel Color Management feature, you can attain reasonable output directly from DEPTH. For color output, it's best to use the CMYK color model within DEPTH (under **F**ile, Pre**f**erences, and on the Color Style dialog box) instead of the RGB color model—check your color printer's documentation for specific hardware configuration advice.

If you're the sort of designer who works across multiple applications to create compound documents, the term "output" applies not only to a printing device, but to the means of transporting a DEPTH object to other applications. And this means understanding a little about how DEPTH creates 3D objects, and this is the reason why you were asked in the last set of steps to make the backface surfaces of the Watermelon style invisible.

As a vector design application, CorelDEPTH creates shading by using objects that are blended from foreground to background colors, almost identical in approach to creating Blend objects in CorelDRAW (see Chapter 5, "Complex Fills and Blend Shading"). These discrete objects can add up when you have a long phrase typed in DEPTH, and when you create or import very complex paths. The key to successfully importing a DEPTH object into CorelDRAW, or PHOTO-PAINT, is to assign only the sides of an object that will be visible in the final design a color, decal, or graduated color fill. Less discrete shapes in the finished object means less information for the export filter to calculate. A long sentence exported from DEPTH can consists of over 9,000 objects, which CorelDRAW will take an eternity to import, hours on end to redraw on-screen, and the size of the CDR file to which it is saved can be larger than a high-quality bitmap image.

Naturally, a DEPTH design that demands that the back or the entire side of a 3D object is shown would require that a style which includes backface information is applied to such an object (unless an invisible object effect is your intention), but you'd be surprised by how often a side of a DEPTH object is hidden from the viewer in the finished design. And we're simply proposing that in these situations, something hidden from view doesn't need to exist, to make exporting DEPTH objects easier.

The Clipboard is an unsatisfactory means of copying a DEPTH object to CorelDRAW, or any other Windows application due to a DEPTH object's inherent complexity. Don't try pasting a Clipboard copy of DEPTH objects, *particularly* not DEPTH's Template Wizard objects, into CorelDRAW. The Windows Clipboard's translation modes for object information makes DEPTH objects even more complex than the original object, and CorelDRAW will grind and stall, and eventually, you'll have wasted time. Instead, we have some suggestions coming up in the following sections that address the best way to include DEPTH creations as part of DRAW and PHOTO-PAINT compositions.

Tips on Editing 3D Objects

No pun intended, but on the surface, it appears that a DEPTH object cannot be edited once the 2D path(s) have been extruded. It's important to remember that DEPTH has *two* modes of design and editing—2D and 3D; when you select an object with the 2D Selection tool (or choose no selection before clicking on the tool), the workspace becomes entirely 2D.

Beyond CorelDRAW!

In either design mode, the Working Plane is actually an object on the page frame within the document. It is a 3D object that can be repositioned (hold Ctrl while you click-and-drag the working plane with the 3D Selection tool), rotated (hold Ctrl while you click-and-drag with the Virtual Track Ball tool), and made invisible (choose <u>V</u>iew, then uncheck <u>W</u>orking Plane). Additionally, you can position the Working Plane relative to an object's sides through the <u>A</u>rrange, Set <u>W</u>orking Plane to commands to make the Working Plane grid align with an object you might have rotated in 3D space.

The most intriguing aspect of editing DEPTH objects, however, is that you can reshape and add subpaths to an existing 3D object to create an entirely different object. The Working Plane auto-aligns to an object's front face—the path upon which the extruded 3D object is based—when editing a 2D path, and DEPTH's design tools allow you to draw and edit the path in what appears to be 3D space.

To make this discussion a little more palpable, the following steps show you how to poke a hole through the watermelon slice in its current 3D state. Actual watermelon slices could use a handle to make carrying them around at a picnic easier, so let's create a prototype, virtual version.

Here's how to reshape the outline path of the watermelon slice to create a slightly different, definitely sillier 3D object:

Editing, Creating, and Combining 2D Paths

1. Click on the Zoom tool, then click on the object (don't try to marquee zoom; it's not a supported feature in DEPTH) until you have a close-up view of the melon slice.

   Zooms you into a field of view in which you can comfortably edit the object. Alternatively, you can select a Zoom resolution by clicking on the zoom size field to the right of the document window's horizontal scroll bar. To adjust your view within the document window, you can click and hold on the toolbox Zoom tool, then select the Pan tool from the Zoom tool flyout and click-and-drag to scroll your document view.

2. Click on the melon slice with the 2D Selection tool.

   The melon slice disappears, the original path you drew reappears, and the Working Plane shifts orientation to offer the same perspective on the 2D path as the current angle of rotation of the 3D melon slice.

3. Click and hold on the Rectangle tool, then choose the Ellipse tool from the 2D Primitives tool flyout menu.

   You'll use the Ellipse tool to create a hole in the melon slice's 2D path.

4. Click-and-drag the Ellipse tool within the melon path until you've created an ellipse about 1/5 the total size of the melon path.

   You design a perspective view of an ellipse; it might look distorted from this perspective, but the ellipse is perfectly symmetrical. The melon slice and ellipse shapes are discrete objects now; the ellipse lies on top of the melon shape. See figure 10.7.

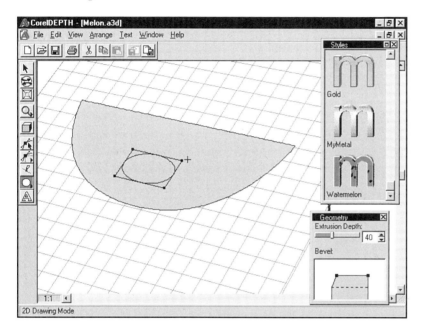

Figure 10.7

It might seem a little disorienting, but you can draw 2D objects in perspective to create paths and subpaths for DEPTH designs.

5. If you feel the ellipse is positioned incorrectly, click on the 2D Selection tool, click on the ellipse, then click-and-drag the ellipse to a different location.

   Moves the path. If you need to move a path drawn with the Bézier tool (not one of the 2D Primitives shapes), click-and-drag with the 2D Selection tool on the path. Be careful not to accidentally select a node instead of the path, or you'll be editing the node instead of moving the path.

6. Click on the 2D Selection tool, then hold Shift and click on the melon slice path.

   Shift adds to the current selection. Both the melon slice and ellipse should be selected now. An indication of a 2D object's selection is that the nodes which make up a 2D path are visible.

Beyond CorelDRAW!

7. Choose **A**rrange, **C**ombine (Ctrl+L, the same as in CorelDRAW).

Combines the ellipse with the melon slice shape to create a shape with a hole in it.

8. Click on the 3D Selection tool.

The mode of the document window changes to 3D; you have a melon slice with a hole carved out of it.

9. Press Ctrl+S (**F**ile, **S**ave).

Saves your finished design.

Tip   Hold the Alt key while clicking with the Zoom tool to zoom out of the active document window.

As with CorelDRAW, every subsequent object you create, or import, into CorelDEPTH becomes the top object of the collection of objects within the document. In figure 10.8, you can see the finished graphics component of the "Bahaman Geometry" poster. The source file for the composition is called GEOMETRY.A3D, and can be found in the EXAMPLES.CHAP10 folder of the *CorelDRAW! 6 Expert's Edition Bonus CD* if you'd like to view and work with it. The poster's text element will be addressed in a section later in this chapter.

Figure 10.8
CorelDEPTH artwork can be as expressive as those designs you create in CorelDRAW, with the added benefit of dimensional realism.

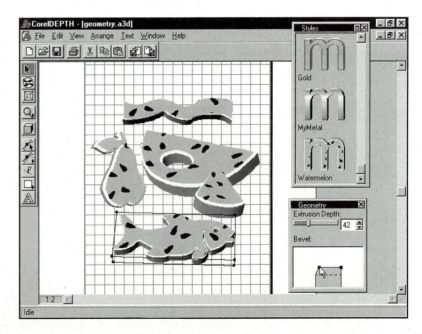

> **➡️ Tip**   In DEPTH's **A**rrange menu, you'll find the To **F**ront and To **B**ack commands, which are essential to creating an order for overlapping 3D objects when you haven't created or imported the elements in sequential order. Like CorelDRAW, the shortcut keys are Shift+PageUp (to front) and Shift+PageDown (to back) for moving selected shapes across a third dimension of your design; if you've memorized the basic DRAW and Windows commands, you'll accomplish a design goal far more quickly.

The GEOMETRY composition is only one example of the possible directions you can take in CorelDEPTH to make appealing, attention-getting artwork. The concept behind applying decals to non-watermelon shapes is borrowed from the surrealist painter Reneé Magritte, who occasionally painted still life scenes containing elements whose textures would normally be found on entirely different objects. With DEPTH, this sort of artistic playfulness comes almost automatically.

Playing with Perspective

The Perspective box, one of the few tools that is not part of the example assignment in this chapter, gives you more control over the dimensional qualities of the entire scene within the printable page in DEPTH.

If you want to direct the viewer's angle of a scene, click on the Perspective Box tool (below the Virtual Track Ball tool on the toolbox), then click-and-drag the rectangle (connected to the four lines that connect the box to the page edges) up, down, or in other directions. Doing this "forces" the perspective of the entire composition (not only the selected objects), and you can display sides of objects without the need to rotate them with the Virtual Track Ball tool. When the Perspective box is positioned toward the top of the page, you can see more of the top edge of objects on the page; the other directions in which you move the Perspective Box provide similar views.

Additionally, to create a wide angle lens effect for your composition, click-and-drag a corner point of the Perspective box toward the center of the page. To "flatten" the composition to suggest a telephoto lens' point of view, click-and-drag a Perspective Box corner away from the center of the page.

Changes in perspective *do* affect the object's physical construction when the composition is exported to other formats, so make certain that what you've created in DEPTH's workspace is the intended final composition.

The Custom Styles on the Bonus CD

To get started on the right foot with CorelDEPTH, you can use the EXPERTS.ADS file in the Bonus CD's EXAMPLES.CHAP10 folder. The 11 preset styles in the Expert's Edition custom Styles Browser are quite unlike those in CorelDEPTH's default Styles Browser. These styles, which you can apply to your 3D creations, will serve you well in a multitude of design situations.

To load the EXPERTS.ADS Styles Browser, follow these steps:

Loading a Custom Styles Browser

1. Before launching CorelDEPTH, copy the EXPERTS.ADS file from the Bonus CD to the DEPTH folder in the Corel 6 folder on your hard disk.

   Copies the file to a location that's easy to locate later.

2. Launch CorelDEPTH, close the Styles Browser by clicking on the Close box on the upper right of the title bar, then hold Ctrl while you choose **W**indow, **S**tyles Browser.

   Indicates to CorelDEPTH that you want a Styles Browser other than the default Styles. This step takes a moment for DEPTH to process, but you'll eventually be presented with the Open Style File dialog box. And you can let go of the Ctrl key at any time now.

3. In the folders window, find the folder which contains the Corel 6 applications, then choose the DEPTH folder, and double-click to open it. Click on EXPERTS.ADS, then click on **O**pen.

   Loads the custom Styles Browser.

If you'd like to create custom Styles of your own, and organize them in your own Browser, don't chose Open, but instead click on Cancel, and DEPTH will display the Create Style File dialog box. Type a unique name in the File **n**ame field, then DEPTH will present you with a new, blank Styles Browser in the workspace that you can populate with original creations.

Similarly, to load the default Styles Browser, close your own—or the Expert's Browser— then while holding Ctrl, choose **W**indow, **S**tyles Browser, and select STYLES.DPS from the DEPTH folder in the Corel 6 folder.

Note Like the file extensions for CorelDEPTH compositions, the DPS or ADS extension can be used to name a Styles Browser. By using the ADS extension, owners of AddDepth on the Macintosh or Windows platforms can share a Styles Browser file you've created.

You'll also notice that there is a Grab button on the Edit Styles window. You can add a style found in a DEP or A3D DEPTH file to your current Styles Browser collection by selecting a 3D object in the design with the 3D Selection tool, clicking on the Grab button on the Edit Styles window, then naming the new Style.

An anomaly can happen with the display of the Styles Browser that appears to "corrupt" the preview icons of Styles. Certain video cards used in combination with CorelDEPTH can cause DEPTH to write a preview in the Styles Browser, that upon reopening DEPTH, makes the Browser's contents look like video noise.

This anomaly has to do with the color depth of your monitor display, and although it doesn't affect the application of a Style to an object, it can make it hard to see what a particular Style looks like before applying it.

> **→ Tip** This problem only appears to occur when you edit and save a Style; DEPTH then writes incorrect visual information to update the Style. To fix the problem, exit DEPTH, and then change video color depth to 256 colors in Win95's Display Properties menu. Then open CorelDEPTH, click on a preview style icon while in Edit Style mode, choose Edit, then click on OK without changing anything in the color Style dialog box. DEPTH then redraws the preview icon, saves the information to file, and you must repeat these steps for every icon that appears corrupted. You can then switch to a higher color mode and work in DEPTH with clean icons in the Styles Browser.

In figure 10.9, you can see that some of the Expert's Styles have been applied to 3D objects, and a selected object is being scaled. CorelDEPTH objects are scaled in exactly the same way as CorelDREAM 3D objects. If you want to distort an object by only resizing height or width, click-and-drag with the 3D Selection tool on a corner selection handle that bounds the object. However, if you want to resize an object proportionately, hold Shift while you click-and-drag away from, or toward the center of the object.

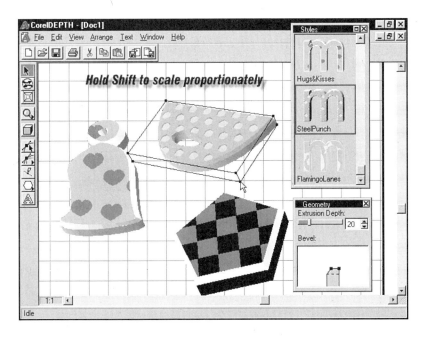

Figure 10.9
Height and Width of a 3D object are adjusted by click-dragging on the bounding box; depth is adjusted from the Geometry Palette.

Beyond CorelDRAW!

Becoming a Corel Mixed Media Designer

The GEOMETRY composition could, in theory, be printed directly from DEPTH, and we could call the assignment finished, but as mentioned earlier in this chapter, computer graphics designers have the opportunity to "mix media"—to place CorelDRAW or PHOTO-PAINT elements next to, behind, or in front of elements created in other applications. And this composition seems to cry out for a sumptuous background and the text that was created earlier.

DEPTH doesn't support the import of bitmap or vector background files; imported graphics can only be used as the model for an object, or a component of a Style. Therefore, a "home" for the composition, and a place where you can continue to add embellishments to the composition, would seem to be PHOTO-PAINT or CorelDRAW.

In this chapter's poster assignment, you'll import the DEPTH composition into DRAW, add a colored background, then export the resulting image to PHOTO-PAINT, where the finished image (the one shown in this book's color plate section) is created.

Refining the Surface of a DEPTH Object

It's important to make certain that the DEPTH exported file (or files) are exactly the way you envision them; an exported 3D object is not easily manipulated after its components are "flattened" to 2D format for DRAW, and other host applications. Occasionally, you'll have a decal surface on an object that doesn't quite show all the details you originally created in the decal WMF resource file; irregularly shaped objects often fail to display the outer edges of a decal design because the surface is rounded, for example.

Therefore, in the following brief example, you'll learn the secret of in-place editing of a decal that's been added as a Style to an object. The MELON.A3D file is in the EXAMPLES.CHAP10 folder of the *CorelDRAW! 6 Expert's Edition Bonus CD* if you'd like some hands-on experience. Here's how to rearrange some of the seeds in a virtual melon slice...

Editing an Imported Decal Image

1. Open the MELON.A3D file in CorelDEPTH from the EXAMPLES.CHAP10 folder of the *CorelDRAW! 6 Expert's Edition Bonus CD.*

   This is a component of the GEOMETRY DEPTH file which contains the melon slice object with the Watermelon Style decal, which you'll modify.

2. With the watermelon slice selected, hold Alt, then click on the 2D Selection tool.

   The Edit Decal dialog box appears.

3. Click on the **F**ront Face radio button if it isn't already highlighted, then click on OK.

   Displays only the 2D paths that make up the basic design of the melon slice, and the imported WMF decal. The Working Plane auto-adjusts to match the angle of rotation the 2D objects display. If you haven't rotated an object whose front face you want to edit, the Working Plane will remain parallel to your view of the document window.

4. With the 2D Selection tool, click on a watermelon seed on the decal foreground, then click-and-drag the seed by about 2 grid markers to the bottom and right of its original position.

   Moves the seed within the decal; changes where the seed will appear on the front face of the melon slice object (see fig. 10.10).

Additionally, you can reshape a foreground path by click-and-dragging on its nodes with the 2D selection tool, and change node properties by using the Convert Point tool on a decal object's path. You cannot, however, add to the decal design, because DEPTH has no 2D paint tools. You can also Copy and Paste a foreground decal element, and by pressing Delete with a foreground element selected, you could make this example a seedless melon.

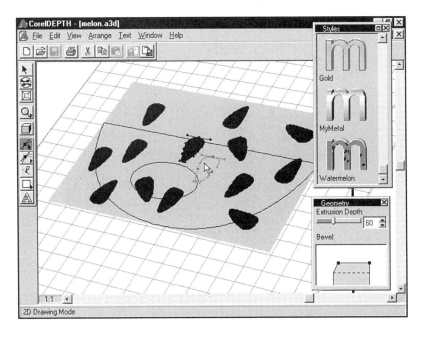

Figure 10.10

Discrete paths in the imported graphic can be rearranged, combined with other objects, and edited to created different paths.

5. Click on the 3D Selection tool.

   Makes changes to the front face of the melon slice; the melon slice is returned to 3D mode.

6. Choose **F**ile, Save **A**s, then save the file as MY-MELON.A3D to your hard disk.

   Saves your work; creates a unique name for the file should you want to use it, or delete it later.

As mentioned at the beginning of this section, MELON.A3D was created by copying the melon slice from the GEOMETRY.A3D file on the Bonus CD. In your own work, you'll want to adopt the practice of breaking a composition into its basic elements, because it makes transportation of copies of the components to other applications easier. Here's some last-minute points to ponder before we move the composition into CorelDRAW, and then on to its final destination, CorelPHOTO-PAINT.

The Benefits of Piecework Exporting

The "Bahaman Geometry" poster example in this chapter consists of more elements than those created in CorelDEPTH. As a designer, with your own work, you have the opportunity of adding manually-created effects and different background schemes to your CorelDEPTH work to flesh out a concept. However, to do this, you need access to other tools; within the context of this example, this means that DRAW and PHOTO-PAINT will make a contribution to "Bahaman Geometry." And this requires hefting the composition up through the export filter and into these other applications.

Let's ponder how importing *every* object in the GEOMETRY composition, in a single file, would impact on the speed of any editing work in CorelDRAW. In a word, it would *stifle* your progress. Unfortunately, DEPTH's **V**iew, **W**ireframe (Shift+F9, the same key command as for wireframe view in CorelDRAW) mode doesn't show the complexity of a design *as it would be imported* into CorelDRAW. You can see 3D outlines of the objects, and work a little quicker in this mode to reposition and rotate objects, but the surfaces you define through the Styles Browser create an enormous number of individual colored shapes that represent shading on objects when exported to other programs. Because you cannot export only a selected object from a DEPTH document but must export the entire document, it makes sense, then, to create separate files for each component of a composition you want to export.

An object copied from a CorelDEPTH file, then pasted to a new DEPTH document window retains its surface style and editability, but more importantly, it retains its angle of rotation, perspective (if any has been created), and its location relative to the document page. Therefore, you "ask" less of the export filter and the host application when you move a DEPTH composition as a collection of files consisting of single objects. This is the reason the text for the example poster has not yet been covered—it's extremely complex, and needs to travel as a separate object to CorelDRAW.

In the following series of steps, we outline the procedure for copying, and breaking down the GEOMETRY.A3D composition into single objects, then we get into how to export, then import the object as a CorelDRAW collection of vector shapes.

Here's how to move the GEOMETRY composition, or one of your own, into another Corel application:

Exporting a Complex CorelDEPTH Composition

1. Open the GEOMETRY.A3D file from the EXAMPLES.CHAP10 folder of the *CorelDRAW! 6 Expert's Edition Bonus CD.*

   This CorelDEPTH file contains all of the graphics elements of the "Bahaman Geometry" poster example.

2. With the 3D selection tool, click on an empty space on the document page, then click on the fish object.

   By default, an opened DEPTH file has all objects selected. Clicking on an empty area deselects the objects, and you've now selected the fish object only.

3. Press Ctrl+C (**E**dit, **C**opy).

   Copies the fish object to the clipboard.

4. Click on the New button on the toolbar (or press Ctrl+N; **F**ile, **N**ew).

   Displays the Document Type dialog box.

5. Click on Create A Blank **N**ew Document.

   A new document window appears on top of GEOMETRY.A3D. You can have as many document windows open in CorelDEPTH as your system memory will allow.

6. Press Ctrl+V (**E**dit, **P**aste).

   Pastes a copy of the fish object into the new document window.

7. Click on the Export button on the toolbox (or press Ctrl+E; **F**ile, Export).

   Displays the Export dialog box.

Beyond CorelDRAW!

8. Choose Windows Metafile (*.wmf) from the Save as type drop-down list, in the folders window, choose a good location on your hard disk for the export, name the file FISH.WMF in the File name field, then click on Save.

CorelDEPTH exports the fish object in the Windows Metafile format, which CorelDRAW can import with greater ease and accuracy than your alternative option, Adobe Illustrator format. See following TIP.

9. Click on the title bar of the GEOMETRY. A3D document window, with the 3D selection tool, click on the pear object, press Ctrl+C, then click on the new document window (containing the fish object), and press Ctrl+V.

Copies the pear object from the GEOMETRY document to the new document.

10. Click on the fish object, then press Delete.

Deletes the fish; the pear is currently the only object in the new document.

11. Repeat steps 7 and 8 with the pear object (name the file PEAR.WMF instead of FISH.WMF, though), then repeat steps 9 and 10 with the other objects which have not been exported yet to the WMF format.

You've exported the compositional elements of the "Bahaman Geometry" to a format CorelDRAW can import, and you haven't used extra hard disk space to store copies of each object in both the CorelDEPTH and WMF formats. When all the objects have been exported, you can close the new document (Ctrl+W), without saving it.

The preceding steps freely ignore the peril of not saving a duplicate of the single objects in DEPTH format; if you ran into a system halt while exporting, you might lose an export. However, the original file containing all the objects is safe and sound by using this technique, and the preceding steps are an economical approach which eliminates hard disk clutter. Digital designers are frequently obliged to perform hard disk housecleaning after an assignment where multiple copies of design elements are exported to different graphical formats. The preceding steps help cut back on the necessity to incessantly tidy up your drives, folders, and files.

 Tip If you're an Adobe Photoshop user, CorelDEPTH files can be directly imported and converted to bitmap format; Photoshop naturally supports its sister application, Adobe Illustrator.

However, the Illustrator (*.ai) export filter in CorelDEPTH includes page size information, and this can cause problems when importing a CorelDEPTH graphic. As a WMF file, CorelDEPTH compositions only include bounding box information about the live objects on the page, but not the page itself.

If you intend to use Photoshop with a DEPTH object exported in the AI format, you should first import the object into CorelDRAW, then export the composition once again in the AI format. This technique strips the AI file of page size information. If you don't perform this step, Photoshop reads the DEPTH exported file page information along with the page's contents (the 3D objects). And you'd then be required by Photoshop to import a 35 MB file or greater simply to convert a small object on the page to bitmap format.

With version 6.00.118 of the Corel suite of applications, the AI export filter in DRAW does not work as well as it does in CorelDRAW version 5. An update is expected from Corel Corp. to solve the filter problems in version 6, but if you need a fail-safe method of working between your Windows applications, and you need it within the next 15 minutes, CorelDRAW version 5.00.F2 is your best bet.

Understanding CorelDRAW!'s Role in Bitmap Image Creation

At some point in your design career, even if you've never used an application other than CorelDRAW, you will question yourself about the prudence of creating *all* designs in the vector format in which DRAW works. CorelDRAW's editing and drawing tools provide precision, smooth scaling to almost any size, and most of the time, the CDR format is the most compact way to store and transport design information. However, DEPTH throws designers a curve—and it's not a vector curve—with respect to the economy and speed with which you can enhance and edit the product of a CorelDEPTH design session.

A vector design, at some point, becomes larger in file size than an equivalent bitmap rendering of the same image information, because of the complexity of the design's curves, and the number of individual objects which comprise the design. When a CorelDRAW file exceeds 1 MB in file size, you'll notice that tools appear to become slow in response, and screen redraws take longer and longer. In very simple terms, this is a sign that the "tools" you are using to accomplish a design task are the wrong ones, and so is the media.

The bottom line is that a DEPTH creation can be edited to a minor extent as a CorelDRAW object, but the finished design is much better off as a bitmap type illustration, saved in CPT, TIFF, Targa, or other bitmap file type. If you plan ahead, as we'll show you in the following sections, you can have the best of both graphics type worlds— you can refine the elements of this poster example in CorelDRAW, then compose the elements into a finished poster with a selection technique or two in PHOTO-PAINT. There is nothing inherently inferior with the output of a bitmap design when compared to a vector design, when you understand some of the rules that govern the construction of bitmap images, which are discussed in the next section.

Beyond CorelDRAW!

Defining Quick Vector-to-Bitmap Conversion Values

Because bitmap images are *resolution-dependent*—bitmap file format construction contains a fixed number of pixels—it's best to decide on a size for the finished bitmap image before exporting a DEPTH design to this graphics format.

The "math" behind calculating a size and resolution for bitmap images doesn't have to be difficult if you use PHOTO-PAINT's **F**ile, **N**ew dialog box. You can type "dummy" values into the boxes; you don't actually use the resulting file or change the size of an existing one, but instead, write down the resulting file size and resolution PHOTO-PAINT provides, then cancel the operation. The values PHOTO-PAINT presents you with can then be used to calculate the ideal dimensions for compositions that are bitmap in construction.

For example, 8.5" by 11" is DEPTH's default size for a document page. If you type these values into the **W**idth and **H**eight fields of the Create a New Image dialog box (**F**ile, **N**ew), at 100 dpi bitmap image *resolution* (the number of pixels per inch in a bitmap image), the resulting file would be 2.7 MB if the image is to be in 24-bit RGB color mode (the best mode for high-quality image output).

A 100 dpi bitmap image might not print well to an imagesetter; imagesetters use lines per inch (lpi) values to determine printing resolution, and in general, the line per inch value should equal half the bitmap file resolution. Which means that a 133 lpi imagesetter would require approximately 266 pixels per inch resolution in a bitmap file to be printed at 1:1 file dimensions.

Another factor enters the picture at this point: how large a bitmap file *can* you create on your system? Although the maximum file size you can create in PHOTO-PAINT is theoretically limited to a combination of free hard disk swap space and available RAM, if you're accustomed to CorelDRAW, and not bitmap image design work, bitmap files which exceed 10 MB on a system with about 16 MB of RAM will "feel" like you're working with molasses when you attempt to edit the work. And there are two solutions to working quickly with bitmap images:

✔ Work with small files which produce medium-quality printed images, or

✔ Buy a motherboard which can hold hundreds of MB of RAM, and populate the motherboard.

Let's stick with the first option above, and conceive of this "Bahamas Geometry" composition as an image that will print well to a personal color printer (whose resolution is typically less than 55 lpi, although non-PostScript printers don't normally measure output in lines per inch). Also, a basic truth when working with bitmap images is that you can achieve a better print if you shrink the dimensions of the bitmap file.

Bitmap image resolution is inversely proportional to image dimensions.

Therefore, a 2.7 MB file, 100 dpi, 8.5" by 11" in dimensions might not have sufficient image resolution to output well to a 133 lpi imagesetter, but the *same image* with 3" by 4" dimensions, 2.7 MB in file size, at 275 pixels per inch will *indeed* output well. You can choose Image, Resample in PHOTO-PAINT when you're finished with the piece, check the Maintain original size check box to ensure that PHOTO-PAINT doesn't *change* any of the pixels in your finished piece, then type a higher Resolution value in the dpi spin boxes. The resampled image contains all of the original image detail, the same file size, and a 2.7 MB bitmap version of a DEPTH design can be manipulated quickly and easily on systems that have a modest amount of system RAM.

> **Tip**   If you don't check the Maintain original size check box when you resample and image, PHOTO-PAINT must interpolate (average, change) original pixel colors to create a bitmap image with fewer (or more) pixels than the number contained in the original. When you resample a bitmap image to create a different file size, you can sometimes distort image content.

Later in this chapter, you'll see the effect of changing pixel count into a bitmap image, and the reason why, on occasion, this is a desired editing technique in your work).

The preceding sections can be a game strategy for your own assignments using DEPTH, CorelDRAW, and PHOTO-PAINT in combination to produce a mixed media creation. In the following section, we'll walk through the exact steps you'll want to take, using the Bahaman Geometry poster as the example image.

Choosing a Background Color for a DEPTH Object in CorelDRAW!

Because there is no way to define a background color other than white in AddDepth, it's not always a good idea to import a DEPTH object directly from DEPTH as a Windows Metafile to PHOTO-PAINT. Exporting of DEPTH 3D objects always results in the flattening of the image content to 2D space, because to date, no other application besides CorelDEPTH can read and edit DEPTH's unique 3D object information.

In the Bahaman Geometry poster, many of the objects display near-white highlights. It's easy to select the exported foreground objects in a program like CorelDRAW, because the WMF imports into DRAW as a collection of discrete shapes. In contrast, a WMF is read into PHOTO-PAINT as a bitmap, where DEPTH's white background, against near-white object edges, is hard to see clearly, and almost impossible to define and separate the foreground design from the background using PHOTO-PAINT's selection tools.

Therefore, it's good to decide at this point what color the background for the finished image shall be. If you look at the color plate for "Bahaman Geometry" in the center of this book, you'll see that the author decided to create a putty, textured background in the finished image. This was accomplished by first adding a pale pink rectangle behind

Beyond CorelDRAW!

each of the DEPTH objects after importing them into CorelDRAW. The rectangle is of sufficiently different color compared to the object edges so that PHOTO-PAINT's Lasso Mask tool can separate the foreground and background areas of the bitmap version of the composition. But pale pink is also close enough in brightness and hue values to the pale edges of the watermelon surfaced objects that the viewer won't see harsh edgework in the finished image.

Let's get the show on the road now with a brief, simple set of steps used to add a background one of the components of the composition, then move on to PHOTO-PAINT where the real magic takes place.

Importing, Editing, and Exporting a DEPTH Object

1. Close CorelDEPTH, launch CorelDRAW, then click on the import button on the toolbar.

   Displays the Import dialog box.

2. Locate MELON.WMF file on your hard disk which you saved earlier, select it, then click on Import.

   CorelDRAW imports the melon slice you exported from DEPTH as a collection of filled vector shapes. If you didn't export the melon slice, MELON.WMF is on the Bonus CD in the CHAP10 folder, along with the other resource files you might need to complete the poster assignment. In figure 10.11, you can see a 2-window view (created by choosing Window, New Window) of the same CorelDRAW document, with MELON.WMF imported. On the surface, the melon looks as though it's made of only 4 or 5 objects, as you might try to design this image using CorelDRAW tools. But in actuality, over 200 objects represent the shading and other details on the imported melon slice.

3. Press F6 (or click on the Rectangle tool), then click-and-drag a rectangle around the melon group of objects, leaving at least 1/2" of rectangle around the border of the melon.

   This is the background portion of the image you'll export to PHOTO-PAINT format.

4. Click on the To Back button on the toolbar (or press Shift+PageDown), click on the color palette's extension button (to the right of the palette), click on the Faded Pink swatch (look at the status bar when you hover your cursor over the palette to see the color names), then right-click on the x on the color palette.

   Sends the rectangle behind the melon group of objects; fills the rectangle with pink; removes the outline property from the rectangle. See figure 10.12.

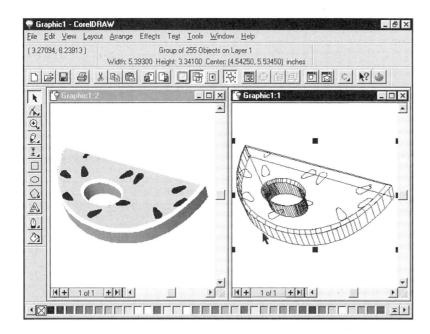

Figure 10.11
DEPTH objects import to CorelDRAW as a large number of objects. It's simpler and quicker to work with DEPTH creations as bitmap images.

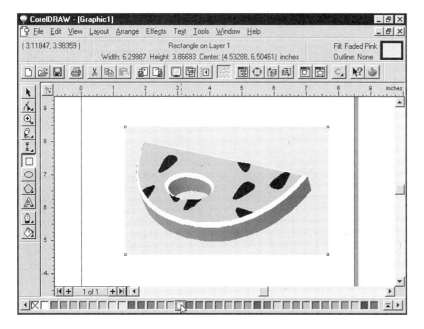

Figure 10.12
Bitmaps don't natively support discrete design objects; you must *create* a background to surround the melon slice export.

III

Beyond CorelDRAW!

5. Double-click on the Pick tool, then click on the Export button on the toolbar.

Selects everything in the document window; opens the Export dialog box.

6. Choose TIFF Bitmap (TIF) from the Save as type drop-down list, choose a good target location on your hard disk for the exported design, check the Selected only check box, name the file MELON.TIF, and then click on Export.

    Displays the Bitmap Export dialog box.

7. Choose 16 Million colors from the Color drop-down list, leave the Size field at the default Width and Height values (1 to 1 should be the drop-down list selection in the Size field), check the Identical Values and Anti-aliasing check boxes, then type 200 in both the Horizontal and Vertical Resolution dpi spin boxes.

    Specifies that the exported graphic has the color capability of 24-bit RGB color, that the dimensions of the exported graphic will be identical to those in CorelDRAW, and that the pixel per inch value shall be 200. We did mention that the finished image was to be 100 pixels per inch, but there's a good reason why you should specify a greater resolution, which will be explained in the section after this example.

Additionally, CorelDRAW 6.00.118, the first release of this version, does *not* appear to support Anti-aliasing, even though the Bitmap Export dialog box sports this option. However, updates to version 6 are expected as of this writing, and it's a good practice to adopt to enable Anti-aliasing in most programs that export or work with bitmap graphics.

8. Click on OK, then click on OK in the TIFF-Color Space dialog box *without* checking the Save in CIELab check box.

    Exports the graphic as a TIFF image to your hard disk. CIELab is a color model available for TIFF images that is structurally different than the RGB mode TIFF image format. The CIELab color model is based around a channel of Brightness and two channels of chromacity, and is generally not applicable to image editing or creation work unless you need to strip only the color values from an image to create a true grayscale version from a color original bitmap image.

9. Close CorelDRAW. You might want to save the graphic of the melon before closing, but the WMF version of the melon is also on the Bonus CD, so this step isn't really required.

Anti-aliasing is to bitmap format images what a piece of sandpaper is to a freshly cut piece of wood. Because bitmap images are resolution-dependent, and pixels are rectangular in shape, a very unaesthetic thing occurs when a picture of anything with a curved shape, such as a watermelon slice, is rendered to bitmap format. In the next section, we'll take a look at how you can manually "force" some anti-aliasing into a vector image that's been converted to bitmap format.

Aliasing and Anti-Aliasing

Aliasing, the placement of "wrong" colored pixels along the border of contrasting color areas in an image, occurs when an application which creates bitmap images fails to calculate the pixels that are needed to create transitional color steps between foreground and background bitmap colors. In the same way as fountain fills appear to be bands of solid colors when you don't have enough fountain fill steps defined, aliased edges in bitmap images are a failure of an application's programming to take a look at the image to be rendered at several different viewing resolutions, and then calculate an average of color values to make up the pixels on the exact edge of an element within a bitmap image.

Obvious, aliased edges in a bitmap are not that hard to correct if you use PHOTO-PAINT's Anti-alias option (which *does* work in version 6.00.118) after making the melon slice, in this example, a floating object within the exported file. By "floating" the foreground, aliased object, then resizing the entire document to half its original dimensions/resolution, you achieve not only anti-aliasing within the melon (around the seeds and rind), but the outside edges of the selected object will also display edge pixels which have transitional tones to smooth your view of the edge from background color to foreground color.

This is the reason why a light color was chosen for the background of the melon in CorelDRAW, and why you were asked to specify 200, not 100 pixels per inch for the resolution of the exported design. In general, it's not a good idea to resize a bitmap image, because doing so tends to blur image details, but you're learning the exceptions along with the rules in this chapter.

Importing and Editing the Melon

MELON.TIF, the sample image in the CHAP10 folder of the *CorelDRAW! 6 Expert's Edition Bonus CD*, is a CorelDRAW export of the WMF version of the original DEPTH object. It's a relatively large image for only a supporting role within a bitmap image—2.8 MB. However, after reducing the image size of the melon slice to half its present resolution to force anti-aliasing to occur, you'll find that working with a file roughly 1/4 its original size (half the height plus half the width) can be accomplished with ease on almost any system with PHOTO-PAINT 6.

Here's how to import the MELON.TIF image, create a floating object from a selection, and create smooth edges in contrasting color areas within the image:

Anti-Aliasing and Object Editing

1. Launch PHOTO-PAINT from Win95's Start menu, then click on the Open button on the toolbar (**F**ile, **O**pen; Ctrl+O).

Beyond CorelDRAW!

Displays the Open an Image dialog box.

2. Choose MELON.TIF from your hard drive in the folder window, or MELON.TIF from the CHAP10 folder on the Bonus CD (if you didn't complete the previous example), then click on **O**pen.

PHOTO-PAINT opens the image. In figure 10.13, a new window has been opened to show the melon bitmap image at two different viewing resolutions. At the 100% viewing resolution (shown on the left), you might be able to see the stair-steppy, aliased edged within the image in this figure. You'll most certainly see the aliased edges on-screen if you load the MELON.TIF image, and at 300% magnification on the right side of figure 10.13, you can see that the bitmap image definitely needs to be filtered.

Figure 10.13
A tell-tale sign that an image is computer-generated is aliased color transitions.

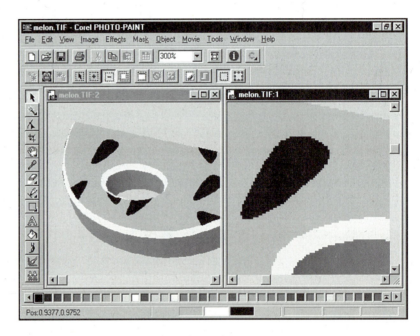

3. Click and hold on the Rectangle Mask tool on the toolbox to access the Mask tools flyout menu, then click on the Lasso Mask tool.

This is one of two tools you'll use to separate the melon slice from the pale pink background. You can create either a freehand (click-and-drag the tool) or a straight line (only click with the tool) bounding path around part of an image you want to select with the Lasso tool.

4. Click single points outside of the watermelon slice areas within MELON.TIF, then double-click when you return to the start point.

The bounding path encloses the melon; double-clicking finalizes the path you've created, and a marquee selection based upon color edges in the MELON image replaces the path. The Lasso Mask tool has automatically defined an accurate selection around the melon. See figure 10.14.

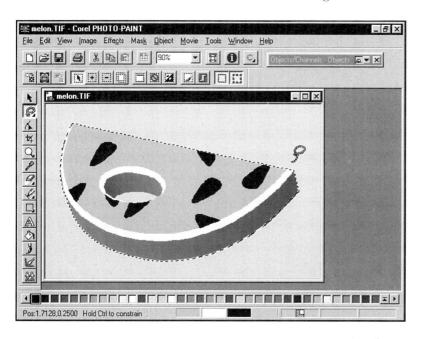

Figure 10.14

Areas of color similarity that are enclosed by the Lasso Mask tool's bounding path automatically become marquee-selected areas.

5. Click and hold on the Lasso Mask tool, choose the Magic Wand Mask tool, then double-click on the Magic Wand tool.

   Selects the tool; opens the Tool Settings Roll-Up for the Magic Wand Mask tool options.

6. Type **1** in the color tolerance slider's number field, then click on the Subtract from Mask button on the Mask/Object toolbar. Do *not* click on the **A**nti-aliasing check box on the Tool Settings Roll-Up. If the Mask Object toolbar isn't on-screen, right-click over the default toolbar and choose Mask/Object from the shortcut menu.

   Reduces the breadth of color range that the Magic Wand will select to an extremely narrow value. This is good in this example, because there are currently no color transition pixels along the edge where the melon meets the background faded pink. And this means that the Magic Wand will only select a solid shade of color, namely the pink area of the background showing through the hole in the melon. The Subtract from Mask feature causes Mask tools to remove an area you define with them from an existing selection. Anti-aliasing is not wanted at this point of editing, because the Tool Settings feature would make the Magic Wand selection imprecise.

7. Click the Magic Wand tool inside the hole area of the melon, then click on the Create Object button on the toolbar.

   Creates a floating object out of the melon slice, which is now hovering above the background of the MELON.TIF image. See figure 10.15.

Figure 10.15
PHOTO-PAINT affords many of the object-oriented features you find in CorelDRAW. The melon object can be repositioned within the image now.

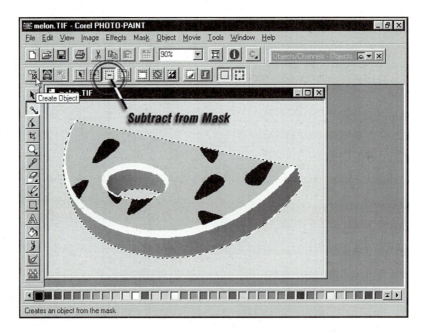

8. Choose **I**mage, **R**esample, type **100** in the **H**orizontal and **V**ertical Resolution spin boxes, make sure Maintain original **s**ize is *un*checked, choose Anti-alias from the **P**rocess drop-down list, then click on OK.

   Reduces the dimensions of the MELON.TIF image by one-half; anti-aliasing removes the harshness from the image edges.

9. Press Ctrl+F7 (**V**iew, Roll-**U**ps, **O**bjects).

   Displays the Objects/Channels Roll-Up.

10. Click on the eye icon to the left of the Background title on the Objects Roll-Up, then choose the Zoom tool, and zoom into the melon's edge. About 300% viewing resolution will do.

Hides the faded pink background object; the melon is surrounded by empty space, and you can seriously evaluate how well resizing the MELON.TIF image produces a smooth anti-aliasing effect, to make the melon appear more dimensional and photographic. If you find the "marching ants"—the marquee selection borders—to be a distraction while you're editing, you can turn them off by clicking on the Show/Hide Object Marquee button, the far right one, on the Mask/Object toolbar. See figure 10.16.

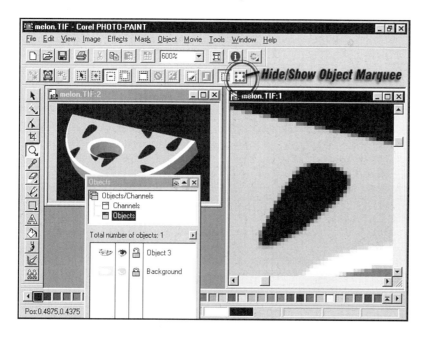

Figure 10.16

Computer images can look as realistic as a scanned photograph, but only by adding unique edge tones through anti-aliasing.

11. Choose **F**ile, Save **A**s, then save the image as MY-MELON.CPT to your hard disk.

   Saves the image at this intermediate stage of completion.

 Note   If you don't have the Mask/Object toolbar visible in PHOTO-PAINT, it will be hard to turn off the object marquee lines using the Show/Hide Object Marquee button!

By default, PHOTO-PAINT installs with the Mask/Object toolbar beneath the Standard toolbar, but if you've accidentally closed it, right-click on the Standard toolbar, then check the Mask/Object field on the shortcut menu.

Additionally, if you want to hide the mask marquees you might have active in an image, the Show/Hide Mask Marquee button is directly to the left of the Show/Hide Object Marquee button on the toolbar.

III

Beyond CorelDRAW!

After you make a floating object from the melon selection, the image file can no longer be saved in the TIFF format; only PHOTO-PAINT's proprietary CPT format can save layered objects. Because the melon doesn't "belong" to the Background image any longer, you can paint on the background, add other layers, and expand the Paper Size (**I**mage, **P**aper Size) of the MY-MELON file to accommodate the other compositional elements for the poster. It's always best to define areas as individual objects in a bitmap image before resizing, especially with the Resample dialog box's Anti-alias feature chosen. In the previous example, if you had resized the original melon image without separating the melon slice from the background first, accurate selection of the melon would have been next to impossible. There are too many unique shades of foreground and background color pixels around the edges of bitmap image details for the Mask selection tools to accurately define an edge after any anti-aliasing.

Basically, there are no more steps in this section that you need to learn to export the other elements of DEPTH's "Bahaman Geometry" poster, but stick around for a moment or two, and we'll show you a few creative tricks for assembling the piece.

Finalizing the Composition

One of the wonderful qualities of PHOTO-PAINT's Objects feature is that you can arrange compositional elements as many times, in as many sessions of PHOTO-PAINT, as you like, as long as the file is saved in the CPT format. If you open MELON.CPT from the CHAP10 folder of the Bonus CD, you'll see the "Bahaman Geometry" composition has been pushed a little further to completion, by adding a background and a burnished dropshadow object to the file. This mini-painting, as you can see in figure 10.17, eventually was increased in dimensions, other DEPTH objects were added by using the same techniques as shown in this chapter, to become the finished poster. We'll show you how to add the 3D text element that you exported from CorelDRAW for use in DEPTH at the beginning of the chapter in the section following this one.

Although this chapter is primarily devoted to CorelDEPTH and CorelMOTION 3D, here is the recipe you can use in PHOTO-PAINT to create MELON.CPT:

✔ **To create the textured background**, scan a real life texture such as some burlap, or better still, use the **E**ffects, Artistic, Canvas, then apply any of the PCX images offered in the dialog box to the Background of the image only. Click on the lock icon next to the melon slice object to ensure that the Canvas effect doesn't accidentally apply to the star of the image. The author used Fractal Design Painter to create the texture, and this news is more of an explanation for the distinctive texture in the sample image rather than a suggestion that the effect is better accomplished through a non-Corel program.

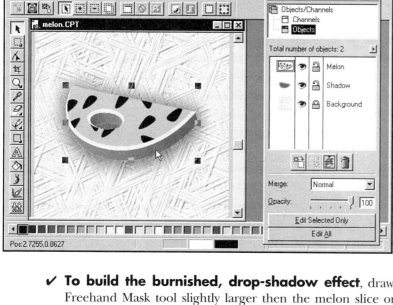

Figure 10.17
The shadow, the textured background, and the melon slice are all individual objects. You can rearrange a CPT file's contents indefinitely!

✔ **To build the burnished, drop-shadow effect**, draw an outline with the Freehand Mask tool slightly larger then the melon slice on the Background object layer. Copy the area, then paste it back into the image as a unique object (Ctrl+C, then Ctrl+V). Fill the new object with a warm brown by using the Fill tool set to 100 Tolerance on the Tool Settings Roll-Up. This produces a solid colored object when you click inside the object marquee with the Fill tool cursor.

To create a soft, blurry suggestion of color, click on the Object Picker tool, right-click over the object, then choose **F**eather from the shortcut menu. For a relatively small file, containing not that many pixels, the **W**idth of the feathered edge for the object should be no more than 20 in the Feather dialog box. You should also choose Soft **E**dges from the drop-down list to make a *subtle*, soft background shade.

✔ **To complete the effect seen in MELON.CPT**, select shadow object on the Objects Roll-Up, click on **E**dit Selected Only, choose Multiply from the Merge drop-down list, then click-and-drag the Opacity to about 80%. Multiply mode accentuates the darker pixels in an object, and hides lighter values from view, which is very similar to the lighting conditions that produce a real life shadow.

To share this image with non–PHOTO-PAINT users, you must first use the Combine command on the Objects Roll-Up (the icon with the stack of layers) to merge the

Beyond CorelDRAW!

objects to the background of the image. Make certain no layers are locked before you do this; locked layers will not be included in the merged image. Once the bitmap image's "special effects" have been removed, it can then be saved in a number of more common file formats such as TIFF or BMP.

Adding the Image Icing to the Poster Cake

Hopefully, you've seen in the previous sections how DEPTH is not confined to the lowly role of a "text extrusion utility." Simply put, you can design away for hours without even glimpsing at a font with what you now know about CorelDEPTH. But to put the capper on the "Bahaman Geometry" poster, we conclude this section with a trick for *individually* manipulating characters in a DEPTH string of text. You can give the effect of animation to motionless letters, and truly command attention with your words.

Here's how to create the final compositional piece for "Bahaman Geometry"…

Importing Text as Graphics

1. In CorelDEPTH, open a new, blank document, then click on the Import button on the toolbar.

   Displays the Import dialog box.

2. Choose Illustrator (*.ai) from the Files of type dialog box, find the BAHATEXT.AI file you created at the beginning of this chapter, click on it, then click on **O**pen. If you didn't export the text from CorelDRAW in the first example in this chapter, you can import BAHATEXT.AI from the CHAP10 folder on the Bonus CD.

   Imports the graphic; the text immediately begins to extrude to the default Geometry Palette depth value.

3. With the graphic selected by default upon importing it, click on a Style Browser icon that suits your fancy.

   Applies the style to all the objects in the imported graphic. Consider applying a Style that has no back face in this example. The file is going to be huge when exported, and you definitely don't want to include faces of the objects that won't appear in the finished piece.

4. While this graphic is still grouped, click-and-drag on the left and right nodes in the Geometry Palette window to create bevel faces for the graphic.

5. Choose **A**rrange, **U**ngroup (Ctrl+U).

Ungroups the graphic; each graphical character can now be individually resized and rotated. See figure 10.18, and see following TIP.

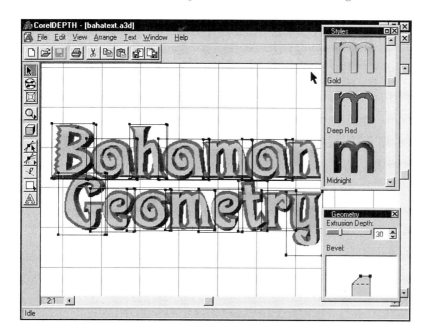

Figure 10.18
Paths that are not combined, and exported in the AI format, can be ungrouped and manipulated as individual objects.

6. With the 3D Selection tool, click on an empty space on the document page, then click on one of the character objects, then with the Virtual Track Ball tool, click-and-drag the object.

   Rotates only the selected object.

7. Press Ctrl+Tab, then select another object.

   Ctrl+Tab toggles between the 3D Selection tool and the Track Ball tool. You can't select a new object with the Track Ball tool.

8. Press Ctrl+Tab, then rotate the object in a unique direction. Make sure you can still see part of the front of the object. See figure 10.19.

   Rotates the object. Be careful when rotating an object the audience is going to read. 3D text is wonderful, but it becomes illegible when rotated or distorted too much.

9. When you have the arrangement of the individual objects the way you want it, click on the toolbox Export button (or press Ctrl+E), then export a copy of your work as BAHATEXT.WMF.

   Saves the design in a format CorelDRAW can import.

Beyond CorelDRAW!

Figure 10.19
If you want the
viewer of you
masterpiece to
actually read the 3D
text, don't rotate so
much that the front
face is hidden!

10. Press Ctrl+S (File, Save), then save the DEPTH design as BAHATEXT.A3D to
     your hard disk.

     Saves the piece in 3D format which you can edit later.

 You can also manipulate individual characters in a text string you've created using
DEPTH's Text tool, but the text must be converted to a graphic first.

Select the text with the 2D Selection tool (not the 3D), then choose **C**onvert to Curves from the Text
menu.

Use the techniques shown in "Becoming a Corel Mixed Media Designer," earlier in this
chapter, to add your 3D text objects to the other watermelon-styled objects. In figure
10.20, you can see the completed composition.

If you think we've taken this 3D stuff as far as it can be taken, you're right. The next
section shows you how to create *4D* stuff!

Figure 10.20
CorelDEPTH does more than create 3D text. It offers the change to *work* with designs in three dimensions.

CorelMOTION 3D: Adding the Dimension of Time to Artwork

CorelMOTION 3D is nothing less than a mini-motion picture studio. Within the program, you'll find props, stagehands, and a workshop where you can make adjustments to actors in a way the Screen Actors Guild in real life probably would not allow!

If you've browsed Chapter 9, and soaked in some of our DEPTH discussions in the first part of this chapter, you're well ahead of the game in understanding how to get the most from MOTION 3D. Like DEPTH and DREAM 3D, MOTION 3D features a complement of design tools, and you can import CorelDRAW paths for use in MOTION 3D. However, MOTION 3D has the capability to render still images as well as animated AVI, MPEG (Motion Picture Expert's Group), and other PC and Macintosh digital film formats.

Adding the dimension of time to a graphic is a serious consideration. Typically, you have more than your hands full creating stunning 2D design work!

To begin the MOTION 3D section, let's begin with a little advice, some facts about digital "flicks," and create a game plan for your adventures in three-dimensional animation.

Beyond CorelDRAW!

So Where Are the Funny 3D Glasses?

The term "3D animation," to be honest, is hype, and not to be confused with the thriller films played in theaters 30 years ago to audiences who had to wear polarized or two-tone cardboard glasses to view the effect. MOTION 3D, like other computer animation programs, offers a stage modeled around 3D space, which you use special tools through your 2D monitor view of the scene to manipulate objects. The file that is the result of an animation session in MOTION 3D produces a series of image frames that are compressed into a single, proprietary file format, that Windows Media Player, and other computer utilities can play back in two dimensions.

You also have the option in MOTION 3D of rendering still frames (not a movie format file), numbered in sequence, in case you want to perform some post-production editing in a painting or video editing application. However, it's up to you and the software you own to then *compile* a movie format file from the rendered still images if you choose not to make a movie file in MOTION 3D.

The quality and screen size of a personal computer animation, such as an AVI, Autodesk FLIC, or other Windows and Macintosh movie formats MOTION 3D supports is somewhat limited. Do *not* expect to render a 1/2 hour, full-screen action adventure—such an effort would require more processing power than a Pentium, an operating system optimized for digital video, and hard disk storage few small businesses can afford or imagine.

However, if your ambition is to become familiar with the *process* of creating computer animation, MOTION 3D's capabilities and features rank at the top of the list of animation applications, and you can indeed generate short flicks that can be used for a wide range of business and leisure purposes.

Creating a 4 or 5 second animation of high quality can be created overnight, quite literally. Like most modeling and rendering applications, a movie-making program requires time to convert the information for the movie file to bitmap format. Each "frame" of the movie must be created pixel by pixel, and this is why animation professionals often start the rendering procedure at the end of a work day... or the beginning of a weekend. By the morning, sometimes Monday morning, the render is complete for the animation, and the creator has something to look at.

Note Have you noticed that most AVI files distributed on the World Wide Web or on CDs don't fill your screen? The problem is not with your monitor. Full-screen—or even half-screen sized—computer animations take longer to redraw on-screen, and the bigger the view, the greater the chatter and jerkiness introduced at playback time.

Despite the confines of a small screen and short air times, computer animations are a lot of fun to create, and generate a *lot* of interest from people who aren't familiar with the PC's capabilities. Businesses are always looking for fresh avenues of advertising, and with a little practice and the information in this chapter, you can add the profession of "mini-movie guru" to your artist's repertoire!

The Virtual Script Call for MOTION 3D

Although MOTION 3D offers all the helping hands required to practically automate the process of creating a flying logo animation, once you've sailed a half dozen logos, you'll soon look for more ambitious projects.

Like traditional directors, you need actors, and you need a story. Try this one on for size: Cactus Todd's, a fictitious restaurant in Cincinnati, Ohio, is famous for their "3-Alarm Chili." The owner, Mr. Cactus Todd, is interested in brightening up his storefront window with an animated display. Putting a monitor in a store window is okay in this example because Cactus Todd's store front faces due north, and besides, this is a fictitious example.

You're given the charge of creating an auto-repeating computer animation that will intrigue lunch time sidewalk traffic, and lure them inside.

Forget about complex storytelling when you create a MOTION 3D animation; the viewer of a computer animation is primarily attracted by two things: the animation itself, and the quality of the graphics. In terms of storytelling in this chapter's example, chili beans and peppers leaping out of a bowl and off stage, and an animated logo are more than sufficient to preoccupy 4 seconds worth of time.

Now that the script has been approved here, it's time to move from script call to making a star.

Creating CorelDRAW! Profiles for MOTION Cast Members

MOTION's Workshop is a separate interface within MOTION 3D which features an Editor's toolbox—a set of vector editing and drawing tools. Although these tools are great for slightly modifying existing shapes, you find them to be limited when you need the control, and precision of CorelDRAW tools. Fortunately, Corel Corp. saw the need for cross-application compatibility, and you can import a path for use as the basis for a 3D object as easily as clicking and dragging a file into MOTION 3D's Workshop window.

Unlike DEPTH, MOTION 3D offers two different ways to create a 3D object from a 2D path: extrusion and lathing. If you worked with the examples in Chapter 9 (which covered CorelDREAM), you might be familiar with the geometric functions of extruding and lathing. Between these two methods of adding a third dimension from

Beyond CorelDRAW!

information about the existing 2D path characteristics, you'd be hard-pressed to conceive of an object that can't be fairly accurately represented in MOTION's stage (called *World Space*).

In figure 10.21, you can see the contents of the CorelDRAW file CACTUS.CDR. Believe it or not, when you dimensionalize these paths in MOTION 3D, they will become the key players in the Cactus Todd animated "short."

Figure 10.21

The paths that can be dimensionalized using MOTION 3D's features are typically easier to create in DRAW than in MOTION's Workshop.

Before continuing, there was some careful planning put into the objects you saw in the previous figure. If you plan to create an animation *similar* to Cactus Todd's mini-movie, the following considerations must be made before launching MOTION 3D:

✔ **What is the size of your finished movie frame?** Your finished "imaging surface" for a MOTION 3D animation will most likely be a computer monitor, unless you've invested heavily in expensive video-to-tape output equipment. About a third of the monitor screen, maximum, will allow folks who don't have a lot of system RAM on their machines to play a 5 second animation without screen jitters or system slowdowns. We've constructed this example animation to 350 pixels wide by 260 pixels in height. This is a fractional proportion of a monitor's dimensions, about 1.3:1. It's also the size of most of MOTION 3D's backdrop images; imitation, flattery aside, also helps one conform to a new program's preferences when creating custom work!

This size should encourage you to design actors for your flick in CorelDRAW of similar size. You'll notice in figure 10.21 that the rulers indicate that the maximum width of the group of paths is about 3.5." If you design to this scale, you won't waste time in MOTION resizing your players.

✔ **How should a CorelDRAW path be constructed for use in MOTION 3D?** As mentioned earlier, there are two ways to make a 2D path into a 3D object in MOTION: through extrusion, the addition of a solid surface "behind" a path in the shape of the path, and through lathing, which is a tad more complicated to explain. In figure 10.22, you can see the path that was labeled "Bowl" in figure 10.21, swept along its left side in a 360° angle. Imagine a lump of clay on a turning wheel being sculpted. In MOTION 3D, you can "turn" a path around an axis to achieve similar results. Unlike CorelDRAW, however, MOTION 3D uses open paths, not closed ones, to lath an object.

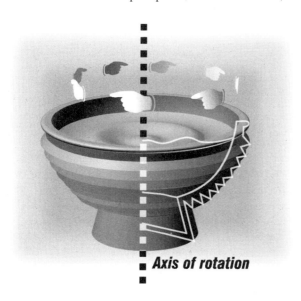

Axis of rotation

Figure 10.22
Through extrusion, lathing, and the grouping of 3D objects, you can sculpt hundreds of different real life objects.

You need to use DRAW's Combine (Ctrl+L) option on subpaths in shapes that are to be extruded (a combined path doesn't produce anything recognizable in MOTION 3D). The pepper in this example, will display holes in areas because the design consists of a path—the outside of the pepper shape—and negative space—the subpaths.

✔ **What about the backgrounds?** Backdrops can be added to an animation scene by importing a bitmap image into MOTION 3D. Backgrounds are more important than they might seem in animations, because like an actual movie stage and CorelDRAW illustrations, there must be something in the background to play against the foreground elements.

Beyond CorelDRAW!

MOTION 3D ships with four excellently designed backdrops, and you'll see how to load them in this chapter. However, only four backdrops might not suit every user's need. We've created a custom backdrop you can load for the Cactus Todd's assignment, and to create your own, you only need to create, scan, or crop a PhotoCD image to the pixel measurement of the Scene Setup you define (so the background is full frame), and use a bitmap resolution of 72 pixels per inch for the backdrop image.

Aside from these considerations, the correct format of path input to MOTION 3D must be created from the CACTUS.CDR sample image, or from your own designs. Paths should be exported from CorelDRAW *before* launching MOTION 3D, so you don't have two resource-intensive applications open at the same time.

Converting Paths to CMX Format

Corel Corp. has for the past two versions of DRAW supported a file format called CMX. The Corel Presentation Exchange is a vector format that supports only the simplest of vector information. You cannot save Blends, PowerLines, or other CorelDRAW "effects" objects in the CMX format with live links between control objects. Because of this limitation, users have been puzzled over what a CMX format is good for.

With the release of MOTION 3D, CorelDRAW users can finally put the CMX format to excellent use. CorelMOTION 3D does not currently support the direct import of CDR files; it is uncertain whether updates to version 6, or later versions will address this. However, importing a CorelDRAWn path to MOTION 3D for lathing or extruding is an easy matter if you export the potential players in an animation as CMX files, with a single path in a file.

In preparation for your trip to Virtual Hollywood, here's an example of how to send ahead the paths needed to create Cactus Todd's stars:

Exporting CMX Files to Win95's Desktop

1. In CorelDRAW, open the CACTUS.CDR file from the EXAMPLES.CHAP10 folder on the *CorelDRAW! 6 Expert's Edition Bonus CD*.

   This file contains all the makings for your cast members in MOTION 3D.

2. Click on the bowl path, then click on the Export button on the toolbar.

   Displays the Export dialog box.

3. Choose Corel Presentation Exchange 6.0 (CMX) from the Save as type drop-down list, type BOWL.CMX in the File name field, and click on the Selected

<u>o</u>nly check box. In the folders window, find your Win95 folder, double-click on it, double-click on the Desktop folder, then click on E<u>x</u>port.

Exports the bowl path to your Desktop as a CMX document. The Desktop is both a screen element and a physical location on your hard disk in Win95. A file icon is now on your Desktop for the bowl export.

4. Repeat steps 2 and 3 with the other objects in CACTUS.CDR; give them appropriate file names, and save them in the CMX format.

Adds to your Desktop collection of future MOTION 3D objects.

5. Close CorelDRAW without saving the CACTUS.CDR file.

Concludes the path export process.

The Desktop might seem like a strange location for exported files, but you'll see in the following section how easy this location makes it to drag and drop the paths into MOTION 3D.

The Casting Call on MOTION 3D's Stage

Except for a virtual doughnut wagon, all the elements for creating a MOTION 3D picture are now waiting outside the application's stage. It's time to assemble the cast, and position them before blocking positions and shouting, "Take 1!"

In the following set of steps, you'll define the scene setting, add the custom backdrop on the Bonus CD, and create the first 3D player, the logo for Cactus Todd's restaurant.

Although Type 1 and TrueType font formats are supported in MOTION 3D through the use of the 3D Text tool, you aren't going to use text in this example. Why not? Because the logo object in the CACTUS.CDR isn't composed of font information; it's a graphical object based upon a *modified* version of Letterset's La Bamba font, edited to produce bolder stems by converting the text to curves and editing the curves with the Shape tool.

Quite frequently, company logos don't belong to a specific typeface family. But the Cactus Todd logo *looks* like a typeface, and it's legible—as a MOTION object, it doesn't matter whether text is text or a graphic.

Here's how to begin Cactus Todd's animation:

Adding Objects to a MOTION 3D Scene

1. Before launching MOTION 3D, copy the TODDBACK.BMP file from the EXAMPLES.CHAP10 folder on the *CorelDRAW! 6 Expert's Edition Bonus CD* to the MOTION3D.BACKDROP folder nested within your Corel 6 folder on your hard disk.

    This is the backdrop image for the Cactus Todd's assignment. By default, MOTION 3D searches the BACKDROP folder for images when you choose the Backdrop option while setting up a scene.

Also, if you didn't copy the CMX files to your Desktop in the previous example, drag and drop copies found in the CHAP10 folder of the Bonus CD to your Desktop now—open a drive window for the Bonus CD, then click-and-drag the files to copy them to the Desktop.

2. Launch MOTION 3D from Windows Start menu.

    Starts the application. Upon starting, MOTION 3D presents a new scene. The objects such as the light, objects you add to the *scene*, and the space of the scene itself are part of the *World*—the *extent* of the scene space.

This might not be the easiest concept to accept, but objects in MOTION's World can be within camera view, or not. Because an object is not seen by a camera view, does not mean that the object ceases to exist, because although out of view, it still exists within the World space.

3. Choose **S**pecial, **E**nvironments (or press Alt+F10), then click on the Backdrop tab in the Environment Properties dialog box.

    Displays a File names list of the backdrops currently in MOTION 3D's BACK-DROP folder on your hard disk.

4. Click on TODDBACK, then click on **O**K.

    Loads the custom background you copied from the Bonus CD into the Camera view window in MOTION 3D. The white outline in the Camera window is the extent of the camera range. This camera range doesn't affect the view of the Backdrop if you zoom the camera in or out of the scene (zooming only works with objects). Chances are the outline isn't perfectly aligned with the backdrop image's borders, so let's correct this now.

5. Choose File, S**c**ene Setup.

    Displays a tabbed menu of options for Rendering, Animation properties, and type of file you want to Save after creating an animation, or simply a still frame.

6. Choose Shade Fast from the Shading **M**ode drop-down list. Click-and-drag the Ray Tracing field's Depth slider toward Low (4 is a good value), uncheck the **T**ransparency check box, uncheck the Constrain **p**roportions check box in the Window size field, type **350** in the **W**idth spin box and 263 in the **H**eight spin box. Choose True color (24-bit) in the Number of colors drop-down list, then click on **O**K.

Specifies that the ray tracing feature shall not perform an incredible number of calculations to create shadows and reflections (you don't need this feature while setting up a scene), that MOTION 3D won't spend time calculating transparency information for objects (there won't be any transparent objects in this animation), and that the Window size (of the Camera window) should match the dimensions of the bitmap background you loaded. See figure 10.23.

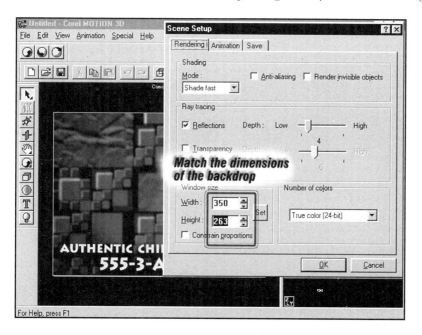

Figure 10.23
Rendering Properties apply to both the preview and the final rendering. Keep requirements modest until your final render.

7. Click on the Extrude Object tool on the toolbox, then click in the Camera window.

Creates a cube, with a default color of lilac.

The cube is not part of the Cactus Todd animation, but an object is required to be in the scene in order to access the Workshop mode in MOTION, where you'll replace the cube's wireframe structure with one of the paths you exported from CorelDRAW. You have to "prime" the Workshop with an object before importing paths. Also, the 4 views

Beyond CorelDRAW!

of the World space can be resized; click-and-drag on a divider if you can't see the whole Camera view. See figure 10.24.

Figure 10.24

Before you can import or edit anything in MOTION 3D, an object has to exist within the scene.

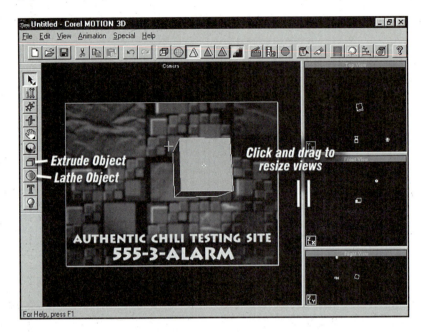

8. Click on the Restore/Maximize button (the middle of the three upper right buttons on the menu bar) in MOTION 3D, then resize MOTION 3D's window until you have a view of your Windows Desktop and the Camera view in MO-TION 3D.

    Allows you to view both the CMX icons on your Desktop, and the Camera window in MOTION 3D.

9. Double-click on the cube in the Camera window. You can use the Vertical Move (the Pick) tool, or the Extrude tool cursor for double-clicking in this step.

    Changes modes in MOTION 3D; you are now in the Workshop, and the cube is a wireframe in the editing window.

10. With the wireframe cube selected, press Delete.

    Deletes the cube wireframe from the editing window.

11. Click-and-drag the TODDLOGO.CMX file from the Desktop to the editing window.

Copies the contents of TODDLOGO.CMX file—the text converted to curves you saw in figure 10.21—to the editing window. See figure 10.25.

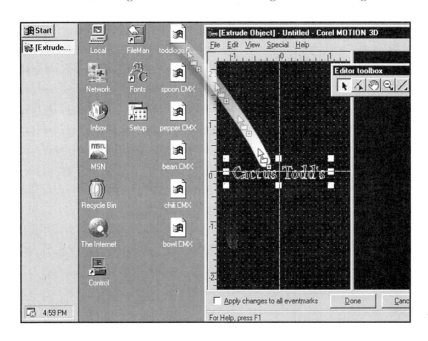

Figure 10.25

A file that contains a path in the CMX format can be copied directly to the editing window of MOTION 3D's Workshop mode.

12. With the Pick tool on the Editor Toolbox (in the Workshop window), center the logo across the vertical and horizontal crosshairs in the edit window. Click on **D**one in the Workspace window, then click on the Restore/Maximize button on MOTION 3D's title bar.

    Defines the relative center of the object; returns you to the Camera and other views of the scene; displays a 3D, extruded version of the Cactus Todd's logo in the Camera view; restores MOTION's window to full size. See NOTE that follows.

13. Click on the Save button on the toolbar, then save the scene to your hard disk as CACTODDS.M3D.

    Saves your work up to this point.

Note Dragging a CMX file from the Desktop to the Workshop's editing window is not the only way to make a MOTION 3D object from a CorelDRAWn path. While in the Workshop mode, you can also choose **E**dit, Insert **N**ew Object from the menu. However, this method requires that you go through at least four dialog boxes to define the type of object, and find it in the folder, then open the file's contents into the editing window.

III

Beyond CorelDRAW!

As you proceed in this section, it will become clear why you need to center 2D paths in the editing window of the Workshop. A path's position on the editing window grid determines both the shape of the 3D object, and the center around which you can rotate the object in scene space later.

Before proceeding to edit the 3D logo object, it's worth noting here that adding text to the backdrop of a MOTION scene is a great way to embellish the final animation without requiring the addition of text as a 3D object in the scene. Todd's fictitious telephone number will remain on-screen for the duration of the animation, and you don't have to worry about it accidentally moving when you create the animation. Objects can't go *behind* the text on the backdrop, but objects appear to bump into it, and can certainly move in front of the backdrop text area.

Editing a MOTION 3D Object

You should now have an extruded logo in the Camera window. It's going to look terrific in the final animation, but at present, it's pointed upward toward the camera (you can't read the lettering), and it's most likely extruded way too deeply, because MOTION assigns a default extrusion depth to all 2D paths.

Here's how to edit extruded objects in MOTION 3D:

Applying Object Transformations

1. With the Vertical (Pick) tool, right-click on the logo, then choose Transform from the shortcut menu.

   Displays the Transform menu for the extruded shape. The Scale tabbed menu is displayed, by default.

2. Type 10 in the **Z** % spin box, click on **A**pply, then click on **O**K.

   Decreases the Z distance—the depth—from front to back on the logo object;
   , returns you to the Camera view window. See figure 10.26.

In modeling and animation programs, 3D space is usually measured using separate coordinates for both objects, and the space in which they exist. X is typically width, measured from screen left to right, Y is the height (measured from bottom to top), and Z represents depth for an object, measured from front to back.

3. Click on the Vertical Rotate tool (beneath the Pan tool on the toolbox), then click-and-drag the logo object in an downward direction until it's more or less facing the camera view.

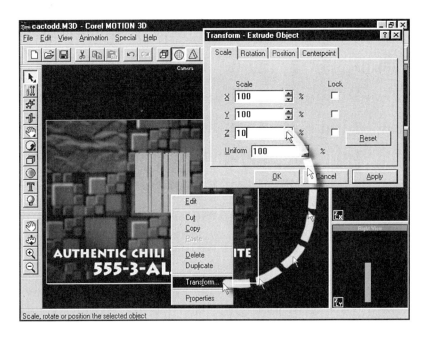

Figure 10.26
You can adjust any of the three dimensions of a MOTION object by specifying different Scale percentages.

Rotates the object along its vertical (X) axis; makes the logo face the front camera view. See figure 10.27. In this example, we've made the logo tilt backwards ever-so slightly to reveal some of the bottom of the 3D object. You might want to do this, too.

4. Press Ctrl+S (**F**ile, **S**ave).

Saves your work up to this point.

Understanding Modes of Previews

As the scene becomes more densely populated with other 3D objects, you might want to switch to Wireframe view in MOTION 3D to work more quickly. MOTION's interruptable preview takes longer to interrupt when there's more to redraw in the scene. On the toolbar, you can see a group of geometric-shaped icons; the group of icons begins above the title "Camera" (on the Camera view window) in the previous figure—10.27. From left to right, these are:

✔ **Bounding box view.** A box is drawn instead of an object on-screen which represents the dimensional extremes of an object.

✔ **Wireframe.** Provides an outline view without surface shading on objects.

Beyond CorelDRAW!

Figure 10.27
Turn the object
around its X axis
with the Vertical
Rotate tool.

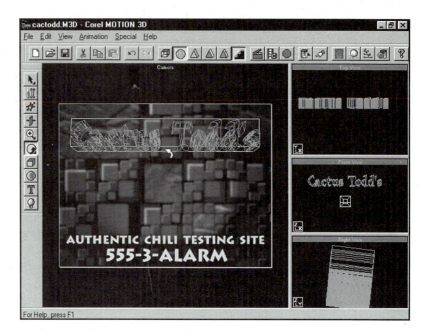

✔ **Shade Faster.** Displays a rough idea of what the object will look like in finished format. No reflections can be seen on the objects, and shadows are primitively rendered. In this mode, it's easiest to select objects you want to move or edit.

✔ **Shade Better.** This is most likely the mode in which you'll want to render a finished animation. However, it is a poor choice of modes in which to work, because screen updates take a lonnnnnng time, even on Pentium 133s.

✔ **Ray Tracing.** This mode should not be used except on occasions when you want to render a still image—not an animation—to file format. Ray Tracing calculates, pixel by pixel, where light sources in the scene reflect, are hidden by, and travel through objects. Ray Tracing is phenomenally accurate and provides the most photorealistic results, but your preview will take sometimes half an hour to update with this mode chosen.

✔ **Anti-aliasing.** Not actually a preview mode. That stairstep icon on the end of the preview mode group on the toolbar provides smoothing between the backdrop and the foreground objects. You can specify anti-aliasing for Shade Faster, Shade Better, and Ray-trace previews, and finished rendered animations and stills.

With any of the modes chosen, you have the option to switch modes on-the-fly. If for example, you've accidentally pressed the Ray-trace button, you can click on the

Wireframe button to prevent the interruptable preview from rendering for minutes on end, thus stopping your work.

Editing Surface Properties

As with most 3D computer graphics, there are two basic properties of an object which constitute what you see on-screen: the shape of the object and its content—the material of which the shape is made.

In MOTION 3D, all new objects are assigned a Plastic Lilac surface. Cactus Todd might prefer a shiny, metallic gold look for his logo, however, so the following steps show how to work with MOTION's Surfaces Roll-Up. Additionally, like CorelDEPTH, you can choose a bevel size for the edge where the extruded object's sides meet the front and back faces. Unlike DEPTH, however, a solid material must be assigned to front, back, side, and bevel faces—you can specify any of a number of different bevel shapes, but the bevel side cannot have a unique color.

Here's how to make the Plastic Cactus Todd's logo look like a proud, chiseled gold ornament:

Assigning Surface and Object Properties

1. Right-click over the 3D logo object, then choose Properties from the shortcut menu.

   Displays the Object Properties tabbed menu.

2. Click on the Bevel tab, choose Straight from the **T**ype drop-down list, click on the Apply bevel on back also check box, then click-and-drag in the preview window until there's a small, 45° side joining the front and side faces in the preview window (the preview window "view" of the selected object is from the top). See figure 10.28.

   Creates a sharp bevel face on every character in the logo object.

3. Click on **O**K, then click on the Surfaces Roll-Up button on the toolbar (to the left of the Help contents button, the question mark) if the Roll-Up isn't already on-screen.

   Applies the changes to the edges of the logo; you're returned to the Camera view window and the Surfaces Roll-Up is displayed.

4. Scroll through the Surfaces Roll-Up, click on Gold, then click on **A**pply.

   Applies a Gold surface (*texture*) to the selected logo object. See figure 10.29.

Figure 10.28
You can add character to a simple extruded object by specifying different types of bevel sides.

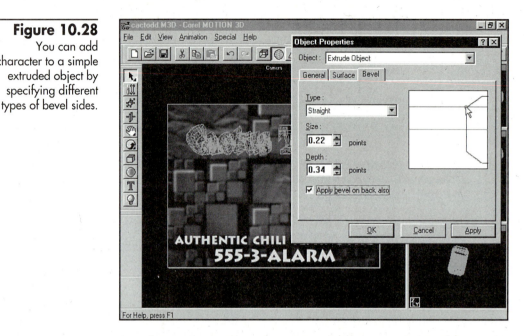

Figure 10.29
You can apply a MOTION 3D preset surface to an object, or create your own, unique surface.

5. Press Ctrl+S (**F**ile, **S**ave).

    Saves your work up to this point.

If you click on Shade Better now, you'll get a better feel for how the logo will look in the finished animation. It should be pointed out here that the metallic preset surfaces don't appear very different than the plastic surfaces when applied to objects, and viewed in a mode other than Ray-trace.

Unfortunately, metal gets a lot of its character from what it reflects, and this requires MOTION 3D to perform calculations to account for what parts of the scene are reflected into every facet of a 3D object. If you turn to the color plate section of this book, you'll see a ray-traced still image of the completed Cactus Todd's scene. This rendering, although it's only 640×480 pixels, at 72 pixels per inch resolution (producing a 1.18 MB file), took over 6 hours to render on a 486 DX2 with 32 MB of RAM. You shouldn't hope to have accurate reflections in a finished animation—which can consist of scores of individual frames—but MOTION 3D, through animating the shading and highlights of an object moving through space, produces a fascinating metallic look for objects without the Ray-trace option.

Adding and Positioning the Other Cast Members

The pepper 2D path, the spoon, and the chili bean path can all be brought into the Workshop editing window using the same techniques described for dragging the logo file off the Desktop and into the editing window. You should do this now before reading the following set of steps.

Put the spoon, pepper, and chili bean CMX files you created in CorelDRAW earlier on Win95's Desktop (or use the CMX files provided in the EXAMPLES.CHAP10 folder of the Bonus CD). After creating a "primer" 3D extruded cube, go to the Workshop window, delete the cube, drag the CMX file into the Workshop window, then click on **D**one to return to the workspace and Camera view window. Use the methods as described with the Cactus Todd logo to change the depth of each of these shapes, then apply a surface of your choice to them. Keep these three objects to the right of the Camera view (click-and-drag them to the right of the scene with the Vertical move tool); we'll show you shortly where their final positions will be in the scene.

The chili bowl and the chili will be dimensionalized through lathing, not extrusion. They must be placed with their axis of rotation (refer to figure 10.22) meeting the vertical crosshair in the editing window in order to be swept along their axis correctly.

Here's how to import, dimensionalize, and position the bowl and the chili for the animation:

Creating and Positioning Cactus Todd's Chili

1. With the Lathe object tool selected from the toolbox, click in the Camera view window, then click on the Vertical move tool.

   Adds a sphere to the scene; switches tools to the Vertical move tool.

2. Double-click on the sphere, then click on the Restore/Maximize button on the title bar after you're in the Workshop mode.

   Opens the Workshop mode window; allows you to see Win95's Desktop.

3. Press Delete, then click-and-drag the BOWL.CMX file you placed in the Desktop folder earlier, into the editing window.

   Deletes the sphere path; copies the chili bowl path to the editing window.

4. With the Editing Toolbox's Pick tool, click-and-drag the bowl path until it's positioned as shown in figure 10.30.

   Aligns the bowl path's left edge with the axis of lathing. The bowl will not be a moving object in the finished animation; if it were, you'd want to position the path so that the horizontal crosshair in the editing window bisects the bowl path. Doing this would make the center of rotation for the resulting 3D object become the center across all dimensions.

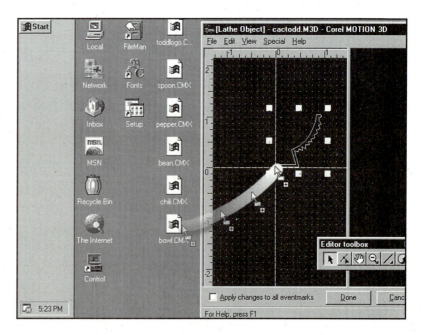

Figure 10.30
The crosshairs in the editing window determine the 3D spatial center of an object.

5. Click on the **D**one button. Do *not* resize the 3D bowl object yet. It shouldn't be too large for the composition, but if it is, you'll address this later.

   Returns you to the Camera view window; a 3D bowl is now in the scene.

6. Perform steps 1-5 with the CHILI.CMX file on the Desktop.

   Adds 3D chili to the scene. Because "replacement" objects for the cube, or sphere, have their spatial origins in identical places to where you've created the original cube or sphere in the Camera view window, chances are that the chili object and the bowl objects are in proportion, but aren't aligned. We fix this now...

7. Click on the Wireframe button on the toolbar.

   Allows you to move quickly through the view windows, because there's less for MOTION 3D to update on-screen.

8. Click-and-drag the window divider so that the Top View window takes up most of the workspace, then click on the title bar of the Top View window.

   Makes the top view window larger; makes Top View the current editing window.

9. With the Vertical move (Pick) tool, click-and-drag the chili object wireframe so it aligns inside the bowl object.

   Aligns two of the three dimensions of the bowl and chili. See figure 10.31.

➤**Tip**   You might want to zoom in or pan the Top view window to better see your editing work. Unlike other Corel applications, MOTION 3D's Zoom tool doesn't have a marquee mode. Instead of click-and-dragging in a window to zoom in, you click and hold the left mouse button to "power zoom." The same technique holds true for the Zoom out tool (in the View flyout menu); the Pan tool works like any other application's Hand tool.

You can also see in figure 10.31, that the View toolbox has been docked beneath the default toolbox, to more easily access all the view tools. To add the toolbox to the left of the workspace, right-click on the default toolbox to display the shortcut menu, then choose the View toolbox from the menu, and click-and-drag it into a docked position.

10. Click-and-drag the window dividers so that you can see the Right View window as the main view, then click on the title bar of the Right View window.

    Makes the right view the predominant view in MOTION 3D.

11. Click-and-drag the chili object so that it's centered within the bowl object (if necessary).

Beyond CorelDRAW!

Figure 10.31
Each window in
MOTION 3D only
provides two-
dimensional access.
Therefore, use more
than one view to
align 3D objects.

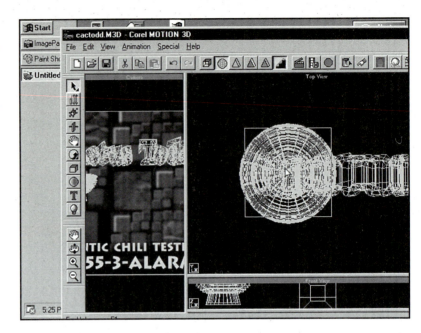

You've aligned the chili to the bowl in all three dimensions of MOTION's scene space.

12. Resize the View windows until the Camera View is once again the main view.

Restores the view in which you'll continue editing.

13. Press Ctrl+S (**F**ile, **S**ave).

Saves your work up to this point.

Working in 3D space is not the easiest of tasks, but think about how astronauts feel...

Creating a Surface for the Chili Object

In the next steps, you'll learn how to define and apply a unique surface to the chili, and in doing so, you can practice a little independent study and define surfaces for all of the object presently in the Cactus Todd's scene.

Unlike DREAM 3D or DEPTH, surfaces are limited to non-textured properties in MOTION 3D. It would require the calculation power of an SGI or SUN workstation to "move" a texture in relation to other objects around in 3D space, but you still have a lot of control over the shininess, color, and other attributes of the objects you make in MOTION 3D.

Here's how to make a chili surface worthy of Cactus Todd's famous eatery:

Creating and Applying Surfaces

1. Click on any of the Surface preview icons on the Surfaces Roll-Up, then click on **E**dit.

   Displays the Edit Surfaces dialog box.

2. Click on **D**uplicate, then type Chili in the **N**ame field.

   Creates a duplicate object you can now edit without fear of messing up the default Surfaces Roll-Up.

3. Choose a brownish color from the Co**l**or drop-down list.

   Makes the Chili surface brown; the preview sphere turns brown.

4. Click-and-drag the specular highlight slider to about 70%, then click-and-drag the remaining sliders to the positions shown in figure 10.32.

   Creates surface characteristics similar to those found in Cactus Todd's chili. Although you'll frequently want to define a texture for a flying logo that's shiny and metallic, other objects, such as the chili and bowl should be non-metallic and not very shiny.

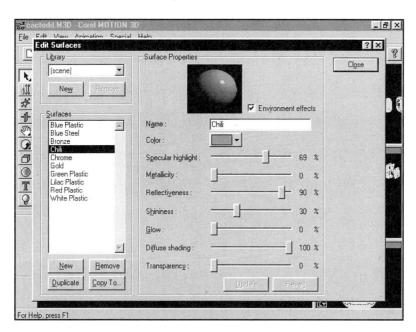

Figure 10.32

Create a surface for an object that has appropriate characteristics. Chili might have liquid highlights, but shouldn't be metallic.

III

Beyond CorelDRAW!

5. Click on **U**pdate, then click on Cl**o**se.

   Adds the Chili surface to the default collection of surfaces. The Surface Roll-Up will only display custom surfaces for a current project; you cannot access the Chili surface from a new scene window.

Because there are now several objects in close proximity in the Cactus Todd scene, it might be hard to select the chili to then apply the new surface. This is why you should label every object in a scene (for quick reference), and why you'll perform the following steps...

6. Click on the Timelines button on the toolbar (to the left of the Surfaces Roll-Up button).

   Displays the Timelines panel. It is here you can select objects in a scene by name, and it's also how you create an animation.

 To name an object through the Timelines panel, right click on the default name of an object, choose P**r**operties from the shortcut menu, then type a name in the **N**ame field.

7. Click on the chili object's name on the Timelines panel. Its default name should be Lathe Object 1 (the chili bowl is Lathe Object, with no appended number).

   Selects the chili object in the scene; the object is now highlighted in the current window view.

8. Click on the Chili surface preview icon on the Surfaces Roll-Up.

   Applies the Chili surface to the chili object. Is it getting chili in here? See figure 10.33.

9. Press Ctrl+S (**F**ile, **S**ave).

   Saves your work up to this point.

How to Block Action in MOTION 3D: The Timelines Panel

The "gang" is all present and accounted for, and they should have appropriate surfaces before we continue with the animation phase of your MOTION 3D work.

In figure 10.34, you can see a view of a well-organized workspace for an animation project. All the objects are in their "first pose," the initial frame of the animation you'll create. You can't see the pepper and the bean in the Camera window, because they're hidden in the chili, and will prance across the screen for the 4 second duration of the animation.

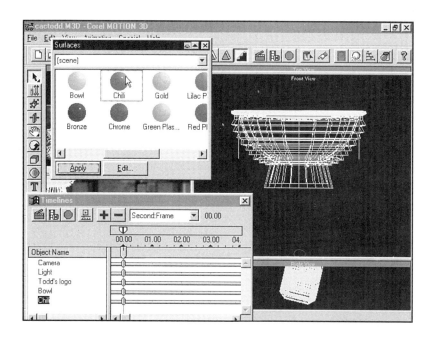

Figure 10.33
If you need to select an object that's obscured by another object, select the object using the Timelines panel.

Figure 10.34
Allow yourself a large view of the main Camera window, but create close-ups in the other view windows, so you can move objects in 3D space as you animate.

Beyond CorelDRAW!

A tidy workspace in MOTION 3D is essential, because you'll need to work between the Timelines panel and the Camera View window, back and forth, to reposition your actors across time.

The process of animation is handled by MOTION 3D; however, you have to define key frames with which MOTION can 'tween (create in-b*etween*) the rest of the animation frames. A *key frame* is a definitive moment in time, where actors (or props) are positioned differently than in the previous key frame. An example of this is an animation of a door closing; the first key frame is a still picture of an open door, and the next key frame is a picture of the door closed. In such an animation, MOTION 3D calculates the number of in-between frames based on the total number of frames you've defined for the movie, then automatically renders the correct number of stills to complete the animation.

It's important that you don't create too many key frames (such as more than 4 per second of final animation), or your animation might run too long, the resulting file size for the animation will be huge, and the animation will run quite slowly.

In figure 10.35, you'll see some callouts for the controls on the Timelines panel you'll use the most the first month or so you experiment with MOTION 3D on your own. We have a detailed explanation of what each feature is for following this figure, and the example to follow shows how to use the Timelines controls to put Cactus Todd's presentation into action.

Figure 10.35
The animation controls on CorelMOTION 3D's Timelines panel.

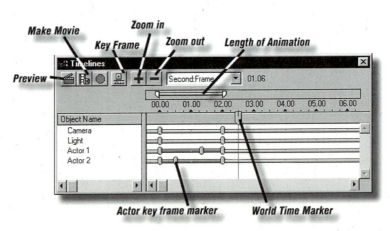

In clockwise order in figure 10.35, beginning with the Preview button—

✔ The Preview button plays back the animation sequence, in bounding box view only, from your current view window. Preview is an essential feature that enables you to see how smoothly your transitions are going, and whether an object bumps into (or bumps through another) object.

✔ The Make Movie button commences the rendering process, and this should be the last button you click in MOTION 3D. But prior to making the movie, you need to define compression options, file format, and number of frames per second. This is explained in the section following these Timelines panel functions.

✔ The Key Frame button creates an event across the Timelines marker area, and advances the movie by the amount you specify in the Scene Setup dialog box, in the Animation menu's frame rate spin box. The Key Frame button should only be clicked after you've moved your actors, camera, and/or lights to their next pose within the "plot" of your movie.

✔ The Zoom in and Zoom out buttons have nothing to do with views of the scene, but instead offer an increased or decreased view of the timeline markers. Suppose you want an event to happen precisely 3 frames after key frame. At 1:1 viewing resolution, the timeline markers are far too large to make this adjustment. In this case, click on the Zoom in button to expand your view of the timelines, position the key frame, then Zoom back out to see the entire timeline.

✔ The length of an animation is up to you (and your system resources), but the animation length marker, the slider that appears to have calipers at each end, tells you how much of the animation will be rendered. By default, all of your animation is rendered to file, but if you want to only render a "slice of time," click-and-drag the animation length markers to the left or right to bracket the part of the MOTION 3D movie you want to render.

✔ The World Time Marker moves your view in the active MOTION 3D window through the entire movie. You can view the position of objects at, say, 2 seconds into the movie, or at any other time in the timeline.

✔ Actor Key Frame marker—whether it's a 3D object, a light, or a 3D object, everything in MOTION's World space has at least one marker along the timeline of the animation. You'll notice in figure 10.35 that the camera and light have a marker at the beginning and end of the timeline, but no intermediate markers, as Actor 1 and Actor 2 do. This means that as the Key Frame button was clicked, these objects weren't moved. Additionally, you can tell when there is no motion for an actor or prop between keyframes when the marker intervals which the marker lies on top of is a default color; the marker intervals turn a deep shade when there is actor motion (an *event*) between markers.

You can speed up the action between frames by moving key frame makers for actors or props closer together, or further apart. To move more than one key frame marker, hold Shift while you select additional markers (see fig. 10.36).

Beyond CorelDRAW!

Figure 10.36
You can speed up the action between frames by moving key frame makers.

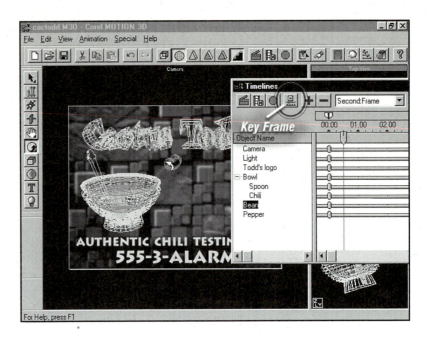

By getting the nitty, gritty details taken care of now, your director's role will be a fun and productive one. It's on to Lights, Camera, You-Know what now!

Keeping Track of Individual Motions

There are one or two ways to animate a scene. This first is to move objects to their coarse key positions between key frames, then go back to the key frames by dragging the World Time Marker back to each key frame, then refining the pose of each object.

The second method is to invest some time that you're sure will be uninterrupted, and place objects in the exact positions you want them every time you click the Key Frame button.

Let's take the second of these alternatives in the following set of steps as we walk through the animation of the Cactus Todd's movie. CACTORS.M3D is located in the CHAP10 folder on the Bonus CD, and this MOTION 3D file contains the actors if you haven't created the scene, and would like to work with it in the following steps.

Animating Your MOTION 3D Scene

1. Select the bean from the chili bowl with the Vertical (Pick tool), then drag it away from the bowl, up toward the spacing between "Cactus" and "Todd's."

Moves the bean in space, but not across time yet. If you have a problem clicking on the bean object, click on its name on the Timelines panel; this selects the object.

2. Click on the Vertical rotate tool, then click-and-drag on the bean in an upward direction.

   Rotates the bean in an upward direction.

3. Click-and-drag on the Cactus Todd's logo in an upward direction with the Vertical Rotate tool.

   Rotates the logo in an upward direction. In Shade Faster view, you can click on an object with any of the Rotate tools to select it; in Wireframe mode, you need to use the Vertical (Pick) tool.

4. Click on the Key Frame button on the Timelines panel.

   Advances the movie by the default value of 1/2 second (or 18 frames, also a default value you'll see how to change in this chapter).

5. With the Vertical move (Pick) tool, click-and-drag the chili bean further to the right, and down, then choose the Vertical Rotate tool, and rotate the bean about a quarter turn.

   You're making the bean jump up and down, and spin through time.

6. Click-and-drag on the pepper hidden in the bowl with the Vertical move (Pick) tool, and position it where the bean used to be.

   You're creating a cascading animation effect; in the final movie, the bean and pepper will merrily alternate positions as they jump from the chili bowl.

7. With the Vertical Rotate tool, click-and-drag on the Cactus Todd's logo in a downward direction.

   You're specifying that the logo will rock up and down as the chili ingredients escape from the bowl.

8. Click on the Key Frame button on the Timelines panel.

   Advances the animation by 1/2 second. See figure 10.37.

9. Click-and-drag the bean out of the camera window with the Vertical move (Pick) tool, switch views to the top view, then drag the bean completely out of frame.

Figure 10.37

Keep some objects in constant motion, and leave others static; the visual contrast helps make the scene easier for the viewer to follow.

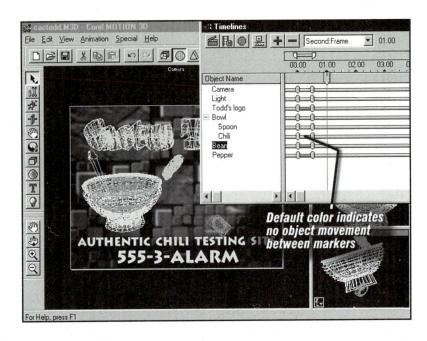

The bean exists the frame. You need to move an object completely out of the frame in order for MOTION 3D's rendering engine to eliminate it from the final render. Otherwise, a corner of an object will remain in the rest of the movie.

10. Click-and-drag the pepper to the bean's former position, then with the Vertical Rotate tool, click-and-drag the Cactus Todd's logo in an upward direction.

   Continues to animate the scene.

11. Click on the Key Frame button on the Timelines panel.

   Adds another key frame to the animation.

12. Press Ctrl+S (**F**ile, **S**ave).

   Saves your work up to this point.

The preceding were the basic steps for creating an animation. The author got a little ambitious with the project, and if you'd like to examine some of the embellishments, open the CACTODDS.M3D file from the CHAP10 folder of the Bonus CD. The bean object and the pepper object were copied to create a richer animation (and a richer chili). You can copy actors (by pressing Ctrl+C, then Ctrl+V), but timeline actions are copied along with the actors. To remove the key frames, click on a marker, then right-click and choose **D**elete from the shortcut menu. Do not, however, delete the first key frame marker for anything; with no key frame markers, a prop or actor doesn't exist, and you delete the object from the file.

To add key frames for a single actor, choose Duplicate from the shortcut menu when you're positioned over the first marker, then click-and-drag the marker to the next key frame point for the other objects. Then move the World Time Marker to this point, position the object the way you want, and repeat these steps for the rest of the movie run time.

To create a looping file—one that begins and ends at the same point, you'll want to duplicate the beginning key frame markers for all moving objects in the scene, then drag them to the end position of the movie on the Timelines panel (delete the markers that exist at the end before positioning the duplicate markers).

Before you shout, "Cut! It's a Take! Print it!," Cactus Todd Productions here needs some film in the camera. Check out the following section before clicking on Make Movie.

Specifying Virtual Film Options

Let's take a trip back to the Scene Setup dialog box now, and define the type of file you'll want to render, the format, and other options. Pre-planning is key to creating a 2 to 3 hour rendering session. If a CorelDRAW file gets corrupted, you've lost a file; but if a MOTION 3D render fails along the process, or you've specified the wrong settings, you've lost a file, and you've lost time.

Here's how to set up the output for the scene you've choreographed. This is sort of buying film before you photograph something...

Defining Rendering Settings

1. Choose File, Scene Setup.

   The tabbed Scene Setup dialog box appears.

2. Click on the Animation tab, then click on the All frames radio button in the Frames to Render field. If you wanted to render only a single frame to BMP, TIFF, or other bitmap format, you'd click on the From radio button, and pick the frame in the movie you want to render.

   The other options in the Animation dialog box are okay at their defaults, but you can change them if you need a more detailed, smoother (larger) animation.

3. Click on the Save tab of the dialog box, then click on Compression Options.

Lists the options available for making your movie smaller. In general, leave this setting at its default of Microsoft Video 1, 75% compression (or specify this option if it's been changed). Animation compression is a trade-off between how well (how smoothly and fast) an animation plays, and the overall visual quality of the movie. Click on OK to return to the main tabbed dialog box.

4. Click on **O**K to exit the Scene Settings dialog box.

Admittedly, the preceding set of steps were a "discovery" example; they taught you more about where to find final rendering parameters than about animation itself.

If you're ready for a slightly more productive, even briefer set of steps, you're all set to click on the Make Movie Button now!

The Steps to Rendering Your Movie

Procedure is what counts at this point more than anything else. You're basically finished with creating the animation; you've only yet to render the file to an animation format.

CACTODDS.AVI is also in the CHAP10 folder of the Bonus CD, if you'd like to play it. It's the result of the steps described in this chapter.

Here's how to launch the rendering in MOTION 3D:

ACTION!

1. Minimize MOTION 3D's window, and turn off any communications, printing, or screen blinkers that might be running in the background of Win95, then restore MOTION 3D's window.

   This is insurance against a system halt while MOTION 3D renders your movie.

2. Click on the Shade Better button on the toolbar, and click on the anti-aliased button.

   Defines a good quality for the movie. These options are also found in the Rendering tab menu of the Scene Setup dialog box. This is why we didn't cover them in Scene Settings earlier.

3. Click on the Make Movie button on the Timelines panel.

   Displays the Make Movie dialog box.

4. Choose the format of the exported (rendered) movie from the Save as **t**ype drop-down list.

We recommend that you choose Video for Windows (AVI), because you can play the movie seconds after it's finished using Win95's Media Player.

5. Click on **S**ave.

   The rendering Movie window pops up, and if you like, you can see the slow-motion rendering process take place.

6. Come back in about a half hour with friends, popcorn, those candies that stick to your fillings, press Ctrl+S, then Alt+F4.

   Your movie is finished, you save the M3D document one last time, and exit MOTION 3D.

7. In Windows Start menu, choose **P**rograms, Accessories, Multimedia, then click on Media Player.

   Loads the Media Player.

8. Choose File, Open, locate the CACTODDS.AVI file in the folders window, click on it, and choose **O**pen.

   Loads the AVI file.

9. Press Ctrl+O (**E**dit, **O**ptions), then click on the Auto-**R**epeat check box, and click on OK.

   Specifies that the movie will play endlessly until you stop it.

10. Click on the Play button on the Media Player.

    Plays the epic saga of Cactus Todd and his famous 3-Alarm chili.

11. Call Todd and try to renegotiate your contract. All movie moguls do this these days.

This chapter is intended as a springboard for achieving quick, satisfying results with MOTION 3D, but the story isn't over yet. There are more features in MOTION 3D that were not covered in this chapter, but you have the basics down now, and with some practice and independent discovery, you'll find more rewards than you can imagine with the extra added dimensions in a most extraordinary design application.

You'll notice that we didn't use fonts once in this chapter. Although DEPTH and MOTION are advertised as 3D font programs, hopefully you've learned that you can paint, draw, and direct, in addition to manipulating text in the programs featured in this chapter.

Beyond CorelDRAW!

Now that you're a little more experienced with the role of virtual director, what do you say to engaging the services of the largest broadcasting company in the world? "Special Effect and Web pages" is right around the page. Are you listening, URL?

Special Effects for Web Pages

The World Wide Web (WWW) is part of the Internet, and it's one of the most exciting, fastest-growing places for artists, writers, business people, students, and even Uncle Fred to hang out. One of the qualities that has made the Web so appealing to artists is that it is a great place to display artwork. It has also provided a lot of work for artists who *design* Web pages and graphics for businesses and other institutions. If you want to be a part of all this graphical activity, you already have the most important tools—your artist's eye and skill, CorelDRAW, and this chapter along with the tools and materials on the *CorelDRAW! 6 Expert's Edition Bonus CD*. In this chapter, you'll learn how to put all the pieces together to create the special kinds of graphics that Web pages use, and how to place the graphics within Web documents.

HTML Documents—The Foundation of the WWW

The WWW is a network of computer systems. The computers that make up these networks are of every kind: PCs, Macintoshes, Unix workstations, and even mainframes. If you've ever tried to share a document or a page layout with someone who uses a different kind of computer than you have, or who uses different software, you know that the process is not an easy one.

One of the characteristics of the WWW that makes it such a special place is that WWW *HTML documents* are hardware and operating system independent. No matter what kind of computer you use, you can create Web documents that can be accessed and easily used by *anyone*, regardless of the type of computer *they* use.

This amazing feat is possible due to the invention of *HyperText Markup Language* (HTML). An HTML document is a simple ASCII or plain text file whose structure is defined using HTML *tags*. Because the tags are also written in ASCII text, the document contains no binary data, and any computer can read the document.

HTML publishing is unlike desktop publishing in that the tags used to format the document do not describe how the document will look. They do not explicitly specify characteristics such as font choice, point size, or even line spacing or justification. Rather, they describe the elements that compose a document and its *relative structure*, how elements are proportioned and located to *other* elements. It is up to a *Web browser* to read and interpret the tags and then render the document to screen. A Web browser is platform dependent—it is *software* that runs on the visitor's computer.

When a person visits a Web site, it is that person's browser software that determines exactly which fonts are used to display the document, and what the point size of body text and headers are. The browser is also responsible for determining where text wraps on-screen and how much space surrounds each element.

If you've used the styles feature in your word processor or desktop publishing program, the concept of using tags to format an HTML document will seem familiar. The difference between HTML tags and word processor styles is that you specify that a style is to be used in HTML, but you don't actually specify the absolute characteristics that make up the style; it is the Web browser that fills in these details.

Because Web browsers are platform-specific software, every Web browser displays an HTML document differently. On a Windows computer, text is often Times Roman or Arial. On a Macintosh, the default font is *neither* Times Roman nor Arial. Also, most browsers allow the user to choose any size typeface they like as their default font. What *is* constant is the *relationship* between elements. If you tag a section of text as a first-level heading, it will be larger and more prominent than a section tagged with a second-level heading; both headings will be larger than the default paragraph text.

However, Web pages can contain more than mere text. They can hold graphics, sound, movies, and Acrobat documents, as well as links to any other document or resource on the Internet. While these items appear to be *in* the HTML document when the document is viewed on the Web, they are not. Only the path (*address*) to the location in which elements are stored is actually in an HTML document. This is very similar in concept to linking graphics rather than embedding graphics in a DTP application such as CorelVENTURA or PageMaker. Again, it is up to the visitor's browser to be able to load and place other elements in their proper place amongst the text.

As a graphically inclined computer user, the lack of ultimate control over every aspect of how a document looks might be initially hard to accept. However, by understanding the Web and its conventions for HTML documents, you gain platform and operating system independence. And with this independence, the audience for your masterpieces becomes the entire Internet community.

Special Graphics Formats for a Special Place

In the same way that text needs to be formatted according to Web conventions, graphics also must undergo some changes and follow the rules before they are suitable candidates for display on the Web.

Everyone loves large, color-rich graphics, but large graphics files take a long time to receive over the slow modems and connections most people use to access the WWW. Visitors to a Web page can get impatient (and irritated) if graphics take too long to download, or if their Web browser doesn't know how to handle the format that the graphics use. Graphics must be small in file size if they are to transfer and display quickly, and they must be in a file format that all types of computers can read.

As a designer, it is up you to bring your skills and your artist's eye along with your own creativity to make every pixel you use in a Web graphic count. Ensuring that all types of computer users can see your graphic as you intend it is easy if you use the right file format—the GIF file format.

The GIF File Format

The Internet community and the HTML standards committees have embraced the CompuServe GIF file format as the standard for Web graphics. GIF is a compact, indexed (256-color) bitmapped file format that was designed to speed the transfer of online graphics. All kinds of computers can read GIF files.

When the GIF89a subformat is used to save an image bound for a Web page, the image can be saved in an *interlaced* format. Interlaced images begin appearing on-screen as soon as they are accessed by a browser. This is an important feature because when a visitor can see a graphic build on-screen, they perceive that the entire process is going quicker than if they had to wait for the entire image to download before it displayed.

III

Beyond CorelDRAW!

Additionally, if the user decides as the graphic builds that the image is unappealing, he or she can save time and move on without waiting to receive the entire image.

GIF format images also have another advantage when used in a Web document. Because GIF is an indexed file format, one color out of the 256 in the image can be designated as a *transparent color*, a color that the Web browser will ignore and not display. When you can have transparency in a graphic, the background can show through parts of the image, which leads to some exciting design possibilities.

The JPEG File Format

The JPEG file format is the only other graphics file format that is currently supported by Web browsers. Only newer versions of browsers such as the Netscape browser or Mosaic-based browsers are capable of handling JPEG images. The HTML 3 proposed specifications and the widely used Netscape extensions to HTML have only recently allowed a limited use of JPEG images in Web documents.

Although the JPEG file format is very compact and can support many more unique colors than indexed color GIFs, JPEG images cannot *interlace* as they download. JPEG images also do not presently support transparency within the context of a Web page, and JPEG images cannot be used for Web page backgrounds.

One typically sees JPEG format images used in combination with an identical, but smaller, GIF image. Visitors to the Web page see the faster loading, smaller GIF image first, and then have the option to choose to take the time to view a larger, more colorful version of the same image that is in the JPEG format.

Creating HTML Documents

In this chapter you'll learn the steps needed to make stunning graphics for your Web pages and we'll make note of the things you should consider when planning your Web page graphics. Although comprehensive documentation of HTML is beyond the scope of this chapter, we've included a fully annotated HTML template on the *CorelDRAW! 6 Expert's Edition Bonus CD*, along with tools and the information you need to produce a home page, complete with an art gallery.

Learn by Example, and "Steal, Steal, Steal!"

As strange as it might seem, the best way for you to learn how to create an HTML document is to put this book down and experiment with an actual HTML document. It is a long-standing and honored tradition on the World Wide Web to "steal from the best." This does not mean that you should plagiarize a person's ideas or otherwise appropriate the graphics or content someone else has posted, but rather to look at how they've used HTML tags to create a page, or an effect on a page that you like. Learning by observing and applying it to your own pages is the quickest and most effective way to learn Web publishing. It also doesn't hurt to find a good HTML reference book or to take advantage of the many HTML primers that are available on the Internet or in an Internet library on an online service.

We've given you a leg up in this process. In the CHAP11/ANNOTATE folder of the *CorelDRAW! 6 Expert's Edition Bonus CD*, you'll find a set of HTML documents, that, if posted on the Web, would comprise the fully functional home page of Gordon Robinson, our semi-fictitious artist in this chapter's example. Gordon's home pages consist of an opening home page (INDEX.HTM); a mini art gallery (GALLERY.HTM) of his work; the documents that branch from the art gallery; and a section that describes who Gordon is, how to get in touch with him, and how expensive his digital creations are (GPART.HTM).

While attractive, Gordon's pages are not to be taken as the last word on how a set of pages should be constructed. We've used a variety of tags and page treatments to show you how HTML documents can be strung together. But we've done more than give you HTML documents; we've put numerous notes in the documents to explain how and why the tags are used, to clarify the syntax and structure of HTML.

You are encouraged to adapt Gordon's home page to suit your own purposes. If you see a layout that you like on one of Gordon's pages, use a text editor or one of the HTML editors on the *CorelDRAW! 6 Expert's Edition Bonus CD* to delete the Gordon text or graphic reference, then insert your own information in its place. As long as you don't accidentally move or add to the tags themselves, you're home free.

If you find it hard to get a good look at the HTML code that makes up Gordon's home page because of all the notes we've placed in the documents, check out the CHAP11/ WEBPAGE folder. The documents you'll find there have been stripped of annotations and only contain what you'd actually use in a functional Web document.

Tools for Editing

Before you put this book down and start examining Gordon's Gallery, you'll need to equip yourself with a few tools. For viewing and editing, you'll find a text editor and an HTML editor in the SHARWARE folder on the *CorelDRAW! 6 Expert's Edition Bonus CD*. See the "What's on the Bonus CD" Acrobat document in the ACRODOSC folder of the Bonus CD for more information on the programs used to view and edit HTML documents.

You'll also need a Web browser to view the documents as they would be seen online. When you installed Windows 95 as your operating system, if you chose to install the Microsoft Network software, you already have Microsoft's Internet Explorer Web browser installed on your system. You do not have to join or sign on to MSN to access the browser. Web browsers are also available for download from CompuServe, AOL, and other online services, and are often found on the disks that online services send in the mail or place in magazines.

Beyond CorelDRAW!

You don't have to be connected to the Internet to view Web pages with a properly installed Web browser. Simply load the HTML file you wish to view into the browser, which is usually accomplished by choosing **F**ile, **O**pen from the menu.

Software is not the only tool you need when building your own Web page. No matter how technically sophisticated communications becomes, it still begins with the concept, and this generally leads us to an image of what we need to communicate. In the next section, you'll learn how images and text work to complement each other on the WWW, as we walk through the creation of the graphical elements required to support the HTML document for Gordon's Gallery.

Creating the Elements of a Web Page

Whether you decide to include *all* type of graphics elements within your Web page or not, there are different graphics *formats* used on the World Wide Web, and the following section shows you how to build buttons, backgrounds, and how to resize and convert copies of your design work.

Creating a 3D Web Page Masthead

Because Web page graphics must be in bitmap format—specifically GIF or JPEG—it would appear that CorelDRAW can play no part in Web graphics creation. However, as you've seen in other chapters in this book, a CDR file can be converted to a typeface, play the star attraction in a MOTION 3D movie, and a CorelDRAW design can indeed be exported to the GIF bitmap graphic file format.

DRAW's combination of sophisticated drawing tools and special effects make it an ideal place to build a centerpiece—a logo—for Gordon's Gallery. The complete Web page will contain graphical elements from both PHOTO-PAINT and CorelDRAW, but DRAW can easily outmatch its bitmap editing counterpart here for the easy creation of clean, exciting graphics.

Before we begin with Gordon's logo assignment in DRAW, let's consider one or two things about image file size when you create and post a Web page. Because the graphics you produce in CorelDRAW are *resolution-independent*, you can scale a design as large or as small as you like—but Web graphics must be of a fixed size, as all bitmap images are.

Platform-independence is the whole idea behind the World Wide Web, and "Netiquette" (*Net*work-based *Etiquette*) is a good starting place for your continuing online adventures. Because many different processors and video drivers are used to browse the Web, it's a good idea to—as they say in the theater—"play to the cheap seats." This means that images you link to an HTML document shouldn't be excessively large in file size *or* dimensions, and you should design around the lowest resolution of screen display: 640 pixels by 480 pixels. The Gordon's Gallery logo, as you'll see in the following section, was designed at about 4 1/4" by 2 3/4" wide; doing this allows users browsing the Gordon's Gallery Web site a view of the masthead without scrolling horizontally or vertically in a Web browser program.

A sort of equivalency chart you can use when exporting a CorelDRAWing as a GIF image, so that it won't occupy more than the first screen in a Web page document, is in order here. If you keep the following guideline in mind *before* you design a piece, it'll mean you won't have to scale or reproportion a design before exporting it.

A display at 640×480 screen resolution, at 72 pixels per inch, displays an image that's equivalent to 6.7" wide and 5" tall when pixel measurement is converted to pixels. Although some video subsystems can display 96 pixels per inch, again, you need to play to the cheap seats when designing a Web graphic, and display inches converted to a larger size when 800×600 and higher video resolutions are used. If you use CorelDRAW's Page Setup dialog box (double-click on the page border in a document to display the box) to define a 6.7" by 5" **L**andscape page, then stay inside the page with your design, allow for the menu and scroll bars that most Web browsers display, and you can't go wrong.

Creating Gordon's Logo

Gordon has an affinity for the art deco style of architecture, and in keeping with his tastes, we'll use the movie marquee signs of the earlier part of this century as an artistic guide for creating the logo. The choice of fonts for the logo, then, becomes fairly important. We've used Kaufmann and Anna ITC in the creation of the logo design, but if you'd prefer to use alternative fonts, feel free.

Part of the visual interest found in Gordon's logo will be the use of CorelDRAW! 6's new Extrude Roll-Up capabilities. Unlike previous versions—and quite like CorelDEPTH—you can now rotate an extruded object in 3D from within CorelDRAW. However, like CorelDEPTH, you must begin a 3D composition by first creating the necessary 2D elements.

Here's how to begin the logo composition:

Creating 2D Logo Components

1. In a new document window, click-and-drag a horizontal guideline from the ruler to about 5" on the printable page, click-and-drag a vertical guideline from the ruler to about 2" on the printable page, then click-and-drag the zero origin box (on the document window's upper left corner) into the page so that it aligns with the intersection of the two guidelines.

   Sets the zero origin for the printable page at the intersecting points.

2. Click-and-drag a second horizontal guideline so that it aligns with the 2 3/4" mark on the vertical ruler, then click-and-drag a new vertical guideline to the 4 1/4" marker on the horizontal ruler.

   The interior of where the guidelines intersect is the live area for the logo design. When it's exported to bitmap format and eventually becomes a Web graphic, the logo will occupy much less than half a screen.

3. Press F8 (or click on the Artistic Text tool), click an insertion point within the guideline rectangle, then type **Gordon**, press Alt and then **0**, **1**, **4**, **6** on the keyboard numeric keypad, then type **s**.

   Spells "Gordon's," the first object in the logo composition. The use of extended characters, such as a typesetter's apostrophe, contributes to a polished look for the design. Use Windows Character Map utility to access or look up other typographic marks contained within digital typefaces.

4. Press Ctrl+spacebar, then press Ctrl+T.

   Toggles the Artistic Text tool to the Pick tool; displays the Character Attributes dialog box.

5. Choose Kaufmann from the **F**onts list, choose Bold from the Style drop-down box, then click on OK.

   Changes the default font for the text to Kaufmann.

6. With the Artistic Text tool, click and insertion point below "Gordon's," then type **GALLERY**.

   Adds the second text element to the design.

7. Press Ctrl+spacebar, then press Ctrl+T.

   Toggles to the Pick tool, then the text is selected; the Character Attributes dialog box is displayed.

8. Choose Anna, Plaza, Busorama, or any other art deco font that's slender in composition from the **F**onts list, then click on OK.

   Changes the font for the "Gallery" word.

9. Click-and-drag on a corner selection handle for the Gallery word, away from the center of the lettering, until the Status Bar says that the font height is about 50 points.

   Scales the "Gallery" text larger; this is the final size for the text in the composition. If you used a typeface other than Anna (which is *not* part of the Corel 6 font collection), make sure that resizing doesn't exceed the space defined by the guidelines.

10. Perform step 9 with the "Gordon's" text.

    Scales the lettering to its final size in the composition.

11. With the Shape tool, click on the "Gallery" text, then click-and-drag the Kerning handle (the right, honeydipper-shaped selection handle) to the right until the bounding box for the text is horizontally extended by about by about 1/3 longer than the original text.

    Extends the kerning between characters. This is why you were asked to choose Plaza or Anna for this example. As you can see in figure 11.1, extra spacing between characters helps convey an art deco look.

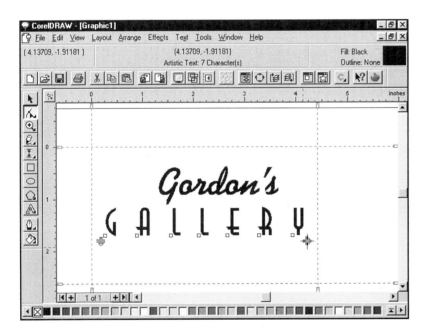

Figure 11.1
You can use character spacing to make a design statement using text elements.

12. Choose **F**ile, Save **A**s, then save the document as GORDLOGO.CDR to your hard disk.

    Saves your work at this intermediate stage of completion.

Quite frequently, you'll find a typeface you'd like to use in a design, but the font is the wrong weight. In the next section, you'll see how to use the contour tool to create custom text.

Contouring a New Font Weight

In Chapter 8, "Creating Your Own fonts," we described the method by which you can create an original logotype from the outline of an existing font. For some reason, the font you always need in a design doesn't come in a wide selection of weights, and Anna, the font used in this example, is no exception. Gordon would like the word "Gallery" to read a little heavier on-screen on his Web page, and the following set of steps show you how to use the Contour effect in combination with the Shape tool, to create the perfect element for this design.

Adding Weight to a Font Outline

1. With the "Gallery" lettering selected, press Ctrl+F9 (or choose Effe**c**ts, Co**n**tour).

   Displays the Contour Roll-Up.

2. Type **0.015** in the Offset field of the Roll-Up, type **1** in the Steps field, click on the Outside radio button, then click on Apply.

   Applies a contour shape around the text, making it appear bolder. See figure 11.2.

Figure 11.2
You can create a new shape that is bolder than the original text by using the Contour effect. Use very small Offset amounts, though.

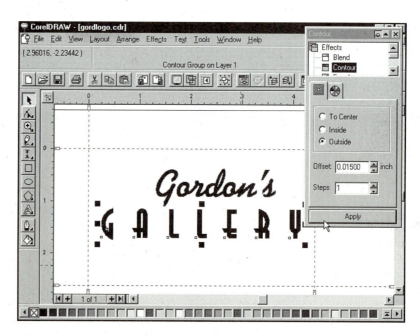

3. With the Shape tool, adjust the kerning (inter-character spacing) of the "Gallery" word if it isn't exactly the way you want it.

Adjusts the spacing; the Contour object changes, also, because it is a dynamically linked object.

4. With the Pick tool, click on the Contour object (not the text), then choose **A**rrange, **S**eparate.

   Two objects are now selected: the text and the contour shape; the link between the shape and the text is broken.

5. Click on a blank space on the printable page, then click on the contour object and click-and-drag it away from the text.

   Moves the object so you can see it and work with it apart from the text. Generally, it's a good idea to keep a copy of a text original in the workspace, in case something goes wrong with an object created from the original. For this reason alone, you'll see the original text in future screen figures.

6. Right-click on the Shape tool, and choose Properties from the shortcut list.

   Displays the properties for the Shape tool.

7. If the value is not at the default of .004, Type **0.004** in the Auto-reduce field, then click on OK.

   Changes the Auto-reduce value to work most effectively in this particular situation. The value of Auto-reduce for the Shape tool can sometimes be too small to substantially remove excess nodes from an outline. You should change this value regularly, depending on the size of the object you're editing.

8. With the Pick tool, click on the contour "Gallery" object, then click on the ungroup button on the toolbox.

   Ungroups the contour shape, and the nodes on the outline of the shape are now editable. Contours make many design chores an almost automated process, but unfortunately, the contour effect produces far too many nodes than are necessary to describe a path, and there is no way in CorelDRAW! 6 to address this, other than manual node editing.

9. With the Shape tool, click-and-drag a marquee around all the nodes in the contour shape, then right-click and choose Auto-Reduce from the shortcut menu, as shown in figure 11.3.

   Reduces the nodes along the contour shape path to (mostly) the essential nodes needed to create the path. If you have functions other than the defaults defined for your mouse buttons, you might want to access the Auto-reduce feature from the Node Edit Roll-Up, which is displayed when you double-click on the Shape tool on the toolbox.

III

Beyond CorelDRAW!

Figure 11.3
The Contour effect
creates overly
complex paths. You
can reduce the
number of nodes
with the Shape tool
and the Auto-reduce
command.

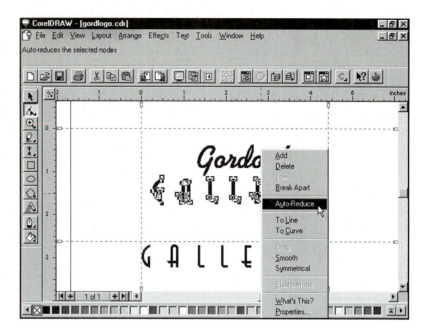

10. Press Ctrl+S (**F**ile, **S**ave)

    Saves your work up to this point.

It should be noted here, well in advance of getting into the Extrude effect, that the Extrude effect creates many linked objects to the original when the 3D effect is applied. Not unlike CorelDEPTH, the Extrude tool must create shading by the addition of objects, and quite frequently produces a number of shaded objects that become hard to work with in a design.

Our hedge against an overly complex Extrude shape, then, begins by keeping the design components as simple as possible. By using Auto-reduce on the contour shape, you've eliminated several objects from the future extrude shape. In the next section, we'll show you how to work with script fonts, and how to reduce their total number of nodes when text is converted to curves.

How to Work with Overlapping Characters

Most fonts that are used for business purposes are from the roman or gothic font families, and you almost never see one of these fonts display negative-spaced characters. If you read Chapter 9, "Working between CorelDRAW! and CorelDREAM," you'll see that in a digital typeface construction, there is a *character space* that surrounds the actual path that represents a character. Typically, the character space provides a "buffer" between characters so words don't feature characters that run together.

However, script fonts are deliberately constructed so that individual characters encroach upon each other's character space, thus creating the look of smooth brush or quill calligraphy. Brush Script, Vivaldi, Kaufmann, and Snell are a few examples of Script fonts that contain information for overlapping characters.

However, the Extrude effect tends to produce weird, sometimes unaesthetic results when applied to a script font, because the effect cannot calculate whether a character intersects another character, falls on top of, or lies beneath its neighbor. To remove all of the Extrude effect's doubt in the matter, the simplest route is to convert script text to curves before editing.

In the following example, you'll see the correct way to convert script lettering to a single curved shape.

Editing a Script Typeface to Its Essentials

1. Click on the "Gordon's" text in the design, then click on the Convert to Curves button on the toolbar.

   Converts the text to curves. If you're using Brush Script, Kaufmann, or other script font in this example, you'll notice that the converted text many have some "negative space"—areas where you can see through to the printable page, where characters overlap. This will ruin the Extrude effect, and its incorrect path construction.

2. Press Ctrl+K (**A**rrange, **B**reak Apart).

   Breaks the converted text into its component subpaths. Now, the counters within each closed character are filled in with their own, separate shapes.

3. Zoom in to the converted text, click on the wireframe view button on the toolbar, then choose **A**rrange, **W**eld.

   Displays the converted text in wireframe view, where you can clearly see the overlapping paths; displays the Weld Roll-Up.

4. Uncheck the Target Object and the Other Object(s) check boxes on the Roll-Up, click on the *o* in "Gordon's," then click on the Weld to button on the Weld Roll-Up.

   Specifies that paths will be welded in this example, and no original object will be duplicated; *o* is selected; cursor changes to huge arrow.

5. Click over the *r* in "Gordon's."

   Welds the outside of the *o* to the *r*; eliminates the overlapping areas.

Beyond CorelDRAW!

6. Repeat step 5 with the other characters that overlap.

   Creates an outer path for the text that contains no overlapping areas. See figure 11.4.

Figure 11.4
Extruded shapes
should be simple.
You can simplify
script text by welding
overlapping,
converted characters
together.

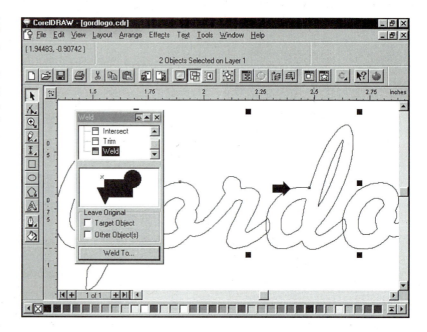

7. With the Pick tool, marquee select all the objects that make up the "Gordon's" lettering, then press Ctrl+L (**A**rrange, **C**ombine).

   Combines the lettering into a single object, with numerous subpaths.

8. Press Ctrl+S (**F**ile, **S**ave).

   Saves your work up to this point.

Note On a whim, I tried this chapter's example with converted text, and then with editable Artistic Text, using the Kaufmann font. The Extrude effect, even through it leaves text objects as text objects, must perform some internal calculations about how many control points (nodes) must be used to define a path to be extruded. Amazingly, the Status Bar told me that over 4,000 nodes were defined for Kaufmann as text, when the text was extruded. However, as an object, not text, the "Gordon's" object contained fewer than 3,000 nodes.

Besides being the only file format for Gordon's logo, the GIF format—the final format for this design—will remove the complexity of the extruded path from the design. As a vector object, the logo will be ponderously complex, but as a bitmap, you'll find the design easy to work with using PHOTO-PAINT's tools.

Adding the '50s Boomerang Look

The final element in the logo, and the one that ties the two text objects together, is an abstract boomerang shape behind the text. 1950s architecture, furniture, and especially the neon signs, were wonderfully experimental pieces, and the period also borrowed heavily from the Art Deco period of art in the 1920s when it came to typography. As a designer, you have the right to create a happy amalgam of period pieces, as long as your eye tells you that the elements work together compositionally.

Here's how to complete the 2D design for Gordon's Web page logo.

Creating Abstract Art with the Bézier Tool

1. Beginning between the *G* in *Gordon's* and *G* in *Gallery*, click and hold on the Freehand Pencil tool, then click on the Bézier tool.

   This is the tool you'll use to create a smooth, curved boomerang shape for the logo design.

2. Click-and-drag the Bézier tool to the right, release the cursor, then click-and-drag at a point that's upward and to the right of the first point you clicked.

   Creates an arc; you're holding on the control point of the arc between the first and second point you clicked.

3. Click-and-drag down and to the right of the second point; release the cursor, then click-and-drag downward and to the right.

   You're describing a triangular shape here, with an indentation on the right side. See figure 11.5 to get a better idea of the abstract shape you're creating here. The points where you click-and-drag are mapped to this figure.

4. Close the path by clicking on your beginning point, then with the Shape tool, click-and-drag on nodes to create a shape that looks more like the one in figure 11.5, if necessary.

   Creates a closed shape that will be an element in the logo design.

Figure 11.5
The Bézier tool is not
the most intuitive of
Corel's tools to use,
but it can produce
wonderful, abstract
shapes.

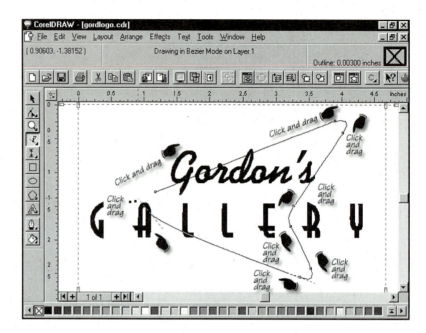

5. Press Ctrl+S (**F**ile, **S**ave).

   Saves your work up to this point.

11ROUGH.CDR is in the CHAP11 folder of the Bonus CD. It contains the elements you've designed in this example. If you'd like to check them out for construction, or use them in the upcoming examples, now is a good time to do so.

Contouring the Abstract Shape

Let it be noted here that the design aspect of Gordon's Gallery is a purely subjective one, and that the steps shown here involve the creation of special effects objects, and the elements for a Web page. If you have design ideas of your own, you should substitute them throughout this chapter. You do, however, need to create a closed path for extruded objects (sorry, open paths can't be extruded), and the objects in the 11ROUGH.CDR document all qualify for extrusion.

Before commencing with the 3D work, let's breeze through a few steps to make the abstract object in the composition into a frame for the text, instead of merely a background. Here's how to use the Contour effect to make easy work of it:

Creating a Contour Frame

1. If you closed the Contour Roll-Up after previous use, press Ctrl+F9.

   Displays the Contour Roll-Up.

2. Select the Bézier curve with the Pick tool, type **.1** in the Offset spin box, type **1** in the Steps spin box, click on the Inside radio button, then click on Apply.

   Creates a second, linked object inside of the Bézier curves.

3. On the Contour Roll-Up, choose **A**rrange, **S**eparate, click on an empty space on the printable page, click on the contour group in the document, then click on the ungroup button.

   Separates the linked contour object from the curve and ungroups the contour shape, allowing you to edit the nodes.

4. With the Shape tool, click-and-drag the nodes to perform whatever refining needs to be done to the inside shape.

   Creates a more aesthetic composition.

As you can see in figure 11.6, the author decided to create straight lines where the extremes of the curve meet. You can reassign node and path segment properties if you've left the right mouse button functions at their defaults in CorelDRAW, by accessing Node Edit commands from the shortcut menu.

5. With the Pick tool, with the contour shape selected, Shift+click on the Bézier curve, then press Ctrl+L (**A**rrange, **C**ombine).

   Combines the inner and outer boomerang shapes to make a frame object.

6. Click on the To Back button on the toolbar.

   Sends the boomerang behind the lettering in the design.

Beyond CorelDRAW!

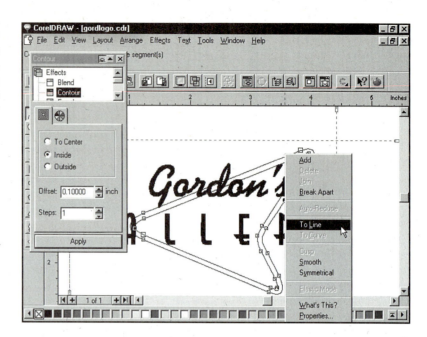

Figure 11.6
Quickly access the
Node Edit Roll-Up's
commands by using
the right mouse
button shortcut
menus.

7. Press Ctrl+S (**F**ile, **S**ave).

Saves your work up to this point.

Thoughts on Colorizing the Logo

Now that you have the logo design laid out, it's time to choose a color scheme for the elements. Unlike printed material, the color space of the World Wide Web is glorious RGB color, so you should definitely indulge your creative whims at this point, and choose some outlandish colors for the logo.

I went with an orange to purple linear fountain fill frame, a red to yellow "Gordon's" text object, and left the "Gallery" lettering a dull but light greenish-blue. These colors seem reminiscent of drive-in signs from a childhood's perspective. When you're designing for the Web, you don't have to concern yourself about the number of steps used in a fountain fill; GIF graphics are confined to a color capability of 256 shades, and 50 steps is more than adequate to convey the graphical idea of a fountain fill.

Working with the Extrude Roll-Up

There are five tabbed menus on the Extrude Roll-Up, three of which we'll work with in the examples to follow. The first menu, the presets, is not of interest with respect to this logo design, because the presets are…presets, and not a true artistic discovery place within CorelDRAW. The Color wheel tab at the right side of the Extrude Roll-Up is the Fills option for extruded shapes. If you want to color the extruded side of an object with a shade other than the front face of the object, the Fills menu provides a quick and easy solution.

In the following set of steps, we'll take a look at the aspects of extrusion depth, angle of object rotation, and the lighting of an object. Unlike the lighting you might define for a scene in CorelDREAM 3D, lighting in CorelDRAW is an object attribute; you can have many extruded shapes on the same page that display different lighting characteristics.

Here's how to extrude the converted "Gordon's" lettering in the design:

Extruding and Shading a Logo Element

1. Press Ctrl+E (or choose Effe**c**ts, E**x**trude).

   Displays the Extrude Roll-Up.

2. Click on the extruded "I" beam on the Extrude Roll-Up.

   Offers options for extrusion depth and vanishing point for the extruded shape.

3. Choose VP locked to Object from the drop-down list.

   Specifies that the vanishing point for the extruded shape will always be relative to the object, and not the printable page. In general, this is the best option for extrusions, because you can then refine objects after they've been extruded without worrying about their relative position on the page.

4. Choose Small Back from the drop-down list.

   Specifies that the back of the extruded shape will be slightly smaller than the front face. This is a good option, because it tends to force perspective, and adds more of a 3D look to an object.

5. Type **2** in the Depth field, then click on Apply.

   Extrudes the "Gordon's" lettering, as shown in figure 11.7. Unless you are extruding objects of, say, more than 5 inches in size, it's a good idea to keep the Depth to a minimal amount. You can create wonderful cubes and cylinders with greater depths, but lettering on a sign such as this logo needs to be more of the "cookie cutter" depth of extrusion.

6. Click on the rotate icon on the tabbed menu.

Beyond CorelDRAW!

Figure 11.7

Figure 11.7

The preview
bounding box
provides a good
indicator of the
depth and direction
of the object to be
extruded.

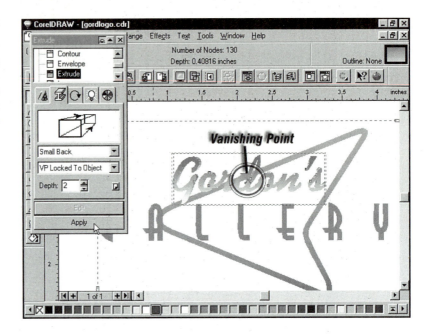

Displays the rotation options for the extruded object. Corel Corp.'s logo on this menu is one, large graphical handle by which you "steer" the angle of rotation for an object.

7. Click-and-drag, gently and slowly, upward and to the right, then click on Apply.

   Rotates the object upward and to the right. The *x* in the lower left of the menu is a reset button. You can return a selected, extruded object to face front by clicking on it. Additionally, you can toggle to a number entry submenu from the rotate menu by clicking on the page icon in the lower right of the menu. On the submenu, you can type values for the counterclockwise rotation of an object along its vertical, horizontal, or depth axis. See figure 11.8.

8. Click on the lighting menu icon.

   Displays the lighting options for the selected object.

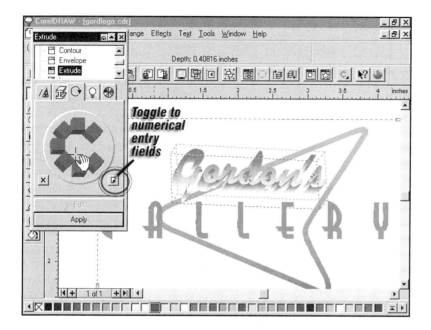

Figure 11.8
Click-and-drag on
the 3D Corel logo,
then click on Apply
to create an angle of
rotation for an
extruded object.

9. Click on the lightbulb button marked with a "1."

   Adds the light to the 3D wireframe preview on the lighting menu.

10. Click-and-drag the circled "1" in the wireframe to the front, top, left position.

    Specifies the angle of lighting as it will be applied to the selected extruded object.

11. Check the Use full color range check box, then click-and-drag the Intensity slider to about 75.

    Adds lighting to the object using the full range of available colors found within the selected object; the "Gordon's" extruded text truly looks dimensional with the aspect of lighting active. See figure 11.9.

III

Beyond CorelDRAW!

Figure 11.9
Extrusion of an object suggests dimension, but accurate lighting makes the object more photorealistic.

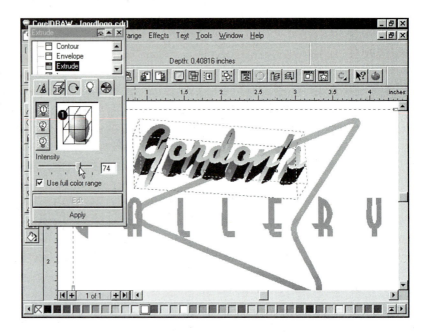

12. Press Ctrl+S (**F**ile, **S**ave).

Saves your work up to this point.

The depth and rotation options on the two menus in the Extrude Roll-Up work in a mutually exclusive fashion. If you've rotated an object, you'll find that the vanishing point options are dimmed on the depth menu. And if you need to change the depth of an extruded shape, you must remove the rotation from it (by clicking on the rotate menu's *x* button) before making changes. For this reason, it's usually best to work from left to right on the Extrude Roll-Up; specify the depth first, then the rotation angle, then add your lighting effects.

Adding the Same Point of View to Other Objects

Because there are so many options for extruding an object, it would seem as though it would be a trial to match the other components of Gordon's logo to the exact lighting, angle of rotation, and extrusion depth of the first object.

CorelDRAW makes it easy, however, for you to copy the attributes of an extruded object, without changing the other properties of the object, such as color.

Here's how to completely dimensionalize Gordon's logo, in less than 2 minutes:

Using the Effects, Copy Command

1. Click on the frame object in GORDLOGO.CDR.

    Selects the object.

2. Choose Effects, Copy, then choose Extrude from.

    Your cursor turns into a gigantic arrow.

3. Click on the extrude side, not the front, of the "Gordon's" lettering.

    Extrudes the frame object to the same depth and angle of rotation as the Gordon's lettering, and with the same lighting effects. See figure 11.10.

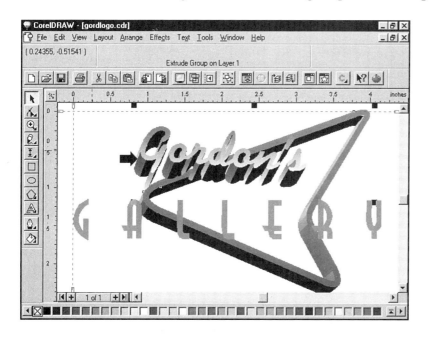

Figure 11.10
You can copy all the aspects of an extruded object to a different object through the Effects, Copy command.

4. Repeat step 3 with the "Gallery" object.

    Extrudes the Gallery object. All three objects are in the same relative position to one another now, but they're aligned in all *three* dimensions.

5. Press Ctrl+S (File, Save).

    Saves your work up to this point.

It's on to one or two embellishments, then it's time to send this composition off across the airwaves... em, *cable*-waves?

Creating Your Own 3D Artwork

Although the graphic looks pretty smart right now, there's no reason why you can't add a touch or two of 2D artwork to enhance it. Because extruded objects are simply a group of 2D shapes drawn with perspective, you can indeed at this point, "go behind" the frame object, and give it a fill. In figure 11.11, you can see that a shape is being created that fits inside of the frame's width. The finished shape is then filled with a uniform, blue fill, and sent to the back of the page. It's not necessary to extrude 2D objects when you cannot see their back or side facets. Additionally, if you read Chapter 5, "Complex Fills and Blend Shading," you already know the source of inspiration for—and the means for creating—the dropshadow text.

Figure 11.11

Elements within a composition that have been extruded can work harmoniously with other elements that *suggest* perspective and depth.

Converting a CorelDRAW! Graphic to a Web Graphic

The final touch needs to be added to the Gordon's Gallery logo, but it's a technical addition rather than an artistic one. The image information read by Web browsers that specifies a transparent color is an explicit RGB color value. In the following sections, you'll see how to create a seamless, tiling background GIF image in PHOTO-PAINT for use as the "WebPaper" for a home page.

When a GIF image has transparent attributes, the specified RGB indexed color in the image simply vanishes on-screen, to display the background wallpaper. Therefore, you need to export the Corel design as a bitmap with a background included; the background color should occur in any of the foreground objects, or the foreground elements will drop out, too. In the GORDLOGO.CDR document on the Bonus CD, we've created a rectangle and placed it behind the other objects, as seen in figure 11.12. Then, values of R:204, G:204, and B:204 were typed into the fields in the Uniform Fill dialog box to produce a light, neutral gray for the selected rectangle. It might seem like a picky thing to choose explicit color values instead of choosing them from a color model, but you'll need to remember these values after the logo is converted to bitmap format. These values are the key to specifying the transparency value.

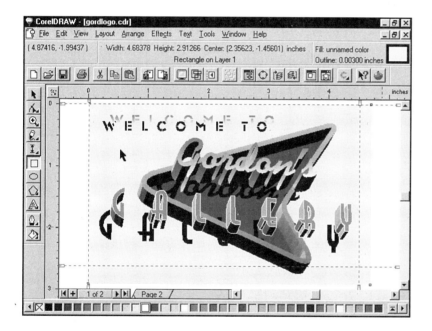

Figure 11.12
Choose a background color for a background shape that you can easily specify later as RGB values, to create a transparent Web page background.

You'll also notice if you open the GORDLOGO.CDR image from the CHAP11 folder of the Bonus CD, that the dropshadows have been given a black fill, a little unrealistic if this were to be a "fine art" illustration, but as you'll see in the following note, the choice of colors was a necessary one.

> **Note** To create a transparent GIF with dropshadow elements that can effectively be used against *any* background pattern or color, the dropshadow can only be black. Shades of gray cannot be included in the foreground design information, because you might have a background whose pattern includes a color that is darker than one of the dropshadow's component colors.

And this makes for an awkward shadow!

Here's how to export the CorelDRAW design to the format used on the Internet Web:

Exporting Graphics from DRAW to the Web

1. With the logo and its gray background selected, choose **F**ile, **E**xport or press Ctrl+H. Choose a location on your hard disk where the Gordlogo file should be saved. In the Save file as **t**ype drop-down box choose TIFF Bitmap (TIF). Put a check mark in the Selected **o**nly check box. Click on the E**x**port button.

   Opens the Export dialog box where you choose the kind of export to be performed (the file format the new file will have, in this case TIF), the name of the file and where it will be exported to. Clicking on the Export button opens the Bitmap Export dialog box.

2. In the **C**olor drop-down list of the Bitmap Export, choose 16 Million Colors if it is not already chosen. In the **S**ize drop-down box choose 1 to 1. From the **R**esolution drop-down box choose Custom. Set **H**orizontal and **V**ertical to 72 dpi. Put check marks in the **I**dentical values and the **A**nti-aliasing check boxes. Your screen should look like figure 11.13. Click on OK only after checking all the options listed here.

   These settings choose the color depth, dimensions, and resolution of the TIFF file. You didn't choose a lower color depth here because the file will be brought into PHOTO-PAINT, which is much more capable than DRAW at producing high quality color reduction. Always set Vertical and Horizontal resolutions to the same dpi, because if they are set to different values your image will be distorted. For Web graphics you only need to set the resolution to the screen's resolution; anything larger will bloat the file and be wasted information. Opens the TIFF-Color Space dialog box.

3. Make sure the Save in CIELab check box is unchecked in the TIFF-Color Space dialog box and then click on OK. The file exports as a TIF and you are returned to the workspace where GORDLOGO.CDR is still on-screen.

   For Web page graphics, you want to stay within the RGB color space, so you don't want to save the TIF in the CIELab color space. The CIELab setting is useful if you are printing the TIF directly to a PostScript Level 2 device, or if you're converting the saved color TIFF to a grayscale bitmap in a paint program.

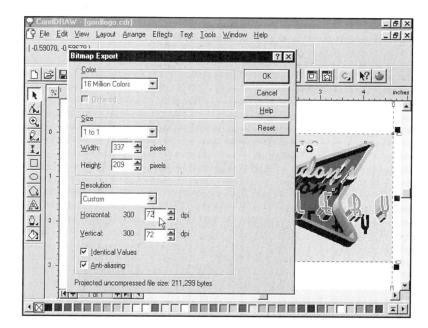

Figure 11.13

Use 72 dpi as the export resolution for RGB TIFF images that will be converted into Web graphics in PHOTO-PAINT.

4. Press Ctrl+S and Alt+F4 or choose **F**ile, **S**ave and then choose **F**ile, E**x**it.

   Saves GORDLOGO.CDR to your hard disk and closes CorelDRAW.

It is possible to create a transparent GIF by exporting from CorelDRAW. However, you have much less control over how color reduction is applied in CorelDRAW than you have in PHOTO-PAINT. In DRAW, you have choices that produce either banding or dithering; in PHOTO-PAINT you can choose to build a special color table that eliminates banding and dithering almost all of the time. Additionally, creating a transparent GIF requires knowing which slot in the indexed GIF image the color you want to pick as the transparent color is stored. In DRAW you have to guess, in part because you have no way of directly sampling the color, but mostly because the image is still a vector and has not been rasterized; colors have not yet been assigned to a color table.

Therefore, to get the most faithful rendition of the GORDLOGO for this Web page, a PHOTO-PAINT session is next on the agenda. Although it is possible in Windows 95 to have several major applications open at one time, CorelDRAW and Corel PHOTO-PAINT demand a lot of your system's resources. It is a good idea to exit one full-featured application before opening the other.

Beyond CorelDRAW!

With the exception of assigning the background color of GORDLOGO.TIF a transparency attribute, we've completed the foreground design aspect of the Web Page assignment. In the next section, we'll turn to discussions on the hows and whys of GIF transparency, and how to create seamless tiling backgrounds for Web pages.

Creating a Transparent GIF Image

Unlike the JPEG format of bitmap images, GIF (Graphics Information Format) images can only contain a maximum of 256 unique values, and you have to *dither* (perform color reduction) on an RGB image to make a legitimate GIF file. However, the HTML specifications include transparency information for GIFs, and this means that you can select one of the 256 color "slots" within the indexed color GIF to drop out when the design is placed above a background tile in a Web page.

There are several versions of the GIF standard; currently, Version 89a Interlaced is used in HTML documents to produce a transparent GIF. CorelDRAW and CorelPHOTO-PAINT support this standard. This section shows you how to create transparent GIFs in PHOTO-PAINT.

Before commencing with the transformation of Gordon's Gallery logo to transparent GIF format, we should explain what an *interlaced* image is. Besides compactness, the GIF image structure allows users to preview a low resolution version of a GIF image. This saves time previewing images available on CompuServe, and when a GIF image is called from an HTML document, an interlaced GIF appears at first to be pixelated, then becomes more refined. The effect is somewhat like focusing a pair of binoculars. When someone jumps to your Web site, all graphics linked to the HTML document are downloaded; this can produce long moments of waiting while the graphics are composed, but interlaced graphics will immediately appear in the audience's Web browser. Additionally, the audience can scroll through the Web document quickly as interlaced graphics build; non-interlaced images can halt document scrolling for moments on end.

The GORDLOGO image is approximately 200 KB when saved as a TIFF, and machines with less than 16 MB of system RAM might force CorelDRAW to take a long time to complete the vector to bitmap conversion process (*rasterizing*). If you'd like to complete the example in this section, but aren't sure whether you have the system "umph," cancel this operation now, and open the GORDLOGO.TIF image, also in the CHAP11 folder of the *CorelDRAW! 6 Expert's Edition Bonus CD*. The GORDLOGO.TIF image is a saved copy of the already-imported graphic.

The secret to creating a transparent GIF image for Web page use lies in the capability of a GIF file to contain a unique color that is read by a Web browser as a "no show" color. This capability is not unique—icons in both Windows and Macintosh desktops can contain transparent colors. However, the trick here is to assign a background color value to the masthead (or your own image) that is unique to the image. The transparent GIF color should have three properties:

✔ It should be close in color to the background color scheme of the intended design.

✔ It should not be a color contained within the design.

✔ The color should be flat—no dithered pixels of other colors within the background.

The intention here is to create as elegant a masthead for the Web page with the limited amount of graphical information as size and the limitations of indexed color allow. However, you must think in *context* of a Web page when designing graphical elements; there will be much for the viewer's eye to focus upon in this composition. Therefore, the trade-off between content and overall design is usually an accepted one in Web documents.

Tip   If you choose a *solid* color background for a Web page, you can include more visual information in a transparent GIF you place within the document. The example in this section shows you how to use PHOTO-PAINT to create a Transparent GIF that can be placed atop *any* background—pattern or not—but should you choose a solid background, you don't have to create a mask to isolate dropshadows and text from the background.

Create the graphic you want to use in either CorelDRAW or PHOTO-PAINT; if you use DRAW, you must export the graphic to bitmap format before finalizing the design in PHOTO-PAINT. Create a solid color background that's the same color value you want to use as a transparency.

In PHOTO-PAINT, choose **I**mage, Con**v**ert To, then choose **2**56 Colors (8-bit). From the Convert to 256 Colors dialog box choose **O**ptimized in the Palette type field and **E**rror diffusion in the Dither type field. The resulting image can then be assigned a transparent background color, and the graphic can be used on a solid background whose color is identical to the image background.

Read the rest of this section for the details on creating transparency information.

Creating Seamless Repeating Tiles

One of the more exciting improvements that Netscape has unofficially added to the HTML language is the capability to tile a bitmap to represent the background of a Web document. The tile covers the background, and a tiling bitmap of small size will quickly redraw in the audience's browsing utility.

Because you are now no longer limited to a solid color background within the framework of an HTML document, people who design Web documents are now discovering a profession—that of "WebPaper Hangers"! However, the most exciting possibility for tiling patterns behind your message lies in the capability of *seamlessly* tiling a background; the pattern appears to endlessly repeat itself without edges.

III

Beyond CorelDRAW!

The EXAMPLES/CHAP11 folder on the *CorelDRAW! 6 Expert's Edition Bonus CD* contains several samples of seamless tiling patterns, and some of the secrets to creating seamless tiles from anything you imagine can be found in Chapter 5.

A Web page background shouldn't compete with the foreground message, textual or graphical, but it should show that the designer wants to convey something fresh and unusual. If you're an artist like Gordon by profession, you probably would like a background that complements the art pieces hung in the virtual online Gallery. Most background tiles on the Web consist of a repeat pattern that tiles either vertically or horizontally—because pixels are rectangular, this is sort of hard to defeat! However, in the next set of steps, you'll see how to create an endlessly repeating *diagonal* tile.

CorelDRAW's Custom Fountain Fills are great for creating many different types of repeat patterns.

Here's how to create a "candy-stripe" effect, using a Custom Fountain Fill, that you can use for Web page backgrounds:

Creating WebPaper

1. In CorelPHOTO-PAINT, press Ctrl+N (**F**ile, **N**ew), then specify the following for the new document: Color **m**ode: 24-Bit Color, Size: Custom **W**idth **2**, **H**eight **2**. Make sure the units in the drop-down box next to **W**idth is set to inches. In the Resolution field set **H**orizontal and **V**ertical **72** dpi**,** pixels/inch. The C**r**eate a partial file and Create a **m**ovie check boxes should remain unchecked. Click on OK.

   Creates a new, blank document, New-1.cpt, if this is the first file you've created in this PHOTO-PAINT session; otherwise it will be New-x, where *x* is another number. New files are numbered sequentially. You'll use New-1.cpt to create a seamless tiling pattern.

2. Double-click on the Fill tool. Then click on the Fountain Fill button (second from the left). Click on the Edit button to the right of the preview box.

   Opens the Tool Settings Roll-Up. Moves to a view of Fountain Fill options. Clicking on Edit opens the Fountain Fill Dialog box.

3. In the **T**ype drop-down box, choose Linear. In the Options field, double-click in the **A**ngle: spin box and enter **-45**. Double-click in the **S**teps: spin box and enter **256**. The **E**dge pad: spin box should remain at 0. In the Color Blend field, click on **C**ustom. See figure 11.14.

   These settings specify a Linear fill made up of 256 steps (maximum allowed), that runs at an angle that's diagonal to the image's side angle. It is important that the angle is a true diagonal–45° or 135°–otherwise the pattern will not tile correctly in the Web browser. Specifying Custom causes the lower part of the dialog box to change. It now displays the preview ribbon, a color palette, and other color controls.

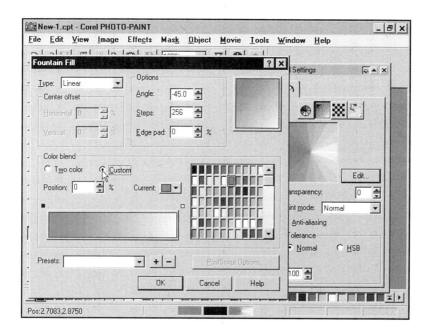

Figure 11.14
Choosing Custom on the Fountain Fill dialog box causes the preview ribbon to display.

4. Click once on the small black box above and to the left of the preview ribbon. Double-click in the Position spin box and enter a value of **0,** if any other value' appeared in the box.

   Causes a dotted line box to appear above the preview ribbon that encompasses the small black square on the left and the small white square on the right, and causes the Position spin box to become active.

5. Click on the Current drop-down box. Click on the Others button at the bottom of the mini-palette.

   This brings up another Fountain Fill dialog box where you can specify color.

6. Make sure that the Color Mo**d**els radio button is selected and that RGB is the selection in the Mod**e**l drop-down box. Enter values of **R**:237; **G**:211; and **B**:236 in the spin boxes. When your screen looks like figure 11.15, click on OK.

III

Beyond CorelDRAW!

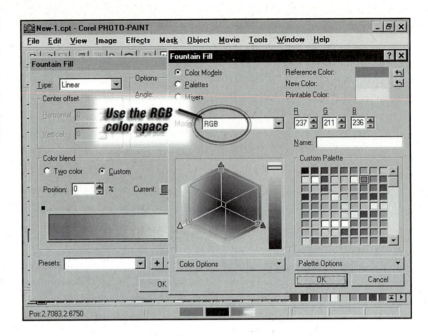

Figure 11.15

Use colors from the
RGB color model
when designing
graphics for Web
pages and other
documents that will
only be viewed
on-screen.

Selects a soft lavender as the starting point of the custom fountain fill. Alternatively, you could select a color by clicking on one of the swatches in the Custom Palette. You are returned to the first Fountain Fill dialog box, and the starting point of the fountain fill changes to light lavender.

7. Double-click on the preview ribbon about half a screen inch from the small black box. The Position spin box will report a new value. Change the value to **12**.

   A black, inverted triangle called a color marker appears at the 12% point above the preview ribbon. This marks the starting point for the addition of the intermediate color, which you specify in the next step. See figure 11.16.

8. Repeat steps 5 and 6 to specify a new color except this time, use the RGB values of **R**:220; **G**:231; and **B**:228, to specify a light, greenish gray. Set another marker using these same **R**:220; **G**:231; and **B**:228 color values at the **62**% point.

   Sets two intermediate steps in the complex fountain fill.

9. Following the same procedures, set two new color markers with RGB values of **R**:19; **G**:15; and **B**:26, (near black) at the **25**% and the **75**% point. At the **50**% and **100**% point set a new color marker with RGB values of **R**:237; **G**:211; and **B**:236, to specify the same light lavender color used at the 0% point.

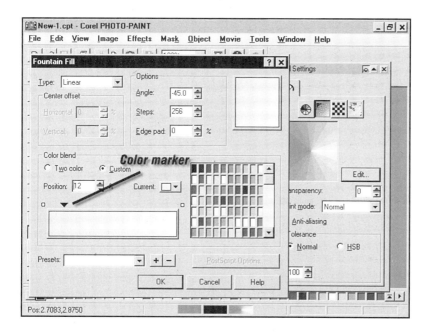

The complex fountain fill should look like figure 11.17. If not, click on each maker and check both the position as reported by the spin box and the color. It is important to create two identical repeats within the pattern, so that the final image can be tiled seamlessly.

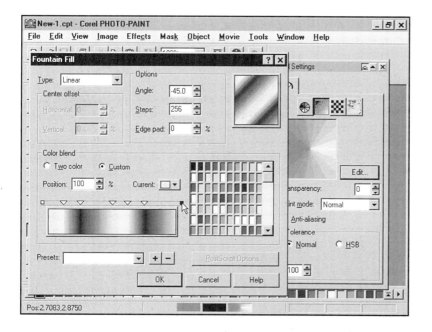

Figure 11.17
A diagonal, custom fountain fill that repeats color transitions within the pattern will create a seamless tile.

Beyond CorelDRAW!

10. Click in the Presets drop-down box and enter **Gordon's Tile** as the name for this fill. Click on the plus button to the right to save the preset. Then click on OK.

Saves the complex fountain fill to the preset with the name Gordon's Tile and becomes the current fill. This preset can be used in both CorelDRAW and in PHOTO-PAINT.

Now that the Gordon's Tile complex fountain fill has been created and saved, it's on to the tile making process.

Creating a Web Page Tile

1. With the Fill tool, click in the New-1.cpt image window.

The entire window fills with the Gordon's Tile fountain fill.

Unless you're planning on reversing text in your Web page, chances are that the current image is a little too intense for using as a background. To fix this...

2. Choose Effects, Color Adjust and then choose Brightness-Contrast-Intensity from the Color Adjust submenu.

Displays the Brightness-Contrast-Intensity dialog box. A copy of your image is displayed in the Original: box on the left and changes you make in this dialog box can be previewed in the Result: preview box on the right.

You'll use these controls to "wash out" the image so that text placed on top of the pattern will be legible and not fight for attention with the text and other graphics placed on top.

3. Click-and-drag the Brightness slider to about **30** or enter **30** in the entry box to the right. Click-and-drag the Contrast slider to the left to about **-60** or enter **-60** in the text entry box. Click on the Preview button. (See fig. 11.18)

Increases the Brightness values and reduces the Contrast in the image. Displays the proposed changes in the Result box on the right. These values were determined by trial and error, if different values look better to you, use them. The goal is to create a pale version of the image that still retains some original color and color transition pattern.

4. If you like what you see in the Result: box, click on OK.

Closes the dialog box and applies the change to New-1.cpt.

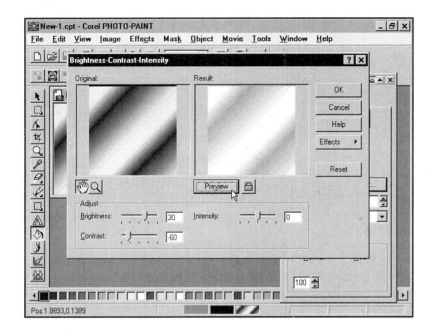

Figure 11.18

Increase Brightness and reduce Contrast in an image to create a light-colored, patterned background for a Web page.

The image looks like it could be improved by increasing the saturation. Increasing the saturation of the colors in the image by a small amount will make the colors appear richer and perkier, without making the image too prominent.

5. From the menu, choose Effe**c**ts, Adjust and then choose Color Tone from the Adjust submenu.

    Displays the Color Tone dialog box.

6. In the **S**tep entry box change the default value of 10 to 5.

    Reduces the amount of adjustment that will be applied. Notice that the thumbnail previews at the bottom of the dialog box change to reflect the reduced amount of adjustment you just specified. See figure 11.19.

7. Click once on the Saturate thumbnail.

    Notice that the Result preview box changes to reflect the increase in saturation you requested by clicking on the thumbnail. You can click on any of the thumbnails to make further corrections if you deem them necessary. If you do, you'll notice that the Result preview box changes again to reflect the additional changes. All changes you make in this dialog box are cumulative.

Figure 11.19
Specify the amount of change that will be applied to the image by moving the Step slider or entering the amount in the Step entry box.

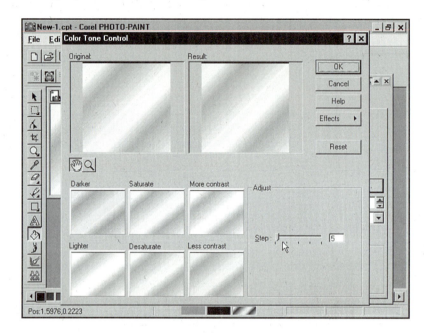

8. Click on OK when you like what you see in the Result: window.

Closes the dialog box and applies the change to New-1.cpt.

The tile pattern might look a little bland now, but you must consider how it fits into the Web page design as an element. With graphics and text piled upon it, its contribution will be a handsome one.

Web page tiling background graphics need to be in the GIF file format. Unlike the TIF or CorelDRAW's CPT file format, the GIF file format is an *indexed* file that is capable of displaying 256 colors. There are many different versions of the GIF file format standard; as of this writing, CorelDRAW's GIF conversion filter works fine for background tiles to be displayed on Web pages and for creating a *transparent* GIF, as does PHOTO-PAINT's GIF export filter. The only problem when using DRAW's GIF 89a export filter is that you have no way to visually select the color; you have to *guess* at the transparency color's index value. There are bound to be very similar colors in an indexed color palette, and PHOTO-PAINT allows you to see the indexed colors as well as the indexed color's numerical component values.

We'll get to creating and using transparent GIF's later in this chapter.

The next steps you need to take to make New-1.cpt a graphic suitable for a Web page background is to reduce the color depth of the image from the RGB 24-bit mode it currently has to 256 colors or 8-bit mode and then save it to the GIF file format.

Saving an RGB Image as a GIF File

1. With New-1.cpt as the active image in the PHOTO-PAINT workspace, choose **I**mage, Con**v**ert To and then **2**56 Colors (8-bit) from the menu.

   Displays the Convert to 256 Colors dialog box.

2. Click on the **O**ptimized radio button, click on the **E**rror Diffusion radio button, then click on OK.

   Reduces the number of unique colors in the image to 256; returns you to the image.

3. Press Ctrl+S (**F**ile, **S**ave).

   Displays the Save an Image to Disk dialog box.

4. In the Save as **t**ype drop-down box, scroll up and choose CompuServe Bitmap (GIF). Name the file MY-TILE.GIF, choose a location on your hard disk, then click on **S**ave.

   Chooses the file format, the name of the file and where the file will be stored when saved. Brings up the Transparent Color dialog box.

5. Make sure the **89**a Format radio button is chosen and that the **I**nterlaced image and the **T**ransparent Color check boxes are unchecked. Click on OK.

89a is the format supported by Web browsers. For wallpaper, there is no advantage to interlacing the tile. You can specify a transparent or drop out color, although it is not customary to do so. The color that would show through is the Background color specified in the HTML document, or the default background color specified by the Web browser software. Clicking on OK saves the image to your hard disk. See figure 11.20.

Beyond CorelDRAW!

Figure 11.20
The finished image can be placed as a Web page background and will seamlessly tile.

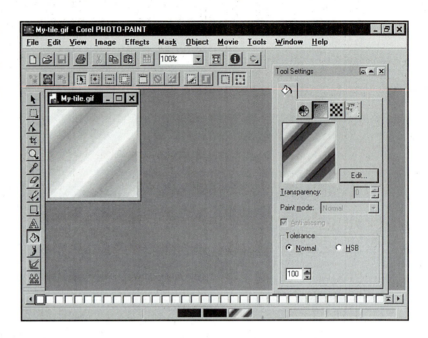

Note The author finds that *error diffusion dithering* produces more eye-appealing results than the alternative option of Ordered dithering color when reducing color in PHOTO-PAINT. Ordered dithering produces a weave of available colors in an Indexed image's limited color range to "fake" original colors that cannot be expressed. And a weave of colors sometimes overwhelms the visual content of an indexed color image, particularly one with as few pixels as a Web page graphic. Additionally, if you choose the **N**one option for dithering, it results in a very harsh image, very unlike the original image, because no approximations are made to simulate original image content.

The Optimized palette option is probably the best choice for retaining as much original color information as possible, because an Optimized color palette for an image emphasizes the predominant tone of the original within a palette of 256 colors. An Adaptive palette takes the first 256 colors it finds in the image, regardless of their predominance in the image. In contrast to the Optimized and Adaptive palettes, a fixed palette such as Uniform always contains the same colors, and these colors might not be the ones present in your design. When you choose Uniform as the palette that Corel PHOTO-PAINT reduces colors to, more often than not, you will notice more dithering patterns as PHOTO-PAINT attempts to approximate original colors.

In figure 11.20, we've tested the MY-TILE.GIF image by creating a bitmap fill from MY-TILE.GIF. To do this, click on the Bitmap Fill button on the Tool Settings Roll-Up and click on the Edit button. In the Full-Color Bitmap Pattern dialog box, click on the

Import button. In the Import dialog box, go to the drive and folder in which you saved MY-TILE.GIF and double-click on the file name to load the bitmap. In the Full-Color Bitmap Pattern dialog box, MY-TILE.GIF becomes the current pattern. Make sure that the Use original size check box is checked and all other settings and check boxes remain at 0 or are unchecked. Click on OK to make all of the settings effective and return to the workspace. Open a new file with any dimensions—New-2.cpt in figure 11.21 is 9" by 10"—then click within New-2.cpt's image window with the Fill tool.

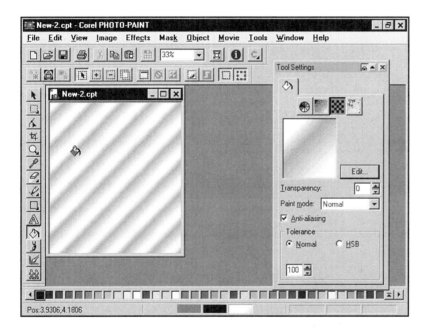

Figure 11.21
You should test a pattern on an image larger than the pattern to see whether you, or the Web audience, can detect pattern edges.

Working from back to front, it's now time to create some elements to go upon this seamless tiling background.

Working with Imported Files in PHOTO-PAINT

1. Launch PHOTO-PAINT. Choose **F**ile, **O**pen or press Ctrl+O. Use the Open an Image dialog box to find and open GORDLOGO.TIF from your hard disk.

   Opens the GORDLOGO.TIF file you created and exported from CorelDRAW in PHOTO-PAINT.

2. With GORDLOGO.TIF the active image in the workspace, choose **I**mage, Con**v**ert To from the menu; then choose **2**56 Colors (8-bit) from the submenu.

Beyond CorelDRAW!

Displays the Convert to 256 Colors dialog box.

3. In the Convert to 256 Colors dialog box, choose **O**ptimized in the Palette type field and **E**rror Diffusion in the Dither type field (see fig. 11.22). Leave the Co**l**ors spin box at its default of 256, then click on OK.

   This action will reduce the color depth of the TIF file from RGB (24-bit, 16 million colors) to the best 256 (8-bit) colors for this image. Any colors that can't be expressed by the reduction in color depth will be "faked" or approximated using the error diffusion method of dithering.

Figure 11.22

Output levels expand the tonal range of the selected image; you can remove absolute black or white from an image with this control.

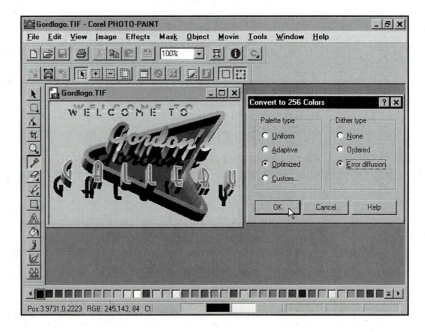

Reducing the color depth from 24-bit to 8-bit also reduces the file size by two-thirds, which brings it closer to an acceptable size for the Web. Saving the color reduced TIF as a GIF will further reduce the file size because GIF is a highly efficient indexed file format that incorporates LZW compression methods.

4. Double-click the Eyedropper tool on the toolbox.

   The Color Roll-Up displays and the Eyedropper tool is the active tool.

5. Click the Eyedropper on GORDLOGO.TIF's light gray background. Be sure to click over an area that is *not* close to the foreground boomerang shape. Look at the first (left) field of the Status Bar. It should read R 204, G 204, and B 204, and tell you that the index number of the background color is 14.

Determines the RGB color specification (formula) for the light gray, and tells you the number of the indexed color value so you can specify this number as the transparent value when you export the image in the GIF format.

Some dithering took place when you reduced the number of colors in this design from a possible 16.7 million (24-bit color), to 256. For this reason, it's important that you take a sample with the Eyedropper tool that's in "the open" within the design. There are three or four neutral gray colors in this image at present; several shades close to, but not exactly the background color exist, because the anti-aliasing process and the color depth reduction process adds these colors to smooth transitions where there are hard color breaks. This is why it's important to specify that the "main" background gray is measured for its index number, and not the "off" grays found as a single pixel fringe around the logo edges are.

6. Choose **F**ile, Save **A**s from the menu. In the Save an Image to Disk dialog box, choose CompuServe Bitmap(GIF) from the Save as t**y**pe drop-down box. The file name automatically changes from GORDLOGO.TIF to GORDLOGO.GIF; keep this name. Click on the **S**ave button.

This is the first stage of saving a file to another file format, in this case you are saving from TIF to GIF. The file will be saved to the same location on your hard disk as the TIF file, unless you specify another location in this dialog box. The Transparent Color dialog box displays after you click on the **S**ave button.

7. In the Transparent Color dialog box, make sure that the 8**9**a format radio button is selected and that the **I**nterlaced image and the **T**ransparent Color check boxes are checked. In the In**d**ex entry box, enter the index number displayed on the Status Bar when you pointed and clicked the Eyedropper tool on the image background. For this example, the index number is **14**. (See figure 11.23.) Click on the **S**ave button.

You have specified that the GIF file about to be created will be in the 89a format, that it will be interlaced and that the color 14 in the file's color index will be ignored and therefore made "transparent" when the resulting file is viewed in a Web browser. Clicking on Save performs the action and changes GORDLOGO.TIF in PHOTO-PAINT's workspace to GORDLOGO.GIF.

Beyond CorelDRAW!

Figure 11.23
Enter the index number of the color you want to become transparent and drop out when viewed in a Web browser.

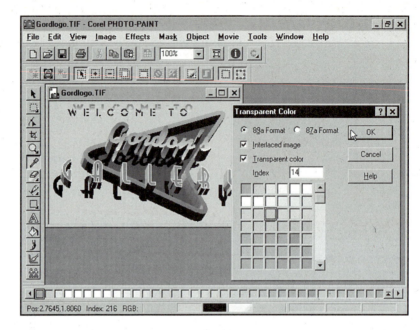

8. Press Alt+F4 or choose **F**ile, E**x**it.

   Closes GORDLOGO.GIF and exits PHOTO-PAINT.

When you've been returned to the workspace nothing appears to change except that now GORDLOGO.GIF is the file that is open. The neutral colored background is still there. You will only be able to see for sure that the gray "is gone" when the image is displayed in a Web browser.

▶**Tip** Always name your Web graphics files with a three-character extension such as .GIF and .JPG, even if you are using long file names. It is not a requirement, but it is a good idea to limit your file names to the 8.3 DOS file naming convention, if for no other reason than it limits the amount of typing and possible error when composing the HTML document. In any case, you must always use a three letter file extension such as .GIF or .JPG, because Web browsers need the extension information.

Gordon's Gallery needs jumps—links within the HTML document to other places within, or outside of the document—so some graphical buttons are the next call to order. In the next section, you'll see how to create handsome Web page buttons, and how to use buttons provided on the *CorelDRAW! 6 Expert's Edition Bonus CD.*

Creating Web Page Buttons

The personal computer took a cue from the 1960s adage, "We live in a push-button society," and today, many software companies, including Corel, advise that "click on anything that moves" is the best way to become familiar with an application. The same is true of Web pages; although links can be specified in a Web Document through the use of underscored text, graphical buttons look more professional, and people can't resist the urge to click on them!

ARTIST.GIF, TO-ART.GIF, HOME.GIF, and BACK.GIF, as seen in figure 11.24, are image files the author made for your Web-creation adventures, and they are located in the CHAP11/STOCK folder of the EXAMPLES folder on the *CorelDRAW! 6 Expert's Edition Bonus CD*. This collection of buttons has already been through the transparent GIF process, with the light gray background specified as the transparent color. If you read Chapter 10, "Adding DEPTH and MOTION," and you own a symbol font or two, you can see that the buttons for a Web page can be extruded WingDings, or font creations of your own.

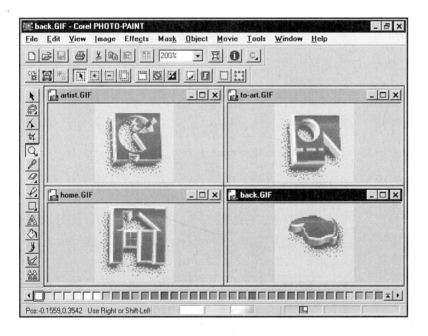

Figure 11.24
The *CorelDRAW! 6 Expert's Edition Bonus CD* ready-to-go buttons you can add to a Web Page document.

➤**Tip**   If you like the Glass, The Boss, and the Whirlpool filters in PHOTO-PAINT 6, you'll love Alien Skin's Black Box version 2 filters. These are new, 32-bit filters that work splendidly with PHOTO-PAINT 6 and include some great new filters such as Dropshadow, Carve and Inner and Outer Bevel.

Creating 3D buttons is a breeze with the new Alien Skin 2 filters.

Suggestions on Creating Your Own Mini-Art Gallery

In our efforts to create handsome Web elements, let us not forget the star attraction of Gordon's Web page—his paintings! Regardless of the finished image size of artwork you create electronically in CorelDRAW (or other applications), Web pictures need to be *small*. We're talking an average of about 100 KB for *un*compressed images; large images posted on the Web frustrate, and eventually lose the audience, whose computers might not have as much processing power or RAM as a graphics professional's.

Let's suppose that you, like Gordon, are an artist who wants a little publicity from his Web site, but more importantly, wants to attract potential customers. If you give the Internet audience just enough of an idea through your imagery to attract them, you can always send them a larger version of your artwork through other routes (like, gasp, the U.S. Mail) once they've gotten in touch with you.

We've created three templates in PHOTO-PAINT CPT format for your use in sizing artwork of your own, or the sample images provided on the *CorelDRAW! 6 Expert's Edition Bonus CD*. We've used the same basic screen "rules" as mentioned at the beginning of this chapter to create the templates THUMBNAIL, L-PORT (larger portrait), and L-LAND (Larger Landscape) found in the CHAP 11 folder of the Bonus CD. Take measurements from them for your own work, and use PHOTO-PAINT's **I**mage, **R**esample command to resize copies of your bitmap format graphics. These template are not the last word in graphics dimensions for the Web, and you may outgrow the need to use them after one or two uses, but it's a pace to start as you begin to evaluate image dimensions for publication in electronic, not physical format.

Typically, there are two different sizes of artwork that Web sites contain: the *thumbnail*, which is often a jump in the document to a larger graphic, and the *larger graphic*. Because many graphics folk are accustomed to designing on-screen for the *printed* page, it's a little hard to embrace the notion that Web graphics should be sized and proportioned for the physical screen, most often the monitor you stare at when you use CorelDRAW. So consider how large CorelDRAW's buttons are, size your Web page graphics and buttons accordingly, and try to make artwork you intend to display on a Web page full size, at 1-to-1 viewing resolution; there's no Zoom tool in a Web browser!

Moving Your Document to the World Wide Web

Before you give your pages to an Internet provider for posting, it's a good idea to preview the document for structure. Do the links within the document take the visitor to the correct section in the document? Do links to *outside* of the document—such as jumps to interesting places you'd recommend to others exist? Have you entered the location of these jump sites correctly? It is very easy to make a typing error in an HTML document; we've provided jump sites in electronic format within the Gordon's Gallery document for this exact reason. If you copy and paste jumps, you are more likely to include accurate information.

Preview and play with the document until it looks the way you want it. We recommend that you load a text or HTML editor containing the HTML code for your Web page in the background while you preview the document in a Web browser. Changes can be made in this way on the fly.

Previewing and Launching Your Web Page

In order to preview your Web page, you must have a browser installed on your computer, and all the elements that make up the document must be stored in the same location on hard disk if the links refer to internal jumps. Storing all of the documents and graphics used for your site in a single folder is highly recommended because it is the most foolproof way to ensure that all elements are present and accounted for, and that your pages will work.

We've now loaded Gordon's Gallery into Netscape Navigator browser by double-clicking on the INDEX.HTM file in the CHAP11/WEBPAGE folder. Figure 11.25 shows how the page described by the HTML code in INDEX.HTM will look to visitors to Gordon's site who use Netscape. It will look similar, but not identical to this when viewed using other browsers, such as Microsoft's Internet Explorer.

Figure 11.25

By understanding the importance of properly sized graphics for the WWW, the text and pictures come together in a well-proportioned composition.

III

Beyond CorelDRAW!

In the previous figure, you can see that the cursor turns into a pointing hand icon when hovered over a link. Netscape's browser, like many browsers, tells the visitor *where* the link will take them. The natural place to go in an artist's document is the graphical section, and you can tell that if you use this link you will go to another document on the same system, because the address displayed on the status line and in the Address: box below the toolbar only change to reflect a new document, not a new address.

If you double-click on any of the HTM documents in the WEBPAGE folder of the Bonus CD, and have installed Microsoft's Internet Explorer, you'll be immediately taken to a "dry run" of Gordon's virtual Gallery. You can see the Gallery Page you are taken to when you click on the jump to the gallery tour. Gordon tells you on this page that the thumbnail images in this mini art gallery have a purpose in addition to looking great. Each of the four thumbnail graphics on this page is a hyperlink to still another page. Graphics, just like the underlined text that brought you to this page, can be tagged as a hypertext link. You can see how Gordon accomplished this if you look at the GALLERY.HTM document in the WEBPAGE folder. The

```
<IMG SRC="art05.gif" ALT="A piece of my artwork" ALIGN="LEFT"
➥HSPACE="10" BORDER="0">
```

tag causes the GIF image of the tricycle to be displayed on this page. But it is the hypertext anchor tags that surround it:

```
<A HREF="lookma.htm"> before and </A>
```

Immediately after the IMG tag, that make the tricycle graphic a hyperlink to another page in the set. Other, similar references compose the rest of the page. Note, however, that the image tags that call the buttons at the bottom of this page are not within a hypertext anchor, and are links themselves. In this case, text is within the hypertext anchor and it is the link visitors click on to make a jump.

If you have an Internet connection *active* while browsing Gordon's Gallery and you click on any of links Gordon lists in figure 11.26 as some of his favorite Internet sites, you will jump to that site. Notice that the status line indicates that the address for the link you are about to click on is not the same as the one displayed in the Address: field toward the top of the browser. When you visit a site you'd like to revisit, use your web browser's bookmark or favorites feature to save the address for you. It's a good way to get the addresses you need to make your own favorites list.

➡ Tip   RESOURCE.HTM, in the EXAMPLES/CHAP11 folder, can be your connection to graphics, graphics services, and CorelDRAW-related places on the WWW. Load the page in your Web browser (usually, **F**ile, **O**pen) and click on any link to go to that site.

You can also add the sites listed in RESOURCE.HTM to your private address book, or use them as jumps within your own Web page.

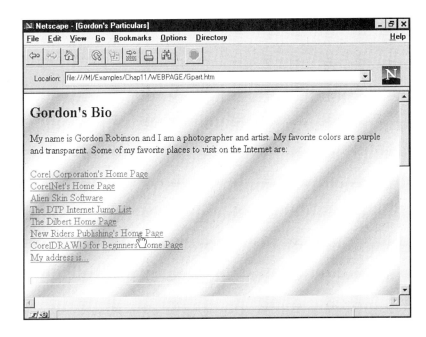

Figure 11.26

Links to outside documents—in a different town, or a different country—are as easily made.

Once you're confident that all the links within your Web page are working correctly, find out if there is a special format or naming convention the Provider who hosts your site requires for posting your Web page. Many Providers will fax you a form with special instructions for submitting the elements that comprise the Web page(s).

The level of proficiency with which you create a Web document largely depends upon the amount of time you have to invest in understanding the structure of HTML. In this respect, the results you get from spending time working with CorelDRAW's features are quite similar. Electronic communications have redefined the meaning of the term "composition," but if you have a talent for creating a meaningful something out of mixed media, the possibilities for becoming not just a Web visitor, but a Web *innovator* can be yours.

Quite simply, the World Wide Web is the cheapest place you can go to advertise your art to…you guessed it—the *world*.

Beyond CorelDRAW!

Symbols

J–K–L

PLUG YOURSELF INTO...

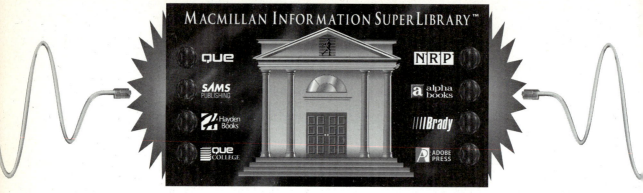

THE MACMILLAN INFORMATION SUPERLIBRARY™

Free information and vast computer resources from the world's leading computer book publisher—online!

FIND THE BOOKS THAT ARE RIGHT FOR YOU!

A complete online catalog, plus sample chapters and tables of contents give you an in-depth look at *all* of our books, including hard-to-find titles. It's the best way to find the books you need!

● STAY INFORMED with the latest computer industry news through our online newsletter, press releases, and customized Information SuperLibrary Reports.

● GET FAST ANSWERS to your questions about MCP books and software.

● VISIT our online bookstore for the latest information and editions!

● COMMUNICATE with our expert authors through e-mail and conferences.

● DOWNLOAD SOFTWARE from the immense MCP library:
  - Source code and files from MCP books
  - The best shareware, freeware, and demos

● DISCOVER HOT SPOTS on other parts of the Internet.

● WIN BOOKS in ongoing contests and giveaways!

TO PLUG INTO MCP: →   **WORLD WIDE WEB: http://www.mcp.com**

GOPHER: gopher.mcp.com

FTP: ftp.mcp.com

WANT MORE INFORMATION?

CHECK OUT THESE RELATED TOPICS OR SEE YOUR LOCAL BOOKSTORE

CAD

As the number one CAD publisher in the world, and as a Registered Publisher of Autodesk, New Riders Publishing provides unequaled content on this complex topic under the flagship *Inside AutoCAD*. Other titles include *AutoCAD for Beginners* and *New Riders' Reference Guide to AutoCAD Release 13*.

Networking

As the leading Novell NetWare publisher, New Riders Publishing delivers cutting-edge products for network professionals. We publish books for all levels of users, from those wanting to gain NetWare Certification, to those administering or installing a network. Leading books in this category include *Inside NetWare 3.12*, *Inside TCP/IP Second Edition*, *NetWare: The Professional Reference*, and *Managing the NetWare 3.x Server*.

Graphics and 3D Studio

New Riders provides readers with the most comprehensive product tutorials and references available for the graphics market. Best-sellers include *Inside Photoshop 3*, *3D Studio IPAS Plug In Reference*, *KPT's Filters and Effects*, and *Inside 3D Studio*.

Internet and Communications

As one of the fastest growing publishers in the communications market, New Riders provides unparalleled information and detail on this ever-changing topic area. We publish international best-sellers such as *New Riders' Official Internet Yellow Pages, 2nd Edition*, a directory of over 10,000 listings of Internet sites and resources from around the world, as well as *VRML: Browsing and Building Cyberspace*, *Actually Useful Internet Security Techniques*, *Internet Firewalls and Network Security*, and *New Riders' Official World Wide Web Yellow Pages*.

Operating Systems

Expanding off our expertise in technical markets, and driven by the needs of the computing and business professional, New Riders offers comprehensive references for experienced and advanced users of today's most popular operating systems, including *Inside Windows 95*, *Inside Unix*, *Inside OS/2 Warp Version 3*, and *Building a Unix Internet Server*.

Orders/Customer Service **1-800-653-6156**   Source Code **NRP95**

New Riders Publishing   201 West 103rd Street ◆ Indianapolis, Indiana 46290 USA

REGISTRATION CARD

CorelDRAW! 6 Expert's Edition

Name _____ Title _____

Company _____ Type of business _____

Address _____

City/State/ZIP _____

Have you used these types of books before?   ☐ yes   ☐ no

If yes, which ones? _____

_____

How many computer books do you purchase each year?   ☐ 1–5   ☐ 6 or more

How did you learn about this book? _____

Where did you purchase this book? _____

Which applications do you currently use? _____

_____

Which computer magazines do you subscribe to? _____

_____

What trade shows do you attend? _____

_____

Comments: _____

_____

_____

Would you like to be placed on our preferred mailing list?   ☐ yes   ☐ no

☐ **I would like to see my name in print!** You may use my name and quote me in future New Riders products and promotions. My daytime phone number is: _____

New Riders Publishing   201 West 103rd Street ◆ Indianapolis, Indiana 46290 USA

Fax to **317-581-4670**   Orders/Customer Service **1-800-653-6156**   Source Code **NRP95**

Fold Here

- -

‖‖‖‖

BUSINESS REPLY MAIL
FIRST-CLASS MAIL PERMIT NO. 9918 INDIANAPOLIS IN

POSTAGE WILL BE PAID BY THE ADDRESSEE

NEW RIDERS PUBLISHING
201 W 103RD ST
INDIANAPOLIS IN 46290-9058